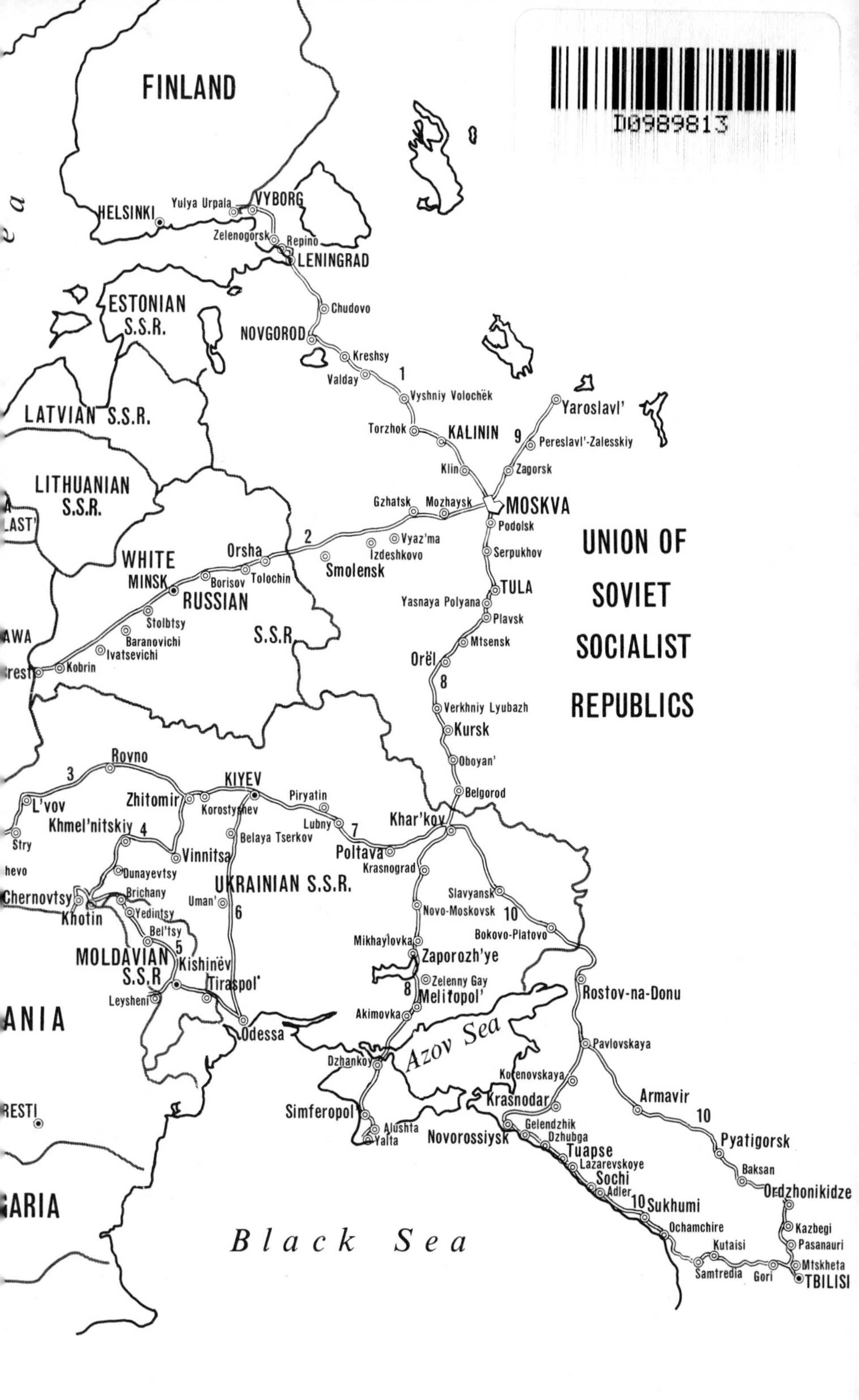
FINLAND
HELSINKI
Yulya Urpala
VYBORG
Zelenogorsk
Repino
LENINGRAD
ESTONIAN S.S.R.
Chudovo
NOVGOROD
Kreshsy
Valday
1
Vyshniy Volochëk
LATVIAN S.S.R.
Torzhok
KALININ
9
Yaroslavl'
Pereslavl'-Zalesskiy
Klin
Zagorsk
LITHUANIAN S.S.R.
Gzhatsk
Mozhaysk
MOSKVA
Podolsk
UNION OF SOVIET SOCIALIST REPUBLICS
2
Vyaz'ma
Izdeshkovo
Orsha
WHITE RUSSIAN S.S.R.
MINSK
Borisov
Tolochin
Smolensk
Serpukhov
TULA
Yasnaya Polyana
Stolbtsy
Plavsk
Baranovichi
Mtsensk
Ivatsevichi
Kobrin
Orël
8
Verkhniy Lyubazh
Kursk
Oboyan'
Rovno
3
KIYEV
Belgorod
L'vov
Zhitomir
Korostyshev
Piryatin
Khmel'nitskiy
4
Lubny
7
Khar'kov
Stry
Belaya Tserkov
Poltava
Vinnitsa
Krasnograd
Dunayevtsy
UKRAINIAN S.S.R.
Chernovtsy
Brichany
Slavyansk
Uman'
6
Khotin
Yedintsy
Novo-Moskovsk
10
Bel'tsy
Bokovo-Platovo
5
MOLDAVIAN S.S.R
Kishinëv
Mikhaylovka
Zaporozh'ye
Tiraspol'
Zelenny Gay
Leysheni
8
Melitopol'
Rostov-na-Donu
Akimovka
Odessa
Azov Sea
Pavlovskaya
Dzhankoy
Korenovskaya
Krasnodar
Armavir
Simferopol'
10
Alushta
Yalta
Novorossiysk
Gelendzhik
Dzhubga
Tuapse
Pyatigorsk
Lazarevskoye
Sochi
Baksan
Adler
10
Sukhumi
Ordzhonikidze
Ochamchire
Kazbegi
Kutaisi
Pasanauri
Black Sea
Samtredia
Gori
Mtskheta
TBILISI

A MOTORIST'S GUIDE TO THE SOVIET UNION

A MOTORIST'S GUIDE TO THE SOVIET UNION

BY

V. E. LOUIS

AND

J. M. LOUIS

PERGAMON PRESS

OXFORD · LONDON · EDINBURGH · NEW YORK
TORONTO · SYDNEY · PARIS · BRAUNSCHWEIG

Pergamon Press Ltd., Headington Hill Hall, Oxford
4 & 5 Fitzroy Square, London W.1

Pergamon Press (Scotland) Ltd., 2 & 3 Teviot Place, Edinburgh 1

Pergamon Press Inc., 44-01 21st Street, Long Island City, New York 11101

Pergamon of Canada, Ltd., 6 Adelaide Street East, Toronto, Ontario

Pergamon Press (Aust.) Pty. Ltd., 20-22 Margaret Street, Sydney, N.S.W.

Pergamon Press S.A.R.L., 24 rue des Écoles, Paris 5e

Vieweg & Sohn GmbH, Burgplatz 1, Braunschweig

First edition 1967

Library of Congress Catalog Card No. 65-16215

2361/67

The use of travelling is to regulate imagination by reality, and instead of thinking how things may be, to see them as they are.

SAMUEL JOHNSON

To I.M.S.,

who is always welcome

CONTENTS

PART I

BIOGRAPHICAL NOTE

JENNIFER LOUIS is an Arts Graduate of Edinburgh University and VICTOR is a qualified lawyer. They are both journalists and write regularly from Moscow for various British and other Western publications. Their work often takes them travelling in the Soviet Union, and when they began to collect material about the different localities they had visited, what started as a hobby became a serious occupation because many places have not been described recently and relevant guide-books are unobtainable. The background of an old monastery in Georgia or an attractive mansion in a quiet country town can only be discovered in rare books.

Until now there has never been a travel guide following the roads open to foreign motorists in the Soviet Union. The authors have been to the places they describe several times, and after working on this book for the past six years they nevertheless checked the data thoroughly to bring it up to date and make the book a reliable guide and companion for tourists in the Soviet Union.

INTRODUCTION

This book is not a collection of personal impressions. In compiling it we hoped to fill the gap between general descriptions of Russia written by visiting tourists and the existing guide-books of individual towns and cities. Few of the latter have been translated into English, and one can find out about many places only by extensive research in reference libraries. Guide-books of the Soviet Union soon grow out of date, for the process of change is exceptionally rapid: new towns and villages appear, and where it is considered necessary old houses and other buildings are completely removed to make way for new streets. Details about present-day Russia will be given to you by Intourist, so we have not described entirely new built-up areas, collective farms, factories, institutes, educational establishments, etc., although these can certainly be visited by the tourists to whose special interests they appeal.

We should like to stress the fact that the roads covered in the book are open to foreign motorists *at the time of writing*; it is essential to check your proposed route with Intourist before you set out, to make sure there will be no official objections to it. The roads themselves are not generally known by their numbers.

The towns described in the book are arranged in the order in which they occur on the roads; those which occur on more than one road are described the first time they are encountered. We have chosen to follow the roads towards Moscow from the border points with the exception of the Moscow–Kharkov–Simferopol–Yalta and the Kharkov–Rostov-on-Don–Ordzhonikidze–Tbilisi ring roads. Ring roads and loops are always described in a clockwise direction, travelling from left to right. We hope that our guide will also be of use to you if travelling in the opposite direction, even though you may have to read the entries in the reverse order.

The description of each town in the book falls roughly into four sections:

(a) *facts:* general description, history, geographical location, population, etc.

(b) *places of interest:* churches, museums, theatres, parks, etc.

(c) *information:* hotels, restaurants, camping sites, shops, etc.

(d) *motorists' information:* filling and service stations, parking, interesting excursions in the vicinity, etc.

We are sorry not to have been able to describe Moscow and Leningrad street by street, but these cities deserve a separate volume which we hope to compile in the future.

This book will also serve as a guide for those who do not come to the Soviet Union as motorists, if they do not include Central Asia or the Baltic countries in their itineraries; and there is certainly much of interest for the armchair traveller.

Before we completed this book we drove thousands of miles along Russian roads, and looked through hundreds of books. We should now like to express our gratitude to Mr. Vladimir Babkin of Intourist, and to Mrs. Danilov and Mr. Henri Bronstein for their generous help in preparing the material. We should also like to thank our publisher, Mr. Maxwell, for his encouragement; he appreciated our idea from his own experience, and shares our trust in the usefulness of this book.

We are much indebted to Mr. C. V. James, Mr. M. Heller and Mrs. P. Chennells for their professional advice and assistance.

We should welcome comments, criticisms and corrections from those who put our guide to practical use (these should be addressed to the Publisher), and in any case we hope that our readers enjoy their travels.

Shchastlivova puti! Have a good trip!

Moscow V. E. Louis and J. M. Louis

HISTORY OF RUSSIA AND OF THE SOVIET UNION

THE Soviet Union consists of 15 republics. The whole country is often referred to as Russia, but this is really the name of the biggest of the republics, the Russian Federation. The Soviet Union is largely based on the former territories of the Russian Empire, and the history of the country as a whole is mainly the history of Russia. The other 14 republics are: the Ukraine, Belorussia, Latvia, Lithuania, Estonia, Moldavia, Georgia, Armenia, Azerbaidzhan, Kazakhstan, Uzbekistan, Tadzhikistan, Turkmenistan and Kirghizia. The country, which is the largest in the world, occupies one-sixth of the world's land mass, 22,402,200 square kilometres (about 8,600,000 square miles). The population numbers 229,000,000 (1965), the third largest population in the world, following China and India. Moscow Time (2 hours ahead of CET) is adhered to by the western part of the Soviet Union.

FACTS AND FIGURES FROM THE COUNTRY'S HISTORY

800–882: The formation of the first Russian state dates from this time. In the south a Slav tribe known as the Polyane founded the Kiyevan state with its centre called Kiyev after Prince Kii of the Polyane. In the north was the Novgorod State: when in 862 Norsemen, led by the Varangians Rurik, Sineus and Truvor, were invited by the Novgorod Republic to come and restore order, one of them, *Rurik*, became the first of the Rurikids to rule in Russia. Their reign lasted until the 17th century.

882: *Oleg*, Rurik's successor, conquered Kiev and this united both the states.

988: *Prince Vladimir of Kiev* introduced Christianity into Russia.

1169: Kiev began to decline in importance. Prince Andrei of Vladimir attacked and conquered Kiev, and proclaimed Vladimir (800 km, i.e. 500 miles, north-east of Kiev), the new capital.

1224: Russia's first encounter with the advance army of Genghis Khan took place in this year, and this was, in fact, the beginning of the Tartar invasions.

1237–1242: The Tartars under Baty Khan conquered Russia and established in the Volga steppes the rule of the "Golden Horde" to which all Russia became vassal and paid tribute.

1380: *Dmitri Donskoi* (Demetrius of the Don), the Grand-Prince of Muscovy, won a considerable battle against the Tartars. The Grand-Princedom of Muscovy had by this time obtained power over most of the older principalities by acting as tax-collector for the

Tartars. Although Dmitri Donskoi's battle was not decisive, the Tartar grip on the country was greatly loosened.

1162–1505: *Ivan III* of Muscovy laid the foundations of the future Russian Empire when, between 1465 and 1488, he annexed the rich and strong city of Novgorod with its vast territories, defied the Tartars by refusing to pay them further taxes and routed the Golden Horde's armies sent against him. This ended the 250-year-long Tartar oppression.

1533–1584: *Ivan IV* (known as "the Terrible"). In 1547 Ivan assumed the title of Tsar (the word is derived from "Caesar") of All the Russias. To Ivan IV goes the credit of building a powerful and united Russian state; during his reign the last of the other independent principalities disappeared from the map of Russia. Ivan IV received his nickname for his severe persecution of the boyars (barons) who possessed great influence in government. Ivan the Terrible organised a special bodyguard known as the "oprichina" which arrested prominent boyars, tried them, and usually executed them for "treason". In 1552 and 1557 respectively the Tartar kingdoms of Kazan and Astrakhan were conquered. In 1582 Russia's conquest of Siberia began.

1598: *Feodor I*, Ivan IV's son, died; he was succeeded by his brother-in-law, *Boris Godunov*, and in 1610 the Interregnum began, caused by the appearance of two false Dmitris, each claiming in turn to be Dmitri, Ivan the Terrible's youngest son who had died in 1591. Both impostors were supported by the Poles. Organised government collapsed and a disastrous civil war ensued.

1613: Kosma Minin, a Russian meat merchant, with Prince Pozharsky gathered an army of volunteers and finally drove the Poles from the country. *Mikhail Romanov* was elected tsar, thus founding the Romanov dynasty.

1645–1676: *Alexei I.*

1676–1682: *Feodor II.*

1689–1725: *Peter I* (*the Great*). Peter I was one of the most outstanding statesmen and warriors in Russian history; he may rightly be called the "enlightener of Russia", for he introduced Western customs, culture and technical achievements into his backward country. He also extended Russian dominion to the southern shore of the Caspian sea, won access to the Baltic, reorganised the national economy, founded a new army and Russia's first large fleet. He founded St. Petersburg (now Leningrad) in 1703, and defeated the Swedish army at the Battle of Poltava in 1709. In 1721 he assumed the Imperial title.

1725–1727: *Catherine I*, widow of Peter I.

1727–1730: *Peter II*, grandson of Peter I.
1730–1740: *Anna Ivanovna*, daughter of Ivan, half-brother to Peter I.
1740–1741: *Ivan VI*, great-grandson of Ivan, the half-brother of Peter I.
1741–1761: *Yelizaveta Petrovna*, daughter of Peter I.
1761–1762: *Peter III*, nephew of Yelizaveta and grandson of Peter I.
1762–1796: *Catherine II* (*the Great*), widow of Peter III. Catherine's reign is notable for the extension of Russian territory after the three partitions of Poland, for victorious wars with Turkey and for the cession of the Crimea and Danubian principalities. During this period Russia became a Great Power.
1796–1801: *Paul I*, son of Catherine II. Paul was unpopular with the nobility and was eventually assassinated in his palace.
1801–1825: *Alexander I*, son of Paul I. In 1812 Napoleon invaded Russia and was defeated.
1825–1855: *Nicholas I*, third son of Paul I. During the short interregnum caused by Alexander I's sudden death, a group of aristocratic officers made the first military attempt to overthrow the autocracy of the tsars, and to change the system of serfdom. This rebellion took place on 14th December 1825, and the rebels were accordingly known as the Decembrists. The uprising was promptly suppressed, and its leaders were hanged or sent to Siberia; but the very fact of its occurrence served as a powerful impetus for the further development of liberal thought in Russia, although its immediate effect was to produce a period of intense persecution and affirmation of the autocratic powers of Tsar Nicholas. In 1853–1856 the Crimean War with England, France and Turkey ended with Russia's defeat.
1855–1881: *Alexander II*, son of Nicholas I. In 1861 the Tsar issued a decree for the emancipation of the serfs, making possible industrial expansion. The Caucasus was conquered and in 1877–1878 the war with Turkey was won, resulting in the liberation of Bulgaria.
1881–1894: *Alexander III*, son of Alexander II.
1895–1916: *Nicholas II* was the last Russian tsar. The Russo-Japanese war (1904–1905) ended with a Russian defeat. In 1905 there took place the first revolution and armed insurrection of the workers, and the establishment of a more democratic form of constitutional monarchy. In 1914 Russia entered World War I. In February 1917 there was the bourgeois-democratic revolution, after which the provisional government was formed; and on 7th November (25th October, by the old calendar) occurred the October Socialist Revolution of workers, peasants and soldiers led by Lenin's Communist Party (the Bolsheviks), after which the Soviet State was established.

1918: The Soviet government moved from Petrograd (Leningrad) to Moscow, which once again became the capital of Russia. The country was in a critical situation and the young Republic had to contend with the opposition of the White Russians (counter-revolutionaries), and with foreign intervention.

1918–1922: Civil War.

1924: Lenin died, and Soviet leadership passed to Stalin.

1929: The first Five-Year Plan of Economic Development, aiming to lay the foundation of socialist economy, was adopted, and the campaign for the collectivisation of farms was launched.

1936: The new constitution was adopted on 5th December.

1939: The 18th Congress of the Communist Party proclaimed that gradual transition from socialism to communism was in progress.

1941–1945: World War II. Russia and her allies defeated the Axis powers.

1945–1950: This was a period of post-war reconstruction.

1953: Stalin died, and Khrushchev was appointed First Secretary. Stalin's close followers were soon dismissed from posts of authority, and by the end of the 1950's they had been labelled the "anti-party" group.

1961: At the 22nd Party Congress it was proclaimed that the foundations of communism will have been fully laid in the Soviet Union by 1980.

1964: Khrushchev was replaced by Leonid Brezhnev and Alexei Kosygin.

SOVIET GOVERNMENT

(1) The Supreme Soviet has two chambers of equal power: the Council (soviet) of the Union and the Council of Nationalities (re-elected every four years). It is the legislative body electing:

(2) the Praesidium, consisting of a president, 15 vice-presidents (one from each Union republic), a secretary and 16 members. The Praesidium is the highest organ of government between sessions of the Supreme Soviet. Nikolai Podgorny is now the president of the Praesidium (1965–).

The Council of Ministers coordinates the work of the Ministries. Its present chairman is Alexei Kosygin (1964–).

THE SOVIET COMMUNIST PARTY

This is the only political party. At least every four years its 9,716,000 (1961) members elect a Central Committee of 175 members, and the Central Committee elects a Praesidium of 11 members, with 5 candidate-members. The present First Secretary is Leonid Brezhnev (1964–).

The Komsomol (abbreviation for the "Young Communist League") is a youth organisation for people between the ages of 15 and 28 assisting in the work of the Communist Party. The movement numbers 19,000,000 members (1961).

The Pioneer organisation, which is the junior branch of the Komsomol, has 17,000,000 children between the ages of 10 and 15 as its members (1961).

PUBLIC HOLIDAYS

1st January: New Year's Day.

1st–2nd May: International Labour Day, celebrated by parades and demonstrations.

7th–8th November: October Revolution Day, so called because the revolution took place on 25th October 1917 according to the old calendar, which differs from the Gregorian calendar by 13 days. This holiday, regarded as the National Day, is also celebrated by parades and demonstrations.

5th December: Constitution Day, commemorating the adoption of the Constitution in 1936.

The Soviet Union also marks 23rd February as Soviet Army and Navy Day, 8th March as International Women's Day (commemorating the 2nd International Conference of Socialist Women which took place in Copenhagen in 1910), Lenin's birthday on 22nd April, and other days for the Air Force, Tank Corps, Railwaymen, etc.

THE RUSSIAN ORTHODOX CHURCH

The Eastern Orthodox Church is the second largest body of organised Christians in the world. It consists of a number of independent and self-governing Churches, among them the Churches of Russia and Georgia and the autonomous Churches of Estonia and Latvia which are also independent except that the appointment of their chief bishops requires the sanction of their Mother Church, the Church of Russia.

When in the 11th century Russia adopted Orthodoxy, the religion had already a thousand years' experience behind it, and so the books, the doctrine, the music and paintings, the monastic system and even the architectural style were taken over as they stood in working order. They were regarded as an integrated whole, already as perfect as may be as the name "Orthodox" even then conveyed; it means "that which guards and teaches the right belief" and admits of no alteration. The rigidity and conservatism of the Russian Church was enhanced by centuries of threat from enemies of other faiths. The only change was the translation of the Greek texts into old Slavonic, and in general language has never been a problem. As the Russian Church spread,

1. Cupola; 2. drum; 3. kokoshniki; 4. tent roof; 5. ribs of tent roof; 6. arcades; 7.–8. pilasters; 9. pilasters with panelled brickwork; 10. basement; 11. gallery arches; 12. rampant arches; 13. chetverik; 14. octagonal pridela; 15. octagonal bell-tower; 16. lunettes; 17. cornice.

so the Arabian and Tartar peoples had suitable translations made for them and the peoples of the north and right across Siberia were provided for in their turn.

As is to be expected, different parts of the country and different times in the history of the Soviet Union have produced variations of the form of ecclesiastical architecture, but it is still safe to say that most Russian churches are built on a rectangular plan and have five domes, with the largest in the middle. If the church is in a good state of preservation the domes may be gilded, painted silver or some bright colour, and surmounted by a Greek cross. The bell-tower, which has no clock, is generally a separate structure standing nearby.

Inside the church the sanctuary is separated from the main body of the building by the Iconostasis, a screen with sacred pictures (icons) painted on it. The icons may be richly framed and decorated, and have a lamp burning before them. Slender wax candles, which are on sale in the church, are also placed before them by the faithful. Of the three doors leading through the Iconostasis, the central one, known as the Holy Door, is used by priests only. The language used during the services is Church Slavonic.

There are no seats in the church and although the services are long the congregation remains standing. The very stance is an act of worship. If, as a visitor, you get tired feet you will not be the first to complain. In 1656 the Archdeacon of Aleppo wrote pathetically, "As for the Muscovites their feet must surely be of iron". The singing, which is always unaccompanied but in which the congregation readily joins, is lead by the choir, dressed in ordinary clothes and usually standing out of sight.

The head of the church is the Patriarch of Moscow and All Russia, and the bishops of Moscow, Leningrad, Kiyev, Minsk and Novosibirsk bear the title of Metropolitan.

Although the Russian Orthodox Church is quite separate from the Soviet State, two government councils have been set up to maintain relations between the state and the religious bodies. These are the Council of the Russian Orthodox Church and the Council of Religious Cults, both of which have their headquarters in Moscow.

The following are among the more usual names of churches in Russia (Церковь (Tserkov') or Храм (Khram) means Church; Собор (Sobor) means Cathedral):

Church of:
- the Annunciation—Благовещенская (Blagoveshchenskaya)
- the Epiphany—Богоявленская (Bogoyavlenskaya)
- the Ascension—Вознесенская (Voznesenskaya)
- the Resurrection—Воскресенская (Voskresenskaya)
- the Apparition of the Virgin—Знаменская (Znamenskaya)
- the Immaculate Conception—Зачатиевская (Zachatiyevskaya)
- the Elevation of the Cross—Крестовоздвиженская (Krestovozdvizhenskaya)
- the Protection and Intercession of the Virgin—Покровская (Pokrovskaya)
- the Transfiguration—Преображенская (Preobrazhenskaya)
- the Assumption—Успенская (Uspenskaya)
- the Holy Trinity—Троицкая (Troyitskaya)
- John the Baptist—Иоанна Предтечи (Ioanna Predtechi)

BELORUSSIA

("*White Russia*"; *Belorussian: Belarus*)

This republic of the Soviet Union is situated in the west of the European part of the country and shares its borders with Poland. It is 207,600 sq.km (81,000 sq.miles) in area, and its population numbers 8,455,000 (1964), of which a quarter live in the towns. The people are a mixture of Belorussians (80%), Russians (9%), Poles (7%), Jews (2%) and others (2%).

The Belorussians are closely related to the Great Russians and the Ukrainians, and they trace their origin from the East Slav tribes, the Krivichi, Dregovichi and others. The language spoken is Belorussian, which is closely akin to Russian and Ukrainian. The inhabitants of the major cities speak mostly Russian.

Until the 12th century the area was under the authority of the Kiyevan state; later the new principalities of Turov-Pinsk, Smolensk and Volynia emerged, and these were incorporated in the 13th and 14th centuries into the Grand Duchy of Lithuania. Russian was the official language spoken until Lithuania's union with Poland in 1569. The whole of Belorussia was taken over by Russia after the Polish partitions of 1772–95.

The first demands for autonomy occurred at the beginning of the 20th century when the revolutionary Hromada ("community") Party (later called the Socialist Hromada Party) was formed. This, however, gained little popular support. Strong Polish and Zionist movements were also active at that time. In 1918, during the German occupation, an independent Belorussian Republic was proclaimed; in 1920 the country was temporarily occupied by the Poles who later partly withdrew, while remaining in possession of the western part. In 1921 the Soviet Belorussian Republic was formed, and it joined the Soviet Union in 1922. The size of the republic was increased in 1924–26 by the addition of adjacent territory to the east, and, in 1939, by the inclusion of Western Belorussia. It suffered a great deal during the First and Second World Wars, especially the latter.

Approximately 25 per cent of the area of Belorussia is covered with forests and about 10 per cent with marshes. The climate is moderate continental.

Belorussia's agricultural products are chiefly grain, potatoes and dairy products. There is pig-breeding too and Belorussia is also the most important flax-growing area in the Soviet Union.

The country's main industries are food production and light industry, wood-processing and engineering. The country also has large resources of peat (about 5,000,000,000 tons), which constitute the main source of fuel for its many power stations. Other mineral resources include lignite, potassium and rock salt.

GEORGIA

(*Russian: Gruzia; Georgian: Sakartvelo*)

This republic, situated in central and western Transcaucasia, shares its southern borders with Turkey. It is 72,000 sq.km (26,900 sq.miles) in area, and its population numbers 4,415,000 (1964), 42 per cent of which lives in the towns. The people are mostly Georgians (63%), but other nationalities include Armenians (11%), Russians (11%), Azerbaidzhanis (4%), Ossetians (3·5%), Abkhazians (2%) and others (5·5%).

The Georgian people are far from being homogeneous, although they speak more or less the same language; some of the various groups of people still preserve definite features peculiar to them in their speech and habits, and some of them, such as the Mingrelians, still use their historical names.

Georgia is one of the oldest countries in the U.S.S.R. A Georgian kingdom of Iberia was known to exist as early as the 3rd century B.C. Christianity came in 318 and since 337 it has been the official religion of the country. The natural wealth of the area and its strategic position drew the attention of various invaders: it suffered conquest and domination by Romans, Byzantines, Persians, Arabs, Mongols, Seljouk Turks, the Ottoman Empire and finally the Persians again. There were times when the country was united and when it included, together with vassal territories, the whole of Trans-caucasia and neighbouring areas. At the end of the 18th century Western Georgia was under Turkish domination and Eastern Georgia under Persian rule. The king of Eastern Georgia sought Russian protection, and then in 1800 his successor ceded his country to Russia, being helpless against the Persian threat.

In 1921 a Soviet republic was established in Georgia, but from 1922 to 1936 it was a part of the Transcaucasian Soviet Federal Republic and only after that did it come to be called the Georgian Soviet Socialist Republic.

The present republic consists of Georgia proper, the Adzhar Autonomous Republic (the population of which is mainly Moslem), the Abkhazian Autonomous Republic and the South Ossetian Autonomous Region.

Climatically the country can be divided into two zones:

(1) Western Georgia (the Abkhazian and Adzhar Autonomous Republics, Imeretia and Mingrelia) has a Mediterranean climate with subtropical vegetation.

(2) Eastern Georgia (South Ossetian Autonomous Region and Kakhetia) has a dry continental climate.

Georgia has the best manganese in the world, and its other mineral resources are coal, iron ore, oil, natural gas and stone. The country's industry includes engineering, metallurgy, oil extraction and refining, manganese- and coal-mining, light food industries. Agriculture is mainly concerned with tobacco, tea, maize, wheat, citrus and other fruit, vines, silk, sheep-, pig- and poultry-breeding.

Georgia's principal towns are Tbilisi (capital), Batumi, Sukhumi, Kutaisi and Poti.

A Note on Georgian Churches

The acceptance of Christianity from Byzantium led to the Georgian Orthodox Church's adoption of Byzantine forms of church architecture. By the 10th–12th centuries a more complex type of church, with three to five elongated aisles and a decorated façade, had evolved. Later still the characteristic Georgian tower developed, drum-shaped and crowned by a many-faceted conical dome. The height of the cone sometimes equalled the width of the drum, but the more recently constructed churches tend to have taller cones.

The interior of the churches has very simple frescoes in imitation of Byzantine style, and there is usually little statuary, although there may be some very attractive decorative stone work (patterned reliefs and borders).

The head of the Georgian Orthodox Church is the Katolikos Patriarch.

Useful Expressions in Georgian

hello	gamardzhobut	yes	ki
how do you do	rogor brdzandebit	no	ara
I am a tourist	me tooristivar	good	kargyet
please	getakhvat	I don't understand	ar mesmis kartuli
thank you	madlobt	good-bye	nakhvamdis

MOLDAVIA

(*Moldavian: Moldova*)

This rebublic of the Soviet Union is situated to the north-west of the Black Sea, on the Rumanian frontier. It is 33,700 sq.km (13,000 sq.miles) in area, and its population numbers 3,242,000, 22 per cent of which lives in the towns. The people are mostly Moldavians, but other nationalities include Ukrainians (15%), Russians (10%), Jews and Gagauz (3·3% each) and others (4·4%). With 85 people per square kilometre, the country has the densest population in the Soviet Union.

The Moldavians, once called the Volokhs by the Russians, speak a Romance language very similar to Rumanian, but use the Cyrillic alphabet. As much as 40 per cent of the language consists of words of Ukrainian origin.

The country has been inhabited since prehistoric times. It is supposed that the Moldavians are descendants of the ancient Thracians, and the Greeks, Romans and Turks had colonies in the area and influenced the country for a considerable time. The Moldavian principality was formed in the 14th century, but from the 16th century the country was under Turkish rule. After the Russo-Turkish war of 1806–12 Moldavia was joined to Russia.

The country is divided in two by the River Dniester, and the territory on the right bank of the river up to the border (formed by the River Prut) came to be known as Bessarabia. From 1918 until 1940 this area was under Rumanian rule and a small autonomous Moldavian republic was created in 1921 within the Ukraine on the left bank of the River Dniester. The Soviet Union never accepted the annexation of Bessarabia and in 1940 she demanded that the Rumanian army leave Bessarabia within four days. Subsequently the Union Republic of Moldavia was formed, comprising both parts of the country.

Moldavia's soil is fertile and the climate very mild, so the country is mainly agricultural and grows wheat, maize, sunflowers, etc.; in viniculture it ranks second in importance in the U.S.S.R.

The country's food and light industries are well developed; its mineral resources are only lignite and stone. The main towns are Kishinev (capital), Beltsy, Tiraspol' and Bendery.

Useful Expressions in Moldavian

hello	norok	good	beene
I am a tourist	ayoo sint tourist	bad	rayoo
please	poftim	I don't understand	noo intseleg
thank you	mooltsoomesk	please fetch an interpreter for me	kemats ve rog oon interpret
yes	da	good-bye	la revedere
no	noo		

UKRAINE

(*Ukrainian: Ukraynia*)

This republic is situated in the south-west of the European part of the U.S.S.R., and shares its western frontier with Rumania, Hungary, Czechoslovakia and Poland. After that of the Russian Federation, its population of 44,636,000 (1964) is the second largest in the U.S.S.R., and in size it is the third largest republic (after the Russian Federation and Kazakhstan), covering an area of 601,000 sq.km (232,100 sq.miles). 46 per cent of the population is urban; the majority are Ukrainians (76%), then come Russians (18%), Jews (2%) and others (4%). By nationality the Ukrainians are Eastern Slavs, closely related to the Russians and the Belorussians.

Since the Kievan period of Ukrainian history distinctive features have developed in the people's speech, and Ukrainian is now considered to be a separate language, although Russian is usually spoken in all the big cities except Lvov.

The Ukraine was the cradle of the Kiev State. It was in Kiev that Christianity was first adopted when Prince Vladimir had his subjects baptized in the river Dnieper in 988. After the Tartar invasion and the decline of the Kiev State (13th–14th century), the Ukraine changed hands several times, being held by Russia and Poland, and devastated—sometimes totally and sometimes in part—by the Crimean Tartars. In the middle of the 17th century the Cossacks (the most militant members of the Ukrainian population at the time) led by Hetman (Cossack military leader) Bogdan Khmelnitskii won independence from Poland and established a state of their own, which occupied the central part of the present-day Ukraine. Then, as the new state could not possibly stand alone, it chose to unite with Muscovy, and the agreement was signed in 1654.

Nationalism and demands for the autonomy of the Ukraine were very strong at the beginning of the 20th century. During the Civil War of 1918–22 the Ukraine was fought over by Germans, White Russians, Red Russians and various separatist groups.

The Ukrainian Soviet Republic was first proclaimed in December, 1917, and in 1922 it was one of the original four republics to form the U.S.S.R. In 1939 the western part of the Ukraine, together with L'vov, until that time under Polish rule, was returned to the republic, followed in 1945 by Transcarpathia which had belonged to Hungary and Czechoslovakia, and in 1954 by Crimea, which had belonged to the Russian Federation.

The Ukraine can be divided into three soil and vegetation zones: (1) Mixed forests on the Belorussian boundary in the north, (2) wooded steppe with oak and beech forests, and (3) steppe. The steppe zones are notable for their predominantly fertile black earth. In the mountain regions of Carpathia and the Crimea there is typical mountain vegetation. The moderately continental climate is much warmer than that of central Russia, and the southern coast of the Crimea has a Mediterranean climate.

The area is highly developed both industrially and agriculturally. Its main industries include engineering, metallurgy, coal-mining, chemicals and the most important sugar industry of the U.S.S.R. The country grows chiefly wheat, barley, rye, oats, sugarbeet and sunflowers, and has many orchards. Cattle, pigs and poultry are also bred. The Ukraine is very rich in natural deposits—coal, iron ore, natural gas, manganese, oil, mercury and other minerals.

The major cities are Kiev (capital), Kharkov, L'vov, Odessa, Donetsk, Dnepropetrovsk and Lugansk.

WHAT TO TAKE

It is worth every tourist's while to consider packing certain items which they will not find readily available in Russia, for instance, stain remover, air freshener, adhesive tape, spare radio batteries, films, and ballpoint refills. These are mainly the products of various firms which have no trade connections with the Soviet Union. Tourists should also remember any medicine to which they are accustomed, e.g. analgetics, indigestion tablets, laxatives, etc.

Chewing gum is not on sale in the U.S.S.R., nor are familiar brands of sweets, so if you enjoy these be sure to bring a small stock, a part of which will be gladly accepted by your new Russian friends. You may also be thankful for a tin of instant coffee and a jar of marmalade.

Along with the above mentioned items, ladies should bring with them a supply of cosmetics and tissues.

Children will probably ask you if you have any coins, match-boxes, stamps or badges to exchange with them.

Smokers are advised to bring a sufficient quantity of their favourite brand of cigarettes or tobacco with them if they do not want to switch to a Russian variety. If you use a lighter do not forget extra flints and some lighter fuel.

For the Car

Motorists should bring a complete set of tools, a towing cable, a pressure gauge, a pump, a spare wheel, a repair outfit if you use tubeless tyres, a good jack and a tyre lever or two, a petrol-can, a spare fan-belt, spare windscreen wiper blades and sparking plugs. It is also advisable to have a set of lamp bulbs and fuses, a set of contact-breaker points for the ignition distributor, a spare condenser, a box of tyre valve interiors and a roll of insulating tape. It would be wise also to have a catalogue of numbered spare parts together with the address of a reliable firm to which you can cable for parts to be sent to you in case of emergency. We should also recommend a canvas bucket for car-washing.

CLIMATE AND CLOTHING

The climate in the part of Russia which is visited by motorists is moderately continental, but graduates to subtropical on the southern shore of the Crimea and in parts of Transcaucasia.

Moscow's temperature averages 18·5°C (65°F) in July. The best weather is between May and September, but thunderstorms are likely during very hot spells. The autumn may be cold and wet, or there may be an "Indian Summer", but this is without fail the "velvet season" in the Crimea and Caucasus. Moscow's winter begins in mid-November, and snow and frosts are likely to last until the thaw at the beginning of April. Leningrad, as it is on the coast, has a milder, wetter climate than Moscow, and Kiev, being further south, is generally warmer.

Other average July temperatures are as follows:

	Centigrade	*Fahrenheit*
Kharkov	20·6°	69°
Kiev	19·3°	67°
Leningrad	17·5°	64°
Lvov	18·7°	66°
Minsk	17·5°	64°
Odessa	22·1°	72°
Sochi	23·0°	74°
Tbilisi	24·1°	75°
Yalta	24·2°	75°

The water at the edge of the Black Sea: 27–29°C; 81–84°F.

In summer light clothing will be sufficient, but tourists should bring at least one warm outfit. A plastic mackintosh and overboots or galoshes will probably also be useful. Evening dress will not be necessary, nor any formal dress or suit for visiting restaurants or theatres in the evening. It is considered very indecent to wear shorts or even a low-cut dress in towns, and these would prevent admittance to any museum or café. Ladies *may* wear slacks, but they are frowned upon. It is best to be conservatively dressed, and to avoid highly pictorial shirts.

MONEY

The Russian rouble is divided into 100 kopeks. There are notes for 1, 3, 5, 10, 25, 50 and 100 roubles, copper coins for 1, 2, 3 and 5 kopeks and nickel coins for 10, 15, 20 and 50 kopeks and 1 rouble. (2-kopeks is a very useful coin to save for use in telephone booths.)

On entering the country tourists have to declare the amount of foreign currency they bring in. They should be careful to save the certificate they are given, as it must be shown on leaving the Soviet Union.

No ordinary Russian shop or restaurant will accept foreign currency, with the exception of a few special "foreign currency counters" in big hotels and at some airports. Money and travellers' cheques must be changed at the bank or in the Intourist hotels where there is a special cashier to deal with it. They will not, however, accept the currencies of other Communist countries.

RATES OF EXCHANGE
(as at 1st May 1965)

Australian pounds (per unit)	2·00 roubles
Austrian schillings (per 100)	3·49 roubles
Belgian francs (per 100)	1·81 roubles
British pounds sterling (per unit)	2·51 roubles
Canadian dollars (per unit)	0·83 roubles
Danish kroner (per 100)	13·01 roubles
Dutch guilder (per 100)	25·01 roubles
Finnish markkas (per 1000)	28·13 roubles
Federal German marks (per 100)	22·64 roubles
Italian lire (per 1000)	1·44 roubles
Japanese yen (per 1000)	2·51 roubles
Mexican pesos (per 100)	7·22 roubles
New Zealand pounds (per unit)	2·50 roubles
Norwegian kroner (per 100)	12·58 roubles
Pakistani rupees (per 100)	18·89 roubles
Swedish kronor (per 100)	17·52 roubles

Swiss francs (per 100)	20·72 roubles
Turkish liras (per 100)	10·00 roubles
U.S. dollars (per unit)	0·90 roubles
Yugoslav dinars (per 1000)	1·20 roubles

SOVIET TRAVEL SERVICES

The Government Tourist Board was inaugurated by the U.S.S.R. Council of Ministers in 1964 and soon afterwards Local Tourist Boards were set up in the principal republics of the Soviet Union. Their task is to develop the tourist industry by opening up new centres, extending facilities and by advertising. They provide information about the U.S.S.R. and about passport, visa and customs regulations.

Their Moscow address is: Marx Prospect 16; tel: 21-61-52

The three Soviet travel agencies are the Tourist Council of the Trade Unions, Sputnik and Intourist. The first organises visits made by Trade Union delegations.

Sputnik is the International Youth Tourist Bureau which specialises in young people's group tours of the Soviet Union. Their most favourable rates are offered to groups of more than 25 persons, but any group of ten or more may purchase a tour. They run twenty or more different tours lasting from 4 to 22 days, provide guides, interpreters, full board, accommodation and transport. They do not deal with individual motorists.

Their address is: Moscow, Lebyazhy Pereulok 4; tel: 23-95-12; cables: Tourbureaumol, Moscow.

Intourist is the largest travel agency in the Soviet Union and deals in all types of foreign travel, both that of visitors to the Soviet Union and that of Soviet citizens going abroad. In the Soviet Union the company owns hotels and restaurants and has offices or representatives in most of the larger towns visited by tourists.

Their Moscow address is: Marx Prospect 16; tel: 92-27-68; cables: Intourist, Moscow. Intourist's offices overseas are:

Austria:	10 Park Ring, Wien 1; 52-15-01
Denmark:	5 Jerbandage, Copenhagen C; Bjen 25-27
France:	10 Rue Desèze, Paris 9e.; Richelieu 47-40
Great Britain:	314 Regent St., London W.1; Museum 1969
Sweden:	21 Sergelgatan, Stockholm C; 21-59-34
U.S.A.:	355 Lexington Ave., New York 16, N.Y.; Murray Hill 2-7607
West-Berlin:	36-B Württembergische Strasse, Wilmersdorf; 91-56-57

Apart from the above, Intourist has agency contracts with more than 400 foreign travel firms throughout the world.

ACCOMMODATION

All accommodation and other services for foreign tourists visiting the Soviet Union are provided through Intourist, which has a wide network of branch offices both in Russia and abroad.

Motorist's tours are usually purchased in advance and may be divided into the following categories:

1. *First Class*—costing 17·10 roubles per person per day and including a hotel room with bath and telephone, three meals a day as per the First Class menu but not including wines and spirits, one half-day excursion daily in one's own car with a guide-interpreter (the full-time services of a guide-interpreter may be provided if application for such service has been made to Intourist at least two weeks before the tourist's arrival in the Soviet Union), free parking near the hotel or in an attended car-park and two pieces of luggage carried free of charge (the cost for each additional piece is 20 kopeks—except at railway stations where it is 30 kopeks).

Hotels have a laundry, a barber's and a hairdresser's shop, and facilities for the repair of shoes and clothing. Charges are made according to the standard price lists; hotel residents need not queue at the hairdresser's in their own hotel. Tipping is officially disapproved of in the Soviet Union, and Intourist employees will certainly not accept gratuities. 10 kopeks is sufficient for taxi drivers, doormen and cloakroom attendants. A waiter might expect 5–7 per cent of the bill (where service is not already charged for). There is no need to tip at filling or motor repair stations.

Because of the increasing number of tourists coming to Russia there is still a lack of hotel accommodation. Nevertheless, Intourist will provide you with a place, but you can hardly expect a choice of hotels, or to be able to change your room. In most large towns that motorists are permitted to visit there is an Intourist hotel; the other hotels belong to the town, and they are often chartered by Intourist to cope with the overflow.

When you arrive the receptionist will ask for your passport. The most important place in the hotel for you is the Service Bureau (or the Administrator's Office) where you will be able to have all sorts of problems solved, from ordering your breakfast (if you do not speak Russian) to getting tickets for theatres.

The hotel staff are, almost without exception, honest, and there is rarely any complaint of theft.

2. *Tourist Class*—costing 11·70 roubles per person per day and including the same services as are provided for First Class except that the hotel rooms are smaller and without a private bath or shower, and the meals must be chosen from the Tourist Class menu.

3. *Business Tour*—costing 7·20 roubles per person per day. This tour is for business men arriving in their own cars. The services provided are the same as for First Class except that excursions are not included.

4. *Camping*—costing 1·35 roubles per day per person which covers the use of camping sites and the facilities provided there, and also one excursion in one's own car with a guide-interpreter for each two days of stay in the Soviet Union.

Motorists are not allowed to camp wherever they like. Some towns have a motel and some a camping site, and others have both. The *camping sites* are usually very pleasant, and far less crowded than their counterparts in the West. They have parking areas, space to pitch tents, water supply and outdoor fire-places. The *motels* differ greatly one from another, some providing accommodation in a small hotel and others having separate chalets. Food and service are always available at the motels.

At the camping sites one can hire all sorts of equipment from tents to tea-spoons, as on the following list:

List of Camping Equipment Available for Hire at the Camping Sites

			COST
Folding camp bed	раскла́душка	raskla′dushka	10 kopeks
Inflatable mattress	матра́ц	matrats′	5 kopeks
Pillow	поду́шка	padush′ka	3 kopeks
Woollen blanket	шерстяно́е одея́ло	sherstyano′ye udeya′la	10 kopeks
Cotton blanket	ба́йковое одея́ло	bay′kovoye udeya′la	5 kopeks
Sheet	простыня́	prostinya′	10 kopeks
Towel	полоте́нце	palatyen′tse	5 kopeks
Pillow case	на́волочка	na′vlochka	5 kopeks
Tent (for 2)	пала́тка 2-ме́стная	palat′ka nadvayikh′	10 kopeks
Tent (for 4)	пала́тка 4-ме́стная	palat′ka nachetyr′ yokh	20 kopeks
Deck chair	шезло́нг	shezlong′	4 kopeks
Folding table and chairs	сто́лик со сту́льями	stol′ik sostool′yami	10 kopeks
Sleeping bag	спа́льный мешо́к	spal′nyi meshok′	20 kopeks
Beach umbrella	пля́жный зонт	plyazh′nyi zont	5 kopeks
Saucepan (any size)	кастрю́ля	kastrool′ya	3 kopeks
Frying pan	сковоро́дка	skavarod′ka	1 kopek
Thermos flask	те́рмос	ter′mos	3 kopeks
Plate	таре́лка	taryel′ka	1 kopek
Glass or mug	стака́н, кру́жка	stakan′, kroozh′ka	1 kopek
Spoon, fork or knife	ло́жка, вилка, нож	lozh′ka, veel′ka, nozh	1 kopek
Kettle	ча́йник	chai′nik	3 kopeks
Milk-can	бидо́н	bidon′	3 kopeks
Electric hotplate and electricity	электропли́тка	elek′tropleet′ka	10 kopeks
Bowl	та́зик	ta′zik	1 kopek

Campers would be well advised to bring a small store of food with them to supplement what they will be able to buy here (instant coffee and packet soups, for example). Detergent would also be useful.

WEIGHTS AND MEASURES

The Soviet Union uses the metric system of measurement. Here are some useful equivalents:

1 pint	0·6 litre
1 litre	$1\frac{3}{4}$ pints
1 kilogram	2 lb 2 oz
1 kilometre	$\frac{5}{8}$ mile
1 metre	$39\frac{1}{4}$ inches
1 hectare	$2\frac{1}{2}$ acres

Gallons	*Litres*
1	4·5
2	9·0
3	13·6
4	18·2
5	22·7
6	27·3
7	31·8
8	36·4
9	40·9
10	45·5
11	50·0
12	54·6

Miles	*Kilometres*
1	1·6
2	3·2
3	4·8
4	6·4
5	8·0
10	16·0
20	32·2
30	48·2
40	64·4
50	80·5
60	96·6
70	112·7
80	128·7
90	144·8
100	160·9

Temperatures are measured in Centigrade. To convert Centigrade to Fahrenheit—multiply by 9, divide by 5 and add 32. To convert Fahrenheit to Centigrade—subtract 32, multiply by 5 and divide by 9.

Air Pressure for motor tyres is measured in kilograms per sq.cm. instead of lb per sq.inch.

14 lb — 1·00 kg	32 lb — 2·25 kg
18 lb — 1·26 kg	36 lb — 2·53 kg
22 lb — 1·54 kg	40 lb — 2·80 kg
28 lb — 1·96 kg	

BUYING FOOD SUPPLIES

How much does this cost?	Ско́лько э́то сто́ит? Skol′ko eta sto′yit?
Write it down, please	Напиши́те пожа́луйста napishee′tye pajal′sta
Give me one kilogram	Да́йте мне оди́н килогра́мм dai′tye mnye udeen′ kilogram′

Bread	хлеб	khlyeb	Tea	чай	chai
Water	вода́	vada′	Coffee	ко́фе	ko′fye
Boiled water	кипято́к	kipyatok′	Apples	я́блоки	yab′loki
			Pears	гру́ши	groo′shi
Milk	молоко́	malako′	Grapes	виногра́д	vinograd′
Butter	ма́сло	mas′lo	Lemon	лимо́н	limon′
Cheese	сыр	syr	Strawberries	клубни́ка	klubni′ka
Eggs	я́йца	yai′tsa	Cucumbers	огурцы́	agurtsy′
Yoghurt	кефи́р	kifir′	Tomatoes	помидо́ры	pamido′ri
Sour cream	смета́на	smeta′na	Ice-cream	моро́женое	maro′zhe-noye
Salt	соль	sol′			
Sugar	са́хар	sakh′ar	Lemonade, fizzy	лимона́д	limonad′
Cold sausage	колбаса́	kolbasa′			
			Wine	вино́	vino′
Ham	ветчина́	vecheena′	Beer	пи́во	pee′vo
Sweets	конфе́ты	kanfye′ti	Soft fruit	я́годы	ya′godi
Chocolate	шокола́д	shokolad′	Fruit	фру́кты	frook′ty

RESTAURANTS

Cafés usually close at 10·00 or 11·00 p.m., and restaurants at 11·00 or 11·30 p.m., although diners are not admitted during the half-hour before closing time. The best restaurants usually accept Intourist meal coupons. Intourist restaurants and a few others have their menus printed in several languages. The fact that there is a price beside some of the dishes indicates that they, and only they, are available.

Recommended Russian Food

ikra′—black caviar (remember to ask for toast [*tost*] and butter [*mas′lo*]
kras′naya ikra′—red caviar (excellent with sour cream, *smeta′na*)
salat′ iz sve′zhikh agoortsov′ so smeta′noi—cucumber salad with sour cream

borshch—beetroot soup
shchi—cabbage soup
rasol'nik—hot soup, usually of pickled vegetables
akrosh'ka—cold soup with a *kvass* base (very refreshing)
(Portions of soup are large, but one may ask for a half-portion)
syom'ga s limo'nom—smoked salmon with lemon
beef Stroga'nov—beef stewed in *smeta'na* with fried potatoes
kutlye'ty po Pajar'ski—good chicken cutlets
kutlye'ta po Ki'yevski—fried rolled breast of chicken (beware of the melted butter inside which is liable to squirt)
pirozh'ki—savory fried rolls with various fillings
bli'ny—small pancakes, eaten with caviar, fish, melted butter, *smeta'na*
aladi'—crumpets, eaten with jam as well as the other things listed for *bli'ny*
pyelmeni'—meat dumplings
stakan' kise'lya—dessert of thickened cranberry juice
gooryev'skaya ka'sha—semolina with various dried fruits
maro'zhnoye—ice-cream, eaten all the year round. Try "assorti" in a special ice-cream parlour.

Wines and Spirits

All alcoholic drinks must be ordered in grammes or by the bottle.

Small glass	100 g
Large glass	200 g
Small bottle (2/3 regular size)	500 g/½ litre
Normal bottle	750 g/¾ litre

Vodka. According to regulations in Russia not more than 100 gr. of *plain* vodka can be served per person per meal. But if you enjoy strong drinks we may suggest you do as the Russians do, namely, ask for a special variety—*Starka*. There are other kinds too, including *Tminaya* (caraway flavour), Lemon vodka ("hunters' vodka"), *Khorilka s pertsem* (Ukrainian vodka with peppers in it), and one of the best is *Yubileinaya* ("Jubilee").

Wine. The best wine comes from the Crimea and the Caucasus. Some names are:

White:	
Dry	*Tsinandali* No. 1
Medium Dry	*Tvishi* No. 19 or *Tetra* No. 26
Red:	
Dry	*Mookoozani* No. 3
Medium Dry	*Hvanchkara* No. 20 (Stalin's favourite) *Oosoohoolaoori* No. 21 or *Kinsmaraooli* No. 22

Champagne:

Dry	*Sookho'ye*
Medium Dry	*Palusookho'ye*
Sweet	*Slad'koye*
Red (not pink) medium dry	*Tsimlyan'skoye*

There are Russian equivalents to Port (*portvein*), Madeira (*madera*) and Vermouth (*vermoot*). In general there is a wide choice of wine from Eastern Europe.

BRANDY AND LIQUEURS. The best brandy comes from Armenia (*armyan'skii kanyak'*). Most liqueurs have French names, but the resemblance to the originals may be slight.

MINERAL WATER. The most common mineral waters are *Narzan* and the slightly salty *Barzhomi*. Fresh water is seldom served at table.

FIZZY FRUIT DRINKS. These include "Limonad" and various other -ades, orange, cherry, apple and pear.

Outside in the street you may buy a glass of *kvass* (fermented bread-water), or plain soda water.

HUNTING AND FISHING

Intourist organises hunting trips for foreign visitors in the Crimean State Hunting Preserve near Yalta, which abounds in deer and roe. The season lasts from September to January.

The cost is 20·25 roubles per day, and this includes meals and transport to and from the hunting reserve, the services of an interpreter at the reserve and of an Intourist representative who will meet tourists at all points of arrival and departure. Experienced huntsmen accompany the hunters; rifles and ammunition are provided if required, and the tourist receives his trophies after the hunt.

Among the fish which can be caught in the rivers of the central part of Russia are perch, pike, carp, roach, "ruff" and "crucian", and in the Volga, in addition to these, there are *zander* (or "pike-perch"). In the Black Sea, particulary in the Odessa region, bullhead, sea perch, mackerel and *stavrida* can be found.

ENTERTAINMENT

Visitors to Russia should apply to the Service Bureau of their hotel for tickets for shows, and the sooner this is done the greater the chance of obtaining tickets. The majority of theatre performances begin at 6·30 p.m., the Circus and concerts at 7·00 p.m., and most performances do not end later than 11·00 p.m. On Sundays there are matinées at 11·00 a.m. Tourists may only know whether or not they have tickets on the day of the performance.

Tickets are priced between 1 and 3 roubles. Tickets can be bought, as well as from Intourist, from "theatre agents" and small booking-office kiosks just inside the Metro stations, or in the street. Tickets bought from these kiosks can be obtained a few days in advance, but it is hard to get any for a "hit" entertainment.

Like most tourists, you will want to see a ballet in Moscow or Leningrad, but do not be disappointed to learn that the ballet season does not include the summer months (end of May to the beginning of September). But during the summer leading dancers often perform separately throughout the country, and sometimes even at open-air shows. Synopses of the best-known operas and ballets are printed in English, and are obtainable at the Intourist Service Bureaux.

The new music and drama festivals are proving immensely popular and we recommend that if possible you arrange your visit to coincide with one of them. "Moscow Stars" takes place in Moscow (5th–13th May) and "White Nights" in Leningrad (21st–29th June). Ask Intourist for a festival programme and book your tickets in advance to avoid disappointment.

Other interesting performances are given at the Puppet Theatre, the various circuses and the "Romany" Gypsy Theatre—the only one of its kind in the world where most of the plays include gypsy dances and songs. Symphony concerts are given all the year round and feature world famous soloists.

Concerts and circus performances usually have one interval, while plays and operas have two or three. These last up to twenty minutes each, and most theatres have a large foyer where the audiences promenade anti-clockwise. Often theatres have an exhibition of theatrical pictures, stage models, etc., and always a buffet and a bookstall. Smoking is allowed only in specified places, and in the entrance foyer. Before curtain-up there is a series of three warning bells; the doors of the stalls are firmly shut after the last bell, but upstairs doors are left open for latecomers.

Outdoor clothing is not allowed in the auditorium. If you have a coat to leave, it is wise to pay the cloakroom attendant 30 kopeks at the same time for a pair of binoculars, no matter how close to the stage your seat. After the performance you will then be able to go to the front of the slow-moving queue to collect your possessions.

Films in Russia are—not surprisingly—practically always in Russian. Sometimes Moscow's "Metropole" Cinema shows foreign films in the original language. You can buy your own ticket, or ask Intourist to help you. In Moscow there is a "Classic" cinema where only old films, including silent ones, are shown. There is circorama too. Non-stop film showing does not exist in Russia, and each ticket entitles you to one film and its attendant newsreel only; the auditorium is emptied between showings. Different films may be showing at a single cinema during the course of the day. The highest ticket price is 50 kopeks. It is strictly forbidden to smoke in the auditorium.

Clubs in the Soviet Union belong to various enterprises and organisations, and there are clubs for professionals (artists, writers, etc.). Some of these have restaurants which are not open to the public, although a Russian friend might invite you there. There are no night clubs, bars or pubs.

Parks are open all the year round. In the wintertime they are used for skiing and skating, and in the summer there are facilities for boating (30 kopeks per hour, plus a small deposit for the safe return of the boat), sports grounds, playgrounds with swings and merry-go-rounds, open air concerts and dance areas. There are also various restaurants, cafés and ice-cream stalls. Entrance to all parks is free, and they remain open till 11·00 p.m. Most large Russian cities have their own zoos and botanical gardens.

SHOPPING

In general the shops are always full of people. GUM on Red Square, and TSUM beside the Bolshoi Theatre are among the biggest department stores in Moscow; in Leningrad there is Gostinyi Dvor opposite the Europa Hotel, and in Kiyev the Central Univermag on the corner of Ulitsa Lenina and the main street Khreshchatik. All have special souvenir departments.

In self-service shops you must surrender your own bag in exchange for one supplied by the shop and then repack your purchases after you have paid. Sometimes, in ordinary shops, you pay over the counter, but the usual way is to find out the price of the article you want, pay for it at the cash desk and return to the counter to exchange your receipt for what you have chosen. In GUM, TSUM or in antique or jewellery shops, where you will most likely be shopping, you must hand over the slip of paper on which your assistant has written the price before paying at the cash desk. It is impossible to have things delivered to your hotel (except food from certain shops) and no shops will undertake the postage of presents.

The larger shops have an information desk where foreign languages are spoken and there are a few shops where foreign currency is accepted, including the chain of Beryozka shops and souvenir kiosks throughout the country.

Shops have varying times for opening and closing, but in general they stay open till 7·00 p.m., being closed for lunch from 2.00 to 3.00 p.m. They are closed on Sunday, and early closing day is on Monday. Food shops on the other hand are open every day and may close for lunch between 1·00 p.m. and 2·00 p.m.

Ideas for Presents

Black caviar (19 roubles per kg, sold in small sealed jars, but it will taste better when you get home if you buy a 2-kg tin and ask for a supply of small empty tins to decant it into for presents on your return); balalaika (5–6 roubles, instructions are available); electric samovar (20–30 roubles); fur hat (5–30 roubles); embroidered skull-cap from Uzbekistan (2–15 roubles); Ukrainian hand-embroidered shirt or blouse (15 roubles upwards); toys; gramophone records (12 in. LP—1 rouble); books (comparatively inexpensive); traditional silver- gilt-and-enamel ware (e.g. tiny fork for lemon or butterballs—1 rouble; child's spoon with animal handle—3 roubles); wood, alabaster or pottery ornaments.

If you would like to visit the markets, you should go as early as possible in the day. You will be able to find in the market good quality fresh fruit, which is often lacking in the hotels. Also on sale there are honey, fresh eggs, and dairy products; there may be various items of local handwork as well. The markets close at 5·00 p.m.

PASSPORTS AND OTHER FORMALITIES

In order to enter and leave the Soviet Union a foreign tourist must have a valid national passport and a Soviet entry visa. Soviet visas are issued free of charge usually within a seven-day period from the time of application to the Soviet Embassy or Consulate in the tourist's own country. The border points through which the tourist enters and leaves the Soviet Union must be those indicated in the Soviet visa.

Foreign tourists' arrivals in the Soviet Union are registered when they first hand over their passports at the first Intourist service point indicated on the visa.

In addition to Soviet visas, it is required that the citizens of most Western European countries obtain visas for the Communist countries through which they will drive on their way to and from the Soviet Union: East Germany, Poland, Czechoslovakia, Hungary, Rumania or Bulgaria; East German visas are obtainable on entry to that country.

Besides an International Driving Permit, *motorists* must bring an international automobile registration certificate of the country of departure, stipulated in the 1926 International Automobile Traffic Convention. Tourists' cars can be brought into the Soviet Union and taken out again without payment of duty on condition that the owner gives a written guarantee to take the car out of the country upon departure. This guarantee is to be handed over to the customs authorities at the Soviet border.

It is forbidden to bring the following into the Soviet Union:

(a) arms and ammunition

(b) printed matter, films, photographs, negatives, drawings, etc. "which are hostile to the U.S.S.R. in political or economic respects".
    Printed matter, plants (fruit, seeds, etc.) and animals are liable to inspection by customs authorities.

It is forbidden to take out of the Soviet Union:

(a) arms and ammunition

(b) precious works of art such as paintings, sculptures and rugs. Antiques (including furniture, icons, musical instruments, etc.), may only be taken out of the country with the permission of the Ministry of Culture and on payment of 100 per cent duty on the value of the article.

Items of value (watches, pearls, jewellery, foreign currency) must be declared and registered on entry to the country in order that they may be taken out when you leave. A camera, cine-camera, wireless, typewriter or musical instrument may be included in one's luggage, and it is permitted to purchase an additional camera in the Soviet Union to take out of the country.

INSURANCE

Many foreign insurance companies are unwilling to insure cars touring in the Soviet Union, or if they do so, their premiums are very high. The Soviet insurance organisation, Ingosstrakh (Upravlenie Inostrannogo Strakhovaniya is their full title), will probably offer you more favourable terms. Their address is Moscow K-12, Kuibyshev Street 11/10 (Cables: Moscow, Ingosstrakh).

The premium for the insurance of motor vehicles depends upon the engine's cubic capacity, as well as upon the time the motorist is staying on Soviet territory.

Third Party Liability insurance may be effected according to the following three categories:

I. (a) injury to and/or death of one person	indemnity 10,000 roubles
(b) injury to and/or death of several persons	indemnity 30,000 roubles
(c) damage or destruction of property	indemnity 3,000 roubles
II. (a) injury to and/or death of one person	indemnity 15,000 roubles
(b) injury to and/or death of several persons	indemnity 45,000 roubles
(c) damage or destruction of property	indemnity 4,500 roubles

III. No limitation to the sum of responsibility.

These insurances may be arranged in any currency. The premium is paid in the currency in which insurance is effected and possible claims will be settled accordingly.

The insurance of motor vehicles and Third Party Liability may be effected before the motorist starts out for the U.S.S.R. by sending Ingosstrakh a letter or a cable in which is indicated:—the model of the car, the engine number, the registration number, the value of the car and the currency in which it is to be insured, the period of staying in the U.S.S.R. and the category of limits desired.

Personal accident insurance may also be effected for the whole time of staying in the U.S.S.R., the premium for this insurance depending on the sum insured and the period of staying in the U.S.S.R.

There are representatives of Ingosstrakh at eight entry points to the Soviet Union, Vyborg, Leningrad, Brest, Uzhgorod, Lvov, Chernovtsy, Kishinyev and

Odessa. They will be glad to be of service to the motorist if he has not taken out an insurance policy before his arrival.

Other socialist countries also have facilities for insurance at their border points.

POST, TELEPHONE, etc.

Any post to be forwarded to Moscow should be addressed c/o Intourist, Moscow (or any other large city), U.S.S.R. The more information on the envelope, the better; e.g. John Brown,
from England,
arriving Moscow
2nd July.

Intourist will keep it for you to collect. Usually post from European countries takes 3–10 days, and from the United States and Canada a week or more. The address *must* be legible.

The London *Times*, *The New York Herald Tribune* (*European edition*) and the *New York Times* can be airmailed to the country, arriving one day late. Locally the *Morning Star* only is available, but there are some Soviet periodicals in English and other languages.

Airmail letters abroad cost 16 kopeks and postcards 14 kopeks. Express rate is an extra 18 kopeks, and ordinary mail 6 and 4 kopeks respectively. *Telegrams and Telephone Calls* abroad are priced as follows:

Country	Telegraph: cost per word ordinary rate †	Telephone: cost per 3 min
Austria	14 kopeks	3 roubles
Belgium	16 kopeks	3·29 roubles
Denmark	12 kopeks	2·88 roubles
Finland	14 kopeks	1·00 rouble
France	15 kopeks	4·35 roubles
Federal Germany	13 kopeks	3·32 roubles
Great Britain	16 kopeks	4·28 roubles
Italy	16 kopeks	4·23 roubles
Netherlands	15 kopeks	2·46 roubles
Norway	14 kopeks	3·44 roubles
Sweden	13 kopeks	2·41 roubles
U.S.A. (New York)	23 kopeks	10·80‡ (Sundays—8·10)
U.S.A. (other cities)	30 kopeks	

† Telegrams may be sent LT or ELT at half-price.
‡ Calls may not be made between midnight and 2·30 a.m.

Parcels involve complications. Incoming parcels are not delivered, but you will be notified of their arrival by post. Customs duty must be paid when they are collected (this may be inexplicably high).

To send parcels out of the Soviet Union do not pack the article at all. Buy a standard wooden box at the post office (the largest size available is approximately 45 cm × 25 cm × 25 cm/18″ × 10″ × 10″). The post office assistants will pack it for you. The maximum weight, including packing, is 10 kilograms (22 lb) and this costs 3·05 roubles to England and 4·74 roubles to the United States. Airmail parcels of similar size and weight cost 16·40 roubles to England and 27·00 roubles to the United States.

Printed matter to be sent by book post will also be packed for you. The cost per kilogram (2 lb 2 oz), whatever the destination, is 45 kopeks.

It is forbidden to send the following out of the Soviet Union by post:—caviar or any food in tins, more than 12 gramophone records in a single parcel, pre-revolutionary editions of any book, and also gold, silver or precious stones.

Local Telephones. Most Intourist hotels have automatic telephones in each room. One should usually dial "8" before the town number needed; frequent regular buzzing means "line engaged". With non-automatic telephones you should ask the operator for "gorod" and wait for a continuous buzzing sound before you dial. In Leningrad the Intourist hotels "Astoria" and "Europa" have a direct connecting line, and you should simply say the name of the hotel to the operator. If you cannot manage to say room numbers in Russian, you may use English or French very slowly, number by number. In case of emergency ask the operator for "Service Bureau" or "administrator".

Telephone kiosks: Put a 2-kopek coin in the slot, lift the receiver, wait for a continuous buzzing and then dial.

Long distance calls: Such calls made from a hotel must be ordered through the Service Bureau; they may take an hour to come through. Otherwise one should go to a long distance telephone office ("peregovornyi punkt"); there one might be asked to pay for 3 or 5 minutes' conversation in advance.

In the larger cities telephone numbers consist of a letter followed by numbers. For those who are not familiar with the Russian alphabet it is probably simplest to substitute the appropriate number for the letter. This is how they appear on the telephone dial:

1	2	3	4	5	6	7	8	9	0
А	Б	В	Г	Д	Е	Ж	И	К	Л

It would be wiser, however, when giving Russians your telephone number to write it down with the proper letter.

FOREIGN EMBASSIES IN MOSCOW

Afghanistan	Ulitsa Vorovskogo 42	tel: 94-17-87
Algeria	Krapivinsky Pereulok 1-a	tel: 23-02-98
Argentina	Ulitsa Lunacharskogo 8	tel: 41-78-20
Australia	Kropotkinsky Pereulok 13	tel: 46-31-24

Austria	Starokonyushenny Pereulok 1	tel: 46-32-00
Belgium	Khlebny Pereulok 15	tel: 95-22-72
Brazil	Ulitsa Gertsena 54	tel: 95-25-23
Bulgaria	Leningradsky Prospekt 20	tel: 51-25-85
Burma	Ulitsa Gertsena 41	tel: 95-75-08
Burundi	Uspensky Pereulok 7	tel: 99-72-00
Cambodia	Sobinovsky Pereulok 5A	tel: 95-80-65
Cameroon	Ulitsa Vorovskogo 40	tel: 94-95-49
Canada	Starokonyushenny Pereulok 23	tel: 41-90-34
Central Africa	Vadkorsky Pereulok 7/37	tel: 50-35-18
Ceylon	Ulitsa Shepkina 24	tel: 81-91-26
Chad	Gruzinsky Pereulok 3, Apt. 289	tel: 53-29-14
Chile	Ulitsa Sadovo-Triumfalnaya 4/10	tel: 99-75-74
China	Ulitsa Druzhby 6	tel: 143-15-40
Congo (Brazzaville)	Lopukhinsky Pereulok 5	tel: 46-55-20
Cuba	Pomerantsev Pereulok 6	tel: 46-13-09
Cyprus	Ulitsa Gertsena 51	tel: 23-21-54
Czechoslovakia	Ulitsa Yuliusa Fuchika 12/14	tel: 53-75-07
Consul:	Ulitsa Yuliusa Fuchika 12/14	tel: 53-75-07
	office hours: Mon.–Fri. 9 a.m.–6 p.m.	
	Sat. 9 a.m.–12·30 p.m.	
Denmark	Ostrovsky Pereulok 9	tel: 41-10-30
Ethiopia	Kropotkinskaya Naberezhnaya 35	tel: 46-80-23
Finland	Kropotkinsky Pereulok 15/17	tel: 46-45-40
France	Ulitsa Dimitrova 43	tel: 31-85-06
Germany (East)	Ulitsa Stanislavskogo 10	tel: 94-00-25
Consul:	Ulitsa Stanislavskogo 20	tel: 94-00-25
	office hours: Mon.–Fri. 8 a.m.–5 p.m.	
Germany (West)	Bol'shaya Gruzinskaya Ulitsa 17	tel: 55-00-30
Ghana	Pogodinskaya Ulitsa 12	tel: 46-40-14
Great Britain	Naberezhnaya Morisa Toreza 14	tel: 31-95-55
Greece	Ulitsa Stanislavskogo 4	tel: 29-22-74
Guinea	Ulitsa Alexeya Tolstogo 13	tel: 94-40-02
Hungary	Ulitsa Vorovskogo 21	tel: 95-20-06
Consul:	Ulitsa Pisemskogo 17	tel: 95-26-29
	office hours: Mon.–Sat. 10 a.m.–12 noon	
Iceland	Khlebnyi Pereulok 28	tel: 94-06-03
India	Ulitsa Obukha 6–8	tel: 97-08-20
Indonesia	Novokuznetskaya Ulitsa 12	tel: 31-95-49
Iran	Pokrovsky Boulevard 7	tel: 97-46-19
Iraq	Pereulok Ostrovskogo 8	tel: 46-27-53
Israel	Bol'shaya Ordinka 56	tel: 33-86-13
Italy	Ulitsa Vesnina 5	tel: 41-15-34

Japan	Kalashny Pereulok 12	tel: 94-25-30
Jordan	Sadovskikh Pereulok 3	tel: 99-43-44
Kenya	Ulitsa Bol'shaya Ordinka 70	tel: 33-86-65
Korea (North)	Ulitsa Stanislavskogo 9	tel: 29-60-13
Kuwait	3rd Neopalimovsky Pereulok 13	tel: 45-08-25
Laos	Ulitsa Kachalova 18	tel: 95-64-67
Lebanon	Sadovo-Samotechnaya Ulitsa 14	tel: 95-20-83
Libya	Merzlyakovsky Pereulok 20	tel: 95-27-65
Luxemburg	Khrushchevsky Pereulok 3	tel: 46-17-27
Mali	Novokuznetskaya Ulitsa 11	tel: 31-22-60
Mauritania	Leninsky Pereulok 93, Apt. 17-18	tel: 38-27-56
Mexico	Ulitsa Schukina 4	tel: 46-79-32
Mongolia	Ulitsa Pisemskogo 11	tel: 95-30-61
Morocco	Ulitsa Gor'kogo 60	tel: 51-23-12
Nepal	Vtoroy Neopalimovsky Pereulok 14/7	tel: 41-94-34
Netherlands	Kalashnyi Pereulok 6	tel: 94-19-85
Nigeria	Ulitsa Kachalova 13	tel: 94-25-00
Norway	Ulitsa Vorovskogo 7	tel: 95-25-20
Pakistan	Sadovo-Kudrinskaya Ulitsa 17	tel: 51-78-39
Poland	Ulitsa A. Mitskevicha 1	tel: 99-00-04
Consul:	Ulitsa A. Mitskevicha 1	tel: 99-00-04
	office hours: Mon.–Sat. 10 a.m.–4 p.m.	
Rumania	Mosfilmovskaya Ulitsa 40	tel: 143-04-20
Consul:	Mosfilmovskaya Ulitsa 40	tel: 143-04-27
	office hours: Mon.–Fri. 9 a.m.–2 p.m.	
	3 p.m.–6 p.m.	
	Sat. 9 a.m.–2 p.m.	
Senegal	Ulitsa Donskaya 40	tel: 32-28-65
Somalia	Spasopeskovskaya Ploshchad' 8	tel: 41-86-24
Sudan	Ulitsa Vorovskogo 9	tel: 21-69-50
Sweden	Ulitsa Pisemskogo 15	tel: 23-22-26
Switzerland	Stopani Pereulok 2/5	tel: 95-53-22
Syria	Mansurovsky Pereulok 4	tel: 46-66-03
Tanzania	Pyatnitskaya Ulitsa 33/35	tel: 31-81-46
Thailand	Eropkinsky Pereulok 3	tel: 46-13-61
Tunisia	Ulitsa Kachalova 28	tel: 52-17-69
Turkey	Ulitsa Gertsena 43a	tel: 95-30-62
Uganda	Sadovskikh Pereulok 5	tel: 99-64-07
United Arab Republic	Ulitsa Gertsena 56	tel: 52-05-37
United States of America	Ulitsa Chaikovskogo 19/23	tel: 52-00-11
Uruguay	Ulitsa Zholtovskogo 28	tel: 99-53-04

Vietnam (North)	Bol'shaya Pirogovskaya Ulitsa 13	tel: 45-10-92
Yemen Arab Republic	Prospect Mira 22	tel: 84-49-17
Yugoslavia	Khlebnyi Pereulok 21	tel: 94-79-02

Travel Agency American Express Ploshchad Sverdlova 2, in Hotel Metropole, Room 384 tel: 25-63-84
American House Club—Kropotkinskaya Naberezhnaya 3 tel: 46-05-89

PHOTOGRAPHY

Photographs and cine-films may be taken during your visit, but you must obtain permission from the administration of factories, railway stations and government offices, before taking pictures of them, and permission is needed to photograph people in service uniform.

It is forbidden to take photographs of any military object, seaports, hydro-electric installations, bridges, scientific research institutions, radio, telephone and telegraph stations, and no photographs should be taken from planes or trains.

It is advisable to bring a supply of film with you, which (if it is not colour film) you may have developed before you leave. Photo-studio "Intourist" is at the Metropole Hotel in Moscow. If you use Soviet colour film it would be best to have it developed before you leave.

TRANSPORT

The most popular form of transport in Moscow, Leningrad and Kiyev is the underground 'Metro'. The fare is 5 kopeks for any distance.

Tickets in Moscow for any distance cost:
bus—5 kopeks,
trolleybus—4 kopeks,
tram—3 kopeks.

Some other towns still work on the fare-stage system. In some large towns public transport operates without a conductor and instead there is a money-box for your fare. Public transport services stop at 1·0 a.m.

Taxis have a chequered pattern on their doors, and when free show a green light in the corner of the windscreen. You can catch a taxi in the street, or at a taxi rank, or call for one by telephone. It costs 10 kopeks to hire a taxi and then the charge is 10 kopeks per kilometre; waiting costs 1 rouble per hour. There are also taxi services which ply to and fro along certain routes; these are called "marshrootnoye" taxis and the charge is 10 kopeks for any distance along the route.

Trains. Most "soft" (i.e. first) class sleeping compartments are designed for 4 people. There are also some for 2, but not on all lines. Check whether your train has a restaurant car, otherwise expect a 20–40 min. stop at large towns when you can visit the restaurant at the station. Each carriage has a conductor who will provide glasses of hot tea and sugar.

Air. Snacks are provided during flights, and hot meals are served on long distance journeys. No refreshments are provided on the Moscow–Leningrad flights.

Sea travel. Tourists can reach Russia by Soviet ships sailing regularly to *Odessa* (or other Black Sea ports) from Marseilles, Genoa, Naples, Athens, Istambul and Varna (Bulgaria), or to *Leningrad* from London, calling in at the Scandinavian capitals en route. Non-Soviet ships also operate on these lines.

It is possible to vary one's tour considerably by making use of the ships which ply between the ports of the Black Sea.

Odessa Port ("morskoi vokzal"), tel: 2-07-86 *or* 9-85-51
Booking Office: Ploshchad' Karla Marksa 1
Administrator: tel: 2-09-54
Inquiry Office: tel: 2-09-44

Yalta "Morskoi Vokzal"—Bul'varnaya Ulitsa 5
tel: 25-35

Novorossiisk "Morskoi Vokzal"—Ulitsa Lenina 10
tel: 23-17 *or* 20-35, ext. 1-24

Sochi "Morskoi Vokzal"—Ulitsa Voikova
tel: 66-2-03 *or* 66-2-52

Sukhumi "Morskoi Vokzal"—Prospekt Rustaveli 16
tel: 7-38

The Cost of Car Ferry Between the Ports of the Black Sea
(in roubles per ton)

Ports	Yalta	Novorossiisk	Tuapse	Sochi	Sukhumi
Odessa	12·90	17·37	18·53	19·70	20·86
Yalta	—	12·13	13·68	14·46	16·21
Novorossiisk	—	—	6·89	8·25	12·13
Tuapse	—	—	—	5·05	9·02
Sochi	—	—	—	—	7·28

Additional costs:

1. Loading and unloading charge of 1·30 roubles per ton at each port.
2. Cargo Tax of 1·44 roubles per ton.

CAR HIRE

Foreign tourists may hire "Volga" or "Moskvich" cars through Intourist. With "Volga" models they may ask for the services of a chauffeur.

The costs of hire in roubles per 24 hours are as follows:

Car	Hire for 1–6 days	Hire for 7–14 days	Hire for 15 days or more	Extra—for every 10 km
(including insurance)				
"Volga"	5·40	4·95	4·50	0·54
"Moskvich"	4·50	4·05	3·60	0·45

In addition there are the following costs to be met:

Petrol (A-72)	54 kopeks per 10 litres
Oil	34 kopeks per litre
Washing	1 rouble

The car should be serviced every 1000 km and Intourist will repay the costs on receipt of the Service Stations' bills.

Cars can be delivered from Moscow or Leningrad to any point on the tourist's itinerary at a charge of 10 kopeks per km.

The main payment should be made in advance, with a final settlement at the end of the tour taking into account the actual times and distances involved.

There is a cancellation fee of 10 per cent of the advance payment.

THE HIGHWAY CODE AND NIGHT DRIVING

Traffic keeps to the right throughout the Soviet Union. The only place where left-hand traffic is strictly observed is within the gates of the British Embassy in Moscow.

In town and any built-up area your speed should not exceed 60 km per hr, (40 m.p.h.), but on the wide streets of Moscow few people observe this rule. In the Soviet Union the main roads take 2 or 3 lines of traffic in each direction, and in towns there is sometimes room for 5 lines (as on the ring-road in Moscow). Most of the new highways are built for a large amount of traffic but so far they are comparatively deserted. The traffic becomes heavier as large towns are approached, and the bulk of it is made up of lorries.

When setting off on a trip it is much better to leave big towns early in the morning so that you can pass through the bottlenecks before the first lorries jam them up. Beware of lorries, especially near a left-hand junction. They rarely have trafficators, and the left door may or may not fly open to warn you that they are going to turn. Use your horn as little as possible, and not at all in built-up areas—but it is often safer to sound it when overtaking and a polite driver will reply.

In some narrow streets in the centres of Moscow and Leningrad it is forbidden to park or to overtake, but in general you can park anywhere you like, without looking for a parking sign. It is forbidden to cross the road and park facing the oncoming traffic. Incidentally many Russian drivers read the international P-for-parking sign as the Russian "R" which looks the same, and think it stands for "razresheno" (permitted)!

Foreign motorists are not encouraged to drive at night. It is a most unpleasant time to drive, partly because there are no dual-carriage ways. The oncoming cars flash their lights to insist that you switch yours off and force everyone to drive in complete darkness. Dipping headlamps is practically unheard of, so even if yours are already dipped, still from a psychological point of view the opposition will resent anything stronger than your sidelights, and you must go very slowly or even stop altogether if you don't want to be blinded. Beware of lorries which may have pulled in at the roadside for the night, and very often switch off all their lights. Sometimes by braking dramatically you can pull up without hitting an unlit fence bearing a sign telling you part of the road is under repair. The sightseeing time you may gain is hardly worth the hazards of night driving.

It is a good rule to avoid "one for the road", whether wine or beer, because in Russia there is no blood test for alcohol—even the smell of a rum-flavoured sweet may be incriminating!

Russian pedestrians are most unpredictable—they will cross anywhere, even when the lights are against them. People will thumb a lift, usually for a very short distance. Long-distance hitch-hiking is non-existent in the Soviet Union.

Note. In *four*-signal traffic lights, left or reverse turns are permissible only when a green light and a green direction arrow are shown.

When traffic lights stay at amber, all traffic should stop to allow an ambulance, fire-engine or any other priority vehicle to pass.

Traffic lights blinking on and off at amber, especially after dark, mean "Caution! Cross-road" or "Road junction".

SIGNS YOU MAY BE GLAD TO SEE

ГОСТИНИЦА	Hotel
РЕСТОРАН	Restaurant
КАФЕ	Café
КАФЕ-МОЛОЧНАЯ	Milk Bar
КАФЕ-МОРОЖЕНОЕ	Ice-cream
СТОЛОВАЯ	Restaurant (cheaper)
АВТОМАТ	Slot Machine (Self-Service Snacks, Telephone Kiosk)
ЗАКУСОЧНАЯ	Snack Bar
БУФЕТ	Buffet
ЧАЙНАЯ	Teas
ЛАРЁК	Small Shop
МАГАЗИН	Shop

ПРОДМАГ	Provisions
СЕЛЬМАГ	Village Store
СЕЛЬПО	Village Store
ПИВО, ВОДЫ, СОКИ	Beer, Minerals, Fruit Juices
ГАСТРОНОМ	Provisions (in town only)
БУЛОЧНАЯ-КОНДИТЕРСКАЯ	Baker-Confectioner
МЯСО-РЫБА	Butcher-Fishmonger
ОВОЩИ-ФРУКТЫ	Greengrocer
МОЛОКО	Dairy
АВТОМАГАЗИН	Spare Parts for Cars
КВАС (хлебный квас)	"kvas"—a refreshing drink of fermented rye-water
ШАШЛЫЧНАЯ	Shashliks
КОЛХОЗНЫЙ РЫНОК	Market
ТУАЛЕТ, УБОРНАЯ	Lavatory
М (мужская комната)	Gentlemen
Ж, Д (женская, дамская комната)	Ladies

Note. In Ukrainian "Ч" is the letter used to indicate the Gents, and in Moldavian it is "Б" for the Gents and "Ф" for the Ladies.

ПОЧТА—ТЕЛЕГРАФ—ТЕЛЕФОН	Post—Telegraph—Telephone

ROADSIDE SIGNS

There are hardly any advertisements beside the roads except those encouraging people to patronise the Savings Banks and to fulfil the various plans. Some of the gayest posters are concerned with overtaking the United States in production.

Here are some notices which might concern the driver:

ОСТОРОЖНО	Caution—Drive carefully
КРУТОЙ СПУСК	Steep Hill
КРУТОЙ ПОВОРОТ	Sharp Bend
ОБЪЕЗД	Diversion
ПРОЕЗД ЗАКРЫТ	Road Closed
ВОДИТЕЛЬ! БУДЬ ОСТОРОЖЕН!	Driver, be careful!
ОСТАНОВКА ТРАНСПОРТА ОБЯЗАТЕЛЬНА	All Traffic, Halt

(This one appears near tram stops, for instance, where pedestrians may suddenly cross the road.)

ОСТОРОЖНО! ПЕШЕХОДЫ	Caution! Pedestrians
НЕПРАВИЛЬНЫЙ ОБГОН ВЕДЁТ К АВАРИИ	Careless Overtaking Causes Accidents
ДО МОСКВЫ 320 КМ.	To Moscow—320 km
ДО ВЯЗЬМЫ 156 КМ.	To Vyazma—156 km
ДО СМОЛЕНСКА 8 КМ.	To Smolensk—8 km
ПОВОРОТ ЧЕРЕЗ 200 МЕТРОВ	Turning 200 metres ahead
РЕМОНТ ДОРОГИ	Road Repairs

GARAGING

Hotels do not provide garages. You have to leave your car in the street unless there is a hotel yard that you can use. If your windscreen wipers can be taken off, remove them and also your wing mirror because otherwise there is a chance that someone else may fancy them as souvenirs. You can be absolutely sure that no one will take your car because there are so few foreign cars in Russia that it would easily be recognised. Stolen foreign cars are unheard of here. It is better, however, to take indoors any luggage you are carrying on the roof, and also to remember to lock the boot, although in an Intourist hotel yard your property will be safe.

Russians generally use a plastic or fabric cover to protect a car standing long in the sun.

Parking in the street is free. Some towns provide an attended car park for the use of foreign tourists.

PETROL AND OIL

Filling stations are situated every 100–150 km (70–100 miles) along the "Intourist roads", and are preceded by warning notices in English 20 km (14 miles) and again 2 km (¾ mile) in advance. Foreign tourists may go to the front of the queue.

The petrol available is of many different varieties:

70- and 72-octane costing 54 kopeks for 10 litres
74- and 76-octane costing 64 kopeks for 10 litres
93- and 95-octane costing 93 kopeks for 10 litres

It is wise to fill up when you can and not to wait until you come to a town as filling stations there may be hard to find, and the type of petrol you prefer even harder.

Russian oil is of good quality, but if you like to use a particular brand for your car be sure to bring enough with you.

Coupons for petrol and diesel fuel are sold in all Intourist offices and agencies. At some filling stations no cash sales are made and coupons only are accepted.

SERVICING

Usually filling stations do not undertake to service cars, nor to overhaul them in any way. There are special garages for this in the major towns, and on the tourist routes there are repair stations every 200–300 km (130–200 miles). It is not possible either in the repair stations or in the shops to obtain any spare parts that are not of Russian production. Intourist guarantee to do their best to help mend or replace parts in case of breakdown, but it would be difficult to deal with some parts at a local factory—a damaged water-pump or ball-bearings, for example. If a Russian mechanic is unable to adapt a Russian spare part, and if Intourist cannot get a substitute made at a factory, you must simply be patient, and send a telegram for spare parts to be flown in for you as soon as possible. Obviously it would be wise to check and change any unreliable parts before setting out.

Except at the service stations, no one will wash your car for you. In large towns Russian car owners are liable to a fine for driving a dirty car. Every big service station has a car-washing department, and so have a very few filling stations. The local drivers manage by filling a bucket in a village just before they enter a large town so that their car will be clean.

Tourists can purchase tickets for servicing and fuel in advance at the following prices:

74-, 93- and 95-octane petrol 64 kopeks, and 93 kopeks respectively for 10 litres.

Motor oil	37 kopeks per kilogram
Diesel fuel	7 kopeks per litre
Car washing	52 kopeks
Servicing	6·40 roubles

GARAGE VOCABULARY

What sorts of petrol have you?
Какóй бензи́н у вас есть?
kakoi′ benzeen′ u vas yest?

I need 40 litres of petrol
Мне нýжно 40 ли́тров бензи́на
mnye noozh′no so′rok leet′rov benzee′na

Have we time to get to … before the evening?
Мы успéем до вéчера доéхать до …?
my uspe′yem do ve′chera doye′khat do …?

Please help us to telephone to Intourist in the town of ...
Пожа́луйста, помоги́те нам позвони́ть в Интури́ст го́рода ...
pazhal'sta, pamaghee'tye nam pazvaneet' v inturist' go'roda ...

May we spend the night here?
Мо́жно нам здесь переночевать?
mozh'no nam zdyes perenochivat'?

Our car has something wrong with it.
У нас испо́ртилась маши́на.
u nas ispor'tilas mashee'na.

We need help with the car *or* We need a breakdown van
Нам нужна́ техпо́мощь
nam noozhna' tekhpo'moshch

The car needs to be towed to a garage
Маши́ну ну́жно отбукси́ровать в гара́ж
mashee'nu noozh'no utbuksi'rovat v garazh'

I need ...
Мне ну́жно ...
mnye noozh'no ...

an oil change, routine maintenance and a wash
сде́лать ТО-1
zdye'lat tay-oh udeen'

the oil changed
смени́ть ма́сло
smeneet' mas'lo

the greasing and lubrication done
сде́лать сма́зку
zdye'lat smaz'ku

the car washed
помы́ть маши́ну
pamy't mashee'nu

the ignition checked
прове́рить зажига́ние
pravye'rit zazhiga'niye

the running of the engine checked
прове́рить рабо́ту мото́ра
pravye'rit rabo'tu mato'ra

the wireless repaired
почини́ть ра́дио
pachineet' ra'dio

my tyre repaired
почини́ть покры́шку
pachineet' pakrysh'ku

the horn repaired
почини́ть сигна́л
pachineet' signal'

the strange noise in the engine investigated
устрани́ть стра́нный звук в мото́ре
ustraneet' stran'nyi zvuk v mato'rye

my battery recharged
заряди́ть аккумуля́тор
zaryadeet' akumulya'tor

the electric wiring checked
прове́рить эле́ктрооборудование
pravye'rit elek'tro-abaroo'dovaniye

my brake-light repaired (side lamp)
почини́ть стоп-сигна́л (подфа́рник)
pachineet' stop-signal' (podfar'nik)

my trafficator repaired
почини́ть индика́тор поворо́та
pachineet' indika'tor povaro'ta

my headlamp repaired
испра́вить пере́дний свет
ispra'vit pyered'nyi svet

my rear-light repaired
испра́вить за́дний свет
ispra'vit zad'nyi svet

this part mended (changed)
почини́ть (замени́ть) э́ту дета́ль
pachineet' (zamyeneet') e'tu dyetal'

the radiator topped up
зали́ть во́ду в радиа́тор
zaleet' vod'u v radia'tor

my tyres pumped up
подкача́ть ши́ны
padkachat' shi'ny

my puncture mended
закле́ить ка́меру
zakle'yit ka'meroo

my wheels changed around
переставить колёса
pyeresta'vit kalyo'sa

my brakes bled
прокачáть тормозá
prokachat' tormoza'

my hand-brake regulated
испрáвить ручной тóрмоз
ispra'vit ruchnoi' tor'moz

the carburettor checked
провéрить карбюрáтор
provye'rit karbyura'tor

Please give me ...
Дáйте мне пожáлуйста ...
dai'tye mnye pazhal'sta ...

a screwdriver	отвёртку	utvyort'ku
a spanner	гáечный ключ	ga'yechnyi klyooch
a hammer	молотóк	molotok'
a pump	насóс	nasos'
a piece of wire	кусóк прóволоки	kusok' pro'voloki
a piece of rubber	кусóк рези́ны	koosok' rezee'ny
a nut	гáйку	ga'iku
a washer	шáйбу	sha'ibu
a jack	домкрáт	domkrat'
a couple of tyre levers	монтирóвки	montirov'ki
some cotton-waste	концы́	kontsy'

Useful Words

engine	мотóр	motor'
exhaust pipe	выхлопнáя трубá	vykhlop'naya truba'
axle	ось	os
brakes	тормозá	tormoza'
clutch	сцеплéние	stseplye'niye
crank	заводнáя рýчка	zavadna'ya rooch'ka
ignition	зажигáние	zazhiga'niye
sparking-plug	свечá	svicha'
valve	клапáн	klapan'
steering-wheel	руль	rool
wheel	колесó	kalyeso'

wing	крыло́	krylo′
bonnet	капо́т	kapot′
boot	бага́жник	bagazh′nik
door	дверь	dvyer
window	стекло́	stiklo′
bumper	ба́мпер	bum′per
gear-box	коро́бка ско́ростей	karob′ka sko′rostei
accelerator	акселера́тор	akselerah′tor
petrol pump	бе́нзонасо́с	ben′zonasos′
fan	вентиля́тор	ventilya′tor
radiator	радиа́тор	rahdia′tor
windscreen wipers	щётки [ники	shchot′ki
main bearings	ко́ренные подши́п-	ko′rennye podship′-
brushes	вкладыши	vkladyshi′ [niki
fuel supply	пода́ча бензи́на	pada′cha benzi′na
idling speed	холостой ход	kholostoy′ khod
cruising speed	сре́дние оборо́ты	sred′niye abaro′ty
racing speed	высо́кие оборо́ты	viso′kiye abaro′ty
oil pump	ма́слонасо́с	ma′slonasos′
oil pressure	давле́ние ма́сла	davle′niye mas′la
filter, air	фильтр возду́шный	filter vozdoosh′nyi
filter oil	фильтр ма́сляный	filter mas′lyanyi
water pump	водяна́я по́мпа	vodyana′ya pom′pa
starter	стартёр	startyor′
distributor	распредели́тель зажига́ния	raspredeli′tel zazhiga′niya
induction coil	кату́шка высо́кого напряже́ния	katoosh′ka viso′kova napryazhe′niya
condenser	конденса́тор	kondensa′tor
generator	генера́тор	genera′tor
distributor points	конта́кты прерыва-теля	kontak′ty preriva′telya
fuse	предохрани́тель	predokhrani′tel
distilled water	дистиллиро́ванная вода́	distiliro′vannaya voda′
electrolyte	эле́ктроли́т	elek′troleet′
acid	кислота́	kislota′
gear, first	переда́ча пе́рвая	pereda′cha per′vaya
second	втора́я	ftara′ya
third	тре́тья	tre′tia
fourth	четвёртая	chetvyor′taya
reverse	за́дняя	zadnyaya
neutral	нейтра́льная	nyeitral′naya

gear lock	фикса́тор	fixa'tor
brake system	тормозна́я систе́ма	tormozna'ya sistye'ma
main brake cylinder	гла́вный тормозно́й цили́ндр	glav'nyi tormoznoy' tsilin'dr
brake shoes	тормозны́е коло́дки	tormozny'ye kalod'ki
brake shoe lining	накла́дки тормозны́х коло́док	naklad'ki tormoznykh' kolo'dok
brake cylinder piston cup	манже́ты тормозны́х цили́ндров	manzhe'ty tormoznykh' tsilin'drov
brake drum	тормозно́й бараба́н	tormoznoy' baraban'
front suspension	пере́дняя подве́ска	pered'nyaya podvyes'ka
front axle	пере́дний мост	pered'nii most
independent suspension	незави́симая подве́ска	nezavi'simaya podves'ka
springs	рессо́ры	resso'ri
steering rod	рулева́я тя́га	ruleva'ya tya'ga
bracket	кронштейн	kronshtein
axle shaft	полуо́сь	plau-os'
main leaf of spring	коренно́й лист рессо́ры	korennoi' leest resso'ry
reduction gear of the rear axle	реду́ктор за́днего мо́ста	reduk'tor zad'nyevo mos'ta
gland	са́льник	sal'nik
washer	прокла́дка	proklad'ka
splint pin	шплинт	shplint
castle nut	корончáтая гáйка	koroncha'taya gai'ka
inspection	техни́ческий осмо́тр	tekhni'cheskii asmotr'
pressure gauge	мано́метр	manometr'
camber angle adjustment	регулиро́вка развáла колёс	regulirov'ka razva'la kalyos'
greasing	сма́зка узло́в и агрега́тов	smaz'ka uzlov' i agrega'tov
hydraulic lifting apparatus	гидравли́ческий подъёмник	gidravli'cheskii pudyom'nik
painting	окра́ска	akras'ka
priming	грунто́вка	gruntov'ka
polishing	полиро́вка	polirov'ka
chrome plating	хромиро́вка	khromirov'ka
straightening	рихто́вка	rikhtov'ka
welding	сва́рка	svar'ka
tinning	луже́ние	luzhe'niye
patching up of scratches	заде́лка цара́пин	zadyel'ka tsara'pin

Here are some additional phrases which you could simply point out to the garage assistant if you do not speak the language.

Can you repair my car?
Мóжете ли вы отремонтúровать машúну?

Here is a list of spare parts (spare parts catalogue) for my car.
Вот катáлог детáлей моéй машúны.

Where can I park my car for repairing?
Кудá мне постáвить машúну для ремóнта?

Is it necessary to jack up the car?
Нýжно ли поднимáть машúну на домкрáт?

The engine will not start.
Мотóр не завóдится.

The engine stalls when idling.
Мотóр глохнёт на мáлых оборóтах.

The engine fails at all r.p.m.
Мотóр рабóтает с перебóями на всех оборóтах.

The engine fires back into the carburettor.
В карбюрáторе раздаю́тся «хлóпки».

The engine stops after running for a short time.
Двúгатель останáвливается пóсле непродолжúтельной рабóты.

The engine is knocking; it vibrates strongly while running.
В двúгателе слы́шен стук, при рабóте чýвствуется большáя вибрáция.

The engine overheats very soon.
Двúгатель бы́стро перегревáется.

The dynamo is not charging.
Генерáтор не даёт зарЯ́дки.

There is no oil pressure.
Нет давлéния мáсла.

Set in spark advance for petrol of lower (higher) octane number, please.
Отрегулúруйте опережéние зажигáния на бóлее нúзкое (высóкое) октáновое чúсло бензúна.

Valve clearance needs to be adjusted; also take out the carbon deposits.
Нýжно отрегулúровать клапáна и снять нагáр.

The engine is smoking.
Двúгатель дымúт.

It is necessary to change rings and adjust idling speed.
Ну́жно замени́ть поршневы́е ко́льца и отрегули́ровать оборо́ты холосто́го хо́да.

Change the speedometer drive, please.
Пожа́луйста, замени́те вал (при́вод) спидоме́тра.

There are knocks in the rear axle when the car starts moving.
При трога́нии с ме́ста раздаю́тся сту́ки в за́днем мосту́.

The rear axle "buzzes" when the car is in motion.
При движе́нии за́дний мост «гуди́т».

Oil is leaking from the reduction gear of the rear axle.
Из реду́ктора за́днего моста́ вытека́ет ма́сло.

... gear slips out when the car is in motion.
... переда́ча «выска́кивает» во вре́мя движе́нии.

... gear meshes with difficulty.
... переда́ча включа́ется с трудо́м.

The gear-box is knocking.
В коро́бке переда́ч слы́шен стук.

The clutch is slipping.
Сцепле́ние пробуксо́вывает.

The clutch operation is jerky.
Сцепле́ние «ведёт».

The door handle does not work well.
у дверцы́ пло́хо рабо́тает ру́чка.

The key does not go into the lock.
Ключ не вхо́дит в замо́к.

This window only goes down half-way.
Э́то стекло́ опуска́ется то́лько наполови́ну.

The door does not close properly.
Дверца́ непло́тно закрыва́ется.

Water comes in here while driving in rain.
При движе́нии в дождь сюда́ проника́ет вода́.

The seat springs have become weak.
Пружи́ны э́того сиде́нья осла́бли.

Touch up here, please.
Закра́сьте, пожа́луйста, вот э́то ме́сто.

Have you any suitable paint for my car?
Есть ли у вас подходя́щая кра́ска для мое́й маши́ны.

Straighten this mudguard, please.
Выпрáвьте, пожáлуйста, э́то крыло.

Only priming here, no painting.
Э́ту повéрхность тóлько загрýнтуйте, но не крáсьте.

The trafficators and stop lights do not flash on.
Сигнáл поворóта и стоп-сигнáл не горя́т.

Adjust the position of the headlights, please.
Отрегули́руйте, пожáлуйста, постанóвку фар.

Change the brake fluid, please.
Смени́те, пожáлуйста, постанóвку фар.

The brakes do not hold well.
Тормозá плóхо дéржат.

The brake fluid leaks from the cylinder of this wheel.
Тормознáя жи́дкость вытекáет из цилиндра э́того колéса.

Adjust the brake shoes, please.
Отреули́руйте, пожáлуйста, тормозны́е колóдки.

The hand brake is out of order.
Ручнóй тормóз не дéйствует.

Wash my car, please.
Пожáлуйста, вы́мойте мою́ маши́ну.

I need a pump (vulcanizer).
Мне нужен насос (вулканизатор).

I need a wrench, number ...
Мне нýжен ключ № ...

Have you these parts?
Есть ли у вас э́ти детáли?

Is it possible to change this part?
Мóжно ли замени́ть э́ту детáль?

How much time will the repair take?
Мнóго ли врéмени потрéбует ремóнт?

For how long shall I have to leave my car?
Надóлго ли придётся остáвить маши́ну?

How much will the repair cost?
Скóлько стóит ремóнт?

THE ALPHABET

Russian letter	English letter	
Vowels	*Vowels*	*Pronounced*
а	a	as *a* in "father" (when in a stressed syllable) or as *u* in "up"
я	–	as *ya* in "yard"
э	e	as *e* in "pet"
е	–	as *ye* in "yet"
и	i	as *i* in "hit"
ы	–	as *e* in "me" pronounced with a strong Midland accent
о	o	as *o* in "hot"
ё	–	as *ya* in "yacht"
у	u	as *u* in "pull"
ю	–	as *u* in "union"
Consonants		
б	b	as *b* in "box"
д	d	as *d* in "dog"
ф	f	as *f* in "fish"
г	g	as *g* in "go"
х	kh	as *ch* in "loch"
ж	zh	as *s* in "pleasure"
к	k	as *k* in "king"
л	l	as *l* in "like"
м	m	as *m* in "man"
н	n	as *n* in "nimble"
п	p	as *p* in "pin"
р	r	as *r* in "arrow"
с	s	as *s* in "miss"
т	t	as *t* in "take"
в	v	as *v* in "vat"
з	z	as *z* in "zebra"
Double Consonants		
ц	–	as *ts* in "eats"
ч	–	as *ch* in "chair"
ш	–	as *sh* in "ship"
щ	–	as *shch* in "cash cheque"
Accent Letters		
ь		soft sign (' in transliterated words)
ъ		hard sign
й		short *i* (as "y" in "guy")

NUMBERS

1	оди́н	udeen′
2	два	dva
3	три	tree
4	четы́ре	chety′rye
5	пять	pyat
6	шесть	shest
7	семь	syem
8	во́семь	vo′syem
9	де́вять	dye′vyat
10	де́сять	dye′syat
11	оди́ннадцать	udeen′atsut
12	двена́дцать	dvyenat′sut
13	трина́дцать	treenat′sut
14	четы́рнадцать	chetyr′natsut
15	пятна́дцать	pyatnat′sut
16	шестна́дцать	shestnat′sut
17	семна́дцать	syemnat′sut
18	восемна́дцать	vosyemnat′sut
19	девятна́дцать	dyevyatnat′sut
20	два́дцать	dvat′sut
21	два́дцать оди́н	dvat′sut udeen′
22	два́дцать два	dvat′sut dva
30	три́дцать	treet′sut
40	со́рок	so′rok
50	пятьдеся́т	pyatdyesyat′
60	шестьдеся́т	shestdyesyat′
70	семьдеся́т	syemdyesyat′
80	во́семьде́ся́т	vo′syemdye′syat
90	девяно́сто	dyevyano′sto
100	сто	sto
200	две́сти	dvye′sti
300	три́ста	tree′sta
400	четы́реста	chety′ryesta
500	пятьсо́т	pyatsot′
600	шестьсо́т	shestsot′
900	девятьсо́т	dyevyatsot′
1000	ты́сяча	ty′syacha

TELLING THE TIME

To tell the time, one must always state the number of hours first, and then the number of minutes. (There is a second way of telling the time in Russian which is more complicated grammatically. 8·20 would be literally "twenty minutes of the ninth".) The simple method given here will be perfectly adequate.

In the evening, especially when giving the times of film performances, train departures, etc., Russians tend to use the 24-hour system (saying 18·45 for 6·45 p.m.).

What is the time?
Кото́рый час?
kato'ryi chas?

It is one o'clock, two o'clock.
Час, два часа́.
chas, dva chas'a

It is five past three (p.m.).
Три часа́ пять мину́т, пятна́дцать ноль пять.
tree chasa' pyat minoot' *or* pyatnat'sut nol pyat

It is twenty to five.
Четы́ре часа́ со́рок мину́т, шестна́дцать со́рок.
chety'rye chasa' so'rok minoot' *or* shestnat'sut so'rok

It is twelve o'clock mid-day, midnight.
По́лдень, по́лночь.
pol'dyen, pol'noch

a.m.	утра́	utra'
p.m.	ве́чера	vye'chera
This morning	сего́дня у́тром	syevod'nya oot'rom
This afternoon	сего́дня днём	syevod'nya dnyom
This evening / Tonight	сего́дня ве́чером	syevod'nya vye'cherom
Night	ночь	noch
Tomorrow evening	за́втра ве́чером	zav'tra vye'cherom
Tomorrow morning	за́втра у́тром	zav'tra oot'rom
The day after tomorrow	послеза́втра	poslyezav'tra
Yesterday	вчера́	vchera'
The day before yesterday	позавчера́	pozavchera'
Last night	вчера́ но́чью	vchera' noch'yu
Early	ра́но	ra'no
Late	по́здно	poz'dno
How long?	как до́лго	kak dol'go?

An hour	час	chas
A minute	минýта	minoo'ta
Half a moment	минýточку	minoo'tochku
In a moment	сейчáс	sichas'

ASKING THE WAY, etc.

Would you please tell me ...
Скажи́те пожáлуйста ...
skazhee'tye pazhal'sta ...

the name of this town (village)?
как называ́ется э́тот го́род (э́та дере́вня)?
kak nazyva'yetsa e'tot go'rod (e'ta dyerevnya)?

the way to the town of ...?
как прое́хать в го́род ...?
kak praye'khat v go'rod ...?

where the Intourist hotel is here?
где здесь гости́ница Интури́ста?
gdye zdyes gastee'nitsa inturis'ta?

where the Intourist camping ground is here?
где здесь ке́мпинг Интури́ста?
gdye zdyes kem'ping inturis'ta?

where there is a filling station here?
где здесь бензоколо́нка?
gdye zdyes benzakalon'ka?

where I can park here?
где здесь стоя́нка?
gdye zdyes stayan'ka?

where there is a grocer's, baker's, market, chemist's here?
где здесь продмáг, бýлочная, ры́нок, апте́ка?
gdye zdyes prodmag', boo'lochnaya, ry'nok, aptye'ka?

where there is a restaurant, café, cafeteria here?
где здевь ресторáн, кафе́, столо́вая?
gdye zdyes restoran', kafay', stalo'vaya?

cinema, theatre, park, museum, church?
кино́, теáтр, парк, музе́й, це́рковь?
kino', tyea'tr, park, moozei', tser'kov?

where there is a lavatory here?
где здесь убо́рная?
gdye zdyes ubor'naya?

if this road is good?
хоро́шая здесь доро́га?
kharo'shaya zdyes daro'ga?

where I can find a garage here?
где здесь како́й-нибудь гара́ж?
gdye zdes kakoy'-niboot' garazh'?

if this is the road to ...?
э́то доро́га на ...?
e'to daro'ga na ...?

how many kilometres it is to ...?
ско́лько киломе́тров до ...?
skol'ko kilome'trov do ...?

Petrol	бензи́н	benzeen'	Turning	поворо́т	pavarot'
Diesel Oil	солярка	solyar'ka	To the left	нале́во	nalye'va
Oil	ма́сло	mas'lo	To the right	напра́во	napra'va
Water	вода́	vada'	Straight on	пря́мо	prya'ma
Highway	шо́ссе	sho'sai	Here	сюда́	syuda'
Road	доро́га	daro'ga	There	туда́	tuda'
Street	у́лица	oo'litsa	Back	наза́д	nazad'
Square	пло́щадь	plosh'chad	Stop	стоп	stop
Lane	переу́лок	pyeryeoo'lok	Forest	лес	lyes
			Field	по́ле	po'lye
Dead-end	тупи́к	tupik'	River	река́	reka'
Town	го́род	go'rod	Lake	о́зеро	ózyero
Village	село́	syelo'	Hill	гора́	gara'
Village	дере́вня	dyerev'nya	Sea	мо́ре	mo'rye
House	дом	dom	Black Sea	Чёрное мо́ре	chor'noye morye
Cottage (in Ukraine)	ха́та	kha'ta			

Filling station	Бензоколо́нка	benzokalon'ka
Distilled Water	Дистиллиро́ванная вода́	distiliro'vannaya vada'
... horse power	. . . лошади́ных сил	... loshadee'nykh sil
Brake fluid	Тормозна́я жи́дкость	tormozna'ya zhid'kost

Who speaks English, French, German here?
Кто здесь говори́т по-английски, по-францу́зски, по-не́мецки?
kto zdyes gavareet' panglee'ski, pafrantsoos'ki, panimyets'ki?

May I have an interpreter?
Мо́жно попроси́ть перево́дчика?
mozh'no papraseet' perevod'chika?

We are tourists from England, America, France, Germany, Italy.
Мы тури́сты из Англии, Аме́рики, Фра́нции, Герма́нии, Ита́лии.
my tooris'ti iz an'glii, ame'riki, fran'tsii, germa'nii, ita'lii.

We are going to the town of ...
Мы е́дем в горо́д . . .
my ye'dyem v gorod' ...

We are coming from the town of ...
Мы е́дем из го́рода ...
my ye'dem iz go'roda ...

I do not understand Russian.
Я не понима́ю по-ру́сски.
ya ne panima'yu paroos'ki.

What is this called in Russian?
Как э́то называ́ется по-ру́сски?
kak e'to nazyva'yetsa paroos'ki?

Yes	да	da	When?	когда́?	kagda'?
No	нет	nyet	Where?	где?	gdye?
Thank you	спаси́бо	spasi'bo	Why?	почему́?	pachimoo'?
Please	пожа́луйста	pazhal'sta	Quickly	бы́стро	by'stra
Hello	здра́вствуйте	zdrav'stvuytye	Slowly	ме́дленно	myed'lenna
			I	я	ya
Good-bye	до свида́ния	dasvidanya	He	он	on
Good	хорошо́	kharasho'	She	она́	una'
Bad	пло́хо	plo'kho	We	мы	my
Much, many	мно́го	mno'go	You	вы	vy
Little, few	ма́ло	ma'la			

FIRST AID

In the Soviet Union medical care is free of charge and motorists who fall ill during their trip are also entitled to free medical care. In case you are unwell, notify an Intourist representative and a doctor will be called immediately. There is no charge for the doctor's visit, but the patient pays for any medicines according to standard prices.

There are First Aid Posts and hospitals at regular intervals along the Intourist routes, and in Moscow there is a special clinic which cares for foreign tourists. Its address is Ulitsa Gertsena 12, and telephone numbers 29-73-23 and 29-03-82. Its staff includes qualified doctors and nurses, and there are X-ray, physiotherapy, dental and other departments.

First Aid Phrases and Vocabulary

I feel ill.
Я пло́хо себя́ чу́вствую.
ya plo'kho syebya' choo'stvuyu

I have a head-, ear-, tooth-, stomach-ache, sore throat.
У меня́ боли́т голова, у́хо, зуб, живо́т, го́рло.
u myenya' baleet' galava', oo'kho, zoob, zhivot', gor'lo

I have a cough, cold, influenza.
У меня́ ка́шель, на́сморк, грипп.
u myenya' ka'shyel, na'smork, grip

I have diarrhoea, constipation.
У меня́ поно́с, запо́р.
u myenya' panos', zapor'

I have broken my arm, my leg.
Я слома́л ру́ку, но́гу.
ya slamal' roo'ku, no'gu

I have burnt my hand, my leg, my finger.
Я обжёг ру́ку, но́гу, па́лец.
ya abzhog' rooku, no'gu, pa'lyets

I have sprained my ankle.
У меня́ растяже́ние ноги́.
u myenya' rastyazhe'niye naghee'

I have a blister.
Я натёр себе́ но́гу.
ya natyor' sibye' no'gu

I have a rash, a swelling.
У меня́ сыпь, о́пухоль.
oo myenya' syp, o'pukhol

She is very tired.
Она́ о́чень уста́ла.
una' o'chyen usta'la

He has a temperature.
У него́ температу́ра.
oo nyevo' temperatoo'ra

What is the matter with you?
На что вы жалу́етесь?
na shto vy zhaloo'yetyes?

Where is the hospital?
Где здесь больни́ца?
gdye zdyes balni'tsa?

Call an ambulance.
Позови́те ско́рую по́мощь.
pazovi'tye sko'ruyu po'moshch

It is necessary to call a doctor immediately.
Ну́жно сро́чно позва́ть врача́.
noozh'na sroch'na pazvat' vracha'

I have lost my appetite.
У меня́ пропа́л аппети́т
u myenya' propal' apeteet'.

Fainting fit	о́бморок	ob'marok
Infection	инфе́кция	infek'tsiya
Burn	ожо́г	azhog'
Inflammation	воспале́ние	vospale'niye
Sprain	вы́вих	vy'vikh
Convulsion	су́дорога	soo'daraga
Fracture	перело́м	pyerelom'
Inoculation	приви́вка	priveev'ka
Anaesthetic	нарко́з	narkoz'
Dressing	перевя́зка	pyerevyaz'ka
Injection	уко́л	ukol'
Nurse	медсестра́	myedsyestra'

Medicines—лека́рства—lekar'stva

An aspirin	а́спирин	as'pirin
First Aid Kit	перевя́зочные сре́дства	pyerevya'zochnyye sryed'stva
Castor Oil	касто́рка	kastor'ka
Disinfectant	дезинфициру́ющее сре́дство	dizinfitseeroo'yushcheye sryed'stvo
Epsom Salts	англи́йская соль	anglee'skaya sol (i)
Iodine	йод	yod
Ointment	мазь	maz
A Pill	пилю́ля	pilyoo'lya
Quinine	хини́н	khineen'
A Bandage	бинт	bint
Cotton-wool	ва́та	va'ta

INTRODUCTION TO THE ROADS

Motorists may enter the Soviet Union from the north, west or south, either by road from Finland, Poland, Czechoslovakia, Hungary or Rumania, or by sea through the ports of Leningrad or Odessa.

One's choice of route naturally depends upon the time one can spare and upon personal interests; it is usually obligatory to plan one's trip beforehand, to notify Intourist of the route, and then keep to it. The ten sections of the roads open to foreign motorists are described below in the same order as that in which they appear in the book, and with the help of a map it will be seen that they can be linked to form a wide variety of different motor tours.

It should be borne in mind that most of the territory open to foreign motorists except the Moscow–Yaroslavl road was under German occupation during the Second World War and suffered serious damage. Because of the occupation there are numerous war memorials, and many military graves and monuments to be seen.

1. *Vyborg–Leningrad–Novgorod–Kalinin–Moscow*

Yulya–Urpala (Finnish-U.S.S.R. border)–Leningrad:
Total length—220 km (137 miles)
Surfaced width—6–7 m (7–8 yd)
Subgrade width—7–10 m (8–11 yd)
Surface—Asphalt-concrete, with some stretches of gravel.

Leningrad–Moscow (Soviet Motor-road No. 10)
Total length—725 km (450 miles)
Surfaced width—7 m (8 yd)
Subgrade width—12–17 m (13–19 yd)
Surface—Asphalt-concrete and concrete.

Motorists have here an opportunity to get acquainted with the two largest cities of the Soviet Union, Moscow and Leningrad. They are the cultural centres of the country with museums and places of architectural interest. The road passes through the ancient city of Novgorod with many lovely churches and through Klin, where Tchaikovsky lived.

2. *Brest–Minsk–Smolensk–Moscow* (Soviet Motor-road No. 1; European Road E-8)

Total length—1054 km (655 miles)
Surfaced width—7–12 m (8–13 yd)
Surface–Asphalt-concrete and concrete.

The most interesting part of the journey from Poland is naturally the visit to Moscow itself. Minsk was rebuilt after the war, and is almost entirely new. The old Russian town of Smolensk has some fine churches.

3. *Uzhgorod–Mukachevo–L'vov–Rovno–Zhitomir–Kiev* (Soviet Motor-road No. 12)

Total length—792 km (492 miles)
Surfaced width—6–7 m (7–8 yd)
Subgrade width—8–9 m (9–10 yd), except in the mountains where it is 7–8 m (8–9 yd).

Instead of going to Uzhgorod from Czechoslovakia one can enter the Soviet Union from Hungary (via Chop), or go from Przemysl in Poland (via Mostiska) straight to Lvov.

From Uzhgorod the road runs through the Carpathian Mountain region, which is one of the most picturesque places in Russia. It is worth stopping for a day in Lvov to see its ancient buildings. Rovno and Zhitomir may not prove very exciting, but tourists will be more than repaid by the richness of Kiev.

4. *Chernovtsy–Khmelnitskii–Vinnitsa–Zhitomir*

Parubnoye (Rumanian-U.S.S.R. border)–Chernovtsy:
Total length—37 km (23 miles)
Surfaced width—6 m (7 yd)
Surface—Gravel, with some stretches of road metal.

Chernovtsy–Zhitomir:
Total length—449 km (279 miles)
Surfaced width—6–7 m (7–8 yd)
Surface—Asphalt-concrete, with some stretches of road metal.

After coming into the Soviet Union from Rumania this road passes through historic towns whose architecture has been influenced by both central Europe and by Turkey. The mosques have not survived, but there are Roman Catholic as well as Russian Orthodox churches. In this area tourists are advised to keep to the main roads through the towns and villages (in many cases there is a map displayed at the entrance to the town). From Zhitomir one may proceed to the Ukrainian capital of Kiev.

5. *Chernovtsy–Kishinev–Odessa*

Total length—520 km (323 miles)
Surfaced width—6–7 m (7–8 yd)
Subgrade width—7–8 m (8–9 yd)
Surface–Asphalt-concrete.

This road crosses Moldavia and leads to its capital, Kishinyov. The language spoken here is similar to Rumanian. There are many vineyards to be seen among the Moldavian farmlands. One should spend at least a day in Odessa; this famous port, now a popular health resort, has some interesting architecture.

6. *Odessa–Uman'–Kiev* (Soviet Motor-road No. 20)

Total length—472 km (293 miles)
Surfaced width—7 m (8 yd)
Subgrade width—9 m (10 yd)
Surface—Asphalt-concrete and cement-concrete.

From Odessa the new Motorway (called here the "Avtostrada") runs North to Kiev through the heart of the Ukraine. As far as the town of Uman, which is known for its lovely Sofievka Park, it avoids all built-up areas, but as it approaches the Ukrainian capital it passes through small villages and towns.

7. *Kiev–Poltava–Kharkov* (Soviet Motor-road No. 13)

Total length—478 km (297 miles)
Surfaced width—6–7 m (7–8 yd)
Surface—Asphalt-concrete with some stretches of road metal.

The most interesting place on this section of the road is Poltava, which is the site of the historic battle for supremacy between Russia and Sweden. If you wish to improve your Ukrainian, you should remember that the Poltavian accent is considered the best. Kharkov, big industrial and educational centre and one-time capital of the Ukraine, has, besides its ancient monuments, interesting examples of Soviet architecture of the early thirties.

8. *Moscow–Kharkov–Simferopol–Yalta* (Soviet Motor-road No. 4)

Total length—1500 km (932 miles)
Surfaced width—7–9 m (8–10 yd)
Surface—Asphalt-concrete.

This road goes southwards through Tula, Tolstoi's Yasnaya Polyana, Orel, Kursk, Kharkov, and Zaporozhye to Yalta on the Black Sea. Motorists will cross through the most populous part of the Soviet Union, and a rest by the sea after this long journey is especially pleasant. From Yalta excursions can be made to the former capital of the Crimean khans, Bakhchiserai; to the imperial palaces of Livadia, to the wine-cellars of Massandra, and also to the historic port of Sevastopol.

9. *Moscow–Yaroslavl* (Soviet Motor-road No. 9)

Total length—260 km (161 miles)
Surfaced width—7–10 m (8–11 yd)
Subgrade width—10–13 m (11–14 yd)
Surface—Asphalt-concrete.

As you must reach Yaroslavl by nightfall, we suggest that you stop first in Zagorsk, the famous monastery that is now the centre of Russian Orthodoxy, then continue to Pereslavl-Zalesky to visit the churches and museums in this town, and then go straight on through Rostov to Yaroslavl. You may like to spend the following day in this ancient town beside the Volga River, and the third day, on your return journey, it is pleasant to stop and enjoy the small town which is still known by its old name of Rostov the Great. This route would certainly satisfy the tourist curious to see as much as possible of the old Russia.

10. *Kharkov–Rostov-on-Don–Ordzhonikidze–Tbilisi–Sochi–Rostov–Kharkov* (using Soviet Motor-roads Nos. 13, 14, 16, 17, 19 and 18)

Total length—3219 km (2000 miles)
Width—variable, because of the mountainous section
Surface—Asphalt-concrete and concrete.

As on any circular route, motorists can travel in either direction. The road is however described in this book in a clockwise direction, leading first to the spas, then along the Georgian Military Highway to Tbilisi, with the return route following the Black Sea coast. From experience it would seem preferable to travel in this direction. The Georgian Military Highway is well worth seeing, but it is certainly not easy driving and it would be best to check any suspected faults in your car before leaving Ordzhonikidze. After driving this way to the Black Sea coast, it is very pleasant to relax there. But if you are short of time and wish to get to the Black Sea resorts as soon as possible, then you must turn right at Pavlovskaya.

PART II

ROAD ONE

VYBORG—LENINGRAD—MOSCOW

VYBORG

Zelenogorsk · Repino · Sestroretsk · Razliv

LENINGRAD

Yam-Izhora · Lyuban · Chudovo

NOVGOROD

Krestsy · Valdai · Vyshny-Volochek · Torzhok

KALININ

Gorodnya · Bezborodovo · Klin · Solnechnogorsk · Khimki

MOSCOW

VYBORG

Finnish: Viipuri—Swedish: Viborg
Population: 51,000 (1959)

The Russo-Finnish border point is actually Yulya-Urpala, near the village of Torfyanovka (peat), and 53 km (33 miles) from Vyborg. Motorists usually drive straight through Vyborg, but with Intourist's permission they may stay in the town overnight. There is a buffet in the town.

Vyborg is situated on the Gulf of Finland about 120 km (75 miles) north-west of Leningrad. Once a trading point between the people of Novgorod and the Karelian hunters, it was founded as a castle in 1293 by Swedish soldiers under Torkel Knutson. It became a town in 1403 by decree of Erik XIII, and at that time it, like many other mediaeval towns, had its own court, council and merchants' guilds. In 1710 Peter the Great managed at the second attempt to take the fortress, and is reported to have said at the time, "Since I have taken this fortress, St. Petersburg is safe at last." The fortress was reinforced during the reign of Anna Ivanovna (1730–40 and the northern part of the town was then called Kron Saint Anne. From 1811 onwards it changed hands several times between Russia and Finland, finally becoming Russian in 1940. It was badly damaged during World War II. After 1940 the Finns were not able to use the Saima Canal, which is of great economic value, but in 1962 the Soviet Union again granted them the right to use it.

The canal, which was built in 1844 to 1859, is 60 km (37 miles) long and links Vyborg Bay through Vyborg seaport with the huge water basin of the Saima Lakes. It has 28 locks, since the water rises 76 m (250 ft). Vyborg is also the junction of five railway lines.

The main thoroughfare is Lenin Prospekt; and Krasnaya (Red) Square has been completely rebuilt. There is a Teachers' Training College and a drama theatre in Vyborg. Among local industries is the manufacture of agricultural machinery.

✿ CATHEDRAL OF THE TRANSFIGURATION *Krepostnaya Street 8*. The cathedral was built in 1787.

CHURCH OF THE DOMINICAN MONASTERY *Vyborgskaya Street*. The monastery was founded in 1318; there used also to be a Franciscan monastery, founded at a later date, in the town.

✿ VYBORG FORTRESS. This was at one time the most formidable stronghold on the shores of the Baltic Sea. Now only ruins remain; it is planned to open a museum here.

CLOCK TOWER *Krepostnaya Street*. The clock tower was put up in 1494.

ROUND TOWER *Torgovaya Square, near house No. 5*. This tower was built in 1547–50 to defend the south-east Kremlin Gate. It was originally outside the fortifications. The bastion known as Panzerlux, which stands near the seaport, was built in 1552 as part of the defences of the newly built section of the town.

PETER I MONUMENT *On the site of the Russian military headquarters*. This monument was erected in 1910 to mark the 200th anniversary of the capture of the town by Peter the Great. The statue by L. Bernshtam was restored in 1955.

LENIN MONUMENT *Red Square*. This monument was designed by Mikatadze and unveiled in 1957.

MON-REPOS PARK *On the shore of the northern bay*. This park was founded in the 18th century by Stupin, who was at that time military governor of Finland. Its 15 hectares (38 acres) are preserved as a typical stretch of northern landscape, and include shady avenues and impressive granite cliffs. The small columned mansion was built in 1820 by the architect Martinelli for Baron Nikolai, the owner of Mon-Repos at that time. On a high granite cliff near the house is a marble obelisk erected in 1827 to commemorate members of the family who fell during the Napoleonic Wars. The family mausoleum is on the Island of Death on the south-western side of the park. Ludvicstein Castle is also at this point.

VYBORG HOTEL AND RESTAURANT *Near the railway station, Leningradsky Prospekt, 19*.

RESTAURANT *At the railway station*.

G.P.O. *Krepostnaya Street*.

FILLING STATION AND SERVICE STATION WITH CARWASH *Near the railway station*. The local Intourist office is also at the railway station.

ZELENOGORSK

Called Terioki until 1948
Population: 12,700 (1959)

This resort was on Finnish territory from 1918 to 1940, on the northern shore of the Gulf of Finland, and is situated in a pine forest. There are many sanatoria and rest homes here. The Zolotoi Plyazh (golden beach) is an excellent sandy bathing beach.

RIVIERA HOTEL

ZHEMCHUZHINA (PEARL) RESTAURANT. There are also many small cafés in the town.

MOTEL *Primorskoye chaussée, 90; 60 km (37 miles) from Vyborg and 150 km (93 miles) from Leningrad*. The motel is situated in a pinewood on the edge of the Gulf of Finland where there is a good bathing beach. It has a restaurant, a café, a telephone, baths and showers, and a service station.

FILLING STATION *Leningradskoye chaussée, 60*. This station has round the clock service.

REPINO

(*Formerly Kuokkala*)

Ilya Repin lived here in the estate he called "Penati" (meaning "Penates") from 1900 until his death in 1930. Born in 1844, Repin was both the most accomplished of the 19th century realists and the most prolific and versatile of Russian artists. He was skilful in expressing character and situation, and particularly in depicting dramatic incidents.

Gorky, Shalyapin, Mayakovsky, Pavlov and other prominent people visited him here in Repino. His house was burnt down during the German retreat, but is now restored and open as a museum. Repin's grave may also be seen in the grounds of the estate.

Among Repin's best known paintings are "The Volga Boatmen", "The Religious Procession in Kursk province", "Ivan the Terrible with the body of his Son" and "Zaporozhye Cossacks Drafting a Reply to the Turkish Sultan".

MOTEL *Pervaya Novaya Street* 8; *at the 47 km milestone (from Leningrad), on the left side of the road*.

This motel is situated in wooded territory 200 m (229 yd) from the Gulf of Finland, and is open from May to September for 140 or 150 people.

VOLNA (WAVE) RESTAURANT *At Wonderful Beach*. This restaurant will supply food directly to the motel.

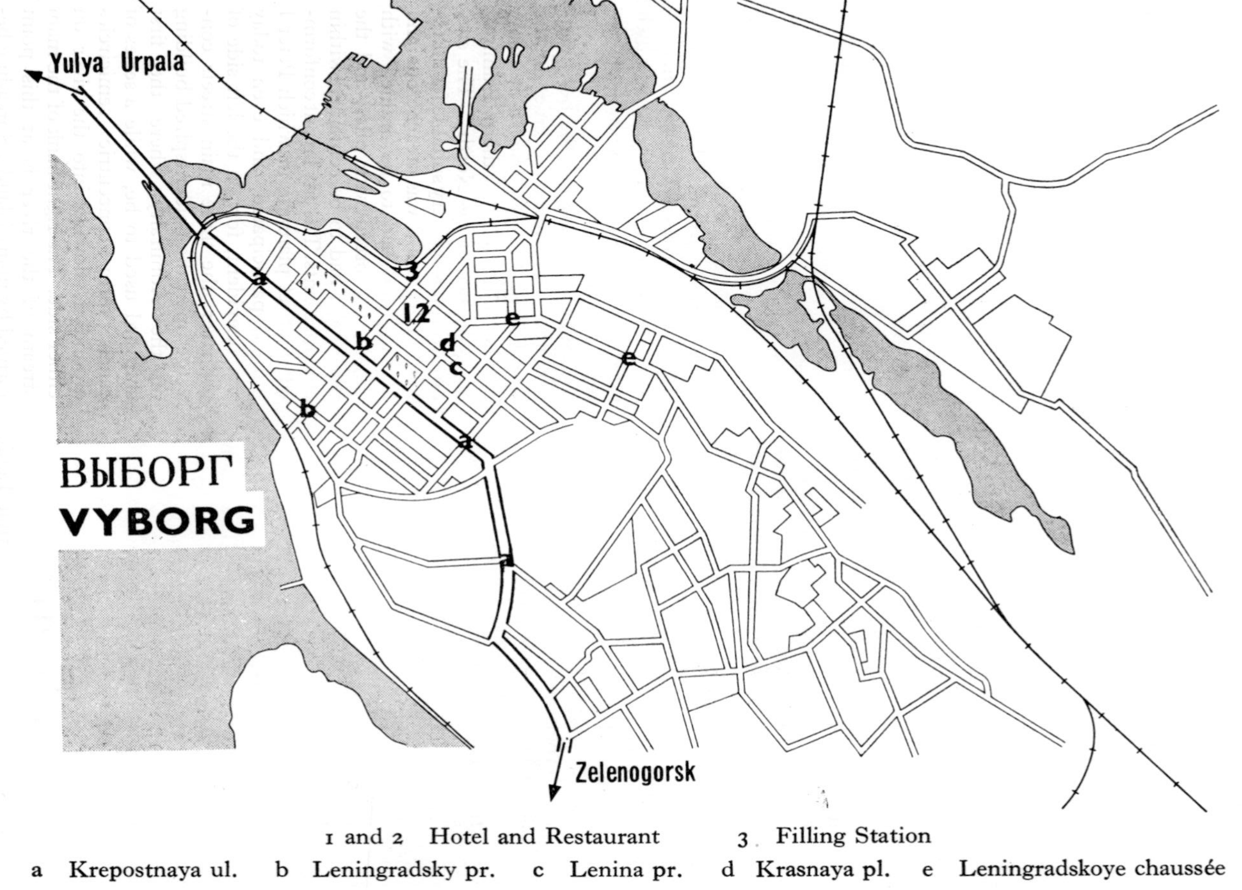

1 and 2 Hotel and Restaurant 3 Filling Station

a Krepostnaya ul. b Leningradsky pr. c Lenina pr. d Krasnaya pl. e Leningradskoye chaussée

Camping Site *Primorskoye chaussée; at the 43 km milestone (from Leningrad), near the sea and 300 m (328 yd) from the main road to the left.*

The furnished tents stand in mixed coniferous and deciduous woodland, and the camping site has a buffet, self service kitchen, showers, and sports grounds.

SESTRORETSK

In 1714 Peter I founded an arms factory near the River Chernaya (black) and the River Sestra (sister) where the town of Sestroretsk now stands. Sestra, for a long time, marked the boundary between Russia and Sweden, and after 1917 the boundary between Finland and the Soviet Union.

Today the place is a resort, sometimes called locally the "Pearl of the North". The beach is one of the best in the country; it is on the Gulf of Finland, by Dubki Park, and is 80 m (80 yd) wide. Lake Razliv also has a beach (between 5th and 6th Tarkanovskaya Street) and a boating station.

Beyond Sestroretsk, at the 41st km from Leningrad there is a colonnade by the road with the inscription "Health Resort Region of Leningrad". The area has been fashionable since the days of old St. Petersburg; now it is a weekend and summer vacation resort for thousands of people from Leningrad.

✿ Dubki Park remains from Peter the Great's time. The name means "oaks", and according to legend Peter planted the trees himself.

✿ Sestroretsk Restaurant *In Dubki Park.*

RAZLIV

It was near this village that Lenin hid from the agents of the Provisional Government in the summer of 1917. He concealed himself in a roughly built hut in the uninhabited area by *Lake Razliv.*

✿ A granite monument to Lenin was built in 1927 by Gegello on the site of the hut.

LENINGRAD

St. Petersburg until 1914,
Petrograd until 1924
Population: 3,000,000 (1959)

Until 1700 when Peter I marched with his army to take back the lands around the mouth of the river Neva from the occupying Swedish forces, Russia had no access to the seas, for Turkey was still holding the Black Sea.

The Peter and Paul Fortress was the first part of Leningrad to be founded, and it guarded this hard-won passage to the outside world. The port which the fortress protected became increasingly important, and the city which grew up around it was declared the capital of Russia in 1712.

Leningrad is among the best-planned and most attractive cities in the world, and this has earned it many names such as "Northern Palmira" and "Venice of the North". The site, however, was not very suitable for building. The ground was treacherous and marshy, and had to be drained with canals, reinforced with piles, and the river itself had to be contained within embankments. The city layout conformed to strict planning in which Peter I himself participated, and even today this is evident, for, on the left side of the river, the three main streets converge upon the golden-spired building of the Admiralty where the first shipyard used to be, while a series of canals form concentric semicircles around it, flowing into the river on either side. The right bank of the main stream of the river is at this point formed by many islands. Spreading behind the Peter and Paul Fortress is Petrogradskaya Storona and nearer the sea is the expanse of Vasilyevsky

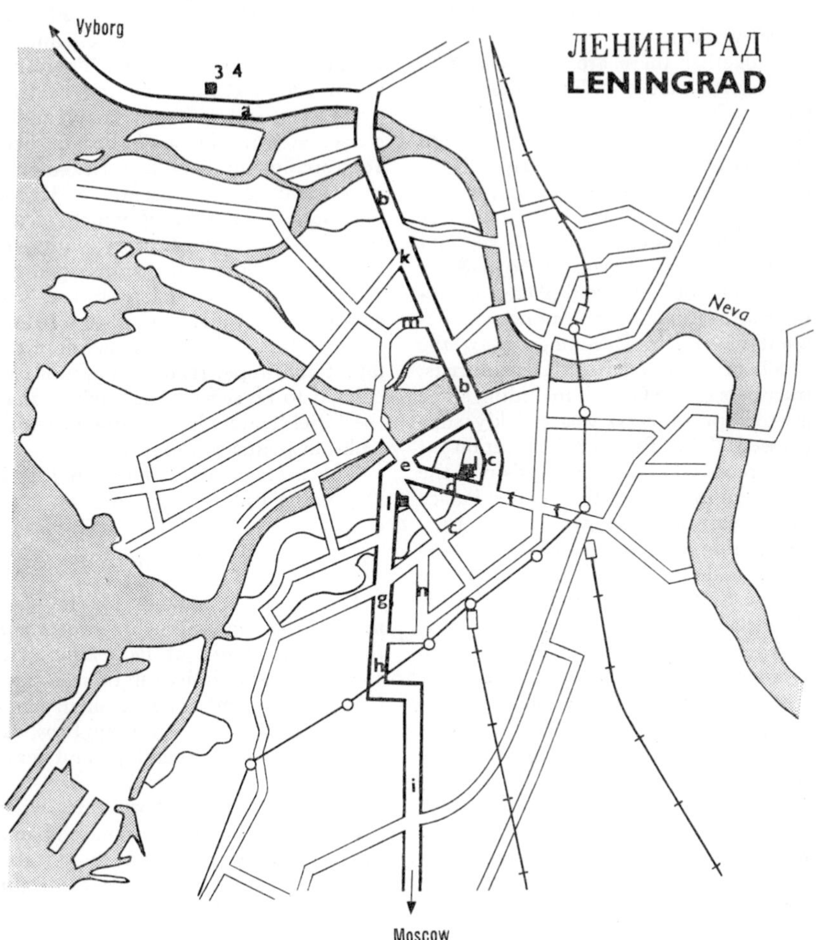

1 Hotels
3 Filling Station
4 Service Station

a Primorsky pr.
b Kirovsky pr.
c Sadovaya ul.
d Brodskogo ul.
e Dvortsovaya pl.
f Nevsky pr.
g Maiorova pr.
h Izmailovsky pr.
i Moskovsky pr.

Ostrov, where Peter I founded the Academy of Sciences and where Lomonosov, Popov, Mendeleyev and Pavlov all worked.

Altogether there are 101 islands in Leningrad, including Vasilyevsky, Krestovsky, Yelagin and Dekabristov, and between them flow the different streams of the Neva. The river Neva itself is 67 km (42 miles) long, 13 km (8 miles) of which are within the city boundaries. Its width within the city varies from 337 m to 592 m (369–648 yd).

The city of Leningrad played a leading role in Russian revolutionary movements. Here, in December 1825, the revolt of the *Dekabristy* (Decembrists, members of the Guard, including some aristocratic officers) was quickly suppressed. The Russian Revolution of 1905 received its bloody baptism in the massacre in front of the Winter Palace in January of that year. The 1917 Revolution first broke out in Leningrad, and the establishment of the Soviet State was subsequently proclaimed here.

After the beginning of the war with Germany in 1914 the name of the city was changed from the Germanic Petersburg to its Russian equivalent, Petrograd (*burg* and *-grad* both meaning *town* or *city*). It has been called Leningrad since Lenin's death in 1924. It is also known as the "cradle of the Russian revolution" and is still spoken of colloquially as "Peter" pronounced in the English way). The city remained the capital of Russia until 1918, when the seat of government was transferred back to Moscow.

During World War II Leningrad was besieged for 29 months; it was subsequently awarded the title of "Hero City" (as were also Odessa, Sevastopol, Stalingrad—now Volgograd, Kiev and Moscow).

Now there are many new blocks of flats, such as those along Moskovskii prospekt, and even whole new regions such as Avtovo. Leningrad is still one of the biggest seaports in the Soviet Union and one of the main industrial centres of the country. Machinery, metals and ships are produced here and light industry includes chemicals, textiles and food products. There are about 270 scientific research centres, over 40 institutes, a university and a conservatoire; the city boasts over 1000 architectural and historical monuments and has 50 museums and 2000 libraries, the largest of which is the Saltykov-Shchedrin Library, with over 13,000,000 books and manuscripts.

Leningrad's television tower was completed in 1962. It rises to a height of 316 m (1037 ft) and is therefore the tallest in Europe. Its total weight is calculated to be seven times lighter than the Eiffel Tower. It is planned to open look-out points to the public.

The average temperature in July is 17·3°C (63°F).

Driving in Leningrad

Leningrad is notable for its geometrical planning, its wide streets and the small amount of its traffic. The spire of the Admiralty can be seen from many points, and is an excellent landmark for motorists; Nevsky Prospekt is the central thoroughfare and leads straight to the Admiralty.

Motorists should take care when turning to drive along the canal embankments, because on some of them traffic keeps to the left instead of the right, which is unusual in Russia.

For a while during the small hours of the morning, after 2 a.m., the Neva bridges are raised for shipping to pass through.

The road into the city from the north (Vyborg) runs along Primorsky Prospekt past the filling and service station and over a bridge to Kirovsky Prospekt which goes straight to the Palace Embankment.

To leave Leningrad for Moscow, motorists should drive from Saint Isaac's Square as far as possible along Mayorov Prospekt and its continuation,

Izmailovsky Prospekt, which passes Izmailovsky Cathedral on the right (near Varshavsky Railway Station), then turn left beside the canal to the first bridge; turn right into the main Moscow road. There is a filling station on this road which provides round the clock service.

NEVSKY PROSPEKT. This is the main street of the city and one of the oldest, founded in 1710 as the main road to Novgorod. Beginning at the Admiralty building it leads to Moscow Railway Station, and then runs further on to the Alexander Nevsky Monastery, covering a total of 4·5 km (3 miles).

Along it were built the banks, the best shops and the palaces of the nobility. No. 9/1, at the corner of Gogol Street, was the Wavelburg Bank, built in 1912 by Peretyatkovich in imitation of the Doge's Palace in Venice and the Medici Palace in Florence. No. 20 was the former Dutch Church (1834–36). On the corner of the Moika Embankment is the white-columned Stroganov Palace, built in 1752–54 by the architect Rastrelli, and constituting one of the best examples of Russian baroque style. No. 22–24 is the former Protestant Church of Saint Peter and Saint Paul, built in Roman style by the architect Bryullov in 1833–38. Opposite the impressive Kazan Cathedral is the former Singer building (1907), with a globe on the top. No. 32–34 was formerly the Roman Catholic Saint Catherine's Church, built by La Mothe in 1763–64 in the form of a Latin Cross. No. 29–31 was the one-time Silversmiths' Row, built in 1784 by Quarenghi, who was also responsible for the erection in the same year of the city hall nearby, later reconstructed. The tower by Ferrezi (1802) was used for fire-watching, and for a "mirror telegraph", linking the Winter Palace by signals with the imperial residence at Tsarskoye Selo (now Pushkin).

Next to the tower at No. 35 is the 230 m (250 yd) frontage of Gostinnyi Dvor; here numerous shops were built into galleries forming a square 1 km (½ mile) around. It was built in 1761 to 1785 by La Mothe. Opposite, at No. 40 to 42, is the former Armenian Church (1770) and a little further down the other side is another big shop, Passage, founded in 1848 and reconstructed in 1900. At the corner of Sadovaya Street is the Saltykov-Shchedrin Library, built partly by Sokolov in 1796–1801 and partly by Rossi in 1828–32, containing statues of Homer, Plato and other famous Greeks. In Ostrovskaya Street in front of the Pushkin Drama theatre is a monument to Catherine II. No. 56 is one of the biggest food shops, formerly called Yeliseyevsky and built in 1903–07 by Baranovsky.

At the point where Nevsky prospekt crosses the Fontanka Canal stands the famous Anichkov Bridge. The present bridge was built in 1839–41, with railings designed by Montferrand. It is chiefly noted for its statues of horses by Peter Klodt; these were begun 10 years before the present bridge was completed. Originally there were two statues, each cast twice and placed at the four corners of the bridge. Then one pair was sent by Nicholas I to the King of Prussia as a present. New casts were made, but again in 1846 Nicholas I sent them away as presents, this time to the King of Sicily. In 1850 Klodt made two different statues to complete the set, and they were accordingly erected on the bridge where they have since stood, except for a time during World War II when they were buried for protection.

By the bridge is the Anichkov Palace, built by order of the Tsaritsa Elizabeth for her favourite, Count Razumovsky, in 1741–50, and subsequently reconstructed. Its garden also faces onto Nevsky Prospekt. The crossroad of the Prospekt with Liteiny Prospekt and Vladimirsky Prospekt is the busiest in the city. The Moscow Station building was designed by Thon in 1851.

DVORTSOVAYA (PALACE) SQUARE. The Winter Palace stands on the north side of the square; opposite is the horseshoe-shaped building built by Rossi in 1819–29 for the tsarist military General Staff and once occupied by the offices of the Ministries of Finance and Foreign Affairs. The 585 m (640 yd) long frontage in strict classical style was decorated by the sculptors Pimenov and Demut-Malinovsky. Their chief work here is the six-horse victory chariot which symbolises the victory of Russia over Napoleon in 1812; this stands on the copy of a Roman triumphal arch which intersects the building. The arch is 28 m (92 ft) high and is now called the Triumphal Arch of the Red Army.

Alexander's Column, in the centre of the square, stands 30 m (150 ft) high and weighs 600 tons. The monument was designed by Montferrand, and was erected in 1834 on the order of Nicholas I in memory of AlexanderI, and also to commemorate the victory over Napoleon. The column of polished red Finnish granite was quarried out of a cliff by the sea—a task that took three years—and in 1832 was brought here on a specially constructed barge. It took 2000 soldiers equipped with complicated pulleys to raise it into position. Orlovsky was the sculptor of the angel which stands on the top, holding a cross and trampling a snake under foot.

On the east side of the square are barracks built in 1840 by Bryullov.

The square itself was the scene of the massacre of January 1905, and it was here that the rebellious troops and workers attacked the Winter Palace, then the headquarters of Kerensky's government, in October 1917.

DEKABRISTOV (DECEMBRISTS') SQUARE. This square takes its name from the 2000 soldiers of the tsarist guard who attempted a *coup d'état* in December, 1825; they gathered here outside the Council of State, beside the river and on the opposite side of the square from the Admiralty. The buildings of the former Senate House and the Holy Synod, joined by a high archway, were built in 1829 to 1834 and constitute the last great architectural work of Rossi. In the grassy park is the famous statue of Peter I known as the Bronze Horseman, of whom Pushkin wrote in his poem entitled *The Bronze Horseman*:

"There, by the billows desolate,
He stood, with mighty thoughts elate,
And gazed."

The solid block of granite upon which the statue stands was transported part of the way on a specially built platform on wheels.

During the summer, boats leave from this embankment on sight-seeing tours of the city.

PETROPAVLOVSKAYA KREPOST' (PETER AND PAUL FORTRESS) *Revolution Square. Open 11–7; closed on Wednesdays.* In 1706 builders began to replace the original earthworks, founded in 1703, with powerful brick fortifications 12 m (40 ft) high; the task was not completed, however, for 35 years, and later the walls were faced with granite slabs. Gradually the fortress lost its military importance and became a prison. The first prisoner held there was Peter I's son, Alexei, who was tortured to death on his father's orders in 1718. From the end of the 18th century the fortress served as a prison for political offenders; the writer Maxim Gorky was imprisoned here in 1905. In 1917 the arsenal of the fortress was used to arm the revolutionaries, and in 1922 the fortress was opened as a museum.

PETROPAVLOVSKY SOBOR (PETER AND PAUL CATHEDRAL). This cathedral was founded in 1712 and planned by Domenico Tressini, but was rebuilt, after a fire in 1753, on architectural plans by Rastrelli and his brilliant pupil Savva Chevakinsky. It is 64 m (210 ft) long and 30 m (98 ft) wide; the slender gilded spire is 120 m (394 ft) high; there is an angel at the top. The clock in the spire was brought from Cologne in 1760. In this cathedral were buried all the rulers of Russia, (with the exception of Peter II), from Peter I to Alexander III after Leningrad became the capital of Russia. The imperial tombs are of white marble, with gilded eagles at the corners. The iconostasis was designed by Zarudnyi in 1726.

PETROVSKIYE VOROTA (PETER GATE). The gates were designed by Domenico Tressini and built in 1717 to 1718. The bas-reliefs of Saint Peter are by Konrad Osner.

NEVSKIYE VOROTA (NEVA GATE). It was through this gate which was built in 1787 that the prisoners passed on their way to the gallows.

MONETNYI DVOR (THE MINT) *To the west of the cathedral.* The mint was originally founded in 1724, but the present building by Voronikhin dates from the 19th century.

GAUPT VAKHTA (ARSENAL). The building now houses the military museum. There are 50,000 exhibits, including weapons, military uniforms and documents.

The city *bathing beach* is below the fortress walls.

DOMIK PETRA (PETER I'S COTTAGE) *Petrogradskaya Storona, Petrovskaya Naberezhnaya 1. Open May–November 12–7; closed on Tuesdays.* The cottage was built in three days in 1703. Peter I lived there only in the summer, so it had no stone foundations and no arrangements for heating. The pine logs were painted to resemble bricks, a device frequently resorted to in the city's early years. The tsar stopped using the cottage altogether when the Summer Palace across the river was completed, and it was only preserved as an interesting historical relic. It is 19 m (62 ft) long and 6 m (20 ft) wide and contains two rooms and a cabinet. It is enclosed within a stone building set up to protect it by Catherine II in 1784.

Inside the cottage is the boat in which the tsar saved the lives of some fishermen on Lake Ladoga in 1690. It is said to have been built by the tsar himself.

The river embankment is decorated with two mythical lion-frogs (Shih Tsa) brought from Manchuria in 1907. There is a bronze bust of Peter I in the garden.

THE ADMIRALTY. The Admiralty was constructed in 1704 as one of the first buildings in St. Petersburg. Originally a shipyard and a fortress, it rose to be the headquarters of Peter I's navy, and now houses various naval offices.

The present building dates from 1806–23 and was designed by the architect A. Zakharov. It is 730 m (800 yd) in length and is adorned with 56 sculptures and 11 large reliefs, symbolising various mythological aspects of the sea, Russia, trade, victory, and so on. Some of them are by the sculptor Shchedrin. The building has a golden roof, and the spire, 70 m (230 ft) high with a ship's weather vane on top, is visible from many different points in the city.

THE SUMMER PALACE *Open May to November 12–8, closed on Tuesdays.* This modest two-storey building in Dutch style was designed by Domenico Tressini in 1710–14. It was used only occasionally during festivities in the gardens.

On each floor there are 6 halls, a kitchen, corridor and servants' room. Notable are the tiled kitchen, the entrance hall with a carved Minerva, the Green Study upstairs and numerous blue-and-white tiled stoves. The statuary by Schlüter and the paintings on the ceilings are still in good condition.

The Coffee House was designed in 1826 by Rossi and decorated with bas-reliefs. The Tea House was designed by the architect Charlemagne in 1827.

SMOLNYI. At one time the Swedish fort of Sabina stood here. The present name comes from *smolnyi dvor* (tar yard); situated by the river, this was a convenient site for the storage of tar for St. Petersburg's shipbuilding industry. But in 1723 the tar was moved elsewhere, and a summer palace was built here for Elizabeth, daughter of Peter I.

When this was burnt down, Elizabeth decided to have a convent for orphans built in its place and in 1748 the architect Rastrelli designed the new baroque-style building, the Cathedral of the Resurrection, (1744–57) which has five domes, the central one of which is 70 m (230 ft) high. The whole group of buildings is reminiscent of ancient Russian church architecture. Catherine II decreed that there should be a school for the daughters of the nobility here, and a widow's house in classical style designed by Giacomo Quarenghi was added to the complex. The school moved here, and the widows were accommodated in the convent building.

In August 1917 the Petrograd revolutionaries took over Smolnyi as their headquarters, and Lenin joined them there on 25th October of that year. His office is still carefully preserved.

Smolnyi is now used as the local headquarters of the Communist Party.

THE STRELKA (*little arrow*) *of Vasilyevsky Ostrov*. The Strelka is the tip of the island nearest to the Peter and Paul fortress. On it are two 32 m (105 ft) high Rostral Columns, designed by Thomas de Thomon in 1806 and decorated with beaks of galleys and figures of naiads. The statues at the foot of the columns personify Russia's commercial waterways, the Neva, the Volkhov, the Volga and the Dnieper. The columns once served as beacons for ships entering the commercial port. Oil was poured into the copper cups at the top and, when it was lighted at dusk, the columns turned into gigantic flaming torches. Now on national holidays gas jets are lit, and the heat from them can be felt by those standing nearby.

On the other side of the road is the former building of the Stock Exchange, designed by Thomon in 1810 to 1816 and surrounded by 44 Doric columns in imitation of the ancient Temple of Paestum in southern Italy. The sculptures on the eastern and western façades are devoted to seafaring, navigation and trade, and on the eastern (main) façade stands a figure of Neptune in a chariot drawn by sea horses, with the Russian rivers Neva and Volkhov symbolically flowing round him. One of the most beautiful views of Leningrad is that obtained from the semi-circular space between the columns. On the left side is the spire of the Saint Peter and Saint Paul Cathedral in the Fortress, and to the right the former palaces along the Neva embankment. The Exchange building now houses the Navy Museum.

✿ CATHEDRAL OF SAINT NICHOLAS *Kommunarov Square 3*. This cathedral was built in 1753–62 by Chevakinsky. This and the following two churches are open for religious services.

CHURCH OF THE TRANSFIGURATION *Radishchev Square 1*. The architect of this church was Stasov.

CHURCH OF SAINT VLADIMIR (or CHURCH OF THE ASSUMPTION) *Petrogradskaya Storona, Blokhin Street 16*.

CHURCH OF THE RESURRECTION *On the north side of Nevsky Prospekt, by Griboyedov Canal*. This church was built in

1883–1907 by the architect Parland in Russian style with ornate decorations, and was modelled on Saint Basil's Cathedral in Moscow. It stands on the spot where Alexander II was assassinated in 1881.

BAPTIST CHURCH *Bolsheokhtinsky Prospekt 5.*

ROMAN CATHOLIC CHURCH *Kovensky Pereulok 7.*

SYNAGOGUE *Lermontovsky Prospekt.*

MOSQUE *At the beginning of Kirovsky Prospekt. Open on Fridays.* The Mosque has two minarets, and its grey stone is decorated with gaily coloured tiles. It was built in 1912 by Krichinsky following the design of the tomb of Tamerlane in Samarkand (dating from the early 15th century).

ALEXANDER NEVSKY MONASTERY *Alexander Nevsky Square. Open 11–7; closed on Thursdays.* According to legend the monastery stands on the spot where Grand-Prince Alexander won a victory over the Swedes and the Teutonic Knights in 1240, after which he was surnamed Nevsky ("of the Neva"). Peter I built a small church on this spot in 1713 and in 1724 brought the remains of Saint Alexander here all the way from Vladimir; a bas-relief illustrating this can be seen in Saint Isaac's Cathedral. In 1750 a silver sarcophagus was made in the St. Petersburg Mint for the ashes of the saint. This was transferred to the Hermitage Museum in 1922.

This used to be the largest monastery in Russia, after the Monastery of the Caves in Kiev. It was built in 1710–16 by Domenico Tressini and had 11 churches and 4 cemeteries; there were also church offices, an ecclesiastical Academy and a Seminary.

The Museum of Urban Sculpture, where the original models of many of the works of art that decorate the city are on display, is now here.

TRINITY CATHEDRAL (TROYITSKY SOBOR). This cathedral was founded by Peter I in 1724, and completed in 1778–90 by Stavrov. It is in classical style, with sculptures by Shubin.

THE GATE-CHAPEL. This was designed by Stavrov in 1783–85.

MITROPOLICHY KORPUS. This was designed in baroque style by Rastorguyev in 1756–59.

The Tower, which stands to the left of the main gate, was built in 1722 by Tressini. Inside, on the first floor, is the Church of Saint Alexander Nevsky and on the ground floor is the Church of the Annunciation, where Suvorov is buried.

The cemeteries are now known as the Necropol, and can be seen on admission by ticket. It was in Lazarevskoye Cemetery that Natalia Alexeyevna, Peter I's sister, was buried in 1716, soon after the foundation of the monastery. Lomonosov and the architects Voronikhin, Zakharov and Rossi are also buried here.

In the Tikhvinskoye Cemetery, to the right of the main entrance, lie the fable-writer Krylov, the musicians Glinka, Tchaikovsky, Borodin, Mussorgsky, Rimsky-Korsakov, the architects Klodt and Stavrov, the writer Dostoyevsky, the poet Zhukovsky, and the physician Dr. Botkin.

Some monuments of artistic interest have been brought for display from other cemeteries to this monastery, including a number by P. Martos.

ST. ISAAC'S CATHEDRAL *Isaakyevskaya Square. Open as a museum 10–5; closed on Tuesdays.* Built in Russian Empire style in 1819–58, and covering 1 hectare ($2\frac{1}{2}$ acres), this is the largest church in Leningrad. The architect was Auguste Montferrand (1786–1858), who was also responsible for the Alexander Column in Palace Square, and for some houses.

The Cathedral, built of granite and marble in the shape of a cross, is 111 m

(364 ft) long and 96 m (315 ft) wide. Its enormous gilded dome is visible from afar, and there is an excellent view of the city and the river from the dome. Special permission is needed to take photographs from there.

The main entrances on the north and south sides have porticos imitating the Pantheon in Rome. Each has 16 great columns of polished red Finnish granite 16 m (54 ft) high and 2 m (7 ft) thick, with bronze bases and capitals. The porticos are decorated with bronze reliefs; there are angels at the corners of the roof and statues of the evangelists and apostles. Altogether there are 350 sculptural decorations on the roof, some of them by Vitali and Klodt.

The interior height of the dome from the floor is 82 m (269 ft), (cf. St. Paul's in London—69 m (225 ft) and St. Peter's in Rome—123 m (404 ft)). From the dome of St. Isaac's swings a pendulum weighing 54 kilograms (over a hundredweight) which moves round 13° each hour.

The four colossal doors of oak and beaten bronze each weigh more than 20 tons and are adorned with sculptures by Ivan Vitali (1794–1855). To the left of the main doors there is a bust of architect Ricard de Montferrand, also by Vitali. The iconostasis is 68 m (223 ft) in length and is made of gilded marble. Vitali was responsible for the Holy Doors in the centre, which are flanked by columns veneered with lapis-lazuli and malachite.

KAZAN CATHEDRAL *Kazanskaya Square. Open 12–6 (Sundays 11–6); closed on Wednesdays.* This cathedral, which now houses the Museum of the History of Religion and Atheism, has a colonnade of 136 columns and is a miniature of St. Peter's in Rome. It was designed by Andrei Voronikhin (1760–1814), and at the time of its construction in 1811 it was the third largest cathedral in the world. It is 79 m (264 ft) high, 72 m (236 ft) long and 55 m (180 ft) wide, built on the plan of a Latin cross in Greek neo-classical style.

To the right of the entrance is the tomb of Field-Marshal Kutuzov, and on either side hang the keys of the towns and cities he captured during his campaigns. Nearby is a memorial to the architect of the cathedral. The building takes its name from the wonder-working ikon of Our Lady of Kazan, which has now been transferred to the Russian Museum. It is worthwhile going down into the crypt to see the exhibits there.

In the square in front of the Cathedral are statues of Kutuzov and of General Barclay de Tolly, who led the Russian army in the 1812 campaign. The statues were designed by Orlovsky in 1831–32.

✿ HERMITAGE MUSEUM *Winter Palace, Dvortsovaya Naberezhnaya 36. Open 11–6; closed on Thursdays.* The first exhibits (Flemish, Dutch and Italian paintings, antique sculptures, objects of Chinese art and golden articles found in Siberia) were collected at the beginning of the 18th century, but the date of the foundation of the Hermitage collection is generally considered to be 1764, when a large collection was acquired in Europe and placed in the Hermitage Pavilion, which had been specially built for the purpose and connected to the Winter Palace. Until the middle of the 19th century the Hermitage was the imperial repository for works of art, and access to it was restricted. During the last 40 years the collection has been tripled and now consists of well over 2,000,000 exhibits in more than 1000 rooms and halls, spreading through four different buildings.

The *Winter Palace*, formerly the imperial residence, was built in 1754 to 1762 by Rastrelli, and after the fire of 1837, it was reconstructed by Stasov and Bryullov. The baroque palace is 200 m (219 yd) long, 160 m (175 yd) wide and 22 m (72 ft high); it has

1057 rooms and halls with an area of 45·516 sq.m (54·437 sq.yd) and 117 staircases. The main staircase of the palace, of white marble, still preserves its 18th century appearance, and many of the halls are of great historical and artistic value, the majority being decorated with skilfully worked Russian (Ural) stone. The Heraldic Hall (1000 sq.m/1200 sq.yd) is interesting, because its chandeliers bear shields with the coats-of-arms of Moscow and St. Petersburg, as well as of all the regions of the Russian Empire.

In the years 1764–67 a special Hermitage Pavilion was built, which later came to be called the *Small Hermitage*, and the first collections were placed here. The Hall in this building is notable for its décor, and the Hanging Garden can be seen from its windows. The Garden is so called because it is laid out on a platform supported by vaults, and thus seems to hang in the air. The layer of earth on the platform is 2 m (6 ft 6 in. deep).

In 1775–84 another building known as the *Old Hermitage*, and notable especially for its interior decoration, was constructed by Felten. In 1788 Quarenghi built a gallery in the Old Hermitage; this is an exact replica of the Raphael Gallery in Rome, and is now of great interest, as the original is in poor condition.

By 1850 one more building had been added to the Hermitage, connected to it by a system of corridors; this is known as the *New Hermitage* and has several halls of special interest, including the Hall of Twenty Columns, with columns of Karelian granite and the white marble Roman Courtyard.

The exhibits in the Hermitage Museum fall into 7 main sections, and are subdivided into 40 smaller sections.

1. History of Russian Culture

7th–13th centuries 1st floor, rooms 5–10
17th-early 18th century 1st floor, rooms 13–18
Second half of the 18th century 1st floor, rooms 20–34
First quarter of the 19th century 1st floor, rooms 35–39 and 48
Russian silverware (17th–20th centuries) 1st floor, room 60
Malachite objects (early 19th century) 1st floor, room 19

This room is known as the Malachite hall, decorated with Ural Malachite of the so-called silky-toned variety. More than 2000 kilograms (2 tons) of stone was used for the columns alone. It was in this hall that the ministers of the Provisional Government were gathered for conference on the eve of the October Revolution, before being arrested by the revolutionary troops.

Russia's Heroic Military Past 1st floor, room 65–67
1812 Patriotic War Gallery 1st floor, room 67

This gallery contains portraits of Russian senior officers who distinguished themselves in the war. The majority of the portraits are by British portrait-painter George Dawe. Nearly all of them were painted from life, as the subjects had been commanded to appear in the artist's studio, each at an appointed day and hour.

St. George's Hall 1st floor, room 68

Alternatively known as the Large Throne-room, this hall with its 48 6 m (20 ft) Italian marble columns decorated with gilded bronze is dominated by a large map of the U.S.S.R. (covering 27 sq.m/300 sq.ft) made of Ural stones and jewels. Moscow as the capital is marked by a diamond hammer and sickle.

2. History of Primeval Culture. (Relics of primeval culture found on the territory of the U.S.S.R.)

Scythian culture and art (7th–2nd centuries B.C.) Ground floor, rooms 6–12.

Culture and art of primeval nomads in the Altai area (Western Siberia). Ground floor, rooms 15–21.

3. History of Oriental Culture and Art (on Soviet territory).

Middle Asia (6th century B.C.–19th century A.D.) Ground floor, rooms 1–16.

Caucasus (10th century B.C.–8th century A.D.) Ground floor, rooms 17–22.

4. Oriental Culture and Art (outside the U.S.S.R.).

Ancient Egypt (4000 B.C.–6th century A.D.). Ground floor, rooms 1–12.

Babylon and Assyria (4000–1000 B.C.) *and Palmyra* (2nd–3rd centuries A.D.) Ground floor, rooms 13–17.

Byzantium (4th–15th centuries) 2nd floor, rooms 39–40.

Near and Middle East: Persia (3rd–18th centuries), Iraq (13th–14th centuries), Syria (13–14th centuries). Egypt (7th to 15th centuries) and Turkey (14–18th centuries). 2nd floor, rooms 41–55.

China (2000 B.C.–20th century), 2nd floor, rooms 18–35.

India (17th–20th centuries) 2nd floor, rooms 36–38a.

Japan (17th–19th centuries) 2nd floor, room 26a.

5. Antique Culture and Art

Ancient Greece (8th–2nd centuries B.C.) Ground floor, rooms 1–4, 8 and 10.

Greek Colonies on the northern shore of the Black Sea (7th century B.C.–3rd century A.D.). Ground floor, rooms 5–7, 9, 10 and 21.

Ancient Italy (7th–2nd centuries B.C.). Ground floor, room 13.

Ancient Rome (1st century B.C.–4th century A.D.) Ground floor, rooms 11–12 and 14–18.

6. West European Art

Mediaeval European Applied Art, (11th–15th centuries) 1st floor, room 1.

Italian Art (13th–18th centuries), 1st floor, rooms 4–33.

Room 11 has two paintings by Leonardo da Vinci, and Rooms 29 and 31 contain 9 Titians.

Spanish Art (16th–18th centuries), 1st floor, rooms 34–35.

In Room 35 are masterpieces by El Greco and Velasquez, among others.

Dutch Art (15th–16th centuries), 1st floor, rooms 37–40.

Flemish Art (17th century), 1st floor, rooms 41–44.

Belgian Art (18th–20th centuries), 2nd floor, rooms 121–123.

Dutch Art (17th–18th centuries), 1st floor, rooms 46–54.

The Hermitage collection includes at least 42 paintings by Rubens, most of which are in Room 42. They include "Perseus and Andromeda", "Philip IV of Spain", "Queen Elizabeth of Spain", "The Union of Water and Earth", "Venus and Adonis", and a statue of Ceres.

Room 43 contains works by Van Dyck including: "The Holy Family", "Self-portrait", "Portrait of E. Jaabach" (banker and art collector), "Charles I of England", "St. Peter", and "Rubens with his son Albert".

There are 21 works attributed to Rembrandt in Room 50 including: "Portrait of Saskia as Flora", "Abraham's Offering", "The Return of the Prodigal Son", "Danae", "The Holy Family", and the "Descent from the Cross".

Dutch Art (19th century), 2nd floor, rooms 124–125.

German Art (15th–19th centuries), 1st floor, rooms 61–69.

Room 64 was originally the Small Throne room, also known as Peter's Hall in Honour of Peter the Great. It was decorated by Montferrand and redecorated after the fire of 1837 by Stasov.

Austrian Art (18th–19th centuries), 2nd floor, rooms 71–73.

French Art (15th–20th centuries), 1st floor, rooms 74–89a and 93–97 and 2nd floor rooms 98–114.

Rooms 111–114 on the top floor have works by Renoir, Matisse, Gauguin and other Impressionists.

Swedish and *Danish Art* (18th century), 1st floor, rooms 90–92.

Finnish Art (19th–20th centuries), 2nd floor, room 70.

English Art (17th–19th centuries), 1st floor, rooms 115–118.

History of *Western European Arms* (15th–17th centuries), 1st floor, room 36.

Western European Silverware (17th to 18th centuries), 1st floor, room 83.

Western European Decorative China (18th century), 1st floor, room 120.

7. RUSSIAN AND FOREIGN MEDALS, BADGES AND ORDERS. 2nd floor, room 2.

RUSSIAN ART MUSEUM *Inzhenernaya Street 4/2. Open 11–6; closed on Tuesdays.* The Museum occupies two buildings, the first being the former Mikhailovsky Palace, among the finest pieces of architecture in Leningrad. It was built in 1819–25 by Rossi, one of the most prominent Russian architects of the period, for Grand Prince Mikhail, son of Paul I. Pre-revolutionary Russian art is housed here now.

The second building (designed by Benois, architect Ovsyanikov) was finished in 1916. In 1948–53 it was rebuilt and re-arranged after severe damage during World War II. Soviet art and temporary exhibitions are to be found here.

The Russian Museum possesses one of the finest collections of Russian art in the country. There are extensive collections of drawings, paintings and engravings, examples of artisan handicraft and folk art and a large collection of ancient ikons. All the greatest masters are represented here, and the collection covers all the important periods and tendencies in the development of Russian art.

KUNSTKAMERA (OR THE ANTHROPOLOGICAL AND ETHNOGRAPHICAL MUSEUM, *with the* LOMONOSOV MUSEUM *in the same building*) *Vasilyevsky Ostrov, Universitetskaya Naberezhnaya 3. Open on Thursdays and Sundays 11–5 and Fridays 11–4.* This massive two-storey building with a tower, a protruding central section and arched façade in baroque style was built by Mattarnovyi, Kiaveryi and Zemstov in 1718–34, and is one of the oldest buildings in the city. Mikhail Lomonosov worked here from 1741–65, and it was the first home of the Academy of Sciences; it was also Russia's first natural science museum, and housed the first library. At one time there used to be an observatory on the upper floor.

Originally known as the Kunstkammer, Peter I referred to the museum as his cabinet of "curiosities, rarities and monsters". The collection developed from art works which Peter I purchased in 1716 in Holland; these were predominantly of Chinese and Indian origin. Added to these were anatomical specimens and a collection of "monsters", mostly freak human and animal embryos. Also on display are Peter I's surgical instruments, porcelain, laquerwork, bronzes, wood-, stone-, and ivory-carvings, and a large globe made in 1754. The collection has since grown into one of the biggest anthropological and ethnographical museums in the country.

PORCELAIN MUSEUM *Obukhovskoi Oborony Prospekt 151/2.*

LENINGRAD ARTISTS' PERMANENT EXHIBITION *Nevsky Prospekt 8. Open 11–7; closed on Sundays.*

HISTORY OF LENINGRAD MUSEUM *Krasnogo Flota Naberezhnaya 44. Open on Mondays, Thursdays, Saturdays and Sundays 11–7 and Tuesdays and Fridays 1–9; closed on Wednesdays.* The house in an 18th century mansion, rebuilt in 1826–27, with a sculptured frieze on the façade by the architect I. P. Martos. The exhibits illustrate the history of the city: St. Petersburg till 1914, then Petrograd, then ten years later, Leningrad. Among the exhibits are models reproducing in detail the transportation of the great rock for the Bronze Horseman statue, a firework display in St. Petersburg at the beginning of the 18th century and other models and dioramas showing the past, present and future of the city. One of the sections is devoted to the siege of Leningrad during World War II.

In front of the museum there is a wall of pink granite erected on the spot where the cruiser *Aurora* was moored on the night of the October uprising.

PLANETARIUM *Krasnaya Street 60. Open Tuesdays and Fridays 4–7 and Saturdays 6–8 from September until 15 June.*

ARCTIC MUSEUM *Marat Street 24. Open 12–6, Mondays 12–4, Sundays 11–5; closed on Tuesdays.*

CENTRAL NAVAL MUSEUM *Vasilyevsky Ostrov, Pushkinskaya Square 4. Open 12–7, Sundays 11–7; closed on Tuesdays.*

ARTILLERY HISTORY MUSEUM *Petrogradskaya Storona, Lenin Park 7. Open 11–6, Sundays 10–7, Mondays 11–3; closed on Tuesdays.*

MUSEUM OF ETHNOGRAPHY OF THE PEOPLES OF THE U.S.S.R. *Inzhenernaya Street 1/4. Open 11–6; closed on Mondays.*

LENIN MUSEUM *Khalturin Street 5/1. Open 11-7, Sundays 10-5; closed on Saturdays.* This museum is the Leningrad branch of the Lenin Museum in Moscow. The exhibits illustrate the activities of the founder of the Soviet state during the pre-revolutionary period and his work in this city during the 1917 revolution; a documentary newsreel is also shown. The museum is located in the Marble Palace built by Rinaldi in 1768–85 as a present from Catherine II to Count Orlov. The walls both inside and outside are of marble, as are the impressive staircases in the museum, and one hall is decorated with 32 different kinds of marble.

PUSHKIN MUSEUM *Moika Naberezhnaya 2. Open 11–5; closed on Thursdays.* The famous poet Alexander Pushkin died here on 29th January, 1837. His flat is kept as it was during his lifetime, and in the courtyard is a monument to him by Didikin (1950).

SUVOROV MUSEUM *Saltykov-Shchedrin Street 41 b. Open 11–5; closed on Wednesdays.* Generalissimo Alexander Suvorov (1730–1800), one of the most respected Russian military leaders, distinguished himself in the Seven Years' War and in the Russo-Turkish wars. Hed is also famed for one of the bravest feats in military history, the march through the Saint Gotthard Pass. The museum was built in 1904 by Gogen, and on the façade is a mosaic copy of the painting by Popov illustrating the Saint Gotthard march.

THE CRUISER *AURORA*. On 7th November, 1917, the *Aurora*, upon the orders of the military Revolutionary Committee, sailed up the river and trained her guns on the windows of the Winter Palace, then used by the Provisional Government. She fired one blank shot which was the signal for the revolutionaries to attack.

Since 1948 the ship has been permanently moored near the Nakhimov Naval College, where she is used for training purposes. The vessel is open twice a week as a museum.

KIROV MUSEUM *Kirov Prospekt 26/28. Open 11–7, Sundays 10–6; closed on Saturdays.*

MUSEUM OF THE REVOLUTION *Kuibyhsev Street 4.*

THE BRONZE HORSEMAN, MONUMENT TO PETER THE GREAT. *Dekabristov Square, by the river.* This statue by E. M. Falconet was unveiled in 1782; Marie Collot, who later became Falconet's daughter-in-law, modelled the tsar's head, and F. G. Gordeyev designed the writhing snake under the horse's hoofs. The statue, 5 m (16 ft) high, stands upon an enormous block of granite weighing 1638 tons. The inscription "To Peter I from Catherine II: 1782" is written in Russian on one side and in Latin on the other.

At Engineer's Castle, there is another monument to Peter the Great, designed by Rastrelli in 1800.

CATHERINE II MONUMENT *Ostrovsky Square.* This statue, 14 m (46 ft) high, by Opekushin, was unveiled in 1873.

NICHOLAS I MONUMENT *Isaakyevskaya Square.* The equestrian statue by P. Klodt, which was unveiled in 1859, is unusual for being balanced on two points only.

RIMSKY-KORSAKOV MONUMENT *In front of the Conservatoire.* Designed by Bogolyubov and Ingal in 1952.

MOSCOW TRIUMPHAL GATES *Moskovsky Prospekt.* These gates were built by Stasov in 1833–38.

NARVA TRIUMPHAL GATES *Stachek Prospekt.* These gates were planned by Quarenghi and reconstructed by Stasov in 1827–34; they commemorate those who defended the country in the 1812–14 war. The arch is decorated with allegorical figures of Glory and with inscriptions enumerating the Guards' Regiments that had distinguished themselves during the war, and the places where decisive battles had been fought.

KIROV MONUMENT *At the entrance to Kirov Stadium, Krestovsky Island.* Pinchuk designed this monument in 1950 in honour of Sergei Kirov (1886 to 1934), a Communist leader who for some time headed the Leningrad Party organisation.

CHERNYSHEVSKY MONUMENT *Moskovsky Prospekt, near Park Pobedy.* This monument to the philospher was designed in 1947 by the sculptor Lishev.

LENIN MONUMENT *By Finlyandsky Railway Station.* This monument by Yevsyev, 1926, is perhaps the best of the many of Lenin, who is shown standing on an armoured car.

PUSHKIN MONUMENTS *In the garden in front of the Russian Art Museum; Pushkin Street.* These two monuments were designed by Anikushin in 1957 and Opekushin in 1884 respectively.

GLINKA MONUMENT *In front of the Conservatoire.* This was designed by R. Bach in 1906.

GRIBOYEDOV MONUMENT *Zagorodnyi Prospekt, Vitebsky Railway Station.* The monument to the writer Griboyedov was put up by V. Lishev in 1959.

WAR MEMORIAL *Piskarevskoye Cemetery, by the main gate.* There are two granite pavilions in this cemetery, with a museum showing life in Leningrad during World War II. At the end of the avenue of graves is a sculpture, by Isayeva and Taurit, of a woman symbolising the Motherland.

WAR MEMORIAL *Serafimovsky Cemetery.* This memorial, unveiled in 1965, is dedicated to the memory of the defenders of Leningrad.

✿ PUSHKIN THEATRE *Ostrovsky Square 2.* Built by Rossi in 1832, in Empire style, this theatre was originally called the Alexandrinsky Theatre in honour of Tsaritsa Alexandra, wife of Nicholas I. The statue of Apollo's chariot is by Pimenov.

Here first-class actors perform modern and classical drama.

Comedy Theatre *Nevsky Prospekt 56.* This theatre has the reputation of being among the best comedy theatres in the country.

Kirov Theatre *Teatralnaya Square 2.* The building by the architect Kavos was completed in 1860 and called the Mariinsky Theatre in honour of Tsaritsa Maria, wife of Alexander II. It was renamed after the prominent Bolshevik, Kirov, in 1935, following his assassination.

At the beginning of the 19th century this theatre was the cradle of Russian ballet; since then Anna Pavlova danced here and Shaliapin sang. More recently, Galina Ulanova started her career here before leaving in 1944 to join Moscow's Bolshoi Ballet Company.

Malyi (Small) Opera Theatre *Iskusstv Square 1.* This building was designed in 1833 by Bryullov, following Rossi's general project for the whole square, and was redesigned in 1859 by Kavos.

The theatre was first called the Mikhailovsky, and this was also the old name for the square in which it stands. Up to 1918 it was occupied by a more or less permanent French drama company. After that date an opera company worked here, and was joined by a ballet company in 1933. Lavrovsky was in charge of the ballet in this theatre before he became the chief choreographer at the Bolshoi Theatre in Moscow.

Gorky Theatre *Fontanka Naberezhnaya 65.* This building was constructed in 1879 by the architect L. Fontan. Maxim Gorky was responsible for the foundation of the present theatre company in 1919.

Komsomol Theatre *Lenin Park 4.* Built in 1939 by Miturich and Makashov, the theatre was badly damaged during World War II, but was soon restored.

Musical Comedy Theatre *Rakov Street 13.* Opened in 1929, this was the only theatre in Leningrad which gave performances throughout the Second World War, even during the siege of Leningrad.

Youth Theatre *Zagorodnyi Prospekt 46.* This theatre was founded in 1921 by A. A. Bryantsev.

Theatre of the Music and Drama Institute *Mokhovaya Street 35.*

Leningrad Philharmonia Concert Hall *Brodsky Street 2.* The building was designed in 1834–39 by P. Jaquet, with a façade by Rossi, to house the Nobles' Club. In 1921 it was given to the Leningrad State Philharmonic Society.

New Concert Hall *Lenin Square 1.*

Glinka Kapella (Choir Hall) *Moika Naberezhnaya 20.* The building was constructed in 1880 by L. N. Benois, but the Choir itself was founded by Peter the Great in 1713. Glinka and Rimsky-Korsakov performed here, as did other famous musicians.

Circus *Fontanka Naberezhnaya 3.* V. A. Kennel designed this building in 1876.

✿ Summer Garden (Letny Sad) *Pestelya Street 2.* The garden lies on an island between the River Neva and the Fontanka, Moika and Swan Canals, and was laid out by Le Blond in 1704–12 in geometrically precise Franco-Dutch style, with fountains fed by the Fontanka River. 79 statues stand in the garden; the statue "Peace and Plenty" was carved at Peter I's special order, and in an allegorical representation of the victory of Russia in the Northern War (1700–21), the fallen lion representing conquered Sweden.

In Peter the Great's day the garden was the centre of the social and political life in St. Petersburg. Among the famous men who have since enjoyed strolling there are Pushkin, the poet Zhukovsky, the fabulist Krylov and the composer Mussorgsky.

The fence that separates the garden from the Neva embankment was designed by Felton and Yegorov and erected in 1770–84. The columns of granite are decorated with vases and urns, and are linked by some of the finest iron casting in the world.

In the garden stands a monument to the fable-writer Ivan Krylov, made by Klodt in 1855, with bronze bas-reliefs illustrating some of his fables.

FIELD OF MARS. This 10 hectare (25 acre) park was used for drilling troops and for firework displays on special occasions. It was formerly known as Tsaritsin Lug (Tsaritsa's Meadow), and it received its present name at the end of the 18th century, or possibly in 1801, when the statue of Generalissimo Suvorov was erected. This statue by Kozlovsky, in which Suvorov is represented as the God of War now stands by the Kirov Bridge. The park was once known for its dustiness and was referred to as the "St. Petersburg Sahara". The walks meet in the centre of the square at the monument of the Victims of the Revolution, designed by Rudnyev in 1919. The epitaphs in blank verse were written by Lunacharsky. One of them, carved in granite, reads:

> "By the will of tyrants
> The nations were tearing each
> other.
> You rose, St. Petersburg toilers,
> And were first to wage a war
> Of all the oppressed
> Against all the oppressors,
> thus to destroy
> The very seed of war itself."

Surrounding the square are the Summer Garden, the Mikhailovsky Garden, Engineer's (or Mikhailovsky) Castle, the former barracks of Paul's Regiment (designed by Stasov), and the marble Palace.

BOTANICAL GARDENS *Petrogradskaya Storona, Professor Popov Street 2. Open 11–6; closed on Saturdays. The hothouse is open 11–4; closed on Sundays and throughout the winter.* These gardens lie on Apothecary's Island; in the time of Peter the Great there was a large plantation of medicinal herbs called the Apothecary's Garden here. It remained so for 100 years, and then became the Botanical Gardens. The Botanical Institute was opened in 1931 and now it also has a museum which is open from 11–6 and closed on Saturdays and Sundays.

ZOO *Petrogradskaya Storona, Lenin Park 1. Open daily, all the year round.*

KIROV PARK *Yelagin Ostrov (Island).* The island takes its name from I. Yelagin, the nobleman to whom it belonged after 1780. From the tip of the island, known as the Strelka (little arrow), there is a look-out point facing out to sea; this was replanned in 1927 and now has a terrace of pink marble with lion carvings on stone pedestals.

The pleasant park was laid out in 1932 and 18,000 trees have been planted in recent years. There is a summer theatre for 1600, a variety theatre, a cinema, exhibition halls, boating stations and a bathing beach. Celebrations in June and July to see the white nights in and out are held in this park.

The central building is the Yelagin Palace, built for Alexander I by Rossi in 1818–22 in Russian classical style. There are also a musical pavilion and kitchen buildings.

KIROV STADIUM *Krestovsky Ostrov (Island).* This Island is the sports centre of Leningrad. Pobedy Park was laid out in 1945, and the Dynamo Stadium was built in 1925. The island also has many sports grounds and boathouses.

Kirov Stadium was built in 1950 on plans by A. Nikolsky. It is unusual in that it was constructed of mud from the bottom of the Gulf of Finland and from the river beds. This was pumped to the site, where it spread out to form an oval crater with sides 15 m (50 ft) high, capable of holding 100,000 people.

PARK POBEDY (PARK OF VICTORY) *Moskovsky Prospekt.* Leningrad has two victory Parks, both founded in 1945. This one covers an area of 70 hectares (175 acres) and contains an Avenue of Heroes decorated with busts of famous men.

The Astoria and the Yevropeiskaya are Intourist hotels.

ASTORIA HOTEL *Gertsen Street 39; tel: 10-00-31.*

BALTĬISKAYA HOTEL *Nevsky Prospekt; tel: 10-77-42.*

YEVROPEISKAYA HOTEL *Brodsky Street 1/7; tel: 10-00-10.*

ROSSIYA HOTEL *Moskovsky Prospekt 163; tel: 98-76-49.*

LENINGRADSKAYA HOTEL *Maiorov Prospekt 10–24; tel: 15-00-31.*

MOSKOVSKAYA HOTEL *Ligovsky Prospekt 43/45; tel: 10-00-16.*

NEVA HOTEL *Tchaikovsky Street 17; tel: 72-14-86.*

OKTYABRYSKAYA HOTEL *Nevsky Prospekt 118; tel: 10-00-01.*

SEVERNAYA HOTEL *Vosstaniya Street 2; tel: 72-04-97.*

INTERNATIONAL SEAMEN'S CLUB *Griboyedov Naberezhnaya 166.*

All Restaurants in Leningrad stay open until midnight.

ASTORIA RESTAURANT *In the Astoria Hotel.*

YEVROPEISKAYA HOTEL RESTAURANT *Brodsky Street 1/7.*

ROSSIYA HOTEL RESTAURANT *In the Rossiya Hotel.*

VOSTOCHNYI RESTAURANT *In the Yevropeiskaya Hotel.*

KAVKAZKY RESTAURANT *Nevsky Prospekt 25.*

METROPOL RESTAURANT *Sadovaya Street 22.*

MOSKVA RESTAURANT *Nevsky Prospekt 49.*

PRIMORSKY RESTAURANT *Petrogradskaya Storona, Bolshoi Prospekt 32.*

SEVERNYI RESTAURANT *Sadovaya Street 12.*

UNIVERSAL RESTAURANT *Nevsky Prospekt 12.*

CHAIKA RESTAURANT *Griboyedov Naberezhnaya 14.*

NEVA RESTAURANT *Nevsky Prospekt 44.*

AVTOMAT (SELF-SERVICE) CAFE *Nevsky Prospekt 45.*

NEVA CAFE *Nevsky Prospekt 30.*

SEVER CAFE *Nevsky Prospekt 44.*

UYUT CAFE *Liteiny Prospekt 28.*

FESTIVALNOYE CAFE *Stachek Prospekt 57.*

SPUTNIK CAFE *Moskovsky Prospekt 171.*

FANTASIA CAFE *Ivanovskaya Street 7.*

BURATINO CAFE *Vosstaniya Street 35.*

PROGRESS CAFE *Nevsky Prospekt, at the corner of Suvorovsky Prospekt.*

YOUTH CAFE *Poltavskaya Street.*

This cafe, where young poets gather and recite, is open in the evenings only.

There are many other cafes and milk-bars along the length of Nevsky Prospekt.

BOLSHOI GOSTINNYI DVOR DEPARTMENT STORE *Nevsky Prospekt, between Sadovaya and Dumskaya Streets.*

APRAKSIN DVOR DEPARTMENT STORE *Sadovaya Street, from Lomonosov Street to Apraksin Pereulok.*

PASSAGE DEPARTMENT STORE *Nevsky Prospekt 48.*

DOM LENINGRADSKOI TORGOVLI DEPARTMENT STORE *Zhelyabova Street 21/23.*

NOVINOK (NOVELTIES) SHOP *Nevsky Prospekt 23.*

GIFT SHOP *Nevsky Prospekt 26.*

SOUVENIR SHOP *Nevsky Prospekt 100.*

ANTIQUES *Nevsky Prospekt 58.*

BOOKSHOP *Nevsky Prospekt 28.*

G. P. O. *Soyuza Svyazi Street 9.*

CENTRAL TELEGRAPH OFFICE *Soyuza Svyazi Street 15.*

SERVICE STATION No. 3. *Novaya Derevnya, 3-Liniya 5; tel: 33-69-30 or 33-87-04. Open 8–11 for overhauls, 9–4·30 for repairs; Closed on Sundays.*

FILLING STATION No. 30. *At the Service Station. Round the clock service.*

FILLING STATION No. 2. *Klinicheskaya Street 10. Round the clock service.*

FILLING STATION No. 3. *Moskovsky Prospekt 100. Round the clock service.*

FILLING STATION No. 12. *Dnepropetrovskaya Street 18.* Diesel oil is also obtainable here.

———— ★ ————

PETRODVORETS (*German: Peterhof*) *can be reached by road or by boat from Leningrad; it is about 34 km (21 miles) away.* The *Grand Palace* was begun in 1715–24 according to plans by Le Blond, but its modest dimensions could not hold the large imperial court, and it was resonstructed and enlarged for the Tsaritsa Elizabeth by Rastrelli in 1746 to 1751. The main building has three storeys and is connected to the wings by galleries. The façade is 268 m (885 ft) long and at the eastern corner of the palace is a church in rococo style with five gilded cupolas built by Rastrelli in 1751. These buildings were burned down during World War II and are under reconstruction, the work proceeding in accordance with drawings, photographs and other documents so that the reconstructed ensemble will be as like the original as possible. The grounds also suffered during the war when 25,000 trees were felled.

The Grand Palace stands on a terrace about 12 m (40 ft) high. The surrounding *park* and *gardens* cover approximately 120 hectares (300 acres). Petrodvorets is known as the Russian equivalent of Versailles: it took 4000 soldiers and peasants to dig the canals. When all the fountains are playing 30,000 litres (7500 gallons) of water flow each second. The system was designed by hydro-engineer V. Tuvolkov. The most famous of the 129 fountains now operative is directly in front of the palace façade, at the head of the grand Cascade; this is the Samson Fountain, where Samson is portrayed tearing open the jaws of a lion from which a jet of water rises 20 m (65 ft) into the air. The lion represents Sweden defeated by Russia at the Battle of Poltava on St. Samson's Day in 1709. Other sights of interest include the Chessboard Cascade, and the *Zontik* (little umbrella) and the *Dubok* (little oak), surprise fountains which shower any unsuspecting visitors who come near.

The *Hermitage* is a two-storey pavilion built for Peter I.

The walls of the dining-room on the first floor are lined with Dutch paintings, and part of the table can sink to the floor below to be cleared and relaid. To the right of the Hermitage is a statue of Peter I, made by Antokolsky in 1883.

The small villa in Dutch style, built in the early 18th century, where Peter I lived while the Grand Palace was under construction, is known as *Mon Plaisir*. The stone wing of this miniature palace was built by Rastrelli and reconstructed by Quarenghi, and inside it is decorated with numerous paintings. The Dutch style garden contains small flowerbeds and exotic trees. *Marly* is the name of the small two-storey house in Louis XIV style built in 1714 by Peter I.

The Pavilions which stand on either side of the canal were designed by Voronikhin in about 1800.

GATCHINA *48 km (30 miles) south of Leningrad.* The Gatchina estate was originally owned by Peter I's sister, Natalia; it changed hands before belonging to Count Orlov, for whom Rinaldi built a palace in 1776–82. The park with the White Lake in its centre was also laid out at that time.

The whole estate was subsequently purchased by Catherine II, and her son Paul who lived there turned the palace into a mediaeval castle with help of the architect Vincenzo Brenna. It acquired moats, drawbridges, battlements and a parade ground in front. The castle was badly damaged by the Germans in World War II, and has not been rebuilt.

The main entrance to the park is through Admiralty Gate. This gate with Corinthian columns was built in 1796 by Brenna. The private Garden in formal French style with a statue of Flora in the centre, was added at the end of the 18th century. The Priory, with an octagonal tower and tapering spire was built by Lvov in 1797–98 on the shore of Black Lake. It was intended for a prior of the Knights of Malta, whose Order enjoyed Paul's special patronage.

Chesma Obelisk at the edge of the White Lake commemorates the victory of the Russian fleet at Chesma, as does the obelisk at Pushkin. It was designed by Rinaldi and is of many different shades of marble.

At the end of the lake is the Island of Love with a Temple of Venus on it.

PUSHKIN

Formerly Tsarskoye Selo (tsar's village), this place was called Detskoye Selo (children's village) after the revolution because the buildings were used as kindergartens, children's hospitals, sanatoria and schools. In 1937 it was again renamed, this time after Alexander Pushkin on the occasion of the 100th anniversary of the poet's death.

The so-called Egyptian Gates mark the entrance to the town. They were designed by English architect, Adam Menelaws, and built in 1828; Menelaws also built a ruined "chapel" and a Turkish elephant house for the Zoo. By the Egyptian Gates stands a monument to Pushkin (1911) by Bernstam.

Yekatерininsky Palace was built for Elizabeth, youngest daughter of Peter I and Catherine II. It was begun by the architects Kvasov and Chevakinsky, completed by Rastrelli. It is now under restoration, having been badly burnt during World War II. A small part of it is now open as a museum from 11–6. This includes the green Dining room, the Light Blue Parlour, the Chinese Light Blue Parlour and other halls which have been completely restored.

Yekaterininsky Park. The surroundinglands were given to Catherine I by Peter I and subsequently gardens, a hothouse, ponds and a zoo were laid out. The park covers 592 hectares (1482 acres).

An obelisk, unveiled in 1771, commemorates the Russian victory over the Turks near the Danube.

The Orlov Column, on an island in the middle of the lake, was erected in 1778 by Rastrelli to commemorate Prince Orlov's victory at Chesma; this was a sea battle where the Russians again beat the Turks.

Cameron's Gallery, built 1779–93 by the Scottish architect Charles Cameron, is adorned with the busts of Greek and Roman philosophers.

The Grotto was designed by Rastrelli.

The Concert Hall on the island was designed by Rastrelli and Chevakinsky.

The Hermitage was built in 1752 by Rastrelli. The Agate Rooms were fitted out by Cameron with agate, jasper and porphyry. These and the Hermitage were used as stables by the Germans during World War II.

Alexander I's Triumphal Arch was built by Stasov in 1817–21 in honour of the Russian victory of 1812.

Vechernyi Zal (evening hall) near the Yekaterininsky Palace was designed by Neyelov in 1796–1810.

The Granite Terrace was planned by Luigi Rusca in 1809.

The bronze fountain, "Girl with a Pitcher" was made by Sokolov in 1810. It was mentioned by Pushkin in one of his poems.

The Alexandrovsky Palace was built by Quarenghi in 1792–96. In the Alexandrovsky Park are the Ruined Kitchen (built of real pieces of ancient ruins brought from Italy), many chinoiseries (the Chinese village and the Chinese summer-house, for example) and the Grande Caprice built by Neyelov in 1770–73.

The Lycée is linked to the Yekaterininsky Palace by an arch over the road. Neyelov erected the building in 1791 and a school for the nobility was opened in here 1811; the poet Alexander Pushkin, who spent his schooldays here was one of the first pupils. The school moved to Kirovsky Prospekt in Leningrad in 1843, after which time it was known as the Alexandrovsky Lycée. The monument to Pushkin in the Lycée Garden was made by Bach in 1909. The Lycée building is open from 11–6, and closed on Tuesdays.

By the Lycée is the Znamenskaya Church, which was built in 1734–47 by the Moscow architect, K. Blank, and was the first stone building in the town.

PAVLOVSK

25 km (15½ miles) south of Leningrad and 3 km (2 miles) from Pushkin. The entrance to the town on the road from Pushkin is marked by cast-iron gates designed by Rossi in 1826. Visitors to the palace, which is open from 11 till 6, should leave their cars by the wooden bridge; it is a short walk across the bridge and up the drive to the palace itself.

This territory was originally the hunting ground attached to the imperial estate of Tsarskoye Selo (3 km/2 miles away). In 1777 Catherine II gave the lands to her son Paul as a site for a country residence, and they then received the name of Pavlovskoye, Paul's Village. In 1782 Charles Cameron was in charge of the planning of the original Grand Palace, which was subsequently enlarged and decorated inside by Quarenghi, Brenna, Voronikhin and Rossi. It now has three storeys and a central dome which rests on 64 columns; the palace was badly damaged during the Second World War, but part of it is now open to visitors. The statue of Paul I in the middle of the main courtyard was designed by Klodt in 1872.

It was also Cameron who supervised the first plans for the surrounding park; now with 600 hectares (1500 acres), it is one of the biggest landscaped parks in Europe. The river Slavyanka was dammed to form a lake, and the trees were planted with special attention to their autumn colours. The park is intersected by avenues and winding paths which lead to pavilions and statues, and which constantly reveal new views of the beautifully landscaped estate.

Apollo's Colonnade on the left bank of the River Slavyanka was built by Cameron in 1780–83, and in the centre is a bronze copy of the Apollo Belvedere. Part of the colonnade collapsed during a flood in 1817, but it was decided to leave the fallen stones to create a more ancient effect.

The Pavilion of the Three Graces, a stone terrace with 16 columns supporting the roof, is also by Cameron (1800–01) and the central statue was carved out of a solid block of marble by Trisconni.

Cameron's Temple of Friendship on the bank of the river is a graceful domed rotunda in Doric style with sixteen white columns, built in 1780 to 1782.

There is a boating station in the park, and an open-air cafe near the palace.

PULKOVO

On Pulkovo Heights, 75 m (246 ft) above sea level, an observatory was founded in 1839 by the astronomer

Struve. Bryullov was the architect of the building which was utterly destroyed in 1941 when it was on the front line of battle; it has since been completely restored.

1 km (½ mile) south of Pulkovo, on the main road, granite obelisks mark the place where the German advance upon Leningrad was halted.

YAM-IZHORA

This village beside the River Izhora was founded in 1712. In 1768 the first Russian vaccination point against smallpox was opened.

Yam-Izhora was fiercely fought over during the 1919 Civil War and during World War II. Beside the road stands a monument commemorating the battle of 23rd June, 1942.

One of the roads to the Imperial Palace of Pushkino (formerly Tsarskoye Selo) branches off from the main road at this village.

LUBAN

Population: 7400 (1960)

The town Luban stands on the River Tigoda, and was first mentioned in writing in 1500. From the middle of the 19th century on, it was a week-end haunt for the citizens of St. Petersburg. It has now a brick works and a veneer factory.

There is a restaurant in the town.

MELNIKOV MONUMENT *In the railway station garden.* Melnikov was responsible for planning the Petersburg–Moscow railway, and this bronze bust to his memory by Yepifanov was unveiled in 1955. There is also a monument to Lenin in Luban.

CHUDOVO

The town of Chudovo was founded at the beginning of the 18th century, during the reign of Peter the Great, as a road station. Its name means "miracle". The Insurrection Glass Works were founded in 1876 and the match factory in 1885.

FILLING STATION *At the 118 km milestone.* Diesel oil is available, and there is round-the-clock service.

KHOLOPYA POLIST and TREGUBOVO

These two villages on the main road between Chudovo and Novgorod, have a history and records going back to 1500. The name of the first means "listing of serfs".

NOVGOROD (New Town)

Population: 61,000 (1959)

The town of Novgorod lies on either side of the River Volkhov which is spanned by a bridge. The two parts of the town are known as the Sophia Side and the Market Side. Novgorod stands on a hill and the surrounding lowlands are flooded in spring.

Novgorod played an interesting part in early Russian history. An old chronicler writes that the northern Slavs were attacked by invaders but after they had combined forces to drive out their enemies there arose internal strife so great that in 862 Slavonic legates went away beyond the sea to the Norse tribe called Rus and said, "Our land is great and fruitful, but there is no order in it; come and reign and rule over us." Three brothers came with their armed followers and the eldest, Rurik, settled in Novgorod. Russia is supposed to have been called after Rurik's tribe.

The city of Novgorod itself was founded over 1100 years ago by the Ilmen Slavs. In 882 Prince Oleg with his Novgorodian army conquered Kiev and transferred the government to that city, but Novgorod continued to grow. In 990 Christianity was accepted there and by the 12th century it was an independent republic. It had fought victoriously as far as the Baltic, traded on the Baltic sea, remained unharmed by the Mongol invaders and was even on good terms with them. Its power had extended to the River Volga and also northwards. Its important place on the trade route between the Baltic and Black seas earned it the name of "Lord Novgorod the Great".

Between 1100 and 1500 there are supposed to have been 230 churches in Novgorod, but still there were numerous fights between the princes of Novgorod, Suzdal and Moscow, and these naturally had an adverse effect on the prosperity of the towns. On one occasion Novgorod was saved by a miracle. The story runs that the army of Andrei Bogolyubsky from Suzdal was besieging the town when the citizens hung a great icon of the Virgin on the town gates. Tears ran down the face of Our Lady and so upset the attacking army that they fled.

In 1471 the armies of Novgorod fell before those of Ivan III and the Tartars. Ivan the Terrible destroyed the last relics of the former prosperity of Novgorod in 1570 when he is said to have butchered 60,000 citizens in order to supress a plan of Novgorod nobles to kill the tsar. For six weeks there was torturing, murders, robberies and fires and, according to the old chronicler, every day hundreds of Novgorodians were thrown into the Volkhov River with their wives and children. The river was choked with corpses and since that time, according to the legend, the water never freezes in that place.

By the middle of the 17th century the population which had once numbered 400,000 had been reduced to about 2000. It is written that after the Swedish war of 1627 there were no more than 850 people left alive. The foundation of St. Petersburg and a succession of disastrous fires completed the ruin of the once flourishing city.

65 out of the 66 more valuable monuments of the town were damaged during World War II, but there still remain more than 40 churches and part of the 12th century earth wall of the town. The two monasteries, Antonovsky and Yurievsky, were built beside the River Volkhov, to the north and the south of Novgorod respectively, in order to protect the city. The main Moscow–Leningrad road crosses Novgorod's there main thoroughfares, Sadovaya Street, Leningradskaya Street and Gorky Street. The latter is lined with new houses and on Pobedy Square the Palace of Soviets and the Communist Party School buildings are to be seen. There is also a monument to Lenin in the square.

There is a pedagogical institute in Novgorod and a History Institute of the Academy of Sciences. The town's industries are mainly concerned with timber (particularly matches), ship repairing and food.

The Kremlin

Rurik built the first kremlin-fortress (called Detinets) in 864 on the site of the present kremlin. Since then it has been reconstructed many times and now the wall, which has nine towers, is 1386 m (about 1500 yds) in circumference, between 8·5 and 10·6 m high (28 ft–35 ft) and 2·7 to 3·3 m thick (9 ft to 11 ft). The kremlin and all the buildings within its wall now form a complex museum. The 47 m (155 ft) Yevfimiev Clocktower was built in 1443 and used to be the city watch tower. Also to be seen are the Archbishop's Palace (15th century), the Pokrov Church (17th century), the Church of Sergei Radonezhsky (15th century), and the Church of Andrei Stratilat (17th century), which is reputed to have been built in a single day. The Sofiiskaya Zvonitsa (15th–17th centuries) is the belfry belonging to the Sofiisky Sobor (Saint Sophia's Cathedral) which dominated all the other buildings.

The Cathedral itself was built with six domes by Greek architects between 1045 and 1052. An earlier Saint Sophia's Cathedral, built entirely of oak with thirteen domes, was burned down in 1045. The new cathedral was built following the pattern of Kiev's Saint Sophia, but in every way simpler (three apses instead of five, wall paintings instead of mosaics, stone and brickwork instead of marble). However, a new feature in this Cathedral was the emphasis laid upon the apses, which became in all subsequent typically Russian architecture the most important external feature.

The central dome of Saint Sophia's is a gigantic copy of the helmet of an ancient Russian warrior, topped by a cross and a bronze dove. Legend has it that Novgorod will stand until the dove flies away. At the west entrance are the famous Sigtuna or Korsun doors, apparently made by Master Riquinius of Magdeburg between 1152 and 1154 for the Bishop of Plotzk, and supposed captured in 1187 from the ancient Scandinavian capital of Sigtuna, where they had served as the town gates. They are about 3·5 m high (12 ft) and made of oak overlaid by 48 plates of bronze. Three of these doors portray scenes from the Old Testament, 23 from the New Testament and 22 are of allegorical or mythological subjects. The inscriptions are partly in Latin and partly in Slavonic, but the latter were probably not added until the beginning of the 15th century.

The original frescoes on the interior walls can be seen in a few places only, for the Cathedral was almost entirely redecorated in the 1830's. Then redecoration was stopped by Nicholas I who occasionally passed through Novgorod, but the painting was renewed in the 1890's. The best frescoes that are left are in the southern part of the building where there are works of the 11th century depicting the Byzantine emperor Constantine and his mother Helen. The few 11th century mosaics are now in the local museum.

In this museum, which is also inside the kremlin, there are many other items of interest. Over 80,000 exhibits are displayed in its 35 halls. There are private letters dating from the 11th to the 15th century and written on birchbark, which were found as recently as 1951; excavations for more are still in progress. More than 200 10th to 15th century houses have been discovered. In front of the museum stands a monument commemorating Russia's 1000th anniversary, designed by the sculptor Mikyeshin in 1862. On the imperial orb kneels a figure of Russia, watched by her guardian angel who leans upon a cross. The six statues surrounding this centre-piece represent the six main periods of Russian history;—the times of Rurik, Saint Vladimir, Ivan III, Dmitri Donskoi, Peter the Great and Mikhail Feodorovich.

There is a second museum in the kremlin, inside the Granovitaya Palata (Facetted Palace), which houses a collection of icons and other articles of value from the churches and monasteries.

By the kremlin wall on the graves of soldiers who died in World War II an Eternal Flame has burned since 1964.

✿ Across the river in the Market (Torg) Side the following four churches are probably of greatest interest:

CHURCH OF IOAN-NA-OPOKAKH *Gertsen Street*. This church was built in 1127–30 and was partly reconstructed in 1453.

USPENIA-NA-TORGU CHURCH *Moskovskaya Street*. This church was built in 1135–44.

GEORGIYA-NA-TORGU CHURCH *Pervomaiskaya Street*.

CHURCH OF THE PARASKEVY PYATNITSI. This church, built in 1207, was reconstructed in 1345 and is at present under restoration.

Apart from these churches in the old trading part of the town, there is an interesting group of buildings in the area known as the Yaroslavovo Dvorishche. The Cathedral of Saint Nicholas, built in 1113 and the oldest church in Novgorod after St. Sophia's, can be seen here. It is, in fact, the only church now used for services and it was elevated to the status of a Cathedral because of this. The principal icon, a circular one depicting Saint Nicholas, is now in the local museum. The story runs that it was originally in Kiev, but Prince Mstislav of Novgorod was fatally paralysed and sent ambassadors to Kiev to fetch the icon which he believed could cure him. On the way home the ambassadors' ship was wrecked, but the icon was found floating in the river. Prince Mstislav recovered his health and, in gratitude, built the church to house the icon.

Also in Yaroslavovo Dvorishche is the Gridnitsa Tower, built in 1472, and alternatively known as Vyechevaya Bashnya; this tower was a local government building, and is an interesting example of early civil architecture. Two other churches of interest can be seen: the Prokopia Church, built in 1529 in Moscow style, and the Zhon Mironosits Church, built in 1510.

Another building of note is the small imperial palace in Gertsen Street used by the tsars as they travelled through Novgorod, and dating from the 18th century. It is supposed to have been built by Kazakov. It is now a House of Culture.

The grave of the Russian poet Gavrila Derzhavin (1743–1816) is inside the kremlin, and there is also a war memorial commemorating those who fell during the liberation of the city in January 1944 after it had been held for 29 months. A second war memorial stands in Yaroslavovo Dvorishche.

DRAMA THEATRE AND CONCERT HALL *These are both located inside the kremlin.*

THE DYNAMO STADIUM. This Stadium can hold 3000 people.

VOLKHOV HOTEL AND RESTAURANT *Tolstoi Street.*

ILMEN HOTEL AND RESTAURANT *Gorky Street.*

3 km (2 miles) south of Novgorod is the Spasa-na-Nereditse. Church, built in 1198, which formerly contained frescoes painted in 1199. The church, however, was completely destroyed in the Second World War and has now been entirely rebuilt.

The Sirkov Monastery, built in 1548, lies 6 km ($3\frac{1}{2}$ miles) to the north-west of the town, while $1\frac{1}{2}$ km (1 mile) north of Novgorod is the Antoniev Monastery, the principal building of which is the Cathedral of the Nativity of the Virgin, constructed in 1117–19, where some interesting frescoes are to be seen.

The other churches which remain in Novgorod are listed below according to their ages:

12th century churches:

GEORGIEVSKY SOBOR *Yuriev Monastery.* This cathedral was built in 1119.

ROZHDESTVA BOGORODITSI-V-SKITU CHURCH *Near the Yuriev Monastery.* This church dates from the 12th century.

BLAGOVESHCHENIYA-V-ARKAZHA CHURCH *On the way to the Yuriev Monastery.* This church was constructed in 1179.

"PIETRA-I-PAVLA-NA-SINICHEI-GORYE CHURCH—(Church of Saint Peter and Paul on Bluetit Hill) *Petrovskoye Cemetery.* This church was built in 1185.

ILIA-NA-SLAVNYE CHURCH *Ilyinsky Pereulok.* The lower part of the church dates from 1198, the upper part 15th century.

UVERENIYA-FOMYI-NA-MYACHINYE CHURCH *To the left of Proletarskaya Street Near White Tower.* This church was built during 12th–15th century.

13th–15th century churches:

NIKOLY-NA-LIPNO CHURCH *At the point where the River Msta joins the River Ilmen.* The church dates from 1292.

FEODORA STRATILATA CHURCH *On the Sophia side, Komsomolskaya Street.* This 13th–17th century church has good murals.

POKROVA (Intercession) CHURCH *Zverin Monastery.* The church was built in 1339.

FEODORA STRATILATA CHURCH *On the market side, Feodorovsky Ruchei Street.* This church was built between 1360 and 1361.

TROITSY CHURCH (TRINITY) *Proletarskaya Street.* The church was built in 1366 and partly reconstructed in the 19th century.

PETRA-I-PAVLA-NA-SLAVNYE CHURCH *Ilyinsky Pereulok.* This church was built in 1367.

SPASA-PREOBRAZHENIYA CHURCH (TRANSFIGURATION OF OUR SAVIOUR) *Pervomaiskaya Street.* The church was built in 1374.

ROZHDESTVA-BOGORODITSY-NA-MOLOTKOVE CHURCH (NATIVITY OF THE VIRGIN) *Molotkovskaya Street.* This church was built in 1379.

ROZHDESTVO-NA-KLADBISHCHE CHURCH (NATIVITY) *On the market side, Rozhdestvenskoye Cemetery.* This church dates from 1381 to 1382.

IVANA BOGOSLOVA CHURCH (SAINT JOHN THE DIVINE) *On the market side, to the north of the earth wall, beside the River Volkhov.*

DMITRIYA SOLUNSKOVO CHURCH *Moskovskaya Street.* This church was built in 1383.

FILIPPA CHURCH *Ilyinskaya Street.* This church was built in 1383–84.

CLIMENTA CHURCH (CHURCH OF SAINT CLEMENT) *Moskovskaya Street.* This church was built in 1386.

NIKOLY BYELOVA CHURCH (SAINT NICHOLAS THE WHITE) *near Zverin Monastery.* This church was built between the 14th to 16th centuries.

PETRA-I-PAVLA-V-KOZHEVNIKAKH CHURCH *Zverinskaya Street.* This church dates from 1406.

VLASIYA CHURCH *Chernyshevsky Street.* This church was built in 1407.

IOANA-MILOSTIVOVA-NA-MYACHINYE *To the left from Proletarskaya Street, near White Tower.* The church was built in 1421.

TWELVE APOSTLES CHURCH *Lev Tolstoy Street.* The church was constructed in 1454.

SIMEONA CHURCH *Zverin Monastery.* Built in 1467.

16th and 17th century churches

BORISA-I-GLEBA CHURCH *On the market side, to the north across the earth wall, beside the River Volkhov.* This church was built in 1536.

NIKITY CHURCH *Moskovskaya Street.* This church dates from 1555–56.

SOBOR-BOGORODITSY-NA-MOLOTKOVE *Molotkovskaya Street.* The cathedral was built in 1557.

TROITSY CHURCH (TRINITY CHURCH) *Dukhov Monastery (Monastery of the Holy Spirit), Molotkovskaya Street.* This was also built in 1557.

SOBOR TROITSY (TRINITY CATHEDRAL) *Dukhov Monastery, Dukhovskaya Street.*

BYELAYA BASHNAYA (WHITE TOWER) *Proletarskaya Street.* This is a 16th century building.

GEORGIYA CHURCH *Pervomaiskaya Street.* This church dates from the 17th century.

ZNAMENSKY SOBOR *Pervomaiskaya Street.* This church was built in 1682 to 1688.

FILLING STATION *Leningradskaya Street 92.* Diesel oil is obtainable here; round the clock service.

SERVICE STATION *Leningradskaya Street 92, on the main road into the town from Leningrad; tel: 10-73. Open 8 a.m. to 4 p.m.*

CAMPING SITE *Near the village of Savino, 11 km (7 miles) south of Novgorod, 219 m (200 yd) to the left of the main road.* There are furnished tents in grounds of 2 hectares (5 acres), and a buffet, self-service kitchen, and post office. The site is on the banks of the Vishersky Canal with a bathing beach and fishing; campers are warne that the mosquitoes may be a nuisance.

KRESTSY

Krestsy (crosses) stands on the River Kholva. This ancient village, first mentioned in the chronicles in 1238 when the Tartars turned back frightened by the swamps and wild forests, was chartered as a town in the 18th century. Now it is no more than a large village.

The experimental forestry estate is a branch of the Timber Extraction Industry Research Institute. Krestsy also has a factory which produces cross-stitch embroidered objects which have won prizes in Paris, Brussels and elsewhere. A cathedral stands in the central square.

Tea is available at a tearoom in the village.

VALDAI

Population: 9,700 (1959)

This small town lies just to the east of the main road. It is surrounded by hills and is situated on the west bank of picturesque Lake Valdai, which forms one of the loveliest landscapes in the central part of Russia. The lake has long been noted for its clear water, and in the language of the ancient tribe that once lived in this place "valda" means "white". The first recorded mention of the town dates it from 1495. It became a domain of the tsars in the 16th century, and received its present name in 1770.

Once Valdai was well known for the making of bells which were marked by the special quality of their resonance. Now there are mechanical, textile and food industries.

SAINT CATHERINE'S CHURCH *On the road, just outside the town.* This is a beautiful little church in rotunda style.

IVERSKY MONASTERY *3 km (2 miles) from town, on the islands in Lake Valdai.* This monastery was founded by Patriarch Nikon in 1652. Its walls, towers and the Cathedral of the Assumption have remained intact since that time.

There is a restaurant in the town.

VYSHNY-VOLOCHEK

Population: 66,000 (1959)

The town is situated on the Vyshne-Volotsky Canal which connects the River Tvertza with the River Msta. The town was formerly the place where ships were pulled over the top of the watershed dividing the Baltic and the Volgo-Caspian basins, and its name, which means "high pulling place", is derived from this. It was used by the Novgorod Slavs as far back as the 7th century. The canal, which was the first artificial waterway to Russia, was begun at the order of Peter the Great, and the house where he lived in 1720 still stands. The canal was built between 1703 and 1709, under the supervision of a Dutch specialist, to connect the

River Volga and the River Neva. During the 18th and 19th centuries it was of great importance; later it was neglected, but now the whole system, which is 538 km (334 miles) in length, is under reconstruction.

Vyshny-Volochek is famous throughout the Soviet Union for being the home town of Valentina Gaganova, Hero of Socialist Labour. She left a good job of her own to work with an unproductive group and by her example raised the level of production of that group. This idea of "leavening" is now used throughout the country. Valentina Gaganova still works at the cotton mill here; she became a member of the Central Committee of the Soviet Communist Party in 1961.

In Viyshny-Volochek much timber is brought down by river to the town's cellulose factories. Other industries include the manufacture of textiles and food products.

✿ CHURCH *Ostashkovskaya Street.* This church dates from the late 18th century.

✿ DRAMA THEATRE *Pervomaiskaya Street.*

✿ HOTEL *Pervomaiskaya Street.*

RESTAURANT *Pervomaiskaya Street.*

✿ FILLING STATION *On the main road, at the 120 km milestone (from Kalinin).* Diesel oil is for sale; round the clock service.

TORZHOK

This very picturesque old Russian town lying on either side of the River Tvertsa is in fact by-passed by the main road, but the turning to it is sign-posted. Founded in the 10th century as a colony of Novgorod, Torzhok became important as a trade centre between Novgorod and Suzdal, and its name comes actually from the word "torg" meaning "trade". In 1238 it held out against the attacks of the Tartars, and some historians think that it was this persistance that saved Novgorod. During its history it changed hands continuously between Novgorod and Suzdal, sometimes even being divided between them; it was ruined by Lithuanians, Tartars and Poles in turn.

A local legend tells how in 1405 the last prince of Smolensk, Yuri, was in exile in Torzhok and fell in love with Juliana, wife of Prince Simeon of Vyazma. When he found that his love was unrequited he killed the unfortunate husband but was himself wounded by the Russian Lucretia, who then fled. Prince Yuri pursued her, put her to the sword and had her body thrown into the River Tvertsa. Afterwards, however, he repented of his evil deeds and spent the rest of his days in penitence in a hermitage in Ryazan.

✿ HOLY TRINITY CHURCH *Respublikansky Pereulok, on the hill.* Services are held in this church which dates from 1564.

CONVENT OF THE NATIVITY OF THE VIRGIN *In the suburbs, beside the River Temak.* This church dates from the 16th century.

BORISOGLEBSKY MONASTERY. The existing church was built in 1781 with money donated by Catherine II.

VOSKRESENSKY (RESURRECTION) CONVENT *On the left bank of the river.* The convent was built in the 17th century.

CHURCH OF THE TRANSFIGURATION. Built in 1714–22, this church is now used as a bakery. It is said that the tomb of Princess Juliana of the legend related above is down in the crypt of this church.

There were at one time about 30 churches in Torzhok. Many of these were destroyed during the war, and most of the remainder are closed or are being used for various secular purposes.

Underground prisons and some interesting architectural details are preserved among the relics of the town's fortifications.

LOCAL MUSEUM *Lunacharsky Street*. This museum is located in what was originally built in 1763 as a small imperial palace, but which was later converted into the Governor's House.

ARTISTIC-HISTORICAL MUSEUM *Museum St*. This museum was founded in 1918.

HOTEL *Tverskaya Naberezhnaya 26*. The town was famous for "Pozharskiye Kotlety", chicken cutlets which were called after the hotel-owner Fedukhin-Pozharsky. It is known that the poet Pushkin stayed here and enjoyed them.

FILLING STATION *On the main road, at the 60 km milestone* (*from Kalinin*). Diesel oil is available; round the clock service.

KALININ

Population: 261,000 (1959)

An old song tells of "Tver, wonderful and charming and dear to my heart ..." Tver, supposedly derived from the old Russian word "tverd", meaning "stronghold", was the name of this ancient town until it was renamed in 1931. Mikhail Kalinin (1875 to 1946) was born in this region. An old Bolshevik, he played an important role in establishing Soviet rule in Central Asia and was Soviet President until 1946.

A Novgorodian trading post originally stood here on the bank of the River Volga, at its confluence with the River Tvertsa and the River T'maka. The town was really founded by Grand-Prince Vsevolod of Vladimir in 1134–81. The main part of the town lay at that time on the left bank of the River Volga and it was not until 1240 that Grand-Prince Yaroslav Vsevolodovich built the wooden kremlin fortress on the right bank. The kremlin stood on the place where the Khimik Stadium is today.

In 1246 Tver was separated from the Vladimir Principality and became independent, its first ruler being Yaroslav, the brother of Alexander Nevsky. In 1327, when the kremlin had grown to be really large and well-fortified, Tver organised the biggest uprising against the Tartars in the whole of Russia at that time. The local Tartar chief, Chol Khan, was torn to pieces; this action cost most of the local population their lives because Khan Uzbek gave 50,000 soldiers to Moscow's ruler Ivan Kalita, and ordered him to punish Tver. This was thoroughly done, and Kalita even brought Tver's largest church bell back to Moscow, the greatest possible humiliation in those times.

Tver survived nevertheless and in the 14th and 15th centuries was well known for the high level of its craftsmanship. The townsmen not only built their own churches, but sent their craftsmen to build churches in other towns too. They made bells and armaments, and at the beginning of the 15th century the local artillery was among the strongest in Russia. Tver minted her own coins and her craftsmen were famous for their jewellery and fine metal work.

The town was represented at the Conference of Churches in Florence in 1439, when the question of inter-church unity was being discussed, and decided not to submit to the authority of Rome. After Novgorod was joined to Moscow in 1478 Tver was surrounded by Moscow's territory, and had no choice but to yield to Moscow when in 1485 Ivan III came with his army to the town. Ivan Mikhailovich, the last prince of Tver, fled to Lithuania. It

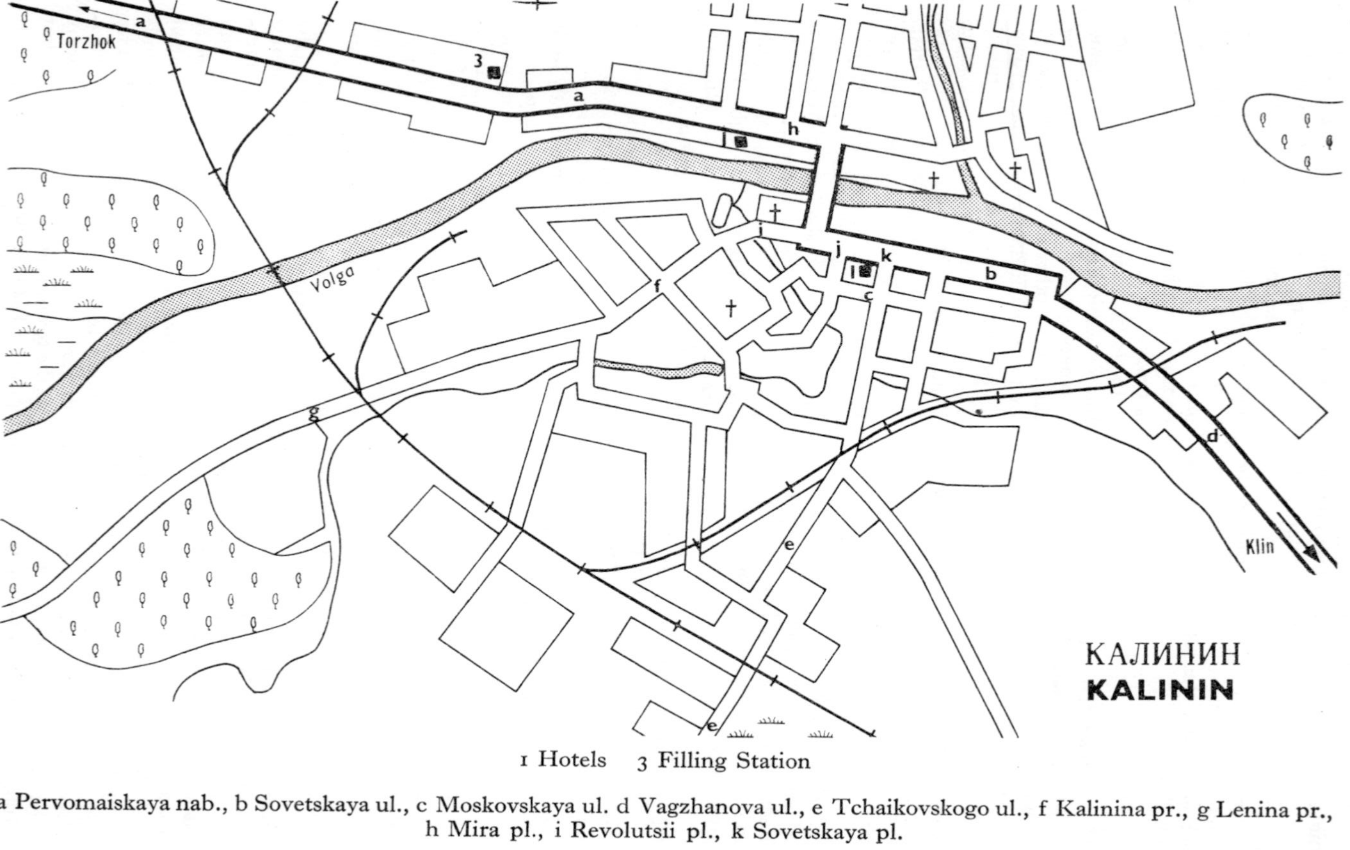

1 Hotels 3 Filling Station

a Pervomaiskaya nab., b Sovetskaya ul., c Moskovskaya ul. d Vagzhanova ul., e Tchaikovskogo ul., f Kalinina pr., g Lenina pr., h Mira pl., i Revolutsii pl., k Sovetskaya pl.

is hard now to believe that Tver was ever the rival to Moscow and had fought her for nearly 200 years for the leadership of the surrounding territory.

When Ivan IV passed through Tver on his campaign against Novgorod in 1569 he sent Maluta Skuratov, a trusted member of his bodyguard, to the Metropolitan Philip (then exiled from Moscow to a monastery in Tver) to ask a blessing before his journey north to punish the citizens of Novogorod. The priest said that he felt able to bless those with good intentions only; Skuratov was frightened to bring such a reply to the tsar and accordingly strangled the old man with his own hands before reporting that he had not found him alive. Ivan the Terrible then lived up to his name and delivered Tver's inhabitants up to the brutality of his soldiers. Over 90,000 people were murdered. Afterwards he put a Christian Tartar, Simeon Begbulatovich, to rule over those who remained alive.

Tver was ruined by the Poles during the Time of Troubles, and in 1763 there was a disastrous fire which demolished most of the buildings. Catherine the Great sent architects to rebuild the town, and among them the famous Matvei Kazakov (1738–1813). As a result Tver became a well-planned town, a "provincial Petersburg" and Catherine the Great herself wrote in a letter, "The town of Tver, after Petersburg, is the most beautiful in the empire." In the 18th century and the first part of the 19th century it was the biggest town on the way from Petersburg to Moscow, and the court used to stop here, thus encouraging a certain degree of smartness. This was particularly evident between 1809–13, a time of real prosperity and growth for the town, when Prince Georgy Oldenburgsky (married to Catherine, Alexander I's favourite sister) was Governor General. In 1860–62 the post of Vice-Governor was held by the famous Russian satirist Mikhail Saltykov-Shchedrin, who had published his *Provincial Sketches* four years earlier. Feodor Dostoyevsky lived here also for some time after his return from exile.

Following the 18th century plan of the town, there are still three main streets radiating from the centre. The central street used to be Millionnaya Street, where the rich people lived and which is now a shopping street. It is still the main Leningrad–Moscow road, but is now called Sovietskaya Street. Along it there are three squares, Pushkinskaya, Pochtovaya ("post office") and Lenina. The latter, formerly Fountain Square, is the most interesting in the town; it contains the Town Hall (1770–80), the House of Nobles (now the local Party headquarters) (1766–70) and a school built in 1786 which is now the Youth Theatre. In the centre of Kalinin is Sovietskaya Square, where demonstrations and parades take place.

Kalinin is the centre of a flax-growing region and is also an industrial centre especially concerned with light industry. There is a cotton mill over a hundred years old, and much of its production is exported. The town also produces rolling stock and textile machinery and there is a large printing works. There are pedagogical, medical and peat institutes, several technical colleges and a Suvorov Military Academy. A new part of the town is now under construction on the left bank of the River Volga. After World War II, when much reconstruction had to be done in the old parts of the town, most of the houses in the centre had two or three storeys added but the 18th century style was preserved.

WHITE TRINITY CHURCH *Engels Street*. Founded in 1563–64, this is the oldest building in the town. There is a plaque on the wall saying the church was built in the time of Ivan the Terrible; some of the icons in the iconostasis date from the 17th century. High up in the building there were secret rooms, and it is said that the blood of those found there and killed long stained the pillars and walls of the church below; this is probably true because it could have trickled through the ventilation holes. The church is open for services.

TRANSFIGURATION CATHEDRAL. This Cathedral was built in 1689–96 following the lay-out of the Uspensky (Assumption) Cathedral in the Moscow Kremlin; like the Moscow Cathedral it has five domes. The bell-tower standing near it was built between 1739 and 1758.

CONVENT OF THE NATIVITY *On the banks of the River T'maka.* The convent dates from the 16th century.

CHURCH OF ELIJAH THE PROPHET *Pervomaiskaya Naberezhnaya.* This church was constructed in the late 18th century.

✿ LOCAL MUSEUM *Sovietskaya Street 3, in the left wing of the Palace. Closed on Tuesdays.* This museum was founded in 1866.

PICTURE GALLERY *In the Church of the Ascension.* The church was built in 1813.

PUTYEVOI DVORETS *Sovietskaya Street 3.* This was built in 1763–75 by Kazakov as a coaching palace for Catherine the Great. It was partly reconstructed in 1809 by Rossi. The central façade is reminiscent of Leningrad's Winter Palace, but is simpler in design. The Palace used to contain a church dedicated to Saint Catherine. The Regional Executive Committee offices are now housed in the building.

There is a group of old houses built by Kazakov on Pervomaiskaya Naberezhnaya, near the Church of Elijah the Prophet and the building of the theological college, now used as a technical college.

The new bridge over the River Volga was completed in 1956.

KALININ STATUE *In front of Putyevoi Dvorets.*

NIKITIN MONUMENT *On the bank of the River Volga.* Afanasy Nikitin was a globetrotter and merchant who went to India via Persia between 1466 and 1473, 30 years before Vasco da Gama. He spent three years there, and died in Smolensk on his way back home to Tver. He wrote a book of his travels called *The Crossing of Three Seas.* His 8 m (26 ft) bronze statue designed by Orlov and Zakharov stands on a red granite pedestal with a Russian ship's figurehead; it is on the left bank near the jetty, supposedly on the spot where he first set sail. It was unveiled in 1955.

OBELISK *In the garden in front of Putyevoi Dvorets.* This obelisk commemorates those who fell during the revolution.

LENIN MONUMENT *Lenin Square.* This statue by Kenig was unveiled in 1959; near it are the graves of those who fell during the Second World War.

KRYLOV MONUMENT. Ivan Krylov (1769–1844) was a writer of fables who spent his childhood and adolescence in Tver. The monument by Shapozhnikov was unveiled in 1959; it stands 7 m (23 ft) high, and around it are eight separate bas-reliefs illustrating his fables.

PEACE MONUMENT *Mir (Peace) Square.* This sculptured group in the town's newest square was unveiled in 1959.

✿ DRAMA THEATRE *Svobodnyi Pereulok 43/18.*

PUPPET THEATRE *Svobodnyi Pereulok 43/18.*

YOUTH THEATRE *Sovietskaya Street 44.* This building was formerly a school built in 1786.

CIRCUS.

KHIMIK (CHEMIST'S) STADIUM *Revolyutsiyi Square*. The stadium, which can hold 11,000 people, stands on the one-time site of Tver's kremlin.

SELIGGER HOTEL AND RESTAURANT *Sovietskaya Street 52; tel.: 3-27-21*.

VOLGA HOTEL AND RESTAURANT *Uritsky Street 37/60*

OREL RESTAURANT *Naberezhnaya Stepana Razina*

RESTAURANT *At the jetty*.

MILK BAR *Uritsky Street 39/65*

CAFE *Komintern Street 104*.

CAMPING SITE *At the village of Emmaus, 18 km (11 miles) south of Kalinin, on the left of the main road*. The site is situated in a 2-hectare (5-acre) clearing in the woods, protected by the trees from rain and sun, and has a buffet, self-service kitchen, post office and a telephone. The River Inga flows nearby.

BANK *Sovietskaya Street 56/35*.

G.P.O. *Sovietskaya Street 56/35*.

CENTRAL MARKET *Kommuny Square*.

DEPARTMENT STORES *Sovietskaya Street 84 and Uritsky Street 35*.

FILLING STATION No. 1 *Pervomaiskaya Naberezhnaya, on the way into Kalinin from the north*. Diesel oil is available; round the clock service.

SERVICE STATION *Burashevskoye chaussée 2. Open 8·30–4·30*.

GORODNYA

This was an ancient Russian settlement, and the remains of an earthen fortress can still be seen, for it was a border town between the territory of Tver and Moscow. At one time experienced fishermen were stationed here for the purpose of supplying the tsar with fresh fish. The village now stretches along the main road for 2 km (1¼ miles).

There is a 15th century church in the village.

TOS

This strange name is an abbreviation for the Peat Experimental Station, which is situated in a nearby pinewood; there is a museum about the peat industry of the Soviet Union in the village.

BEZBORODOVO

The name of the village means "beardless". The so-called Moscow Sea, which appeared after the Moscow-Volga Canal was completed, and which covers an area of 327 sq.km, lies nearby. Many villages were transferred from the bottom of the "sea", as was also the town of Korchev (Population: 4000).

This region is well known as fishing and hunting territory. The road runs close beside the river and the Moscow Sea.

KLIN

Population: 53,000 (1959)

The name of this town which stands on the River Sestra ("sister") is first recorded in 1234. In 1482 it became part of Muscovy, and in 1572 Ivan the Terrible left it to his son, Ivan, after which it passed to the Romanovs. Klin was made a district town in 1785. It has factories making synthetic fibre, glass and thermometers.

There is an old arcade of shops in the town.

16th CENTURY CHURCH *On the territory of the Uspensky (Assumption) Monastery, which was closed in the 18th century*. The church, built in the style of Moscow baroque, dates from 1712.

TCHAIKOVSKY MUSEUM *Chaikovsky Street 48. Open 11–5; closed on Wednesdays*. The Composer Peter I. Tchaikovsky lived in this region from 1885 until 1893, and his home was actually in this house between 1892 and 1893. He himself wrote of his affection for the place, "I have become so attached to Klin that I cannot imagine myself living anywhere else ... I am unable to do justice to the charm of the Russian village, the Russian landscape and this silence which I need most of all". He wrote his 6th ("Pathetic") Symphony, the 3rd Piano Concerto and the music for the "Nutcracker" and "Sleeping Beauty" ballets here.

When the composer died, his brother, Modest, decided to make the house a museum, so it was first purchased from the owner by Tchaikovsky's servant, Sofronov, and then bought by Modest Tchaikovsky and the composer's nephew, V. Davydov. The former died in 1916 and the house passed to the Russian Musical Society; it was protected by government charter and became state property in 1921. It was looted by the Germans during World War II, but anything of value had previously been evacuated, and the house was restored in 1944.

The two-storey building is furnished and decorated as it was in the composer's lifetime, and contains his books, paintings, grand piano and other personal possessions. Modest Tchaikovsky wrote a three-volume biography of his brother, and the material he collected for this purpose formed the basis of the Tchaikovsky archives now amounting to almost 50,000 items and still used for research.

There is a Restaurant in the town.

FILLING STATION AND SERVICE STATION *Just outside the town, on the road to Moscow.*

SOLNECHNOGORSK

The present name of the town means "sunny hill"; it was earlier known as Podsolnechnoye—"sunflower".

At the beginning of the 17th century attempts were made to link the River Moskva and the River Volga at this point. Senezhskoye Lake is an artificial lake which resulted from a continuation of these attempts in 1826 to 1850.

CHURCH *Near the main road.* This church dates from the 18th century.

The large building in the village is the House of Culture.

KRUKOVO

Near this village one of Moscow's satellite towns is under construction. The site covers 750 hectares (1875 acres) and some of the capital's larger factories will be transferred here.

CHERNAYA GRYAZ

The name of the village means "Black mud". The present hospital building was once a posting station of the St. Petersburg–Moscow road.

SHEREMETIEVO

The airport used for international flights to and from Moscow is here.

KHIMKI

Khimki is Moscow's port on the Moscow–Volga Canal. The Canal was constructed between 1932–37 and connects the River Moskva with the Upper Volga. It has a total length of 129 km (80 miles), a depth of 5·5 m (18 ft) and a width of 85·5 m (94 yd). Ships can now sail to the capital from the Baltic, White, Black, Azov and Caspian Seas. The canal is also Moscow's chief source of water.

The Northern River Station is in a park of 48 hectares (120 acres). Seen from a distance, the two-storey building by Rukhlyadev with its light arcades and galleries looks itself like a river steamer. It is 152 m (167 yd) long and its spire is just under 80 m (300 ft) high.

"VOLGA" RESTAURANT. This restaurant specialises in freshwater fish dishes.

BATHING BEACH.

DYNAMO CLUB HOUSE AND WATER SPORTS FACILITIES.

Tourists with time to spare should go by boat on an excursion along the canal and back (5 or 6 hours). On Saturdays larger vessels leave for the Moscow Sea, returning on Sunday evening. These have de luxe cabins and cabins for one, two, three and four persons. There is a restaurant on these boats.

MOSCOW

Population: 6,390,000 (1962)

Moscow is the capital of the Russian Federation as well as of the U.S.S.R.

According to a little known legend, Moscow was founded by Japhet's sixth son, Mosokh; Mosokh's wife was called Kva and so the place was given the name Moskva. Mosokh and Kva had a son and a daughter, whom they named respectively Ya and Vuza. It is said that from these names the River Yauza, Moscow's second largest river, took its name.

Long ago it was known as the sacred city of the Russians, the city of "white walls", and often in Russian poetry and songs it was referred to as "Matushka Moskva"—Mother Moscow. During the last century it was sometimes called "Brides' Fair" because of the society marriage market.

Moscow was founded by Prince Yuri Dolgoruky of Rostov-Suzdal as a southern border settlement. Prince Yuri, in spite of his Russian name and the important place he occupies in Russian history, had in fact a considerable admixture of foreign royal blood in his veins, for his mother Christina was the daughter of the Swedish King Ing. Moscow was first mentioned in the Russian chronicles in 1147 when Dolgoruky wrote to his friend, Prince Svyatoslav, "Come to me, brother, to Moscow". At the beginning of the 13th century Moscow became the capital of a small principality, vassal to Rostov-Suzdal, and during the years of Tartar rule it gradually climbed to the highest position among the Russian principalities, absorbing many of its immediate neighbours, because of its advantageous geographic position and also because of the wily policy of its Grand Princes.

In the 14th century Moscow became the capital of the Grand Principality of Vladimir, and later of Muscovy. Its importance grew enormously after the early 14th century when the seat of the Metropolitans (later Patriarchs) of the Russian Orthodox Church was transferred here from the old Church capital of Vladimir. In 1453, when the Turks took Constantinople, a monk in Pskov wrote of Moscow, "Two Romes have fallen, but the third one stands". This occured during the reign of Ivan III; he had married Sophia, niece of the last Byzantine emperor, and considered himself their heir. This was his reason for adopting the double-headed eagle as his arms.

The Tartars reached the city on several occasions and last attacked it in 1591.

In 1712 St. Petersburg became the imperial capital but nevertheless the status of Russia's second capital was retained by the older city. Pushkin wrote:

"And Moscow bowed to the
new capital
As the Queen Dowager bows
to the young Queen ..."

Fires have raged in Moscow on several occasions during its history, and especially severe was the fire of 1812 when Moscow was for a short time under French occupation. The rebuilding that took place after this was mostly in brick.

MOSCOW RING ROAD

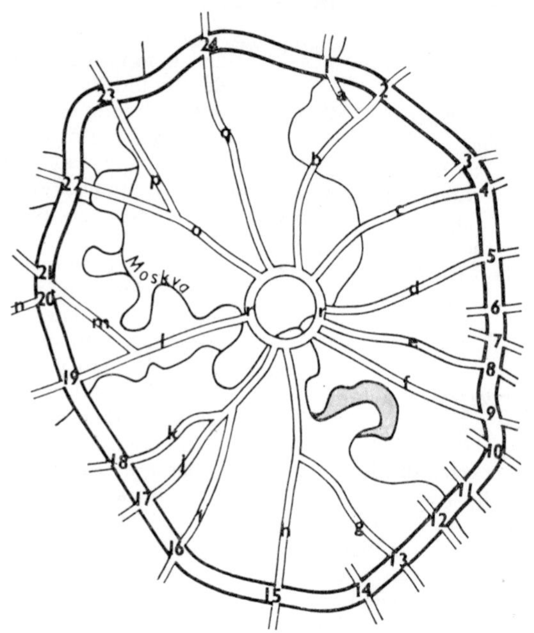

1 Ostashkov,
2 Yaroslavl,
3 Abramtsevo,
4 Shchelkovo,
5 Gorky,
6 Krutitsy,
7 Kosino,
8 Ryazan,
9 Lyubertsy,
10 Sovkh. Belye Dachi,
11 Dzerzhinsk,
12 Besedy,
13 Kashira,
14 Bulatnikovo,
15 Simferopola,
16 Kaluga,
17 Kiyev,
18 Borovsk,
19 Minsk,
20 Uspenskoye,
21 Rublevo,
22 Volokolamsk,
23 Leningrad,
24 Dmitrov.

a Ostashkovskoye chaussée,
b Yaroslavskoye chaussée,
c Shchelkovskoye chaussée,
d Gorkovskoye chaussée,
e Ryanzanskoye chaussée,
f Novoryazanskoye chaussée,
g Kashirskoye chaussée,
h Podolskoye chaussée,
i Kaluzhskoye chaussée,
j Kiyevskoye chaussée,
k Borovskoye chaussée,
l Minskoye chaussée,
m Rublevskoye chaussée,
n Rub. usp. chaussée,
o Volokolamskoye chaussée,
p Leningradskoye chaussée,
q Dmitrovskoye chaussêe,
r Sadovoye Koltso.

Since the Middle Ages Moscow has been an important trade and craft centre and it was here that the first large manufacturing establishments appeared at the end of the 17th century. In the middle of the 19th century machines were introduced into Moscow's industry (at that time chiefly concerned with textiles); these innovations were followed by the industrial boom of the 1890's.

The first Russian Revolution of 1905 was famous for its battles here, especially that in the Presnya region. It was of this that Vladimir Lenin wrote, "It trained the ranks of the fighters who were victorious in 1917".

Soon after the 1917 revolution Moscow was re-established as the official capital of the country. Now it is one of the world's largest cities, and the political, industrial, economic and cultural centre of the Soviet Union. It is also the chief railway and road junction. During World War II the German army was dangerously near the city and in 1965 Moscow was acclaimed a Hero City, sharing the honour with Odessa, Sevastopol, Volgograd (Stalingrad), Kiev and Leningrad.

Moscow has developed from the centre (the Kremlin) outwards in concentric circles. Present-day construction keeps to this form and new streets are being laid out so that they will make another circle. The circular bypass around Moscow lies at an average distance of 25 km (16 miles) from the centre and marks the city boundary. The ring is 109 km (68 miles) long, and crosses 14 main highways leading from the city. The territory within the bypass ring is 87,500 hectares (218,750 acres), while the area of Greater Moscow (including the green belt) is 265,000 hectares (662,500 acres).

Driving in Moscow

Moscow is the busiest city in the country as far as the traffic is concerned, and although the wide streets and enormous squares could easily cope with more traffic, even so at peak hours the central streets are very busy.

As everywhere in the Soviet Union, it is essential to look out for unsuspecting pedestrians, who frequently ignore the rules despite all warnings. It is wise to slow down at crossroads even though there may be a green light.

As a rule U-turns can only be made at the places indicated.

In case you are lost, the Sadovaya Ring serves as a landmark and will always lead you to a more or less familiar place, such as the crossing with Gorky Street at Mayakovsky Square.

The main highways leading from the Sadovaya Ring are:

(1) Varshavskoye (Warsaw) chaussée from Danilovskaya Square towards the south (via Butovo Camping Site).

(2) Kutuzovsky Prospekt from Chaikosvky Street (On Sadovaya Ring, near the American Embassy) to Minsk.

(3) Gorky Street which leads to the Leningradskoye chaussée and to Leningrad and

(4) Prospekt Mira from Kolkhoznaya Square to Yaroslavl.

THE CENTRE OF MOSCOW

(*Russian: "Krasnaya Plohchad"*)

Red Square is the main square of the city, where demonstrations and military parades take place. Its present name dates from the 17th century; in Old Russian the word "krasnaya" meant "beautiful". The architectural ensemble of the square as it now is consists of Saint Basil's Cathedral to the south (with the Minin and Pozharsky Monument in front of it), the Kremlin Wall with the Lenin Mausoleum to the west, the Historical Museum to the north and GUM—the State Department Store—on the east side. Close to Saint Basil's is the Lobnoye Mesto, a

МОСКВА MOSCOW (MOSKVA)

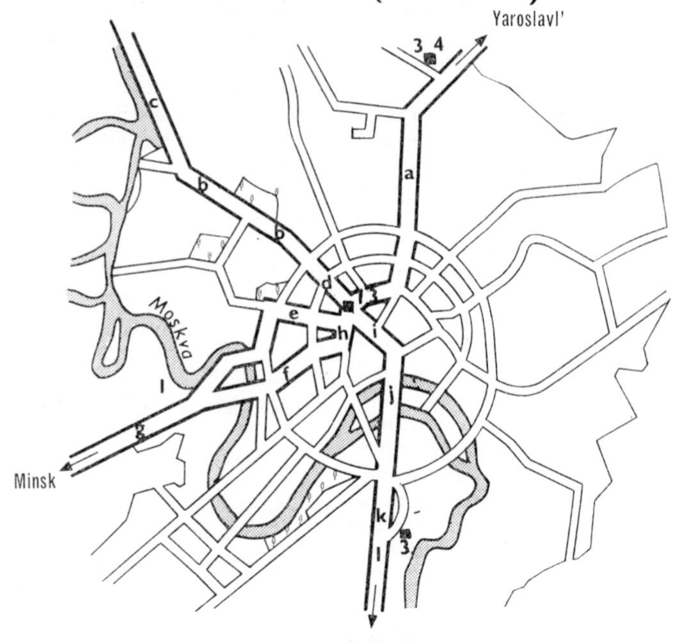

1 Hotel 3 Filling Station 4 Service Station.

a Pr. Mira,
b Leningradsky pr.,
c Leningradskoye chaussée,
d Ul. Gorkogo,
e Ul. Gertzena,
f Ul. Arbat,
g Kutuzovsky pr.,
h Manezhnaya pl.,
i Krasnaya pl.,
j Ordynka,
k Lusinovskaya ul.,
l Warshawskoye chaussée.

round platform of white stone from which the Tsar's edicts and sentences were once proclaimed.

Two streets run out of Red Square to the east. They go through the old part of Moscow called *Kitai-Gorod*, the "Moscow City" of the 16th century, which was encircled by a stone defence wall; some remains of the wall can be seen from Marx Prospekt near the Metropole Hotel. After the 14th century, Kitai-Gorod was the site of numerous small shops and markets and later banks and offices appeared in it. *25th-October* (formerly Nikolskaya) *Street* runs from the north-east corner of Red Square into Kitai-Gorod. No. 9 of this street is the Zaikono-Spassky ("Behind-the-Icon-of-the-Redeemer") Monastery founded in 1600. The Slavic-Greek-Latin Academy, the first higher educational establishment in Russia where Lomonosov, the famous 18th century Russian scholar, studied, was here. At the other end of GUM, *Kuibyshev* (formerly Ilyinka) *Street* runs out of Red Square and forms the main thoroughfare of Kitai-Gorod; banks, offices and several ministries are situated on this street. On the right-hand side, half way along the street from Red Square is the building of the former Moscow Exchange (built in 1873–75 and now the All-Union Chamber of Commerce). Behind Saint Basil's Cathedral, *Razin* (formerly Varvarka) *Street* runs parallel to the two streets already mentioned. In it are several old churches of minor architectural interest, and also the so-called Boyar's House, reconstructed from the ruins of 17th century building by Richter in 1859. To the right of Razin Street beside the river, the Rossiya hotel is under construction. It is to be one of the biggest hotels in Europe.

REVOLUTSIYI SQUARE adjoins Red Square to the North. It is bounded by the Lenin Museum, a Metro station and the older part of the Moskva Hotel. To the east of Revolution Square is *Sverdlov Square* (formerly "Teatralnaya"); Yakov Sverdlov (1885–1919) was a prominent Bolshevik and one of Lenin's closest collaborators. During the last years of his life he was the titular head of the young Soviet State. On one side of Marx Prospekt Sverdlov Square is bounded by the Stereo-Cinema and the Metropole Hotel (built at the beginning of the 20th century and decorated with a majolica panel by Vrubel'). On the other side of the Prospekt the square is surrounded by a Metro station and three theatres, the Children's Theatre and the Bolshoi and Malyi Drama Theatres.

PROSPEKT MARKSA is in fact the new name (1961) for some of the oldest streets in the city. Beginning from *Dzershinsky Square* the Prospekt runs downhill to cross *Sverdlov Square* (where the theatres are) and runs between the Moskva Hotel (built in 1932–35 by Schusev and having on its 15th floor an open-air café, "The Lights of Moscow", with a good view over the city) and the impressive building of the Council of Ministers (built in 1932–35 by Langmann). This part of the Prospekt was formerly known as Okhotnyi Ryad ("hunters' row") and was once a market street. To the right is *Gorky Street* and on the far side of Gorky Street next to the National Hotel, is Intourist's head office; it was built by Zholtovsky and was once used by the American Embassy.

On the other side of Marx Prospekt is *Manezhnaya Square*, the place where, during national festivities, there is open-air cinema, music, folkdancing demonstrations and informal dancing. Marx Prospekt goes on to pass between the Manege and the old buildings of the University as far as the Lenin Library.

Behind the Bolshoi Theatre and running parallel to Marx Prospekt is *Kuznetsky Most* ("Blacksmith's Bridge") so-called because blacksmiths from the Royal Arms Foundry lived here in the 14th–15th centuries). It is one of the busiest streets of the city and is full of shops. It is crossed by *Neglinnaya Street*, under which the small River Neglinka, which was bricked over at the beginning of the 19th century, flows. No. 12 Neglinnaya St. is the State Bank of the U.S.S.R., built at the end of the 19th century by Bykovsky and rebuilt in 1930–31 by Zholtovsky.

BULVARNOYE KOLTSO *The Boulevard Ring*. The area between the modern boulevards and the Kremlin was known in the 16th and 17th centuries as the White Town, and this was where the boyars and nobles, as well as those in permanent court service, lived. The defence walls and towers were pulled down between 1750 and 1792 and the boulevards were planted. The Boulevard Ring, though known as a ring, does not yet in fact form a complete circle.

From the Moskva open air swimmingpool the boulevard ring leads to *Arbatskaya Square*; the Praga Restaurant stands at the corner of this square and is famous for its dome, which is one of the best in the city. The monument on the boulevard at this point is dedicated to the writer Gogol. The twisty streets, especially to the left, form the largest section of the old nobles' quarters that has survived. *Prospekt Kalinina* to the right is easily recognized by the Moorish-style building which once belonged to the family of the textile-king Morozov; today it is the House of Friendship. To the left Prospekt Kalinina runs through the construction sites of new buildings which are replacing the old.

ALONG BULVAR' Suvorova No. 8a is the House of Journalists, built in 1760. On the other side of the boulevard is the house where Gogol' died in 1852, and an old monument to him stands in the courtyard. The point at which *Gertsen Street* crossed the boulevard is known as *Nikitskive Vorota* ("gates"), still called after the old gates of the town which once stood here. To the right in Gertsen Street is the Tchaikovsky Conservatoire. A Monument to botanist Timiryazev (wearing an Oxford University gown because Oxford had conferred an honorary doctorate upon him), stands at the beginning of *Tverskoi boulevard* once the most elegant and fashionable promenade in Moscow. The other end of this boulevard crosses *Gorky Street* and Pushkin's monument is in the centre of the square called after him. Admirers still bring tributes of flowers here, fulfilling the poet's prophesy that:

> "My verses will be sung throughout all Russia's vastness,
> My ashes will outlive and know no pale decay ..."

Ulitsa Chekhova leads out of the square beside the Russia Wide-Screen Cinema. To the right is Pushkinskaya ulitsa which contains some of Moscow's older theatres.

The next square on the boulevard ring is *Petrovskiye Vorota* with *Petrovka Street* to the right running straight down to the *Bolshoi Theatre*. Branching off to the right from Petrovka Street is *Stoleshnikov Pereulok*, an old trading street and the centre of a busy shopping area. Closer to the Ring is the former Petrovsky Abbey with a cathedral built in 1691. The street running off the left of the Boulevard Ring is *Karetnyi Ryad* ("Coachbuilders' Row"), marked by the Hospital building designed by Kazakov; the Hermitage Garden is on this street. Further along, *Trubnaya Square* was formerly known for its bird market, which was later transferred to *Konnaya Square*. The River Neglinka flows beneath the square and the street to the right still bears its name; down this street on the right side is the Uzbekistan Restaurant, which has tables out in the garden.

The steep hill which comes next along the Ring and leads to *Rozhdestvensky boulevard* (Nativity) was once a real problem for horse-trams. The walls of the old monastery from which this part of the boulevard takes its name can be seen on the right. At *Sretenskiye Vorota* the Ring is crossed by *Sretenka Street* with many shops on its left side. The gardens on this part of the Boulevard Ring are always crowed with children and in good weather it becomes an informal open-air club for playing chess and domi-noes.

Kirov Street crosses the next square. To the right is the Central Post Office and there are many shops on the ground floor of the old office buildings. Opposite the Post Office is the curious Chinese-style building of the Tea Shop (1896) and nearby is the tower of the former Church of the Archangel Gabriel, built by Zarudnyi in 1707 and called "Menshikova Bashnya" after Peter I's favourite; before one disastrous fire it was taller than the highest bell-tower in the Kremlin. Farther down this street there is a special record shop.

There is a statue to the writer Griboyedov at the beginning of the *Clear-Pond Boulevard.* Boats can be hired on ponds.

From Pokrovskiye Vorota, *Bogdany Khmelnitsky Street* on the right runs all the way to Red Square (partly through *Kuibyshev Street*; to the left is *Chernyshevsky Street* with a rococo building of 1766 known, because of its abundant decoration, as "Chest-of-Drawers House". The wide space along the boulevard was formerly a parade ground in front of the military barracks built in the 1830's.

Next comes the last section of the Boulevard Ring which bears the name of the Yauza River. The 22-storey apartment house, with a 32-storey tower, was built in 1949–52 by Chechulin and Rostovsky; it is 173 m (568 ft) high.

One can return to the beginning of the Boulevard Ring at the Moskva Swimming Pool by going along the embankment of the Moskva River to the right of this skyscraper, along the Kremlin Embankment with a pleasant view of Saint Basil's Cathedral from the river side; opposite the Kremlin walls, on the other side of the river, are the restored bell-towers of churches and among the former merchants' houses is a well-preserved yellow-painted building with trees behind its iron gates; it is occupied by the British Embassy and has the only English pub in the country (frequented by the local foreign colony) on the top floor of the lefthand block. By Krymsky Bridge, further along the Kremlin side of the river, is American House which has a bar open in the evenings.

SADOVOYE KOLTSO (THE SADOVAYA RING).

This is Moscow's widest street. The city's old circular earth wall was pulled down at the beginning of the last century, and the gardens in front of the small houses there gave the new street its name ("sad" being the Russian word for "garden"). Trees were planted along the middle of the boulevard, but were removed in the 1930's leaving the wide street (in some places over 60 m/66 yd) so much appreciated by motorists today.

Crossing *Gorky Street* by the Mayakovsky Underpass, Sadovaya runs down to *Samotechnaya Square* (if one sets off in a clockwise direction) with *Tsvetnoy* "flower") *boulevard*, once a flower market, where the circus, the panorama cinema and Moscow's central market now are, to the right. The boulevard to the left leads out to the Soviet Army Theatre and Museum.

The next square is *Kolkhoznaya*; to the left *Prospekt Mira* runs out to the Economic Achievements' Exhibition and Ostankino Palace. To the right is *Sretenka*, one of the oldest shopping streets; there is an antique shop near the corner. Further along Sadovaya on the left stands the impressive hospital building by Quarenghi and Nazarov (1792–1807). On the same side is a Le

Corbusier-style building designed by the Russian architect Schusev in 1933, and now housing the Ministry of Agriculture. To the right is *Kirov Street*, with a genuine Le Corbusier building, and close to it stands another built in the early 30's in the same style. Among the 18th century houses of the nobility, No. 42 was designed by the architect Kazakov.

In *Lermontov Square*, popularly known by its old name of *Krasnye Vorota* ("red gates"), is a 24-storey skyscraper office building, 133 m (436 ft) high, built in 1952 by Dushkin and Mezentsev. To the left the road goes through *Komsomolskaya Square* with Moscow's three busiest railway stations, and then out to Sokolniki Park. The Leningradskaya Hotel, a 26-storey skyscraper, is on this square; it is 136 m (446 ft) high, built in 1953 by Polyakov and Boretsky.

Next, Sadovaya itself turns to the right leading to Kursk Railway Station on another square. Beyond the square, on the left of Sadovaya, there is a beautiful mansion built by Gillardi in 1829–31. Sadovaya then crosses the Yauza River, a tributary of the River Moskva, runs through a tunnel, across a bridge over the River Moskva itself and on through the region where petty merchants used to live. *Zatsepa Street* (one of the sections of Sadovaya with a name of its own) has a market, and opposite in a quiet side-street is the Bakhrushin Theatre Museum. On the left of *Dobryninskaya Square* Varshavskoye chaussée begins; this is the road to the south and the one for sightseers going to Kolomenskoye and Tsaritsino.

At the next square, *Oktyabrskaya*, where *Leninsky Prospekt* begins, Sadovaya runs through an underpass. The impressive stone arch on the left is the entrance to Gorky Park where there is a fun fair. The 700 m (770 yd) long Crimean Suspension Bridge is one of the best designed in the city. On the other side of the river an overpass links *Komsomolsky Prospekt* (to the left) with *Metrostroyevskaya Street* on the way to *Marx Prospekt*. The long yellow-washed buildings on the right were constructed by Stasov in 1830 as a food depot. The road to the left from *Zubovskaya Square* leads to Novodevichy Convent; to the right is *Kropotkinskaya Street*, with many nobles' houses of the last century in it. All the area between this part of Sadovaya and the inner Boulevard Ring was the old aristocratic region of Moscow, and the narrow winding by-streets with their quiet mansions still retain an atmosphere of old Moscow.

Further along Sadovaya on the right towards *Smolenskaya Square* is a green-painted house, No. 18, formerly the home of millionaire Morozov. The 27-storey skyscraper (171 m/561 ft) on the right houses the Ministries of Foreign Affairs and Foreign Trade, and was designed by Gelfreikh and Minkus in 1951. Also to the right is Arbat Street, traditionally one of the busiest shopping streets in Moscow. Sadovaya emerges from the next underpass near the American Embassy, a tall building on the left; Kalinina Prospekt, which leads into the Moscow Minsk road, branches off to the left beyond the tunnel. The 22-storey (160 m/525 ft) apartment house built by Posokhin and Mndoyants in 1954 on *Vosstanya Square* has a group of food shops on the ground floor. To the right is the once fashionable *Vorovsky Street*; many of its mansions are now occupied by foreign embassies. Next to it *Gertsen Street* leads down to the Kremlin. To the left from Sadovaya, where a road runs downhill to the Moscow Zoo, is a house with columns, designed by Gillardi in 1813.

On the right side of Sadovaya past the square is the tiny red house (No. 6) of the Chekhov Museum; the famous Russian writer lived here during the 1880's. On the opposite side of the street is Moscow's Planetarium. To the left approaching *Mayakovsky Square* is the Peking Hotel and on the right, at the corner of *Gorky Street* is the Tchaikovsky Concert Hall.

The total length of the Sadovaya Ring is 16 km (10 miles).

ULITSA GORKOGO (*Gorky Street*) is Moscow's central thoroughfare. It was formerly known as Tverskaya, because it was the road which led to Tver (now Kalinin), and then on to St. Petersburg. It begins at the crossroad with *Marx Prospekt* opposite the Kremlin, and has now not much in common with the old Tverskaya Street; only a few of the original buildings remained after the street was reconstructed in the 1930's, and in some parts the width of the street was doubled to its present 40 m (44 yd). The National Hotel on the corner has a modern extension under construction. No. 4, 6, blocks A and B, were built by Mordvinov in 1936, as were also No. 15–17 in 1939–40. The Central Telegraph building was designed by Rerberg in 1927.

Some of the small streets now join Gorky Street through arches in the big buildings that line it on both sides. On *Sovietskaya Square* there is a monument to Yuri Dolgoruky, the founder of Moscow. The City Hall in this square was built in 1782 by Kazakov for Moscow's Governor-General. In 1946 architect Chechulin moved the main edifice 11 m (12 yd) back and added two more storeys. Opposite is the Marxism-Leninism Institute (designed in 1927 by Chernyshev) with a monument to Lenin by Merkurov. No. 10 was known as Philippov's Bakery; it was built by Eichewald in 1912 and is still Moscow's best baker's shop. No. 14 is "Gastronom No. 1" and probably the only shop in Moscow which is still unofficially known by the name of its former owner—Yeliseyevsky; its ornate decorations deserve a visit.

At the point where Gorky Street crosses the Boulevard Ring is *Pushkinskaya Square*. The formal garden with Pushkin's statue has now been laid out in place of the former Strastnoi Abbey. At the other end of the square is the Rossiya Cinema, one of the largest cinemas in the country. Near this, in *Chekhov Street*, is the elegant Church of the Nativity (1781). The *Izvestia* editorial offices and printing works (on the square itself) were built in 1927 and at one time the building was among the highest in Moscow. When Pushkin described this street as he knew it he mentioned the lions on the gates of No. 21, once the aristocratic English Club. Almost opposite, at No. 22, is the new nine-storey Minsk Hotel.

Mayakovsky Square, with a statue of that poet, lies where Gorky Street crosses the Sadovaya Ring. One corner is occupied by the Tchaikovsky Concert Hall, built in 1940 by Chechulin and Orlov. The Peking Hotel across the street can be identified by its Chinese writing. There is a monument to the writer Maxim Gorky (after whom the street was named in 1935) on *Belorusskaya Square*. The semi-circular building is the railway station, built in 1870, and beyond the bridge, over the railway, is *Leningradsky Prospekt*.

LENINGRADSKY PROSPEKT is a continuation of *Gorky Street*, which ends at the Belorussian Railway Station.

Many new buildings were put up here before the Second World War, when it became a fashionable residential area. The Sovetskaya Hotel and Restaurant (Leningradsky Prospekt 32) was once known as "Yar", the best restaurant outside the city. It has now been partly reconstructed.

Further on are the Dynamo Stadium, the second largest in Moscow, and the Helicopter Station marked by two tall blocks. Near the Dynamo Stadium is the Petrovsky Palace, built by Kazakov in the 18th century to look like a battlemented fortress; the tsars frequently resided there, and it was from there that they drove into Moscow to be crowned. The Palace is now the home of the Zhukovsky Air Force Academy. All Saints' Church nearby was built in 1736.

The road to Leningrad is to the right of the large underpass; motorists should keep straight on to reach the Arkhangelskoye Museum.

Near the underpass is the site where a 25-storey skyscraper is under construction. It is to be used for the offices of Gidroproyekt, the organisation responsible for designing hydro-power stations.

PROSPEKT MIRA. *Prospekt Mira*, which branches out from the Sadovaya Ring at *Kolkhoznaya Square*, was so named after the 1957 Youth Festival in Moscow. Once populated by middle-class merchants, it still has some old buildings, but these are now dominated by huge apartment houses.

At No. 28 is Moscow's oldest Botanical Gardens, once known as the "Apothecary's Garden", and transferred here by the order of Peter I in 1706 from its former position beside the Kremlin wall.

Riga Railway Station (designed by Diderix in 1899) once marked the end of the city. Since 1964 the soaring space-rocket monument has formed a striking landmark, seen from far along the Prospekt. The whole region beyond the bridge changed in the late 1930's, at the time of the construction of the Agricultural Exhibition (now known as the Exhibition of Economic Achievements). The turning to the left, approaching the Exhibition, is the way to Ostankino. On the right an 18th century aqueduct and the five-domed Tikhvinskaya Church (17th century) can be seen.

The Prospekt then comes to *Yaroslavskoye chaussée*, which leads via Zagorsk Monastery to the town of Yaroslavl on the Volga.

LENINSKY PROSPEKT. *Lenin Prospekt* begins from *Oktyabrskaya Square* on the Sadovaya Ring, and follows part of the old road (*Dimitrov Street*) from the centre of Moscow to the town of Kaluga; it was along this route that Napoleon's army retreated in 1812.

The Warsaw Hotel stands on the corner of the Sadovaya Ring. On the right side of the *Leninsky Prospekt* are the new buildings of the Mining, Steel and Oil Institutes. Then there are the Town Hospitals, built by Bovet in 1828–32; close to these is the former Prince Golitsyn Hospital, designed by Kazakov in 1796–1802. There are gardens in front of the Hospitals.

On the next square is a side entrance to Gorky Park and the former *Neskuchnyi Sad* which is now part of the main Park. No. 14 is the former Alexandrinskii Palace built by Iyekht in 1842; the gates are decorated with Vitali's sculptures, "Seasons of the Year". The Palace is now used by the Academy of Sciences, and indeed this Prospekt is popularly known as the Prospekt of Science because so many research institutes are located on it.

The next turning to the left leads to the Donskoi Monastery.

In 1940 the imposing crescent of buildings by Arkin marked the entrance to the city; their position shows how Moscow has grown since then. Beyond them a new shopping centre is developing with big stores such as "The House of Shoes" and "The House of Fabrics" and farther on, the Moskva Department Store. The roads crossing the Prospekt lead to the University and the South-West part of the city (to the right), while to the left is the Cheremushki Region with experimental blocks of flats. When this part of the city is complete, this new area will nearly equal the territory of the whole of old Moscow. The houses are built in separate neighbourhood units for 25,000 inhabitants, each on an area of 36–50 hectares (90–125 acres).

The new houses and shops extend

further along the Prospekt which turns into the highway leading to Vnukovo Airport.

KOMSOMOLSKY PROSPEKT. *Komsomolsky Prospekt* begins at *Krymskaya Square*, at the road bridge over the Sadovaya Ring. Most of the buildings now lining it are new, but among the old ones at the beginning are the Church of Saint Nicholas (1679–82) and the three-storey military barracks (1807–09).

Komsomolsky Prospekt is one of the city's newest thoroughfares, and it links the centre of Moscow with the Lenin Stadium, the University and the growing South-Western Region, interesting for its contemporary town-planning and architecture. After the Lenin Stadium, the road crosses the Moskva River by a double-decker bridge; the lower part of the bridge carries a line of the Metro.

KUTUZOVSKY PROSPEKT. *Kutuzovsky Prospekt* was named after the famous Russian Field-Marshal. It starts from Kalinin Bridge with the Ukraina Hotel to the right. New blocks of flats have replaced the old suburbs of *Dorogomilovo*; the part of the street by the underpass was mostly built up before World War II. Here is Moscow's foreign currency grocery store. There are more new apartment houses at the end of the Prospekt. The fork to the right leads to Fili-Mazilovo, now one of the city's busiest construction sites. In Fili is the wonderful Pokrova Church, built in 1693–94.

Kutuzovsky Prospekt eventually turns into the Moscow–Minsk road and a motel stands at the point where it crosses the circular by-pass.

THE KREMLIN WALLS. Moscow's Kremlin occupies an irregular triangle of ground covering 28 hectares (69 acres), part of which rises 40 m (130 ft) above the River Moskva. The red-brick battlemented wall is over 2 km (1¼ miles) in circumference and in some places as much as 19 m (63 ft) high. It was erected during the reign of Ivan III, and was reinforced with 20 towers, five of which are also gates to the stronghold. Those which since 1937 have been decorated with red stars are marked with asterisks.

The main gate to the Kremlin is that opposite St. Basil's Cathedral on Red Square. It is known as the *Spasskiye* ("*Redeemer's*") *Gate**, and was built in 1491 by Pietro Antonio Solario of Milan. In 1625 the Scots architect, Christopher Galloway, added the Gothic tower and a clock was installed; the chime of the biggest of the bells in the tower clock is broadcast, as is that of Big Ben. The bell, which weighs over two tons, was cast in 1769 by Semyon Mozhukin.

The next gate in order round the Kremlin (in an anti-clockwise direction), is the *Nikolskye Gate** (near the Historical Museum) which was blown up by Napoleon in 1812 and rebuilt in 1820. At the corner of the wall is the *Sobakina Tower;* this was built so solidly partly because it contained a secret well (important in time of siege), and also because it concealed a way out to the Neglinnaya River which now flows underground, but which used to run along beside the Kremlin wall. The *Trinity Gate**, linked by a bridge over the Alexandrovsky Garden to the white-washed Kutafia Tower, was built in 1495. At 80 m (262 ft) it is the highest of all the towers. The mounds beside the wall further along the Garden are the remains of *earthworks* constructed by Peter the Great in 1707 when Charles XII of Sweden planned to attack Moscow. The *Borovitskiye* ("*forest*") *Gate** comes next; it stands on the spot where Yuri Dolgoruky first settled in the dense pine forest. It was through this gate that Napoleon entered the Kremlin, and it is the one usually used by visitors. At the corner nearest Kamennyi ("stone") Bridge is the round

*Water-Hoist Tower**, so called in 1633 when craftsmen found a way to raise water from the river and convey it along an aqueduct to the Kremlin palaces and gardens. It was badly damaged in 1812 and has been repeatedly restored since its foundation in 1488. The southern wall of the Kremlin follows the river back to the next bridge and to Red Square again.

KREMLIN. The central square of the Kremlin is Cathedral Square where the three principal cathedrals are situated. The USPENSKY (ASSUMPTION) CATHEDRAL was built in 1475–79 by the Italian architect Aristotle Fioravanti, who had spent many years in Russia studying the architecture of the ancient cities. The cathedral was built in the style of the Uspensky Cathedral at Vladimir, and it became Russia's principal church. The Tsars were crowned here, and the cathedral served as the burial vault of the Moscow metropolitans and patriarchs. It is built of white stone and its grandeur is equalled only by its simplicity; at the time of its completion it was an architectural wonder. Inside the cathedral are 16th–19th century murals and the Monomakhs' Throne, a wonderful example of wood-carving which was made in 1551 and which belonged to Ivan the Terrible. The iconostases of the cathedral have such precious icons as the "St. George" (early 12th century) and the "Trinity" (13th century). During the Napoleonic invasion the French soldiers turned the cathedral into a stable, using the old icons as firewood. They carried off as much as 288 kilograms ($5\frac{1}{4}$ cwt) of various golden articles and about 5,000 kilograms (5 tons) of silver, much of which was lost during the subsequent retreat, and which has not yet been recovered.

THE BLAGOVESHCHENSKY (ANNUNCIATION) CATHEDRAL was built in early Moscow style in 1484–89 on a 14th century white-stone foundation laid down by builders from Pskov. It had three cupolas at first but in 1562–64 it was rebuilt after a fire; six gilded cupolas were added to it and it then became known as the "Golden-topped". The top two rows of the iconostasis include icons by Theophanes the Greek, Andrei Rublyov and Prokhor from Gorodets. The frescoes were done in 1508 by Feodosi. The cathedral served as the Tsar's private church. Other works of art on display in the South Gallery include the 13th century "Golden-Haired Christ", the 14th century "Cloaked Christ", the 15th century "Transfiguration" and the 16th century "Our Lady of Vladimir".

ARKHANGELSKY (ARCHANGEL MICHAEL'S) CATHEDRAL was built in 1505 to 1509 by an Italian, Aleviso Novyi. The ground plan of the cathedral is rectangular and is designed in Russian style with traces of Italian influence. The exterior has more decoration than that of the other two cathedrals. The murals inside depict several historical, as well as religious and battle scenes, and scenes from everyday life. The carved wooden iconostasis is 13 m (43 ft) high, and the "Archangel Michael" icon on it is supposed to have been painted by the painter Rublyov. From 1340 until 1700, first the smaller church which stood on this site, and then the cathedral itself, served as the burial vault of the Grand-Princes of Moscow and the Russian tsars, and among those buried here are Dmitri Donskoi, Ivan III and Ivan the Terrible.

The *Belltower of Ivan the Great*, which unites the various buildings of the Kremlin into a single architectural ensemble, is one of the most remarkable structures built in the 16th century world. First built in 1532–43, it was rebuilt in 1600 and crowned with an onion-shaped cupola covered with gilded copper. It is 81 m (265 ft) high, and when it was first built, it served as a watchtower from which all Moscow and the vicinity within a radius of 30 km (19 miles) could be observed. It has 21 bells altogether, and the main bell weighs 63 tons. *The Tsar Bell* which stands on a stone pedestal near the belltower is the biggest bell in the world. It was cast in the Kremlin in 1733–35, weighs more than 200 tons, is 6 m (20 ft) high and 6·6 m (22 ft) in diameter. The bas-reliefs on its surface were by Rastrelli and represent Tsar Alexei Mikhailovich and Tsaritsa Anna Ivanovna. After its completion the bell remained where it had been cast, but during the Kremlin fire of 1737, probably due to the heat and to the cold water which extinguished the flames, several cracks appeared and a large piece weighing 11½ tons broke off. Only in 1836 was it raised from the pit in which it lay; the architects Montferrand and Lebedev were responsible for the operation. It was then placed as it stands today, with the broken piece beside it.

Not far from the Tsar Bell is the *Tsar Cannon* which has the largest calibre of any gun in the world. It was cast in bronze in 1586 by the famous Russian craftsman, Andrei Chokhov, and was the biggest cannon of its day. It weighs 40 tons and is 5·3 m (17 ft 6 in.) long, with a calibre of 890 mm (35 in.) and a barrel 15 cm (6 in.) thick. A special carriage was required to fire it, but its present carriage was cast in 1835 especially for display purposes.

Also outside Cathedral Square, and behind the Blagoveshchensky Cathedral, is the *Church of the Twelve Apostles and the Patriarch's Palace*. The Church was built in 1655–56 and served as the patriarch's private church. The buildings now house the Museum of 17th century Applied Art; the exhibits were taken from the reserve of the State Armoury Museum (see below) and include books and items of tableware, clothing and household linen.

The Great Kremlin Palace was built in 1838–49 from designs by Thon, and was used as the residence of the imperial family during their visits to Moscow. It is now a governmental building where the Supreme Soviets of the U.S.S.R. and of the Russian Federation meet.

To the east of the Great Kremlin Palace stands *Granovitaya Palata*, or the "Hall of Facets", so-called because of the shape of the stone facings on the side nearest Cathedral Square. Built in 1473–91 by the Italian architects Marco Ruffo and Pietro Antonio, it is actually a large low-vaulted chamber, the roof supported in the middle by a rectangular pier. The iron ribs of the vaulting are gilded and there are inscriptions in Slavonic lettering on the vaulting.

The ARMOURY, or Oruzheinaya Palata, is the oldest Russian museum and the place where the Tsars' regalia and ambassadorial gifts are kept. It is open (for group excursions) at 9.30, 11.30, 2.30 and 4.30, and is closed on Fridays. Tickets are best obtained through Intourist.

Arms, armour and valuable objects from the country's chief armouries and storehouses were collected and the present building was put up in 1849 to 1851 after the completion of the Great Kremlin Palace.

The display opens with a large collection of Russian and foreign arms and armour (Hall 1). Of special interest here are the collection of helmets (Stand 1) of which the oldest was made in the 13th century and is said to have belonged to Prince Yaroslav (father of Alexander Nevsky). Here, too, is the helmet of little Prince Ivan, son of Ivan the Terrible, killed at the age of 28 by his father in an outburst of anger. On the same stand are examples of Russian chainmail, followed by a collection of battle-axes and maces. Russian arquebuses and German and Dutch muskets of the 16th and 17th centuries are on display on Stand 2. A collection of ceremonial armour, among which Tsar Mikhail's helmet should be noted for its finish, is on Stand 3. There is also a collection of Russian and oriental sabres, among which are those of Minin (Egyptian-made) and Prince Pozharsky (Persian-made); these men together headed the army which drove the Poles out of Moscow in 1613. On Stand 4, together with a small collection of Indian arms, is the large Greek quiver which belonged to Tsar Alexei, his Oriental sabre and a heavy (1·2 kg/2 lb 10 oz) golden mace presented to him by the Persian Shah Abbas. Also in this hall are Russian arms of Peter the Great's time and trophies of the Swedish War (Stand 5), European suits of armour of the 15th–17th centuries, a collection of pistols of the 16th century (Stand 6) and Russian and European arms and firearms of the 17th–18th centuries (Stands 7 and 8).

In Halls 2 and 3 gold- and silverware of the 12th–19th centuries is displayed. Of special interest in Hall 2 is the collection of Russian and foreign clocks and watches of 16th–19th centuries. The gilded copper watch in the form of a book belonged to Ivan the Terrible, and the wooden watch was made in the 19th century by Russian craftsmen. In Stand 26 in Hall 3 there is a collection of 18th–20th century jewellery. There is a silver egg, on the outside of which a map of the Trans-Siberian Railway is engraved; inside is a golden clockwork model of a train with a platinum engine, the carriages having inscriptions—"Smokers' Compartment", "Ladies Only", "Clerics", etc. The windows are crystals and a tiny ruby serves as a lantern.

Precious vestments of priceless silk, velvet and brocade, woven and embroidered with gold and encrusted with jewels and pearls are on display in Hall 4. They belonged to the Moscow Tsars, Patriarchs and Metropolitans.

A large collection of foreign golden and silver objects, mostly ambassadorial gifts to the Russian Tsars, is to be found in Hall 5.

In Hall 6 is the Russian Tsars' regalia. Stands 48–52 have on display the Tsars' thrones, the oldest of which is the one, veneered with carved ivory, that belonged to Ivan the Terrible. Also of interest is the throne of the first years of Peter I's reign, when he shared the power with his elder brother, Ivan. The throne has two seats in the front and one hidden seat behind the back, where the Regent (their sister Sophia) usually sat and prompted the young Tsars the right answers to the ambassadors' questions. Here, too, is the throne covered with thin plates of gold and studded with 2200 precious stones and pearls, presented to Tsar Boris Godunov by Shah Abbas of Persia, and the throne of Tsar Alexei (also of Persian work), decorated with 876 diamonds and 1223 other stones. Of the crowns, the oldest is the "Cap of Monomakh" which dates from the 13th century and was altered in the 16th century. Anna Ivanovna's Imperial Crown is encrusted with numerous diamonds and a large ruby. Stands 60 and 61 are devoted to Russian and foreign orders and medals.

Hall 9 contains equipages; the oldest here is an English carriage said to have been presented to Tsar Boris Godunov by Queen Elizabeth I of England. The most picturesque carriage in the hall is the French rococo one, with paintings by Bouchet, presented by Count K. Razumovsky to Elizaveta Petrovna in 1754. A new section of the museum has been opened to show the presents made to the Soviet Union by foreign countries.

The new PALACE OF CONGRESSES was built 15 m (49 ft) down into the ground—a depth equal to the height of a 5-storey house—so that it would not be higher than the rest of the Kremlin ensemble. Designed by Mikhail Posokhin and completed in 1961 for the

22nd Soviet Communist Party Congress, it is now used for concerts and by the company of the Bolshoi Theatre; some ballets were especially produced for this stage. International congresses also meet here.

SAINT BASIL'S CATHEDRAL *Red Square. Open 10.30–5.0, Mondays 10.30–2.30; closed on Tuesdays.* The Cathedral of the Intercession, or Saint Basil's, as it is more usually known, was built in 1555–60 by the order of Ivan the Terrible to commemorate the conquest of the Tartar city of Kazan on the Volga. It was built by Barma and Posnik (—some new historical research indicates that both names may have belonged to one person). Ivan the Terrible planned to build a cathedral composed of 8 subsidiary churches, each dedicated to the saints on whose days he won his battles. The architects however preferred nine and planned them all with different designs. The exotic grandeur of the exterior makes this cathedral one of the best examples of old Russian architecture.

The first room of the museum inside gives the history of the building the story of its construction and specimens of the materials used. In the 16th century the crypt was used as the State Treasury; in 1595 two nobles planned to rob the treasury, first diverting the city guard by starting fires at different points of the suburbs. Their plan was, however, a failure and they were executed. Among the more interesting sights of the cathedral are the iconostasis of the Trinity Church, the "Entry into Jerusalem" icon in the church of that name and the interior decoration of the Church of Saint Alexander of Svir.

In 1588 a church was built close to the cathedral, and dedicated to the memory of a holy man called Basil, a Muscovite who had exercised a certain amount of influence on Ivan the Terrible. It was from this church that the cathedral took its more popular name.

NOVODEVICHY CONVENT *Bolshaya Pirogovskaya Street 2, near Sportivnaya Metro Station. Open May 1st—Sept. 1st 11–5.30; Nov. 1st.—Apr. 30th. 11–4.30; closed on Tuesdays and the last day of each month, early closing on Mondays.* This is one of the most interesting historical and architectural monuments in Moscow. It was founded in 1524 by Grand-Prince Vasili Ioanovich to commemorate the union of Smolensk and Moscow. It formed a stronghold on the road to Smolensk and Lithuania and was a convent for ladies of noble birth; Evdokiya, Peter the Great's first wife, and Princess Sophia, his rebellious sister, both spent part of their lives here and both are buried here.

The buildings that remain date mostly from the 16th century.

THE SMOLENSKY CATHEDRAL. This cathedral, built in 1525, was dedicated to Our Lady of Smolensk. Its architect was Aleviz Fryazin. The wooden iconostasis has 84 wooden columns and the icons dating from the 16th and 17th centuries were painted by the best Muscovite masters. The cathedral is open as a museum and contains objects of Russian craftsmanship (both ecclesiastical and secular) of the 16th and 17th centuries, including wood- and metalwork, paintings, fabrics, and embroidery. There is also a large collection of 16th and 17th century books, beautifully illuminated and illustrated, leather-bound and decorated with gold, silver and jewels. Beneath the cathedral is a large crypt.

THE CHURCH OF THE ASSUMPTION. This church was built in 1687. It is open for religious service.

TRANSFIGURATION GATE CHURCH. The gate-church was built in 1688.

The *Belfry* stands 72 m (237 ft) high. It was completed in 1690, and constitutes one of the best examples of 17th century tiered architecture.

The towers and walls surrounding the convent also date from the 17th century.

There is a separate entrance to the cemetery from the boulevard running beside the convent. The famous writers Gogol and Chekhov are buried here, as is also Stalin's wife, Aliluyeva. At the present time prominent statesmen, artists and generals are still laid here.

The following churches are among those open for services in the capital: (Daily services at 10 a.m. and 6 p.m.).

THE PATRIARCHAL CATHEDRAL OF THE MANIFESTATION OF CHRIST *Spartakovskaya Street 15*. The cathedral was built in 1835–45 and contains, among other treasures, the Kazan Virgin icon, the Virgin of Tikhvin icon and a sacred relic, the shrine of Saint Alexis, Metropolitan of Moscow in the 14th century, which was transferred here from the Assumption Cathedral in the Kremlin.

THE ASCENSION CHURCH *Sokolniki Square*. This church was built in 1914, but it possesses many old icons, including the wonder-working Virgin of Iberia (Iberia was the old name for the country of Georgia).

THE TRANSFIGURATION CHURCH *Preobrazhenskaya Square*. This church was built in 1746, and contains the wonder-working icon of the Virgin of Healing.

THE CHURCH OF THE LAMENTERS *Bolshaya Ordynka 20*. This church was built in 1787 and contains the wonder-working icon "The Joy of All Afflicted".

ASSUMPTION CHURCH *Novo-Devichy Convent*.

CHURCH OF SAINT NICHOLAS *Komsomolsky Prospekt, Teplyi Pereulok 1/2*. The church was built in 1679; it contains the wonder-working icon of the "Countenance of Sinners" Virgin.

THE CHURCH OF THE HOLY MARTYR, JOHN THE WARRIOR *Dimitrova Street 46*. The church was built in 1712, and contains the icon of the Holy Martyr.

THE CHURCH OF THE RESURRECTION *Brusovsky Pereulok*. The church was built in 1629.

THE CHURCH OF THE RESURRECTION *Aksakovsky Pereulok 20*. This church was built in 1683.

ALL SAINTS' CHURCH *Leningradsky Prospekt, Sokol*. This church was built in 1736.

THE CHURCH OF THE ARCHANGEL GABRIEL *Telegrafnyi Pereulok No. 15a*. This church was built in 1704–07.

CHURCH OF SAINT PIMEN *Novovorotnikovsky Pereulok 3*. The church was built in 1848.

EVANGELICAL CHRISTIANS' (BAPTISTS') MEETING HOUSE *Malyi Vuzovsky Pereulok 3. Meetings at 6 p.m. on Tuesdays, Thursdays and Saturdays, and at 10 a.m. and 6 p.m. on Sundays.*

OLD BELIEVERS' CATHEDRAL *Rogozhsky Pereulok 29*.

ARMENIAN CHURCH *Malaya Dekabrskaya Street 27*.

SAINT LOUIS' ROMAN CATHOLIC CHURCH *Markhlevsky Street 7*. This church was designed by Gilliardi, and built in 1827–30.

MOSQUE *Vypolzov Pereulok 7*. The midday service is recited on Fridays at 1 p.m.

SYNAGOGUE *Arkhipov Street 8. Daily services at 10 a.m. and one hour before sundown.*

MOSCOW UNIVERSITY. Moscow University was founded in 1755 (in the reign of Elizaveta Petrovna) by Russia's great scientist and encyclopaedist, Mikhail Lomonosov, and is named after him.

It is now the largest university in the country and has over 22,000 students attending its 14 faculties. It is housed in many buildings in the city; the oldest are on either side of Gertzen Street, where it joins Marx Prospekt. One of these was built by Kazakov and restored by Gillardi after the fire of 1812. The other was designed by Gillardi in 1835 and has a monument to Lomonosov by Ivanov (1876) in front of it.

On Lenin Hills is the new 32-storey skyscraper with four 18-storey wings designed by Rudnyev and completed in 1953. The building, including the spire, is 240 m (787 ft) high and the main façade is 450 m (492 yd) long. To inspect all the premises here one would have to walk nearly 150 km (93 miles). The monument to Lomonosov is by Tomsky (1954). In the grounds of the university are a botanical garden and an observatory.

From Lenin Hills' "look-out" terrace there is an excellent panorama of Moscow. Lenin Stadium lies on the other side of the river; close to it on the left is Novo-Devichy Convent, the Kremlin is on the horizon straight ahead and the skyscrapers stand out from the rest of the city's buildings.

THE METRO, MOSCOW'S UNDERGROUND RAILWAY. The Metro is the pride of the city, the apple of the Muscovite's eye. Its three main lines crossing in the centre are linked by a circle line crossing them each in turn. This basic spider-web plan follows the layout of the city itself.

In all the system is well over 100 km (60 miles) long, has about 80 stations and carries over 4,000,000 passengers daily. The first line was opened in 1935 and new construction is always in progress.

The Metro works perfectly from a technical point of view; the escalators, the air-conditioning and the passenger tunnels are all well planned.

The dêcor of each station is a separate work of art; some give the impression of a palace, with soft lights shining on the marble columns and intricate mosaics. Each line has its characteristic features; the noble simplicity of the Sokolniki–Gorky Park Line is in contrast to the extravagant grandeur of the Circle Line. One of the most impressive stations is Mayakovskaya, named in honour of the poet Mayskovsky, whose statue stands in the square above. Here the columns are of stainless steel and red marble, and the mosaics on the ceilings were made from paintings by A. Deineka, a well-known artist in the Soviet Union.

SCHUSEV RUSSIAN ARCHITECTURE MUSEUM *Kalinin Prospekt 5. Open 10–6, Wednesdays and Fridays 12–8; closed on Tuesdays.* Academician Schusev (1873–1949) was a well-known Soviet architect who designed, among other things, the Lenin Mausoleum. The Museum covers the principal periods and trends in Russian architecture from 1037 to the present day.

DONSKOI MONASTERY *Donskaya Square 1. The Architecture Museum is housed in this monastery—open 11–6; closed on Monday and the last day of every month.* The monastery was founded by Tsar Feodor in 1592–93 to commemorate Moscow's deliverance from the Crimean Khan, Kasi-Gerei, in 1591. A small church of this date still stands but the rest of the present-day buildings and the walls were put up between 1680–1730.

The name came from the icon of Our Lady which was carried by Prince Dmitri Donskoi's army.

The museum is located in the Cathedral (1684–98) and contains original projects and models by famous Russian and Soviet architects. The display is very similar to that of the Schusev Museum. The six-tiered, carved iconostasis was made in the 17th century by craftsmen from the Kremlin.

In the monastery grounds there is a church open for services, and the cemetery contains many monuments to nobles. In the former private church and chapel of the Princes Golitsyn (built in 1809) are Russian monumental sculptures of the 18th and 19th centuries. The horsedrawn chariot and figures along the paths are from the Moscow Triumphal Arch which was dismantled and is to be rebuilt on a new site.

ANDREI RUBLYOV MUSEUM *Pryamikov Square 10. Open 12–5, on Mondays and Thursdays 2–7, Tuesdays 11 to 3; closed on Wednesdays.* The museum is inside the walls of the former Spaso-Androniyev Monastery, founded in 1360 by Saint Alexei and its first abbot, Andronik, whose name it bears. On its territory is the city's oldest cathedral, the Spassky Cathedral (1420 to 1427). Arkhangelskaya Church was built in 1691–94, and the walls and towers also date from the second half of the 17th century.

Andrei Rublyov and another famous icon painter, his teacher Daniil Chornyi are buried in the monastery.

TRETYAKOV GALLERY *Lavrushinsky Pereulok 10. Open 10–8 (ticket office open till 7;) closed on Mondays.* The foundation of this collection was laid in 1856 by the art collectors brothers Pavel and Sergei Tretyakov, who presented the gallery to the city in 1892.

In the forecourt is a copy of Yevgeny Vuchetich's sculpure "Swords into Ploughshares", presented to the United Nations by the Soviet Union. The Gallery contains an impressive collection of Russian art from early icons to the most prominent Soviet artists of the present day. Highly valued is the country's best collection of the so-called "peredvizhniki" (members of the Society of Travelling Art Exhibitions), who displayed their realistic works in many towns in the 1870's.

Hall 1–6: Mostly portraits by 18th century Russian artists.

Hall 7: *Ivanov (1806–58)* "The Appearance of Christ to the people" (Ivanov spent about 20 years on this canvas; and there are many of his preliminary sketches in this hall). *Bryullov (1799–1852)* "The Rider".

Hall 11: *Perov (1833–82)* "Hunters at Rest", "The Troika" (Children pulling a barrel of water through the snow).

Hall 12: *Ivazovsky (1817–1900)* "The Black Sea", "The Seaside".

Hall 13: *Savitsky (1844–1905)* "Railway Repair Work".

Hall 14: *Kramskoi (1837–87)* "Christ in the Wilderness", a portrait of Leo Tolstoi, a portrait of Pavel Tretyakov, and "The Stranger".

Hall 15: *Ghe (1831–94)* "Peter I Questioning Tsarevich Alexei in Peterhof", "Golgotha".

Hall 16: *Savrasov (1830–97)* "The Rooks Have Come".

Hall 18: *Pryanishnikov (1840–94)* "Episode from the War of 1812" (Russian peasant women taking French soldiers prisoner), *V. Makovsky (1846–1920)* "Failure of a Bank". *Yaroshenko (1846–98)* "Life Everywhere" (Pigeons feeding from a convict train).

Hall 19: *Shishkin (1832–98)* "Morning in a Pinewood" (bears in the forest), "A Corn Field". *Kuindjy (1842–1910)* "Night on the Dnieper".

Hall 20: *Polenov (1844–1927)* "Granny's Garden", "Overgrown Pond".

Hall 22: *Vasnetsov (1848–1926)* "Alyonushka" (illustration of a fairy tale), "Ivan the Terrible".

Hall 23: *Vereshchagin (1842–1904)* "Deification of War". This artist is best known as a painter of battle scenes.

Hall 24: *Surikov (1848–1916)* "The Execution of the Streltsy" (... on Red Square), "Boyarinya Morozova".

Halls 25–26: *Repin (1844–1930)* "Princess Sophia in Novo-Devichy Convent", "Ivan the Terrible and his Son" portraits.

Hall 27: *Levitan (1861–1900)*, famous for his landscapes. "Eternal Peace" (small church in the distance), "Golden Autumn", "Evening on the Volga"; *Serov (1865–1911)* "Girl with Peaches". *Antokolsky (1843 to 1902)*, sculptor, "Ivan the Terrible" (marble), "Peter I" (bronze).

Hall 28: *Ancient Russian Art*—icons and frescoes from Ancient Kiev, Rostov-the-Great, Suzdal, Tver, Novgorod and Pskov. "Assumption" (12th century)—Novgorod, "Epiphany" (12th century)—Novgorod, "Our Lady of Vladimir" (12th century) from the Assumption Cathedral in the Moscow Kremlin where it was revered as a miracle-working icon.

Hall 29: *Ancient Art of Moscow. Rublyev (d. 1430)* "Trinity" icon, "Apostle Paul". *Ushakov (1626–86)* "Our Lady of Vladimir".

Hall 30: *Vrubel (1856–1910)* "The Demon", "Pan", "Nightfall". *Konenkov (1874)*, sculptor. "Stone Crusher" (bronze).

Halls 31–51: Works of Grabar, Konchalovskii, Rerich, Sariyan, Brodsky, Golubkina, Ioganson, Kustodiev, Yuon, Gerasimov, Reshetnikov, Neprintsev, and Prorokov among others. Political cartoons by Yefimov are displayed in Hall 43.

LENIN MAUSOLEUM *On Red Square, by the Kremlin walls. Open 1–4, on Sundays 12–5; closed on Mondays and Fridays. To avoid standing in the long queue, tourists should ask Intourist to arrange a special time for an accompanied visit.* The body of Vladimir Lenin whose real name was Ulyanov (1870–1924), founder of the Communist Party and of the Soviet State, lies here. Stalin's body also lay in the mausoleum from his death in 1953 until 1961, when it was removed by popular demand, and buried near the Kremlin wall among other Communist Great.

The building of the mausoleum was constructed in 1930 by Schusev and is generally agreed to be well-planned, harmonising with the older structures surrounding the square. Members of the government stand on the platform on the mausoleum to watch the parades which take place on the square.

LENIN MUSEUM *Revolyutsiya Square 4. Open 11–7; closed on Mondays.* The museum was opened in 1936 following a resolution taken by the Central Committee of the Soviet Communist Party. Its 22 halls contain several thousand exhibits, covering the main periods of the life and work of Vladimir Ilyich Lenin, founder of the Soviet State. Among the exhibits are Lenin's personal belongings such as a desk with secret drawers, a coat with bullet-holes (which were the result of an attempt on his life) and his car. A newsreel of 1917–24, in which he appears and speaks, is shown.

The museum is located in the Duma ("parliament") Building, constructed in pseudo-Russian style in 1890–92, its red brick harmonizing with the Historical Museum beside it.

MARX-ENGELS MUSEUM *Marx Engels Street 5.*

HISTORICAL MUSEUM *Red Square, 1/2; Open 10.30–5.30 on Mondays, Thursdays and Sundays and 12–7 on Wednesdays, Fridays and Saturdays; closed on Tuesdays and on the last day of each month.* The building was constructed in 1874–83 by Sherwood and Semyonov, under the influence of 17th century Russian architecture. The museum was initiated by Moscow University, and with 300,000 exhibits is now the biggest repository of historical material and documents tracing the origin and history of the peoples of the Soviet Union from 300,000 years back until the end of the last century.

PUSHKIN ART GALLERY *Volkhonka Street 12. Open 10.30–8; closed on Tuesdays and the last day of each month.* The collection was founded by Professor Tsvetayev and was supported by private donations. The present building was put up for it in 1895–1912 by Academician Klein; it was first of all known as Alexander III's Museum.

After the Hermitage in Leningrad this is the largest Museum in the country. Its greatest pride is its large collection of Ancient Egyptian art. Ancient Greece and Rome are also well represented, but mostly by copies.

The picture gallery is noted for paintings by Botticelli, Ribera, Murillo, Rembrandt, Rubens and Van Dyck. One of the most treasured sections is the French collection which includes works by Poussin, Watteau, Greuze, David, Delacroix, Courbet, Cézanne, Renoir, Degas, Monet, Gauguin, Matisse, Picasso and Van Gogh.

MANÈGE EXHIBITION HALL *Marx Prospekt.* This building by Bovet (1817) was designed as a riding school, and was outstanding in the 19th century for its construction, having a broad roof-span (55 m/60 yds) without supporting pillars. Russian and foreign exhibitions of art, textiles, furnishings, glass, etc. are held here.

HISTORY AND RECONSTRUCTION OF MOSCOW MUSEUM *Novaya Square 12. Open on Mondays 10–3, Wednesdays and Fridays 2–9, Thursdays and Sundays 10–5, Saturdays 10–6; closed on Tuesdays and the last day of each month.* The Museum is housed in the former Church of Saint John the Baptist, built in 1825. It was founded in 1896 and gives an outline of the history of Moscow's rise, telling the part it played in different periods of Russian history.

The reconstruction section deals with the modernization of the public services, building programmes, etc.

The display of presents received by the city of Moscow on its 800th anniversary in 1947 is of interest.

POLYTECHNICAL MUSEUM *Novaya Square 3/4. Open on Tuesdays, Thursdays and Saturdays 1–8, Wednesdays, Fridays and Sundays 10–5; closed on Mondays.* This museum contains a large collection of technical and scientific exhibits, including some on space exploration, and has a technical library within it.

The building itself was constructed in Russian style in the 1870's from plans by Monighetti.

DARWIN MUSEUM *Malaya Pirogovskaya Street 1. Open 10–5; closed on Sundays.*

NATURAL HISTORY MUSEUM *Gertsen Street 6. Open 9–4; closed on Sundays.*

TIMIRYAZEV BIOLOGICAL MUSEUM *Malaya Gruzinskaya Street 15. Open 10–6, Wednesdays and Fridays 12–8; closed on Mondays.* Kliment Timiryazev (1843–1920) championed Darwinism in Russia; his work as a botanist was chiefly concerned with photosynthesis.

REVOLUTION MUSEUM *Gorky Street 21. Open 12–8 Mondays, Wednesdays and Fridays, 10–6 Tuesdays, Thursdays and Sundays; closed on Saturdays.* The house was originally built in 1780, but was rebuilt in classical style after the Moscow fire of 1812. From 1831 until the revolution it was used as a club for noblemen and called the English Club. The six-inch gun in the yard was used by revolutionary troops to fire on the Kremlin in October, 1917. Opened in 1926, the 37-hall museum is the repository of relics and mementoes of the revolution. The exhibition starts with the history of the first workers' organisations in the 19th century. Some of the halls display presents from foreign countries.

KUTUZOV'S HUT MUSEUM *Kutuzovsky Prospekt 38. Open 10–7; closed on Mondays.* Here in 1812 the Russian Council of War, headed by Field-Marshal Mikhail Kutuzov, decided that it was necessary to retreat from Moscow in order to save the army. The painting by Kivshenko (1880) shows the Council in session.

BORODINO BATTLE PANORAMA *Near Kutuzov's Hut. Open 11–7; closed on Fridays.* The cylindrical building which is 42 m (45 yd) in diameter was built to commemorate the 150th anniversary of the historic Battle of Borodino in August, 1812, when Napoleon's Great Army suffered a serious defeat. The canvases of the panorama were painted in Munich by Roubaud (1856–1912) who came from Odessa, and was also responsible for the Sevastopol Panorama. They are 14 m (46 ft) high and the circumference of the cylinder they form is 115 m (126 yds) round. They had never been displayed in a permanent building till 1962.

LEO TOLSTOI MUSEUM *Kropotkinskaya Street 11. Open 11–5, Mondays 10–3, Wednesdays and Fridays 2–8; closed on Tuesdays.* This is, perhaps, not so interesting as the other Tolstoi Museum.

TOLSTOI'S MOSCOW HOME *Lev Tolstoi Street 21. Open 10–4.30; closed on Tuesdays.* Sixteen rooms of this house are preserved as they were during the time that Tolstoi lived here with his family, from 1882 till 1909.

CHEKHOV MUSEUM *Sadovo Kudrinskaya Street 6. Open 11–6, Wednesdays and Fridays 2–9; closed on Tuesdays and Sundays.* On the door of the house can be seen the original brass plate reading: "Dr. A. P. Chekhov".

DOSTOYEVSKY MUSEUM *Dostoyevsky Street 4. Open 11–6, Mondays 10–4, Wednesdays and Fridays 1–9; closed on Tuesdays.*

GORKY'S HOUSE *Kachalova Street 6/2.* Maxim Gorky lived here from 1931 to 1936.

GORKY MUSEUM *Vorovskova Street 25a. Open on Tuesdays and Fridays 1–8, on Wednesdays, Thursdays and Sundays 10–5 and on Saturdays 10.30–4; closed on Mondays.* Books, letters, manuscripts and photographs illustrate the writer's life.

GLINKA MUSEUM *Gertsen Street 13, in the building of the Conservatoire. Open 9–5.30; closed on Sundays.*
The display includes a collection of musical instruments.

DUROV MUSEUM *Durov Street 4. Open 11–5, Thursdays 10–3, Sundays 10–5; closed on Fridays.* This museum is named ofter the famous Russian animal tamer and circus clown, Vladimir Durov (1863–1934). A variety of animals perform in the hall of the Animal Theatre (seating 120) on Saturday at 1.0 p.m. and on Sunday at 11,1 and 3.

ORIENTAL MUSEUM *Obukh Street 16. Open 11–6, Wednesdays and Fridays 2–9; closed on Mondays.* The museum was opened in 1918 after several private collections including the Schukin collection of oriental fine-arts were taken over by the state. This collection has grown and now, besides exhibits from India, China and Japan, it has interesting pieces from the Soviet East.

EXHIBITION OF RUSSIAN DECORATIVE FOLK ART *Petrovka Street 28.*
Open 12–7; closed on Tuesdays and on the last day of the month. The choice collection is beautifully displayed and includes textiles, lace and embroidery, wood carving, decorative metal work and tiles.

The exhibition is housed in the *Vysoko-Petrovsky Monastery*. Dmitri Donskoy founded a monastery here, in the village of Vysoki, to commemorate his victory over the Tartars at Kulikovo; the name Vysoko-Petrovsky was bestowed during rebuilding by Grand Prince Vasili Ivanovich and three additional churches were built by Peter I at the end of the 17th century. The monastery is in a good state of preservation and forms one of the largest complexes of old Russian architecture in the centre of Moscow. The part known as Naryshkin's House is of particular interest. It also dates from the 17th century and 22 rooms have been restored.

HANDICRAFT MUSEUM *Stanislavsky Street 7. Open 11–5; closed on Saturdays.* Samples of traditional lace and embroidery work, wood and bone carvings, lacquer boxes, etc. can be seen in this museum.

PUSHKIN MUSEUM *Kropotkinskaya Street 12/2. Open on Saturdays 1–7.30, Sundays 11–5.30.*

SKRYABIN MUSEUM *Vakhtangov Street 11. Open 1–5, Tuesdays, Fridays and Saturdays 3–7; closed on Wednesdays.* The well-known Russian composer and pianist Alexander Skryabin (1871–1915) lived and died here.

BAKHRUSHIN THEATRE MUSEUM *Bakhrushin Street 31/12. Open 12–7, Wednesdays and Fridays 2–9; closed on Tuesdays.* This museum was founded in 1894 by the theatre-lover and collector whose name it now bears, and it is located in his house.

BUILDINGS EXHIBITION *Frunzenskaya Naberezhnaya 30.* There are pavilions here as well as exhibits in the open air.

SOVIET ARMY MUSEUM *Kommuny Square 2. Open 10–7 on Tuesdays and Fridays; 12–8 on Wednesdays and Thursdays; closed on Mondays.* The museum is devoted to the history of the armed forces of the Soviet Union, and the museum building was completed in 1965.

The periods most fully represented in the museum are the years of the Civil War and of World War II. The display starts with the story of the workers' combatant groups of the 1905 revolution. While preparing for the armed uprising of 1917, the Bolshevik party established the "Red Guards", the core of the future Red Army. The appropriate decree was signed by Lenin on 28th January, 1918; the official celebration date is 23rd February. On display are hand-grenades, swords and Maxim machine-guns—often the only weapons of the first Red Army units; and also some handmade weapons used by the Siberian guerillas. The stands show personal belongings of some outstanding Red Army commanders, such as Chapayev, Frunze and Budyonnyi. Among the exhibits of the years 1922 to 1939 are pictures of the first people to be awarded the title of Hero of the Soviet Union; these were pilots who rescued 100 members of the polar expedition on the icebreaker "Chelyuskin".

The remainder of the exhibits refer to the conflicts with the Japanese (1937) and the Finns (1939–40), and the greater part to World War II. The display ends with exhibits demonstrating the present state of the Soviet Armed Forces,—modern small arms, models of modern tanks, a self-propelled rocket launcher, etc.

Outdoors, in the museum grounds, is an armoured train, some tanks, planes and other large exhibits.

The museum used to be in the next door building, founded in the 18th century and rebuilt following Gillardi's plans in 1802. In 1812 it was damaged by fire, and was again reconstructed in classical style by Gillardi and Grigoryev. The building housed Catherine the Great's School for young ladies of noble birth. It is now Soviet Army House.

THE U.S.S.R. EXHIBITION OF ECONOMIC ACHIEVEMENTS. This is located in the north-western part of Moscow, the main entrance being on Prospekt Mira, on the way to Ostankino and the Camping Site. The exhibition occupies a territory of 216 hectares (553 acres) and includes about 80 large pavilions and many smaller structures. There is a 5 km (3 mile) circular road with various forms of public transport, including small buses, open car-trains and motorbike taxis.

There are pavilions built in the architectural styles of the different Soviet republics, and there are many large pavilions devoted to different branches of agriculture, industry and science. Among them are the pavilions "Atomic Energy for Peaceful Purposes", "Education", "Science", "Machine Building" (a domed pavilion where there is a display of Russian cars), and "Radio-Electronics". The exhibition grounds also include a circus, a circorama cinema and an open-air theatre. Of the many restaurants and cafes, the best is the Zolotoi Kolos ("Golden Ear") Restaurant.

In front of the North Gates entrance is a stainless steel statue by Vera Mukhina, "Worker and Farm-Woman", designed for the Paris Fair of 1937. By the main entrance is a 90 m (295 ft) monument, with a museum inside, to commemorate Soviet space exploration. In front of it is a seated statue of Tsiolkovsky.

LENIN LIBRARY *Kalinin Prospekt 3*. With an overall fund of 21,000,000 titles, this is the country's largest library, and it always receives one copy of each book printed in the Soviet Union. The rare books and manuscripts section has a collection of early documents, and also many first editions and old manuscripts, both foreign, beginning with Gutenberg, and Russian, dating back to the time of Russia's first printer, Fedorov (d. 1587).

The library building was designed by Schuko and Gelfreikh in the 1930's. Close to it is the old part of the library in a beautiful building, designed by the architect Bazhenov in 1786, where there was once a museum bequeathed to the State by Count Rumyantsev. It is also known as Pashkov House after its owner, who was a descendant of Peter I's batman.

FOREIGN LITERATURE LENDING LIBRARY *Petrovskiye Liniyi 1*.

READING ROOMS *Razin Street 12*.

OSTROVSKY MONUMENT *Sverdlov Square, in front of the Malyi Theatre*. Alexander N. Ostrovsky (1823 to 1886) was a popular satirical playwright, and is regarded as the founder of Russian drama. The monument to him by N. Andreyev was erected in 1929 in front of the theatre where his plays were, and still are, staged.

WORKER AND FARM-WOMAN STATUE *At the entrance to the Exhibition of Economic Achievements.* This gigantic statue created in 1937 by V. Mukhina was on show at the Soviet Exhibition in Paris in that year.

LENIN MONUMENT *Sovietskaya Square, in front of the Marxism-Leninism Institute.* This statue by S. Merkurov was exhibited at the New York World Fair in 1939 before it was erected here in 1940.

GORKY STATUE *By the Belorussky railway station.* Designed by Ivan Shadr and made from his sketches by Mukhina, Zelenskaya, and Ivanova, the statue was unveiled on 10th June, 1951.

GOGOL STATUE *Arbatskaya Square.* This statue of Nikolai Gogol (1809–52) by N. Tomsky was erected in 1952.

LOMONOSOV MONUMENTS *In front of the Old University building, Marx Prospekt and in the courtyard of the New University Building on Lenin Hills.* Mikhail Lomonosov (1711–65), was the scientist and encyclopedist who founded Moscow University in 1755. The statue on Lenin Hills is by N. Tomsky, and was erected in 1954.

YURI DOLGORUKY STATUE *Sovietskaya Square.* Prince Yuri Dolgoruky founded Moscow in 1147, and the foundation of this commemorative equestrian statue was laid to mark the 800th anniversary of the event. It is by S. Orlov.

CHAIKOVSKY MONUMENT *Gertsen Street, in front of the Conservatoire.* This seated statue of the composer was designed by V. Mukhina and erected in 1954.

MAYAKOVSKY MONUMENT *Mayakovsky Square.* This statue of Vladimir Mayakovsky (1893–1930), poet and playwright, was designed by A. Kibalnikov and erected in 1958.

DZERZHINSKY MONUMENT *Dzerzhinsky Square.* This statue of Felix Dzerzhinskii (1877–1926), revolutionary and statesman, was designed by Vuchetich in 1958.

REPIN MONUMENT *Bolotnaya Square.* This statue of artist Ilya Repin was created by M. Manizer in 1958.

SECHENOV MONUMENT *Bolshaya Pirogovskaya Street 2/6.* Ivan Sechenov (1829–1905) is known as the father of Russian physiology; he was a professor of both St. Petersburg and Moscow Universities. This statue erected in 1958 is by L. Kerbel.

GRIBOYEDOV MONUMENT *Kirovskiye Vorota, Chistoprudnyi Boulevard.* Alexander Griboyedov (1798–1829) is famed for his single play, *Woe from Wit,* which was rejected by the censor and only staged two years after he was murdered while serving as Ambassador to Persia. The statue of him by N. Manuilov was erected in 1959.

KARL MARX MONUMENT *Sverdlov Square.* This monument to the philosopher by L. Kerbel was unveiled to mark the 22nd Soviet Communist Party Congress in 1961. The street in front of it was renamed Marx Prospekt at the same time.

MININ AND POZHARSKY MONUMENT *On Red Square, in front of St. Basil's Cathedral.* This statue by I. Martos was erected in 1818 in memory of the meat merchant Minin and Prince Pozharsky, respectively the organiser and the leader of the army which ejected the Poles from Moscow in 1612.

GRENADIERS OF PLEVNA MONUMENT *Ilyinskiye Vorota.* This monument, designed by V. Sherwood, was erected in 1887. It had been built with funds colected by the survivors of the grenadiers who fought at the Battle of Plevna (1877) during the liberation of Bulgaria.

PUSHKIN MONUMENT *Pushkin Square.* This statue by A. Opekushin was erected to the poet's memory by popular subscription in 1880.

LERMONTOV MONUMENT *Lermontov Square.* This 5 m (15 ft) statue by Brodsky was unveiled in 1965 to commemorate the 150th anniversary of the poet's birth.

PIROGOV MONUMENT *Bolshaya Pirogovskaya Street.* This monument to Nikolai Pirogov, surgeon and scientist, by V. Sherwood was erected in 1897.

FEODOROV MONUMENT *Teatralnyi Proyezd.* Ivan Feodorov was the first Russian printer, and the date on the pedestal, 19th April, 1563, is that on which the printing of the first Russian book was begun. The statue by S. Volnukhin was erected in 1909.

TOMBSTONES OF THE SOVIET UNION'S OUTSTANDING LEADERS *Beside the Kremlin wall, on Red Square.* Here lie Sverdlov, Frunze, Zhdanov, Dzerzhinsky, Kalinin, Stalin and others.

OBELISK *In Alexandrovsky Gardens, beside the Kremlin wall.* In commemoration of the 300th anniversary of the House of Romanov, this obelisk was engraved with the names of the Russian tsars. After the revolution these were eradicated, and now the obelisk bears the names of Marx, Engels, Marat, Danton, Plekhanov and Spartacus among other revolutionaries and philosophers.

TIMIRYAZEV MONUMENT *Nikitskiye Vorota.* This monument to the naturalist and follower of Darwin was designed by Merkurov and erected in 1923.

VOROVSKY MONUMENT *At the crossing of Kuznetsky Most and Dzerzhinsky Street.* The memorial to the literary critic and diplomat, who was assassinated in Switzerland in 1923, was erected in the year following his death by M. Kats.

SHEVCHENKO MONUMENT *in front of the Ukraina Hotel, Naberezhnaya Shevchenko.* Taras Shevchenko is the best known Ukrainian poet (1814–61) and this statue was unveiled in 1964 to mark the 150th anniversary of his birth.

TSIOLKOVSKY MONUMENT *at the foot of the soaring rocket monument on Prospekt Mira.* Konstantin Tsiolkovsky (1857–1935) was a pioneer in the theory of cosmic travel and rocketry.

PALACE OF CONGRESSES *Kremlin, entrance for performances through the white-washed Kutafia Gate (by the Manège) which leads to the Trinity Gate (Troyitskiye vorota).* The Palace, which seats 6000, was completed in 1961.

BOLSHOI THEATRE *Sverdlov Square.* This theatre was formerly known as the Great Imperial Theatre; after a fire in 1854 it was rebuilt by Cavos and can now seat over 2000. The theatre is famous for the statue of Phoebus in the Sun Chariot above the ionic portico. The theatre company is known all over the world for its incomparable ballet, and Russian and foreign operas are also in its repertoire. The orchestra, too, is one of the best in the country.

STANISLAVSKY AND NEMIROVICH-DANCHENKO MUSICAL THEATRE *Pushkinskaya Street 17.* This ballet and opera theatre can seat 1400 and is called after the popular Russian actor and director. Its company ranks second only to the Bolshoi Theatre in Moscow.

MALYI ("LITTLE") DRAMA THEATRE *Sverdlov Square 1/6*. (*Affiliated Theatre —Bolshaya Ordinka Street 69*). This theatre, built by Bovet and reconstructed by Thon in 1841, was formerly the Little Imperial Theatre. It has been well known for many years for its staging of Russian classical plays, especially those by the satirist Ostrovsky, a statue of whom stands by the entrance. Plays by other Russian and Soviet playwrights as well as those translated from other languages are in the current repertoire. The theatre can seat over 1000.

MKHAT OR GORKY ARTS THEATRE (DRAMA) *Proyezd Khudozhestvennogo Teatra 3*. (*Affiliated Theatre Moskvin Street 3*). This theatre was founded in 1898 by the famous Russian actor and director, Stanislavsky (1863–1938) and Nemirovich-Danchenko (1858–1943). They staged Chekhov's and Gorky's plays here with a team of leading actors, and it was here that Konstantin Stanislavsky developed his theories, based on the realistic traditions of the Russian theatre, which became known as the Stanislavsky method. After the production of Chekhov's "The Seagull", they chose this bird as their emblem and it now decorates the curtain. This theatre and the Malyi theatre are the country's leading drama theatres.

VAKHTANGOV DRAMA THEATRE *Arbat Street 26*. This theatre is called after Stanislavsky's pupil, Evgeny Vakhtangov (1883–1922).

PUSHKIN DRAMA THEATRE *Tverskoi Boulevard 23*.

MAYAKOVSKY DRAMA THEATRE *Gertsen Street 19*.

CENTRAL SOVIET ARMY DRAMA THEATRE *Kommuny Square 2*. This theatre, designed by Alabyan and Simbirtsev in 1934–38, is built in the shape of a huge five-pointed star. The main auditorium can seat 1800 and the second one 470.

YERMOLOVA DRAMA THEATRE *Gorky Street 5*. This theatre is called after the famous Russian actress, Maria Yermolova (1853–1928).

LENIN KOMSOMOL DRAMA THEATRE *Chekhov Street 6*.

SATIRE THEATRE *Malaya Bronnaya Street 2*.

CENTRAL PUPPET THEATRE *Gorky Street 32a (and in the summer often in the Hermitage Garden Summer Theatre)*. This theatre is often known simply as Obraztsov's Theatre, after its founder and present director. This master's shows for adults are well worth seeing, and the excellent performances even break through the language barrier.

ROMANY THEATRE *Pushkinskaya Street 26*. This is the only gipsy theatre in the world, and many of the performances include gipsy songs and dances.

SOVREMENNIK ("CONTEMPORARY") THEATRE *Mayakovsky Square 1/19*. This is one of the youngest of Moscow's theatres, as regards both the age of the company and the average age of the actors.

OPERETTA THEATRE *Pushkinskaya Street 6*. This theatre can seat nearly 2000; musical comedies are staged here as well as traditional operettas.

VARIETY THEATRE *Bersenevskaya Naberezhnaya 20/2*.

KREMLIN THEATRE *In the Kremlin, entrance from Spasskiye Vorota (gate) on Red Square.* This theatre, which should not be confused with the Palace of Congresses Theatre in the Kremlin, has no permanent company.

GRAND AND SMALL HALLS OF THE TCHAIKOVSKY CONSERVATOIRE *Gertsen Street 13.* There is a monument to the composer in front of the Conservatoire.

CHAIKOVSKY CONCERT HALL *Mayakovsky Square.*

KOLONNYI ZAL ("HALL OF COLUMNS") *In the House of Trade Unions—Pushkinskaya Street 1.* The building, constructed by Kazakov in 1785, was once a club for the nobility. It contains a large hall, judged the most beautiful in Moscow, with columns of white marble.

CIRCUS *Tsvetnoi Boulevard 13.*

PLANETARIUM *Sadovaya-Kudrinskaya Street 5. Open 9–8.30; closed on Tuesdays.*

Some of Moscow's Cinemas

STEREOKINO *Sverdlov Square 3/6.*

CIRCORAMA *At the Exhibition of Economic Achievements.*

RUSSIA *Pushkinskaya Square.*

MIR PANORAMA CINEMA *Tsvetnoi boulevard 11.*

OLD FILMS *Gertsen Street 23.*

METROPOLE *Sverdlov Square 2.*

Foreign language films are sometimes shown here.

✿ GORKY PARK *Krymsky Val 9. Open 9–midnight.* This is the most popular park in the capital. It lies along the River Moskva, and its territory of 120 hectares (300 acres) includes one of the city's oldest parks, the Neskuchnyi Sad ("Gay Garden"); here beyond the Zelenyi Teatr ("Green Theatre"—open air, seating 10,000). The park also boasts amusements, sports grounds, a boating station, a chess club, a shooting gallery, restaurant, cafes, a beer hall, and several exhibition halls.

SOKOLNIKI PARK. Sokolniki Park is called after the falconers ("sokolniki") who used to live here and attend the tsars' hunting parties. For over a hundred years it was a popular place to go for picnics, and the nobility used to drive their coaches along the avenues. It has become widely known for the American, Japanese, British, French and other national fairs held here. Each country has added to the exhibition site's equipment and accommodation; the largest pavilion is 168 m (184 yd) long and 56 m (61 yd) wide.

In the park are also an open-air theatre seating 5000, an amusement park, a shooting gallery, bicycles for hire, restaurants and cafes. The park covers a territory of 612 hectares (1530 acres) and includes part of an ancient forest.

IZMAILOVO PARK *Open 10 a.m.–11 p.m.* One of the biggest parks in the world, this covers 1180 hectares (2950 acres) and includes large stretches of pine forest. It was once the manor of the Romanov family and a favourite resort of the tsars. Here, in a disused storehouse Peter I found the old boat which is now known as the "grandfather of the Russian fleet" and kept in a museum in Leningrad. There is an amusement park, an open-air theatre, and several cafes.

HERMITAGE GARDEN *Karetnyi Ryad 3. Open 10–10.* This small garden in the centre of the city has retained its popularity since the 1890's. During the summer season there are concerts and performances by variety and puppet theatres, and several cafes and a restaurant.

BOTANICAL GARDEN *Prospekt Mira 26.*

ACADEMY OF SCIENCES' BOTANICAL GARDEN *Ostankino.* The territory of 360 hectares (900 acres) includes an attractive park and some forest land.

ZOO *Bolshaya Gruzinskaya Street 1.*

HIPPODROME RACECOURSE *Begovaya Street 22. Races on Wednesdays, Saturdays and Sundays at 5 p.m. and Sundays also at 1 p.m.* The racecourse was founded in 1883. Its gates are decorated with figures of people and horses by K. Klodt, the grandson of the architect P. Klodt, which resemble the latter's famous sculptures on Anichkov Bridge in Leningrad.

There are about 500 horses in the stables, and there is a totalisator and a restaurant.

LENIN STADIUM *In Luzhniki, near Komsomolsky Prospekt.* The complex was built in 1955–56 by Vlasov, Rozhin and other architects. The large sports arena can seat 103,000. Major national and international football matches and sports meetings are held here. The Lenin Monument in front of the arena is by Manizer and was in the Soviet Pavilion at the Brussels World Fair.

The small sports arena seats 15,600, and the outdoor swimming pool 13,000, while the Palace of Sports can take over 17,000. There is also a Children's Sport Area and many other sections for tennis, basket-ball, volley-ball, etc.

DYNAMO STADIUM *Leningradsky Prospekt 36.* This is Moscow's second largest stadium, and can seat 60,000.

THE MOSKVA OPEN-AIR SWIMMING POOL. This pool can take 20,000 people daily, and the warm water with warm currents of air blowing over it make the pool useable all the year round.

There are *bathing beaches* at Serebryanyi Bor (Silver Grove) and at Khimki, and at the recreation area beside Klyazma Reservoir are boats for hire, restaurants, cafes and bathing beaches.

ALTAI HOTEL *Susokolovskoye chaussée 38; tel: 84-05-91.*

ARMENIA HOTEL AND ARARAT RESTAURANT *Neglinnaya Street 4; tel: 90-06-90.*

BALCHUG HOTEL AND RESTAURANT *Sadovnicheskaya Naberezhnaya 1/15; tel: 31-60-88.*

BERLIN HOTEL AND RESTAURANT *Zhdanov Street 3; tel: 90-08-50.* This is an Intourist Hotel, and was formerly called the "Savoy".

BUCHAREST HOTEL AND RESTAURANT *Balchug Street 1; tel: 33-00-20.*

BUDAPEST HOTEL AND RESTAURANT *Petrovskiye Liniyi 2/18; tel: 94-88-20.*

KIEVSKAYA HOTEL AND DNIEPER RESTAURANT *Vtoroi Bryansky Pereulok 16; tel: 43-40-00.* This hotel is beside the Kiyevsky railway station.

LENINGRADSKAYA HOTEL AND RESTAURANT *Kalanchovskaya Street 21/40; tel: 90-11-40.* This 28-storey hotel stands near the Leningrad, Yaroslavl and Kazan railway terminals.

METROPOLE HOTEL AND RESTAURANT *Sverdlov Square 2/4; Service Bureau tel: 25-66-54.* This is an Intourist hotel.

MINSK HOTEL AND RESTAURANT *Gorky Street 22; tel: 99-22-11, 99-12-15/16* (service bureau).

MOSKVA HOTEL AND RESTAURANT *Marx Prospekt 2; tel: 92-10-00.*

NATIONAL HOTEL AND RESTAURANT *Gorky Street 1/17; tel: 29-99-17.* This is an Intourist Hotel.

OSTANKINO HOTEL AND RESTAURANT *Botanicheskaya Street 29; tel: 83-87-00.* Situated at some distance from the centre of the city, this hotel is near Ostankino Palace, the Botanical Gardens and the Exhibition of Economic Achievements.

PEKING HOTEL AND RESTAURANT *Bolshaya Sadovaya Street 1/7; tel: 51-10-00.*

SOVIETSKAYA HOTEL *Leningradsky Prospekt 32; tel: 53-15-87.* This hotel is near the Dynamo Stadium and the Hippodrome Racecourse.

SPORT HOTEL *Luzhniki; tel: 44-08-23.*

TOURIST HOTEL *Selskokhozyaistvennaya Street 17/2; tel: 81-30-00.*

TSENTRALNAYA HOTEL AND RESTAURANT *Gorky Street 10; tel: 29-85-89.*

UKRAINA HOTEL AND RESTAURANT *Kutuzovsky Prospekt 10/9; tel: 43-30-30.* There are 1025 rooms in this 32-storey hotel on the bank of the River Moskva.

URAL HOTEL *Stoleshnikov Pereulok 18; tel: 94-05-65.*

VARSHAVA (WARSAW) HOTEL AND RESTAURANT *Oktyabrskaya Square 2/1; tel: 31-12-05.*

YUNOST (YOUTH) HOTEL AND RESTAURANT *Frunzensky Val 36; tel: 45-00-18.*

ARAGVI RESTAURANT *Gorky Street 6.* This restaurant specialises in Georgian cuisine. The following may be recommended:

Satsivi—poultry in spicy sauce
lobio—butter beans in spicy sauce
kharcho—spiced meat soup
osetrina na vertelye—spitroasted sturgeon
tsiplyata tabaka—roast spring chicken, flattened between hot stones
shashlik po kharski (or po Kavkazsky)—pieces of mutton roasted on a skewer koopati—Georgian sausages

ARARAT RESTAURANT *Neglinnaya Street 4;* This restaurant has Armenian cuisine including:

solyanka—soup
forel' v tyestye—trout in pastry
shashlik
chebooreki—outsize Cornish pasty
tolma—vine leaves stuffed with rice, meat and prunes.

BAKU RESTAURANT *Gorky Street 24;* This restaurant has Azerbaijani cuisine, which is closely akin to Turkish, including:

dovta—sour-milk-and-meat soup
pilaff (choose from 23 different varieties)
golubtsy—meat balls wrapped in vine leaves
piti—thick mutton broth with potatoes, Caucasian peas and herbs

BERLIN RESTAURANT *Pushechnaya Street 6, in the Berlin Hotel.*

BUDAPEST RESTAURANT *Petrovskiye Liniyi 2, in the Budapest Hotel.* The restaurant has mainly Hungarian cuisine.

HERMITAGE RESTAURANT *Karetnyi Ryad 3.*

METROPOLE RESTAURANT *Sverdlov Square 2, in the Metropole Hotel.*

MOSKVA RESTAURANT *Marx Prospekt 2, in the Moskva Hotel.*

NATIONAL RESTAURANT *Gorky Street 1, in the National Hotel.* The bar upstairs serves whisky and other drinks for payment in any convertible currency.

PEKING RESTAURANT *Bolshaya Sadovaya Street 1, in the Peking Hotel.* This restaurant has Chinese cuisine.

PRAGA RESTAURANT *Arbat Street 2*. This restaurant with a pleasant open-air terrace on the roof, specializes in Czech cuisine.

SOFIA RESTAURANT *Mayakovsky Square*. The restaurant has Bulgarian cuisine.

SOVIETSKY RESTAURANT *Leningradsky Prospekt 22, in the Sovietsky Hotel.*

TSENTRALNYI RESTAURANT *Gorky Street 10*. All sorts of traditional Russian dishes are served here.

UKRAINA RESTAURANT *Kutuzovsky Prospekt 10, in the Ukraina Hotel;* Ukrainian cuisine is a speciality, and includes:

Ukrainian borshch
vareniki—tiny dumplings filled with meat, rice or vegetables or various fruits.

UZBEKISTAN RESTAURANT *Neglinnaya Street 29, where some of the tables are in the open air.*

The Uzbek cuisine includes:

mastava—meat and rice soup
logman—meat and noodle soup
maniar—soup of minced meat, eggs and dumplings
muntyi—big, meat-filled dumplings
tkhum-dulma—Scotch eggs
shashlik
pilaff

VARSHAVA RESTAURANT *Oktyabrskaya Square 2/1, in the Varshava Hotel;* Polish cuisine.

YUNOST (YOUTH) RESTAURANT *Frunzensky Val 36, in the Yunost Hotel.*

AELITA CAFE *Oruzheinyi Pereulok 45.*

ARARAT CAFE *Neglinnaya Street 4.*

ARCTICA CAFE *Gorky Street 4.*

ARFA CAFE *Stoleshnikov Pereulok 9.*

ARTISTICHESKOYE CAFE *Proyezd Khudozhestvennogo Teatra 6.*

DRUZHBA (FRIENDSHIP) CAFE *Kuznetsky Most.*

KRASNYI MAK CAFE *Stoleshnikov Pereulok 20.*

MOLODYOZHNOYE (YOUTH) CAFE *Gorky Street 41.*

NATIONAL CAFE *Gorky Street 1, in the National Hotel.*

OGNI MOSKVY (LIGHTS OF MOSCOW) *Marx Prospekt 2, in the Moskva Hotel on the 15th floor.*

✿ GUM (Pronounced "Goom" and meaning State Universal Stores) DEPARTMENT STORE *Red Square*. Now the country's largest shop, GUM was built by Pomerantsev in 1888–94 in pseudo-Russian style as commercial arcades for nearly 1000 small shops. The three parallel aisles are 250 m (275 yd) long, and the building has three storeys. There is a souvenir shop by the fountain in the middle of the central aisle, and the gramophone record department is also on the ground floor. On the 2nd floor is the foreign currency Fur Shop; for details of this and other foreign currency shops, see below:

TSUM (pronounced "Tsoom") DEPARTMENT STORE *Street Petrovka 2*. This large shop beside the Bolshoi Theatre was built in Gothic style for Muir and Merrilees store by Klein in 1909. There is a souvenir counter and a gramophone record department.

PETROVSKY PASSAGE DEPARTMENT STORE *Petrovka 10 and Neglinnaya Street*. The shop runs right through the block.

MOSKVA DEPARTMENT STORE *Leninsky Prospekt.*

DETSKY MIR (CHILDREN'S WORLD) DEPARTMENT STORE *Marx Prospekt 7.*

TOYS: HOUSE OF TOYS *Kutuzovsky Prospekt 14.*

BERYOZKA (BIRCH) SOUVENIR AND JEWELLERY SHOP *Gorky Street.*

"WANDA" POLISH NATIONAL GIFT SHOP *Petrovka Street.*

GIFTS: *Gorky Street 4 and Stoleshnikov Pereulok 13/15.*

HANDICRAFTS: (Wood and Stone): *Petrovka Street 10 and Kutuzovsky Prospekt 17.*

EMBROIDERED GOODS: *Stoleshnikov Pereulok 11.*

PORCELAIN AND POTTERY: *Stoleshnikov Pereulok 5/20 and Kirov Street 8/2.*

JEWELLERY: *Petrovka Street 8 and Stoleshnikov Pereulok 14.*

PERFUME: *Marx Prospekt 2, in the building of the Moskva Hotel.*

ANTIQUES: *Gorky Street 46, Arbat 19 and Sretenka Street 31.*

RUGS: *Gorky Street 10 and Petrovka Street 10.*

PICTURES, GRAPHICS, etc.: *Gorky Street 46B.*

BOOKS (IN FOREIGN LANGUAGES): *Kuznetsky Most 18.*

SECONDHAND BOOKS (IN FOREIGN LANGUAGES): *Gertsen Street 24.*

SHEET MUSIC: *Neglinnaya Street 14, 2nd floor, Gertsena Street 13 and Gorky Street 15.*

CAMERAS AND PHOTOGRAPHIC GOODS: *Gorky Street 41 and 25 and Petrovka Street 12 and 15 (Cine-shop: Leninsky Prospekt 62/1).*

WINES AND SPIRITS: *Stoleshnikov Pereulok 7, which branches off from Petrovka Street.* French brandy and Cuban rum are for sale here.

CENTRAL MARKET: *Tsvetnoi Boulevard.*

Duty-free shops, accepting payment in any convertible currency:

GASTRONOM (food supplies, whisky, gin and American cigarettes) *Kutuzovsky Prospekt 21.*

BERYOZKA DEPARTMENT STORE (souvenirs, transistor radios, watches) *Luzhnetsky Proyezd 25a, near Lenin Stadium.*

VNESHPOSYLTORG CLOTHING STORE: *Fersman Street 5, up Lenin Prospekt, then left opposite Moskva Department Store.*

VNESHPOSYLTORG FUR SHOP

ART SHOWROOM (for trade sales only; applied art, collectors' china, icons, folk art work and handicrafts) *Gorky Street 15.*

U.S.S.R. BANK FOR FOREIGN TRADE *Neglinnaya Street 12.*

G.P.O. *Kirov Street 26.*

CENTRAL TELEGRAPH OFFICE *Gorky Street 7.*

PARKING. Parking in the streets and squares is free, but there are some attended car-parks. Intourist will give you details if you wish to leave your car for a considerable time.

SERVICE STATION No. 7 *Prospekt Mira, Vtoroi Selsko-Khozyaistvennyi Prospekt 6; tel: 83-06-31 and 83-16-38. Open 8–11 (lunch hour 1–2); open on Sundays 8–2.*

FILLING STATION *By the Metropole Hotel.*

FILLING STATION No. 15 *Metrostroyevskaya Street, Vtoroi Zachatyevsky Pereulok; Diesel oil obtainable; round the clock service.*

FILLING STATION No. 18 *Danilovskaya Square. Round the clock service.*

FILLING STATION No. 22 *Plyouschikha Street 44. Round the clock service.*

Filling Station No. 24 *Leningradsky Prospekt, near the Airport Metro Station. Round the clock service.*

Filling Station No. *42 At the Service Station. Round the clock service.*

Lenin Museum at Gorki. The village of Gorki lies 34 km (21 miles) outside Moscow. The museum is open from 11–7 and closed on Tuesdays. The house was built in 1830 and stands in a park of 70 hectares (175 acres), which has 100–150 year-old oaks and a number of ponds. Just before the revolution the estate belonged to Reinbolt, Mayor of Moscow. Lenin and his family lived here from time to time from the autumn of 1918 until his death here on 21st January 1924.

Many of the rooms in the museum remain as they were during Lenin's lifetime. In the garage are old motor cars including Lenin's Rolls-Royce which was adapted for use in heavy snow by the addition of caterpillar wheels.

Arkhangelskoye *16 km (10 miles) from Moscow; to get there motorists should leave Moscow by Leningradsky Prospekt, then Volokolamskoye chaussée and then fork left to Petrovo-Dalniye chaussée. Open 11–5; closed on Mondays and Tuesdays.*

The main complex of the estate was built at the end of the 18th century for Prince Golitsyn by the French architect, Chevalier de Huerne. In 1810 it was bought by Yusupov, one of the richest Russian landlords and a descendant of the Tartar Khans. At one time he was the director of the Imperial Theatres and of the Hermitage Museum; frequently travelling abroad to choose and buy works of art for the Imperial family, he used this opportunity to add to his own collection. The palace still contains many pictures by old European masters (Tiepolo, Rotari, Hubert Robert, Roslin and others), tapestries and numerous marble sculptures. The study contains royal and noble family portraits. Also on display are examples of fabrics, china and glassware which were manufactured on the estate.

The palace is surrounded by a French park, the avenues of which are lined with numerous statues and monuments to commemorate royal visits, and there is also a monument to Pushkin, who enjoyed his visits there. In the western part of the park is a small pavilion known as the "Temple to the Memory of Catherine the Great", here depicted as Themis, goddess of justice.

The two buildings at the end of the park were built much later (by Apushkov in 1934–37) for a sanatorium, but they do not detract from the attractiveness of the original architectural ensemble. There is a delightful view over the Moskva River from the ballustraded terrace at the end of the park between the sanatorium buildings.

The Estate Theatre, on the right side of the main road a little beyond the main entrance, was built in 1817 to seat 400 by serf-architect Ivanov, and the well-preserved stage decorations were done by the Italian artist, Gonzaga; the performances were given by serfs.

Instead of returning to Moscow by the same road, motorists can drive farther on to Ilyinskoye (there is an eating house here) and take the turning to the left which leads to the Mozhaisk–Moscow highway, and continue straight on when the Minsk–Moscow road joins this road. The road enters Moscow by Kutuzovsky Prospekt past the Ukraina Hotel.

Kuskovo Palace Museum *About 10 km (6 miles) from Moscow along Ryazanskoye chaussée. Open 10–7; closed on Tuesdays and the last day of each month.* First mentioned in 1510, the architectural ensemble of the present Kuskovo dates back to the 18th century when it was the summer residence of the Sheremetiev family, one of the oldest Russian noble families whose members were statesmen and soldiers.

The Palace itself was built by serfs between 1770 and 1779, and it has been a museum since 1918. It contains about 800 objets d'art, including one of the best collections of 18th century Russian art in the country. Among other items are 200 portraits. The rooms of greatest interest from an artistic point of view are the White Hall, the dining room, the children's room, the oak-panelled study, the bed-room, the drawing room, the vestibule and the tapestry gallery.

The gardens were laid out in French style, and in the park are several small houses of interest, including the Hermitage (where tables set for dinner were raised from the ground floor to the dining room on the first floor), the Dutch House (where the blue-and-white and pink-and-white tiling deserves mention), the Italian House and the Grotto.

Also known as the State Museum of Ceramics, Kuskovo houses one of the best collections of Russian porcelain. There is also china, majolica and glass, and a considerable number of the pieces are of Chinese, French, German and English origin.

OSTANKINO PALACE MUSEUM *Pervaya Ostankinskaya Street 5. Open 11–6; closed on Tuesdays and Wednesdays.* The Ostankino Estate came into the hands of the Sheremetiev family in the mid-18th century; it possessed 825,000 hectares (2,062,500 acres) and 210,000 serfs, having an annual income of 1,500,000 roubles and was at that time one of the richest estates in Russia. The palace was built between 1792 and 1797 and the existing park and lands were substantially replanned. The palace was so grand and so striking by contrast to the shabby peasants huts of a nearby village that, during a celebration to which many guests were invited, the huts were hidden by huge screens on the top of which burning torches were placed.

The palace was built by serfs, who were also responsible for the tastefully decorated interiors. The serf architects responsible for the construction were Argunov, Mironov and Dikushin, and they were advised by Camporesi, Nazarov, Quarenghi and Blank, all prominent architects of that day. The wood-carvings, ceramics and parquet are all beautifully finished; in every room the parquet is of different design, executed in various costly materials, (amaranth, rose-wood and ivory).

There is a fine collection of 17th and 18th century art, rare carvings, crystal, porcelain and fans.

In the 18th century the theatre in the centre of the palace was very important, and its company included about 200 actors, singers, dancers and musicians. Best of all was the serf-actress Parasha Kovalyova, who had been taken into the company as a girl. She came from a blacksmith's family, and was marked by unusual beauty, great talent and goodheartedness. Count Sheremetiev fell in love with her and later married her. One of the streets in Ostankino bears her name.

Trinity Church, just to the left of the main entrance of the palace, was built in 1683 by the serf-architect Pavel Potekhin. In the park behind the palace is a café and there are boating stations both here and on the lake in front of the palace.

Not far away a 500 m (1640 ft) television tower, which is to have a look-out point and a restaurant high up in it, is under construction.

KOLOMENSKOYE *Kashirskoye chaussée.* Its existence first recorded in 1399, this was once the favourite summer residence of the Grand-Dukes of Moscow and later of the Russian Tsars. One of the earliest and most interesting of the churches is the beautiful church of the Ascension; it was built in old

Russian "tent" style in 1532, and at the time of its construction it was taller than any other church in Russia. In it there is a 16th century iconostasis which has been partly rebuilt, and the Belfry dates from the beginning of the 16th century. Saint John the Baptist's Church, in nearby Dyakovo, was also built in the middle of that century. Both these churches influenced the design of Saint Basil's in Moscow.

The Royal Estate was an impressive complex with a wonderful wooden palace which Catherine the Great demolished in 1767 because it was in a state of decay. (There is a model of it in the museum.) Only the Main Gate and Clock Tower and the Water Tower are now left of the complex.

Peter the Great spent some of his childhood here, and this is the reason why the log cabin (1702), in which he once lived in Archangelsk, was transferred to this place. Other examples of wooden architecture are the Prison Tower from Siberia (1631), the Defence Tower from the White Sea (1690), and a 17th century Mead Brewery from the village of Preobrazhenskoye, near Moscow.

The 17th century Kazan Church, with five onion-shaped domes, is open for services.

The Museum is housed in the former domestic quarters of the estate, and contains displays illustrating the peasant war waged by Ivan Bolotnikov in 1606–07, and the "Copper" Mutiny of 1662, so-called because of the Tsar's decree that copper coins be accepted for the value of silver. There are also exhibitions of Russian wood-carving, metalwork and ceramics, open from 10–7, and closed on Tuesdays. There is an open-air café on the estate.

TSARITSYNO. This lies about 20 km (12½ miles) from the centre of Moscow, along the *Kashirskoye chaussée*, branching off from the main road south to the Crimea and passing the turning to Kolomenskoye and Domodedovo Airport.

It is one of the loveliest localities in the environs of Moscow, being situated in hilly country intersected by ravines. An extensive wood has been turned into an English-style park with numerous lakes and ponds. In 1775 Catherine the Great ordered that a palace be built here. In ten years' time it was nearly completed; Bazhenov had designed it in Moorish-Gothic style, but Catherine did not like it and commanded that it be pulled down again. The job was then given to Kazakov, but the palace (still keeping to the original style) was never finished. The war with Turkey and subsequent financial difficulties prevented its completion.

The Entrance Bridge has survived well, and there are some pavilions scattered in the park. The most remarkable are the round Temple of Ceres, the Milovida Pavilion and the romantic Ruined Tower. There is a café and a boating station on the estate.

ROAD TWO

BREST—MINSK—SMOLENSK—MOSCOW

BREST

Formerly Brest-Litovsk

Population: 74,000

This border town stands on the right bank of the River Mukhovets, at the point where it flows into the River Bug.

It has been known as a fortified town since 1017. From then onwards it was frequently fought over by the Poles, Lithuanians and Russians. In 1240 it was completely devastated by the Tartars, but was already rebuilt by 1275. It became Lithuanian in 1319, Polish in 1569, Russian in 1795, and again Polish from 1919 until 1939. In 1596 the council which established the Uniate Church met here. These Christians, also known as the Greek Catholics, acknowledged the Pope as their head but retained the Russian Orthodox church.

When Brest became Russian in 1795, its position on the western border of the country increased its strategic and trade importance. It was decided to build a really strong fortress there, but this plan was delayed because of the Napoleonic Wars, and only in 1830 did Nicholas I approve a plan for the proposed fortress. The then existing pentagonal castle was demolished in 1831, and the town itself was transferred in 1833 to a site 5 km (3 miles) to the east. Between 1838 and 1842 this whole area was under construction. The fortress and its outer defences were situated on four islands in the River Bug. Surrounding the whole structure was an earth wall 10 m (33 ft) high. The central citadel had a two-storey barrack square, 1·8 km (over a mile) in circumference and with walls 2 m (6 ft) thick, which could hold over 12,000 soldiers. During its history the stronghold was reinforced several times.

The peace treaty of Brest-Litovsk was signed here on 3rd March, 1918. This was a separate treaty between Russia and Germany, by which Russia gave up much of her former territory, including the Baltic countries and the Ukraine, and also demobilised her army. The Soviet government withdrew from the treaty unilaterally when Germany was defeated.

The fortress withstood the German attack in 1941 for about a month, when all the surrounding area had fallen and the German front line had advanced far to the east. In 1965 the town was acclaimed a "fortress-hero" in recognition of its valour. There is now a museum in the fortress in commemoration of this brave stand, which has since been described in many poems and in books. The Museum is open 11–4, and closed on Mondays.

Today Brest is a major transportation centre. Five railway lines meet there, and it is the frontier town on the Moscow–Warsaw line. It also stands on the Dnieper-Bug Canal. It has various food and light industries, and there is a pedagogical institute in the town.

✠ SEMYONOVSKY CHURCH *On the main road through the town.*

✠ LOCAL MUSEUM *Lenin Street.*

✠ DRAMA THEATRE *Lenin Street.*

✠ BUG HOTEL AND RESTAURANT *Lenin Street 2.*

BYELORUS RESTAURANT *At the crossing of Pushkinskaya Street and Sovietskaya Street.*

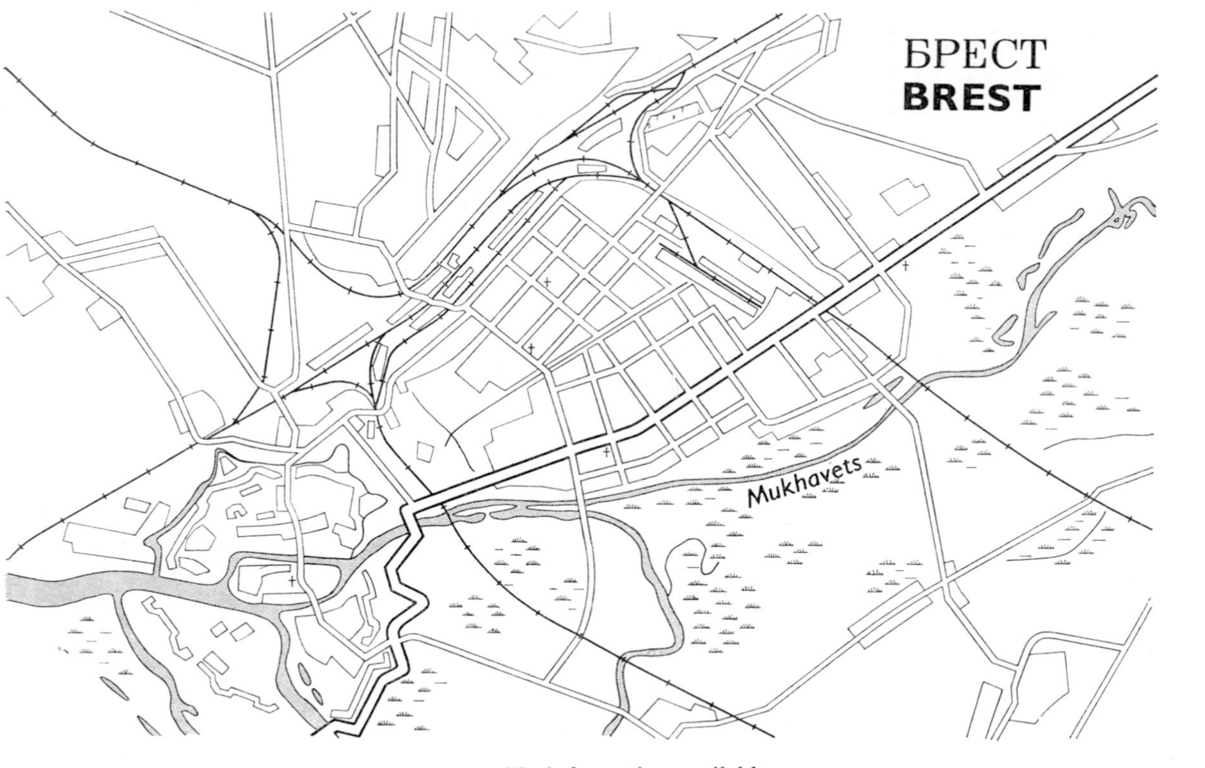

No information available.

FILLING STATION *Moskovskoye chaussée, at the 3/105 km milestone. Open 9 a.m.–11 p.m.*

REPAIR STATION.

KOBRIN

Population: 20,000

Kobrin stands on either side of the River Mukhovets. The first recorded mention of the town was in 1287, and in different periods of its history it has belonged to the Poles and to the Lithuanians. It was here, on 15th July, 1812, that the Russians gained their first victory over Napoleon. Its industry today is mainly concerned with food products.

SAINT ALEXANDER NEVSKY CATHEDRAL *On the main street.* This dates from the 19th century.

CHURCH OF SAINT PETER AND SAINT PAUL *In the cemetery.* This wooden church was built in the 15th century.

SUVOROV MILITARY HISTORY MUSEUM *Suvorov Street 16.* The famous Russian generalissimo Suvorov lived in Kobrin from 1797 to 1800.

VICTORY MONUMENT. This monument was unveiled in 1912 to commemorate the centenary of the victory over Napoleon.

SUVOROV PARK *In part of Suvorov's former estate.* There is a bust of the generalissimo in the park, and the lime trees date from his time.

BYELORUS HOTEL AND RESTAURANT *Svoboda Square.*

BERYOZA

Population: 5,000 (1957)

The name of the town means "birch tree". The remains of the Catholic monastery here were used as a large prison when the town was in Polish hands. It was again used as such, and as a concentration camp, by the Germans in World War II.

Building materials are produced here.

HOTEL AND RESTAURANT *Lenin Street.*

IVATSEVICHI

FILLING STATION *at the 917/137 km milestone.* Diesel oil is obtainable here as well as petrol; limited servicing and repairs undertaken; round the clock service.

BARANOVICHI

Polish: Baranowicze

Population: 58,000

This town lies 3 km (2 miles) off the main road. It was founded as a railway station in 1870, and, with six lines, it is still an important junction. Before the war half the population was Jewish. Industry here is mostly concerned with food products.

INTERCESSION CATHEDRAL *Kuibyshev Street.* The mosaics in this cathedral date from the beginning of the 20th century.

LOCAL MUSEUM.

HOTEL.

RESTAURANT *On the central square.*

STOLBTSY

Stolbtsy is 1·5 km (1 mile) from the main road.

FILLING STATION *At the 268 km milestone (from Brest), by the turning to the town.* Diesel oil is obtainable here; open daily from 8 a.m. to midnight.

DZERZHINSK

Formerly Koydanovo
Population: 7500 (1959)

The former name of this town derives from that of the Tartar leader, Koydan, whose army was defeated here in 1249 just as one of his predecessors had been in 1241. The place was known in the 12th century.

The town was renamed after Felix Dzerzhinsky (1877–1926) who was born in the region, in the village of Petrilovichi. His father was a mathematician of Polish gentle stock. A well known Communist, Dzerzhinsky founded the Cheka, the secret police.

The town's main industries are cutlery and food products.

MINSK

Byelorussian: Mensk
Population: 509,000 (1959)

This city is located in the centre of the Republic of Byelorussia, of which it is the capital. It stands on the River Svisloch, 20–30 m (22–33 yd) wide at this point, and unnavigable, and at the same time it is situated at the crossing of important railway lines between Moscow–Brest and Vilnius–Kiev. Its name comes from the word "menyat" (to change) and refers to its importance as a trading post.

The town is one of the oldest in Russia. It was first known to be mentioned in 1067, when it belonged to Prince Vseslav of Polotsk and stood on the ancient river trade route which linked the Black Sea to the Baltic. The River Svisloch was navigable at that time. From the beginning of its history Minsk has been ruined again and again. In 1084 it was utterly demolished and, according to an old chronicle, "not a single body nor a single beast" remained alive. This devastation was the work of Vladimir Monomakh, who was wreaking revenge on the citizens of Minsk for having burned down Smolensk. Minsk was under Polish rule, and then under Kiev's, but in 1101 it became the capital of an independent principality. In 1326 it became subject to Lithuania and in 1499, when it had already risen to being an important commercial and cultural centre of that state, the Magdeburg Law was introduced into the local city government. In 1505 it was invaded and ruined by the Tartars. Later, in 1569, it formed a part of Poland after Lithuania's union with that country, and in 1793 the region passed to Russia. In 1796 Minsk was proclaimed the provincial capital and then was again ruined, this time by Napoleon. In 1835 Nicholas I signed a decree which stated the few places in which Jews were allowed to live; Minsk was one of these, and until the Second World War the population was in fact half Jewish. Not only was Minsk many times in history devastated by wars and invasions, but it was also ruined by recurrent fires; in 1881, for instance, half the city was burned to the ground. These catastrophes, however, did not halt its ever increasing economy. Development was especially rapid after the completion in 1874 of the railway which followed the old trade routes. Minsk soon grew to be one of the centres of trade with the West.

On 1st January, 1919, The Belorussian Soviet Republic was organised and Minsk was proclaimed its capital. During World War II 80 per cent of the houses were destroyed. Russians call Minsk "the town of partisans", for during the war partisans killed many German Officers in command of the region, including their leader.

Minsk is unique among the Capital cities of the Soviet Union for having been ruined over and over again, and yet still dominating the region. It is now a completely new town, rebuilt on the wartime ruins. As there were no outstanding valuable historical monuments, no attempt was made to try

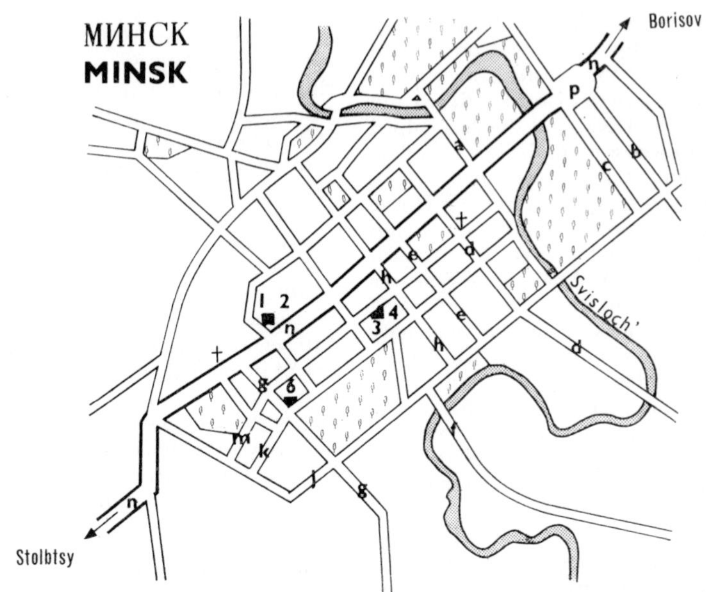

1 and 2 Hotel and Restaurant 3 Filling Station
4 Service Station.

a Ul. Yanki Kupaly,
b Ul. Zakharova,
c Ul. Frunze
d Ul. Krasnoarmeyskaya,
e Ul. Engelsa,
f Ul. Voroshilova,
g Ul. Sverdlova,
h Ul. Lenina,
j Ul. Ulyanovskaya,
k Ul. Kirova,
m Ul. Karla Marksa,
n Leninsky Prospekt.

to restore the old parts of the town, as was done in Warsaw. The territory of Minsk, covering 9000 hectares (22,500 acres), is about twice the size it was before the war. The central street of the town, Leninsky Prospekt, called Zakharievskaya Street before the Revolution, crosses Minsk from north-east to south-west. As it was utterly destroyed during the war, it was widened from 14–19 m (46–63 ft) to 48 m (52 yd) when it was reconstructed. It is about 8 km (5 miles) long. The governmental houses, theatres, museums, shops, hotels and institutes are concentrated in the centre of the town. The main Prospekt is crossed by Leninskaya and Komsomolskaya which are the streets most worthy of note, and, like the other central thoroughfares, are lined with 4- and 6-storey buildings. On the same Prospekt are Pobedy (victory) and Tsentralnaya Squares, where the Minsk counterparts of the Moscow Red Square parades (which take place on the national holidays of 1st May and 7th November), are usually held. On Central Square is the Trade Unions' Palace of Culture; this has a Hall of Columns and also contains a theatre, the stage of which is a replica of that of Moscow's Bolshoi Theatre. Close to the Square is a big, old garden with a monument to Yanko Kupala (1882–1942), Belorussia's most popular poet, usually known by his pseudonym (his real name was Ivan Lutsevich); the monument by Azgur was unveiled in 1949. When the central streets were rebuilt they were planted with 20- and 30-year-old trees, and this has helped to give them a more mellow look than they would otherwise have had.

The Belorussian Government House is an 11-storey building on Lenin Square, designed in 1935 by Langbard. The Belorussian Academy of Sciences was founded in 1922 and reorganised in 1929. Minsk is also a university town; Lenin university, which has eight faculties, was opened in 1921. Besides this there are 12 different institutes and a total of about 35,000 students. The Polytechnical Institute is the second major educational establishment.

The Beloruss Film Studio is in Minsk, and the capital of the republic is also one of the biggest industrial centres of the Soviet Union. When it was reconstructed after the war, over 100 big industrial enterprises were built, and Minsk now produces 25 per cent of all Belorussian manufactures. These include the biggest Russian lorries (40- and 60-ton), tractors, motorcycles, radios, watches, textiles, leather and food products.

The population is now mainly Belorussian, Jewish and Russian.

There are in Belorussia many burial mounds and barrows, which date mainly from the 10th–12th centuries. In a field by the village of *Grushevski*, near Minsk, there are some excavations made between 1945 and 1951. Here the old territory of a fortress ("Zamchishche") was discovered; part of the main street is discernible with traces of some houses and a 12th century church.

✿ BERNARDINE CONVENT *Bakunin Street 4*. Built in the 17th century and situated in the oldest part of Minsk, this convent is now used to house the town archives.

CATHEDRAL OF THE HOLY SPIRIT *Bakunin Street 3*. This is one of the four churches open for religious service in Minsk, and is where the Bishop officiates. The cathedral was built in the 17th century. Its most precious possession is a miracle-working icon of Our Lady; the age of the icon is uncertain, but according to legend it was placed by Prince Vladimir in the Desyatinaya Church in Kiev, where it remained for 500 years. Then, in the 15th century, when the town suffered one of its periodic raids by the Tartars, it was thrown into the river Dnieper. In 1550 an unusual radiance was noticed by the inhabitants of Minsk in their own river Svisloch, and the icon was found and rescued.

THE CHURCH OF SAINT CATHERINE *Ostrovsky Street*. Built in 1611 and at first known as the Church of St. Peter and Paul, this church is also now used to house the town archives.

✿ CALVARY CEMETERY GATES *At the end of Opansky Street*. These gates were built in 1830 and are decorated with sculptures.

THE GOVERNOR'S HOUSE *Svobody Square*. The Jesuits had a college in Minsk from 1650 until they were expelled in 1820; and they used this building during the 18th century. Since 1932 it has been the building of Minsk Conservatoire.

SYNAGOGUE *Shkolny Pereulok*.

MASON'S LODGE *Muzikalnyi Pereulok 5*. This 3-storey house was built in the 18th century; in the second part of the 18th century it was the meeting place for the Northern Torch Lodge. This was declared illegal in 1822 as were all Lodges in Russia.

WORLD WAR II MUSEUM *Svobody Square 23*. Also known as the Museum of the History of the Great Patriotic War, this museum has 25 halls.

BELORUSSIAN ART MUSEUM *Lenin Street 20.* Here are canvases by Ivazovsky, and also by Shishkin and Repin, both of whom lived and worked in Belorussia for some time. The Museum is open 11–7, and closed on Thursdays.

LOCAL HISTORY AND FOLKLORE MUSEUM *Revolyutsionnaya Street.*

YANKO KUPALA MUSEUM *Yanka Kupala Street.* The Museum is open 10–5, and closed on Fridays.

YAKUB KOLAS MUSEUM *Lenin Prospekt 66.* The Museum is open 9.30–3.30, and closed on Saturdays.

MUSEUM OF THE FIRST CONGRESS OF THE RUSSIAN SOCIAL-DEMOCRATIC PARTY *Lenin Prospekt.* This building is a replica of that in which the Social Democrats met in 1898; the original was burned down. The Museum is open 11–6, and closed on Fridays.

THE MINSK LENIN LIBRARY. This Library has 2½ million books on its shelves.

LENIN MONUMENT *On Lenin Square in front of the Belorussian Government House.* The monument was designed by Manizer.

WAR MEMORIAL *Pobeda Square.* This great obelisk was erected in memory of the soldiers and partisans who fell in World War II. It was built in 1954 by Zaborsky and Korol. It stands 38 m (125 ft) high, and on top is a model of the highest Soviet military award, the Order of Victory. At its foot burns the Eternal Flame.

✿ BOLSHOI THEATRE *Parizhskoi Kommuny Square 7.* This opera house was built in 1935, and was designed by Langbard who was also responsible for the Belorussian Government House. Besides opera and ballet, it also shows performances of the Capella Belorussian Choir and the Belorussian Folk Choir. The Puppet Theatre is located in the same building.

YANKO KUPALA BELORUSSIAN THEATRE *Engels Street 23.* This was built in 1890 by Kozlovsky.

GORKY RUSSIAN DRAMA THEATRE *Volodarsky Street 5.* This was once a synagogue.

YOUTH THEATRE *Engels Street.*

PUPPET THEATRE *Lenin Prospekt 23.*

TRADE UNION PALACE OF CULTURE *Lenin Prospekt 25.*

CIRCUS *Lenin Prospekt.*

DYNAMO STADIUM *Kirov Street.* This stadium seats 40,000 people.

WINTER SWIMMING BATHS *Near Kolas Place.*

✿ GORKY PARK *Pervomaiskaya Street 17.* This park was founded in 1880 as the Governor's garden and covers 26 hectares (65 acres). It contains fountains, a monument to Maksim Gorky, an exhibition hall, and an open-air theatre seating 1800.

CHELUSKINTSEV PARK *Lenin Prospekt, beside the main road to Moscow.* This park was founded in a pine forest in 1930. It has an area of 45 hectares (112 acres) and contains a children's railway, an open air stage, a café, and war graves decorated by the statue of a mourning woman.

BOTANIC GARDENS *Lenin Prospekt* 80.

The gardens cover 106 hectares (265 acres).

VICTORY PARK *Zalivnaya Street.* With a territory of 204 hectares (510 acres), this is Minsk's largest park. It has two boat-hire stations, a restaurant and billiard hall.

✿ BELORUSS HOTEL AND RESTAURANT *Kirov Street 13; tel: 2-59-81.*

MINSK HOTEL AND RESTAURANT *Lenin Prospekt 11; tel: 9-23-62. The Intourist office is in Room 600; tel: 2-29-92 and 9-22-35.*

SPUTNIK HOTEL AND RESTAURANT *Chvalov Street 34.*

PERVAYA SOVIETSKAYA HOTEL *Komsomolskaya Street 13.*

VTORAYA SOVIETSKAYA HOTEL *Volodarsky Street 6.*

NEMAN RESTAURANT *Lenin Prospekt 22.* This restaurant is called after a Lithuanian river.

ZARYA (dawn) RESTAURANT *Lenin Street 2.*

RADUGA RESTAURANT *Privokzalnaya Square.*

CHAIKA (seagull) RESTAURANT *Tolbukhin Street 3.*

LETO (SUMMER) RESTAURANT *Pervomaiskaya Street* 8.

VESNA (SPRING) CAFE *In the department store, Lenin Prospekt 21.*

TEATRALNOYE CAFE *Gorky Street 34.*

CAMPING SITE *18 km (11 miles) west of Minsk, 110 m (110 yd) to the left of the main road coming from Brest.* The camping site is situated in a pinewood and has excellent facilities including a restaurant, a shop, a self-service kitchen, hot showers, a verandah-lounge, a post office, telephone and souvenir kiosk. Motor inspection trench. Next to the Camping Site is a second Filling Station; Diesel oil for sale; open 8 a.m. to midnight.

✿ G.P.O. *Lenin Prospekt 10.*

CENTRAL TELEGRAPH OFFICE *Engels Street 44.*

DEPARTMENT STORE *Lenin Prospekt 21.*

CHILDREN'S WORLD STORE *Lenin Prospekt 12.*

PODARKI (GIFT) SHOP *Volodarsky Street 22.*

SPORTS SHOP *Lenin Prospekt 16.*

PICTURE SHOP *Lenin Prospekt 19.*

MOTOR AND BICYCLE SALEROOM *Lenin Prospekt 40.*

JEWELLER'S SHOP *Lenin Prospekt 22.*

FLORIST'S SHOP *Lenin Prospekt 19.*

✿ SERVICE STATION *Karl Marx Street 18; tel: 2-02-81 or 2-04-93.* Open daily from 8 a.m. till midnight.

FILLING STATION *At the same address as the Service Station and open for the same hours.* Diesel oil is obtainable here.

★

MINSK SEA *16 km (10 miles) from town.* This reservoir was completed in 1956; it is possible to bathe here.

BORISOV

Population: 59,000 (1959)

Borisov stands on the River Berezina. It was probably founded in 1102 by Boris, Prince of Polotsk, who gave it his name. From the 14th century until 1795 it belonged to Lithuania-Poland, and was a fortress. It became a town in 1563.

Now the town has a river port and a good timber industry. Paper, matches, pianos and hardware are made here. The main thoroughfare is Revolutsii Prospekt.

✿ CATHEDRAL OF THE RESURRECTION (VOSKRESNYI SOBOR) *Svoboda Square.* This cathedral was built in 1870.

CHURCH OF SAINT ANDREW *Near the Cathedral.*

✿ There is a town park and a stadium.

✿ EATING HOUSE.

FILLING STATION *On the main road, at the 631 km milestone (from Moscow), and at a distance of 73 km (45 miles) east of Minsk.*
The town is a little off the main road, the turning to it being at the 630 km milestone (from Moscow).

★

Not far from Borisov, on the River Berezina, there is a beaver reservation, while 13 km (8½ miles) upstream is Studyonka, one of the places where in November 1812 the survivors of Napoleon's retreating army spent three desperate days attempting to cross, and where in fact 30,000 French soldiers lost their lives.

TOLOCHIN

This is a small town near the main road. Its name was first recorded in 1433.

CHURCH OF THE INTERCESSION (TSERKOV POKROVA). The church is now Russian Orthodox, but was originally Roman Catholic.

HOTEL.

TEAROOM *On the main street.*

YURTSEVO

FILLING STATION *At the 495 km milestone (from Moscow).* Diesel oil is for sale here; open daily from 8 a.m. to midnight. This filling station is at a distance of 117 km (73 miles) from Smolensk.

SMOLENSK

Population: 146,000 (1959)

Once known as "the key and gate of Russia", Smolensk is attractively situated on either side of the River Dnieper. It was first mentioned in a document of 863 and was the chief town of the large Slav tribe known as the Krivichi. It stood on the ancient north-south trade route, linking the Baltic and the Black Sea. In 882 Prince Oleg conquered Smolensk on his victorious way from Novgorod to Kiev and made it a part of the principality of Kiev, but after 1054 it continually changed hands and was attacked in turn by Tartars, Muscovites, Lithuanians and Poles.

The town became independent in the early 12th century and flourished under the rule of Prince Rostislav, the grandson of Prince Vladimir Monomakh. A terrible epidemic of plague and cholera was recorded in 1388 as having left no more than ten survivors. A large Lithuanian army led by Prince Vitovt besieged the town for two months in 1404 before it fell, and then it remained in Lithuanian hands for 110 years. In 1653, after the third war with Poland, Smolensk became Russian again.

Napoleon was in the town twice during his Russian campaign in 1812. As he was finally leaving he gave orders that the kremlin should be blown up, and accordingly gunpowder was placed under all the towers. 8 were destroyed but the rest were saved. At that time only 600 people remained alive in the town, but it quickly recovered and grew into a small industrial centre, becoming especially active when the railways were opened.

The old part of the town is enclosed by a wall 5 km (3 miles) in length, and lies amid trees on the steeply sloping left bank of the river. The walls date from 1596–1602 when they were built by Boris Godunov from plans by F. S. Kon. They are 5·5 m (18 ft) thick and 15·2 m (50 ft) high, and originally boasted 38 towers of which today only 16 remain. Once the walls were known as "the precious necklace of Russia". Parts of it are to be seen in many places in the centre of the town; some towers are now enclosed by the Park of Culture and the Kutuzov Garden. Also in the town park is part of the great 17th century earth wall.

Reconstruction work is now taking place in Smolensk, and the old houses in the streets leading to Smirnov

1 and 2 Hotel and Restaurant 3 Filling Station

a Bolshaya Sovietskaya ul.
b Ploshchad' Smirnova
c Ploshchad' Karla Marksa
d Ul. Lenina
e Ul. Oktyabr'skoi Revolyutsiyi

Square in the centre of the town are interspersed with new buildings. Perhaps the most spectacular street is Oktyabr'skoi Revolyutsiyi, particularly at the point where it is crossed by Dzerzhinsky Street. One of the biggest buildings is the post-war House of Soviets, on Karl Marx Square. The old Kievskoye Chaussée was recently renamed Prospekt Yuriya Gagarina. In the south-west part of the town are the new Ryadovka and Popovka regions, the latter designed to provide accommodation for 50,000.

Smolensk has four colleges, including those for medicine and teachers' training, and the various local industries include machine building, woodwork and clothes manufacture.

✿ Cathedral of the Assumption (Uspensky Sobor) *Sobornyi Dvor 5, on a hill to the south of the bridge.* This huge five-domed building dominates the whole town. When Napoleon walked into it he was so struck by its splendour that he took off his hat and set a guard to protect the building from his own men. It was founded at the beginning of the 12th century and was destroyed by the Poles in 1611. Reconstruction began in 1677 under Alexei Korolkov of Moscow, the idea being to create a monument to the heroic defence of Smolensk against the Poles in 1609–11, and the plans resembled those of the great Moscow cathedrals. Work on it stopped completely when the east wall collapsed in 1679 but was started again in 1732 under the architect Shedel.

The Cathedral is in use today. It stands 69·7 m (229 ft) high and is 42·6 m (140 ft) in width; the central dome is built of wood and is decorated. The iconostasis of gilded lime-wood stands 10 m (33 ft) high; ten people worked for 12 years to complete it. The principal treasure is a wonder-working icon of the Virgin, said to have been painted by Saint Luke for the ruler of Syria. Afterwards the icon went to Jerusalem and Constantinople, and came to Russia when the Emperor Constantine gave it to his daughter Anna on her marriage to Prince Yaroslav. It was brought to Smolensk in 1103; the original was stolen in 1923 and the present one is a 16th century copy, equally revered and standing upon a stone platform. Other valuable icons are those of our Lady of Vladimir, brought to Smolensk in 1445, and of Our Lady of Jerusalem, painted probably as early as the 12th century. Also to be seen here is a shroud, dated 1561, embroidered with a picture of the Entombment. This formerly belonged to the Uspensky (Assumption) Cathedral in Moscow's Kremlin, but was stolen by Napoleon in 1812 and recaptured in Smolensk where it then remained.

CHURCH OF SAINT PETER AND SAINT PAUL ON GORODYANKE CHURCH *Near the railway station, towards Kashin Street*. Dating from 1146, this is the oldest church, and indeed the oldest building, in Smolensk. It was built in the Kievan style, but was changed and reconstructed until the 18th century.

CHURCH OF SAINT JOHN THE DIVINE (TSERKOV IVANA BOGOSLOVA) *Krasnoflotskaya Street, near the bridge*. Built in 1173 and reconstructed in 1770, the church is in the Kievan style and is similar to the Church of Saint Peter and Saint Paul.

SVIRSKAYA CHURCH *Malaya Krasnoflotskaya Street, near the river Smyadinka*. Also known as Saint Michael's Church, this was built in 1191–4 as a court cathedral by Prince David Rostislavich, whose tomb is inside. It was heavily damaged in World War II.

LOCAL HISTORY MUSEUM *Lenin Street 9*. The most interesting exhibits here come from the ancient barrows of which there are 3000 at Gnezdovo, near Smolensk. The barrows mostly date from the 10th century and scientific excavation began in 1868.

LOCAL NATURAL HISTORY MUSEUM *Sobornyi Dvor 7*.

ART GALLERY *Krupskaya Street 7*. This collection is housed in a building specially designed in 1905 for a Museum of Ancient Russia. The Gallery is open 10–7 and closed on Fridays.

✿ 1812 MONUMENT *At the entrance to the Park of Culture*. This huge monument commemorating the defenders of Smolensk against the French was designed by Antoni Adamini, cast in St. Peterburg and unveiled in 1912, the centenary of the victory.

SOPHIA REGIMENT MONUMENT *On the earth wall in the Park of Culture*. The Sophia Regiment was one of those engaged in the defence of Smolensk in 1812; this monument to it was unveiled 100 years later.

MONUMENT WITH EAGLES *Kutuzov Garden*. This is an interesting symbolic monument. One eagle prevents a man dressed as an Ancient Gaul from attacking the nest with his sword, and the other guards the nest while preparing to attack the marauder from behind: the great rock symbolises Russia and the two eagles, the 1st and 2nd Russian armies.

KUTUZOV MONUMENTS. In the central walk of the Kutuzov Garden there is a bust of Field Marshal Kutuzov, unveiled in 1912; the other Kutuzov monument, this time in a standing position, is on *Bolshaya Sovietskaya Street*. By Motorilov, it was unveiled in 1954. Both commemorate the liberation of the town from Napoleon.

GLINKA MONUMENT *In the Glinka Garden, locally known as "Blonye".* This bronze statue of the composer Mikhail Glinka (1804–57) was unveiled in 1885. Phrases of the composer's music are included in the iron fence around the statue. Glinka was born in the province of Smolensk.

✪ DRAMA THEATRE *Karl Marx Street 4.*

PUPPET THEATRE *Lenin Street 5a.*

PHILHARMONIA CONCERT HALL *Bolshaya Sovietskaya Street 18.*

SPARTAK STADIUM *Dzerzhinsky Street.* This stadium can seat 12,000.

PARK *Lenin Street.*

✪ SMOLENSK HOTEL AND RESTAURANT *Glinka Street 9/30; tel: 3-18-25.* This hotel has an attended car park.

ROSSIA HOTEL AND RESTAURANT *Karl Marx Street 2/1; tel: 3-17-42. Intourist office tel: 3-16-53.*

CAMPING SITE *1½ km (1 mile) to the left of the main road, coming from Brest, at the 384 km milestone, a little distance before the Filling Station.* Situated in woodland, the site has a café, a self-service kitchen, showers, washbasins, a shop, a post office, and a telephone.

ZARYA (dawn) CAFE *Kommuny Street 2/2.*

SPUTNIK CAFE *Nikolayev Street.*

OTDYKH (rest) CAFE *Glinka Garden.*

✪ G.P.O. *Oktyabrskaya Revolutsiya Street.*

CENTRAL BOOKSHOP *Bolshaya Sovietskaya Street 18.*

DEPARTMENT STORE *Gagarin Prospekt 1.*

BERYOZKA SOUVENIR SHOP *Kommunisticheskaya Street 22.*

SOUVENIRS OF SMOLENSK *Lenin Street 11/1.*

JEWELLERS *Bolhaya Sovietskaya Street 33.*

TOBACCONIST *Lenin Street 10.*

✪ SERVICE STATION *Khlebozavodsky Pereulok 16. Open 8 a.m.–10 p.m. in winter and 8 a.m.–6 p.m. in summer.*

FILLING STATION *On the main road, near the 384 km milestone.* Diesel oil obtainable, round the clock service. Motorists are advised to fill here without waiting to refuel in Smolensk. Small repairs are also undertaken here.

When driving from Brest on the main Moscow road it is suggested that motorists do *not* leave the mainroad at the first signpost for Smolensk (saying "Smolensk—32 km"). They should take the next turning to the right (by the filling station), which is only 8 km (5 miles) from Smolensk, and much easier going.

———— ★ ————

TALASHKINO *13 km (8 miles) off the main road, along the Roslav chaussée; please notify Intourist before making this trip.* Here, on the former estate of Princess Maria Tenisheva, stands Teremok, a wooden house built in 1901–03 in Russian fairy-tale style after a design by Malyutin. Teremok is now a museum containing 2000 different items of folk art; the wood carvings are of especial interest. Beside Teremok is a small family chapel built in 1902. Over the entrance is a large mosaic of Christ. The artist Rerikh helped design and decorate the chapel and many other prominent Russian artists including Vosnetsov, Vrubel, Polenov and Serov lived and worked here to revive Russian folk art. The museum is open 10–4 on Wednesdays and Sundays.

IZDESHKOVO

FILLING STATION *At the 270 km milestone from Moscow.* Diesel oil is also on sale here; round the clock service.

VYAZMA

Population: 34,100 (1959)

First mentioned in a manuscript of the 11th century, Vyazma stands on the river Vyazma, a tributary of the River Dnieper. Until the 18th century it was a town of great military and economic value, and was seized several times by the Poles and the Lithuanians, especially during the Time of Troubles. During Napoleon's retreat in 1812 it was burnt down.

Once numbered among the biggest dairy centres of Russia, Vyazma now has machine-building and food industries and also a car repair works. Perhaps its best known products are jam-filled biscuits called "Vyazemskiye Pryaniki".

TRINITY CATHEDRAL *Nagornaya Street.* This cathedral dates from the 17th century and contains a copy of the wonder-working icon, the Holy Virgin of Iberia. It is open for religious services.

There are various other monasteries and churches in the vicinity dating from the 17th century and now used for secular purposes.

HOTEL *25 Oktyabrya Street.*

RESTAURANT *Sovietskaya Place.* Vyazma lies to the south of the main road.

GZHATSK

Population: 10,500 (1959)

This town on the River Gzhatsk was founded at the beginning of the 18th century by Peter the Great as a river port on the grain supply route to the newly-built St. Petersburg. As it was very difficult to get people to settle there, some rich merchants were imprisoned, and freed only after they had agreed to live in the Gzhatsk river port.

The port has now lost its importance. The town produces flax and plastics; its most recent claim to fame is that it was the home of astronaut Yuri Gagarin, whose parents still live there. The school where Gagarin studied now bears his name.

RESTAURANT.

FILLING STATION *At the 174 km milestone (from Moscow).* Diesel oil sold here; round the clock service.

REPAIR STATION.

PETRISHCHEVO

ZOYA KOSMODEMYANSKAYA MONUMENT *At the 86 km milestone (from Moscow), beside the main road.* Zoya Kosmodemyanskaya came from Moscow. She was a partisan who was captured in 1941 in the village of Petrishchevo, 5 km (3 miles) to the south of this point, and at the age of 18 was hanged by the Germans. Her execution took place in the village square, in the presence of the inhabitants. Even while the rope was around her neck she shouted out, "I am not afraid to die, comrades. It is happiness to die for your own people". She was posthumously decorated with the award of Heroine of the Soviet Union, and on her monument is the inscription "To the Immortal Heroine of the Soviet Union—1923–1941".

GOLITSINO

FILLING STATION *At the 44 km milestone (from Moscow).* Diesel oil is available here.

MOZHAISK

Mozhaisk lies 5 km (3 miles) off the main road. It is one of Russia's oldest cities, first mentioned in a document of 1231. From 1239 until the middle of the 15th century it was the centre of an autonomous princedom. At the beginning of the 17th century during the Time of Troubles, it was the scene of military actions.

The remains of the Luzhetsky Monastery (16th–17th century) are in Mozhaisk. Saint Nicholas's Cathedral was built in the 19th century.

✿ Near Mozhaisk is the *Borodino Museum*, open 10–6. The way to the museum is along a side road which leaves the main Minsk–Moscow road at the 96 or 108 km milestone.

The museum, founded in 1903, is now located in a building specially erected in 1912 to commemorate the 100th anniversary of the famous 15-hour battle between the French and Russian armies on 26th August, 1812. Napoleon's army suffered a heavy defeat which decided the outcome of the whole campaign. In front of the building are busts of the Russian generals, Barclay de Tolli and Bagration, made by Azgur in 1948.

The collection in the museum includes guns, pictures and personal relics.

There are 34 monuments scattered over the Borodino Field, most of them erected in 1912 to mark the 100th anniversary and dedicated to Russian Field-Marshal Kutuzov and other soldiers, and to whole regiments. There is also a monument to French soldiers and officers, and new memorials which commemorate the Russo-German fight in the autumn of 1941.

BAKOVKA

This is one of the popular places for Muscovites to have a *dacha* (country house). A number of writers have their *dachas* in the nearby village of Peredelkino. Boris Pasternak lived here until his death in 1960.

As you approach the Moscow Ring Road you will see a *motel* to your right. It has a restaurant and there is a filling and service station here. If you wish to go to the Butovo Camping Site without going into the city, turn to the right and continue along the Ring Road to Varshavskoye chaussée. The Ring Road itself marks the boundary of Moscow.

KUNTSEVO

The town of Kuntsevo has been known since 1454; it now lies within the boundary of Moscow.

✿ There is a restaurant on the main street. 3 km (2 miles) along the road to Moscow, and to the right of the road, stands "Farewell Hill", so named because it was the usual place to see relatives off on a long journey. It was on this hill that Napoleon waited in vain for the keys of the city of Moscow.

Kutuzovsky Prospekt leads straight into the centre of Moscow.

MOSCOW

See Road 1 on page 103.

ROAD THREE

UZHGOROD—MUKACHEVO—LVOV ROVNO—ZHITOMIR—KIEV

TRANSCARPATHIA

Russian: Zakarpatiye

The name of this region means "beyond the Carpathians", but it is also called the Ukrainian Caucasus.

Nearly a million people live here: 80 per cent of them are Ukrainians but there are also Russians, Hungarians, Jews, Rumanians and Slovaks. Their occupations are timber- and wood-working, wine-making and horticulture, and only 28 per cent of them live in the towns.

For over a thousand years, from the time when, at the beginning of the 11th century, the Hungarians took it from the state of Kiev Rus, Transcarpathia was outside Russia. In the 16th century it was attacked by the Turks, and then the region was divided into two parts: Uzhgorod, which was under the rule of the Hapsburgs, and Mukachevo, which belonged to Transsylvania. Early in the 18th century the whole Carpathian country, together with Hungary, was under Austrian rule. Count Schönborn was the most influential landlord in the area. The Hungarian revolution of 1848–49 also affected Transcarpathia, and in the mid-19th century Austria stimulated the building of factories there. After the fall of the Austro-Hungarian Empire, Transcarpathia passed to Czechoslovakia.

When the Germans attacked Czechoslovakia in March, 1939, Hungary again took this territory. After World War II, in June 1945, the Soviet Union and Czechoslovakia signed an agreement by which this region passed to the Soviet Union, and in the following year it was united with the Ukrainian Republic.

Since the early 1960's Soviet oil from the Volgo-Caspian area has flowed through the Druzhba pipeline to refineries in Eastern Europe.

CHOP

This town is an important railway junction on the Soviet border with Czechoslovakia and Hungary.

✿ Hotel and Restaurant.

UZHGOROD

Ukrainian: Uzhorod,
Czech: Užhorod,
Hungarian: Ungvár
Population: 53,000 (1965)

The town is situated in the foothills of the Carpathian mountains, on either side of the River Uzh ("grass-snake"; Uzhgorod: "grass-snake town"). Situated in a vine-growing region, the ancient coat-of-arms of the town bears a vine with two bunches of golden grapes.

Known in the chronicles since the 9th century, it is one of the oldest Slavonic towns, and today its industries include the manufacture of veneered furniture, bricks, tiles and food products.

There are mineral springs of the carbonic acid type in front of the main university building, in Gorky Park, and in Podgradsky and Protsky Streets.

✿ Uzhgorod Castle *Kremlovskaya Street 27*. The castle dates from the end of the 9th century, and the Slav prince Laborets lived here until he was executed in 903 by the invading Hungarians. In 1312 Uzhgorod, with its castle, was given by the Hungarian King Karl Robert to the Italian Count Drugget, and the Drugget family held it until 1692, during which period "1598" was engraved over the entrance gate. After this, the castle was sold to Count Berceni. In the 17th century it was seized several times during local disturbances.

In 1649, in the Roman Catholic chapel in the park, the local Orthodox Church signed a union with Rome which marked the foundation of the Uniate, or Greek Catholic, Church. The present castle has a 16th century façade; it was reconstructed in 1598 and in 1653 to suit the requirements of new military techniques. In 1703 it was captured by rebellious peasants led by Ivan Betzei. Later in the 18th century the castle lost its military importance, and when the upper storey of the main castle building was burned down in 1728, it was not rebuilt. In 1775 it was presented to the Bishop of Mukachevo. Soon after that a seminary was opened in the castle and was only closed in 1944.

There are extensive dungeons and cellars in the castle, and from the top of the eastern tower there is a good view of the valley of the river Uzh; in fine weather the ruins of Nevitzkoye Castle can be seen. In the castle garden stands a bronze statue of the mythological Hungarian bird known as the "Turul". Originally the castle had a moat on three sides of it, the fourth side being naturally protected by a steep hill.

✿ RUSSIAN ORTHODOX CATHEDRAL *On the way to the castle.* This was built in 1646, originally as a Roman Catholic Cathedral.

GREEK CATHOLIC CHURCH *Oktyabrskaya Street.*

SAINT PAUL'S CHURCH (RUSSIAN ORTHODOX) *Moskovskaya Naberezhnaya.* This church was built in 1932 to ocmmemorate the Russian soldiers who fell in the Carpathians in World War I.

CALVINISTS' CHURCH *Sovietskaya Street.*

✿ MAIN BUILDING OF THE UNIVERSITY *Gorky Square.*
The university, founded in 1946, now has more than 4000 students attending its seven faculties. Its other buildings are in Lenin Square and Oktyabrskaya Street.

UNIVERSITY LIBRARY. This building was originally founded in 1644 as the residence of the Uniate Bishops of Transcarpathia; it was reconstructed in 1848 in baroque style, and encloses an interesting old sundial.

LOCAL EXECUTIVE BUILDING *Lenin Square.* This huge building was put up between 1934 and 1936.

TOWN COUNCIL BUILDING. This was built in 1809 in baroque style and is now used for newspaper offices.

LOCAL MUSEUM *Kremlovskaya Street 27, inside the castle. Open 11–7; closed on Wednesdays.* There are sections of natural history and local handicrafts in the museum.

PICTURE GALLERY *Kremlovskaya Street 27, inside the castle. Open 11–7; closed on Mondays.* Opened in 1948, this gallery now contains the works of Russian and Ukrainian artists.

THE PYRAMID MEMORIAL *Karl Marx Square* and the MONUMENT *Leningradskaya Naberezhnaya.* These two memorials were built in memory of those who fell in World War I.

FENZIG MONUMENT. This monument is in memory of a local poet.

The iron statue of Hercules in the park near the castle was cast in Uzhgorod.

HEROES' CEMETERY *Geroyev Street.* There are a number of beautiful memorials here.

UKRAINIAN DRAMA THEATRE *Teatralnaya Square.* This theatre dates from 1907.

PHILHARMONIA CONCERT HALL *Teatralnaya Square* This Hall was formerly a synagogue; the Transcarpathian Folk Choir sings here.

SPARTAK SUMMER SWIMMING POOL *Roshcha Gogolya Street in Gorky Park.*

UZHGOROD'S AVANGARD STADIUM. The stadium can seat 10,000.

GORKY PARK *On the right bank of the river Uzh, on the north side of Castle Hill.* The park contains playgrounds, an open air stage, sports pavilions, a library, a dance floor, a pets' corner and a children's railway, the "Small Carpathian Railway", opened in 1947 and running for 1200 m. (¾ mile) along the river bank.

BOTANICAL GARDEN. Here there are more than 3000 plants including many that are only to be seen in this region. Tropical and subtropical plants can be seen in the hothouses.

VERKHOVINA HOTEL AND RESTAURANT *Teatralnaya Square 5; tel: 87-46.*

KIEV HOTEL AND RESTAURANT *Koryatovicha Square 1; tel: 34-24.* Part of the restaurant is in the open air.

KONDITERSKAYA CAFE *Sholokhov Street 4.* There are two other cafés in Suvorov Street.

GIFT SHOP *Suvorov Street 10.*

JEWELLER'S *Suvorov Street 8.*

FILLING AND SERVICE STATION *Sovietskaya Street 148, on the way into town.* Diesel oil is available; open daily 9 a.m.–10 p.m.

DUBKI CAMPING SITE AND MOTEL *6 km/4 miles from town.*

NEVITSKOYE CAMPING SITE *10 km/6 miles from town.*

SEREDNE

The name of this village means "in the middle". On the right as one enters the village the remains of the local castle can be seen. Seredne is famous for its wine, which is reputed to be the best in the Carpathians.

THE RUSSIAN ORTHODOX AND ROMAN CATHOLIC CHURCHES are of no particular historical interest.

TEAROOM *On the main street.*

POST OFFICE *On the main street.*

RUSSKOYE

There is an unusual Russian Orthodox church on the left of the main road.

MUKACHEVO

Hungarian: Munkács,
Czech: Mukačevo
Population: 50,000 (1964)

The town stands on the river Latoritsa. It was first mentioned in 903 when the Hungarians came there as invaders. In 1242 it was ruined by the Tartars but by 1445 it had recovered sufficiently to become a self-governing town. Czechoslovakia held it after 1919 and in 1938, along with the rest of the region, it again passed into Hungarian hands.

There is a large furniture factory in the town as well as tobacco and food-processing factories, a factory where skis are manufactured, and a textile mill.

PALANOK CASTLE *On the top of a hill just outside the town, to the south.* This is the oldest monument in the town, it dates from the 14th and 15th centuries and stands 68 m (223 ft) high. The well is 85 m (279 ft) deep. In 1782 the castle was turned into a prison. It is now under repair.

In the river valley are the remains of a 17th–18th century fortress.

WOODEN RUSSIAN ORTHODOX CHURCH *Bogomoltsa Street.* This church was built in the nearby village of Shelestovo in 1777, and was brought here in 1927 as an example of early architecture.

CONVENT *Podgorod region.* The convent dates from the 18th century.

ROMAN CATHOLIC CHURCH *Mir Street.* This church was built in the 19th century.

MONUMENT TO THE SOVIET ARMY AND LOCAL PARTISANS *In the central square.*

RUSSIAN DRAMA THEATRE *Mir Street.*

PARK *On the left bank of the River Latoritsa.* The park has an open air swimming pool.

ZVEZDA HOTEL AND RESTAURANT AND UKRAINA CAFE *Mir Street 16.*

CHINADEYEVO

The road follows the valley of the River Latoritsa. Wood-working is the principal industry here.

The Russian Orthodox Church in the village is of no particular historical interest.

TEAROOM *On the main street.*

Just outside Chinadeyevo on the road to Lvov in a park to the left stands Count Schönborn's red-roofed palace, built in the 1890's and now used as the Karpati Sanatorium.

SVALYAVA

Population: 12,000 (1965)

Svalyava was first mentioned in writing in the 13th century. Today its inhabitants are mainly engaged in wood-working, experimental trout breeding, and in bottling the mineral water from the numerous local springs. Just before reaching the village, on the way from Mukachevo, on the right side of the road is a spring one may sample.

HOTEL.

Nearby is "Polyana" (clearing), the largest health resort in the Carpathians.

NIZHNIYE-VOROTA

This town is 450 m (1500 ft) above sea level. Its name means "lower gates", and it is not far from here to the main Carpathian Mountain range and to the Veretsky Pass which is 845 m (2775 ft) above sea level. Here the first few log cabin type wooden houses are to be seen.

There is an experimental agricultural station in Nizhniye-Vorota, carrying out research on mountain farming.

18th CENTURY CHURCH.

ROMAN CATHOLIC CHURCH *On the main street.*

BESKID RESTAURANT *Opposite the Roman Catholic Church, on the main street.*

POST OFFICE.

THE PASS itself is the border of the Transcarpathian region.

PEREVAL ("PASS") RESTAURANT.

In August gentians grow beside the road on the slope down to the valley of the river Stryj on the other side of the Pass.

KLIMETZ

ROMAN CATHOLIC CHURCH. This wooden church with silver domes has an unusual oriental look. There are services held in it on Sundays.

ORAVA

To the left of the road to Lvov stands a similar church to that in Klimetz.

KOZEVA

On the right of the road, going through the village towards Lvov, stands another wooden church, built 1939, and this time Russian Orthodox. The road crosses the River Butivlya.

STRYJ

This town dates from 1396. It has a rolling stock repair works, and its other industries include machine building, woodcutting and the manufacture of glass and food products.

RUSSIAN ORTHODOX CHURCH *Nevsky Street.*

ROMAN CATHOLIC CHURCH *Kastyolnaya Street.* Services take place here; there is a statue of Our Lady in front of the church.

LOCAL MUSEUM *Dzerzhinsky Street 15.*

SHEVCHENKO PARK *Dragobuich Street.*

HOTEL.

PRIKARPATIYE RESTAURANT *Lenin Street 8.*

KONDITERSKAYA CAFE *Mitskevich Street 21.*

SELF-SERVICE CAFE *Mitskevich Street.*

G.P.O. *Pochtovaya Street.*

NIKOLAYEV

Ukrainian: Mikolayiv

In 1570 Nikolai Tarlo, a Polish noble, was given permission by King Sigismund Augustus to found this town.

CHURCH *Lenin Street.*

PARK.

DRUZHBA (FRIENDSHIP) HOTEL AND CAFETERIA *Zhdanov Street, near the main road into the town from Stryi.*

TEAROOMS *Lenin Street and Pervomaiskaya Street.*

MOSTISKA

Mostiska lies on the Soviet side of the Polish-U.S.S.R. border, on the road that comes in from Poland via *Przemysl.*

LVOV

Ukrainian: Lviv,
Polish: Lwów,
German: Lemberg
Population: 440,000

The name of the town means "lion". These beasts feature on the coat-of-arms and also frequently in the decorative metal- and stone-work of the town.

Lvov stands near the River Poltva, a tributary of the River Bug, and the river also flows under part of the town. In the past Lvov was important for its position on the Black Sea–Baltic Sea trade route, and now it is the centre of the large region known as Galitsia.

It was founded in about 1256 by the Rusian prince Danil Romanovich who called it after his son, Lev (lion). In 1387 it was captured by Roman Catholic Poland and was so held until, in 1772, it was taken by Austria. It was returned to Poland in 1918 and in 1939 passed to Russia. There are many architectural relics to be seen.

Most of the Polish people have now been repatriated, so the greater part of the town's inhabitants are Ukrainians, and the language spoken is Ukrainian. There remain many elaborate palaces and mansions built by

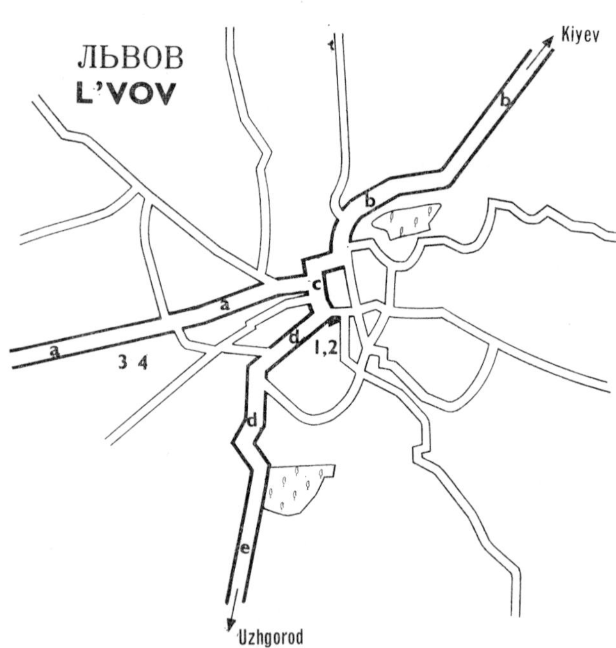

1 and 2 Hotel and Restaurant 3 Filling Station 4 Service Station.

a Ul. Gorodetzskaya, b Ul. 700-letiya Lvova, c Pl. Mitzkevicha, d Ul. Franko, e Striiskoye chaussée

members of the Polish nobility and now housing various institutes, colleges, libraries and offices. These include:

COUNT POTOTSKI'S PALACE *Kopernik Street 15*. This was built in the 19th century and is now used by the Geological Institute.

LOCAL GOVERNMENT OFFICES *Universitetskaya Street*. Built in 1871–81, these are now the university buildings.

THE RATHAUS *Rynok 1*. Dating from 1827–35, the Rathaus is now used by the Town Council.

Lvov has a total of 12 scientific institutes besides other research establishments.

The main industries of the town, besides the manufacture of buses, are connected with machine building, radios and food products. There is also an interesting pottery; the greater part of its products are sold in Moscow and Kiev but it is possible through Intourist to visit the factory and to purchase articles there, as well as buying them in the local shops.

The old part of the town has narrow streets lined with rococo and baroque style houses, and especially interesting are the 16th century houses fronting onto Market Square. No. 14, built in 1600, is decorated with a winged stone lion; this was taken from the coat-of-arms of Venice, for the house once belonged to the Venetian Consul Massari.

GUNPOWDER TOWER *Podvalnaya Street 13*. This was built in 1554–56 and is now the House of Architects. Nearby is the King's Armoury, built in 1639, where the town archives are kept. The Town Arsenal dates from 1554–55; on the south wall is a coat-of-arms taken from the demolished town walls in 1799. Nearby it are the remains of a 15th century tower.

Besides these civil buildings Lvov has a great wealth of churches, both Roman Catholic and Russian Orthodox, some dating from as far back as the 13th century.

SAINT YURI'S ROMAN CATHOLIC CATHEDRAL *Bogdan Khmelnitsky Square*. This was designed by Bernard Meretini in 1744 and completed in 1770. It was later converted for Russian Orthodox use and is still open for services. On the façade is an equestrian statue of Saint Yuri Near by stands the baroque METROPOLITAN'S PALACE, built in 1761. The belltower and walls also date from the 18th century, and in the belltower hangs the oldest bell in the Ukraine, cast in 1341.

ARMENIAN CATHEDRAL *Armyanskaya Street 7*. This was founded in 1363. There is also a 1571 belltower here and the house where the Armenian Archbishops resided in the 16th century. In the courtyard is an 18th century column with a statue of Saint Christopher on it.

WOODEN CHURCH *Krivchitskoi Street*. This was built in 1763 and brought here in 1930 from the Ukrainian village of Krivky as an example of folk architecture.

CHURCH OF SAINT NICHOLAS *Bogdan Khmelnitsky Street 28*. This church was constructed between the 13th and the 18th centuries. Russian Orthodox services are now held here.

SAINT ONUFRIA MONASTERY *Bogdan Khmelnitsky Street 34*. There is a 17th century church where Russian Orthodox services are held, and the belltower and walls are 17th–19th century. Ivan Feodorov, the first

Russian printer, is buried here. He produced his first book in 1563 in Moscow, and then fled from that region to continue his work in Lithuania and Poland. He died in 1583.

PYANITSKAYA CHURCH *Bogdan Khmelnitsky Street 63*. This church was built in 1645 and has a very old iconostasis.

CHURCH AND CONVENT OF THE BENEDICTINES *Vechevaya Square*. The architect of these buildings, put up in 1595–1628, was Pavel Rimlyanin.

CISTERCIAN CHURCH AND MONASTERY *Vossoyedinyeniya Square*. The monastery was built between 1600 and 1630. In the Church there are frescoes and 18 wooden altars with decorative carving of the 18th century.

SAINT MARTIN'S ROMAN CATHOLIC CHURCH *Dekabristov Street*. This Church was built between 1630–1736.

SAINT VOITSEKH ROMAN CATHOLIC CHURCH *Dovbush Street*. This church dates from 1702.

BELLTOWER OF THE CHURCH OF THE HOLY SPIRIT *Kopernik Street 36*. The belltower is 18th century work.

SAINT LAZARUS' ROMAN CATHOLIC CHURCH *Kopernik Street 27*. The Church was built in 1635–40. Nearby, in the same street, is a dried-up well guarded by two stone lions from the former Mayor's House.

CASIMIRA ROMAN CATHOLIC CHURCH *Krivonosa Street 1*. This Church dates from 1660.

CLARISSA ROMAN CATHOLIC CHURCH *Lenin Street 2*. This 18th century church is decorated with frescoes.

SACRAMENTARIAN CHURCH AND CONVENT *Akademik Pavlov Street*. An 18th–19th century building.

ROMAN CATHOLIC CATHEDRAL *Rosa Luksemburg Street*. Although this cathedral is used for services, the building dating from 1370–1480 is still incomplete. It contains 18th century frescoes and many decorative carvings and statues of the 17th and 18th centuries. The chapels and 65 m (214 ft) high Gothic tower were added from the 16th to the 18th century. The Campiani Chapel was founded by the ruthless pawnbroker, Campiani, who became Mayor of Lvov at the beginning of the 17th century. It is made of red, pink, white and black marble and was eventually completed by the founder's son. The Boim Chapel, built 1609–17 in baroque style, belonged to a family that originated in Hungary; one of its members was private secretary to the Polish King Stephan Batory.

CHURCH OF THE ASSUMPTION (USPENSKY SOBOR) *Russkaya Street*. This is one of the most beautiful churches in Lvov. In 1527 the original church was burnt down and a new one was built; this was in turn burnt to the ground in 1571 and money was collected to rebuild it. It is recorded that the Russian Tsar Fyodor gave 200 sables, 200 martens, 50 golden coins and 35 roubles, because it was a stronghold of the Russian Orthodox Church in Poland. The present building was errected in 1590–1629. In the yard in the same Renaissance style is a 66 m (216 ft) high belltower dating from 1572–78. In it is a bell called "Cyril" which was cast locally in 1783 and which weighs nearly 5 tons. On the outside walls of the church is a sculptured frieze of Biblical scenes. In the main dome inside are the carved stone coats-of-arms of Russia, Moldavia and Poland. There are also 18th century sculptures and 17th and 18th century icons. The stained glass windows were recently installed. Among its many other treasures, the church has a silver cross made in 1638. Russian Orthodox services are held here regularly.

ROMAN CATHOLIC CHURCH OF MARIA SNEZHNOI *Snezhnaya Street.* Inside this 16th–19th century church there is an 18th century statue of the Virgin Mary.

CHURCH AND MONASTERY OF THE BAREFOOT CARMELITES *Sovietskaya Street 20.* In this monastery dating from 1634 the remains of some 18th century frescoes are to be seen.

ROMAN CATHOLIC CHURCH OF THE HOLY SPIRIT *Sovietskaya Street 32.* This church with a baroque façade was built between 1642 and 1692.

CHURCH OF THE DOMINICAN MONASTERY *Stavropigiskaya Square.* This church, founded in 1748, was designed in baroque style by Jan Vitte and was reconstructed in 1956. Inside there are some 18th century sculptures and a memorial by the Danish sculptor, Thorvaldsen. Near the church are Gothic cloisters of the 16th century and other monastery buildings.

SAINT MAGDALENE'S ROMAN CATHOLIC CHURCH *Mir Street 10.* The church is of the 17th–18th century and contains some interesting carving and sculptures of the 18th century. Catholic services take place here.

JESUIT MONASTERY AND CHURCH *Teatralnaya Street 11/13.* The monastery dates from 1610–35; inside there are 18th century wood-carvings and 17th and 18th century frescoes.

SAINT BRIDGET'S ROMAN CATHOLIC CONVENT *Chapayev Street 24.* This 17th century convent was turned into a prison in 1792.

HOLY TRINITY ROMAN CATHOLIC MONASTERY *Sherbakov Street 2.* The main church, founded in 1745, has a 17th century marble altar. The church has been converted for Russian Orthodox use. The north building of the monastery now belongs to Lvov University.

HISTORICAL MUSEUM *Rynok 4/6. Open 11–7; closed on Wednesdays and Sundays.* Of the two houses now used by the museum, the "Black House" (Polish: "Cziarna Kamienca") belonged to the Anchovsky family. The other was built by an Italian architect for a Greek merchant and was bought in the 17th century by the Polish King Jan Sobieski. In this house an "eternal peace treaty" was signed with Russia in 1686. The former throne room is now used for a display of present-day industry.

UKRAINIAN ART MUSEUM *Dragomanov Street 42. Open 11–7; closed on Mondays.* There is a good collection of 14th–18th century icons here.

PICTURE GALLERY *Stefanik Street 3. Open 12–7; closed on Mondays.* Among its 10,000 paintings are some works of Rubens, Titian, Goya, Tintoretto and the Russian classics.

LENIN MUSEUM *Lenin Prospekt 20. Open 10–7; closed on Mondays.*

ETHNOGRAPHICAL AND HANDICRAFTS MUSEUM *Lenin Prospekt. Open 11–6; closed on Mondays.*

NATURAL HISTORICAL MUSEUM *Teatralnaya Street 18. Open 11–5; closed on Mondays.*

IVAN FRANKO MUSEUM *Franko Street 152. Open 10–7; closed on Tuesdays.* Ivan Franko was a famous writer.

YAROSLAV GALAN MUSEUM *Gvardeiskaya Street 18. Open 12–5; closed on Wednesdays, Fridays and Saturdays.* Galan was a Ukranian political writer, murdered in 1949 at the age of 47.

MITSKEVICH MONUMENT *Mitskevich Street, opposite the Intourist Hotel.* The sculptors of this statue to the Polish poet Adam Miczkiewicz (Mitskevich) were Popiel and Parashuk, and it was unveiled in 1905.

IVAN FRANKO MONUMENT *In front of the university building.* The monument was unveiled in 1964.

LENIN MONUMENT *Lenin Prospekt,* This monument by Merkurov was unveiled in 1952.

TANK MONUMENT *Lenin Street.* The T-34 tank commemorates the Soviet Tank Corps which liberated Lvov in 1944.

KILINSKY MONUMENT *Stryjsky Park.* Kilinsky was a revolutionary Warsaw cobbler.

KHOLM SLAVY (Hill of Glory) *near Lychakovsky Park.* Here, marking the graves of those who fell during World War II, is an eternal flame and architectural and sculptural complex, constructed in 1946–1952.

In Rynok Square, near the Rathaus are four fountains dating from the end of the 18th century; which have figures of Diana, Adonis, Neptune and Amphitrite.

✿ FRANKO OPERA AND BALLET THEATRE *Torgovaya Square.* The theatre was built between 1897 and 1900 and designed by Gorgolevsky in the Renaissance style. It seats 1100.

ZANKOVETSKAYA URKAINIAN DRAMA THEATRE *Ukrainskaya Street 1.* This theatre was built in classical style in 1837–42.

RUSSIAN DRAMA THEATRE *Gorodetskaya Street 6.*

GORKY YOUTH THEATRE *Gorky Street 11.*

PUPPET THEATRE *Galitsky Street.*

SUMMER THEATRE *Khmelnitsky Park, Dzerzhinsky Street 43.*

CONCERT HALL *Franko Street 25.* The choir of Lvov is called "Trembita".

✿ FRANKO PARK *Universitetskaya Street, opposite the main university building.* The park dates back to the 16th century; and it has a summer restaurant.

STRYJSKY PARK *On the road leading to the town of Stryj.* Stryjsky Park is one of the loveliest parks in Europe, and its 56 hectares (140 acres) also take their place among the richest arboreta in the Soviet Union. The park, which has children's railway and permanent exhibition halls, was opened to the public in 1877.

PRINCE'S HILL The remains of the 14th century VYSOKY ZAMOK ("high castle") fortress can be seen here. There is also a stone monument to Maxim Krivonos, the Cossack colonel who seized the fortress in 1648.

KHMELNITSKY PARK *Dzerzhinsky Street.* There are in the park a monument to Lenin, exhibition pavilions, a summer theatre seating 6000, and a restaurant.

LENIN PARK This park encloses the graves of Russian soldiers who fell in the First and Second World Wars, and has an eternal flame which has burned on the Hill of Glory war memorial since 1958. There are statues including one of a woman symbolising the motherland.

LYCHAKOVSKOYE KLADBISHCHE (Cemetery) *Mechnikov Street*. Since the 16th century many monuments to the nobility have been erected in this cemetery. There is one to Ivan Franko, and the graves of other Polish and Ukrainian artists and writers are also here.

BOTANICAL GARDEN *Scherbakov Street.*

HIPPODROME RACECOURSE *Stryjskoye chaussée.*

SPARTAK SWIMMING POOL *Instrumentalnaya Street 49.*

KOMSOMOLSKOYE LAKE *3 km (2 miles) out of town on the road to Vinniki.*

GLINOVNAVARIA LAKE *16 km (10 miles) from Lvov.* This lake has a sandy beach.

INTOURIST HOTEL AND RESTAURANT *Mitskevich Square 1: tel: 2-89-36 or 2-97-10.*

LVOV HOTEL *Lenin Prospekt 13.*

PERVOMAISKAYA HOTEL AND RESTAURANT *Lenin Prospekt 21; tel: 2-97-50.*

UKRAINA HOTEL AND RESTAURANT *Mitskevich Square 4; tel: 2-87-49.*

KIEV HOTEL *Chapayev Street 15.*

DNIEPER HOTEL *Pervomaiskaya Street 45.*

VARSHAVSKAYA HOTEL *Vosoyedineiniya Square 5.*

PRIKARPATSKAYA HOTEL *Nalivaiko Street 6.*

NARODNAYA HOTEL AND RESTAURANT *Kostushko Street 1; tel: 1-24-06.*

KOLKHOZNAYA HOTEL *Vossoyedineniya Square 14.*

LETO (SUMMER) RESTAURANT *Gorky Street 17.*

MOSKVA RESTAURANT *Mitskevich Square 7.*

PERVOMAISKY RESTAURANT *Lenin Prospekt 17.*

CAMPING SITE *at Dublyany, 12 km (7½ miles) east of Lvov, on the main road toward Rovno.*

G.P.O. *Slovatsky Street 1.*

COMMISSION SHOPS *Shevchenko Prospekt 3, near Intourist Hotel and Volovaya Street 11.*

JEWELLER'S *Mitskevich Square and Lenin Prospekt 29.*

GIFT SHOP *Kopernik Street 1.*

ARTS AND CRAFTS *Mitskevich Square near Intourist Hotel.*

TAXI RANKS *Komsomolskaya Street 5, Lenin Prospekt 22 and at the railway station.*

FILLING STATION AND SERVICE STATION *Fetkovich Street 34, near the central railway station.*

FILLING STATION *Kovelskaya Street 67.*

ZAPYTOV

There is a white Roman Catholic church on the right side of the road.

BUSK

Busk was founded in the 9th century. It was once a stronghold with two castles, but these have been completely ruined.

IVAN FRANKO PARK.

TEAROOM *On the main road.*

EATING HOUSE *On the left as you leave the village.*

OLESKO

THE CATHEDRAL This was founded in the 14th century, and reconstructed and enlarged several times.

THE FORTRESS This was the birthplace of Polish king Jan Sobieski III.

HOTEL.

RESTAURANT.

BRODY

Population 12,200

The name means "fords" and indicates that this town stands in swampy territory. It was first mentioned in writing in the 12th century, and it now has saw-mills, a fruit cannery and weaving and carpet industries.

THE CASTLE-FORTRESS This dates from 1630.

SAINT GEORGE'S CHURCH *Near the fortress.* This church was built in the 16th–18th century.

ROMAN CATHOLIC CHURCH *Main Street.* This church was built in 1596.

SYNAGOGUE *Bazaar.* This is a 17th century building.

In place of a theatre, visiting theatre companies perform in the HOUSE OF CULTURE *Kotsubinsky Street 7.*

PERVOMAISKY (MAYDAY) PARK *Krasnaya Armiya Square.*

HOTEL *Lenin Street.*

RESTAURANT *Bogdan Khmelnitsky Square.*

TEAROOM *Lenin Street.*

CHERVONOARMEISK

formerly Radziwilow

The town is now named after the Red Army. The inhabitants are mainly employed in the food industry.

RUSSIAN ORTHODOX CHURCH *On the main street.* The church dates from the end of the 19th century.

HOTEL *On the main road.*

TEAROOM *On the main road.*

VERBA

"Verba" means "willow".

DOROZHNYI HOTEL AND RESTAURANT *Beside the road, which is in fact the meaning of "dorozhnyi".* This hotel is recommended to tourists.

DUBNO

Population: 18,500 (1959)

This place, which stands on the river Ikva and which became a town in 1498, belonged from the 14th century until 1619 to the noble family of Ostrozhsky. Dubno became Soviet in 1939. Its industry is mainly concerned with the production of machinery, food and textiles. There is also a sugar factory here.

BERNARDINE MONASTERY. A 17th century building.

CARMELITE MONASTERY. This monastery dates from 1660.

SAINT ELIJAH'S CHURCH *Oktyabrskaya Street.*

CHURCH OF THE TRANSFIGURATION *On Kempa Island in the river Ikva.*

CASTLE RUINS *Zamkovaya Street.* This castle dates from 16th–17th century.

LOCAL MUSEUM *Shevchenko Street.*

DRAMA THEATRE.

HOTEL *Lenin Street.*

RESTAURANT *Oktyabrskaya Street 16.*

ROVNO

Population: 57,000 (1959)

The town has been known as a trading point since 1282, and in the middle ages it belonged to Polish and Lithuanian nobles. In the middle of the 18th century it was the setting of Prince Lyubomirsky's brilliant court. In 1793 it passed to Russia, but between 1921 and 1939 it was again in Polish hands. The town became the provincial capital in 1939.

Rovno's main street is Lenin Street. There are two colleges, for hydro-engineering and teachers' training, in the town.

Food products and high voltage electrical apparatus are both manufactured here, and under construction is a linen mill which will be among the largest in Europe.

SAINT ANTHONY'S CATHEDRAL *Lenin Street.*

WOODEN CHURCH *Shevchenko Street.* This was possibly built at the end of the 17th century.

SAINT PETER AND SAINT PAUL ROMAN CATHOLIC CHURCH *Lenin Street.*

RESURRECTION RUSSIAN ORTHODOX CHURCH *Lenin Street 41.*

LOCAL MUSEUM *Krasnoarmeiskaya Street 32. Open daily 10–5.* There is a monument to Nikolai Kuznetsov, a partisan hero who was formerly an engineer from the Urals. During the war he captured a German general from behind the enemy lines, and uncovered a plot against the Allied leaders. This monument to him was unveiled in 1961.

MUSIC AND DRAMA THEATRE *Teatralnaya Square.*

CHILDREN'S RAILWAY *Lenin Street.*

ROVNO HOTEL AND RESTAURANT *Lenin Street 112; tel: 23-02.*

UKRAINA RESTAURANT *Lenin Street, opposite the hotel.*

RESTAURANT NO. 2. *Oleko Dundich Street.*

REPAIR STATION *In the second street on the right from the hotel along the Kiev road.* Cars can be garaged in the yard at night.

PETROL STATION *Liebknecht Street 14, at the bus station on the way to Kiev.*

KORETS

Population: 3400 (1959)

Korets stands on the River Korchik. It has a sugar factory and brick works.

CONVENT OF THE HOLY TRINITY *Lenin Street 56.* There are more than 200 nuns here. Of the three churches the oldest is that of St. Nicholas.

CATHOLIC CHURCH. Services are also held here.

CASTLE RUINS.

DRAMA THEATRE *17-Sentyabrya Pereulok.*

HOTEL *Lenin Street.*

TEAROOM.

Korets has a very busy Sunday market.

NOVOGRAD-VOLYNSKY

Novograd-Volynsky stands on the River Sluch. It has been known since 1257 and now has machine-building and food industries.

CHURCH.

SYNAGOGUE.

Ruins of the CASTLE-FORTRESS belonging to the Princes Ostrozhsky, and built in the 14th and 15th centuries.

LYESIA UKRAINKA MUSEUM *Lyesia Ukrainka Street.* Lyesia Ukrainka was the pseudonym of Larisa Kosach-Kvitka (1871–1913), the writer and poetess, who was born in this house.

PARK.

HOTEL *Karl Marx Street.*

EATING HOUSE *Lenin Street.*

TEAROOM *Lenin Street.*

ICE CREAM PARLOUR *At the crossing of Lenin Street and Karl Marx Street.*

BRONIKI

Tearoom on the main road.

ZHITOMIR

Population: 105,000

The town stands on the River Teterev ("blackcock"), a tributary of the River Dnieper, and has a local spa spring. The surrounding area is rich in red, white and pink granite which is quarried and transported to many parts of the Soviet Union. Both Moscow University and the Lenin Mausoleum are built with this granite.

Above the river are high cliffs and one rock is called "Golova Chatskovo" (Chatsky's head). The legend runs that Chatsky, a rich Polish knight, after being defeated in battle, jumped in full armour with his horse down into the river.

Zhitomir is first mentioned in the chronicles in 1240 as having been ruined by the Tartars. It is supposed to have been founded in 884 as the centre of the Zhitichi slav tribe, from whom it took its name. It was under the Lithuanian rule in the 14th century, and in 1569 passed to Poland. In 1793 Zhitomir became Russian, and the centre of the Volyn Province.

Besides being the centre of the Soviet hop-growing industry, Zhitomir has an engine repairing works and factories for musical instruments and electro-measuring apparatus. Under construction is what will be one of the largest linen mills in the U.S.S.R. There are agricultural and teachers' training colleges.

Six churches are open to visitors; the rest are of no particular historical interest.

SAINT MICHAEL'S CHURCH *Lenin Street 14.* This church dates from 18th century.

CATHOLIC CHURCH *Kooperativnaya Street.* Both this church and Saint Michael's are used for worship. Close to the Catholic Church is the very beautiful Zamkovaya Gora (Castle Hill).

CATHEDRAL OF THE TRANSFIGURATION *Karl Liebknekht Street 14.*

CHURCH OF THE ASSUMPTION *Podolskaya Street 19.* This cathedral was built in 1752.

SYNAGOGUE *Kommunisticheskaya Street 8.*

OLD HOUSE. This late 17th century house was formerly the magistrate's office.

LOCAL HISTORY MUSEUM *Starovilskaya Street 13. Open daily 10–6.*

NATURAL HISTORY MUSEUM *Lenin Street 4. Open 10–6.*

DRAMA THEATRE *Pushkinskaya Street.*

PUPPET THEATRE *Gorsoviet Street.*

a Korostenskaya b Glavnaya
c Berdichevskoye

PHILARMONIA CONCERT HALL *Gorsoviet Street.*

LENKOMSOMOL STADIUM.

✿ BOTANICAL GARDENS.

KAPITOVKA BATHING BEACH AND QUAY *5 km (3 miles) from town.* Since the construction of the Zhitomir Power Station a lake has appeared on the eastern side of the town.

✿ HOTEL *Lenin Street.*

ZHITOMIR HOTEL AND RESTAURANT *Karl Liebknecht Street 10. Tel: 16–69.*

PERVOYE MAYA (MAYDAY) RESTAURANT *Karl Marx Street.*

CAFE *Karl Marx Street.*

✿ G.P.O. *Lenin Street 16.*

✿ FILLING STATION *Lenin Street and then turn right.* High quality petrol is not stocked here.

CAMPING SITE *5 km (3 miles) out of town at Polesye on the road to Kiev.* The "Polesye" Restaurant is here too, and also another filling station, providing round the clock service.

KIEV

Kiev has long covered a series of wooded hills on the right bank of R. Dnieper.

"Away above me, towering high,
Old Kiev guards her river.
At the steep wood's foot doth Dnieper lie,
His water rippling silver".

Now the city has an area of 75,000 hectares (about 300 sq. miles) including the industrial district of Darnitsa which has grown up on the left bank of the river. This region is connected with the rest of Kiev by the Paton Bridge (opened 1953).

Kiev is said to have got its name from the first prince of the Slav tribe, the Polyani, who lived in this area. He was called Ki, and with his brothers he founded the town on an eminence. In 864, after these rulers, Askold and Duir made themselves masters of the region. The city-state of Kiev first grew and prospered from 882 until 1169. Mostly due to the hilly site, the town's early development was unusual. It consisted of three separate settlements. The Upper City (Staro–Kiev) overlooked Podol, the name meaning "low" and which was the trading area close to the Dnieper. The third settlement was also on high ground above the river, but set at some distance behind Staro–Kiev; this was Pechersk, where the natural caves were first used by hermits and later formed the base of the Monastery of the Caves. In spite of these divisions, Kiev was strong enough to become capital of the country, the trading centre of eastern Europe and even rivalled Constantinople in splendour. Its importance gave rise to a Russian proverb, reminiscent of "All roads lead to Rome", saying, "Your tongue will lead you to Kiev".

The year 988 is the one in which Christianity came to Russia but Prince Vladimir's choice of Christianity for a national religion was not made easily. It was said that he was a violent man, "insatiable in vice" and a fanatical heathen who had offered thousands of human sacrifices. He was also a thinker and, although there is no record of his reasons for seeking a new religion, it is fairly clear that as an intelligent monarch he saw for himself that the peoples who remained outside the world's great religions never achieved any degree of culture, civilisation or political power. The legend runs that Vladimir's lively mind considered which religion would suit him and his people best. The Jewish faith was admirable, but the thought that its followers had been scattered throughout the earth for their sins distressed the Russian prince. Islam he rejected on the grounds that total abstinence was incompatible with survival in a cold climate. Roman Catholi-

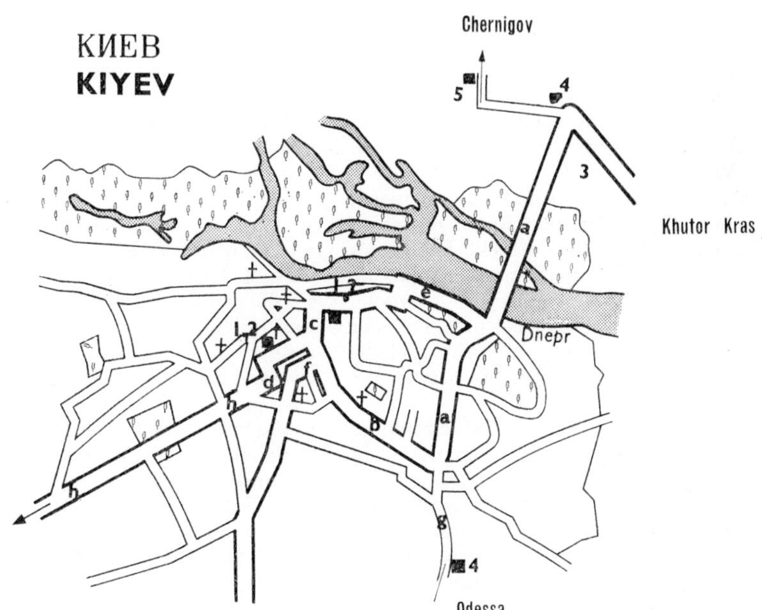

1 and 2 Hotel and Restaurant
3 Filling Station
4 Service Station
5 Camping Site

a Pr. Druzhby Narodov
b Krasnoarmeyskaya ul.
c Kreshchatik
d Bulvar Shevchenko
e Dneprovsky spusk
f Ul. Lenina
g Pr. 40-letiya Oktyabrya
h Brest-Litovskoye chaussée

cism he could not accept because he himself would have had to be subservient to the Pope. The emissaries Prince Vladimir sent to find out about the Greek Orthodox Church reported: ". . . the Greeks led us to the edifices where they worshipped their God; and we knew not whether we were in heaven or on earth. For on earth there is no such splendour or such beauty, and we are at a loss how to describe it. We only know that God dwells there among men, and their service is fairer than the ceremonies of other nations. We can never forget that beauty". Accordingly Vladimir was baptised, married the Princess Anna, no less a person than the Greek Emperor's sister, and adopted Christianity as the religion for the country as a whole. Mass baptisms took place in R. Dnieper even in midwinter, and Prince Vladimir was canonised for his part in the conversions.

There were many rival city-states and constant wars between them. In 1169 Kiev gave way to the city of Vladimir, and the title of capital was lost. At this early date Moscow had hardly been thought of; it was only a very small settlement. After its early period of glory Kiev fell into a decline, was devastated and plundered by the Tartars in 1240 and was later again badly damaged by invading Lithuanians and Poles. It was indeed completely under Lithuanian rule between 1320 and 1455. It only recovered after the unification of the Ukraine and Russia in 1654 when it was proclaimed that they "should be one for ever". Kiev then became a city of merchants and many magnificent buildings were erected in the 17th and 18th centuries, a large number of them in baroque style. It spread along the river and its original three settlements were quickly surrounded by houses and other buildings but it was not until the 19th century that the three separate parts were fully merged into one. In 1797 Kiev was elevated to the status of provincial centre and in 1798 the first of the annual contract fairs was held there. These brought merchants to Kiev from all over Europe but the city's growth was temporarily halted by a series of fires, the most disastrous of which was in 1811. It raged for several days and Podol, the most densely inhabited part of Kiev, suffered badly. This is one reason for the lack of ancient monuments in that region; the other is that it was an area never surrounded by adequate defences and which had always been subject to terrible devastation by any invaders.

In May, 1812, the general reconstruction of the city began, and by the middle of the 19th century the central part of Kiev had wide, well-planned streets with plenty of attactive buildings lining them. Throughout the 19th century Kiev acted as the administrative and economic centre of the south-west part of the Russian Empire, as well as the hub of the Ukrainian literary and national movement, and in the 1870's its importance grew further when it was linked by rail with Moscow, Odessa and other cities. By 1917 its population had reached half a million.

After the October Revolution and during the 1917–20 Civil War, Kiev was the seat of several transitory Ukrainian governments. It was occupied by the Germans for a short while in 1918. In spite of its commercial importance, it was nevertheless Kharkov that was the capital of the Ukraine when the country joined the Soviet Union in 1922, and not until 1934 was the seat of government transferred to Kiev.

In spite of severe damage during the Second World War, when 195,000 Kievans lost their lives, and the drastic rebuilding necessary after it, the three old divisions of the city still exist, and have retained their individuality. Each of the big thoroughfares too has a character of its own. Kreshchatik is the city's central street and its busiest. In the old days the site of the street was a deep, wooded valley crossed by ravines. It was known as Kreshchata (meaning "crossed") and from this the street's present name derives. The street is less than a mile long but over 350 buildings were destroyed in this part of Kiev during the war. Afterwards its width was doubled and it was completely rebuilt. A very few of the old houses remain among the modern buildings of hotels, offices and shops. No. 8 was the Petersburg Bank (architect, Benois), No. 10 was the Volgo-Kama Bank and No. 15 was and still is an arcade of shops; both the latter were designed by Andreyev and all three date from 1911–14.

Kirov Street runs through the Staro-Kiev part of the city, between Kreschatik and the riverside parks. Here the building of the Ukrainian Parliament stands out with its six-columned portico and its great glass dome. It was built in 1939 and designed by architect Zabolotny. Next to it and surrounded by ornamental iron railings is the former Tsar's Palace, built in 1742 following Rastrelli's designs but enlarged and reconstructed in 1870. It is used partly by the Supreme Soviet and partly as a guest house for important visitors to the Ukrainian capital. This area is still known by its ancient name of Lipki (lime trees). It used to be the old aristocratic quarter and a number of the nobility's ornately decorated mansions remain.

Volodimirska Street runs parallel to Kreshchatik on the side furthest from the Dnieper. Most of the ancient monuments of Kiev are to be found along its length. Apart from the best known, including the Golden Gate and St. Sophia's Cathedral, is also No. 54, the Presidium of the Ukrainian Academy of Sciences, built in the 1850's by Beretti. No. 57, now the Lenin Museum, was built as a pedagogical museum by architect Alyoshin in 1911; it was reconstructed in 1938. The red building at No. 58 is the University (architect Beretti, 1837–42). There is a good view of this from Bul'var Tarasa Shevchenko. The Boulevard has an avenue of poplars, but many of the other streets of Kiev are lined with great chestnut trees and it is partly to the abundant summer greenery that the city owes its beauty.

Apart from the usual forms of public transport, a funicular railway runs down from Volodimirska Girka to Podol. Kievans are proud to have the Soviet Union's third underground railway; the stations already operating in their Metro are called Vokzal, Universitetskaya, Kreshchatik, Arsenalnaya, Dnieper, Polytechnical Institute and Bolshevik.

Local industry, which began its most rapid development when Kiev became the capital of the Ukraine, produces among other things building materials, machinery, ships, food products and clothing. Besides the University (founded in 1834) there are nineteen institutes in Kiev.

Kiev is unlike most of the ancient cities and towns of Russia in that there are no obvious remains of a kremlin or a fortified citadel. The ruins of the Golden Gate are almost the only reminders of the way the city had to fight for its life.

The Golden Gate—in the centre of the town, at the crossing of Volodimirska Street and Polupanov Street. These two parallel walls were built of brick and stone in 1037 by Yaroslav the Wise to support the main entrance arch into the earthen-walled city of Kiev. The arch was surmounted by the small Church of the Annunciation and its construction is said to have been inspired by Constantinople's Golden Gate.

THE MONASTERY OF THE CAVES (*Peshcherskaya Lavra*—so called from the word *peshchera* meaning "cave")—*Sichneve Povstannya Street 21. Open 10–5; closed on Tuesdays.* (Please note that the caves themselves are only open from 12 noon till 5.) Every visitor to

Kiev should certainly try to go to see this monastery of which it was written,

"Where the darkness of the silent caves
Is lovelier than the royal halls".

It was founded in 1051 by two monks, Anthony and Theodosius, and through the centuries underground churches were built. In some cases the caves were natural and then the monks themselves excavated further. Some of the members of the community lived their lives there underground and when they died their bodies remained in their cells. Due to the chemical properties of the soil and the temperature the bodies became mummified and they are still to be seen. "The whole Orthodox world bows before the relics of the saints of the monastery; in times past and today, undiminished their blessing emanates upon all who come to their tombs in faith and love". From the time of Peter the Great and throughout the 18th and 19th centuries almost all the tsars and tsarinas came to Kiev and made lavish gifts to the Lavra and to the other monasteries and churches of the city.

The entrance gate is surmounted by the TRINITY CHURCH (1108) which has frescoes and a wooden iconostases of the 18th century. The walls of the Upper Monastery, built between 1698 and 1701, run from this gateway around the territory. The five-domed ALL SAINTS' CHURCH (17th century) is at another gateway. The main court of the Upper Monastery centres around the ruins of the Uspensky Sobor (ASSUMPTION CATHEDRAL), built 1073–1089 and blown up in 1941 by the Nazis. Most of the surrounding houses date from the 18th century. In some, before the revolution, were the printing works of the monastery which turned out their first book in 1617. The architectural complex of the Upper Monastery is completed by the monastery belltower, at 96·5 m (316 ft) (which height includes the cross) the highest in Russia, built in 1731–45 by the St. Petersburg architect, Shedel. In 1956–61 it was completely restored and the dome regilded. A flight of 374 steps leads to the top of the tower. In spite of the fact that the tower was built in comparatively recent times there is nevertheless a legend about its construction. It is said to have been erected by 12 brothers now buried in the caves. During construction the tower is supposed to have sunk slowly down into the earth, thus obviating the use of scaffolding or ladders. When it was completed it sprang out of the earth again in a single night, quite of its own accord.

The Nearer Caves, or ST. ANTHONY'S CAVES, contain 73 tombs and 3 underground churches and the Further Caves, or ST. THEODOSIUS'S CAVES, 47 tombs and another three churches. They are both quite separate from each other and the entrance to the second series of caves is reached by walking along a covered gallery. The belfry of the Further Caves was built in the 18th century by a serf-architect called Stefan Kovnir who also designed one of the houses in the Upper Monastery and who helped to design the big belfry. From 1926 to 1964 the whole territory was open to the public as a museum, with monks caring for it and acting as guides. On entering the caves visitors were asked to purchase a small candle instead of an admission ticket. Now however the monks have gone, there is electric light throughout and the insides of the caves have been painted. At the time of writing it is only possible to visit the Nearer Caves. The mummied bodies still have their names attached, but many of them are further described on new anti-religious plaques. The most famous tomb of all is probably that of the chronicler Nestor (d. 1115).

Near the walls of the refectory are the graves of the Cossack leaders, Kotchubei and Iskra, executed by Ivan Mazepa (1645–1709) in 1708 because they informed Peter the Great of the Ukrainian *hetman's* plan to separate the Ukraine from Russia with the help of Charles XII of Sweden and the Zaporozhye Cossacks; the plan was defeated the following year when the Russian army won the Battle of Poltava.

A BRANCH OF THE KIEV HISTORICAL MUSEUM—*inside the Monastery. Open 10.30–6; closed Mondays.* Here are examples of 17th–20th century fabrics and 16th–19th century handwork, and also wood carvings, metalwork and ceramics, all displayed to demonastrate Ukrainian art work. Particularly interesting are the *krashenki*, intricately painted eggs to be exchanged at Easter time. Some rooms are also reserved here for temporary art exhibitions.

THE UKRAINIAN THEATRE MUSEUM is also here, inside the Monastery.

A little to the north of the monastery stands the early 12th century church of SPAS-NA-BERESTOVE (the Redeemer-in-the-Birchwood). The church is open as a museum. The eastern part dates from 1640–43 and contains frescoes of that time. The older part was formerly a sepulchre for the princes of Kiev and in 1157 Prince Yuri Dolgoruky, who had founded Moscow ten years earlier, was buried here; the grey marble tomb now commemorating him was installed in 1947. It weighs six tons.

✿ VYDUBETSKY MONASTERY on the higher bank of River Dnieper, south of the Monastery of the Caves and in part of the territory of the Academy of Sciences' Botanical Garden. This architectural complex was founded in 1070–77 by Prince Vsevolod, and there is a story attached to its unusual name. After the mass conversion of Kievites to Christianity, the powerful pagan idol, Perun, was thrown into the Dnieper. He was carved out of wood but his head was silver and his beard of gold and apparently the weight of the metal kept him underwater. For some time his distressed followers ran along the river bank shouting, "Vydubai—come out of the water, O God!" and a mile farther down he did in fact rise to the surface but there was much confusion and fighting on the bank as the newly baptised Christians were all for letting him continue his journey downstream. It was from the shouts of "vydubai" that the whole area was thereafter known as Vydubichi, as was the monastery also.

Of ST. MICHAEL'S CATHEDRAL (1070–1088) only the western side remains but it has good frescoes. The other side of the building fell to ruin in the 15th and 16th centuries following a landslide. ST. GEORGE'S CHURCH (1696–1701) is a five-domed masterpiece of Ukrainnian architecture. The refectory dates from the beginning of the 18th century and the belfry was built in 1730. Between St. Michael's and St. George's is the grave of Konstantin Ushinsky (1824–70), Russian teacher and educationalist. The buildings have recently been restored and some are used as storehouses.

MIKHAILOVSKY-ZLATOVERKHY MONASTERY (St. Michael-with-the-Golden-Roof) *Geroyev Revolutsiyi Street, near Volodimirska Girka.* The monastery was founded in 1051 and its cathedral founded by Prince Svyatopolk in 1108 is Kiev's second most important 11th century construction after Sofiisky Sobor. Part of a mosaic of the Last Supper remains.

SOFIISKY SOBOR (ST. SOPHIA'S CATHEDRAL) *Volodimirska Street 24. Open 10-6; closed Mondays.* The cathedral was dedicated in 1037 by Prince Yaroslav the Wise in gratitude for the victory he gained on this site (at the time an open meadow outside the city walls) over the Pechenegi, an invading tribe from the east. It was here that the first library in Russia was organised and the country's earliest historical chronicles were written. The cathedral's form was inspired by St. Sofia's in Constantinople but it is a good combination of the traditional style of wooden buildings and the principles of stone buildings. Interesting mosaics and frescoes are to be seen in the central part of the cathedral and in the main dome. The latter is decorated with a mosaic representation of Christ the All-Ruler, the Pantokrator—not the realistic Christ of the Gospels, but a being very closely akin to the other two members of the Trinity. The archangels surrounding him are dressed in the costume of the imperial court at Byzantium and hold the symbols of the imperial office, the orb and standard. In the apse of the cathedral is the magnificent Virgin Orans, again a symbolic figure in mosaic. She is neither the Queen of Heaven nor the Mother of God, but a symbol of the earthly Church interceding for mankind. Both the figure and the splendid golden background survived the ups and downs of the cathedral so that a legend grew up about the wall's indestructibility and the Virgin Orans became an increasingly important object of worship. In the cathedral's central aisle is a portrait of members of Yaroslav the Wise's family and on the walls of the southern and northern towers are pictures of entertainment, hunting and battle scenes. In the north-eastern part of the cathedral is a marble tomb where in 1054 Yaroslav the Wise was buried. The iconostasis is of local 18th century work.

The cathedral was partly ruined by Tartars and Mongols and was further damaged while the Poles and Lithuanians were ruling the region. It was restored in 1636 and its present day appearance dates only from the first half of the 18th century, when six new domes were added. After the unification of the Ukraine and Russia in 1654, it was in this cathedral that the Kievites pledged their oath of loyalty. It was here also that in 1709 Peter the Great celebrated his victory over the Swedish army at Poltava.

Of the 18th century buildings, the most outstanding is the 78 m (256 ft) belltower, erected between 1744 and 1852. Also interesting is the Zaborovsky Vrata ("gate") built in 1746 as the main entrance to the metropolitan's house and decorated with elaborate detail and stucco ornament. At present it has lost its original proportions as the ground level has risen considerably during the past 200 years. The cathedral's surrounding wall was built in the 1740's.

Now the Sofiisky Sobor is a museum which also displays the architecture of other old Russian towns and local archeological finds and all the precincts are kept as an architectural and historical reservation.

Very near St. Sophia's, and also on Volodimirska Street, is the site of the ancient DYASITINNAYA CHURCH but no trace of it remains today.

ANDREYEVSKAYA TSERKOV (ST. ANDREW'S CHURCH) *Andreyevsky Spusk.* This church was built in 1744–53 in baroque style by Rastrelli, renowned court architect of St. Petersburg and master of the baroque. It stands on Andreyevsky Hill, the highest point of Old Kiev, overlooking Podol, the river and the plain to the east, where according to tradition the Apostle Andrew who first preached the Gospel in Russia erected a cross.

The church stands on a terrace reached by a broad flight of steps. It was built at the command of Peter the Great's religious daughter, Elizaveta. It is outstanding for its perfect proportions as well as for the way in which it makes use of the hilltop upon which it stands. Today the domes are silvered and the walls washed in turquoise and white. Inside the iconostasis is interesting; it was made under the guidance of portrait-painter Antropov. Services are held in the church.

VOLODIMIRSKY SOBOR (ST. VLADIMIR'S CATHEDRAL) *Shevchenko Boulevard 20.* This cathedral with seven cupolas was built in Byzantine style in 1863–96 by Beretti and Gernhardt to commemorate the 900th anniversary of Christianity in Russia. Sparro was another architect who participated later. The completed building shows a diversity of styles which resulted from frequent changes of plan. The original idea was to follow the lines of ancient Russian architecture. It is 49 m (161 ft) long, 28 m (92 ft) wide and 50 m (164 ft) in height. The windows are framed with fine stone ornamentation. The walls bear some interesting murals in imitation of Byzantine style. The decorations were carried out under the supervision of Professor Prakhov, a specialist in the history of art, and include some paintings by famous Russian artists, Vasnetsov and Nesterov among others. In the central aisle is a painting called "the Christening of Russia" showing Prince Vladimir and Princess Olga. The paintings were restored after World War II. It is worth while attending a service here to hear one of the best Church choirs in Russia.

ST. NICHOLAS'S CATHEDRAL near Askold's Grave (q.v.) overlooking the Dnieper, but situated a little higher and nearer to the Monastery of the Caves. Built in 1696 and a good example of the Church architecture of that date.

ST. CYRIL'S CHURCH *Frunze Street 103.* This church was founded in the northern outskirts of Kiev in 1146 as the main church of St. Cyril's Monastery, itself founded in 1140 by Prince Vsevolod. It has been restored several times and its present shape dates from the 18th century reconstruction by Beretti. The 12th century frescoes were restored by Prakhov and Vrubel. It now serves as the Pavlov Mental Hospital and is closed to visitors.

ST. FLOR'S (FLOROVSKY) CONVENT—*Podol, Florovska Street 6/8.* This convent dates from the foundation of the Church of SS. Flor and Laura near Kiselevka Hill in the 16th century. It was exceedingly prosperous at the end of the 18th century but a disastrous fire in 1811 burned down most of the buildings. The Church of the Ascension (Voznesenskaya) (1732) is open for services. Opposite stands the 17th-18th century refectory. The bell-tower was built between 1740 and 1821. The Resurrection Church, which is white with six columns, was built in 1824 by Melensky for the use of the hospital; it is now closed as is also St. Nicholas's Church.

CONVENT OF THE INTERCESSION (POKROVA) *Bekhterevsky Pereulok 15, near Artyema Street.* The convent was founded in 1889, and in the same year the Pokrovskaya Church was built. In St. Nicholas's Church (1896–1911) is the miracle-working icon of Our Lady of Pochayev. In the summer of 1964 there were 238 nuns resident here. Some of the buildings on the convent's territory are used by a state hospital.

Of two other churches, both in Podol, the BRATSKAYA—or EPIPHANY—CHURCH (1710) is closed but the CHURCH OF THE PROPHET ELIJAH is open for services.

SYNAGOGUE—*Shekoivtska Street 25.*

✿ MUSEUM OF EASTERN AND WESTERN ART *Repina Street 15. Open 10–5; closed on Fridays.* The collection includes paintings by Bellini, Rubens, Franz Hals and Velasquez.

HISTORICAL MUSEUM (*founded 1899*)—*Volodimirskaya Street 2. Open 10–6; closed on Wednesdays.*

RUSSIAN ART MUSEUM—*Repina Street 9. Open 10–6; closed on Fridays.* The section on Russian art from the 12th to the

17th century includes icons of the Novgorod, Moscow and Stroganov schools. The 18th–19th century period contains works by Bryullov, A. Ivanov, Shishkin and Repin. The first quarter of the 20th century is represented by the works of Vrubel, Serov and Korovin among others. Another section shows Soviet Russian art. There is an interesting collection of 18th–20th century porcelain, glass and crystal.

UKRAINIAN ART MUSEUM *(built in 1898–1900) Kirov Street 29. Open 10–5; closed on Fridays.* Academician Nikolayev supervised the construction. The building was supposed to resemble an ancient Greek temple and the huge granite steps, 17 m (over 50 ft) wide, which lead to the main façade have lions at each side. The six-columned portico in antique style is decorated with a sculptured group called "The Triumph of Art". The first of the two sections of the display is devoted to Ukrainian art of the 15th–19th centuries while the second contains works by Soviet Ukrainian artists.

SHEVCHENKO MUSEUM *Shevchenko Boulevard 12. Open 10–5; closed on Tuesdays.*

SHEVCHENKO'S HOUSE *Shevchenko Pereulok 8a. Open 10–5.30; closed on Fridays.* The poet lived here during the spring and summer of 1846.

LENIN MUSEUM *Volodimirskaya Street 57. Open 10–7; closed on Mondays.*

THEATRICAL MUSEUM *Sichneve Povstannya Street 6. Open 10·30–5; closed on Mondays.*

PLANETARIUM *Cheluskintsiv Street 17.* This is housed in what was formerly a Roman Catholic church.

ST. VLADIMIR MONUMENT *In the park on Volodimirska Girka at the northern end of the main street, Kreshchatik.* Overlooking the river and holding aloft a cross is a statue of Prince Vladimir, erected in 1853. The statue was cast in bronze by Klodt (famous for his horses on the Anichkov Bridge in Leningrad) after a design by Demut-Malinovsky. Prince Vladimir is shown in the dress of an ancient Russian warrior standing bareheaded in thanksgiving as he gazes at the water of the Dnieper below where he was instrumental in the mass baptism of his people. The statue stands 4·5 m (15 ft) high and weighs about 6 tons. The unusual chapel-like pedestal is covered with cast-iron plates. On the pedestal above the bas-relief depicting the baptism of Rus is the old seal of Kiev. The height of the statue and the pedestal together is 20·4 m (67 ft).

At the bottom of Volodimirska Girka is another monument dating from 1802 and commemorating the conversion of Russia to Christianity.

BOGDAN KHMELNITSKY MONUMENT *In the centre of Bogdan Khmelnitsky Square opposite St. Sophia's Cathedral and near the spot where the Kievites took their oath of loyalty to Russia in 1654.* Khmelnitsky (1593–1657) was the Cossack *hetman* who freed the Ukraine from the Poles and later subjected it to the Moscow State. The fine, rearing equestrian statue of him was cast in bronze by Mikeshin in 1888. It is 10·85 m (35 ft) high and so placed that it can be seen from three different directions. The mace Khmelnitsky holds is a symbol of his power as *hetman* and it points to the north, to Moscow.

TARAS SHEVCHENKO MONUMENT *In the park also bearing his name, in front of the University.* The statue is by Manizer and was unveiled in 1939.

IVAN FRANKO MONUMENT *Franko Square, near the Ivan Franko Theatre.* The statue of the writer and public figure was unveiled in 1956.

LENIN MONUMENT *Shevchenko Boulevard.* The statue is by Merkurov and was unveiled in 1946.

SCHORS MONUMENT. *At the crossing of Shevchenko Boulevard and Kominterna Street.* Nikolai Schors (1895–1919) was a Red Army commander who became a hero of the Civil War. The equestrian statue which stands 6·5 m (21 ft) high was made by Lysenko, Sukholodov and Borodai and was unveiled in 1954. The upper edge of the red granite pedestal bears a bronze cornice and a frieze depicting episodes from the history of the Red Army.

ARSENAL WORKERS' MONUMENT *at the crossing of Kirova Street and Sichneve Povstannya Street.* The cannon mounted on a pedestal of red granite was unveiled in 1922 to commemorate the workers of the Arsenal Plant who fell during the Civil War of 1917–18. There is another monument to these workers in Radyansky Park; it takes the form of a red granite urn hung with crepe and standing on a black marble pedestal which bears the inscription, "To the Eternal Glory of the Fighters for Freedom".

ASKOLD'S GRAVE AND WAR MEMORIAL. *These are located in one of the most beautiful parts of Kiev in the park which is also called Askold's Grave.* In 1809–1810 the architect Melinski built a rotunda where according to legend Askold, Prince of Kiev, was buried in 882. On the upper part of the park, near the rotunda, is the grave of an unknown warrior of World War II and as a memorial there stands a tall obelisk and an everburning torch. The obelisk stands 27 m (88 ft) high and the memorial was completed in 1957. A good motor road runs through the park.

VATUTIN MONUMENT *In Radyansky Park, Kirov Street.* General Nikolai Vatutin (1901–44) died heavily wounded in Kiev after the liberation of the city. The monument by Vuchetich was unveiled in 1948. The 4·7 m (16 ft) sculpture is of grey granite and stands over the General's grave. On the pedestal is an inscription reading, "To General Vatutin from the Ukrainian People".

PUSHKIN MONUMENT *In front of the entrance to Pushkin Park.* The bronze sculpture by A. Kovalyev stands 3·5 m (11ft) high and the total height of the monument is over 7 m (about 23 ft). The black granite pedestal carries an inscription, "To Pushkin from the Ukrainian People". The monument was unveiled in 1962.

✿ SHEVCHENKO OPERA AND BALLET THEATRE (founded in 1962) *Volodimirskaya Street 50.* This building was designed in 1901 by the architect Schretter. It seats 1650.

IVAN FRANKO UKRAINIAN DRAMA THEATRE *Franko Square 2.* Built in 1898.

LESYA UKRAINKA RUSSIAN DRAMA THEATRE *Lenin Street 5.* Lesya Ukrainka (1871–1913) was a great Ukrainian poetess.

MUSICAL COMEDY THEATRE *Chervonoarmiiskaya Street 51a.*

YOUTH THEATRE *Rosa Luxemburg Street 15/17.*

PUPPET THEATRE *Rustaveli Street 13.* This building was once a synagogue.

PHILHARMONIA CONCERT HALL *Kirov Street 16.* This was built in 1882 by Nikolayev as the Merchants' Hall.

ZHOVTNEVY (OCTOBER) PALACE OF CULTURE *Zhovtnevy Revolutsii Street 1.* Constructed in 1838–42 by Beretti as a School for Girls of Gentle Birth, this building with its classical colonnade stands on a hill top. It was restored and enlarged in 1953–57 and its hall, which can seat over 2000, is one of the largest in the capital and is used for concerts.

CIRCUS *Peremoghi Square.* Built 1958–60.

CINERAMA *Rustaveli Street 19*. Built in 1958, this was the first cinerama in the Soviet Union.

HIPPODROME RACECOURSE *Suvorovskaya Street 5*.

DYNAMO STADIUM *Kirov Street 3*. This was built in 1934–36 to accommodate 30,000 spectators. There is a restaurant.

STADIUM *Chervonoarmiiska Street 51b*. This occupies a territory of 53 hectares (130 acres) and the main stadium seats 60,000. Nearby is a Palace of Sport, opened in 1960 and called locally "Crystal Palace". With accommodation for 12,000 it is the largest covered arena in the Soviet Union.

SWIMMING POOL *Vozdukhflotskoye chaussée 32*.

ZOO (founded in 1908) *Brest-Litovskoye chaussée 80*.

ACADEMY OF SCIENCES BOTANICAL GARDEN *Vidubetska Street 11*.

FOMIN BOTANICAL GARDEN *Komintern Street 1*. Founded in 1841, these gardens cover 22 hectares (54 acres).

UKRAINIAN ECONOMIC EXHIBITION *Sorokorichya Zhovtnya Prospekt*. This is a permanent exhibition in the southern suburbs of the city. It is laid out in grounds of 300 hectares (750 acres), more than half of which is park land.

Kiev is lucky to have another beautiful stretch of natural park land close to the centre of the city. It runs along the hilly wooded slopes above the river. There are really a number of parks here, but they run into each other imperceptibly. The most northerly is Volodimirska Girka (Vladimir's Hill) Park where there is the St. Vladimir Monument and an open-air cinema seating 1500. Pionersky (Pioneer) Park is reached by a flight of steps from *Lenkomsomola Square* and contains amusements, a cinema and a concert platform. Pershotravnevy (First of May) Park was laid out in 1747–55 as the tsar's park adjoining the palace. There is a bandstand with 2000 seats, an open-air theatre, amusements and the Cuckoo Restaurant. Radyansky (Soviet) Park, laid out in the 19th century, is opposite the tsar's palace and contains a children's village and a playground. The last of the parks is called Askold's Grave. Lower down beside the river runs Park Lane, closed to motor traffic on summer evenings when it is usually crowded with pedestrians. In the autumn the local fruit and flower show is held here, near the statue of the horticulturist, Michurin. Also on Park Lane is an open-air theatre for 4000. Its amphitheatre makes use of the 19th century wall of Kiev fortress. Higher up the slope, but still inside the park area, runs a good motor road with an excellent view across the river. One can get on to it by driving from the clover-leaf at Paton Bridge along the embankment road and taking the first large left fork up the hill.

TRUKHANIV ISLAND in River Dnieper, and reached by a suspension bridge for pedestrians, opened in 1957. This is Kiev's most popular bathing beach.

PUSHKIN PARK (1899) *Brest-Litovskoye chaussée*. There are groves of beech, pine, birch and other trees.

LENKOMSOMOL PARK—*also on Brest-Litovskoye chaussée*. There is a monument to the young Communists of the 1920's. Boats for hire. Nearby is another park, the Park of the 22nd Party Congress, where there is an open-air theatre for 2000.

GOLOSEYEVO FOREST—*on the left of the main road leading to the Ukrainian Economic Exhibition*. There are lakes and ancient trees, and also a 160-hectare (400 acres) park with sports grounds and an open-air theatre.

CHILDREN'S RAILWAY *In the Syrets district of Kiev.* The engine and six coaches run for 3 km (2 miles) along a track that was opened in 1953. The railway is staffed by schoolchildren.

DNIEPER HOTEL AND RESTAURANT *Lenkomsomola Square, Kirova Street 2; tel: 29-65-69.*

MOSKVA HOTEL, RESTAURANT AND CAFE *In the skyscraper on Kalinina; tel: 9-00-15.*

INTOURIST HOTEL AND RESTAURANT *Lenin Street 26; tel: 5-11-21.*

MIR (PEACE) HOTEL AND RESTAURANT *Goloseyevsky Forest.*

DESNA HOTEL *Shevchenko Boulevard 3.*

LENINGRADSKAYA HOTEL AND RESTAURANT *Shevchenko Boulevard 4; tel: 5-71-01.*

UKRAINA HOTEL AND RESTAURANT *Shevchenko Boulevard 5; tel: 4-50-19.*

KIEV HOTEL AND RESTAURANT *Volodimirskaya Street 36.*

TEATRALNAYA HOTEL AND RESTAURANT *Lenin Street 17; tel: 5-50-45.*

ABKHAZIYA RESTAURANT *Kreshchatik 42.*

DYNAMO RESTAURANT *Kirov Street 3, at the Dynamo Stadium.*

LEIPZIG RESTAURANT *Volodimirskaya Street 30.* Specialises in German dishes.

SPORT RESTAURANT *Chervonoarmiiska Street 22.*

STOLICHNY RESTAURANT AND SELF-SERVICE CAFE *Kreshchatik 5.*

METRO RESTAURANT AND CAFE *Kreshchatik 19.*

RECORD RESTAURANT *Suvorovskaya Street 5.*

OSTROVOK (ISLAND) RESTAURANT *At the Economic Achievements Exhibition.*

Restaurants Open in Summer only:

POPLAVOK (FISHING FLOAT) RESTAURANT *Nabere-zhnoye chaussée.*

PRIBOY (SURF) RESTAURANT *Rechnoi Vokzal* (wharf).

CUCKOO RESTAURANT *Pershotravnevy Park.*

RIVIERA RESTAURANT *Parkovyi Pereulok.*

AUTOMAT SELF-SERVICE CAFE *Sverdlov Street 30.*

MILK BAR *Kreshchatik 15.*

CHERVONI MAK (RED POPPY) CAFE *Kreshchatik 8.*

SNEZHINKA (SNOWFLAKE) CAFE *Kreshchatik, near Tolstoy Square.*

POLISH LEGATION *Karl Liebknecht Street 28.*

CZECH LEGATION *Polupanov Street 3.*

G.P.O. *Kreshchatik 22.*

MAIN DEPARTMENT STORE *Lenin Street 2, at the corner of Kreshchatik.*

PODARKI (GIFTS) SHOP *Karl Marx Street 9 and at the corner of Kreshchatik and Shevchenko Boulevard.*

JEWELLER'S *Kreshchatik 19 and 52.*

PORCELAIN *Kreshchatik 34.*

UKRAINIAN HANDICRAFTS *Chervonoarmiiska Street 23 and Kirova Street 93*

DOM KNIGI (BOOKSHOP) *Kreshchatik 30.*

BESSARABKA COVERED MARKET *Shevchenko Boulevard.* The building designed by Gai was put up in 1910.

MARKET *Vorovsky Street 17.*

TAXI RANKS. Central—*Chervonoarmiiska Street 7/18, and also Peremoghi, Vokzalnaya Square and Chervon Square,*

✿ Motel (under construction) *in Darnitsa.*

Camping Site *2 km (1¼ miles) from town, on the left side of the Kiev-Kharkov road, in Darnitsa region.* Follow the arrows carefully from the roundabout on the Kharkov road; the site is on the left side of R. Dnieper on Chernigov Chausêe. Café, self-service kitchen, showers, laundry.

Filling Station *near the Exhibition of Economic Achievements. Diesel oil is available. Open 8–5; closed on Sundays.*

Filling Station No. 8 *by Paton Bridge, on the right bank of R. Dnieper. Open 8–4; closed on Sundays.*

Service Station *Lenin Street 46*

★

In Lukianovka, in the suburbs of Kiev, near the site of the old Jewish cemetery, is Babi Yar where in the autumn of 1941 over 100,000 people (mostly Jewish) were killed and buried in a tank trap. Yevgeni Yevtushenko wrote a poem about the massacre including these lines:

"Wild grasses rustle over Babi Yar.
The trees look down sternly, like judges.
Everything here shrieks silently
And, taking off my cap,
I feel how gradually I am turning grey".

(trans. Max Hayward)

It is planned to place a memorial tablet here, and to turn the whole area into a park.

Mouth of R. Desna 1 hr by motor-boat up River Dnieper is as pot ideal for swimming, sunbathing and fishing.

Zhukiv Island *20 km (12½ miles) down River Dnieper, on the left side of the river.* Nearer the right bank lies Rybachy Island which has been famed for its fish since the 16th century; the Lakes Koncha and Zaspa form a State Fish Reservation. A good road runs back to Kiev.

Puscha-Voditsa *20 km (12½ miles) from the centre of the city.* Here is the Ukraine's biggest natural park, covering 750 hectares (1875 acres). Part of it used as a holiday resort and there are many sanatoria.

Novo-Petrivtsy. This village stands near the point where the Soviet troops crossed River Dnieper prior to liberating Kiev; there is an impressive war memorial-museum, which was opened in 1958 on the site of the HQ of the Red Army's 1st Ukrainian Front in the autumn of 1943. Tanks, guns and trenches remain there and on the monument is the inscription, "Glory to the Liberators of Kiev". In the village of Novo-Petrivtsy itself is a monument to the commander, General Nikolai Vatutin. The area can be reached by river or by road.

Vyshgorod—This village near Novo-Petrivtsy is the site of Kiev Hydro-power Station, under construction at the time of writing. When the dam is finished, the reservoir it forms will stretch back 100 km (60 miles) and will average 15 km (9 miles) across. The shore of the new Kiev Sea will form a recreation area.

The power station will have a capacity of over 500,000 kilowatts but the unusual thing about it is that about a mile upstream will be a hydro-accumulator station run on pumped-storage. Its capacity of 200,000 kilowatts will be brought into use in the evenings to counteract the increased demand for power then. The stored water will flow into the main stream and then pass through the main dam.

Kaniv—This town is 149 km (93 miles) downriver from Kiev. The way passes pretty Ukrainian villages including Tripillya where a settlement of primitive man of IVth–IInd millennia B.C. was discovered giving rise to the term Tripolyan Culture. Another village of historical interest is Vitachiv which was once a strongly fortified point where merchant vessels assembled in armed convoys to sail on down the river to the Black Sea. Kaniv itself was first mentioned in 1149 and its St. George's Church dates from the time of Kiev Rus. The Cathedral of the Assumption was built in the early 12th century. The town's chief claim to fame however is that 4 km (2½ miles) away is the burial place of Taras Shevchenko, who is often simply called Kobzar which is the Ukrainian for "bard". The celebrated poet visited this place in 1859 and thought of settling down here but his plans never materialised and he died in St. Petersburg in March, 1861, and was buried there. Shortly after the funeral, his friends, carrying out his last wish, conveyed his remains to Kaniv where he was reburied in May, 1861, on the picturesque slopes of the right bank of the Dnieper.

The grave and the surrounding area of 1360 hectares (3400 acres) of woodland now form a national park. The bronze monument to Shevchenko by Manizer was unveiled in 1939. There is also a two-storey museum where in ten halls are displayed documents, pictures and sculptures connected with Shevchenko, copies of his publications and some of his water colours.

✿ TARAS'S HILL HOTEL AND RESTAURANT.

ROAD FOUR

CHERNOVTSY—KHMELNITSKY VINNITSA—ZHITOMIR

CHERNOVTSY

Khotin · Kamenets-Podolsky · Shatava · Dunaevtsi

KHMELNITSKY

Medzhibozh · Letichev · Litin

VINNITSA

Komsomolskaya · Berdichev

ZHITOMIR

(see Road Three, page 168)

CHERNOVTSY

Ukrainian: Chernivtsi,
Rumanian: Cernauti,
German: Czernowitz
Population: 146,000 (1959)

The town stretches for 12 km ($7\frac{1}{2}$ miles) along the banks of the River Prut. The whole territory is famous for its beech-trees (pronounced "buk" in Russian) and from these it gets its alternative name of Bukovina.

The town's name was first recorded in 1408, and it was founded at the beginning of the 15th century near another small town, Chern, only the remains of which are to be seen today. Earlier, in the 10th and 11th centuries, the territory was part of Kiev Rus, and in the 12th and 13th centuries part of the Volyn Princedom. In the first half of the 13th century the place was invaded by Tartars and Mongolians who stayed there for over 100 years. From the middle of the 14th century it was a part of the state of Moldavia, so that from the 16th century onwards it was indirectly under Turkish rule. After the Russian–Turkish peace treaty of 1774 the territory passed to Austria. Chernovtsy became a town in 1786 and the capital of Bukovina in 1849. The area went to Rumania in 1918 and finally to Russia in 1940, after which it was united with the Ukrainian republic.

Many of Chernovtsy's buildings were designed by Austrian architects. Those in Tsentralnaya Square date mostly from the 19th century. The town's main street Lenin Street (formerly known as High Street), is one of the oldest in the town; another is Russkaya Street which runs for 6 km (4 miles) from Tsentralnaya Square. Again, most of the buildings on the street are 19th century.

Chernovtsy has a university, founded in 1875, and a medical institute. Its main industries are connected with food, textiles and machine building.

The population includes many Ukrainians and Jews. One can even hear Jewish spoken on the streets—an unusual thing in large Soviet towns.

✿ CATHEDRAL *Lenin Prospekt.*

CHURCH *Russkaya Street.*

CATHOLIC CHURCH *Lenin Prospekt.*

CHURCH OF SAINT NICHOLAS *Volgogradskaya Street.* Built of wood, this is the oldest church in Chernovtsy.

✿ RATHAUS *Tsentralnaya Square.* This building dates from 1843–47, and is now used by the Local Executive Committee.

LOCAL MUSEUM *Kobilyanskaya Street 28. Open 10–5; closed on Wednesdays.*

KOBILYANSKAYA LITERATURE MUSEUM *Dmitrov Street 5. Open 10–4; closed on Tuesdays.* The Ukrainian writer, Olga Kobilyanskaya (1861–1942), lived here for more than 50 years.

FEDKOVICH LITERARY MUSEUM *Kotsubinsky Street 2. Open 10–5; closed on Tuesdays.* This building in University Park in the suburbs of Chernovtsy was built in 1864–82 by the Czech architect Josef Hlávka (1831–1908), and was formerly the residence of the Bukovina Metropolitans. It is in a mixed style, showing Byzantine and Mauritanian elements. Damaged in 1944, the main part of the building is still under restoration. Yuri Fedkovich (1834–88) was a Ukrainian writer who lived here at one time. The Museum occupies five rooms of the building; some faculties of the University are also housed here. In the park there is a monument to the architect Hlávka.

ЧЕРНОВЦЫ

CHERNOVTSY

1 and 2 Hotel and Restaurant

a Sovietskaya pl. b Tsentral'naya pl.
c Leninskii pr., d Russkaya ul.

PLANETARIUM *Gorky Street 12.* The Planetarium stands in the grounds of the Local Museum.

LENIN MONUMENT *Tsentralnaya Square.* The monument was unveiled in 1951.

VICTORY OBELISK *Sovietskaya Square.* It is in this square that parades and mass meetings take place. The 22 m (73 ft) high granite obelisk designed by Petrashevich was unveiled in 1946 to commemorate the victory of World War II.

TANK MONUMENT *Gagarin Square.* This tank on a stone block was the first to enter the town on the occasion of its liberation in 1944.

MEMORIAL OBELISK *Kalinin Park.* This obelisk commemorates the officers who fell here during the Second World War.

KALININ PARK *Dzerzhinsky Street 1.* This park, opened in the 1830's, is the town's largest. It contains an open air theatre seating 2200, and at the entrance to the park stands a monument to Kalinin which was unveiled in 1956.

UNIVERSITY BOTANICAL GARDEN *Fedkovich Street 11, near Kalinin Park.* This garden was founded in 1877 and now coveres 3·7 hectares (9¼ acres).

DYNAMO STADIUM *Leningradskaya Street 1.*

KOBILYANSKY UKRAINIAN MUSIC AND DRAMA THEATRE *Teatralnaya Square 1.* This theatre was built in 1904–05 by the Viennese architects Fellner and Helmer who also designed the opera houses in Vienna and Odessa. The façade is decorated with figures from Greek mythology, and the walls with busts of Goethe, Schiller and Beethoven, among others.

PHILHARMONIA CONCERT HALL *Pobeda Square 10.*

KIEV HOTEL AND RESTAURANT *Lenin Prospekt 11; tel: 39–10.* There is an Intourist Bureau here, tel: 51–48.

RADYANSKA HOTEL *Universitetskaya Street 34.*

CHERVONA BUKOVINA HOTEL AND CAFE *Tsentralnaya Square 7; tel: 40-05.*

DNIESTER HOTEL *Kobilyanskaya Street.*

MOTEL AND CAMPING SITE *Novoselitskaya Street 3½ km (1¼ miles) east of Chernovtsy.* The site has a beach and a cafê.

G.P.O. *Pochtovaya Street.*

CENTRAL DEPARTMENT STORE *Lenin Prospekt.*

BOOKSHOP *Sovietskaya Street.*

ARTS AND CRAFTS *Tsentralnaya Square.* The town is famed for its woodcarving.

FILLING STATION *Bolshaya Storozhenetskaya Street near Konovskaya Street.*

SERVICE STATION *Novoselitskaya Street 2 km (1¼ miles) east of Chernovtsy; tel: 54-96. Open daily 9–5.*

———— ★ ————

GORA TSETSINO *7 km (4½ miles) out of town.* On the top of this mountain, which is 541 m (1800 ft) high, are the remains of a 14th century fortress.

GORECHA. This is another suburb of Chernovtsy, on the high bank of the River Prut. The remains of a monastery church built in 1767 with money donated by Catherine the Great stands here, and there are some frescoes to be seen in the church. By the river at this point there is a sandy bathing beach.

KHOTIN

Pronounced "hotin"

Khotin was perhaps named after Khotizon, a tsar of ancient times. Another possibility is that the name is derived from the Russian for "we want", and that this gave the Turks the idea of renaming the Moldavian Tigin, Benderi, meaning "I want".

The town stands on the right bank of the River Dniester. The first fortifications were built in the 14th century by the Genoese to guard the trade route. Later it changed hands several times between the Moldavians, the Turks and the Poles. In 1718 the Turks reinforced the fortress with the help of French engineers. Khotin became Russian with the rest of Bessarabia in 1812, but was in Rumanian hands from 1918 to 1940. The town's industries are leather work and food.

✿ TEAROOM *On the street running parallel to the main road and lying to the left of it.*

At the entrance to the town is a map, and tourists are asked to keep to the main road.

KAMENETS-PODOLSKY

Population: 38,200

This extraordinarily lovely old town is situated on either side of the winding ravine through which the River Smotrich flows at the base of precipitous grey cliffs. Its records go back to the 12th century, when it was part of the Volin Princedom. It was ruined by the Turks and the Lithuanians, then became a Polish stronghold, and has been in Russian hands since 1795. Local industry produces machinery, textiles, tobacco and food products, and the town has agricultural and teachers' training colleges.

✿ TURKISH FORTRESS *Muzeinyi Spusk, on an elevated position in the west of the town.* Built between 14th and the 17th centuries, the fortress was used as a prison in the 19th century. Now it houses the historical museum; entry tickets are on sale in the Dominican Monastery. Opposite the fortress the Turkish Bridge crosses the River Smotrich.

The following are to be found in Staryi Gorod (old town):

TOWN BASTIONS—15th–16th century.

RUSSIAN GATES—16th century.

RATHAUS—16th century.

✿ SAINT NICHOLAS CHURCH—14th century.

DOMINICAN MONASTERY—14th–18th century.

SAINT PETER AND SAINT PAUL ROMAN CATHOLIC CHURCH—16th century. The minaret dates from the time of the Turkish domination from 1672 and 1699.

ROMAN CATHOLIC CATHEDRAL—16th to 18th century.

WOODEN CHURCH—1799.

✿ SHEVCHENKO DRAMA THEATRE *Shevchenko Street.*

✿ BOTANICAL GARDEN *Leningradskaya Street.*

LENIN PARK *Shevchenko Street.*

✿ HOTEL *Shevchenko Street.*

UKRAINA RESTAURANT *Kotovsky Street.*

SHATAVA

✿ To the right of the main road stands a church with an interesting dome.

DUNAYEVTSI

✿ RUSSIAN ORTHODOX CHURCH *Shevchenko Street.*

✿ TEAROOM *Shevchenko Street.*

✿ FILLING STATION *In the centre of the town, at the bus station.*

KHMELNITSKY

Known as Proskurov until 1954
Population: 62,000

The town was renamed after Bogdan Khmelnitsky in 1954 to commemorate the 300th anniversary of the Ukraine's union with Russia.

It is situated in the fertile region of Podolia, where the River Ploskaya joins the River Bug.

It was first mentioned in writing in 1433. Four hundred years later, when Nicholas I was passing through the town one autumn day with 12 yoke of oxen to pull his carriage, he scarcely managed to get through the mud. Today, besides many provincial buildings typical of the last century, there is an impressive new building of the House of Soviets in the town centre. The main thoroughfare, which is lined with new buildings, is 25th-Oktober Street.

The town contains factories for machine building, food processing and the manufacture of synthetic fur.

✿ RUSSIAN ORTHODOX CHURCH *In the central market place.* This church dates from the 19th century.

✿ LOCAL MUSEUM *Rosa Luxemburg Street 66.* There is a 1941–45 War Memorial, and on Vokzalnaya Square a monument to Bogdan Khmelnitsky.

✿ MUSIC AND DRAMA THEATRE *Gagarin Street, close to the House of Soviets.*

DYNAMO STADIUM *25th-Oktober Street.*

PHILHARMONIA CONCERT HALL *Kotovsky Street.*

✿ KOTSUBINSKY PARK AND FRANKO PARK *Both have their main entrances on 25th-Oktober Street and lie beside the rivers.*

✿ PODOLYE HOTEL AND RESTAURANT (INTOURIST) *Gagarin Street, near the House of Soviets.*

TSENTRALNYI HOTEL AND RESTAURANT *25th-Oktober Street 15.* Khmelnitsky cutlets are a local speciality.

✿ G. P. O. *Lenin Street.*

GIFT SHOP AND JEWELLER'S *25th-October Street 31.*

MEDZHIBOZH

The town lies to the left of the main road, but is not open to tourists. From the turning which leads to it, however, the 16th century Turkish fortress can be seen clearly. There is also an Orthodox Church in Medzhibozh.

LETICHEV

Close to the main road are the ruins of a monastery, and further back on the left stands a church.

LITIN

✿ LITERATURE AND ART MUSEUM *Svoboda Street 17.*

✿ HOTEL *On the main street.*

TEAROOM *On the main street.*

VINNITSA

Population: 121,000 (1959)

The town stands on the South Bug river. It was founded in the 14th century and first belonged to Lithuania, becoming Polish in 1569, and Russian in 1793. At the beginning of the 17th century the first stone houses, a catholic church, and a school were built in the centre of the town and surrounded by a stone wall. The historical museum and the archives are now there.

Vinnitsa has pedagogical and medical institutes, and its main thoroughfare is Lenin Street. The town is noted for its food processing and its light industry; it has electro-technical and fertiliser factories, and in the surrounding region sugar-beet is both grown and refined.

✿ DOMINICAN MONASTERY *Lenin Street.* This monastery was built in 1634, but was converted in 1774 into a Russian Orthodox church, where religious services are still held today.

MURI JESUIT MONASTERY. Built in the 17th–18th centuries, the building originally consisted of a fortified monastery-house. Now only the ruins remain.

CAPUCHIN MONASTERY *Lenin Street.* This monastery was founded in 1760 and is now closed.

SAINT GEORGE'S CHURCH *Starye Kutora.* This wooden church was built in 1726.

LOCAL MUSEUM *In "Muri", entrance from Volodarsky Street 6.* There is a kremlin made of sugar on display in this museum.

KOTSUBINSKY'S HOUSE *Deputatskaya Street 13.* Where the Ukrainian writer Kotsubinsky was born and lived as a child.

LYALYA RATUSHNAYA MUSEUM. This museum is in the house of the young local partisan who died bravely during World War II. Her mother still lives there. There is another similar museum beside the South Bug river.

In KOZITSKY CHILDREN'S PARK there is an obelisk commemorating World War II, and a monument to those who fell during the 1917–19 Civil War. Another monument of granite on the left bank of the river commemorates the victory of the Cossack Colonel Ivan Bogun over the Poles in 1651. It was unveiled in 1954.

The town park has a summer theatre seating 3000, a stadium, and permanent exhibition pavilions.

SADOVSKY MUSICAL AND DRAMA THEATRE *Dzerzhinsky Street 13.*

PHILHARMONIA CONCERT HALL

UKRAINA HOTEL AND RESTAURANT *Lenin Street.* The Intourist office is in this hotel—tel: 46–56.

VINNITSA HOTEL AND RESTAURANT *Lenin Street.*

G.P.O. *Kozitsky Street, where it crosses Lenin Street.*

FILLING STATION AND REPAIR STATION *Kievskaya Street 26.*

CAMPING SITE *10 km (6½ miles) north of the town.* This is one of the best of its kind in the Soviet Union, pleasantly situated in a pinewood, with good service and a cafê. The site is about 1 km (½ mile) from Hitler's wartime headquarters. The construction of these headquarters was finished in June 1942, and Hitler and Goering were there for some time in 1943. Then the retreating Germans blew up everything. There were underground living rooms, a cinema, a garage and a dining hall,—now only Hitler's swimming pool can be seen among the distorted blocks of reinforced concrete and the remains of the asphalted roads.

5 km (3 miles) before coming in to Vinnitsa from Khmelnitsky is the village of Vyshenky. 1 km (½ mile) from the main road is the museum of the famous Russian surgeon, Nikolai Pirogov, in the house where he spent the last 20 years of his life.

KOMSOMOLSKAYA

TEAROOM *On the main street.*

BERDICHEV

Population: 53,000 (1959)

Berdichev stands on the River Gnilopyat, a tributary of the Dnieper. It has been known since the 14th century, and there are some ancient underground tunnels running beneath the town. After 1842 it grew in importance as a Ukrainian trading centre. Until the Second World War the population was predominantly Jewish.

The town is situated in the centre of a sugar-growing area, but apart from the food industry there are also machine building, textile and furniture industries.

Berdichev has a teachers' training college.

BAREFOOT CARMELITE MONASTERY. This monastery was founded in 1627, supressed in 1864 and is now in ruins.

TRINITY CHURCH *Zagrebelya.* This church dates from the end of the 18th century.

RUSSIAN ORTHODOX CHURCH OF SAINT NICHOLAS *Karl Liebknecht Street 7/12.* The church was built in 1908; religious services are still held there.

SAINT BARBARA'S ROMAN CATHOLIC CHURCH *Karl Liebknecht Street.*

In 1850 Honoré de Balzac was married in this church to a local lady of noble birth, Evelina Ganskaya. Her family estate lay in the village of Verkhovnya, a little to the east of Berdichev. The house is now an agricultural college but one room is preserved as a Balzac museum.

THE BUILDING OF THE MAIN SYNAGOGUE *Poperechnaya Street.* This now houses a textile factory.

16th–17th CENTURY FORTRESS *Karl Liebknecht Street.*

LOCAL MUSEUM *Komsomolskaya Street 23, in the monastery grounds.*

SHEVCHENKO PARK *Karl Liebknecht Street.*

HOTEL *Lenin Street.*

UKRAINA RESTAURANT *Karl Liebknecht Street 11.*

G.P.O. *Sverdlov Street.*

ZHITOMIR

See Road 3, on page 168.

ROAD FIVE

CHERNOVTSY—KISHINEV—ODESSA

CHERNOVTSY

(see Road Four, page 187)

Boyany · Lipkany · Brichany · Yedintsy · Rishkani
Beltsy · Orgeyev · Leusheny · Kotovskoye

KISHINEV

Aneny · Bendery · Tiraspol

ODESSA

CHERNOVTSY

See Road 4, on page 187.

BOYANY

✿ There is a church of no particular historical interest on the main street.

✿ TEAROOM *On the main street.*

LIPKANY

✿ ROMAN CATHOLIC CHURCH.

✿ TEAROOM *Sadovaya Street.*

BRICHANY

Population: 10,000

This town, picturesquely situated in the slopes of the hills, is the centre of an agricultural region.

In the town's records it is written that on 20th June, 1891, there was an extraordinary storm lasting for an hour and a quarter when hailstones fell the size of a hen's egg.

Brichany produces dairy products and vodka.

YEDINTSY

✿ RESTAURANT *In the main street.*

CAFE *In the main street.*

The rolling open country of this part of Moldavia is reminiscent of Salisbury Plain.

RISHKANY

This village stands on the River Kopochanka which has a series of small ponds used for fish breeding.

Fruit is dried here, and cheese and wine are made.

BELTSY

Population: 67,000 (1959)

The town stands on the River Reut, which floods the district in the spring and autumn, and gives the town its name of "bog".

The history of Beltsy goes back to the 15th century, and in the 1750's it became known for its permanent fair. Now it is the second most important Moldavian city. It has a teachers' training college, and its industries are concerned with wine, food and sugar refining.

✿ RUSSIAN ORTHODOX CHURCH *Leningradskaya Street.*

✿ There is an obelisk in memory of the heroes of the Second World War.

✿ MOLDAVIAN AND RUSSIAN MUSICAL AND DRAMA THEATRE *Lenin Street.*

✿ MOLDAVIA HOTEL *Dostoyevsky Street 12.*

DNIESTER RESTAURANT *Lenin Street.*

After leaving Beltsy the road follows the valley of the Reut river and then slowly climbs the Bessarabian Hills to Kordy (429·5 m—1408 ft), their highest point.

ORGEYEV

Population: 12,000

The town of Orgeyev stands beside the River Reut. It was first mentioned in writing in 1400, but the ruins of an earlier Dacian fortress known as Pietrodava, stand near the town. The fortress was also called Orkhey ("fortress"), and from the end of the 13th century the Turkish governor of the northern part of Bessarabia resided there. One hundred years later Orgeyev became the capital of the Moldavian princedom. In 1812 it passed to Russia.

БЕЛЬЦЫ
BEL'TSY

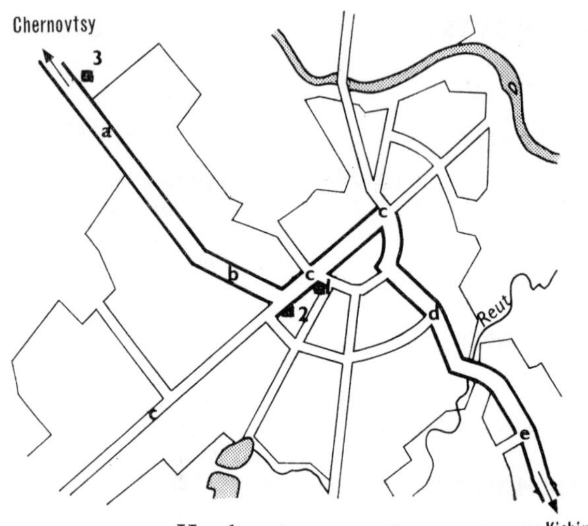

1. Hotel 2. Restaurant
3. Filling Station

a Ul. Artema, c Ul. Leningradskaya,
b Ul. Kotovsk, d Ul. Kishinevskaya,
e Ul. Orgeyevskaya

Local industry is concerned with tobacco, textiles and food products.

SAINT DMITRY'S CATHEDRAL *Kishinyevsky Proyezd.* This cathedral was built by the Moldavian Gospodar ("ruler"), Vasilyi Lupa, who ruled Moldavia between 1634 and1654.

VASILYI LUPA STATUE *In a square near the Cathedral.*

LENIN MONUMENT *Lenin Prospekt.*

PUSHKIN OPEN-AIR THEATRE *In Pushkin Park.*

STADIUM.

HOTEL *Krasnoarmeiskaya Street.*

VESNA (SPRING) RESTAURANT *Main Street, which is the road running through the town.*

LEUSHENY

Pronounced lay-oo-sheni

Leusheny lies on the Soviet side of the Rumanian–U.S.S.R. border, on the Bucharest motor road.

TEAROOM.

FILLING STATION.

KOTOVSKOYE

This village was formerly called Gancheshti, but was later renamed after the Civil War hero Kotovsky who was born here in 1889. Kotovsky's father worked as a mechanic in a local distillery. Local industry is mostly concerned with food production.

Kotovsky Museum.

Kotovsky Monument.

Eating House.

KISHINEV

(Pronounced Kishinyov)
Rumanian: Chisinau
Population: 214,000 (1959)

The name of the capital of Moldavia is supposed to come from Kishla Noue ("kishla" means "sheepfold"). The city was founded in 1420, and was for a long time the property of the Holy Sepulchre Monastery and it is sometimes thought that the name might have come from the Turkish word for "monastery village".

The city stands on the River Bik. It has an average summer temperature of 20–23°C (68–74°F) and is warm in in the autumn.

In 1812, when Moldavia was united with Russia, there were only 7000 people living in Kishinev. The population decreased again when from 6th–8th April 1903 there was a severe Jewish pogrom, but it has since increased greatly.

Kishinev is divided into two parts, the old town with small, winding streets down by the River Bik, and the new town, which occupies the upper part of the territory beginning from Lenin Prospekt, which was formerly called Alexandrovskaya Street after Tsar Alexander II. In this part of the town the streets are better planned and the houses, which are mostly one-storey buildings, were the private mansions of merchants and businessmen.

Kishinev was in Rumanian hands from 1918 until 1940 and during World War II 76 per cent of the residential buildings were destroyed. In 1953 the 3·5 km (2¼ mile) long Lenin Prospekt was reconstructed and office blocks of three and five storeys were put up. The building with a statue of Mercury (the god of trade) on the façade is the State Bank. The central part of the Prospekt, between Pushkinskaya Street and Gogolevskaya Street was extended to five times its original width and was called Pobeda (Victory) Square. A monument to Lenin was erected, and it became the Red Square of Kishinev, where parades and demonstrations take place. The new Moldavian government building is under construction in this square.

The suburbs of Kishinev, especially Benderskaya and Skulyanskaya, have become the industrial regions of the capital and account for half Moldavia's industry. The food industry is the most important, but there are also factories for the tobacco, textiles and machine building industries. A new part of the city was built in the suburbs after the war. Kishinev has a branch of the U.S.S.R. Academy of Sciences (opened 1961), some scientific research institutes, a university with eight faculties and 7000 students, medical, agricultural and pedagogical institutes, and a conservatoire.

Russian Orthodox Cathedral of the Nativity *Lenin Prospekt, opposite the Lenin Monument in the city centre.* The cathedral was built in 1836. The cathedral's belltower (1840) was designed by architect Zaushkevich, who was also responsible for the Victory Arch nearby. Originally known as Holy Gate, the arch is decorated with 16 Corinthian columns and supports the town clock. The big bell weighs almost 7 tons and was cast from melted-down Turkish guns captured during the Russo-Turkish wars. It was only renamed Victory Arch after World War II, when commemorative plaques were added.

Mazarakievskaya Church of the Nativity of the Virgin *In the old part of the town.* This church, built in 1152, is called after a Greek, Vasilyi Mazaraki, who donated the money for its building. He vowed he would do so

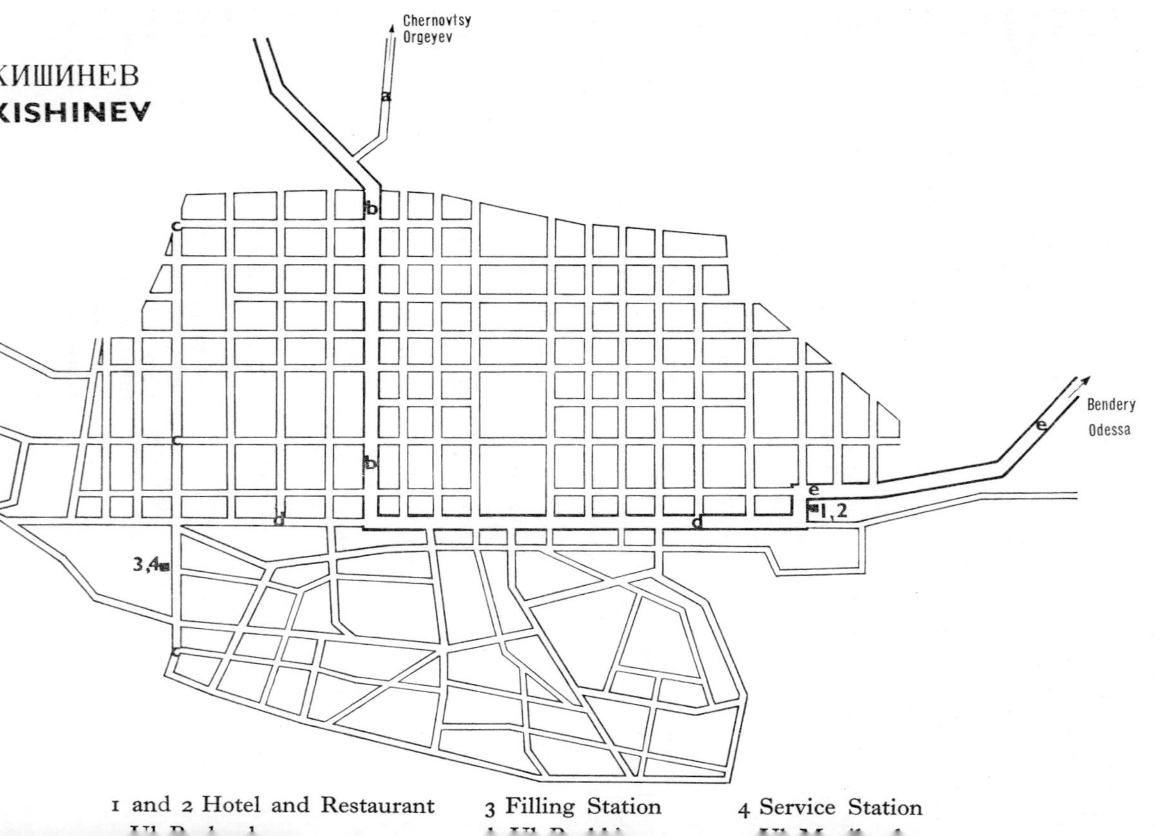

1 and 2 Hotel and Restaurant 3 Filling Station 4 Service Station

if his innocence was proved for he had been in trouble because he was a Christian in the service of the Turkish Sultan. The walls of the church are 1·4 m (4 ft 6 in.) thick.

SYNAGOGUE *Near Armyanskaya Street.*

PUSHKIN MUSEUM AND PUSHKIN'S HOUSE *Antonovskaya Street. Open 11–6; closed on Mondays.* Pushkin lived in exile in Kishinev between 1820 and 1823, and it was here that he began to write "Eugene Onegin".

FINE ARTS MUSEUM *Lenin Prospekt 115. Closed on Tuesdays.* The 5000 exhibits are displayed in 14 halls, and they include Russian art dating from the end of the 18th to the beginning of the 20th century, and also Soviet, Moldavian, Western European (16th to 19th centuries), and applied art. The Western European section has examples of Italian, Dutch, Flemish and German masters.

LOCAL MUSEUM *Pirogov Street 82. Open 12–7; closed on Wednesdays.* The museum, founded in 1889, is located in a house built in 1905 in Mauritanian style; it has a good collection of carpets and national costumes.

ISKRA MUSEUM *Podolskaya Street 39. Open 11–6; closed on Wednesdays. Iskra* (spark) was the name of the first Bolshevik newspaper, published illegally here in 1901–02 by the Social Democratic Party.

KOTOVSKY AND SERGEI LAZO MUSEUM *Komsomolskaya Street 31. Open 11–6; closed on Tuesdays.* These were heroes of the Civil War, both born in Moldavia.

LENIN MONUMENT *Pobeda Square, just opposite the Cathedral.* This 12 m (40 ft) high monument is by Merkurov and was unveiled in 1949.

8*

KOTOVSKY MONUMENT *Kotovsky Square.* This equestrian statue by the Moldavian sculptors Dubinovsky and Kitaika was unveiled in 1954. Grigory Kotovsky (1881–1925) was a hero of the Civil War, born in Moldavia, in the village now called Kotovskoye after him.

STEFAN THE GREAT MONUMENT *At the entrance to Pushkin Park where Gogol Street crosses Lenin Prospekt.* Stefan was called "the Great" despite his small stature, for his victories over the Turks. He was Moldavian Gospodar (ruler) between 1457 and 1504, and during that time the country remained independent. This monument by Plamadeala was unveiled in 1927.

PUSHKIN MONUMENT *In Pushkin Park.* Unveiled in 1885, this bust is by Opekushin who designed the Pushkin statue in Moscow.

KOMSOMOL MONUMENT *Molodezh Prospekt.* This 15 m (46 ft) high statue is by the sculptor Dubinovsky and the architect Naumov. During World War II this part of the town was the region of the Jewish ghetto.

MOLDAVIA OPERA HOUSE *Lenin Prospekt 79.*

PUSHKIN MUSIC AND DRAMA THEATRE *In the same building as the Opera House.* All performances here are in Moldavian.

CHEKHOV RUSSIAN DRAMA THEATRE *28th-June Street.* This theatre used to be a synagogue.

PHILHARMONIA CONCERT HALL *At the corner of Komsomolskaya Street.* Performances are given by symphony orchestras, the famous Doina choir, the Zhok National Dance Ensemble, the Fluerash Orchestra of National Music.

PUPPET THEATRE *In the Likurich (glow-worm) Theatre, Fontanaya Street 7, at the corner of Kotovsky Street.*

YOUTH THEATRE *At the same address as the Puppet Theatre.*

✿ PUSHKIN PARK *In the centre of the town.* This Park is famous for its Writers' Walk with statues of Rumanian and Moldavian classical writers. The main gates of the park are on Lenin Prospekt.

KOMSOMOLSKOYE OZERO (YOUNG COMMUNIST LEAGUE LAKE). Here there is a bathing beach and a boat hire station. An impressive flight of 250 steps with waterfalls leads down to the water. In the park is an open-air theatre for 7000 and also a parachute tower, a dance floor and other attractions. There are two restaurants, the Otdykh (rest) and the Chaika (seagull)—the latter on a floating raft. The park covers 96 hectares (240 acres).

MOLDAVIAN EXHIBITION OF AGRICULTURAL AND INDUSTRIAL ACHIEVEMENTS *On the banks of Komsomolskoye Ozero.*

BOTANICAL GARDENS *Boyukansky Spusk.*

RESPUBLIKANSKY STADIUM *Benderskaya Street.* The stadium seats 30,000 people.

✿ KISHINEV HOTEL AND RESTAURANT *Negruzzi Boulevard 7; tel: 47-18.*

MOLDOVA HOTEL AND RESTAURANT *Lenin Prospekt 81a.*

DNIESTER CAFE *Komsomolskaya Street 56.*

DRUZHBA (FRIENDSHIP) CAFE *Lenin Prospekt 62.* A national dish worth trying is "mititeyi", small sausages containing spice and onions.

CAMPING SITE *27 km (17 miles) north of Kishinev.*

✿ G.P.O. *Lenin Prospekt 134.*

KOLHOZNYI RYNOK *At the corner of Benderskaya Street and Lenin Prospekt.* This newly-built market in the centre of the town sells peasant ware and national handicrafts as well as food.

DEPARTMENT STORE *Lenin Prospekt 136, at the corner of Pushkinskaya Street.*

PODARKI (GIFT) SHOP *Komsomolskaya Street, at the corner of Lenin Prospekt.*

JEWELLER'S *Lenin Prospekt 85.*

COMMISSION SHOP *Pushkin Street 36.*

MAIN TAXI RANKS *Gogol Street, at the corner of Lenin Prospekt, Zhukovskaya Street, at the corner of Lenin Prospekt* and *by the hotels and the railway station.*

✿ SERVICE STATION *Mogilevsky Street 23, at the main taxi garage.*

FILLING STATION *On the road from the town to Odessa, Gagarin Prospekt.* 12 km ($7\frac{1}{2}$ miles) from Kishinev, in the valley of the River Bik, work is now in progress on the Kishinev Sea, a reservoir covering 900 hectares (2250 acres).

ANENY

✿ There is a tearoom by the main road in this large village on the road to Odessa.

BENDERY

Population: 58,000 (1960)

The town stands on the River Dniester. In Slav chronicles the town was known as Tungati. The Genoese built a fortress, then known as Tigin, in the town in the 16th century. Tigin shared the fate of the rest of Moldavia and fell under the Turks, who gave the town its present name which in Turkish means "I want". In 1708 the Turks enlarged the Genoese citadel and surrounded it with an eight-bastioned wall. During the several Russo-Turkish wars it passed from one side to the other, finally becoming Russian in 1812. The fortress was abandoned in 1897, and is now closed to the public. Like Kishinev, the town was later under Rumanian rule and passed back to Russia in 1940.

Today Bendery manufactures textiles and food products.

CATHEDRAL *Lenin Street.*

SYNAGOGUE *Suvorov Street.*

LOCAL MUSEUM *Dzerzhinsky Street.* There is a monument to the 55th Podolsk Regiment who helped drive theTurks out of Bessarabia.

OPEN-AIR THEATRE.

MOLDAVIA HOTEL AND RESTAURANT *Lenin Street.* The Intourist road runs through the outskirts of the town.

TIRASPOL

Population: 62,000 (1960)

The name Tiraspol means "the town on the Dniester". Tiraspol was founded in 1795 and was a trade centre on the way to Odessa from Kishinev. Small merchant houses remain in the town. Between 1929 and 1940, when Kishinev and other parts of Moldavia belonged to Rumania, Tiraspol was the capital of the country. Now it is Moldavia's third town, both in size and importance.

The main street is 25th-Oktober Street. Tiraspol has a teachers' training college, and its industry is concerned with dairy products and other foods, wine, mining equipment, packing cases, glass jars, furniture and clothing.

SREDNYA (MIDDLE) FORTRESS *Outside the town.* Built in 1792, the fortress was so called because it stood in the middle of a line of fortifications. Now only ruins remain.

LOCAL MUSEUM *25th-Oktober Street.*

OLD BELIEVERS' CHURCH *Rosa Luxemburg Street.*

TANK MONUMENT *In the main square.* This monument was erected in memory of 15 officers of a Tank Regiment in the Second World War.

POBEDA PARK.

TOWN BATHING BEACH AND BOAT HIRE STATION.

MOLDAVIA HOTEL *25th-Oktober Street 114.*

DNIESTER RESTAURANT *25th-Oktober Street at the corner of Shevchenko Street. Closed between 4 and 5 p.m.*

VOLNA (WAVE) CAFE *Sverdlov Street.*

MOLODYOZNAYA (YOUTH) CAFE *On the Embankment.*

MILK BAR *25th-Oktober Street.*

SHASHLIK BAR *On the Embankment.*

FILLING STATION *Energetikov Street 14.*

Round the clock service.

REPAIR STATION.

ODESSA

Population: 700,000 (1965)

Ukrainian: Odesa

Odessa is the Ukraine's second largest city. It is situated 30 km (18½ miles) north of the mouth of the River Dniester, and the central part of the city stands on a plateau divided by three ravines, Quarantine, Military and Water Ravine. The city now covers them all. Odessa's coat-of-arms bears Saint George and the Dragon an a gold field and a four-fluked anchor on a red field.

In the middle ages the settlement and port of Kotsubievo sprang up on this site. It flourished because of its proximity to the mouths of the Dniester, Danube, Dnieper and South Bug

ТИРАСПОЛ
TIRASPOL'

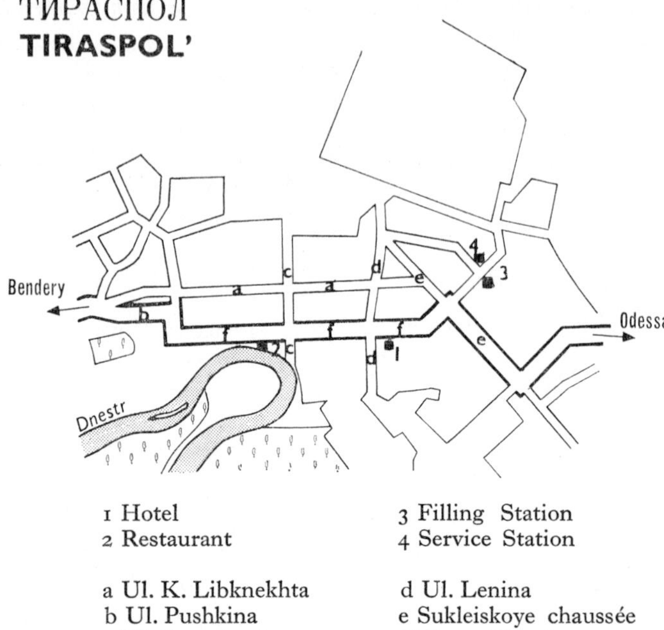

1 Hotel	3 Filling Station
2 Restaurant	4 Service Station
a Ul. K. Libknekhta	d Ul. Lenina
b Ul. Pushkina	e Sukleiskoye chaussée
c Ul. Shevchenko	f Ul. 25 Oktyabrya

rivers, which brought goods from the steppes and the northern regions. It was chiefly important for exporting grain, mainly through Italian merchants. The city was destroyed by the Tartars and then rebuilt under the name of Khadzhibei. It regained its importance as a trading centre, and then the Tartars were succeeded by the Turks, who in 1764 built a fortress called Yeni-Dunia ("new light"). In 1789, during the third Russo-Turkish war, Russian troops led by the Napolitan de Ribas captured the fortress and the town together with the entire region between the rivers Dniester and Bug. By the Yasi Peace Treaty of 1791 the captured area was finally declared to be Russian. Alexander Suvorov built a new fortress in 1792–93 and the foundations of the present naval port were laid in 1794 under the supervision of Vice-Admiral de Ribas and on the order of Catherine the Great. The following year the town was given its present name of Odessa after the ancient Greek settlement of Odessos then believed to have been located on one of the estuaries (*limany*) near the River Bug, although recent research denies the existence of such a settlement at any time. In 1803 some German colonists settled near Odessa to farm, and their successors lived there in the villages until the Second World War.

At this point the history of Duke Richelieu becomes interwoven with that of the city of Odessa. Duke Richelieu Armand Emmanuel du Plessis (1766-1822), a descendant of the famous cardinal of the time of Louis XIII, came to Russia at the beginning of the French revolution, and remained a devoted follower of Louis XIV. At the end of her reign, Catherine the Great put him in command of her Cuirassier Regiment. He fell from favour under Paul I and went to Vienna. However, when the throne passed to

Alexander I in 1801, the new tsar gave an order that the privileges given to Odessa by Catherine the Great be returned for a period of 25 years, and in 1803 the tsar recalled Richelieu and made him the Mayor of Odessa, with great independence of action and local power. Through him one fifth of all the Odessa customs duty was paid in to the town treasury; as a result banks, theatres and institutes were built, street lighting was installed, and under his guidance the town grew five times larger.

When Louis XVIII became King of France in 1814 he offered Richelieu a high governmental post. The latter accepted, leaving his country house and his pension to the city of Odessa. The city was nevertheless neglected after his departure and its development slowed down considerably, but Richelieu fully intended to go back again. On learning of his death in 1822, Alexander I told the French Ambassador, "I mourn Duke Richelieu as a real friend who always spoke me the truth. His merits will be eternally commemorated by the gratitude of all honest Russian people".

From 1816 Count Langeron was Mayor of Odessa. The new city grew rapidly because of the speed of building, the privileges afforded to the population and the establishment of a *porto franco* in 1822. In 1854 the city was bombarded by the Anglo-French fleet for 12 hours but was successfully defended. Its development continued and it gradually acquired its European aspect. By 1881 it had risen to be Russia's greatest port through its trade turnover, which still dealt largely in grain. Its industrial growth was also considerable, and by 1900 it ranked third after Moscow and Saint Petersburg in the number of its industrial concerns.

In 1875 the first Marxist working organisation "the South Russian Union of Workers" was formed; this was the first revolutionary political organisation in Russia. During the 1905 revolution the workers of the city were joined by the mutineers of the *Potemkin*, a battleship of the Black Sea Fleet. After the suppression of the uprising, the pogroms began, and as a result more than 13 per cent of the total population of 600,000 (including many of Jewish origin) fled the city. Odessa suffered greatly during the civil war of 1917–20 when it changed hands several times. One third of the city's houses were destroyed and the population decreased considerably; it was not until after the famine of 1921–22, when at last renewed sea traffic again brought trade with foreign countries, that the city began to revive.

In 1941 Odessa endured a 69-day siege by Nazi troops, suffered heavy damage, and after World War II was, together with Leningrad, Sevastopol and Volgograd (formerly Stalingrad), given the title of Hero City by decree of the Presidium of the Supreme Soviet.

Today Odessa is the port of the Slava (glory) Antarctic Whaling Fleet. It boasts 16 colleges and 23 technical training centres, more than 70,000 students making it the fifth largest educational centre of the Soviet Union. The city's heart is October-Revolution Square; in the past this was a place for merry-making on public holidays, and now parades and demonstrations take place. The suburbs of Moldavanka and Vorontsovka in the west, Melnitsy in the south-west and Peresip in the north are now integral parts of the city.

✿ USPENSKY (ASSUMPTION) CATHEDRAL *Sovietskoi Armiyi* (or *Preobrazhenskaya*) *Street*. This five-domed cathedral was built in 1855–69. Its façade is a mixture of Russian and Byzantine styles. The belltower is 47 m (154 ft) high. A memorial plaque tells that during the German occupation in World War II a certain Georgi Dubakin raised a red flag on the top of the cathedral. Services take place in the cathedral which has a miracle-working icon of Our Lady of Kasperovskaya.

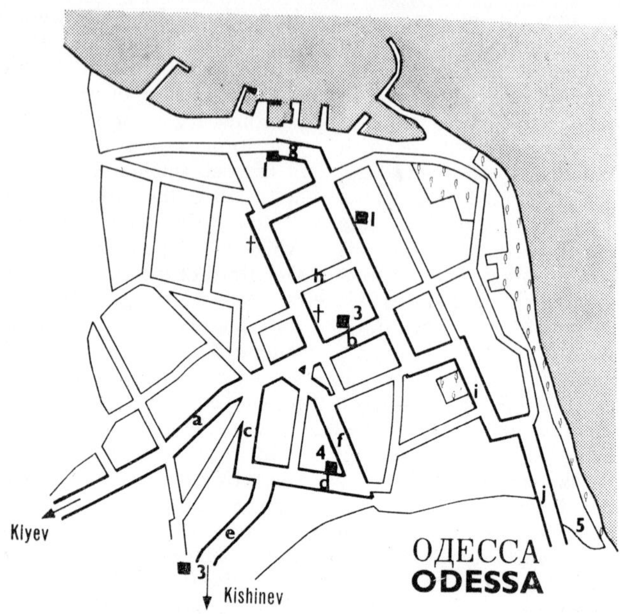

1 Hotel 3 Filling Station
5 Camping Site

a Ul. Ordzhonikidze
b Ul. Chkalova
c Ul. Commitetskaya
d Ul. Mizikevicha
e Ul. Moissenko
f Ul. Mechnikova
g Primorsky bulvar
h Ul. Pushkinskaya
i Ul. Sverdlova
j Novo Arkadiyskaya doroga

ILYA PROROKA (ELIJAH THE PROPHET) CHURCH *Pushkinskaya Street 79*. This church, built in the second part of the 19th century, is also open for religious services.

SAINT PETER'S CHURCH *Khalturina Street 5*. Services take place at this Roman Catholic church.

KIRCHE, THE LUTHERAN CHURCH *Ostrovidov Street. Closed.*

GREEK ORTHODOX CHURCH *Karl Marx Street. Open.*

There are other late 19th and early 20th century churches in Odessa, but they are of no historic interest and are all closed.

✿ ODESSA FORTRESS *In Shevchenko Park (formerly Alexandrovsky Park)*. The old tower and wall remain from the military fortress built by Suvorov in 1793.

PRINCE VORONTSOV'S PALACE. This building by Boffo in classical Russian style was built in 1826–27 and it became the Palace of Pioneers in 1936.

The white lighthouse in the port also bears Vorontsov's name.

POTEMKIN STAIRS. This flight of stairs completed in 1841 was built narrower at the top than at the bottom to give an illusion of greater length. The first step is 21 m (69 ft) wide and the top step (the 192nd) is 12·5 m (41 ft) wide. From the top only the landings are visible, and from the bottom only the steps. The stairs are called after the battleship which took part in the uprising of 1905. They lead to Primorsky (formerly Nikolayevsky) boulevard which, at over a 100 years old, is one of Odessa's main streets and still most popular promenade. One of the cannons used in the Crimean War stands on it. It came from the English frigate *Tiger*, and was brought up from the bottom of the sea. Beside the Stairs is a funicular railway.

THE CITY HALL. This 19th century building is decorated with statues of Mercury and Ceres, and the large clock on the main façade has figures of Day and Night.

CATACOMBS. There are many entrances and exits, but most are on the slopes of Mount Shevakhovo. Most of the caves were formed early in the 19th century when the sandstone was quarried to build up the growing city, and later they were used by smugglers. Numerous revolutionaries hid in the caves during the Civil War of 1917–20, and an underground printing shop was also hidden in them. During World War II the catacombs were a headquarters for partisans. The tunnels run for a total of more than 800 km (500 miles). In some places they are very narrow and in others several metres wide; even now new corners are still being discovered, with the remains of soldiers and their munitions in them.

ARCHEOLOGICAL MUSEUM *Kommunarov Square. Open 10–8; closed on Wednesdays.* This museum, dating from 1825, shows the history of the people living on the northern shore of the Black Sea from ancient times until the 13th century, and also has one of the largest collections of ancient Egyptian relics in the Soviet Union, as well as material from the ancient Greek settlements on the Black Sea.

HISTORICAL-ETHNOGRAPHICAL MUSEUM *Open 9–5; closed on Saturdays.* This museum is divided into two parts: the historical section at Khalturin Street, 4, in the former Commercial Club, and the Geological and Natural History departments—Lastochkin Street 24.

MARINE MUSEUM *Zastochkina Street 6. Open 10–5; closed on Tuesdays.*

MUSEUM OF EASTERN AND WESTERN ART *Pushkinskaya Street 9 (formerly Italian Street). Open 11–5.30; closed on Wednesdays.* This two-storey building was erected in 1856 by the architect Otton for a merchant called Abaza. It contains 18 halls, and the exhibits fall into three groups:—*antique*—mostly copies, *western European art*—including original works by Rubens, Rembrandt, Veronese, and Murillo, and *oriental art*—Persian miniatures and handicrafts from China, India and Japan.

PICTURE GALLERY *Korolenko Street 5a. Open 11–4; closed on Wednesdays.* Russian artists of 18th and 19th centuries, Soviet art and graphics are displayed here.

RICHELIEU MONUMENT *At the head of the Potemkin Stairs.* This figure of the Duke, shown wearing a Roman toga, was cast in Paris in 1828 by Martoss, Dean of the Saint Petersburg Academy of Art. Part of the pedestal was broken by a cannonball during the Anglo-French bombardment, and was restored with an artificial cannonball remaining for all to see. Inside the biggest stone in the pedestal were placed the most important medals and coins minted during the reigns of Louis XVI, Catherine II, Paul, Alexander I and Louis XVIII, all of whom Richelieu had served, as well as a medal of Napoleon I and a bronze medal cast in Paris to commemorate the great man's death.

VORONTSOV MONUMENT *Sovietskaya Armiya Square*. This bronze statue was cast in 1863 in Munich by Brugger. The Prince is shown on a pedestal of Crimean porphyry decorated with bas-reliefs of battles.

PUSHKIN MONUMENT *At the end of Primorsky Boulevard, opposite the town hall*. Under the bust of the poet by sculptor Polonsky is written "To Pushkin from the Citizens of Odessa". The dates 1820–24 engraved on the upper part of the pedestal indicate the years when Pushkin lived in exile in Odessa. The monument was unveiled in 1888.

GRIGORY VAKULINCHUK MONUMENT *Tamozhnaya Square, near the port*. This monument commemorates one of the organisers of the mutiny on the Potemkin who was killed by one of the officers, and whose funeral became the excuse for a mass demonstration. The monument with his bust on a pedestal of red granite stands 6 m (20 ft) high. It was unveiled in 1958.

POTEMKIN UPRISING MONUMENT *Karl Marx Square*. The monument by Bogdanov commemorates the uprising of 1905 and was unveiled in 1965.

KOTOVSKY MONUMENT *Kotovsky Street*.

OBELISK TO THE UNKNOWN SEAMAN *Shevchenko Park*. An eternal flame burns beside the obelisk.

✿ OPERA AND BALLET THEATRE *Lastochkina Street 8*. This theatre was designed in 1884–87 by Hellmer and Fellner, two Viennese architects, and resembles the Vienna Opera House and the Dresden Court Theatre. On the Italian Renaissance style façade are busts of Glinka, Gogol, Griboyedov and Pushkin. The interior is in Louis XVI style, and the ceiling of the auditorium is decorated with scenes from Shakespeare's *A Midsummer Night's Dream*, *As You Like It*, *Hamlet*, and *A Winter's Tale*. The theatre seats about 1600. It was damaged by fire in 1925 and then restored. It suffered again with the rest of the city during World War II. Tchaikosky, Rubinstein, Glazunov and Rimsky-Korsakov all conducted here in their day.

OCTOBER REVOLUTION UKRAINIAN DRAMA THEATRE *Paster Street 15*.

IVANOV DRAMA THEATRE *Karl Liebknecht Street 48*.

MUSICAL COMEDY THEATRE *Karl Liebknecht Street 50*.

OSTROVSKY YOUTH THEATRE *Chaikovsky Pereulok 12*. This theatre is called after the Russian playwright.

PHILHARMONIA CONCERT HALL *Rosa Luxemburg Street 15*. This building, dating from 1899 and originally the merchant stock exchange, is one of the best pieces of architecture in Odessa. It was designed by Bernardazzi in Florentine Gothic style. The ceiling is painted to symbolise trade and industry.

NEZHDANOVA CONSERVATOIRE *Ostrovidova Street*. David Oistrakh, Emil Gilels and many other leading Soviet musicians graduated from this conservatoire.

CIRCUS *Podbelsky Street 25*. This circus is one of the best in the Soviet Union.

✿ SHEVCHENKO PARK. Formerly Alexandrovsky Park and now named after the famous 19th century Ukrainian poet, this 90 hectares (225 acres) park has an excellent view of the Black Sea and has its own bathing beach, Komsomolskaya Beach. There is a monument to Bogdan Khmelnitsky, who united the Ukraine and Russia in 1654. Also in the park are the Avangard Stadium which can seat 40,000 and is one of the largest in the Ukraine, an open air theatre, boat hire stations and the University observatory and planetarium.

POBEDA (VICTORY) PARK *Perekopskaya Pobeda Street.* This Park was formerly called Dukovsky Gardens. There is a swimming pool here, and a permanent local Economic Achievements Exhibition.

CHARLES DARWIN GARDEN *Near the Opera House.* This garden was once known as Palais-Royale.

ZOO *Near Ilyich Park. Open daily.*

HIPPODROME RACECOURSE *Bolshoi Fontan, Chetvertaya Stantsiya.*

✿ ODESSA HOTEL AND RESTAURANT *Primorsky Boulevard 11; tel: 2-60-87.* Formerly the London Hotel, this is now run by Intourist.

KRASNAYA HOTEL AND RESTAURANT *Pushkin Street 15, at the corner of Kondratenko Street; tel: 2-14-22.* This is also an Intourist hotel.

BOLSHAYA MOSKOVSKAYA HOTEL *Deribasovskya Street 29.*

SPARTAK HOTEL *Deribasovskaya Street 25.*

PASSAGE HOTEL *Sovietskaya Armiya Street 34.*

TSENTRALNAYA HOTEL *Sovietskaya Armiya Street 40.*

MORYAK (SEAMAN) HOTEL *At the port.*

YOUZHNYI (SOUTH) RESTAURANT *Khalturin Street 12.*

UKRAINIA RESTAURANT *Karl Marx Street 12.*

KIEV RESTAURANT *Martynovsky Square.*

TEATRALNYI RESTAURANT *Sovietskaya Armiya Street 36.*

PRIMORIYE RESTAURANT *Tiraspolskaya Street 1.*

CHERNOMORSKY (BLACK SEA) RESTAURANT *Karl Marx Street 23.* This hotel has an open air restaurant.

Alice Parusa YOUTH CAFE *Deribasovskaya Street 20.*

ICE CREAM PARLOUR *Lenin Street 5.*

TWO OTHER CAFES *Lenin Street 57 and 19.*

MOTEL *In Arcady Region, on Gagarin Plateau.*

CAMPING SITE *Near the Motel.*

✿ BANK *Lenin Street, at the corner of Deribasovskaya Street.*

G.P.O. *Gorky Street 12.*

CENTRAL TELEGRAPH OFFICE *Sadovaya Street 3.*

INDIAN LEGATION *Kirov Street 31; tel: 28-851.*

DEPARTMENT STORE *Pushkin Street 75/73.*

PODARKI (GIFT) SHOP *Deribasovskaya Street 33.*

BERYOZKA SOUVENIR SHOP *Deribasovskaya Street 19.*

BOOK AND MUSIC SHOP *Deribasovskaya Street 25.*

✿ INTOURIST CAR PARK *Right beside the bottom of Potemkin Stairs.* This car park is for the use of those staying in hotels.

FILLING STATION No. 8. *Chkalov Street 70. Open daily 7.30 a.m.–8 p.m.* Diesel oil is available here. Motorists going north are advised to leave Odessa with full tank, and possibly with some spare cans of petrol, as the first filling station on the Odessa–Kiev Motorway is at Uman.

FILLING STATION No. 9. *Vtoraya Zastava.* Diesel oil is for sale here; round the clock service.

SERVICE STATION *Mechnikov Street 57a. Open daily 8 a.m.–4 p.m.*

———— ✶ ————

Odessa's estuaries (*limany*) are former river mouths which have become separated from the sea by sandbanks; through evaporation they have turned into saline-bitter lakes of varying degrees of salt concentration. The water contains more magnesium, lime, iodine and brome than sea water, and the mud is rich in sulphur, which is efficacious in the cure of rheumatic, nervous and skin diseases. Besides these natural assets the sea itself is very shallow and is quickly warmed by the sun. There are over 30 sanatoria and 15 rest homes in this part of the Black Sea coast.

LERMONTOVSKY RESORT *Lermentovsky Pereulok*. The resort is located within the city boundaries. It stands on a high plateau from which a 220 m (720 ft) slope with terraces leads down to the sea. There is a large park and sanatoria for rheumatics.

Beyond Shevchenko Park and the Komsomolsky Beach the western resort region begins. *Langeron*, near Shevchenko Park, was called after Count Langeron who took the place of Richelieu as Mayor of Odessa in 1816. There is a good bathing beach, and behind it, in Chernomorskaya Street, are many sanatoria.

After *Otrada* comes the park of *Arkadiya*, running along the sea shore. This is the most popular place near Odessa and the most picturesque. Some parts of this region, along the shore, are known as *Minor Fountain* (malyi fontan), *Middle* (sredny) *Fountain*, and *Major* (bolshoi) *Fountain*—but these names have nothing to do with fountains. They simply indicate Odessa's problems with its fresh water supply in the 19th century. There were Artesian wells (*fontany*) here. Malyi Fontan region lies between 1st and 7th Stantsiya, Sredny Fontan between 7th and 9th, and Bolshoi between 10th and 16th. There is an exceptionally good beach at Bolshoi Fontan, called Golden Beach.

There is a summer theatre, a restaurant and many sanatoria in what were formerly private villas. Near Primoriye Sanatorium are the Medicinal Baths. Here also is one of the entrances to the catacombs.

✿ USPENSKY MONASTERY *Mayachny Pereulok 6, Bolshoi Fontan.* The Monastery was founded in 1824 and today 40 monks live there while 50 students attend the seminary. There are vineyards in the grounds and the Patriarch usually spends the summer here. *St. Nicholas's Church* was built in the 1840's and *Uspenskaya Church* in 1892.

CHERNOMORKA *18 km (11 miles) from Odessa.* The name of this resort means "Black Sea"; it was formerly the German settlement of Lustdorf. The beach of quartz sand is one of the best in the Odessa region and there are many sanatoria here, including a special one for children suffering from ossical tuberculosis. There is a café in the resort.

Malodolinsky was also at one time a German colony; known as Klein Liebenthal. The *liman* here is 10 km (6½ miles) long and 1 km (½ mile) wide.

The road from Odessa to the eastern resorts leads through the seaside suburb of Peresip to *Shevakhovo* on Mount Shevakhovo. It is 11 km (7 miles) from the centre of the city. Here, too, is *Luzanovka* with two parks, Verkhny and Nizhny. The beach is wide and sandy; at a distance of 50 m (55 yd) the sea is not more then 2 m (6 ft) deep. There is a large children's sanatorium called Ukrainian Artek at this point.

KUYALNITSKY RESORT *13 km (8 miles) from the centre of Odessa.* Formerly known as Andreyevsky after Dr. Andreyev who founded the first medical establishment here in 1833, Kuyalnitsky stands beside *Kuyalnitsky Liman.* This is 30 km (19 miles) long, up to 2–3 km (1¼–2 miles) wide and 2·2 m (7 ft 3 in.) deep. It is divided from the sea by a 2 km (1¼ mile) wide sandbank and has the most concentrated salt solution of any of the Odessa *limany* (4·5–27 per cent). There is a summer theatre and a restaurant and also sanatoria, mudbaths and a mineral spring used for bathing and drinking.

Near the village of Kholodnaya Balka, 21 km (13 miles) from Odessa, is *Khadzhibeyevsky Liman*, 34 km (21 miles) long, 2·5 km (1½ miles) wide and, in the southern section, 10·5–14 m (34–46 ft) deep. The salt solution is weaker than that of many of the other limans, 2·5–12 per cent. There is a park, beach, café and mudbaths on the *liman*.

ROAD SIX

ODESSA—UMAN—KIEV

ODESSA

(see Road Five, page 203)

UMAN

Belaya Tserkov · Grebyonki · Ksaverovka · Sokolovka · Vasilkov

KIEV

(see Road Three, page 170)

ODESSA

See Road 5, on page 203.

UMAN

The town stands beside the River Uman in a hilly locality on the eastern branch of the Avratin Hills, and is a little to the west of the Odessa–Kiev Motorway.

Uman was founded in the early 17th century, and from 1718 belonged to Count Potozky, at which time it was judged one of the best towns in the western Ukraine. In the peasant rising of 1768, known as the "Uman slaughter", Uman was razed to the ground and over 18,000 of the inhabitants, mostly Poles and Jews, were killed.

The town has a pedagogical college, and Pototsky's house is now an agricultural college. In the town is a flour mill and brickworks. Various food products are also prepared.

SOFIEVKA PARK The park and gardens date from the 18th century. Sofievka was formerly a country house built by Count Felix Pototsky for his wife Sophie, in 1793. There were no buildings there previously. The park covers 89 hectares (220 acres). At the main entrance to the park is an iron gate with two classical style guard towers. The main avenue is lined with horse-chestnuts and ends with the Flora Pavilion in Doric style. Pools and waterfalls were made using the water of the little River Kamenka. There is 23 m (75 ft) in difference between the height of the Upper and the Lower Pools. The area between the two pools is called the Champs Elysées and, among other artificial structures, it contains the Caucasian Mount. In the Upper Pool is the artificial Isle of Love with a small pavilion, and in the centre of Lower Pool stands Serpents' Fountain, 20 m (65 ft) high. Over the Lower Pool is the Belvedere Cliff whose side view resembles a human profile, and in the western part of the Pool stands the Cliff of Death, weighing over 200 tons. It is said that during the work it fell down and crushed many serfs, killing 300 outright. There is also the so-called Dead Lake, surrounded with a granite embankment and 100-year-old trees. From this flows an underground river, the Styx, through a 224 m long (245 yd) granite tunnel, leading to an open wooden canal, the Amsterdam Lock. This river sometimes dries up through lack of water. There is another fountain called the Seven Springs, and the farther end of the Lower Pool joins the Valley of the Giants, filled with great disordered rocks. In this valley are the Three Tears Waterfall and the Column of Mourning. In the park there are many grottoes dedicated to Fear and Doubt, Diana and Venus among others, and a part of the park is known as the English Park. It is open daily.

LOCAL MUSEUM *Oktyabrskaya Street 33. Open 10–5; closed on Wednesdays.*

LENIN MONUMENT *Lenin Square.*

IVAN CHERNYAKHOVSKI MONUMENT *Karl Marx Street.* This commemorates a general killed in the Second World War.

KOTOVSKY MONUMENT *Sovietskaya Street.*

KOTOVSKY GARDEN There is a monument here to the soldiers who established Soviet power in Uman.

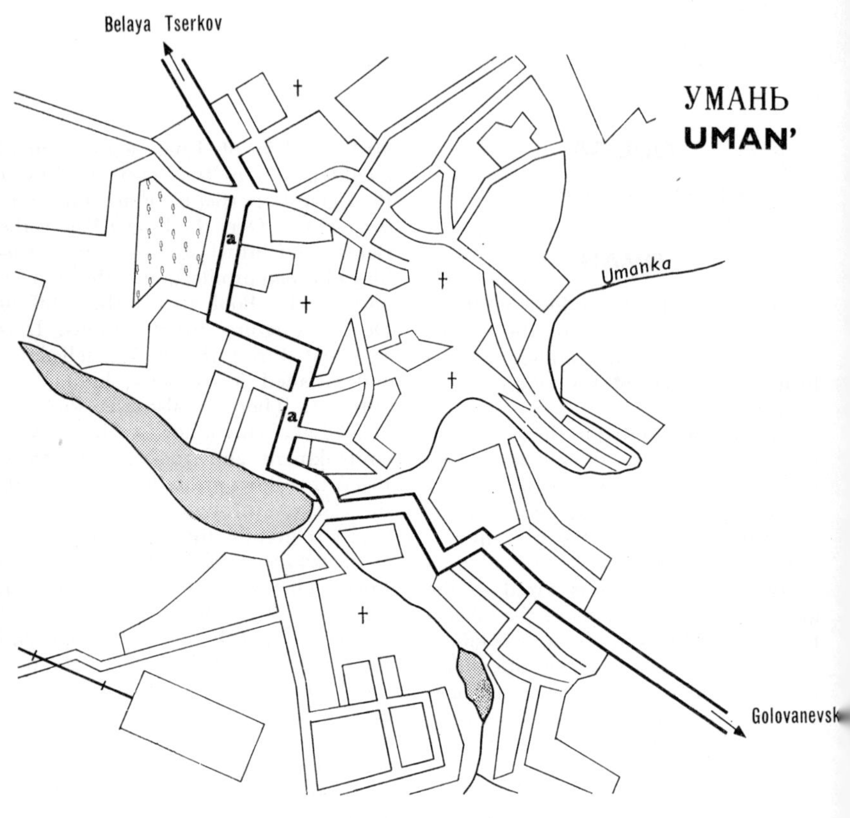

a Dvortsovaya ul.

UMAN HOTEL AND RESTAURANT *Lenin Square 21/32; tel: 23-45.*

DRUZHBA (FRIENDSHIP) RESTAURANT *by the entrance to Sofievsky Park.*

EATING HOUSE *Lenin Square.*

CAFETERIA *Sovietskaya Street 13, to the left down the street from the hotel.* Breakfasts are provided here.

G.P.O. *Sovietskaya Street 17.*

TELEGRAPH OFFICE *Engels Street 8.*

BANK *Kolomenskaya Street 16.*

DEPARTMENT STORE *Sovietskaya Street, at the corner of Lenin Square.*

FILLING STATION *At the 203 km milestone, on the left side of the main Motorway.* Round the clock service.

REPAIR STATION *At the 203 km milestone, on the right side of the main motorway. Open 8 a.m.–4 p.m.*

BELAYA TSERKOV (White Church)

Population: 71,000 (1959)

The town, which lies off the main Odessa–Kiev Motorway, was founded in the 11th century, and stands on the site of the ancient town of Yuriev, ruined by the Mongols in 1240. Only a part of a white stone church remains, and it is from this that the town takes its name. Between 1570 and 1793 it was under Polish rule.

In the centre of Belaya Tserkov is an arcade of shops built in the 19th century. The central Lenin Square, however, is quite new and has a hotel, shops, and a monument to Lenin.

There are agricultural and teacher's training institutes in the town, and the First of May Factory produces agricultural machinery. Among the town's other important products are bricks, furniture, footwear and clothing.

SAINT NICHOLAS' CHURCH. The church was built in 1706.

LOCAL MUSEUM *Zamkovskaya Street 15, on Castle Hill. Open 10–6; closed on Wednesdays.* This museum has historical and natural history sections, and some relics of the Ukrainian-Polish battles of 1648–54. It stands where the castle-fortress once stood, and the remains of some of the walls are to be seen. At the entrance to the museum stands the statue of an Amazon.

HOUSE OF NOBLES. This is a long 18th century building with a columned façade.

WAREHOUSES. The three-storey 18th century building is 100 m (110 yd) long.

ALEXANDRIA PARK *In the Western part of the town.* This is a very beautiful park, laid out on 200 hectares (500 acres) of land beside the River Ros at the beginning of the 19th century by the serfs of Countess Branitskaya. The park contains 110 different species of trees.

SAKSAGANSKY DRAMA THEATRE

HOTEL AND RESTAURANT *Lenin Street.*

GREBYONKI

This village has a café beside the main road.

KSAVEROVKA

This new village, founded in 1959, consists mainly of brick-built houses.

TEAROOM.

SOKOLOVKA

There is a café beside the main road in this village.

VASILKOV

Population: 20,000 (1959)

Vasilkov was founded in 988 by Prince Vladimir Svyatoslavich. The remains of the town walls can be seen, and in the 11th century the palace of the Grand Duke Vladimir was built here. Vasilkov was under Tartar and Lithuanian rule and then until 1775 belonged to the Pecherskaya Lavra (monastery) of Kiev.

The town is prettily situated, and is famous for its pottery factory which makes the traditional Ukrainian pottery vases, sheep, etc. These have been exhibited in various countries of Europe. The town also produces refrigerators and leather.

CHURCH OF SAINT ANTONY AND SAINT THEODOSIUS. The church was built in 1756–59 in the style of Rastrelli and dedicated to the Saints who founded the Pecherskaya Lavra in Kiev.

Another green-domed church, built in the 19th century but of no particular architectural interest, stands back from the main road.

HOTEL *Lenin Street.*

RESTAURANT *On the main road.*

KIEV

See Road 3, on page 170.

ROAD SEVEN

KIEV—POLTAVA—KHARKOV

KIEV

(see Road Three, page 170)

Borispol · Piryatin · Lubny · Khorol

POLTAVA

Chutovo · Vasilevka

KHARKOV

KIEV

See Road 3, on page 170.

BORISPOL

This small town was founded in 1602. It has a park and a stadium, and its main function today is to supply the city of Kiev with fruit and vegetables.

Outside the town are some ancient burial mounds.

FILLING STATION *On the main Kiev–Kharkov road.*

PIRYATIN

Piryatin stands a little off the main road. It was first mentioned in writing in 1155. Between 1647 and 1764 it was known as a Cossack town, and a Cossack regiment was stationed here.

It has now a flour mill and other varieties of the food industry.

FILLING STATION *Round the clock service.*

RESTAURANT.

LUBNY

Population: 29,000 (1959)

This town stands on the River Sula, a tributary of the River Dnieper. First mentioned in the chronicles in 1107, Lubny was one of the border strongholds of the princedom of Pereyaslavl. In the 1720's the first chemist's shop in the Ukraine was opened here and the first herb garden was planted out beside it. Now an experimental station where exotic herbs and roots are cultivated has grown up on this spot. Lubny's industrial enterprises produce machinery, cement mixers, cranes and furniture.

LOCAL MUSEUM *Lenin Street 55.*

There is a drama theatre under construction.

HOTEL *Lenin Street.*

RESTAURANT *Sovietskaya Street.*

KHOROL

The town of Khorol stands on the River Khorol. It was first mentioned in the chronicles in 1083, and it was here that the Princes of Kiev, Svyatoslav and Igor fought the Tartar Khan Konchak.

There is a distillery here, and branches of the food industry.

Khorol is just off the main road.

POLTAVA

Population: 141,000 (1959)

Near this town is the battlefield where the Russian army under Peter the Great defeated the Swedes under Charles XII on 27th June, 1709. The battle concluded the great War of the North and established the position of Russia in Europe. When Catherine the Great and Alexander I each visited the battle-field, soldiers demonstrated the manoeuvres of the two armies.

SPASSKY CHURCH (CHURCH OF THE SAVIOUR) *On the crossing of Parizhskoi Kommuny Street and Dzerzhinsky Street.* This church, built 1705 to 1706, is the oldest in the town.

CHURCH *Oktyabrskaya Street.*

LOCAL MUSEUM AND KOTLYAREVSKY LITERARY MUSEUM *Lenin Street. Open 10–5; closed on Wednesdays.*

ART MUSEUM *Dzerzhinsky Street 11. Closed on Fridays.*

KOROLENKO LITERARY MUSEUM *Korolenko Street 1.*

PANAS MIRNYI MUSEUM *Mirnyi Street 56.*

HISTORY OF THE BATTLE OF POLTAVA MUSEUM *7 km (4½ miles) out of town. Open 10–5; closed on Wednesdays.* Not far from the Battle Museum is a 7·5 m (25 ft) granite cross unveiled in 1894 marking the grave of the Russian soldiers.

About ½ km (¼ mile) from this cross is the Russian monument in memory of the Swedish soldiers who fell in the battle. This was unveiled in 1909 to commemorate the 200th anniversary of the battle. A second monument to the Swedish soldiers brought from Sweden and unveiled on the same date, is to be seen 3 km (2 miles) from the Battle Museum.

GLORY MONUMENT *In the centre of October Park in Poltava.* This monument is 11 m high (36 ft) and made of pig iron surmounted by a bronze eagle turning towards the battlefield. It was designed by Tomon, and unveiled in 1811.

KELIN MONUMENT *Pervomaisky Prospekt.* This monument was erected to Colonel Kelin, commander of the fortress, in commemoration of the 200th anniversary of the Battle of Poltava.

PETER THE GREAT MONUMENT *Near Spasskaya Church.* This monument was erected on the spot where Peter the Great rested after the battle.

✿ GOGOL DRAMA AND MUSICAL THEATRE.

PUPPET THEATRE *Vantsetti Street 8.*

✿ HOTEL POLTAVA AND RESTAURANT.

POLTAVSKAYA LESNAYA HOTEL *On the main road.*

POLTAVA RESTAURANT *Lenin Street 16.*

VORSKLA RESTAURANT *Named after the River Vorskla on the highway coming into town from Kiev.*

✿ FILLING STATION *On the main road, 337 km (210 miles) from Kharkov. Round the clock service.*

REPAIR STATION *Kirov Street 2.*

CHUTOVO

✿ EATING HOUSE.

VASILEVKA

✿ The fortress in this village was built between 1736 and 1738.

KHARKOV

Pronounced "harkov"

Population: 930,000 (1959)

When driving southwards from Moscow, motorists can bypass Kharkov by taking a left turn directly onto the main Simferopol road.

The city is built on a plateau in the midst of the black earth region of the Ukraine. Three rivers, the Lopan, the Udy and the Kharkov, flow through it. Although it probably took its name from the river Kharkov, legend records that a certain Cossack called Kharko or Khariton lived here, until he was drowned in the River Donets, and that it was called after him.

The town of Kharkov dates from about 1656, when the fortress was built to protect Russia's southern border, particularly from the Crimean Tartars. There was probably some sort of settlement here before this, but no evidence of it remains. During the Cossack insurrection, Kharkov remained loyal to the tsars, who in return granted the town various privileges. Later, at the end of the 18th century, an earth wall with towers was built to surround the expanding town.

Before the foundation of the university in 1805, two men in particular

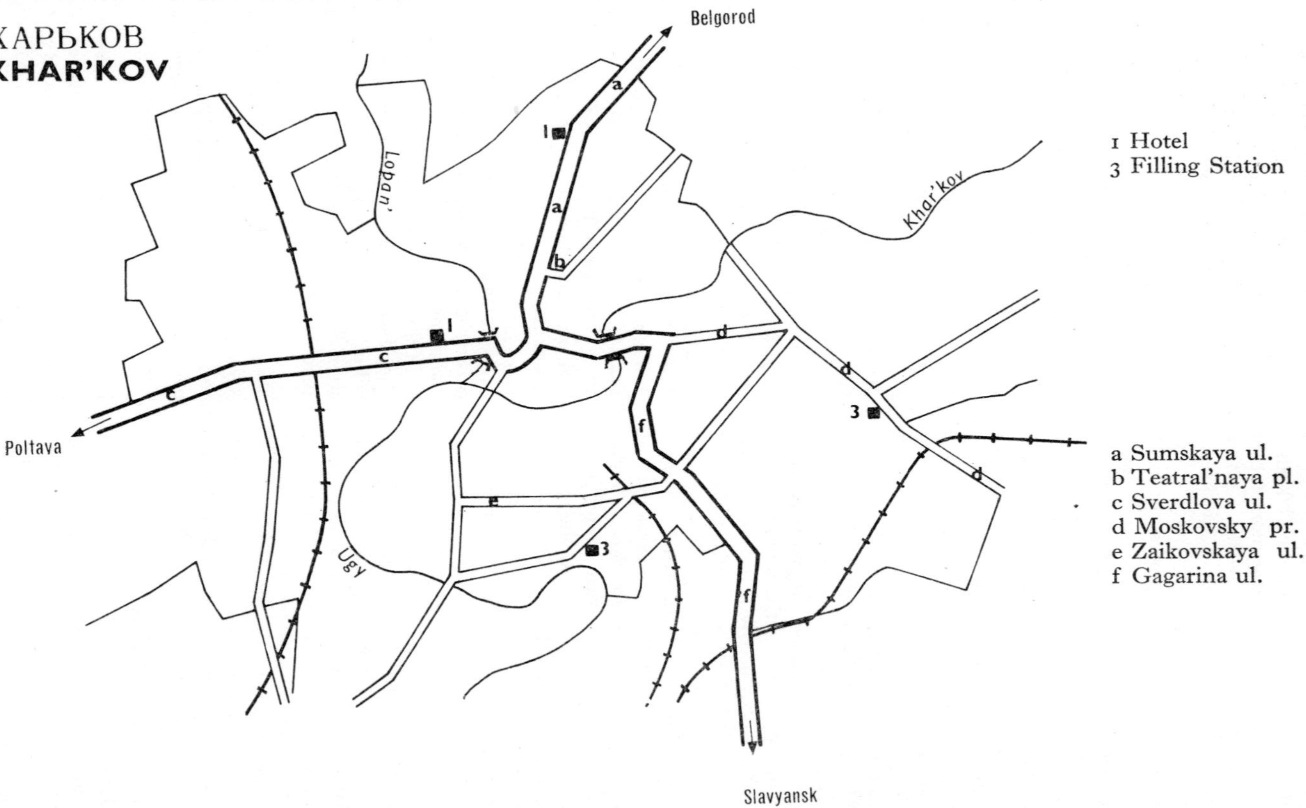
ХАРЬКОВ
KHAR'KOV
1 Hotel
3 Filling Station
a Sumskaya ul.
b Teatral'naya pl.
c Sverdlova ul.
d Moskovsky pr.
e Zaikovskaya ul.
f Gagarina ul.
Belgorod
Poltava
Slavyansk
Khar'kov
Lopan'
Ugy

were closely concerned with the problems of education in the Ukraine. Grigori Skovoroda (whose name means "frying-pan") (1722–94) was a philosopher who spent most of his life as an itinerant teacher of morals and was one of the chief sources of modern Russian Intuitivism. Grigori Kvitka-Osnovyanenko ("Kvitka" means "flower" in Ukrainian) (1778–1843) was an author and playwright. The present-day university has 10 faculties and over 100 Chairs. 12,000 students study in it and it contains 200 fully equipped laboratories. Kharkov has a total of 100,000 students because, besides the university, there are 22 other higher educational establishments and 57 scientific research institutes.

Kharkov has one of the most picturesque entrances of any Russian town. Approaching the town from the direction of Moscow, a wide tree-lined road leads to Sumskaya Street which is lined with cafés, restaurants, shops and old buildings, and leads to the centre of the town. One of the oldest parts of the city is Universitetskaya Gorka. This was originally surrounded by a wooden palisade, and at the end of the 17th century brick buildings were erected: the Pokrovsky Cathedral and the Uspensky Cathedral. Dzerzhinsky Square is one of the largest in the world and covers an area of 11 hectares (27½ acres). The buildings around it were constructed between 1929 and 1933 and form an interesting complex. One of them is known as the House of Projects and was designed by S. Serafimov; another, the House of Industry, built by the architects S. Serafimov and S. Kravets, is, with its 18 storeys, the first Soviet skyskraper. It was badly damaged during the Second Warld War, when the city changed hands five times, and is now occupied by the University.

Until 1934 Kharkov was the capital of the Ukraine, but this honour was then restored to ancient Kiev. It has long been one of Russia's major railway junctions and is the administrative centre of the great iron and coal mining industries of southern Russia. Its huge engineering industry produces locomotives, tractors, aircraft, agricultural machinery and turbines, and there are various light industries as well.

✿ POKROVSKY CATHEDRAL *Universitetskaya Street*. The basic plan of this cathedral, built in 1689, is that of the old wooden Ukrainian churches, but the details are Russian. Its domes are coloured blue.

USPENSKY CATHEDRAL *Universitetskaya Gorka*. This stands on the site of a 17th century cathedral which was destroyed by fire in 1733. The present cathedral was erected between 1821 and 1841 by the architect Vasiliyev, and is 89·5 m (294 ft) high. It was badly damaged during World War II, but has since been restored.

BELLTOWER *Universitetskaya Gorka*. The architects Vasiliyev and Thon designed this picturesque tower in 1841 to commemorate Russia's victory over Napoleon. It is 89·5 m (294 ft) high and the foundations are 14 sazhen (98 ft) deep.

ANNUNCIATION CATHEDRAL *Engels Street, down the hill from the old town and across the river*. This cathedral was built in 1901 on the site of earlier churches, and was restored in 1950. It is built of brick in neo-Byzantine Style after St. Sophia in Istambul. It holds 4000 people.

THREE SAINTS' CHURCH *Zaikovskaya Street*. This church was built in 1915, and services are held here; part of the church is used by the Old Believers and contains some old icons.

ROMAN CATHOLIC CHURCH *Gogol Street*. There are, besides those mentioned, a number of other churches, mostly of the 19th and 20th centuries, of no particular historical interest.

Yekaterinsky Palace was built between 1767 and 1776, in Russian classical Empire style. It is now used as an administrative building of the University.

HISTORICAL MUSEUM *Universitetskaya Street. 10 and another nearby building. Open 10–6; closed on Tuesdays.* The displays illustrate the past history of the city and the more recent development of its flourishing industry. Other sections are devoted to the Civil War and to World War II.

FINE ARTS MUSEUM *Sovnarkomovskaya Street 11. Open 11–7; closed on Fridays.* This museum contains works of Repin, who was born nearby in Chuguyev, including his "Zaporozhe Cossacks writing a letter to the Sultan". The museum has 19 halls, with the first section devoted to Russian and Ukrainian pre-revolutionary art. It also shows icons of the Novgorod, Pskov, and other schools dating from the 16th century. The second section covers Soviet art.

PLANETARIUM *Kravtsov Pereulok 13.*

PUSHKIN MONUMENT *Teatralnaya Square.* The monument was erected in 1904, and designed by B. Edwards.

KARAZIN MONUMENT. This monument was erected in 1905 and designed by Andrioletti. Vasili Karazin (1773–1842), "the Lomonosov of the Ukraine", founded Kharkov University in 1805. It was the first university in the Ukraine and the second in Russia, and Karazin first received permission from Tsar Alexander I to organise it. He collected the necessary money from the nobles and merchants of Kharkov. Having left a letter in the palace at the time of the accession of the tsar explaining his ideas and hopes for the future of Russia, he was then summoned to Saint Petersburg where he discussed educational problems with the tsar.

GOGOL MONUMENT *Sumskaya Street.* This monument was erected in 1909; the author's autograph is on the lower part of the pedestal.

KOTSUBINSKY MONUMENT *In the garden at the crossing of Pushkinskaya and Chernishevsky Streets.* Mikhail Kotsubinsky (1864–1913) was a Ukrainian writer.

SHEVCHENKO MONUMENT *Sumskaya Street, at the main entrance to Shevchenko Park.* The 16·5 m (54 ft) high statue and its base by M. Manizer were erected in 1935. The 16 subsidiary statues represent the history of the Ukrainian people.

LENIN MONUMENT *Dzerzhinsky Square.* This monument by Oleinik and Vronsky was unveiled in 1963.

MONUMENT TO REVOLUTIONARIES *Sovietskaya Square.* Unveiled in 1957.

RUDNEV MONUMENT *Rudnev Square.* Nikolai A. Rudnev (1894–1918) was a hero of the Civil War.

LYSENKO OPERA HOUSE *Rymarskaya Street 19.*

MUSICAL COMEDY THEATRE *Karl Marx Street 28.*

KRUPSKAYA PUPPET THEATRE *Krasin Street 3.*

PUSHKIN RUSSIAN DRAMA THEATRE *Chernyshevsky Street 11.*

REGIONAL DRAMA THEATRE *Sverdlov Street 18.*

SHEVCHENKO UKRAINIAN DRAMA THEATRE *Sumskaya Street 9.*

CIRCUS *Krasnovo Militsionera Street 17.*

PHILHARMONIA CONCERT HALL *Sumskaya Street 10.*

UKRAINA CONCERT HALL *Shevchenko Garden.* This modern building, seating 2000, was opened in 1965.

✿ HIPPODROME RACECOURSE *Pervomaiskaya Square.*

AVANGARD STADIUM *Plekhanovskaya Street 65.*

DYNAMO STADIUM *Dinamovskaya Street.* There is a swimming pool in the stadium.

ZOO *Sumskaya Street 35.*

GORKY PARK *Sumskaya Street 81.* There is a monument to Gorky here, and also a children's railway.

BOTANICAL GARDEN *Klochkovskaya Street.* This garden belongs to the University.

SHEVCHENKO PARK *Sumskaya Street.*

✿ KHARKOV HOTEL, RESTAURANT AND CAFE *Dzerzhinsky Square, tel: 3-05-20.*

INTOURIST HOTEL AND RESTAURANT *Sverdlov Street 4; tel: 2-22-46.*

NEW INTOURIST HOTEL AND RESTAURANT *Lenin Prospekt 21.*

YUZHNAYA (*South; Called Pivdenna in Ukrainian*) HOTEL AND RESTAURANT *Karl Marx Street 30.*

LUX RESTAURANT *Sumskaya Street 3.*

TEATRALNAYA RESTAURANT *Sumskaya Street 2.*

DYNAMO RESTAURANT *In the Dynamo Stadium.*

CENTRAL CAFE *Rosa Luxemburg Street.*

VARENIKI (DUMPLINGS) BAR *Sumskaya Street 14.* These small dumplings are a national Ukrainian dish. They may be filled with various things including cottage cheese, potato or fruit.

CAMPING SITE *18 km (12½ miles) along the main road to Simferopol, on the left, in a shady oak wood.* On a territory of more than 2 hectares (5 acres) are showers, washbasins, a laundry, a self-service kitchen, a café and verandah-lounge; a shop, souvenir and newspaper kiosks, a post office and a car wash.

✿ G.P.O. *Privokzalnaya Square 1.*

BANK *Teatralnaya Square 1.*

DEPARTMENT STORE *Rosa Luxemburg Street.*

COMMISSION SHOPS *Engels Street 29 and Sverdlov Street 4.*

JEWELLER'S *Tevelov Street 16 and Sumskaya Street 3.*

✿ FILLING STATION *Moskovsky Prospekt 94 and Gagarin Prospekt (Diesel oil for sale here).*

REPAIR STATION *Botanichesky Pereulok 2.*

ROAD EIGHT

MOSCOW—KHARKOV—SIMFEROPOL YALTA

MOSCOW

Butovo · Podolsk · Molodi · Chekhov · Serpukhov

TULA

Tula · Yasnaya Polyana · Schekino · Plavsk · Chern
Passkoye-Lutovinovo · Mtsensk

OREL

Orel · Kromy · Verkhny Lubazh · Fatezh

KURSK

Oboyan · Belgorod

KHARKOV

Merefa · Krasnograd · Natalino · Novo-Moskovsk · Levshino-Mikhailovka
Zaporozhye · Zeleni-Gai · Melitopol · Akimovka

THE KHERSON ROAD

Askania-Nova · Kakhovka · Novaya Kakhovka · Kherson

THE CRIMEA

Dzhankoi · Timiryazevo

SIMFEROPOL

Alushta · Gurzuf · Massandra

YALTA

Livadia · Oreanda · Gaspra and Koreiz · Miskhor · Alupka · Simeiz
Foros · Baidar Gate · Sevastopol · Sapun-Gora · Severnaya Storona
Hersones (Korsun) · Bakhchiserai · Chufut-Kaleh · Katchi-Kalen
Tepe-Kermen · Mangup-Kaleh

MOSCOW

See Road 1, on page 103.

BUTOVO

This village is 24 km (15 miles) south of Moscow and the Camping site is 500 m (550 yd) aside from the main road. It is situated on hilly ground among pine trees, and is very dry owing to the sandy soil. There is a self-service kitchen, a buffet, and shops.

As the site is only 300–400 m (330 to 440 yd) from Butovo Railway Station visitors can conveniently leave their cars behind if they do not wish to drive in the city itself.

PODOLSK

Population: 124,000 (1959)

Podolsk stands on the River Pakhra, near which there are large marble and limestone quarries.

In 1781 it became a town and was given a coat-of-arms with crossed pickaxes, symbolising the inhabitants, work in the quarries. At the end of the last century a Singer sewing machine factory was built; this was later enlarged and is still working today. Podolsk itself has grown into an industrial centre with factories producing concrete and machinery.

THE TROITSI SOBOR (TRINITY CATHEDRAL). This cathedral dates from the 18th century.

LENIN MUSEUM *Moskovskaya Street*. This is in a house where Lenin's family lived for some time during the 1890's.

EATING HOUSE.

MOLODI

This village is some distance south of Podolsk, on the main road to the south and contains a picturesque church dedicated to Saint Peter and Saint Paul.

CHEKHOV

This town was formerly known as Lopasnya, and stands beside the river of that name. It has been known historically since the 12th century, and it was near here that the Russians defeated the Crimean Tartars in a battle in 1572. It was renamed after the writer, Anton Chekhov, in 1954. The town has a woodworking factory, and under construction is the biggest printing works in Europe.

CHURCH OF THE IMMACULATE CONCEPTION. This dates from the 19th century.

EATING HOUSE.

Melikhovo 13 km (8 miles) from Chekhov. It was here that Anton Chekhov (1860–1904) lived on his own estate between 1892 and 1898. He was responsible for building the local school, and during the cholera epidemic here he resumed his work as a doctor. There is now a museum on the estate, and among other exhibits is the wooden platter upon which the peasants presented him with bread and salt (an old Russian custom) upon the occasion of the opening of the school.

The Chekhov Monument was erected on the Melikhovo Estate in 1951. Chekhov wrote the *Seagull* while living here.

SERPUKHOV

Population: 105,000 (1959)

The town stands on the River Nara, which is a small tributary of the River Oka, and it dates from 1328. Down the River Nara, on either side, stood two fortresses; these were the Vladichny Convent, founded by Metropolit Alexei in 1362, and the Vysotsky Bogoroditsy Monastery, founded by Saint Sergius of Rodonezh in 1373. The fate of Serpukhov was linked with that of Moscow, but the Princes of Serpukhov still had their own independence to a certain extent in the 14th and 15th centuries and minted their own money. Like many other Russian towns, Serpukhov was destroyed several times by the Tartars and later by the Lithuanians.

In 1556 by the order of Ivan the Terrible it was built up into a powerful fortress with a stone wall and towers replacing the original fortifications of earth and oak. Its situation made it one of the strategic points on the Oka thoroughfare, protecting the road to Moscow from the encroachments of the Tartars. At the end of the 18th century Tsar Paul I ordered the defences to be dismantled; this was duly done, and now only remains of the earth wall and some parts of the Kremlin walls can be seen.

Today Serpukhov is an important centre of the chemical and machine-building industries and has several large textile mills.

The local churches, all of different styles, can be seen from the top of the Kremlin Hill.

✿ TROITSKY (TRINITY) CATHEDRAL. This cathedral was built in 1380 by Prince Vladimir Andreyevich. It was reconstructed in 1714 and is still open for religious services.

CHURCH OF SAINT NICHOLAS THE WHITE *Kaluzhskaya Street 26*. This church was built in 1649 and reconstructed in 1835.

CHURCH OF THE PROPHET ELIJAH *Volodarsky Street*. This church was founded in 1748 and is open for services.

USPENSKY (ASSUMPTION) CHURCH. This church was built in 1851.

VLADICHNYI CONVENT. The walls with four towers remain; these were built in the 16th century and reconstructed in the 18th century.

VYSOTSKY BOGORODITSY MONASTERY. The 15th century cathedral, reconstructed in the 17th century, still stands and the remains of the walls with towers of 1664 can be seen.

✿ LENIN MONUMENT *On the central square.*

HISTORY AND ART MUSEUM *Chekhov Street 87*. This is located in a house built in the 1870's. The museum was founded in 1920, to house the local nobility's collections of icons and western European works of art, which had passed to the museum after the revolution.

✿ DRAMA THEATRE *Chekhov Street 58/27.*

✿ MOSKVA HOTEL AND RESTAURANT *Lenin Square.*

TULA

Population: 345,000 (1959)

Tula is an industrial town lying on either side of the River Upa, a tributary of the River Oka. It lies 180 km (112 miles) south of Moscow and covers an area of over 10,000 hectares (40 sq.miles), measuring 9 km (6 miles) from north to south. Like most old Russian towns it is built on a plan of concentric circles centering on the kremlin. The present-day layout of the town was planned in the middle of the 19th century, and now there are as many as 570 streets.

The first records of Tula date from 1146, and the town was developing at the same time as Moscow, which it protected from the Crimean Tartars. Tula itself suffered much from their invasions.

Iron deposits were discovered in the vicinity in the 16th century, and the first gun factory was established in 1632 by a Dutchman named Vienius. The town's period of prosperity dates from 1712 when Peter the Great founded the Imperial Small Arms Factory here. This was built under the superintendence of an Englishman, Trewheller, and is situated near the Kremlin. It supplied Russia with her arms for many years, and is still in operation. Napoleon planned to capture Tula and so to disarm Russia; in World War II the Germans had a similar plan, but although they managed to seize part of the town they failed to capture it all.

Tula iron-workers have long been famous for their craftsmanship, and a favourite story by the 19th century Russian writer Leskov tells how at the beginning of the 19th century a present of a life-size metal flea was sent to the tsar from England to show the skill of British metal-workers. The tsar sent it to Tula to a certain Master Levsha ("left-handed") who, to prove that his skill was greater than that of the British made for the flea a set of "horseshoes" which could only be seen through a magnifying glass.

Besides the local iron ore, coal has been mined from valuable deposits nearby and has also added to the town's prosperity.

Tula is famous for being the place where sweet biscuits called *Tulskie Pryaniki* are made, but more important are the "Tula ware" objects made of brass, such as samovars, and of nickel-plate, iron and steel, especially knives. The so-called "Tula-work" consists of black enamel inlaid with silver, and is often imitated elsewhere.

The main streets of the town are all near the kremlin, including the principal *Lenin Prospekt*. On *Mendeleyev Street* stands the Lenin Library, built in classical style with massive columns. Tula's main square is *Chelyuskintsev* to the south-west of the kremlin; on this square stands a huge Palace of Pioneers, reconstructed from the original town hall, which contains a planetarium and a concert hall for 500. Close to the kremlin wall on the other side of the square, is a technical school, and in the centre is a statue of a Soviet soldier with a rifle. Nearby in Revolutsiya Street is one of the biggest maternity hospitals in Russia with 280 beds, and not far away in Dennisovsky Pereulok are the remains of the palace which belonged to the factory owners the Levintsevs; its magnificence can now only be judged by the baroque gates, built in the middle of the 18th century, which are still standing. The Luginin Palace, now housing the Pedagogical Institute, stands near the crossing of Mendeleyev Street and Lenin Prospekt. Mendeleyev Street leads to the horseshoe-shaped Sovietskaya Street which is the town's second most important thoroughfare and which was built to follow the line of the old earth wall in the 18th century. This street runs through Vosstanie Square where stands a huge bronze monument to Lenin and where parades and demonstrations take place. Near is Pioneer Garden Square, where a church used to stand. The busiest spot in Tula is at the crossroad of Sovietskaya Street and Lenin Prospekt. Lenin Prospekt is 4 km ($2\frac{1}{2}$ miles) long and passes to other garden squares, *Gogol Square* and *Pushkin Square* where Pushkin's bust was unveiled in 1889.

In Lenin Prospekt 44 is the House of Officers, formerly the House of Nobles, which contains a Hall of Columns with room for 800 people—a replica of the famous Hall of Columns in Moscow. Opposite this building is another garden square with the graves of soldiers who fell during the Russian Civil War of 1918. Nearby Gogol Street was the street of Tula's nobility; it has been partly reconstructed but many original houses remain. A number of Russian writers have lived in this street.

Not far from Komsomol Park is the beginning of *Oktyabrskaya Street* where, beside Chugunnyi Most (Pig-iron Bridge), stands the 18th century Nikolo Zaredskaya Church.

The south-east of the town, the Novotulsky Region, is the newest part, built to house the metal factory workers. Although it belongs to Tula, there are 4 km (2½ miles) of allotments between these two parts of the town.

Tula's industrial station for the underground gasification of coal, is one of the biggest in the world, as well as in the Soviet Union; the coal is burnt below ground, and the gas supplies many Tula factories.

THE KREMLIN stands on *Vosstaniye Square* in the centre of the town. It is rectangular with a perimeter of over 1 km (¾ mile) enclosing an area of 6 hectares (15 acres). It is about 985 ft long and 630 ft wide. Its architecture is characteristically Russian; it was built between 1514 and 1521, and in spite of restorations in 1784 and in 1824 it has changed little during the past 400 years. The walls are 3 m (10 ft) thick and about 13 m (43 ft) high, built of limestone with battlements of brick. There are 4 corner towers with 5 square towers between them.

Within the walls stands the *Uspensky Sobor* (Cathedral of the Assumption), founded in the 16th century, but reconstructed in Russian baroque style between 1742 and 1744. It is famous for its frescoes which were painted by artists from Yaroslavl, and which repeat the motifs of the ancient churches of Yaroslavl, Vladimir and Moscow. The technique used is quite outstanding, and they are considered to be the finest examples of old Russian fresco work. Some of the frescoes illustrate the Song of Solomon.

Another church within the kremlin walls is the Bogoyavleniya (Epiphany) Church, built in the middle of the 19th century.

Outside the kremlin, but close to the western wall, is the Church of the Annunciation, built in 1692 and typical of the older Russian churches.

✿ CHURCH OF THE USPENSKY MONASTERY *At the crossing of Mendeleyev Street and Lenin Prospekt.* This church was built in the 19th century.

✿ LOCAL MUSEUM *Sovietskaya Street 68.*

ART MUSEUM *Lenin Prospekt 44.*

MUSEUM OF THE HISTORY OF ARMS *Lenin Prospekt, on the main Moscow–Yalta road just opposite the Kremlin. Open 11–3; closed on Mondays.* This museum, established in 1724, contains collections of Russian arms of all ages and includes many miniatures. There are also some foreign arms on display, and the museum is well worth a visit.

VSEVOLOD RUDNEV MONUMENT *At the entrance to Tula from Moscow.* Rudnev (1855–1913) was commander of the man-of-war *Varyag*, famous for its lone stand against the Japanese fleet in January 1904 when the Japanese war began. The monument was unveiled in 1956 to commemorate the 50th anniversary.

✿ GORKY DRAMA THEATRE *Lenin Prospekt 51.*

YOUTH THEATRE *Kominterna Street 10.*

PUPPET THEATRE *Sovietskaya Street 78.*

ZENITH STADIUM *In the eastern half of the kremlin territory.*

✿ KOMSOMOL PARK. This park was laid out in 1895 on an area of 45 hectares (111 acres). It has many oak and lime trees and in the centre of the park is the so-called Pushkin Oak. There is also a summer café, a dance floor, a musical variety stage, and a monument which commemorates the Soviet soldiers who died in 1941.

SEZHENSKY FOREST. This is another favourite playground for the people of Tula.

CENTRAL HOTEL AND RESTAURANT MOSKVA *Sovietskaya Street 29.*

TULA HOTEL AND RESTAURANT *Lenin Prospekt 96.*

FILLING STATION *On the main road leading out of the town to the south, by the bus station. Round-the clock-service.*

YASNAYA POLYANA

Yasnaya Polyana ("sunlit meadows") was the birthplace and beloved home of Count Leo Tolstoi (1828–1910). Of it he wrote, "Without Yasnaya Polyana I can hardly think of Russia or of my attitude to her".

The estate lies 1·5 km (1 mile) from the main road, the turning being marked by a bust of the writer. At 201 km (125 miles) south of Moscow, a visit here may count as a day trip from the capital.

Tolstoi would probably have died in Yasnaya Polyana as well as spending most of his life there if, ten days before his death, he had not left home and caught pneumonia, so that he died at a small railway station not far away. His grave surrounded by nine oaks is in the park, on Staryi Zakaz Hill.

Preserved in the house are portraits of the writer by Repin and Kramskoy (the latter painted in 1873 while Tolstoi was working on *Anna Karenina*), a library of 22,000 books in more than 20 languages of which Tolstoi himself spoke 13, a phonograph presented by Edison, an English-made grandfather clock, and a portrait of the real Anna Karenina. The desk at which Tolstoi's wife transcribed *War and Peace* many times is in her bedroom. The other simple furnishings remain much as they were during Tolstoi's lifetime.

There is now a literary museum in the building where Tolstoi organised a school for the peasants, and one of the curators is his last secretary, Valentin Bulgakov.

The museum Ticket Office is by the main gates of the estate. The museum is open 9–5; closed on Wednesdays.

RESTAURANT AND CAFE *just outside the gates of the estate.*

SCHEKINO

This is one of the oldest mining towns in the Moscow coal basin.

The German General Guderian's panzers were defeated here in December 1941.

PLAVSK

Plavsk stands on the River Plava; the town contains a machine-building factory.

SAINT SERGEI'S CHURCH. This church dates from the end of the 18th century.

RESTAURANT *Near the church.*

FILLING STATION.

CHERN

Chern lies on the left bank of the River Zusha. The town was founded in the time of Ivan the Terrible, and was first mentioned in the chronicles in 1578 as a guard post on the Russian defence line against the Tartars.

There are two 19th century churches on the hill, one of which is the Church of the Intercession.

SPASSKOYE-LUTOVINOVO

SPASSKOYE-LUTOVINOVO—*Motorists should turn off the main road north of Mtsensk, at the 303 km milestone (from Moscow) where there is a bust ot the writer Ivan Turgenev and a signpost indicating the way to his former estate, 6 km ($3\frac{1}{2}$ miles) from the main road.*

The Turgenev family estate is now a branch of the Orel Museum. There are 8 halls of exhibits in the Exile's House, where Turgenev was exiled in 1852–53 by the order of Nicholas I for writing an unsuitable obituary on the death of writer Nikolai Gogol. Although after 1855 Turgenev spent many years abroad, mostly in Germany and France, this place, where his family had moved when he was three years old, was nevertheless his favourite. In a letter written in France to a Russian friend he said, "When you are next in Spasskoye give my regards to the house, the grounds and my young oak tree—to my homeland". Turgenev's oak tree is still to be seen.

The main part of the house was burned down in 1906, but the remaining side wings and other buildings have been restored to their appearance of 1881 when Turgenev was last here. Some of his works, including the novel *Rudin*, were written here, and *Fathers and Sons* and *A Nest of the Gentry* were completed here.

The park was laid out in 1808. Some of the avenues were planted in the figure "XIX" signifying that it originated in the 19th century. The longest avenue is of limetrees, forming the "I" of the number.

Along the avenues there are wooden boards with quotations from the writer's works, for he is known in Russia as one of the most competent of nature writers. One avenue leads to a pond, called *Savinsky Prud* after Maria Savina (1854–1915), an actress who took parts in his plays. On the estate are a church and a mausoleum, built at the beginning of the 19th century.

MTSENSK

This town, first mentioned in writing in 1147, stands on the River Zusha. In the 14th century this was the border town between Lithuania and Moscow; it passed from hand to hand several times and was looted by the Tartars. By the 18th century it had grown in importance as a trade centre and today its industry is mainly concerned with food products; there is also a large iron foundry.

✿ THE CHURCH OF THE SAINT PETER AND SAINT PAUL MONASTERY. This church dates from the 17th century.

✿ HOTEL. This hotel is recommended for motorists and has a large carpark.

MTSENSK RESTAURANT *Open 7 a.m. till midnight.*

BUFFET *Open 10 a.m.–7 p.m.* The town of Mtsensk is in fact off the tourist road, but, at 310 km (193 miles) from Moscow, Mtsensk is a good place to stop at; if one leaves Moscow in the afternoon to avoid the traffic, one can spend the night at the hotel in Mtsensk and then set out from there in the early morning.

✿ SERVICE STATION *At the 310 km milestone (from Moscow) tel: 2-00. Round the clock service.*

FILLING STATION *At the Service Station.* Diesel oil supplied as well as petrol; round the clock service.

✿ CAFE *By the road at the 328/1071 km milestone.*

✿ OBELISK *To the right of the main road at the 439/1050 km milestone.* This commemorates General Gurtiev who lost his life here in 1943.

OREL

Pronounced ahr-yol and meaning "eagle"

Population: 152,000 (1959)

The town stands at the confluence of the River Oka and the River Orlik. It was founded in 1564 in the reign of Ivan the Terrible when it was a border fortress of the Muscovite State against the Crimean Tartars. It was said that once, when a group of Tartar invaders were in these parts, an eagle fell like a stone onto the Khan who led them. After a short fight between them the eagle, pouring blood, rose into the air and then folded its wings and plunged down into the river. The Khan, however, was also wounded and fled with all his men from the River Oka. Ivan the Terrible heard this legend and decided to name the new fortress after the eagle.

Orel was an especially important border fortress because it was on the main route by which the Tartars came north to attack Moscow. It was ruined by the Poles at the beginning of the 17th century, and in the 1660's was again devastated by the Tartars; in 1673, after a tremendous fire, it was transferred to a new site known as Yamskaya Hill. It played a useful role in the extension of Russia's dominion further south, and after that life became more peaceful in Orel. The fortress remained until 1702.

On 7th June, 1884, it is recorded that Orel was again badly damaged by fire. Its trade at this time was in grain, hemp, eggs and poultry. In the 1860's Orel served as a place of exile for Polish insurgents and later a central prison was built to accommodate prisoners on their way to Siberia.

The present lay-out of the town dates from 1779 when Orel became the district capital, and, according to new plans, was divided into three parts, each part containing a certain area where it was forbidden to build. Thus originated the three main squares, Komsomolskaya (formerly Kromskaya), Promyshlennaya (formerly Vozdvizhenskaya) and Poleskaya Squares. Near Lenin (formerly Market) Square, arcades of shops were built in 1849.

The town was the scene of much fighting in 1943 and was largely destroyed. When it was liberated on 5th August 1943 a salute was fired in Moscow; this was the first of such salutes which afterwards heralded the liberation of all the larger cities and towns in turn.

Orel now stretches 11 km (7 miles) from the north to the south. From Lenin Square the main Moscow–Simferopol road runs along Moskovskaya Street and Komsomolskaya Street which are the busiest in the town. Most of the buildings here are of post-war construction.

The quiet Normandiya-Neman Street is called after the French squadron who fought with the Russians for Orel in the Second World War.

Lenin Street is among the oldest in Orel with many pre-revolutionary houses. There is a pedagogical institute in the town, and the local House of Soviets stands on Lenin Square.

Orel is an important railway junction and its industries include the manufacture of machinery for agriculture, road making, and the textile, footwear and food industries. Leather, food products, watches and clocks are also produced.

✿ SAINT NIKITA'S CATHEDRAL *Rabochy Pereulok 18*. This church was built in 1775.

CHURCH OF THE ARCHANGEL MICHAEL *Sacco and Vantsetti Pereulok*. This church was built in 1801 in Russian classical style.

SAINT NICHOLAS-ON-THE-SAND CHURCH *Normandiya-Neman Street*. This church was built in 1790, is closed and of no particular historical interest.

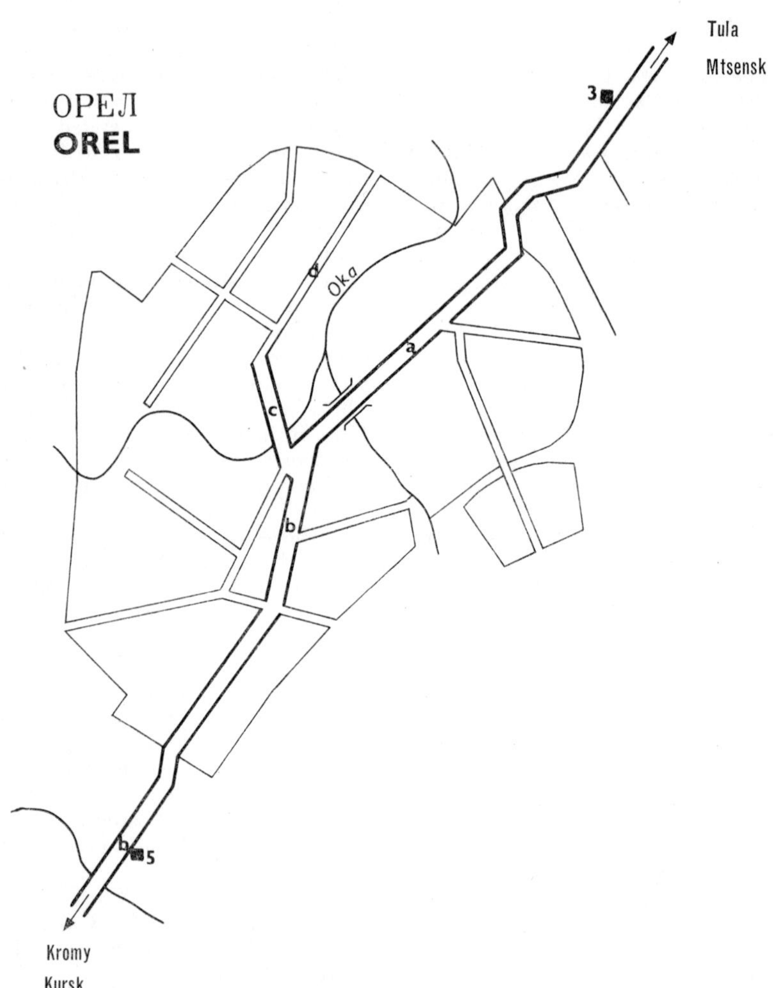

3 Filling Station 5 Camp Site

a Moskovskaya ul. b Komsomolskaya ul.
c Lenina ul. d Gorkogo ul.

SMOLENSKAYA CHURCH *Normandiya-Neman Street*. This church is also of little interest. It is of 19th century construction.

TURGENEV MUSEUM *Turgenevskaya Street 11. Closed on Fridays*. This museum is located in the house which belonged to landlord Trubitsyn; Turgenev never lived here although he was born in Orel.

MUSEUM OF LOCAL WRITERS *7th-November Street 24. Closed on Fridays*. The building was the home of the historian and writer Timofei Granovsky.

Many of the streets of Orel are named after writers and poets who were born or lived here. Among them are Ivan Turgenev, Leonid Andreyev, Nobel prizewinner Ivan Bunin, Granovsky, Leskov, Fet, Prishvin and others whose names mean much for any admirer of Russian literature. The Writers' Museum is in a hilly part of the town, and the region around is known as "the nest of the gentry". Many old houses typical of Russian nobles'homes have survived. Leskov, talking about the importance of Orel in Russian literature, said that his birthplace, "with its shallow waters nourished for the motherland more Russian writers than any other Russian town". Local enthusiasts used to call Orel the literary capital of Russia.

LOCAL MUSEUM *Moskovskaya Street 1/3*.

PICTURE GALLERY *Saltykov-Shchedrin Street 33*.

LENIN MONUMENT *Lenin Square in front of the House of Soviets*. The sculpture by Tomsky was unveiled in 1949.

POLIKARPOV MONUMENT *In the garden on Moskovskaya Street*. Nikolai Polikarpov (1892–1944), an aeroplane designer, was born in Orel.

MEDVEDEV MONUMENT *Moskovskaya Street*. Mikhail Medvedev (1887–1919) was a civil war hero.

TANK MONUMENT *Tankistov Garden*. A tank marks the grave of those who fell here in World War II; an eternal flame burns here.

GURTEV MONUMENT *Gurtev Square*. Major-General Gurtev was killed during the liberation of Orel in 1943.

TURGENEV DRAMA THEATRE *Teatralnaya Square*. Founded in 1815, this is one of the oldest theatre companies in the country. It was organised as a theatre of serf-actors by Count Kamensky on his estate 12 km ($7\frac{1}{2}$ miles) from Orel. The Count was a real tyrant, and used to sit in his box with a book in front of him in which he wrote down each mistake the actors made. Nearby hung an assortment of whips, and during the interval he would select one of these and go backstage to beat those who had displeased him. Their cries could even be heard by the audience. Nevertheless the company thrived and in 1817 it is recorded that during six months 82 productions were staged, including 18 operas, 15 dramas, 41 comedies, 6 ballets and two tragedies; the playwrights included Shakespeare, Schiller, Beaumarchais and the Russian classics, and there were also works by local serfs. Productions were extremely lavish, with costumes of silk and velvet. The theatre is described in the writings of Leskov. The building now used by the company was built in 1779 and was originally occupied by the Town Council.

PUPPET THEATRE *Moskovskaya Street 1/3, in the 18th century building of the Epiphany Church*.

PARK *Gurtev Square, beside the River Orlik*. There is a summer theatre there.

CHILDREN'S PARK *In the centre of town, where the rivers Orlik and Oka meet and where the fortress once stood*.

The region beside the River Tson, a tributary of the River Oka, called Botanika,

5 km (3 miles) from the town centre, it is one of the most beautiful in the area. The Orel Exhibition of Economic Achievements, and a fruit-farming research station are here.

HIPPODROME *Near Troitskoye Kladbishche.*

OREL HOTEL AND RESTAURANT *Pushkin Street 5; tel: 32-89.*

ROSSIYA HOTEL AND RESTAURANT *Saltykov-Shchedrin Street.*

OKA RESTAURANT *Lenin Street 16.*

ORLIK RESTAURANT *Komsomolskaya Street 228.*

DRUZHBA (FRIENDSHIP) CAFE *Moskovskaya Street.*

G.P.O. AND TELEGRAPH OFFICE *Gorky Street 43.*

BANK *Teatralnaya Square.*

DEPARTMENT STORE AND SOUVENIRS *Moskovskaya Street 5.*

FILLING STATIONS *By the main road as it enters and leaves the town.*

REPAIR STATION *At the entrance to the town, by the main road.*

TSON RESTAURANT *Out of town on the way to the camping site.*

CAMPING SITE *3 km (2 miles) south of Orel, off the main Moscow–Simferopol road, 300 m (330 yd) to left.* Telephone, hot showers; car wash and repair ramp. 300 m (330 yd) from the Camping Site are places on River Tson for fishing and bathing. Buffet (open till 10 p.m.) and self-service kitchen.

KROMY

Founded in 1147, Kromy is best known for being the centre of a battlefield during the Time of Troubles. The battle of 1604 is depicted in Mussorgsky's opera *Boris Godunov*. On this occasion the followers of the first pretender Dmitry made the existing fortress their stronghold. Boris Godunov sent 80,000 troops to capture it. The defenders were few but they held out, and eventually the Tsar's general defected to Dmitry's side.

It was near Kromy that two years later, in 1606, Ivan Bolotnikov, leading rebellious peasants and Cossacks, defeated the tsarist army.

Another battle was fought here during the Civil War in 1919. During World War II the place was so ruined that the inhabitants could hardly recognise the places where their houses had stood.

Kromy is in Russia's most important hemp-growing area.

SAINT NICHOLAS'S CHURCH *By the main road.* This church was built in the 19th century and is open for service.

LENIN MONUMENT.

OBELISK to the memory of those who fell in the Civil War; unveiled in 1949.

CAFE *Karl Marx Street, the main road.*

FILLING STATION.

VERKHNY LUBAZH

FILLING STATION *At the 456 km milestone (from Moscow). Round-the-clock service.*

FATEZH

Fatezh was founded in the 17th century on the frontier line against the Tartars. There are branches of the food industry here and the remains of *Pokrovsky Cathedral* and of the 19th century *Saint Tikhon Church* still stand.

TEAROOM *To the right of the main road coming in from Moscow.*

KURSK

Population: 230,000 (1964)

"Kursk" comes from *Kuropatka*, the Russian word for partridge, and three of these birds were pictured on the old coat-of-arms.

The town is situated on two hills on the right bank of the River Tuskari, a tributary of the River Seim. It was founded in the 9th century and was first mentioned in a document of 1095. The Mongols destroyed it in 1240; later it belonged to Lithuania for many years and an important trade in grain, linen, leather and apples grew up. It was eventually annexed to the principality of Moscow, and in the 16th century became another of the defence points on Russia's southern border.

At the beginning of the 18th century when the Russian border was moved farther south Kursk fortress lost much of its importance. Administrative buildings were built upon its site and in 1798 Kursk became a provincial capital. There are still many houses of typical 19th century Russian architecture, among them the former House of Nobles at 4, Verkhne-Naberezhnaya St. and the manege (now a cinema) at 51, Dzerzhinskova St. An even older part of Kursk can be seen on Pionerskaya and Zolotorevskaya streets where Romodanovsky House (1649–80) and the 17th century Trinity Church stand. There might have been more to see had it not been for the fighting and enemy occupation here during the second World War.

Lenin Street is the main thoroughfare and the road followed by motorists passing through the town. The best shops are here and it leads into Krasnaya (red) Square where there is the hotel and the impressive buildings of the House of Soviets (1948), the town-hall and the Local Economical Council. The monument to Lenin by Manizer was unveiled in 1956. There are pedagogical, medical and agricultural institutes in Kursk and local factories produce electrical apparatus, synthetic fibre, rubber, glass, textiles and food products. The Kursk region is famous for its nightingales and for its Antonovka apples which ripen at the end of September.

✿ ST. SERGE'S CATHEDRAL *Gorky Street*. The cathedral was built in 1752–78 following a project by Rastrelli. Inside is a carved iconostasis, 18 m (60 ft) high, and a Bible dated 1693.

CHURCH OF THE SIGN OF OUR LADY Formerly the cathedral church of the Znamensky Monastery, 43 m (141 ft) high and built in 1816–28. The distinctive silver dome stands out clearly as one drives down Lenin Street. The round brick tower nearby which dates from the 1790's was part of the monastery wall. The church now houses the October Cinema.

TRINITY CONVENT *Gorky Street 13*. Here remain the bell tower and Upper Trinity Church (1695). The buildings are now used to house the local archives.

ST. NIKITA'S CHURCH *near Moskovskiye Vorota*. This church is open for service.

ST. CATHERINE'S CHURCH *Engels Street 7, behind the filling station.*

✿ LOCAL MUSEUM AND PLANETARIUM *Lunacharsky Street 4. Open 10–4.*

MOSKOVSKIYE VOROTA *Karl Marx Street at the entrance to Kursk on the main road from Moscow.* The name means Moscow Gates, and originally there was a triumphal arch here to commemorate the visit of Alexander I in 1823, but now only the gateposts remain.

UFIMTSEV MUSEUM *Semenovskaya Street 13*. Anatoli Ufimtsev (1880 to 1936) was a Kursk-born inventor and aeroplane engine constructor. His first claim to fame was when in 1898 he blew up a miracle-working icon in the cathedral of the Znamensky Monastery with a time-bomb. He was sent to Siberia and the monks set up a copy of the original icon in the hopes that it would also work miracles. Ufimtsev built the windmill that stands beside his house and the house itself is used as a club for young technicians.

PICTURE GALLERY *Sovietskaya Street 3.*

DZERZHINSKY MONUMENT *Dzerzhinsky Square.*

BOROVYKH'S BUST *in the park* is a memorial to the pilot, Andrei Borovykh, Kursk-born and twice made a Hero of the Soviet Union.

✿ PUSHKIN DRAMA THEATRE *Perekalsky Street 1.*

SUMMER THEATRE *Lenin Street, in the 1st-May Garden opposite the Kursk Hotel.*

PUPPET THEATRE *Lenin Street 99.*

✿ DYNAMO STADIUM *Lenin Street 36.*

TRUDOVYE REZERVY STADIUM *Lenin Street 58.* There are places for 17,000. The local ACRICULTURAL EXHIBITION is open between September and November. *It is near the Camping Site.*

✿ TSENTRALNAYA HOTEL *Lenin Street 2; tel: 6-70-84.*

KURSK HOTEL AND RESTAURANT *Lenin Street 4; tel: 3-31-92.* There is an Intourist bureau at this hotel. There is also a courtyard carpark which is guarded at night.

SEIM RESTAURANT *Solyanka Street 6, near the Camping Site.*

CAFE *Lenin Street 4.*

Local delicacies include Kursky Salat (salad of chicken, butter and apple) and Gavyadina-Po-Kursky (rolls of beef stuffed with egg, rice and butter and then deep-fried).

✿ G.P.O. AND TELEGRAPH OFFICE *Krasnaya Square.*

BANK *Lenin Street 83.* Kursk's coat-of-arms with the partridges can be seen on the façade.

DEPARTMENT STORE *Lenin Street 12.*

JEWELLER'S *Lenin Street 2.*

✿ FILLING STATION *Engels Street 3, on the right on the way out of town towards Kharkov.*

REPAIR STATION *Karl Marx Street 31a.*

CAMPING SITE *A little out of town 200 m (220 yd) off the main road to the left south of Kursk; tel: 22-05.* The tents and bungalows are in a pine-wood. There are a buffet, a self-service kitchen, a post office, a souvenir kiosk, and an international telephone. Carwash and repair trench.

300 m (330 yd) from the Camping Site beside the River Seim is Solyanka Park which has facilities for fishing, bathing, and boats for hire.

OBOYAN

Oboyan stands on the River Psyel. It was founded in 1650 on the edge of "no man's land" as part of the Russian defences against the Tartars. In 1779 it had risen to the status of regional town; its coat-of-arms bore a polecat, for there were many of them in the vicinity. Today its industry is mainly concerned with food products.

✿ TRINITY CATHEDRAL *On the main street.* This cathedral, built in the 19th century, is open for religious services. There are also two other churches of no particular historic interest, and both are closed.

HOTEL AND EATING HOUSE *On the main street.*

TEAROOM.

FILLING STATION *At the 583 km milestone (from Moscow).* Diesel oil is available here.

OBOYAN RESTAURANT *By the petrol station, at the entrance to the town from the direction of Moscow.*

BELGOROD

Population: 72,000

The name of this town means "white-town". Belgorod is situated on the right bank of the Northern Donets river with its white chalk cliffs, and it commands a wide view of picturesque landscape. It is known that there has been a town on the site of Belgorod since the 13th century. In the 17th century it was the centre of the defence line on Russia's southern border. The new part of the town was heavily damaged during World War II and now the town centres round Revolutsiya Square. The chimneys of Belgorod's cement factory, one of the largest in Russia, can be seen from miles away. There is also a cannery in the town.

CHURCH OF THE ANNUNCIATION *Popov Street.* This church was built in the 19th century.

BAPTISTS' CHURCH *Narodnaya Street.*

LOCAL MUSEUM *Frunze Street 42.*

LENIN MONUMENT *Revolutsiya Square.*

APANASENKO MONUMENT *Near the railway station.* General I. Apanasenko was killed during the liberation of Belgorod from the Germans in World War II.

TANK MONUMENT *To the north of Belgorod, at the 624 km milestone from Moscow.* The tank, a T-34, stands on a granite block on the east side of the road. It commemorates those who fell here in battle in 1943.

STADIUM *By the main road.*

HOTEL.

BELGOROD RESTAURANT *Revolutsiya Square 1.*

UROZHAI (HARVEST) RESTAURANT *Parkovaya Street.*

BELGOROD CAFE AND ICECREAM PARLOUR *On the main road, at the corner of Khmelnitsky and Narodnaya Streets.*

CAMPING SITE *1 km (½ mile) to the left of the main road just to the south of the town.*

The site covers 3 hectares (7½ acres). There is a buffet, self-service kitchen, hot showers, a laundry, a post office, a telephone, a sports ground equipped for volleyball, a carwash and an inspection ramp.

FILLING STATION *By the main road, near the camping site.*

KHARKOV

See Road 7, on page 222.

MEREFA

Population: 26,000 (1959)

This town standing on the River Merefa has glass works, brick works and spirit factories.

KRASNOGRAD

Population: 15,000 (1959)

When it was founded in 1731 as part of the Ukrainian defence line, this town was known as Belevskaya Fortress. Later in 1797 it was renamed Konstantinograd after Grand Duke Konstantin Pavlovich. Its name was changed to Krasnograd in 1922.

The town stands on the River Berestenaya and manufactures food products.

SAINT NICHOLAS'S CHURCH. This church was built in the 19th century.

LOCAL MUSEUM. Ruins of the fortress built to withstand the Turks and the Crimean Tartars still remain.

DRAMA THEATRE.

RESTAURANT.

NATALINO

The village lies 10 km (6 miles) south of Krasnograd on the main road.

CAFE.

POST OFFICE.

FILLING STATION *Karl Marx Street 24, at the 110 km milestone from Kharkov.* Diesel oil is available here; round the clock service.

NOVO-MOSKOVSK

This town on the River Samara has been nicknamed "the bicycle city" for there are so many to be seen that it seems as if each worker has one.

In 1736 a military settlement was founded here on the site of the Cossack village of Samarchik. In the second half of the 18th century the town of Yekaterinoslavl was founded as the district centre of the newly acquired Black Sea region of Russia. However, the position was badly chosen as two rivers flooded it, and in 1782 the town was rebuilt on the right bank of the River Samara. In 1794 the site was again changed and the present day one selected. The town was then named Novo-Moskovsk, meaning New Moscow.

At present local industry includes a tin factory which supplies most of the canneries in the Soviet Union.

SAINT NICHOLAS THE HERMIT MONASTERY. The Monastery was founded in 1672, and the buildings are now used as an old people's home.

TRINITY CATHEDRAL *Torgovaya Square.* This wooden cathedral has green domes, and is said to have been built between 1773 and 1781 without a single nail being used in its construction.

RESTAURANT *Torgovaya Square.*

LEVSHINO-MIKHAILOVKA

RESTAURANT.

CAMPING SITE *At the 265 km milestone from Kharkov and 22 km (14 miles) north of Zaporozhye; near the filling station to the right of the main road.*

The site is among trees, in typical Ukrainian steppeland. Buffet, showers, self-service kitchen.

FILLING STATION *Near the Camping Site.* Round the clock service.

ZAPOROZHYE

(Formerly Alexandrovsk)

Population: 530,000 (1964)

In the 15th and 16th centuries the Ukrainian Cossacks settled in Zaporozhye Sech on the Island of Khortitsa in the Dnieper. The Island is 12 km long and 2·5 km wide ($7\frac{1}{2} \times 1\frac{1}{2}$ miles) and can be reached today from the old town. There are sanatoria and children's camps there now. The 600-year-old oak which legend maintains is the one under which the Zaporozhye Cossacks wrote their challenging and insulting letter to the Turkish Sultan can be seen 5 km (3 miles) outside the town at Verkhnyaya Khortitsa, Gogol Street. It is certainly the oldest tree in the Ukraine and the girth of its trunk measures 6·32 m (20 ft 9 ins). It is also said that in 1648 Bogdan Khmelnitsky addressed his warriors here with an appeal that in battle against the Poles they should be as strong and firm as this oak tree.

In 1770 a fortress was founded here as part of the defences against the Turks. In the 1806 the settlement that had grown up along side was called Alexandrovsk. Later, when the border with Turkey was at the edge of the Black Sea, this fortress lost its importance and the demobilised soldiers settled in the town. The records say that before 1917 there was only one three-storey house in the town and nine with two storeys. No more than 120 were brick built. The old name of Zaporozhye (which means "beyond the rapids") was given to the town for the first time in 1921.

Zaporozhye saw much fighting in 1918–19 and 70% of the town was ruined during the occupation from 1941 to 1943, but it finally recovered by 1949. With the development of industry a new town grew up, 10 km (6 miles) from the old one. Its first streets were laid out in the 1930's and it grew up as a model socialist town with multi-storey houses and wide avenues—Metallurgov Prospekt is over 30 m (33 yds) from side to side. Among other factories here is Zaporozhstal, a huge steel mill. Apart from metal, the town produces "Zaporozhets" baby cars and a variety of food products.

The main thoroughfare of the town proper is Lenin Prospekt which runs from Yuzhny Vokzal, through Svoboda Square, Sovietskaya Square, Oktyabrskaya Square and Mayakovskaya Square for a distance of over 15 km ($9\frac{1}{2}$ miles). The old and the new parts of the town are linked by a one kilometer long causeway, 30 m (33 yds) wide and 33 m (108 ft) high. The local population is 68% Ukrainian and $25\frac{1}{2}$% Russian, the rest belonging to any of thirty different nationalities, including Tartars, Jews, Greeks, Bulgarians, Georgians and Poles.

Navigation on the Dnieper used to be impossible because of the rapids. The first attempt to avoid them was made in the 18th century, and in the 19th some by-passing channels were built. The river was finally made navigable along the whole of its course by the construction of the Dnieper Hydro-electric Station (known as Dneproges). This was the first big hydropower station to be built in Russia. The plans were begun in 1905 and the construction in 1927. Many foreign firms were consulted before its completion in 1932, and the General Electric Company supplied most of the equipment to build up its 558,000 kilowatt capacity. Alexandrov was the Russian engineer-hydrologist and Vesnin headed the team of architects. The dam is 760 m (831 yds) long and 62 m (203 ft) high. There are 47 sluices. Three-quarters of the whole construction was destroyed during the war and it took three years after the war before it again began to produce any current. It had regained its former capacity by 1950. The completion of a second power house on the left bank of the river will double the power output of Dneproges.

LOCAL MUSEUM *Lenin Prospekt 59.*

TANK MONUMENT *Soviet Square.* This is the first tank that entered the town when it was liberated.

LENIN MONUMENT *At the end of Lenin Prospekt.*

GLINKA MONUMENT *Lenin Prospekt 183, outside the concert hall;* designed by Strakhov.

STEEL SMELTER'S STATUE *Near the Palace of Culture.* This statue by the local sculptor, Vlasenko, stands 4·5 m (15 ft) high. It was unveiled in 1959 as a symbol of the city's industrial might.

REVOLUTIONARIES' MONUMENT *In the garden in Svoboda Square.*

SCHORS DRAMA THEATRE *Lenin Prospekt 41.*

GLINKA CONCERT HALL *Lenin Prospekt 183.* Built in 1952 with seats for 860.

CIRCUS *In Metallurg Park.*

BATHING BEACHES *At Zhdanov Prospekt.*

Metallurg Park has a stadium for 23,000 spectators.

DNEPRO HOTEL AND RESTAURANT *Lenin Prospekt 202; tel: 64-51.* Intourist have their office here.

TEATRALNAYA HOTEL AND RESTAURANT *Chekista Street 23; tel: 9-73-09.*

YUZHNAYA HOTEL *21st-Partsyezda Street*

TAVRIYA RESTAURANT *Lenin Prospekt.*

SICH RESTAURANT *Lenin Prospekt 234.*

ZOLOTOY KOLOS RESTAURANT *Sotgorodka Market.*

PIVDEN RESTAURANT *Gorky Street.*

CHAIKA (SEAGULL) RESTAURANT *On Khortitsa Island, in an oak grove near the river.*

BANK *Lenin Prospekt 48.*

G.P.O. *Sverdlov Street 21.*

BOOKSHOP *Lenin Prospekt 38.*

ANTIQUE SHOP *Lenin Prospekt 196.*

UKRAINA DEPARTMENT STORE *Lenin Prospekt 147.*

GIFT SHOP *Lenin Prospekt 192.*

TAXI RANK *Lenin Prospekt 151.*

FILLING STATION *Near the entrance to the town.*

ZELENYI - GAI

HOTEL.

RESTAURANT.

REPAIR STATION AND FILLING STATION *At the 57 km milestone from Zaporozhye.* Diesel oil is obtainable here; round the clock service.

MELITOPOL

The name means "Honey Town"
Population: 95,000

Before the revolution the village was called Novo-Alexandrovska. It stands on the River Molochnaya ("Milky River"). In the early 19th century this part of the steppe was practically uninhabited until the members of various religious sects—Molokans and Dukhobors among others—began to settle here

Now Melitopol is famed for its fruit growing, particularly white cherries and apricots, and for its experimental horticultural farm. There is a teacher's training college, and one for electromechanics. Local industry includes the manufacture of Diesel engines and the engines for Russian baby cars, machine building and the bottling of mineral water.

CHURCH OF THE DECAPITATION OF JOHN THE BAPTIST *Karl Marx Street.* This church was built in the 19th century.

LOCAL MUSEUM *Dzerzhinsky Street 25.*

BOGDAN KHMELNITSKY MONUMENT *Bogdan Khmelnitsky Prospekt.*

GORKY PARK *Parkovaya Street.*

STADIUMS.

MELITOPOL HOTEL AND RESTAURANT *Karl Marx Street.*

LENINGRADSKAYA HOTEL *Schmidt Street.*

YIUZHNY (SOUTH) RESTAURANT *At the entrance to the town from Moscow.*

VESNA (SPRING) RESTAURANT *On the main road.*

G.P.O. *Karl Liebknecht Street 86.*

AKIMOVKA

RESTAURANT.

FILLING STATION *At the 145 km milestone from Zaporozhye.* Round the clock service.

NOVA-ALEKSEYEVKA

Here is a turning to the right which leads for 190 km (118 miles) through Askania-Nova, Kakhovka and Novaya Kakhovka to Kherson.

ASKANIA-NOVA

Population: 6000 (1964)

This village lies 61 km (38 miles) by good road from Novo-Alekseyevka. It is best known for its wild life reserve.

The territory of 50,000 hectares (125,000 acres) was purchased in 1828 by a German noble, Duke Angalt-Ketenski, and he founded a small settlement in 1841, naming it after his native estate of Askania in Germany. The steppe was used for breeding sheep and horses. But the estate really became profitable when it was sold to another German family, the Falz-Feins, who, with up to 400,000 sheep, became known as "sheep-breeding-kings" in the southern Ukraine.

In 1874 Friedrich Falz-Fein founded his little zoo which was called the Tierpark. Soon he began to buy animals from different parts of the world, ostriches from Africa, emus from Australia, zebu and antelopes from India. Then, from being a simple collection, the zoo took on scientific aims, the acclimatisation of animals and the preservation of rare species from extermination. The Ivanov Institute of Hybridisation and Acclimatisation was founded in 1932 and called after Mikhail Ivanov (1871–1935), an Academician who was responsible for breeding fine-fleeced sheep and also a variety of pig which does well on the Ukrainian steppe. The Institute's main work is the domestication of valuable wild animals and cross-breeding them with other domestic animals. Wars have taken heavy toll of the zoo's population. During the Civil War the zebra hybrids were used to pull gun carriages and after the German occupation (1941 to 1943) only 20 per cent of the animals were left.

Now there are about 100 different species of animals and birds including 4 kinds of zebra, 6 different antelopes, 3 types of ostrich, 5 kinds of swans and both American and European bison. The animals are all either cloven-hoofed or members of the horse family, pride of place belonging to the Przevalsky wild horse from Mongolia. Animals and birds are handed over to other zoos in the Soviet Union and exchanges are made with zoos in foreign countries. The local hospital is making useful experiments with antelope milk in curing ulcers and various illnesses.

Special permission is required to see the animals living free on the open steppe.

NATURAL HISTORY MUSEUM AND ZOO *Askania-Nova, both open from 8–4.*

BOTANICAL GARDEN *Open from 9 till 7.* The garden was laid out between 1887 and 1902 when seeds and plants were mainly brought from Odessa and Riga. The landscaping was by Dufresne, a French landscape gardener, and the territory covers 68 hectares (170 acres) including a beautiful lake with an island and a grotto of stone. 120 different trees and bushes have been acclimatised on the dry Tavrida steppe and the garden is often called an "emerald oasis".

At the entrance stands a water-tower built in 1892–93 in Gothic style. Here also is a monument to 16 paratroopers shot on this spot in 1941.

HOTEL AND RESTAURANT *Krasnoarmeiskaya Street.*

KAKHOVKA

Population: 19,000 (1959)

Kakhovka lies on the left bank of the River Dnieper. It was founded in the 18th century on the site of the Tartar fortress of Islam-Kermen.

In Soviet times it was of greatest importance during the Civil War when it was used as the bridgehead before the capture of the Crimea in 1920,—when the Crimean peninsula was the last stronghold of the anti-Bolshevik army.

The principal industries are car-repairing, food production and the manufacture of electro-welding equipment.

CHAPEL *Pushkinskaya Street 94.*

LOCAL MUSEUM *Lenin Street 12. Open on Tuesdays, Thursdays and Saturdays, 10–7.* Most of the exhibits illustrate the story of the attack on nearby Perekop in November, 1920, which preceded the taking of the Crimea by the Red Army.

BUST OF THE POET PUSHKIN *Pushkinskaya Street.* Pushkin visited Kakhovka in 1820 and the bust was unveiled in 1937.

FRUNZE MONUMENT *on the embankment of the "sea" (which is in fact a reservoir).* Mikhail Frunze was a famous Bolshevik who was a commander on the southern front during the Civil War. The monument, with an inscription reading, "From the Inhabitants of Kakhovka", was unveiled in 1957.

There is a *bathing beach* and a *boat-hiring station.*

TAVRIYA HOTEL AND KAKHOVKA RESTAURANT *Karl Marx Street 138.*

TOURIST RESTAURANT *Outside the town, beside the road leading on to Novaya Kakhovka.*

G.P.O. *Karl Marx Street.*

BANK *Karl Marx Street 118.*

DEPARTMENT STORE *Lenin Street.*

BOOKSHOP *Lenin Street.*

FILLING STATION *By the road leading out of town.*

NOVAYA KAKHOVKA

Population: 20,000 (1959)

In 1950 the decision was taken to build a new hydro-power station on River Dnieper 10 km (6 miles) away from the old town of Kakhovka. So it was that on the site of the little village of Kluchevoye where a few fishermen used to live, New Kakhovka was founded.

Construction of the hydro-power station began in 1951 and continued for five years. The gigantic reservoir, now known as the Kakhovka Sea, was not completely filled until 1957. It covers an area of 2,150 sq km (820 sq miles), has an average depth of 8·4 m (27 ft) and a maximum depth of 36 m (118 ft) and its capacity is 18·2 cu km. The reservoir stretches from Novaya Kakhovka to Zaporozhye and is used for the irrigation of the southern Ukraine and the northern part of the Crimea.

The hydro-power station is of 312,000 kilowatt capacity, and supplies the Dnieper area and the Donbas coal-mining region. It is situated on the Dnieper Rapids, 90 km (56 miles) upstream from the mouth of the River Dnieper.

The town stands on the river's left bank, connected by rail and road via the dam with the opposite bank. It was built as an example of a new type of planning; the streets follow the sweep of the river and are lined with two- and three-storey houses. The residential, working and shopping areas are on the higher ground while the lower slopes leading down to the river are all parks. Wide stone steps lead down from the impressive Palace of Culture through the park to River Dnieper where there is a bathing beach and a boating station.

The town's principal street is Dneprovsky Prospekt and the chief local industries are food production and electro-machine building.

War Memorial *Dneprovsky Prospekt*. Commemorating those who fell in the Civil War and during World War II.

Civil War Memorial *near the dam, on the Novaya Kakhovka side.*

There is a *Summer Theatre* in the park; *Energiya Stadium* can seat 5000.

Druzhba (Friendship) Hotel and Restaurant *Dneprovsky Prospekt 14, tel: 21-00.*

Tavriya Restaurant *Dneprovsky Prospekt.*

G.P.O. and Telegraph Office *Lenin Street 24.*

Bank *Dneprovsky Prospekt 15.*

The road from Novaya Kakhovka to Kherson runs over the top of the dam and then along the opposite side of River Dnieper.

TYAGINKA

Saint Nicholas Church. This church was built at the end of the 19th century but is now closed.

KHERSON

Population: 200,000 (1964)

The town stands on the high right bank of River Dnieper, about 24 km (15 miles) upstream from where it empties into the Black Sea. In the spring the river floods nearby to a width of 15 miles and forms numerous small rivers so that the area is known as Kherson's Venice. The population of the town is mainly composed of Ukrainians, Russians and Jews.

Like Odessa, Kherson stands above a maze of catacombs which vary in depth from 4 to 11 m (13 to 37 ft). It is believed that these date from the time of the greatest activity of the Zaporozhye Cossacks. They were then used by smugglers and members of religious sects, and finally served as emergency exits from the fortress above.

Kherson was founded in 1778 at the instigation of Prince Gregori Potemkin, from 1774 to 1776 the favourite of Catherine II. The town was laid out on the site of old fortifications and called Kherson after the ancient Greek colony of Khersones in spite of the fact that the latter did not stand here at all. Its ruins were found near Sevastopol in the Crimea and have been excavated. The initial work on Kherson was conducted by General Ivan Hannibal (1737–1801), grandfather of the poet, Alexander Pushkin. After a few years a fortress was constructed as well as a large shipyard. The building went ahead so quickly that when Catherine the Great visited the town eight years after its foundation she wrote: "there is a mass of people, apart from the military, and they speak almost all the languages of

Europe". The speed of Kherson's growth was accelerated after Potomkin's idea of making it a free port was adopted.

The present day Black Sea Fleet can trace its origins back to the old shipyard. The 66-gun frigate *Glory of Catherine* was completed here in 1783 and Kherson itself was the fleet's first base. In 1783–84 the shipyard was run by the famous Russian Admiral, Fyodor Ushakov, and it was from here that in 1787 and 1792–94 Generalissimo Alexander Suvorov conducted operations against the Turks.

In 1803 Kherson was designated provincial centre and grew in importance through being the point of export of corn and wool. It enjoyed the unique advantages of being close to the Black Sea and also beside a large navigable river. Russian merchants and foreign firms opened their offices here and, until the foundation of other ports,—Nikolayev and more particularly Odessa, Kherson grew and prospered. Then the new ports took a great deal of its trade and only after 1890, when the river had been deepened allowing ocean vessels to call in, did Kherson really revive.

For a long time the town's industries were of secondary importance but now Kherson has a highly developed shipbuilding industry. There are also agricultural machinery factories (combine harvesters for maize are their most important product) and large food-producing plants, among them the largest food cannery in the Ukraine. The textile combine, one of the biggest in the whole country, covers an area of 100 hectares (250 acres) near River Dnieper. Part of the town's industry is located on Quarantine Island, where there are also a variety of sports facilities and boat hiring stations.

Modern Kherson is one of the Ukraine's regional centres. New buildings line the main street, Prospekt Ushakova, as they do Suvorova Street and Pobedi Square. Prospekt Ushakova is divided into two equal parts by Svobodi (liberty) Square, and among the new buildings along its length still stands the old 17th century fire-watching tower. Suvorov Street is closed to traffic. It was a market street in the old days and now most of the ground floor accommodation is used for shops. The street is a popular place for strolling in the evening. On the corner of Lenin and Kommunarov Streets are the impressive buildings of the one-time *Duma* (town hall), built in 1906 and now used as the local Party headquarters. Also here is the old law court (1893). Another venerable thoroughfare that has retained its importance is Perekopskaya Street which runs beside the Dnieper for 12 km (7 miles). Some old aristocratic mansions remain here, including the two-storey house formerly used by the Governor. It is marked by a plaque commemorating the revolutionary events which took place here. Among the town's larger establishments are the Naval School (1834), the Tsuryupa Agricultural College (1874) and the Krupskaya Pedagogical College (1917).

Kherson was occupied by the Germans from August 1941 until March 1944, but after the war it was quick to recover. The town's holiday facilities are good and it is said to have 300 sunny days a year. The fame of the local melons and water-melons is an additional attraction to visitors.

✿ THE FORTRESS *Perekopskaya Street, by the river, a little to the north-west of the town.* It was abandoned as a military stronghold in 1835 but the earth walls and the Moskovskiye and the Ochakovskiye Gates are preserved as examples of 18th century fortifications. Besides the building of the former arsenal there also remains here the Church of Our Saviour (1781). One of the inscriptions reads: "Dedicated to the Saviour of Mankind by Catherine II". The empress's favourite, Prince Potemkin, was buried here but her son, Paul I, ordered that the tomb be secretly opened in 1798. Potemkin's remains were removed and the vault blocked up again. There are a number of valuable icons in this church, two of which by the portrait-painter Borovikovsky (1757–1825) represent Catherine II and Prince Potemkin. The building is now used to store books belonging to the local library but with special permission it can be visited. The six sculptures set in niches in the outside wall are by Zamarayev (1758 to 1823). Most of the monuments and tombstones are of those who fell during the 1788 siege of the nearby Turkish fortress, Ochakov.

GREKO-SOFIISKAYA CHURCH *Krasnoflotskaya Street 13*. This church is dedicated to the Nativity of the Virgin but usually referred to as the Greek Church. Its iconostasis of carved walnut, made in Cyprus, is famous although four rows of new icons have taken the places of the originals. The church was built in 1780 and is open for services.

CATHEDRAL OF THE HOLY SPIRIT (SVYATODUKHOVSKY) *Dekabristi Street*. This cathedral is alo open for services. It was built in 1835 and is often called Privoznaya (brought-in) Church because it stood near the market where goods were sold that had been brought into town.

LOCAL MUSEUM *Ushakov Prospekt 16. Open 10–5; closed on Wednesdays*. Among other items are objects which belonged to the Scythians and Sarmatians from the ancient Greek colony-town of Olvia. A more modern treasure is the Key of the City of Potsdam, a Soviet Army trophy.

NATURAL HISTORY MUSEUM *Gorky Street 5. Open 10–5; closed on Wednesdays.*

ART PAVILION *Svoboda Square.*

YURI GAGARIN PLANETARIUM *Suvorov Street 29*. Built in 1960.

HOWARD'S HOUSE *Suvorov Street 14*. John Howard (1727–90) was an English philanthropist and prison-reformer who caught typhus while visiting a local hospital here and never recovered. In 1890, on the centenary of his death, a memorial plaque was affixed to the house on the second floor of which he used to live. As well as the house, an obelisk of grey granite on Ushakov Prospekt remains here to his memory. It was erected on the order of Alexander I in 1828 and bears a plaque saying, "Howard died on January 20th, 1790, in his 63rd year". Howard was once Mayor of Bedford, and there is a bust of him in Westminster Abbey.

LENIN MONUMENT *Lenin Street.*

KARL MARX MONUMENT *In Marx Garden.*

BUST OF SUVOROV *Suvorov Street*. The bust, a copy of an old one by Rukavishnikov, was unveiled in 1950. The two-storey house where the generalissimo lived between 1792 and 1794 stands at *Suvorova Street 3*.

BUST OF SHEVCHENKO *In the Oak Grove*, the trees of which were planted in 1964 to commemorate the 150th anniversary of his birth.

USHAKOV MONUMENT *Ushakov Prospekt*. The monument to Admiral Fyodor Ushakov (1744–1817) is by Kravchenko and Chubin and was unveiled in 1957.

MUSICAL AND DRAMA THEATRE *Gorky Street 7.*

LENIN PARK *Ushakov Prospekt*. This is Kherson's oldest park. It was laid out at the end of the 18th century and known as Alexander Park.

An ancient oak stands in the centre and outside the main gate is a statue of Lenin.

LENKOMSOMOL PARK *Perekopsk Street, near the old fortress.* The 19 m (63 ft) obelisk honours the first Young Communists of the town. There is an amusements area here and the Otdikh (rest) Café.

PERVOMAISKI HOTEL AND KHERSON RESTAURANT *Lenin Street 26.*

The local Intourist office is here, tel: 44–85. A new Intourist hotel is under construction on Svoboda Square.

DNIEPER RESTAURANT *At the sea port.*

OGONYOK (little light) CAFE *Ushakov Prospekt 30/1.*

MINUTKA CAFE *Suvorov Street 1/13.*

G.P.O. *Gorky Street 54.*

BANK *Komsomolskaya Street 21.*

TELEGRAPH OFFICE *Druzhby Street 4.*

DEPARTMENT STORE *Ushakov Prospekt 26/2.*

CENTRAL BOOKSHOP *Svoboda Square 1.*

GRAMOPHONE RECORD SHOP *Suvorov Street 14.*

JEWELLER'S *Suvorov Street 22.*

MARKET *Perekopsk Street.*

FILLING STATION *Near the market, Perekopsk Street.*

The *Avangard Stadium* can seat 30,000. On Quarantine Island is one of the oldest *yacht clubs* in the Ukraine, founded in 1907. Also on the Island is a good *bathing beach,* just as there is on either bank of the river.

Not far from Kherson, but on the opposite side of the Dnieper, is the small holiday resort of *Tsurupinsk.*

THE CRIMEA (KRYM)

Pronounced "Kreem"

Population: 1,202,000

Motorists' Notes: The places of interest in the Crimea are described in the order of which the motorist will come to them if he follows the recommended route from Simferopol through Alushta to Yalta, and then back to Simferopol through Bakhchiserai.

N.B. It is necessary to inform Intourist before setting out for Bakhchiserai.

Enchanting region! Full of life
Thy hills, thy woods,
  thy leaping streams,
Ambered and rubied vines,
  all rife
With pleasure, spot of fairy
  dreams!
Valleys of verdure, fruits and
  flowers,
Cool waterfalls and fragrant
  bowers!
All serve the traveller's heart
  to fill
With joy …

Pushkin

The earliest recorded inhabitants of the peninsula were the Taurians of the coastal mountains and the Scythians who grew corn in the inland steppes. The capital of the Scythian kingdom was Neapolis, near modern Simferopol. In the 6th century B.C. Greek colonies began to grow up at various points along the coast, but Eastern Crimea fell into Roman hands and by the 4th century A.D. was a part of the East Roman Empire. In the 3rd century A.D. the so-called Crimean Goths settled along the southern coast, and some remains of Slav culture of a similar date have also been found there. The Greek settlements fell under Byzantine influence and were eventually destroyed by the Great Migrations.

In the 13th century Genoese colonies were founded, and at the same time

Mohammedan Tartars invaded the north of the peninsula, and the Genoese possessions fell to them in 1475. The stormy period of Turkish rule ended when in 1783 Catherine the Great forced the last khan to abdicate and converted the Crimea into a Russian Province.

During the next hundred years there were several wars with Turkey, and with each war more Tartars left the Crimea. At the end of the 18th century as many as 300,000 left, and when the hundred years were over only 60,000 remained. Soon after this most of the Christian Greeks were moved from the Crimea to the region north of the Sea of Azov, and Russian colonisation of the Crimea was speeded up by the discovery of the agreeable southern climate. At the beginning of the 19th century courtiers and nobles were already building luxurious palaces beside the sea.

Soviet power was established in 1920, marking the end of the Civil War in Russia. The Crimea had been the last refuge of the members of aristocratic families which had mansions there. Today, in Yalta's Marine Park stands an obelisk bearing the words:

"The beautiful villas and mansions, formerly the property of wealthy landlords and capitalists, and the palaces of the former tsars and grand-dukes shall be used as sanatoria and health centres for industrial and agricultural workers".

This is a quotation from the decree signed by Lenin in December 1920.

Soon after the Crimea was liberated from German occupation in 1944 the last of the Tartar population was transferred to the Tartar Republic on the Volga and to the Middle Asian Republics. Russians and Ukrainians from territories badly war-damaged moved down to the Crimea. Ten years later the peninsula passed from the administration of the Russian Federation to that of the Ukraine. There are signs and notices to be seen in the Ukrainian tongue, but the principal language now used there is Russian.

By 1965 the River Dnieper will have been diverted; instead of flowing into the Black Sea, to the north-west of the Crimean peninsula, it will flow through the 368 km (245 miles) long North Crimean Canal to Kerch on the shore of the Sea of Azov. From Dzhankoi a system of canals will spread to irrigate the dry Crimean steppe.

The Crimea is also famous for the sieges of Sevastopol (Sebastopol) 349 days during the Crimean War, and 250 days during 1941–42, after which it was proclaimed a Hero Town.

DZHANKOI

The town stands ½ km from the main road. It is the Crimea's largest railway junction, but there is little of interest to tourists. Local industry deals principally with food, and there is a factory where vegetables and fish are canned.

✿ HOTEL *Krimskaya Street 53.*

HOTEL *Kalinin Street 17.*

RESTAURANT AND CAFE *Rosa Luxemburg Street 5.*

RESTAURANT *Dzerzhinsky Pereulok 5.*

✿ G.P.O. *Krimskaya Street 57.*

TIMIRYAZEVO

✿ RESTAURANT.

✿ FILLING STATION *81 km (50 miles) north of Simferopol; round the clock service.*

SIMFEROPOL

Population: 189,000

Simferopol stands picturesquely beside the River Salgir. It is the capital of the Crimea and covers the site of the ancient Scythian town of Neapolis (3rd–4th century B.C.), where the Scythian king Skilur resided. In the 16th–17th centuries the Tartar town of Ak-Metchet (White Mosque) stood here, with the residence of Kalgar Sultan. After the annexation of the Crimea to Russia in 1783, the name of the town was changed to Simferopol, a combination of two Greek words meaning "collective city", because it was the home of people of different nationalities.

Parts of the former Scythian capital have been excavated, and there are also settlements of primitive man, such as Chokurcha Cave, to be seen in the vicinity.

The industries here are mainly connected with food and tobacco, using the products grown in the region. One factory makes rose and lavender oil. Beside this there are machine building and electrical goods factories. There are also medical, agricultural and teachers' training colleges in Simferopol.

Leninsky Boulevard runs for about 1 km from the railway station to the centre of the town, and a monument to Lenin stands on it. During the summer season some of the central streets—including Pushkinskaya Street and its surrounding by-streets—are closed to traffic and used only by pedestrians.

LOCAL MUSEUM *Pushkinskaya Street 18. Open 10–3; closed on Wednesdays.* The museum contains the Tavrica Library, called after the old name for the Crimea, which has some 50,000 books on the Crimea. The Neapolis excavations are also a part of the museum. These are to be found just off the main Alushta road, near the town; a signpost saying "1 km" points the way. The remains of the old defence walls are there, together with some houses, a mausoleum and tombs with frescoes.

PICTURE GALLERY *Karl Liebknecht Street 35, open 10–4; closed on Tuesdays.*

Apart from the Lenin monument already mentioned there is a Turkish obelisk at the crossing of Zhukovsky and Liebknecht Streets. This was unveiled in 1842 to commemorate the liberation of the Crimea from the Turks in 1771. On the bank of the River Salgir is a monument to Suvorov, marking the site of the Russian military camp which was there in 1777. Another war memorial is a T-34 tank in Pioneer Garden, on Karl Marx Street; this commemorates the liberation of Simferopol in 1944.

GORKY DRAMA THEATRE *Pushkinskaya Street 15.*

UKRAINIAN MUSIC AND DRAMA THEATRE *Mendeleyev Street 3.*

PUPPET THEATRE.

SIMFEROPOL RESERVOIR *3 km along the Alushta road.* There is a bathing beach and there are also boating facilities.

YUZHNAYA (SOUTH) HOTEL *Karl Marx Street 7.*

SIMFEROPOL HOTEL *Kirov Street 22.*

VOKZALNAYA (STATION) HOTEL *At the station.*

ASTORIA RESTAURANT *Karl Marx Street 16.*

AIRPORT HOTEL *At the airport.*

SIMFEROPOL RESTAURANT *Karl Marx Street 2.*

DOROZHNYI (ON-THE-ROAD) RESTAURANT *At the station.*

OTDYKH (REST) RESTAURANT *Kirov Garden.*

CHAIKA (SEAGULL) RESTAURANT *Beside the reservoir.*

CAFE *Karl Marx Street 15.*

G.P.O. *Karl Marx Street 17.*

TELEGRAPH OFFICE *Rosa Luxemburg Street 11*. Helicopters fly between Simferopol and Yalta, taking 25 mins, at a cost of 5 roubles. Trolleybuses run to Alushta and Yalta. There is a bus service to Yalta, and taxis are also available.

The old coast road was built over 130 years ago by Russian soldiers. The last part, leading to Yalta, was full of twists and bends; for instance, on a 4 mile stretch near the Kastel Mountain there were 220 sharp bends. In 1961 the road was lagely reconstructed so that the part in question has now no more than 7 corners.

SERVICE STATION *Michurin Street 55; tel: 1-66. Open 8 a.m. to 4 p.m.*

FILLING STATION *Michurin Street 55* (*at the same address as the service station*). Diesel oil is available; round the clock service.

★

PEREVAL (PASS) MOTEL *31 km (19½ miles) farther along the main road from Simferopol (17 km/10½ miles from Alushta)*. This Motel is 766 m (2513 ft) above sea level, and between July and September, when it is very hot down by the sea, it is never more than 24°C. (75°F) by day and 20°C (68°F) by night up here. It stands near a trolleybus route which reaches Alsuhta in 25–30 min. The motel has a restaurant, a carpark and a carwash.

ALUSHTA

Pronounced "alooshta"

This place, at the southern end of the valley of the mountain rivers Ulu-Uzen and Demergi, was originally called Aluston, meaning "Valley of Winds". It was founded by the Byzantine Emperor Justinian, and stood until 13th century. Remains of the Byzantine fortifications are still to be seen. In 14th century Aluston was rebuilt by the Genoese; it grew into a considerable town and was ruled by a council until 1475 when it passed into Turkish hands. In 1783 it was joined to Russia with the rest of the Crimea, and was proclaimed a town in 1902.

There are 15 sanatoria and rest homes in the Alushta region. The Alushta, Kastel and Taurida State Farms grow grapes for wine, and make the wine themselves. The local vineyards were first laid out by German settlers in 1826.

The promenade is officially called after Lenin, but it is generally known simply as the *Naberezhnaya* (Embankment). The best shops are here, and in Tavricheskaya Street. The Alushta Geophysical Station (founded 1952) is in Partizanskaya Street.

The bathing beaches at Alushta are among the best in the Crimea. Recommended are those opposite the Slava (glory) Sanatorium and below the Naberezhnaya, as well as the town beach.

A stone tower in Genueskaya Street remains from the 6th century Aluston fortress, and the Genoese towers stand on the ruins of part of the old fortress.

On Revolution Square there is a monument to the members of the local government who were shot in 1918.

GOLOVKINSKY MONUMENT *Rabochy Ugolok, at the foot of Mount Kastel.* This is a monument to the hydro-geologist who worked in the Crimea 1886–1897.

MAGNOLIA HOTEL *Naberezhnaya 1.*

TAVRIDA HOTEL *Lenin Street 22.*

PENSIONAT-ALUSHTA MOTEL *Rabochy Ugolok* (*workers corner*). Parking place, repair station and spare parts available; cabins and tents, showers, restaurant, café, shops, hairdresser, G.P.O., telephone, good bathing beaches. Workers' Corner is 3 km (2 miles) from town. It was formerly known as "Professors' Corner", being founded in 1872 when some professors built their houses there.

VOLNA (WAVE) RESTAURANT *Naberezhnaya 1.*

POPLAVOK (FISHING FLOAT) RESTAURANT *Naberezhnaya.*

G.P.O. *15th-April Street 1.*

PODARKI (GIFT) SHOP *Naberezhnaya 2.*

MARKET *Tavricheskaya Street 29.*

★

12 km (8 miles) back along the Simferopol road is the *Kutuzov Fountain*; it was here in 1774 that the famous Russian field-marshal, as a 26-year-old colonel, fought the Turks and lost the sight of an eye. The fountain was built to his memory in the 19th century and was reconstructed in 1957.

Special permission is necessary to visit the *Zapovednik*—the 75,000 acre nature reserve which was established in 1923 on the former imperial hunting territory. There are 36 species of animals including Crimean deer, roe deer and wild sheep (imported in 1913 from Corsica) and 135 species of birds. Interesting plants include the Crimean edelweiss. The Zapovednik is 18 km (12 miles) from Alushta and it is here that the Intourist organise hunting expeditions.

FILLING STATION AND SERVICE STATION *At the Motel, Rabochy Ugolok, 2 km* (1¼ *miles*) *from the centre of Alushta.*

GURZUF

On an inland rock stand the remains of an ancient Byzantine fortress called Gurzuvit, dating back to the time of Justinian I (6th century). This fortress was taken by the Genoese, and reconstructed and reinforced by them in 14th–15th centuries. When the Crimea had become Russian, Catherine the Great gave Gurzuf to her favourite, Prince Potemkin. Today there are many sanatoria at Gurzuf, including that of the Ministry of Defence, and the town is a favourite haunt for artists.

To the west of the valley is a rocky bulge known as "Eagle's Eyrie", where whiteheaded griffon-vultures nest. To the north-east is the 565 m (1800 ft) Ayu-Dagh (Bear Mountain) where there are the relics of an ancient Tauridian settlement and also of a Genoese settlement. The legend of Ayu-Dagh is as follows:

Once upon a time when no one lived in the Crimea except bears and panthers, the bears were ruled by a very large and cunning old bear. From time to time they would go out on forays to see what they could steal, and one day they found a wreck upon the shore. Wrapped in a bundle was a tiny baby girl, the sole survivor of the shipwreck, and they took her back to their den and cared for her.

She grew up into a beautiful maiden with a singing voice so sweet that the bears would happily listen to her songs from morning to night. One day after a wild storm she was walking along the shore. She was alone because the bears had gone off hunting, and she found a small boat which had been washed up by the angry waves; lying exhausted in the bottom of the boat was a handsome young man. She helped him to a hiding place and nursed and fed him there in secret. He explained that he had been sold into slavery and decided to run away, but had been caught in the storm.

The maiden grew to love him dearly and they planned to sail away together; they made mast and sails, and one night set out across the sea. The old bear noticed the young girl's absence and rushed down to the sea, waded in and began to drink and drink; the other bears joined him and did likewise until the strong current they made brought the little boat back to the shore. Then the maiden sang to them again so sweetly of her love that they stopped drinking and let them sail away. But the old bear stood where he was in the sea, looking out to the horizon, and after thousands of years he can still be seen, his body full of caves, his shaggy fur changed to thick woods and his head a great cliff.

There is another legend of Gurzuf, this time attached to the two Odolar Rocks which are to be seen in the sea near the coast. They are the remnants of a cape which once existed, rising 40 m (130 ft) above the sea. The story runs thus:

Long ago when Gurzuf was no more than thick forest there was a strong fortress on the top of Bear Mountain. There the twin brothers Prince George and Prince Peter lived. They loved each other dearly, fought and played side by side, and were never apart, for on her deathbed their mother, the Princess Helen, had asked them to revere the memory of their father and never to quarrel. Their most valued servant was the green-bearded Nimpholis; when he raised his sword in his long arms, hundreds fell, and when he breathed the grass was flattened and little waves appeared on the sea.

One night he came to the brothers and said that he had to leave them, but he gave them two presents "not to be used for any evil purpose, nor to gain anything by force". When he had gone they opened the two mother-of-pearl caskets and in one found an ivory stick with a label: "Raise me and the seas will open; lower me and you will learn the secrets of the seas"; in the second casket was a pair of silver wings and the message, "We will carry you wherever you wish".

Soon after this, news was brought to them of twin sisters of great beauty, and the brothers vowed to win their love. They hurried to the town where the maidens lived, slew the inhabitants and carried off their prizes, but instead of love they were shown scorn. They hoped to change matters by showing off their magic powers, but when they all flew together amidst the clouds and lightning, Nimpholis's voice told them to return and the sisters laughed at their obedient cowardice. Then they entered the sea to visit the Sea King; again Nimpholis called to them to turn back, but the brothers feared the sisters would jeer at them again, and so went on until the King of the Sea killed them all with two waves of his trident. The bodies floated to the surface and were united to form twin rocks as a reminder of the sad end of all attempts to force the human heart to love.

✿ The 40 acre PUSHKIN PARK was laid out by the Duc de Richelieu. Pushkin stayed in the original chateau when he visited the Rayevsky family in 1820. Today the park contains a very large sanatorium belonging to the Ministry of Defence, and other buildings, some dating from the end of the last century and others added at different times between 1936 and 1953. The fountains here are reputedly the most beautiful in the Crimea; one called "Night" is to be found in front of Block 2, and the others are "Mother Love", "Rachel" and "Nymph". Also in the park is Korovin House, built in 1911 for the Russian artist and landscape painter Konstantin Korovin; Soviet and foreign artists now come here for holidays.

In 1959 the International Youth Tourist Centre was opened to the west of Pushkin Park.

✿ RESTAURANT *Leningradskaya Street 1.*

✿ CAR PARK (WITH ATTENDANT) *Zelenaya Street.*

G.P.O. *Leningradskaya Street 12.*

★

Artek, the large holiday centre for children belonging to the Pioneer organisation, is not far from Gurzuf. Altogether 24,000 children come each summer including foreign visitors. The territory stretches for 7 km ($4\frac{1}{2}$ miles) along the coast, and the accommodation is divided into 4 camps. More buildings are now under construction. In the grounds are the Pushkin Rock, grottoes and a monument in memory of the poet.

MASSANDRA

Today liqueurs, wines and champagne are made in this town. Wine making began in Massandra in 1785, and by 1850 the vineyards had been extended along the entire southern coast of the Crimea, the wines gradually taking the place of foreign wines on the Russian market, and even winning recognition at international exhibitions. It was here that, at the end of the 19th century, Prince Golitsyn, a friend of tsar Alexander I and Minister of Education from 1816 to 1824, began to build up his collection of wines. The collection is still preserved, having been saved from invading armies on two occasions, in 1920 and 1941–43.

In 1897 a cellar was excavated in the mountain side to hold 3,500,000 litres (nearly 1,000,000 gals) apart from storing 1,000,000 bottles of wine. Radiating from a central hall are 7 tunnels, each 150 m (160 yd) long and 4–5 m (13–16 ft) in width, and there is a constant temperature of 10–12°C (50 to 54°F) in the cellar.

The grounds of the Magarach Institute come right down to Massandra. This experimental nursery was founded 130 years ago and now possesses 700 different types of vines from all over the world, besides several thousand hybrids.

To the east of Massandra along the coast lie the Nikitsky Botanical Gardens, laid out in 1812 by the botanist, Christian Steven. The three parks cover over 60 acres, and there are more than 1000 species of trees and shrubs. Also of interest is the rich herbarium with over 80,000 plants.

At the entrance of the Botanical Gardens stands the Sechenov Medical Research Institute where the possibilities of curing tuberculosis in the Crimea are investigated.

MASSANDRA HOTEL *In Massandra Park, open in summer only.*

CAMPING SITE *In Massandra Park among the pine-trees.* There is an inexpensive restaurant, a café, shops and a do-it-yourself kitchen; showers, a post office, a telephone, sports grounds, a service station and a car wash.

RESTAURANT *In Massandra Park.* Massandra also has a good bathing beach.

SERVICE STATION *Massandra Park, near the Camping Site; tel: 37-25. Open 8 a.m.–4 p.m.*

YALTA

Population: 34,100 (1956)

Yalta—the name means "shore" was originally an ancient Greek settlement. It lies in a broad amphitheatre between two rivers, River Vodopadnaya (waterfall) to the west, and River Bystraya (rapid) to the east. The surrounding mountains are between 1200 m (3900 ft) and 1400 m (4550 ft) high, and in the valley the average temperature in July is 24°C (75°F).

All the passenger ships sailing to the Crimea and the Caucasus come to Yalta's port, and so do the local boats which ply to and fro along the Crimean coast. The quay from which the latter leave is opposite the central Polyclinic.

Yalta was first mentioned in writing at the beginning of the 12th century by an Arabian geographer as the Byzantine port and fishing village of Dzhalita. In the 14th century it was known as the Genoese colony of Etalita. In the 15th century it passed into Turkish hands, and remained under Turkish domination until it became Russian at the end of the 18th century, when it grew in size and was surrounded by prosperous estates. In 1837 there were already many villas in the district, and it was fairly well known; then, by the order of Nicholas I who was there at the time, Yalta was proclaimed a town, and by the end of the 19th century it had become a favourite resort.

In 1854, during the Crimean War, French ships under Admiral Changarnier landed and their crews robbed the local population.

There are about 80 sanatoria in the Yalta region and perhaps as many as 20 holdiay homes. 40 of the sanatoria are in Yalta itself and there are also two research institutes in the town.

Motorists' Notes: Most of the streets in Yalta are narrow and many are one-way streets; some, including the Promenade, are entirely closed to motor traffic.

Franklin D. Roosevelt Street, formerly Bulvarnaya Street, leads from the port to the centre of the town and is one of Yalta's oldest streets. A small bridge over the River Bystraya links it with the Promenade, officially Lenin Promenade, but known simply as *Naberezhnaya.* The resort Polyclinic, built in 1912 as the Villa Helen, stands here; it has 60 surgeries and supplies all kinds of medical help and advice.

The central part of the Promenade joins the Town Garden, which was laid out in the 1880's.

From the Oreanda Hotel the Promenade leads to Primorsky (Marine) Park where there is a 12·5 m (40 ft) monument to Gorky, unveiled in 1956. There is another Gorky statue and an obelisk bearing Lenin's decree at the entrance to the park. This has a column of 10 m (32 ft 6 in.) and was unveiled in 1951. There is a monument to the writer Chekhov (unveiled 1953) to be seen in the park, and the local film studios are there as well.

At the end of Primorsky Park, where Yalta runs into Livadia, stands the huge building of the Rossia Sanatorium, built in 1957. The former Rossia Hotel (1875), now the Bolshevik Sanatorium, is behind the Ukraina Restaurant.

A 12·5 m (40 ft) statue of Lenin, which was unveiled in 1954, stands at the end of the Promenade.

✿ THE ALEXANDER NEVSKY CATHEDRAL. *Sadovaya Street 2.* This cathedral was built in 1902, with an exterior in old Russian style and an interior in Byzantine style; it is open daily for visitors.

✿ LOCAL MUSEUM *Pushkin Street 21. Open 10–4, closed on Wednesdays.* This is housed in what was formerly a Roman Catholic church, built in 1914 in late English Gothic style.

CHEKHOV MUSEUM *Kirov Street 112. Open 10–4, closed on Tuesdays.* This is in the house to which Chekhov moved in 1898 and where he lived until his final illness in 1904. It is in the village of Chekhovo (formerly Autka).

HISTORY AND ARCHEOLOGY MUSEUM *Zagorodnaya Street 3; open 10–5. Closed on Wednesdays.*

LITERARY MUSEUM *Pavlenko Proyezd 10; open 10–5 on Thursdays, Saturdays and Sundays only.*

WINE-TASTING HALL *Litkens Street 1. Open 11–8.* Lectures on Crimean wine production, followed by sampling, are given in this hall.

Fisherman's Club *Sverdlov Street 3.*

Chekhov Theatre *Litkens Street 13.*

Philharmonia Concert Hall *Litkens Street 13.*

Oreanda Hotel Restaurant and Cafe (Intourist) *Kommunarov Street. Restaurant open 12 noon 11–30 p.m.; café open 8.0 a.m.–2.0 p.m. and 4.0 p.m.–11.0 p.m.* This hotel is 30 m (33 yd) from the sea.

Ukraina Hotel and Yalta Restaurant *Botkin Street 18. Restaurant open till 11.00 p.m.*

Primorskaya (Marine) Hotel and Restaurant *Sverdlov Street 13. Restaurant open till 11 p.m.*

Yuzhnaya (South) Hotel and Restaurant *Franklin D. Roosevelt Street 10–12; tel: 28-68. Restaurant open till 11 p.m.*

Gnyozdishko (Little nest) Hotel and Restaurant *Kirov Street, near Chekhov Museum; tel: 3-37-50.*

Yalta Hotel *Sadovaya Street 4.*

Tavrida Hotel and Restaurant *Lenin Street 22; tel: 2-12.*

Krym Hotel and Restaurant *Kommunalnaya Street 1.*

Ukraina Restaurant *Promenade 34. Open till midnight; also rooftop self-service restaurant, open 8.0 a.m. to 6.0 p.m. after which there is service until midnight.*

Priboi (Tide) Restaurant *Primorsky Park; open till 1.0 a.m.*

Leto (Summer) Restaurant *Primorsky Park; open noon 1.0 a.m.*

Otdykh (Rest) Restaurant. This open-air restaurant is on the roof of the main building of the seaport.

Aquarium Restaurant *Moskovskaya Street.* The restaurant bridges one of Yalta's small rivers.

Ukraina Cafe *Promenade 34.*

Avtomat Cafe *Promenade 10. Open until 9.0 p.m.*

Motel *Lomonosov Street 25. Beside the River Vodopadnaya.* Hotel, tents, showers, inexpensive restaurant; service station, filling station, carpark, carwash. The motel is situated among cypresses, plantains and other southern trees.

Nagornyi Park *On Darsan Hill.* This park was only recently planted, and commands a good view over Yalta and the bay.

The local bathing beaches are to be found at Kommunarov Street, Massandrovskaya Street, Zheltyshevka Street, Lechebnyi Plyazh (medical bathing) and Primorsky Boulevard. However, the best beach in the Crimea is the Zolotoi Plyazh at Miskhor, and Intourist is responsible for a section of it.

G.P.O. *Lenin Street 34.*

Photographer's *Promenade 10 and Kalinin Garden. Open daily, 10–6.* There are two markets, Tsentralnyi Rynok and Pushkinsky Rynok.

Taxi Ranks *Pushkinsky Rynok; Krymsky Proyezd, near the Seaman's Franklin D. Roosevelt Street, near the harbour.*

Filling Station *Ushelnoye, Kievskaya Street on the main road into Yalta and Engels Street 1. The latter is always open.*

Service Station and Carpark *Ushelnoye, Engels Street 6; tel: 35-40.* The Promenade is closed to traffic, and it is here that the best shops are to be found, as well as the best restaurants and cafés.

The west road out of Yalta, leading to the southern coast of the Crimea, is signposted "To Sevastopol".

6 km (4 miles) from Yalta, near Livadia, the road divides into the Upper Road (Verkhnaya Doroga) and the Lower Road (Nizhnaya Doroga). The first links *Oreanda*, *Gaspra* and *Koreiz* and the second runs along the coast through *Miskhor* (past Zolotoi Plyazh) and *Alupka* to *Simeiz*. At the point where the road divides there stands a statue called "Friendship", depicting three figures striding forward.

Yalta is also the starting point for the return route to Simferopol via *Bakhchiserai*; Intourist's permission is necessary before setting out upon this road.

LIVADIA

At the end of the 18th century Livadia was a Greek village called Ai-Yan-Su (St. John's Spring), but in 1860 the territory was bought for the imperial family and the place was again given its original name of Livadia (meadow). The present day buildings took the place of older palaces which were entirely demolished, with the exception of the small Byzantine-style belltower and the Byzantine-style Church of the raising of the Cross. This church was built in 1866 and is decorated with frescoes by Monighetti and Professor Grimm.

The 1945 Yalta Conference was held here, but Livadia is now a sanatorium.

THE WHITE PALACE. The large palace known as the White Palace, was built in 1911 from designs by Krasnov as a summer residence for Nicholas II. The three-storey palace which is now Sanatorium No. 2 belonged to Baron Frederiks, the tsar's chamberlain, and the third large palace was built in new Renaissance style for the tsar's suite. Like the White Palace, these were designed by Krasnov. All three buildings were completed between April 1910 and September 1911. 2500 people helped in the construction, sometimes even working at night by the light of bonfires and torches.

The White Palace was built in the early Italian Renaissance style, the main motifs in the design being taken from Florence. The marble was carved by Italians and the marble decorations around the doors are taken from motifs by Raphael. The palace itself is built of white Inkerman granite quarried near Sevastopol. There are two inner courtyards, one in Moorish style and one a copy of the Monastery court of Saint Mark's in Florence. There are altogether 60 rooms in the White Palace. The 1945 conference was held in the white hall, which is now used as the sanatorium dining hall. It was in this palace that President Roosevelt and the American delegation stayed. The windows of the palace are so planned that they each look onto a different view, and the indoor frames are designed to look like picture frames. On a balcony on the left side of the façade is a gargoyle copied from Notre Dame in Paris.

Opposite the entrance is a small marble column inscribed in Arabic, a present to the tsar from the Shah of Persia. There is also a Moorish fountain of exquisite workmanship with "Livadia" written upon it in Arabic. It is built over a natural spring and the water still flows. On a platform in front of the palace are Roman benches of 1st–3rd centuries A.D. and an ancient red Roman well.

From the southern corner of the third palace runs the Tourists' Path (formerly the Tsar's Path), a mile in length and leading to a semicircular columned shelter overlooking Oreanda.

In the park is an open air theatre seating 1000 people.

Livadia State Farm Vineyards were organised here in 1922, based on the former imperial vineyards and wine cellars.

FILLING STATION *In the village. Round the clock service.*

OREANDA

Oreanda stretches right down to the sea; its name is derived from a Greek word meaning "boundary". Nicholas I purchased the territory, and in 1852 an imperial palace was built here. This was burned down in 1882 and the remains were used in the construction of the Church of the Pokrova Bogorodits which the Academician Avdeyev designed in Byzanto-Georgian style. The interior mosaic decorations are by Salviazzi of Venice.

The park is magnificent, with ponds shaped like the Black and Caspian Seas and the Sea of Azov.

Oreanda is divided naturally into two parts, upper and lower. Lower Oreanda Sanatorium, built in 1948–58, is a most impressive building. The third block of this institution has an indoor swimming pool, 18 m (23 yd) long and 2·5 m (8 ft) deep, filled with warmed sea water.

GASPRA and KOREIZ

The boundaries of these places are hard to define, as, like the other southern Crimean villages, they ramble over the mountainsides. Gaspra takes its name from the Greek word for "white".

Leo Tolstoi visited this spot in 1901 and 1902 and stayed in what is now known as the "Yasnaya Polyana" Sanatorium, named after Tolstoi's estate near Moscow, and there is a memorial plaque to Tolstoi by the front door. The writers Gorky, Korolenko, Kuprin and Chekhov visited him here. The grey stone palace in Alexandro-Gothic style was built in the 1830's by Prince Golitsyn who called it his "romantic Alexandria". The architect was Elson (also responsible for Leningrad's Saint Isaac's Cathedral) and the construction was supervised by the Englishman Henry Hunt, who had previously supervised the construction of Vorontsov's palace at Alupka.

Soon after the construction was completed Princess Golitsyna, accompanied by hundreds of attendants, moved there, taking half a year over her journey from Saint Petersburg, from where she was banished. She was slightly demented, and spent her time in the Crimea preaching Christianity to the Crimean Tartars whom she tracked down with a Bible in one hand and a whip in the other. She was locally known as the "old she-devil".

In the park is a grotto and a pond shaped like the Black Sea.

THE YUSUPOV PALACE. This is a horseshoe-shaped building standing in its own park. It was designed by a local architect, Eshliman, and was completed in 1904. The Soviet delegation to the 1945 Yalta Conference stayed here, and today it is used by the Soviet Union's foreign guests. Nearby is a pool in the shape of a fallen leaf.

THE SUBKHI SANATORIUM. This sanatorium, named after a Turkish Communist, has a fishpond decorated with marble capitals, brought from excavations in Greece or Italy.

THE ROSA LUXEMBURG SANATORIUM. This sanatorium, named after the German Communist, is now a children's sanatorium. Its fine park is known as "the Second Nikitsky Botanical Garden", and contains a marble well decorated with exotic birds and other sculptures. The well, whose steps are guarded by two ancient lions, was supposedly brought from Greece. Also of interest is the rock called the White Head or Napoleon's Head.

Cape Ai-Todor is a rock standing 26 m (85 ft) high, covered with shrubby growth and crowned with a lighthouse.

INEXPENSIVE RESTAURANT No. 17.

G.P.O. *Gaspra, Stroi Gorodok.*

MISKHOR

Miskhor takes its name from the Greek words meaning "middle town". It is 12 km (8 miles) from Yalta and is considered to be the warmest resort on the southern coast of the Crimea. Its park, which was laid out in 1790, is worthy of note. It contains over 300 species of trees, and stretches over level ground from the beach to Kommunari Sanatorium.

There are a great many sanatoriums in Miskhor, some housed in new buildings and some in the former royal palaces.

✿ KRASNOYE ZNAMYA (RED BANNER) SANATORIUM. This has an unusual Moorish appearance, with its battlements, silver domes and coloured mosaics. When it was the palace of the Grand-Prince Peter Nikolayevich it was called Dulber (beautiful). It was designed by the architect Krasnov, who also planned the tsar's palace of Livadia, and was built in 1895–97. In 1938 a second sanatorium building, designed to harmonise with the original palace, was constructed nearby.

SOSNOVAYA ROSHA (PINE GROVE) SANATORIUM. This sanatorium is surrounded by 100-year-old trees. A small hunting lodge remains near it.

UKRAINA SANATORIUM. This is the largest in Miskhor. It has an indoor swimming pool and provides bathing all the year round.

THE DNIEPER SANATORIUM. This stands near the Ukraina Sanatorium. It is built in the style of a Swiss chalet, and was originally the Hara Estate. In the park is an unusually shaped Greek courtyard with 12 marble columns, a central fountain and a Spanish vase supposed to be over 2000 years old. It was brought from Greece at the beginning of the 20th century at the wish of the Greek princess who was married to one of the Romanovs. On the way to the lighthouse, on the highest point of the promontory, is a lookout place with a wide view. In 1959 a special lift, 61 m (208 ft) high, was constructed from the beach to the cliff-top. A new part of the sanatorium, recently constructed, is a pier with summer sleeping accommodation.

THE ZHEMCHUZHINA (PEARL) SANATORIUM. This sanatorium belongs to the Ministry of Defence, and it situated in a valley. From it a road runs up to the Swallow's Nest high on the cliffs, which drop sheer from this point to the sea. The villa was built in 1912 for Baron Steingel, a German oilman, who called it his "Castle of Love". The engineer Sherwood designed it in Gothic style, following, it is supposed, the architectural plan of a mediaeval castle on the Rhine. In spite of its precarious situation, the villa survived the severe earthquake of 1927 when a piece of the cliff collapsed. It is at present under restoration.

Another vantage point for a view is Kapitansky Mostik (the Captain's Bridge). This lookout place is 70 m (228 ft) above sea level and is reached after a climb of 315 steps. Looking down one can see the Sail Rock from which seagulls and cormorants dive for fish, and also a sculptured eagle with its wings spread.

Near by is the Kichkinei (tiny) Palace, one of the palaces formerly belonging to the Romanov's. It is built in Eastern style, its towers like little minarets. The architect Tarasov designed the palace just before the outbreak of World War I, and it now houses a children's sanatorium.

Near the sanatorium is a winding path called Kurpati, which may be translated in many ways, among them Girl's Path. It was constructed in 1936 on territory formerly belonging to the tsar. There is a solar energy installation nearby.

ZOLOTOI PLYAZH (GOLDEN BEACH). This is the best place for bathing on the southern coast of the Crimea. It is 70 m (216 yd) wide and stretches for 400 m (434 yd) along the shore. This is also the site of the Intourist bathing beach. Here is the legend of the origin of the bright pebbles.

The last of the Turkish khans named Hadji-Ahmed-Aga lived in Yalta with his son Del-Balta ("Mad Axe"). Together they robbed the local population, but were defeated in battle in 1771 by the Russians, and planned to flee across the sea to Turkey. The waves, however, refused to bear them, and the wrecked ships with the dead bodies and the rich booty of gold and silver were scattered upon the shore. Since that time it has been known as the Golden Beach.

At the west end of Miskhor there is a pavilion called the Tourists' Shelter which commands a fine view towards Alupka and the Vorontsov palace.

In the sea there is a statue of a mermaid (rusalka in Russian), which illustrates another Miskhor legend:

When the Crimea was still under the rule of the Turkish sultan there lived in the village of Miskhor a lovely maiden called Arza. While she was fetching water on her wedding day she was kidnapped by the wicked Ali-Baba and his pirate band, and taken to Istanbul to be sold to the sultan. A year later she escaped with her tiny baby boy and committed suicide in the Bosphorus. That very day a mermaid appeared at Miskhor. She is still supposed to return annually on the day of the kidnapping to visit the spring and drink the water there.

Altogether there are three statues—a girl fetching water beside a natural spring, an evil turbanned gentleman watching her and a mermaid with her baby on a low rock in the sea. Bernstam was the sculptor.

RUSALKA (MERMAID) RESTAURANT *In Miskhor Park*

MISKHOR RESTAURANT (INEXPENSIVE) *Near the quayside.*

INEXPENSIVE RESTAURANT NO. 22. *By Zolotoi Plyazh.*

G.P.O. *In Miskhor Park.*

SOUVENIR SHOP *In a pavilion on the Esplanade.*

PHOTOGRAPHERS *Miskhor Krymskaya Street 2. Zolotoi Plyazh.*

BOATS FOR HIRE *Miskhor beach; also for hire, deckchairs, cameras, games, towels.* Boats coming from Yalta call in at Miskhor, and for motorists there is a good car park near the beach.

ALUPKA

The beach here is pebbly and the high cliffs culminate in the jagged 4210 ft Ai-Petri.

Alupka's visitiors have included Gorky and Mayakovsky.

The item of greatest interest here is the Vorontsov Palace, situated in a 100-acre park where over 200 exotic and decorative plants and abundant rocks have been used in skilful landscaping. In the upper section of the park stand three great trees, a Mexican pine, a Lebanon cedar, and an Italian pine.

The palace was built between 1828 and 1846 by the owner of Alupka, Count (later Prince) Mikhail Vorontsov (1782–1856). The stone was quarried on the estate, and the quarry itself is now known as the "Alupka Chaos".

Vorontsov was brought up in England, and returned to Russia at the age of 18. He was a favourite of both Alexander I and Nicholas I, and was appointed Governor-General of the Novorossia Region. Because he was a confirmed Anglophile his contemporaries called him "Lord Warrensoff"—all the more so when he decided to build his palace in imitation of an English mansion. The project of the palace was drawn up by Edward Blair, from Britain, and the construction was carried out under the English architect, Henry Hunt.

Marble was brought from Italy and masons and sculptors came from Italy to work on it. The walls are of diorite, and are so strong that they have withstood earthquakes. The architectural pattern of the palace follows in silhouette the outline of the Ai-Petri mountain behind it. The architecture itself unites in modern form elements of late English Gothic, English Elizabethan and eastern style of India. The northern façade is primarily of English inspiration and the southern of Indian. The south entrance bears a close resemblance to the portal of the Great Mosque in Delhi; the frieze decorating the portal has an Arabic inscription, six times repeated—a quotation from the Koran saying "There is no happiness, but it comes from Allah". Altogether the decorative work on the palace took almost 10 years to complete.

The three pairs of marble lions beside the steps were specially carved in Italy under the supervision of sculptor Bonanni, and were copied from Canova's lions which decorate the tomb of Pope Clement XII in Rome.

The palace contains over 150 rooms; inside there is a museum containing some copies of famous paintings, and also a number of Dutch, French, English, Ukrainian and Russian originals. Among them is a portrait of Vorontsov himself, and in the winter garden a bust of William Pitt the younger can be seen.

It was in this palace that Mr. Churchill and the members of the British delegation stayed during the 1945 Yalta conference.

✿ Magnolia Hotel *Letchikov Street 23.*

Alupka Restaurant *Kirov Street 2.*

✿ G.P.O. *Voikov Street 26.*

There is a carpark near the main bus stop.

SIMEIZ

This is the most peaceful resort of all, and lies at the end of the southern coast of the Crimea. In 1885 the village was visited by Tolstoi, and the Ukrainian writer M. Kotsubinsky lived here from 1895–97.

The local vineyards provide grapes for the Massandra Trust's wine cellars which are located on the outskirts of the village. Here Crimean Tokay, Muskat, Kagor and other wines are made.

Simeiz is a favourite health resort for the relief and cure of pulmonary tuberculosis, and has many sanatoria.

The fine bathing beach is protected by towering rocks, the highest being Loshadinaya Golova (Horse's Head) 1325 m (4100 ft). The Koshka ("Cat" —from its shape) Mountain rises 259 m (840 ft) above sea level. Remains of the ancient Tauri tribe have been found on the mountain top in 70 barrows hidden amidst dense juniper shrubbery. There are also ruins of Tauri houses and a small fortress. Opposite the Koshka Mountain is the Panea Rock where the remains of Byzantine walls are to be seen. Beside the sea is Swan Cliff, 85 m (276 ft) high, and at its foot lie the remains of the Monk Cliff which fell during a severe storm in 1931. In the sea, closing in the Simeiz bay, is a 50 m (162 ft) high rock called Diva ("maiden").

The Koshka Mountain, the Monk Cliff and the Diva rock are all connected in the following legend of Simeiz:

Long ago there lived a wicked man who enjoyed a life of lust and pleasure. However, as he grew older he repented of this life and went to live as a hermit, eventually gaining the reputation of being the holiest monk in this part of the world. His undeserved honour made the devil and the evil spirits very angry; and so the devil came to the old man's cave in the form of a cat and sang songs of love and the joys of family life until the monk took it by the tail and flung it out of the cave. Another day an evil spirit took on the shape of a lovely girl and appeared in the monk's net while he was fishing on the shore. She embraced the old man and he remembered his past life which has so long been forgotten. The devil and the evil spirits laughed to see his real nature showing itself, but the good spirits of the place were angered at such disrespect for all that human beings hold dear and sacred. They turned all three to stone, thus creating the maiden rock, and, standing back from that, the monk cliff, and overlooking the whole valley, the hunchbacked cat mountain, in the shape that the devil had chosen for himself.

✿ SIMEIZ OBSERVATORY. This was founded in 1900, and is open to visitors on Tuesdays and Fridays, from 12 noon to 2.0 p.m. Ist is advisable to obtain permission from Intourist before making the visit.

THE KRASNYI MAYAK (RED LIGHTHOUSE) SANATORIUM. This sanatorium is situated in the centre of Simeiz. It was formerly the Villa Xenia, built in Gothic style in 1911. A little higher up there is a second building belonging to the Sanatorium. It is in Moorish style and was built in 1925.
The main street of Simeiz is Lenin Prospekt.

✿ INEXPENSIVE RESTAURANT *Sovietskaya Street.*

CAFE *Lenin Prospekt.*

✿ G.P.O. *Sovietskaya Street.*

The Intourist road ends at Simeiz. The next village along the coast is *Opoloznevoye* ("landslide"). It is so called because in 1786 the territory nearby slid slowly down into the sea carrying with it villages, churches and a fortress.

At the time of writing it is not permitted to travel to Sevastopol in one's own car; this must be left in Yalta and an Intourist car be hired to make the journey to Sevastopol and back.

The Sevastopol road, wider than that leading to Simeiz, runs from the north-west of Alupka. After a steep hill it comes to *Foros.*

FOROS

Cars may be parked on Red Cliff in front of the BYZANTINE CHURCH which was built in 1892.

THE FOROS SANATORIUM can be seen from beside the sea. The side road which leads down to the Sanatorium has 80 bends over a distance of 7 km ($4\frac{1}{2}$ miles).

A little further to the west lies Sarich Cape, 85 m (280 ft) high. Its name means "cloth of gold" and it is the most southerly point both of the Crimean peninsula and of the European part of the Soviet Union.

BAIDAR GATE

There is an excellent view from this cliff top, 527 m (1653 ft) above sea level. The Gate was built in antique style in 1848 after a way had been blasted through the solid limestone. It was named after the nearby Baidari Valley (now known as Orlinovskaya Valley)—17 km ($10\frac{1}{2}$ miles) long, 10 km ($6\frac{1}{2}$ miles) wide and traversed by the Little Chornaya River. In the past people used to climb on a rock to the south-west of the Gate to watch the sun rise.

SEVASTOPOL

Population: 148,000 (1959)

The name "Sevastopol" means "town of glory", and it was appropriately made a Hero City after World War II.

The harbour has an average depth of 20 m (65 ft) and is the best harbour in the Black Sea. The Northern Bay divides the town into the Northern and Southern Sides (Severnaya and Yuzhnaya Storona). On the Southern Side are Gorodskaya Storona (City Side) and Korabelnaya Storona (Ship Side), which are in turn divided by the deep and wide Southern Bay.

In 1774 Prince Potemkin recognised the outstanding shape of Sevastopol Bay for use as a fortress and a port. The port was accordingly laid out in 1784 on the site of the Tartar village of Akhtiar. Stone for the building was taken from the ancient town of Hersones, and the admirals Ushakov and Mackenzie were also instrumental in the founding of the city. In 1804 Sevastopol was proclaimed the main port of the Black Sea Fleet.

Sevastopol was almost wholly destroyed during the siege of 1854–55, after which only 14 buildings remained intact. After the Crimean War Russia was forbidden to possess a Black Sea Fleet or to use Sevastopol as a fortress; this restriction lasted until 1871, after which the city was again fortified. The commercial port was closed in 1890.

During the 1905 revolution 15 ships of the Black Sea Fleet joined in the revolt in Sevastopol. About 6000 seamen were arrested, making 40 per cent of the total number of men, and Lieutenant Shmidt, who was leading the revolt, was shot with other seamen. There is a monument over their grave.

The siege of 1941–42 during the Second World War lasted for 250 days and again 97 per cent of the city was laid waste.

Today Sevastopol has the biggest brick and tile factory in the Crimea and also produces other building materials, food products, textiles and shoes. There are two stadiums, two boating stations and two yacht clubs in the town.

SAINT PETER AND SAINT PAUL CATHEDRAL *Lunacharsky Street 34.* This cathedral was built in Doric style in 1843 and rebuilt after the Crimean War. It resembles the Temple of Theseus in Athens and has 44 columns on the façade. It is now used as a House of Culture.

VLADIMIRSKY CATHEDRAL *On the town hill.* Half ruined during World War II, this cathedral is the burial place of 4 Russian admirals, Kornilov, Istomin, Nakhimov and Lazarev, whose names are inscribed on black marble plaques on the outside wall. The cathedral was founded during the 1854 Crimean War; the crypt where the admirals are buried was opened in 1881, and the rest in 1888. The architect Thon designed it in Byzantine style, and its interior marble columns were brought from Italy. The cathedral is now to be restored and used as a sepulchre for famous Russian seamen.

THE TOWER OF WINDS *Opposite Vladimirsky Cathedral.* This is all that remains of the old building of the Marine Library. It is a copy of the marble tower of the same name in Athens, and the upper frieze displays bas-reliefs of Greek mythological heroes.

GRAFSKAYA PRISTAN (COUNT'S QUAY). This is a broad stone staircase with a 12-columned portico dating from 1846, called after Admiral Count Voinovich who commanded the Black Sea Fleet in the 1840's.

BLACK SEA FLEET MUSEUM *Lenin Street 11. Open 10–5; closed on Mondays.* Founded in 1869, this is one of the oldest museums in the country. The building by A. Kochetov was constructed in 1895. The figure "349" on the façade commemorates the duration in days of the siege of 1854–55, and the guns also date from that time.

SEVASTOPOL PANORAMA *Istorichesky Boulevard; open 9 a.m.–8 p.m.; closed on Mondays.* This circular building, completed in 1905, contains a painting by the artist Roubaud of Munich illustrating the storming of Sevastopol by the British and the French on 6th June 1855. The painting is 115 m (126 yd) in length and 14 m (46 ft) wide. Roubaud was an Academician of the Petersburg Academy of Fine Art, who, having collected his material, went to Munich to create the Panorama in a specially constructed circular building. His work was badly burnt in 1942 but the building was reconstructed and the painting copied and recreated; this formidable task was carried out under the guidance of Academicians Yakovlev and Sokolov-Skalya, and was completed on 16th October, 1954.

PICTURE GALLERY *Nakhimov Prospekt 9. Open 12–6; closed on Tuesdays.* Opened in 1927, this gallery contains Russian classical paintings by Repin, Ivazovsky, Shishkin and Levitan, among others. The section on Soviet art includes works by Brodsky and Grabar. The Western European section has 14th–17th century Italian, Dutch and Flemish masters, and among them a "Madonna and Child" by Rafael, and canvases by Giordano, Ruysdael, Rubens and Sneyders.

KOVALEVSKY BIOLOGICAL STATION OF THE ACADEMY OF SCIENCES *Primorsky Boulevard. Aquarium and museum open 10–4; closed on Mondays.*

KAZARSKY MONUMENT *Matrosky Boulevard.* Captain Kazarsky distinguished himself during the naval war of 1828 against the Turks. His ship was the brig *Merkury*.

COUNT TOTLEBEN STATUE *Istorichesky Boulevard.* This statue by Bilderling was unveiled in 1909. The pedestal depicts part of the bastion where soldiers are laying mines.

NAKHIMOV MONUMENT *Nakhimov Square.* The original statue by Bilderling and Schröder was unveiled in 1898 but was destroyed by the Germans, and the existing one is a copy.

THE EAGLE COLUMN *Primorsky Boulevard.* The column stands on an artificial rock close to the shore. Designed by Adamson, it was unveiled in 1904 to commemorate the Russian warships which sunk in the harbour mouth on the 11th September 1854 in an attempt to block the way. The column, surmounted by a bronze eagle with outstretched wings, is now used as the symbol of the city. At the time of the Crimean War the story was told of one of the ships which would not sink, in spite of being holed and then shot at by her sister ships. At last, a sailor went aboard her again and returned with her icon and she went down immediately.

LENIN MONUMENT *On the highest point of the town hill.* This monument by Bondarenko stands 2·5 m (70 ft) high.

GORKY MONUMENT *Lunacharsky Street, in a small garden opposite the Cathedral of Saint Peter and Saint Paul.*

LIBERATION MONUMENT. This can be seen from Primorsky Boulevard; there are the Constantine and Mikhail Batteries and the monument to the soldiers who fell in the liberation of Sevastopol in 1944.

✿ LUNACHARSKY THEATRE *Nakhimov Prospekt 6.*

CIRCUS *Korabelnaya Storona, near the "Sevastopol" wide-screen cinema.*

BATHING BEACH *Primorsky Boulevard.*

✿ SEVASTOPOL HOTEL AND RESTAURANT *Nakhimov Prospekt 8; tel: 25-65.*

PRIMORSKY (MARINE) RESTAURANT *Lenin Street 8.*

VOLNA (WAVE) RESTAURANT *Primorsky Boulevard, by the sea.*

EATING HOUSE *Bolshaya Morskaya Street 8.*

✿ G.P.O. *Bolshaya Morskaya Street 21.*

✿ FILLING STATION *Oleg Koshevoi Street 1. 24 hour service.*

MALAKHOV KURGAN

This ancient burial mound, which is what *Kurgan* means, is 4 km (2½ miles) from the town centre. The town was called after a Captain Malakhov who spent many days and nights drinking in its inns. The plateau, the highest point in the neighbourhood of Sevastopol, is 350 m (383 yd) long by 149 m (163 yd) wide and its seizure in 1855 decided the fate of the rest of the town. The turrets from which the guns were fired have been restored. Three admirals met their deaths on and around the Kurgan; cannonballs fatally wounded Kornilov, and blew off Istomin's head, while Nakhimov was shot in the temple.

✿ ADMIRAL KORNILOV MONUMENT. This was designed by Bilderling and Schröder, and erected in 1895. The admiral is depicted at the moment when he was struck by the fatal bullet and uttered the words: "Defend Sevastopol". To the right, below, is a figure of the sailor Koshka (see below). The monument is under restoration.

On the Kurgan is a monument to the Soviet airmen who died in 1944, and there is also an eternal flame burning on the grave of the Unknown Sailor.

KOSHKA MONUMENT *Near Malakhov Kurgan.* The sailor Pyotr Koshka, whose name appropriately means "cat", participated in numerous reconaissance sorties, and was famed for going into the enemy trenches and putting their guns out of action. He survived the war, though his grandson, Pavel Kucher, fell here in 1942.

SAPUN-GORA

This hill is 6 km (3½ miles) along the road to Simferopol. There is a diorama by the artist Maltsev depicting the storming of the hill in May 1944.

✿ THE GLORY MONUMENT commemorates those who fell during World War II.

SEVERNAYA STORONA

Here, 10 km (6 miles) from the centre of Sevastopol, is the common grave of 127,587 of those who fell in the 1854–55 defence of Sevastopol. Saint Nicholas's Church was built of white Inkerman stone in 1870; it stands 20 m (65 ft) high, and is built in the shape of a pyramid and surmounted by a cross. The interior is decorated with mosaics in Byzantine style, and 38 black marble slabs list the regiments and naval divisions involved in the defence of Sevastopol and also the names of the commanding officers. There are 117 different war memorials and monuments in the vicinity.

HERSONES

Russian: Korsun

Hersones lies 3 km (2 miles) southwest of Sevastopol. Its name means "peninsula", and it is also appropriately known as the "Russian Pompeii". On a headland by the sea are the remains of a town which bear the marks of the three main periods of its history, Ancient Greek, Roman and mediaeval Byzantine, and the ruins of 2000-year old walls whose grandeur was once described by Pliny, are to be found there. The town was founded in the 5th century B.C. by colonists from Heraclea in Bithnyia; it was an important trading centre and was known in old chronicles as Korsun. Political exiles were often sent here and it was here, in exile in the 1st century A.D.

that Pope Clement died. The Byzantine Emperor Justinian II was banished here at the end of the 7th century. The town was taken in the 10th century by Prince Vladimir of Kiev, who, so it is said, adopted the Christian religion on this spot. Its trade with Russia ceased at the time of the Mongolian invasion. It suffered at the hands of the Lithuanians in 1397, and then became completely desolated under the Turks.

The site has been under excavation since 1772. The stones of Hersones were used for building Sevastopol and Odessa until a stop was put to the entire destruction of the historic place. The excavations are proving very valuable; some of the finds have been sent to the Hermitage Museum in Leningrad, some to the Historical Museum in Moscow and some remain in the Hersones Local Museum (founded in 1892). Ancient streets, a square, a theatre, and 6th century mosaic floors in excellent condition have been discovered.

✿ In 1888 a monastery planned by Grimm was constructed here, its principal building being a copy of the ancient Church of Saint Serge in Istanbul.

✿ THE HERSONES MUSEUM *Open 10–5; closed on Mondays.* This museum contains a rich numismatic collection.

BAKHCHISERAI

"The Palace of Gardens"

Motorist's Notes: The suggested return route from Yalta to Simferopol via Bakhchiserai is 111 km (74 miles). We repeat that it is necessary to notify Intourist before travelling this way. The road runs over the Ai-Petri Mountain and the scenery is very picturesque. The Silver Pavilion is a look-out point at the 16/56 km milestone. There is a parking place to the right of the Yalta–Bakhchiserai road, and a 50 m (55 yd) walk leads up to the Pavilion with a remarkable view of Yalta and the sea. For hundreds of years people have enjoyed climbing to the top of Ai-Petri to watch the sunrise. There is a restaurant on the summit at the 22/50 km milestone and also a meteorological station and another look-out point.

Bakhchiserai lies on the River Churyuk-Su (rotten water). It dates from 1501, when the Crimean Khans transferred the capital from Khan Mengli-Gerai. The Khans resided here until 1783. The town is divided into the old part and the new; only the main street is partly built with new houses.

✿ KHAN'S PALACE (KHAN-SERAI): *Open 9–4, closed on Wednesdays.* The Palace is the home of the local History and Archeology Museum.

All silent now those spacious halls,
And courts deserted, once so gay
With feasters thronged within
their walls,
Carousing after battle fray.
Even now each desolated room
And ruined garden luxury breathes,
Gold listens, shrubs exhale perfume.
The shattered casements still
are there
Within which once, in days gone by,
Their beads of amber chose the fair,
And heaved the unregarded sigh.

Pushkin

The 16–18th century palace consists of a number of buildings, including the Harem, now inhabited by waxworks. The Fruit Room was designed by a Persian artist, Omar, in the 18th century. There is a pleasant garden, a falcon tower and a mosque dating from the middle of the 18th century. The cemetery of Khan Gerai's dynasty is also to be seen. During its history the palace has been partly burned and robbed, but it was rebuilt for Catherine the Great's visit in 1783, and was restored again in 1837 for Nicholas I to see. This restoration, however, was not well done, and only in 1900 was restoration carried out with consideration for the past and not simply for oriental style.

In the palace is the famous Fountain of Tears, built in 1756, which inspired Pushkin and the Polish poet Miczkiewicz. This is its story:

The Khan Krim-gerai was well known for his cruelty; it was he who ordered the death of all the boys of his family who stood higher than the hub of his chariot wheel, so that no one would seize power from him. People said that instead of a heart he had a lump of wool. However, when he fell in love with Delarai, a slave girl, he realised that he had indeed a living heart. Delarai could not return his love and soon died of sorrow.

Krim-gerai grieved deeply; he asked the Persian craftsman, Omar, to "make a stone that will continue my grief through the centuries, that will cry as only a man's heart can". Omar thought that if the stony heart of the khan could weep, then so could a stone, and he made a marble fountain and carved flower petals with a human eye in the centre from which would fall heavy drops like human tears, day and night till the end of time. Omar carved a marble snail on the fountain too, to symbolise the khan's doubt of the use of his life to him—or of his laughter and sadness, his love and his hatred.

✿ HOTEL AND RESTAURANT *Lenin Street 93.*

RESTAURANT *On the road to Simferopol.*

INEXPENSIVE RESTAURANT *Lenin Street 77.*

✿ G.P.O. *Pochtovaya Street 18.*

TELEGRAPH AND TELEPHONE *Lenin Street 75.*

✿ Beside the main road, near Bakhchiserai, are a number of round domes. These are 15th–18th century mausoleums in the old Tartar cemetery.

A few kilometres from Bakhchiserai along the Simferopol road, near the village of Partizanskoye (18 km/12 miles from Simferopol), is the Crimean Observatory. Here, in memory of Academician Schein, the biggest telescope in Europe with a mirror 2·6 m (8 ft) in diameter has been installed.

Bakhchiserai's local museum is also responsible for 14 ancient cave towns in the vicinity. The following are probably of greatest interest:

USPENSKY-PESHCHERNYI-MONASTYR

Directions: About 1 mile from Bakhchiserai, past the village of Staroselye on the road to Chufut-Kaleh. The road is fairly good.

This is a cave monastery, no longer inhabited, located in the mountainside. In it are a Cathedral of the Assumption of the Virgin, and four churches dedicated to Saint Constantine and Saint Helen, Saint Mark, Saint George and Saint Innocent. The monastery existed before the Turks came to the Crimea, and the legend of its foundation goes thus:

> Once upon a time a dragon appeared in the mountains, and devoured many of the villagers and their cattle. The rest fled down into the valley, and in despair prayed to the Virgin Mary to help them. Then a strange light appeared upon one of the heights and shone there for three or four days. The sheerness of the cliff-face made it impossible to climb up so 84 steps were cut in the rock. At the top was found an icon of Our Lady with a lamp burning before it, and nearby the fearful dragon lay dead. The people carried the icon down to the valley in gratitude—but it returned to its former position of its own accord; after several attempts to move it was decided to found a church there on the cliff top, and so a cave was dug and dedicated to the Virgin and soon a monastery grew up around it. The icon's fame spread

far and wide, and it was revered not only by the Crimean Greeks, but also by the Tartars and even the Turkish Khans.

The monastery was active until the Russians came to the Crimea, but when the Crimean Greeks were transferred to the Sea of Azov in 1778 they took the icon with them and the monastery lost much of its magnetism. It was, however, rebuilt in 1850. Visitors can climb the 84 steps cut in the cliff, and get a good view of Bakhchiserai and Jehosophat's Valley.

CHUFUT-KALEH

Directions: There is room to park cars at the Uspensky-peshchernyi Monastery and from there the walk to Chufut–Kaleh is a little over a mile. The path leads to a nutgrove at the end of which there is a fountain, and from here a path leads up the mountain to the gate of Chufut–Kaleh.

Chufut-Kaleh, also known as the Jewish Fortress, is a dead city perched on a narrow limestone plateau. Possibly it is the most interesting of all these cave towns; it is also the easiest of access. The former inhabitants belonged to the Jewish sect called the Karaites or the Qaraites. These are disciples of the letter of the Law of Moses, adhering to Judaism without accepting the Talmud and other holy Jewish books, or the traditions of the Elders. The place was inhabited from the 17th century and the last family left the town in the 1870's. The fortress, however, and the town, were known of in the 14th century.

Today Chufut-Kaleh is a town of dead streets and ruined houses. The remains of synagogues can be seen and in the centre is a mausoleum built in Moorish style in 1437. This was erected by a khan to his daughter who, according to legend, heard her father coming while she was in her lover's arms, and threw herself over the cliff.

KATCHI-KALEN

Directions: Katchi-Kalen lies 9 km (6 miles) to the south of Bakhchiserai, opposite the village of Bashtanovka.

Katchi-Kalen was a cave monastery dating from the 9th–10th centuries. The caves were hewn from the living rock. There are many of them at different levels, joined by steps and bridges.

TEPE-KERMEN

Directions: Tepe-Kermen is 7 km (5 miles) to the east of Bakhchiserai.

The name means "hill fortress". There are over 200 caves, on 18 different levels, linked by streets and galleries. Inside are as many as 10,000 rooms and the ruins of several churches including one dating from 9–10th centuries.

MANGUP-KALEH

Directions: This is 67 km (45 miles) from Yalta and 20 km (14 miles) south of Bakhchiserai, near the village of Tankovoye. In this village there is a house with a spire, now used as a children's home; cars may be left here. Mangup-Kaleh is 7 km (5 miles) further on. From here a bad road leads to the villages of Krasnyi-Mak and Zalesnoye, and from there a path leads up the mountain to the cave town.

Mangup-Kaleh was founded in 5th to 6th centuries. The Basilica of Saint Constantine and Saint Helen, dating from the time of Justinian, was discovered in 1912–13. In the 14th century the town was the capital of the Gothic princedom and was known as Doros or Theodoros. In 1745 it was sacked by the Turks and deserted by its inhabitants.

There is a well-preserved Turkish fort to be seen, and among the ruins are the remains of a two-storey palace in the Acropolis, a Christian church, a Tartar mosque and a Karaite synagogue.

ROAD NINE

MOSCOW—YAROSLAVL

MOSCOW

(see Road One, page 103)

Babushkin · Mytishchi · Pushkino · Novaya Derevnya
Bratovshchina · Rakhmanov

ZAGORSK

Novoye · Glebovskoye

PERESLAVL-ZALESKY

Slobodka · Petrovsk · Rostov-Veliky · Karabykha

YAROSLAVL

MOSCOW

See Road 1, on page 103.

BABUSHKIN

Formerly known as Losino-ostrovskaya (elk island), this village was royal hunting ground from the 15th to the 17th centuries. It was renamed after M. Babushkin, a Soviet pilot who was made a Hero of the Soviet Union for his polar flights in the 1930's; it is now a suburb of Moscow.

MYTISHCHI

Population: 99,000 (1959)

The old Russian word *mit* means "customs duty", and there was once a *mytnaya izba* (small customs checking point) at this spot, where pilgrims halted on their way to the monastery at Zagorsk.

The place was first mentioned in writing in the 16th century. It is now part of Greater Moscow, and since 1805 has been one of the major sources of the Moscow water supply, the present water supply system having been modernised in 1924. Mytishchi's heavy industry includes the biggest factory for rolling stock in the country.

PUSHKINO

The village of Pushkino lies 32 km (20 miles) from Moscow. Called after *pushkari* (gunners), it has been known in the records since the 16th century. It was here that the company of the Moscow Arts Theatre held their first rehearsal in 1898.

✿ The Church of Saint Nicholas. This church was built in 1692 and reconstructed in 1861, and contains some old icons.

NOVAYA DEREVNYA

The name means "new village".

✿ The church was built at the beginning of the 20th century.

✿ Just beyond this village on the right side of the road, at a distance of 36 km (22½ miles) from Moscow, is a café.

BRATOVSHCHINA

In 1623 Ivan the Terrible built a palace in this village, which was a convenient stopping place on the way to the Troitsko-Sergievskaya Monastery. Nothing remains of the palace today.

✿ The Church of the Annunciation. This church was built in the 16th century.

RAKHMANOV

✿ Vozneseniya (Ascension) Church. This church dates from the 17th century.

ZAGORSK

Population: 74,000 (1959)

This town, situated on the River Koshura and the River Glimitza, received town status in 1917. Until 1930 it was called Sergiev, and was then renamed after Vladimir M. Zagorsky (1883–1919), a revolutionary well known for his political work who was killed by an anarchist's bomb.

Zagorsk is a centre of the handmade toy industry and is particularly renowned for its carved woodwork. Its other factories produce agricultural machinery, furniture and textiles.

✿ The Troitsko-Sergievskaya Lavra (Trinity Monastery of Saint Sergius). This monastery is one

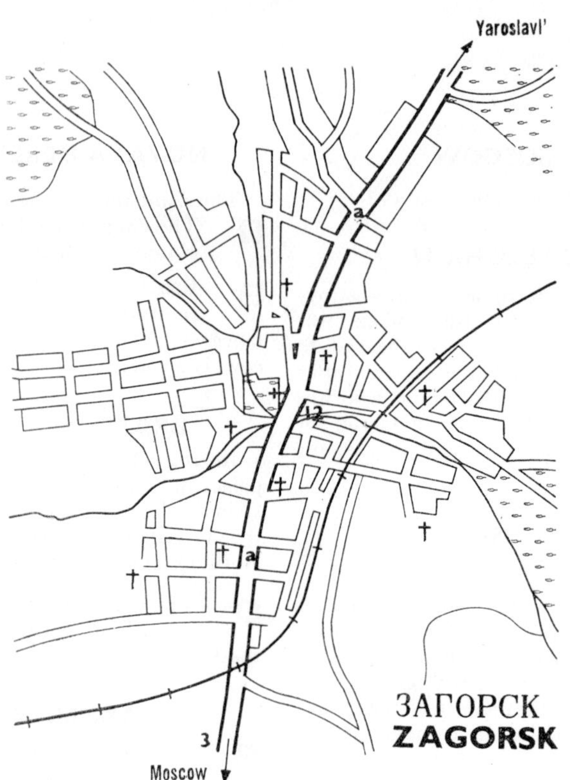

1 and 2 Hotel and Restaurant 3 Filling Station
a Prospekt Krasnoi Armii

of the most important architectural and historical monuments of mediaeval Russia, and is also the centre of Russian Orthodoxy today. Founded in 1340, it soon rose to be the religious capital of northern Russia. Its founder, Saint Sergius (1319?–1392) whose name it bears, was the son of an impoverished noble from the small town of Rodonezh, which was in 1610 completely ruined by the Poles. Saint Sergius also founded other monasteries around Moscow and in other towns, and monks from Zagorsk continued his work; they were responsible for the founding of the Solovyetsky Monastery on an island in the White Sea. The history of Russia in mediaeval times is closely connected with that of Zagorsk monastery, for Sergius was a very influential person and played an important role in Grand-Prince Dmitri's rousing of the Russian people against the Tartars; the Russian princes and soldiers were blessed by Abbot Sergius before the battle of Kulikovskaya against the Tartars in 1380.

In 1408 the whole region, including the monastery, was again devastated by the Tartars, and afterwards the Abbot Nikon found Sergius's body uninjured among the smoking ruins of the monastery, a sure sign of his sanctity. Abbot

Nikon managed to rebuild the monastery by using much of the treasure he had been able to save.

The monastery grew very rich and became the second most important educational centre in Russia after Kiev. Its reserve of figthing men numbered 20,000, and in 1513 the strong fortress wall, 1 km (½ mile) in circumference, 1·5 m (5 ft) thick and with nine towers was built. In 1608–10, during the Time of Troubles, the monastery was besieged for 16 months by 30,000 Poles, but although there were only 1500 men to defend it, it never surrendered.

The fate of the whole of Russia was dependent upon the outcome of the siege. In 1612 an army headed by Minin and Pozharsky halted at Zagorsk for rest and blessing before they set off southwards to liberate Moscow from the Poles, and in 1682 and 1689, during the mutinies of the royal Streltsy guards, the boy-tsars Peter and Ivan were sheltered here. Zagorsk remained an important fortress defending Moscow until the end of the 17th century.

TROITSKY (TRINITY) CATHEDRAL. This cathedral was built between 1422 and 1427, with a single dome in the Suzdal-Vladimir style. Its frescoes date from the 16th century, and there are many icons of value and interest among those in the second, third and fourth rows of the iconostasis. The icon of the Holy Trinity is a copy of the one painted by Andrei Rublev especially for this cathedral; the original is now in Moscow's Tretyakov Gallery. The Cathedral was erected on the site of the wooden Church of Saint Sergius which Abbot Nikon had built over the founder's grave; the body of Saint Sergius which is still visited by pilgrims, lies inside the cathedral in a dull silver sarcophagus presented by Ivan the Terrible. The silver canopy over it weighs 409 kg (8 cwt) and was a gift from the Empress Anne. The porch was added to the southern wall of the cathedral in the 18th century.

CHURCH OF THE DESCENT OF THE HOLY SPIRIT. This church built in 1476–77 by architects from Pskov, stands to the east of Trinity Cathedral. The top of its single dome was once used as a watchtower.

CHURCH OF SAINT NIKON. This church, adjoining the southern wall of Trinity Cathedral, was built in 1548 and reconstructed in 1623.

USPENSKY (ASSUMPTION) CATHEDRAL. This cathedral reminds one, by its size and its shape, of the Uspensky Cathedral in the Moscow kremlin. It was built in the reign of Ivan the Terrible to commemorate the capture of Kazan and Astrakhan from the Tartars, and was consecrated in 1585. The frescoes were painted in 1684 by local and Yaroslavl artists. Near the West Door of the Cathedral, outside, is the tomb of Boris Godunov, his wife and two of his children. The five domes of the Cathedral are painted blue and are decorated with golden stars.

THE GATEWAY-CHURCH. This church, which is decorated with frescoes, was built at the end of the 17th century.

SMOLENSKY CHURCH. This church is called after its principal icon, Our Lady of Smolensk. With its wide entrance, the church resembles a decorative rotunda. It was designed in 1746–48 by Prince Ukhtomsky.

BELFRY. This stands near Smolensky Church and, although founded in 1741, was the last of the whole ensemble to be completed, being finished only in 1769. It was designed in baroque style by Rastrelli and Prince Ukhtomsky; it stands 98 m (322 ft) high and has five tiers. At one time it boasted forty bells.

REFECTORY. This refectory stands by the monastery's southern wall. It was built in 1686–1692 in baroque style, is 73 m (240 ft) long, and gaily painted.

SAINT SERGIUS'S WELL. Just outside the Uspensky Cathedral stands a small chapel, built at the end of the 17th century to cover the well. Many of the pilgrims who still visit the monastery bring bottles to fill with holy water.

THE HOSPITAL BUILDINGS with the Church of Saints Zosim and Savvati, built in 1635–37, are the oldest of the secular structures in the complex.

✿ CHERTOGI. Built at the end of the 17th century and gaily decorated with paintwork and coloured tiles, this building was once the tsar's Palace. The interiors date from the 1740's and one of the halls has a painted ceiling depicting the victories of Peter the Great. The building, which lies near the northern wall of the monastery, now houses the Theological College (founded 1749) and an Ecclesiastical Academy.

THE METROPOLITAN'S HOUSE. This is an 18th century building which was reconstructed from the 17th century cells of the archimandrites. Stoves decorated with 17th century coloured tiles can be seen inside.

The vestry and adjoining monastery buildings now house an interesting museum. The collection is displayed in the order in which it was presented to the monastery, and includes gifts from Russian nobles and the Tsars Ivan the Terrible and Boris Godunov. The museum contains one of the richest collections of Russian ecclesiastical art with some icons by Simon Ushakov (1626–1686). Besides 18th and 19th century portraits, there are collections of 17th to 19th centuries furniture, pottery, china and glass. The fabrics are French and Italian of the 14th and 15th centuries, and there are Persian, Syrian and Turkish tissues of the 17th century. The Russian handicrafts displayed include carving, fabrics, costumes, embroidery, metalwork and toys. There is a small souvenir stall where local woodwork may be purchased. *The museum is closed on Fridays and on the 30th of each month.*

TOY MUSEUM *Krasnaya Armiya Prospekt 136.* This is the only museum of its kind in the Soviet Union. It was founded in 1918 and has a rich collection of toys dating from the Bronze Age to the present time, many of them of local production. There is a laboratory in the town where scientific research on toys is carried on.

PALACE OF CULTURE *In the centre of the town.* This columned building, completed in 1954, is the largest Palace of Culture in the Moscow region.

✿ OTDYKH (REST) RESTAURANT *On the main road, opposite the entrance to the monastery.*

NOVOYE

This village is 119 km (74 miles) from Moscow. Its church was built in the 18th century.

GLEBOVSKOYE

Glebovskoye is 126 km ($78\frac{1}{2}$ miles) from Moscow.

✿ The CHURCH OF SAINT GLEB, built in the 18th century, is now closed.

HOLY CROSS CHAPEL *7 km ($4\frac{1}{2}$ miles) before Pereslavl-Zalesky.* The chapel, which stands on the left side of the road, was erected on the order of Ivan the Terrible in 1557 when he was returning from the consecration of a new church in Pereslavl with Tsaritsa Anastasia, and she gave birth here to their son Fedor. The chapel dates from that time. It was restored in 1889.

PERESLAVL-ZALESKY

The town was established at the mouth of the River Trubezh in 1152 by Yuri Dolgoruky who had previously (in 1147) founded Moscow. In 1302 the Pereslavsky princedom was united with Moscow, and became a great trading centre, flourishing especially in the 16th and 17th centuries. Most of the surrounding lands belonged to the monasteries which then numbered more than 50. The English traveller, Fletcher, listed Pereslavl as one of the 16 greatest towns in Russia.

In 1688 Peter the Great found an English boat in Moscow, and because there was not enough room to sail it there he went to the Pleshcheyevo Lake at Pereslavl. Here he organised a shipyard, studied navigation, and within a few months had built other vessels which formed the basis of the future Russian navy. The first parade of the fleet took place in 1692 and Peter's relatives, foreign ambassadors, clergy, and a regiment of soldiers from Moscow came to the opening ceremony. Peter then went on to build sizeable ships in Archangel, Voronezh and the Baltic, and when he returned to Pereslavl in 1721 he had to reproach the authorities for letting his ships get into a state of decay. They were looked after for another 60 years but in 1783, 87 of them were destroyed by a fire.

✿ BOTIK MUSEUM *Near the village of Veskovo, 3 km (2 miles) from Pereslavl. Open 10–4; closed on Tuesdays.* This museum was formerly part of the Botik Estate, where there is now a wooden palace, a triumphal arch at the entrance which was built in 1852, a monument to Peter the Great designed by Campioni in the same year, some of his naval guns and a museum with relics of the flotilla. Only one ship, the *Fortune* remains.

✿ GORITSKY MONASTERY *Kardovsky Street, reached before entering the town on the way from Moscow; an arrow pointing to the left shows the way to the white-walled monastery. Open 10–4; closed on Tuesdays.* A wooden monastery was founded here in the 14th century but nothing remains of it, and the present complex dates from the 18th century. The Holy Gates were built in the 17th century. The Uspensky Sobor (Cathedral of the Assumption) dates from 1757, as does also its iconostasis which is known to be of Moscow workmanship. The belltower was put up at the same time but the refectory is a little older. Both the Local Museum and Picture Gallery are housed in this monastery; the Gallery contains mainly the works of Academician Dmitri Kardovsky (1866–1943) who was born in this region. The Tsar Gates from Vedenskaya Church were exhibited in 1867 in Paris where they won a medal. The plaster mask of Peter the Great was taken from the living tsar in 1719 by Rastrelli. Falconnet's original model for the "Bronze Horseman" is also in the museum.

THE CATHEDRAL OF THE SAVIOUR AND THE TRANSFIGURATION. This cathedral was built in 1152 and restored in 1894. At the beginning of the 13th century it was the burial place of the local princes. The frescoes were done at the time of the restoration and so are of little historic interest.

THE CONVENT OF SAINT NICHOLAS. This convent was founded in 1392, and its principal church was built between 1690 and 1721.

CONVENT OF SAINT THEODORE. This convent was founded in 1551. The Cathedral of Saint Theodore Stratilata was built in 1557 by order of Ivan the Terrible in memory of the birth of his son Theodore.

The Vedenskaya Church (1710), the Kazan Church (1714) and a belltower (1705) are also here.

DANILOV MONASTERY *Bolshaya Krestyanskaya Street.* This monastery was founded in 1508, and its Trinity Cathedral with 17th century frescoes was built in 1532. Other buildings include

All Saints' Church (1687) and a two-storey refectory (1695). The little Pokhvali Church was completed in the same year as the refectory.

Many of the other churches around the town are now all that remain of the surrounding monasteries.

SMOLENSKAYA CHURCH *Hilovaya Street.* This church was built in 1697–1705.

NOVI-VLADIMIRSKY CATHEDRAL. This cathedral was built in 1745 together with the Peter and Paul Church near it.

SIMEONOVSKAYA CHURCH *Rostovskaya Street.* The church was built in the style of Rastrelli in 1771.

SOROKOSVYATSKAYA (FORTY SAINTS) CHURCH *Rybnaya Sloboda* (*fish quarter*). This church was built in 1775.

POKROVSKAYA (INTERCESSION) CHURCH *Pleshcheyevskaya Street.* Built in the 18th century; this is the only church in Pereslavl at which services are held.

ALEXANDR NEVSKY CHURCH *Nagornaya Sloboda.* This church was built in 1746.

CHURCH OF THE METROPOLITAN PETER *Sadovaya Street 5.* This church was built in 1585 and restored in 1889 and again in 1957.

THE KREMLIN. The town's earthen walled kremlin was founded in 1152–1157; the wall is 2·5 km (1½ miles) long.

HOTEL AND RESTAURANT *Rostovskaya Street 7.*

BOOKSHOP *Rostovskaya Street 8.*

FILLING STATION.

★

NIKITSKY MONASTERY *On the way out of the town on the road to Yaroslavl, in the Nikitskaya Sloboda.* The monastery was founded in the 12th century, but the stone buildings were added only in 1561–64 on the order of Ivan the Terrible; the Nikitsky Cathedral was built at this time. Close to the Cathedral is the Blagoveshchensky (Annunciation) Church with a huge 17th century refectory and a belltower built in 1668. Near the monastery by the road is a small cemetery with an octagonal chapel founded in 1702 on the site of the miraculous healing of Prince Mikhail of Chernigov in 1186.

SLOBODKA

CHURCH OF ST. NICHOLAS *standing back from the road, on a hill on the right.* This white-painted church was built in the 18th century and is open for services.

PETROVSK

This town is justly proud of its fine birch grove.

CHURCH OF THE TRANSFIGURATION *by the cemetery on the way into the town.* This is a 19th century church.

CHURCH OF ST. PETER AND PAUL.

RESTAURANT *Sovietskaya Street.*

SERVICE STATION.

★

Before entering Rostov, a bad side road to the left leads to the interesting *wooden church of St. John the Baptist* (1689). It is open 10–5; closed on Wednesdays.

FILLING STATION *on the left side of the road before entering Rostov.*

ROSTOV VELIKY (or Rostov Yaroslavsky)

Population: 29,000 (1959)

This town was called Rostov the Great to distinguish it from the town of Rostov-on-Don. Founded before the days of Rurik, it is one of the most ancient towns in Russia. It is situated on Lake Nero and was first mentioned in the chronicles in 862 and was called after Prince Rosta. The local merchants traded with Scandinavia in amber and silver coins from the Arabian east, exchanging them for honey, fur and grain. Christianity was officially accepted in 989, when the local inhabitants were divided into groups of about ten and fifteen and forced to bathe in the lake. Priests from Byzantium sailed around on rafts, and boats and gave one Christian name to each group. Paganism, however, did not die out completely for some years.

Rostov was first called the Capital of the North, then in the 12th century it received the title of Great because its territory and population were no less than those of ancient Kiev and Novgorod. As it grew wealthier, the number of its churches increased until it was said:

"The Devil went to Rostov
But the crosses scared him off!"

In 1207 Rostov became the capital of a separate princedom, which, like other parts of Russia, was under Tartar rule in the 13th and 14th centuries. It came into the possession of Moscow under Dmitri Donskoi in 1474. At the end of the 16th century it grew in importance as a town on the trade route between Moscow and the White Sea, and in the 17th century it was invaded by Poles and Lithuanians; it was ruined and sacked by them, and among the rich booty was a golden sepulchre weighing 100 kg ($1\frac{1}{2}$ cwt), stolen from the Uspensky Sobor and presented to a Polish lady.

The earth wall, the remains of which can still be seen, was built in 1631–33.

The town now has an area of 50 sq km and its industry includes the production of chicory coffee, and food (especially treacle), linen and enamel work which has been manufactured here since the 19th century. The main streets are Proletarskaya, Lenin and Sverdlov. The Agricultural College has a botanical garden of its own.

THE KREMLIN. The Kremlin, until the mid 19th century called Rostov Metropolia, is surrounded by a wall with ten round towers. Its territory is a rough rectangle covering 2 hectares (5 acres), and it differs from other Russian kremlins and monasteries in that it has no main cathedral dominating the other buildings. Its churches are good examples of Russian 17th century architecture and were built under the aegis of Metropolitan Ion Sisoyevich between 1667 and 1691. The wall and towers were built not for military defence, but simply to guard the Metropolitan's palace. When the ecclesiastical centre moved to Yaroslavl little more building of interest took place here.

The Kremlin has two gate-churches. The *Church of the Resurrection* (1670) on the north wall has five domes and gates known as the Holy Gates; the southern door is decorated with allegorical paintings. The *Church of Saint John the Divine* is in the west wall. This church has some interesting canopies above the choir stalls. Both gate-churches contain well preserved wall paintings and old frescoes restored in 1954, and both have holes in the west walls which held empty jars to improve the acoustics.

THE CHURCH OF THE SMOLENSK MOTHER OF GOD. This church built in 1693, is painted in brightly coloured triangles.

THE CHURCH OF THE REDEEMER. This church also has pot-holes in the walls; and its iconostasis has been replaced by a screen with five arches.

In the complex of civil buildings is the METROPOLITAN'S PALACE (1672–80) and a series of halls. The BYELAYA PALATA (white palace) was built in 1670 to accommodate the tsars. There is now a museum inside it.

The Kremlin was damaged by a hurricane in 1953 but has since been restored.

USPENSKY (ASSUMPTION) CATHEDRAL *Outside the Kremlin.* This cathedral was founded in 1214 and consecrated in 1230. It was built on the lines of Moscow's Uspensky Cathedral, but its present appearance dates from 15th to 16th centuries. To the left of the Holy Door is the wonder-working icon, the Vladimir Virgin, painted in the 11th century by Alimpi. The four-domed belfry of the cathedral (1680–82) is 32 m (105 ft) long and 17 m (55 ft) high. It has four arched openings and the 13 bells play 4 tunes; the heaviest, the Sisoi Bell, weighs 32,000 kg (about 32 tons).

CHURCH OF SAINT GREGORY *Near the Kremlin.* This church was built in 1670.

THE SAVIOUR-IN-THE-MARKET-PLACE CHURCH. This church was built in 1690 and now houses the town library.

CHURCH OF THE ASCENSION. *To the south-east of the Kremlin.* Built in 1566, this is a typical Moscow-style church.

EPIPHANY CATHEDRAL *In the eastern suburbs of the town.* This cathedral was built in 1554 as part of the Abraham Monastery, which was founded at the beginning of the 11th century, and was the oldest in Russia.

SPASO-YAKOVLEVSKY MONASTERY (JACOB MONASTERY) *In the western surburbs of the town, on the banks of the lake.* This monastery was built during the 17th to 19th centuries and the original wall is still standing. Inside is the Zachatyevsky (Immaculate Conception) Cathedral (1686) and Saint Dmitri's Church (1794–1801), designed in classical Russian style. Close to the monastery is the Church of the Transfiguration; this was built in the 17th century as the cathedral of a now-vanished 13th century monastery.

Services are now conducted in Saint John's Church, *Dekabristov Street* and Saint Nicholas's Church *Gogol Street.*

✿ LOCAL MUSEUM *In the Kremlin Halls and the former Church School. Open 9–5; closed on Wednesdays.* This museum was established in 1883 when the kremlin was first restored. There is an interesting collection of presents made to the monasteries, and of porcelain, icons, and woodcarving of the 16th–20th centuries. There is also a small prison cell called the "stone sack".

✿ HOTEL AND EATING HOUSE *Karl Marx Street, near the Kremlin.*

BERYOZKA RESTAURANT.

✿ PARK *Beside the lake.* There is a boat hire station here.

★

There are some more churches and remains of monasteries around the town, among them, the Borisoglebsky Monastery—24 km (15 miles) from Rostov. This was built in the 16th century as a fortress against Uglich and has strong wall with towers and two gates. The oldest churches inside are the cathedral of 1524, its outside decorated with remarkable tiles, the Church of the Annunciation (1527) and Saint-Sergius-over-the-Gate (1545). There is also a belltower.

KARABYKHA

This town was the birthplace of the Russian poet Nikolai Nekrasov (1821–1878), who spent most of his life in the Yaroslavl region.

✿ NEKRASOV MUSEUM *In the poet's former estate.*

YAROSLAVL

Population: 407,000 (1959)

Yaroslavl stands on either side of the river Volga, at the point where the river Kotorosl flows into it, and where the Volga is nearly 1 km (½ mile) wide. The town covers an area of 170 sq km, stretches along the river for about 26 km (16½ miles) and reaches inland on either side for about 9 km (5½ miles).

Yaroslavl is the oldest town on the Volga, first mentioned in writing in 1071 and said to have been founded by Yaroslav the Wise (1019–54) in about 1024. The town emblem is a bear rampant with a halberd on his shoulder. According to the legend, when Yaroslav the Wise first came to the place where he later founded the town, the local inhabitants let a bear out of its cage to chase him away, and Yaroslav killed it with his halberd. Now lorries made in the town have a bear on the bonnet.

Early in the 13th century Yaroslav established the first school in northern Russia. In 1238 the town was sacked and burnt by the Tartars, and in 1463 the principality of Yaroslavl was united with Moscow, when Prince Alexander Brukhatyi, "the Paunch", exchanged his ancestral princedom with Tsar Ivan III for some land near Moscow.

During the reign of Ivan the Terrible trade relations were established with western Europe through the White Sea. Yaroslavl then became prominent as an important British trading station for commerce with the near east and the Volga, and it began to attract foreign investments. During the Time of Troubles it was the temporary capital of the country. It was badly damaged by the Poles and the Cossacks and then, in the middle of the 17th century, was rebuilt and grew in commercial and industrial importance. An 18th century poet wrote:

"Athens in ancient time boasted
of its sciences;
Other towns were proud of the art
of their hands
—But you have all these in one".

Under Catherine II, in 1777, the town was made a provincial capital. Eventually the Baltic ports took much of its trade, but until the opening of the Moscow-Volga Canal in 1937 Yaroslavl continued to be Moscow's Volga port.

Today Yaroslavl is a big industrial town; apart from making cotton and linen fabric in one of the oldest factories in Russia, it also produces synthetic rubber, motor tyres, lorries, Diesel engines, electro-machines, chemicals and leather, and processes tobacco and oil. There are three institutes, pedagogical, medical and technological, in the town.

The oldest part of the town is the Strelka (arrow), where the River Kotorosl flows into the Volga. This is where the kremlin once stood, and where one of the oldest civil buildings, the house of the Metropolitan, built in 1690, still survives.

The centre of Yaroslavl is Sovietskaya Square (formerly Illinskaya Square) with the Church of Saint Elijah in the centre. The houses around the square were built as regional government buildings in 1781–85. From this square run two streets, Kirovskaya and Bolshaya Oktyabrskaya, which end in two towers, Znamenskaya, dating from 1660, and Uglichskaya (1646), both built as lookout towers on the town's old earthen wall. The Pervomaisky (formerly Kazansky) Boulevard, in the centre, is a favourite place for the local inhabitants to take the air. Yaroslavl is probably the best place for visitors who wish to see old Russian churches because it was not damaged at all during World War II. In the centre of the town there are many typical Russian mansion houses which add to the special charm of the place.

The churches include several of the 16th and 17th centuries which are really of considerable interest. In particular the Yaroslavl frescoes are unique for the colossal area they cover; Moscow churches are smaller and consequently have less interior wall space. Most of the churches in the town were built by the merchants. Yaroslavl is also noted for having the best woodcarvings in Russia.

✪ SPASO-PREOBRAZHENSKY (TRANSFIGURATION OF OUR SAVIOUR) MONASTERY *Podbelskov Square 25*. This monastery was founded at the end of the 12th century, and in 1787 it was converted into an archbishop's palace. The wall was built in the first half of the 17th century to replace the original wall. It is 2·8 to 3 m (9 ft 3 in.—9 ft 10 in.) thick and 188 m (895 yd) in circumference. The Holy Gates at the entrance were built in 1616, and the frescoes inside the archway illustrating Saint John's apocalyptic vision were painted in 1664. Within the walls is the Transfiguration Cathedral, built in 1516 by Moscow architects. It was one of the most revered and rich cathedrals in Yaroslavl and has through the years been altered several times. The frescoes were painted in 1563–64 by three Moscow and two local artists; the whole of the western wall depicts the Last Judgement. Some frescoes were added in 1782. It was in this monastery in 1795 that the manuscript *The Tale of Igor's Campaign* was found, a mediaeval epic which provided the subject for the opera *Prince Igor*.

Besides the Cathedral, the monastery also comprises the Church of Yaroslavl Miracle-workers (1831), now used as a cinema and lecture hall, the 16th century refectory, the 16th century belltower (reconstructed in the 19th century) and the monks' cells of the 16th and 17th centuries. Restoration began in 1958 and is still in progress. Part of the local Museum and the Art Museum are now located in the monastery.

NIKOLY NADEINA CHURCH *Narodnyi Pereulok 2a*. This church was built in 1620–22 but has suffered much alteration; some of the frescoes inside, done in 1640, are reminiscent of miniatures stuck to the wall. The 18th century iconostasis is said to have been constructed following a sketch by Fedor Volkov, the founder of the Russian national theatre in 1750. (His company was the first to stage *Hamlet* in Russia).

ROZHDESTVA KHRISTOVA (NATIVITY) CHURCH *Malaya Fevralskaya Street 1*. This church was built in 1644 and reconstructed in the 19th century.

The frescoes were painted by local artists in 1683. There is a 17th–18th century iconostasis and the mid-17th century belltower is one of the loveliest examples of its kind in Yaroslavl.

THE CHURCH OF ELIJAH THE PROPHET *Sovietskaya Street in the centre of town*. This church is very well preserved. Its frescoes were completed in 6 or 7 months in 1680–81; they are divided into five horizontal strips, the first showing Christ arisen, the second the Gospel story of Christ's life on earth, the third the lives of the Apostles, the fourth the Life of Elijah (to whom the church is dedicated), and the bottom one the life of Elijah and his disciple Elisha. The iconostasis dates from the 18th century, and the tsar's and patriarch's pews were brought here from another church in 1930. This is the most impressive church in Yaroslavl and certainly the one in the best condition. It is now a museum; if it is closed tourists should apply to the museum authorities in the Spaso-Preobrazhensky Monastery to have it opened.

Group of CHURCHES IN KOROVNIKI *Portovaya Naberezhnaya 2*. The church of Ioan Zlatoust (John the Golden-

Tongued) was built in 1649 and is one of the most picturesque churches in Yaroslavl. It has a 17th century iconostasis and frescoes painted in 1732–1733 by local artists. The outside of the altar window is decorated with coloured tiles. The smaller church is Vladimirskaya Church (1669), and between the two churches stands a 17th century octagonal belltower; it is 37 m (122 ft) high and is known as the "candle of Yaroslavl".

CHURCH OF SAINT MICHAEL THE ARCHANGEL *Pervomaiskaya Street 67*. This church was built in 1657–80 and has a belltower. Its frescoes were painted by local artists in 1731; they are divided into nine strips and give the impression of a brightly coloured tapestry.

CHURCH OF SAINT NICHOLAS THE WET *Chaikovsky Street 1*. The church was built in 1665–72, copying the Church of Ioan Zlatoust, and the outside of the altar window is framed with coloured tiles in the same way. The frescoes were completed in 1673; on the left side of the fresco of the Last Judgement on the west wall, among a group of sinners, are depicted foreigners in 17th century European dress and Persians in turbans. At the same address is Tikhvinskaya Church (1686).

DMITRI SOLUNSKY CHURCH *Bolshaya Oktyabrskaya Street 41*. This church was built in 1671 and altered in the 18th and 19th centuries. The frescoes were painted by local artists in 1686.

SPASA-NA-GORODU CHURCH *Pochtovaya Street 3*. The church was built in 1672 and decorated with frescoes by local artists in 1693; of these the most interesting are the two lower strips which show processions, and battles between the larger towns.

NIKOLA-MELINKY CHURCH *Stachek Street 60*. The church was built in 1672 and the frescoes were completed by Yaroslavl artists in 1707. On the northern wall is shown the invasion by Tamerlane, and the carrying of the holy icon from Vladimir to Moscow. Even in the dirty fresco one can see in the background Saint Basil's Cathedral and the Ivan Veliky Belltower in Moscow.

VLADIMIRSKAYA CHURCH *Rybinskaya Street 44*. This church was built in 1670–78.

IOANA PREDTECHI-V-TOLCHKOVYE (SAINT JOHN THE BAPTIST) CHURCH *Kotoroslnaya Naberezhnaya 69*. The whole population of the region round about contributed either physically or monetarily to the building of this church in 1671–87. With its 15 domes it is very grand, and is the best church of 17th century Yaroslavl. The bricks imitate woodcarvings and the impression is that they are made of wood. There are also many coloured tiles in its decoration. The frescoes painted in 1694–95 took only 5 months to complete and they are among the best of their time. Instead of the usual Last Judgement on the west wall there are six illustrations to the Song of Songs. There is an 18th century iconostasis, and the belltower was built in about 1700.

FYODOROVSKAYA CHURCH *Yaroslavsky Street 74*. This church was built in 1687 and contains frescoes painted by local artists in 1715; they are like illustrations to fairy tales, showing the details of secular life in Peter the Great's time. Battles, architecture, ships etc. are depicted.

NIKOLY PENSKOGO CHURCH *Malaya Proletarskaya Street 59*. The church, together with its belltower, was built in 1691.

BOGOYAVLENIYE (EPIPHANY) CHURCH *Podbelsky Square*. Built 1684–93, the façade of the church is decorated with tiles. The frescoes by local artists date from 1693, and there is a 17th century iconostasis of beautifully carved wood with icons of the same date.

NIKOLI RUBLENOV CHURCH *On the site of the kremlin.* The church was built in 1695; it contains no frescoes.

BLAGOVESHCHENIYE (ANNUNCIATION) CHURCH *Volzhskaya Naberezhnaya 51.* The church was built in 1688–1702. The 18th century domes resemble flower buds; the frescoes were painted by local artists in 1709.

PETER-AND-PAUL CHURCH *Peter-and-Paul Park.* Built in 1736–42 in honour of Peter the Great by the owner of a Yaroslavl textile factory of which the tsar was the patron, the church is in the Saint Petersburg baroque style of the 18th century and resembles the Peter-and-Paul fortress in Leningrad. The belltower stands 57 m (187 ft) high. The church is now used as a club.

ILIINSKO-TIKHONOVSKAYA CHURCH *Volzhskaya Naberezhnaya 5.* This church was built in 1825–31 and is now in a bad state of repair.

CATHEDRAL OF THE KAZAN MONASTERY *Pervomaiskaya Street 19a.* Built in 1845, this cathedral is used to house the regional archives.

✿ HISTORICAL AND LOCAL MUSEUM *Sovietskaya Square 19/1. Open 10–5; closed on Saturdays.*

ART MUSEUM *Chelyuskintsev Square 2. Open 10–5; closed on Tuesdays.*

PLANETARIUM *Trefolev Street 20. Open 11–7; closed on Tuesdays.*

NEKRASOV MONUMENT *On the embankment.* The famous poet Nekrasov spent most of his life in this region. His home at Karabykha, 16 km (10 miles) south of Yaroslavl, is now a museum. This monument was unveiled in 1958.

LENIN STATUE *Krasnaya Square.*

OBELISK *in the garden opposite St. Elijah's Church.* This obelisk commemorating Civil War heroes was unveiled in 1958.

✿ VOLKOV DRAMA THEATRE *Volkov Square.* The theatre was built in 1911.

PUPPET THEATRE *Komitetskaya Street 8*

CONCERT HALL *Komitetskaya Street 11*

✿ BUTUSOV TOWN PARK *Chaikovsky Street.*

✿ VOLGA HOTEL AND RESTAURANT *Kirov Street 10.* The local Intourist office is in Rooms 201 and 202; tel: 2-12-58.

TSENTRALNAYA HOTEL *Volkov Square.*

YAROSLAVL HOTEL AND MEDVED (BEAR). RESTAURANT *Svoboda Square 2.*

MOSKVA RESTAURANT *Komsomolskaya Street 1.*

EVROPA CAFE *Svoboda Street 1.*

KONDITERSKAYA CAFE *Volzhskaya Naberezhnaya 43a.*

CHAIKA (SEAGULL) CAFE *Lenin Street 26.*

ROSSIA CAFE *Chkalov Street 23.*

MILK BAR *Pervomaiskaya Street 19.*

✿ G.P.O. *Podbelsky Square 22/28.*

YAROSLAVL DEPARTMENT STORE *Svoboda Street.*

BOOKSHOP *Komsomolskaya Street 5.*

GIFT SHOP *Svoboda Street 16.*

TAXI RANK *Krasnaya Square, tel: 2-51-23.*

✿ FILLING STATION.

SERVICE STATION.

★

Just south of Yaroslavl, beside the main road, is Krestovskaya Church. During an epidemic of cholera a cross was erected here, and after the spread of the disease stopped short of the town the church was built in thanksgiving.

ROAD TEN

KHARKOV—ROSTOV-ON-DON ORDZHONIKIDZE—TBILISI—SOCHI ROSTOV—KHARKOV

KHARKOV

(see Road Seven, page 222)

Chuguyev · Izyum · Slavyansk · Artyomovsk · Debaltsevo Bokovo-Platovo · Novoshakhtinsk · Novecherkassk

ROSTOV-ON-DON

Bataisk · Krylovskaya · Pavlovskaya · Kropotkin · Armavir Nevinnomyssk · Mineralniye Vody · Zheleznovodsk · Pyatigorsk Yessentuki · Kislovodsk · Baksan · Chegem · Nalchik · Beslan

ORDZHONIKIDZE

Chmi · Larsy · Gveleti · Kazbegi · Sioni · Kobi · Gudauri · Mleti Kvesheti · Passanauri · Ananuri · Zhinvali · Natakhtari · Mtskheta

TBILISI

Igoyeti · Gori · Urbnisi · Ruisi · Aradyeti · Khashuri · Surami · Shorapani Zestaphoni · Kutaisi · Samtredia · Zugdidi · Ilori · Ochemchire · Dranda Gulripshi · Sukhumi · Esheri · Novyi-Afon · Gudauta · Mussera · Pitsunda Ritsa · Gagra · Gantiadi · Adler · Khosta

SOCHI

Dagomyss · Loo · Lazarevskoye · Ashei · Tuapse · Novo-Mikhailovskoye Dzhubga · Arkhipo-Osipovka · Pshada · Divnomorsk · Gelendzhik Kabardinka · Novorossisk · Afipskaya · Krasnodar Korenovskaya · Rostov-na-Donu

KHARKOV

See Road 7, on page 222.

CHUGUYEV

Chuguyev lies a little off the main road. It was founded in 1638 and was formerly a Cossack regimental town. The arcades of shops date from the early 19th century and the former town magistrate's office from the end of the 18th century. Among the more impressive of the old houses is the town hall (now used as the House of Pioneers) on Rosa Luxemburg Street.

The town produces building materials, tractor parts and agricultural machinery.

✿ INTERCESSION CATHEDRAL built between 1826 and 1834.

PREOBRAZHENSKAYA (Transfiguration) CHURCH *Oktyabrskaya Square.* Built in the 19th century, and open for service.

✿ REPIN MUSEUM *on the second floor of the House of Culture, Krasnikh Bortsov Square.* Chuguyev was the birthplace of artist Ilya Repin (1844–1930) and he did much of his work here. The paintings displayed are reproductions. There is a bust of Repin by Manizer just in front of the House of Culture; it was unveiled in 1956.

✿ HOTEL AND RESTAURANT *Kharkov Street.*

On the outskirts of the town, coming into it from Moscow, there is *good bathing* in the River Sverski Donets.

IZYUM

Population: 36,000 (1959)

The turkic word *Izyum* means raisin; the town was once a Tartar fortress, but is known to have been a Russian settlement since 1571. In 1681, on the initiative of Colonel Grigori Donets from Kharkov, it was made a town and became an important point on the line of defence against the Crimean Tartars. There is a good view over the town and beyond from the top of Kremyenets Hill (177 m/582 ft) which slopes right down to the river; in the time of Ivan the Terrible guards kept a lookout from the hill for Tartar movements. In 1663 the tsar's huntsmen in charge of the imperial hunting reserve lived in Izyum.

Local industry makes building materials and food products, and there is a railway engine repair works.

✿ THE TRANSFIGURATION CATHEDRAL. This cathedral was built in 1684.

CHURCH OF SAINT NICHOLAS *Sverdlov Street.* This church was built between 1809 and 1823.

✿ LOCAL MUSEUM *Sverdlov Street 12. Open 10–6; closed on Tuesdays.* In the courtyard are twelve stone "bahby", the idols once used by the nomads of the steppes.

LENIN MONUMENT.

TANK MONUMENT. This monument was erected in memory of Lt.-General P. V. Volokh who was killed in 1943.

✿ KREMYANETS HOTEL *Staro-Pochtovaya Street 19, beside the main road.*

SEVERNYI DONETS RESTAURANT *Paromnaya Street, beside the main road.*

The local market, in the upper part of the town, is a large one typical of those in the Ukraine.

★

2 km ($1\frac{1}{2}$ miles) out of town, on the road to Moscow, is the small village of *Peski* (sand).

TRANSFIGURATION CHURCH *Moscow Street*. This was reconstructed and enlarged in 1903.

There are pinewoods and good bathing in the River Seversky Donets; there is another bathing place near the oak plantations 18 km (11 miles) beyond the town in the other direction.

SLAVYANSK

Population: 83,000 (1959)

In 1676 a town and fortress called Tork was founded beside the river Torets. In 1784 the town was renamed Slavyansk, "town of Slavs".

The discovery of medicinal properties in the waters of the three lakes, Slepnoe, Rapnoe and Veisovo, has led to the development of Slavyansk as a health resort. There are many sanatoria in the area, and cures are effected with mineral waters and also with mud.

From the 17th century onward the town has been known for its salt production, and now it also has large farms for breeding fish and ducks, and a local pottery. When Chekhov visited the town in 1887 he wrote: "There is a barber's shop and a clock mender's, so one can expect that in a thousand years there will be a telephone in Slavyansk".

OLD PARK.

RESTAURANT.

FILLING STATION *At the 168 km milestone on the main road.* Here there is also a restaurant for tourists, while the town itself lies some distance off the road to the west. The filling station provides round the clock service.

ARTYOMOVSK

Population: 61,000 (1959)

The town, which was formerly known as Bakhmut and which stood beside a river so called, was renamed in 1924 in honour of Artem, the party nickname of Fedor Sergeyev (1883–1921), who was an active Communist before and after the revolution.

The place has been used for salt mining since the 16th century, and the town was founded in the 17th century. To begin with a small fortress was built here and Cossacks were responsible for defending the place and for supplying the country with salt. The salt was of especial importance to the Russians who had previously had to buy their salt from the Crimean Tartars. Even today half the salt used in the Soviet Union comes from Artyomovsk. Coal was discovered here in the 18th century, and the town now produces plaster of Paris and food products as well as salt. The local champagne factory has its cellars in the abandoned plaster of Paris mines.

GEOLOGICAL MUSEUM *At the crossing of Lenin Street and Profinterna Street.*

MONUMENT TO ARTEM.

THEATRE.

HOTEL.

RESTAURANT.

Artyomovsk lies a little aside from the main Kharkov–Rostov road.

LUGANSKOYE

19TH CENTURY CHURCH.

TEAROOM.

DEBALTSEVO

Population 32,000 (1959)

This town is one of the more important railway junctions of the Donbas area. Its machine-building factory produces equipment for the metallurgial, coke and chemical industries.

BOKOVO-PLATOVO

RESTAURANT.

FILLING STATION *At the 306 km milestone. Round the clock service.*

ANTRATSIT

Antratsit means literally "anthracite" and this small town fully lives up to its name. Growing rapidly among the coal mines, it has only recently reached town status.

CAFE *Beside the main road.*

NOVOSHAKHTINSK

Population: 104,000 (1959)

Formerly known as Comintern, the town was renamed Novoshakhtinsk meaning "new coalmines". It was founded after the revolution and is one of the Soviet Union's coalmining centres. Most of the population are employed in the mines, but there are also chemical and building materials industries.

EATING HOUSE *Beside the main road, to the left.*

SIREN (LILAC) CAFE *By the road that leaves the town.*

FILLING STATION *By the road that leaves the town, near the café.*

NOVOCHERKASSK

Population: 94,000 (1959)

The town stands on a high hill dominating the rivers Tuzlov and Uksai. It was founded in 1805 by the Cossacks, and the settlement soon became their centre and a Russian stronghold on the River Don. It is well known to Russians as the Don Cossacks' capital. During its early years the town received material help and considerable privileges from the government.

There are buildings which remain from these times including the Cossack headquarters, some 19th century barracks and a number of attractive, small houses once owned by rich Cossacks.

There are veterinary, hydro-technical and hydro-chemical institutes in Novocherkassk.

VOZNESENSKY SOBOR (Ascension Cathedral) *Yermak Square.* The architects Zlobin and Yashenko designed this cathedral in Byzantine style, and it is one of the best examples ot its kind in Russia. It was built between 1891 and 1905 and is 74·5 m (245 ft) high, 77 m (252 ft) long and 62 m (203 ft) wide while the diametre of the cupola measures over 21 m (70 ft). It can hold a congregation of 5000 and was formerly the Don Cossack Army's Cathedral. Pictures of life in the army decorate the choir stalls. The cathedral is open for service.

ST. KONSTANTIN'S CHURCH.

ST. GEORGE'S CHURCH.

HISTORY OF THE DON COSSACKS MUSEUM *Sovietskaya Street 38. Open 10–5; closed on Tuesdays.* Here is an interesting collection of banners and a two hundred-guinea English sword presented on 8th June, 1814, to Hetman Count Platov for "consummate skill, brilliant talents and undaunted bravery" in "securing the liberties, the repose and the happiness of Europe." Matvei Platov (1751 – 1818) was a general who was famous for his fights with Napoleon's army. During the retreat of the French, he led the Cossack regiment and recaptured Smolensk, seized Danzig (1813) and Namur (1814). He went to London where the presentation of the sword was made and where he left his uniform in exchange. The museum also contains the works of a 17th century English clock which was captured from the Turkish fortress of Azov in 1695. Local excavations of one of the burial mounds near Novocherkassk in 1864 brought to light the much-prized golden items worked by the Sarmats in the 2nd century B.C. Most of the collection is now in the Hermitage Museum in Leningrad, but some originals and a number of copies can be seen in Novocherkassk museum.

Near the Don Cossack's Museum is the GAUPTWACHTER, THE GUARD HOUSE, built in 1853 and also the old wooden building of the POSTING INN which was used by Pushkin (1820) and Lermontov (1840).

ATAMAN PALACE (1863) *Beside Lenin Garden.* This now serves as the town hall and the local Party Headquarters.

GREKHOV MUSEUM *Grekhov Street 124. Open 11–5; closed on Mondays, Wednesdays and Fridays.* Mitrofan Grekov (1882–1934) was a well-known Soviet artist who painted military pictures and battle scenes. The museum is in his house.

LENIN MONUMENT.

YERMAK MONUMENT *Yermak Square.* The monument by Mekeshin and Beklemeshev was unveiled in 1904. The various inscriptions read, "To the Don Ataman Yermak Timofeyevich, Conqueror of Siberia, in memory of three hundred years of the Don Army from the grateful decendants—1570–1870"; "He lost his life beneath the waters of the Irtish on 5th August, 1584"; "Russia, History and the Church together accord honour to Yermak's undying memory" (-Karamzin, Russian historian) and " ToYermak from the Don Cossacks,—1904". The Siberian campaign lasted from 1581 to 1584.

BAKLANOV'S TOMBSTONE *Yermak Square.* Yakov Baklanov (1809–1873) was a Cossack general and writer.

The two *triumphal arches* of Novocherkassk were erected in 1817 to mark the triumphal return of Ataman Platov and his Cossacks from Paris after the defeat of Napoleon. There are other personal memorials to Platov and to Cossack Stepan Razin who was the leader of a peasant revolt in 1670 to 1671 and who became a popular hero of Russian folklore.

✿ DRAMA THEATRE *Karl Marx Street 16.*

A NEW THEATRE is under construction inside the walls of the old Law Court (1909) *Sovietskaya Street.*

✿ PARK *Karl Marx Street 7.*

TRUD STADIUM *Podtelkov Street.*

✿ HOTEL *Podteklov Street 90.*

YUZHNAYA RESTAURANT *Moskovskaya Street 1.*

DRUZHBA (FRIENDSHIP) RESTAURANT *near the entrance to the town, approaching it from Moscow.*

✿ BANK *Moskovskaya Street 9.*

TELEGRAPH OFFICE *Podtelkov Street 102.*

✿ FILLING STATION *near the entrance to the town, approaching it from Moscow.*

Motorists passing through Novocherkassk should take the opportunity of seeing the *Yermak Monument* and the big *cathedral. As you climb up the hill on the way in to the centre of the town, passing the triumphal arch, turn left at the roundabout (instead of following the sign to Rostov which points to the right).*

ROSTOV-ON-DON

Population: 650,000 (1963)

In the 18th century a fortress was built beside the River Don to withstand the Turks. It was called after Saint Dmitri Rostovsky, and from this fortress the city got its name. When Alexander I approved the town plans in 1811, "on-Don" (Na Donu) was added to the name to distinguish it from Rostov Yaroslavsky, an ancient Russian town north-east of Moscow. In Russian the city is often called "the Gate to the Caucasus".

Rostov stands at the meeting place of roads running from the Ukraine, the Volga region, Siberia and the central regions of the country to the northern Caucasus and Transcaucasia. It is 46 km (25 miles) from where the River Don flows into the Sea of Azov, and it spreads for more than 12 km (17½ miles) along the high right bank of the river. Since the completion of the Volga-Don Canal its port has grown in economic importance, for it is now connected with five seas. The canal links the Don with the Volga near Volgograd (formerly Stalingrad)

РОСТОВ-НА-ДОНУ
ROSTOV-NA-DONU

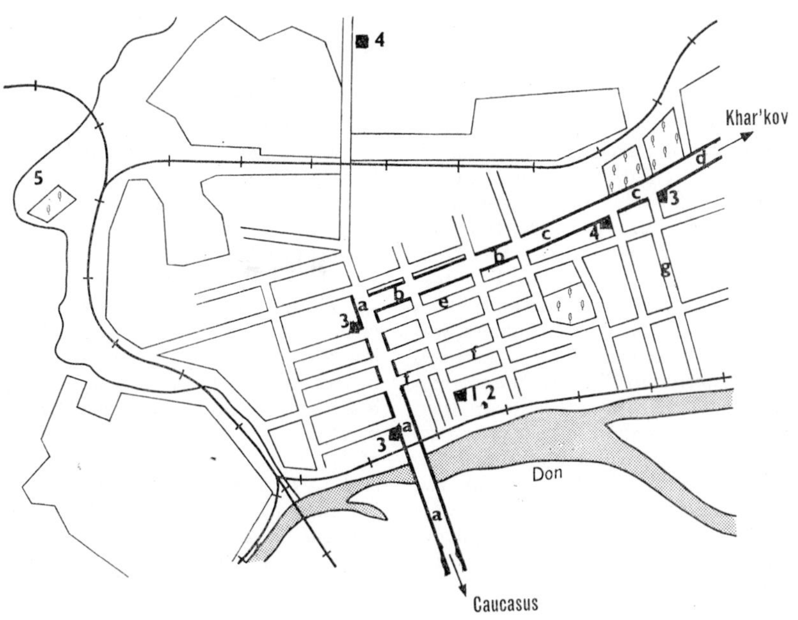

1 and 2 Hotel and Restaurant
3 Filling Station
4 Service Station
5 Camping Site

a Budennovsky pr.
b Malyuginoy ul.
c Oktyabrskaya ul.
d Novocherkasskoje chaussée
e Krasnoarmeyskaya ul.
f Ul. Engelsa
g Teatralnyi projezd

and is 100 km (63 miles) long. The first attempt to build such a canal was made by the Turks in 1569, and from the time of Peter the Great onwards there were repeated plans to build it; it was finally constructed between 1947 and 1952.

The port was established in 1749 by the order of Elizaveta Petrovna, and was then known as Temernik. It was an important place for trading in the Sea of Azov and in the Black and Mediterranean Seas, and was founded as a customs point. The fortress dated from 1761. In 1779 Armenians were transferred here from the Crimea and it was they who founded the township of Nakhichevan to the east of the fortress. The name was taken from that of the ancient Armenian capital ruined by the Tartars in the 13th century. The new Nakhichevan was absorbed by growing Rostov in the 1920's.

Important foreign trade began to develop in Rostov, and the settlement which had become a large economic centre, was declared a town in 1797. The port's freight traffic was the third greatest in Russia. Goods destined for shipment to Turkey, Greece, Italy and even England sailed down the Don. Foreign merchants encouraged Rostov's growth. Among others Sidney, James & Co., an English company, was established here in 1778. The garrison was transferred in 1835 and the fortress was later demolished. The town then grew rapidly as the region's industrial and agricultural potential began to develop, overtaking the Urals in the output of both coal and metal. The railway link with Moscow was completed in 1871 and that with Ordzhonokidze (then called Vladikavkaz) in 1875. Its standards of hygiene, however, did not rise with its rapid growth and at the turn of the century it took third place, after Calcutta and Shanghai, for the number of its deaths by cholera.

Rostov played its part in Russian revolutionary history; 30,000 workers went out on strike in 1902. During the Civil War it was one of the White General's stongholds and the Germans occupied the city for some time in 1918. They also held it twice during the Second World War.

Today Rostov is the administrative and economic centre of a region of 100,000 sq. km (38,460 sq. miles), equal to the combined territories of Belgium, Holland and Denmark, and is one of the granaries of Russia. There are 20 project organisations here, making plans for the factories of the Caucasus and other parts of Russia. The University was founded in 1869 in Warsaw and was transferred to Rostov in 1915; it now has 6 faculties. There is a statue of Lomonosov by Aleschenko in the garden in front of the main building. There are besides many institutes, including an institute of agricultural machinery; machinery of this sort has been produced here in Rostov since 1898, and this institute has 10,000 students. Rostov's main industrial development dates from 1846, and it now has tobacco, food, shoemaking, textile, aircraft and shipbuilding industries. The wine-making factories offer a selection of table wines. One of the Soviet Union's most famous is a local sparkling red wine. Often called red champagne here, its real name is Tsimlanskoye Igristoye. One of the largest Soviet factories to produce agricultural machinery, the Rostselmash factory, was built in 1930. Rostov now produces 86% of Russia's combine harvesters and 70% of her cultivators and seeding machines, and one of the newest colleges is a factory-institute where students who work at Rostselmash attend lectures. Rostov's 25 libraries contain more than 2,000,000 books.

A number of Soviet writers have lived and worked here, among them Alexandr Fadeyev and Vera Panova. Mikhail Sholokhov, best known for his "Quietly Flows the Don", still lives in the village of Veshenskaya, about 200 km (120 miles) from the town.

Engels Street (formerly Bolshaya Sadovaya) begins at Temernitsky Bridge, near the railway station. It is the main street and most of the buildings of interest are to be found along its 3 km (two-mile) length. The 11-storey block of flats at the beginning of the street was completed in 1958. Many of the larger pre-revolutionary buildings were also built as flats, not always in the best of taste. One merchant-landlord, Cherikov, argued with his architect about the decoration of a 6-storey block. He wanted two large columns on the façade, but the architect said that they would spoil the proportions of the Renaissance-style house. Cherikov replied, "Who is paying you, the Renaissance or me?" and the columns were put up.

The crossroads of Engels Street and Budyonnovsky Prospekt is known as the architectural entrance to the town because it has one of the most impressive architectural ensembles of Rostov. Nearby is Gorky Park behind which can be seen the western façade of the Town Hall (1896–99). Engels Street runs next to Dom Sovietov Square. The House of Soviets was built between 1929 and 1941. It was partly burned down during the war, but now its reconstruction is almost complete. In the square is a fountain with two stone lions by the sculptor Vaide, dating from 1917. Nearby stands the huge building of the Bank (1910).

Engels Street ends in Teatralnaya Square, which was once at the edge of the town and had a sign saying "Border". Now it is the biggest square in Rostov and the place where sports parades and public festivities are held. In the 1930's some houses, and also the Gorky Theatre (1930–35) built by the architects Schuko and Gelfreich, were still designed in the constructivist style much in favour immediately after the revolution, when all forms deriving from the past were cast aside. This style was soon to be officially condemned and these buildings are among the last of their kind. The Gorky Theatre is unusual in that it has two halls in one building; the main auditorium seats 2200 and the smaller concert hall seats 550. The building is situated on a hill and its white "forehead", which can be seen for miles around, forms part of the silhouette of the city. It was damaged during World War II and reconstructed in 1963.

Further east begins the part of Rostov originally known as Nakhichevan. The continuation of Engels Street is called Pervaya Sovietskaya Street, and ends in Karl Marx Square, where a monument to the philosopher was unveiled in 1935. It was in this Square that Catherine II's decree was read. The monument to her memory has been removed. In Frunze Garden opposite is a War Memorial dedicated to all those who perished in World War II, and near this is an Eternal Flame. Running parallel to the full length of the north side of Engels Street is the Pushkin Boulevard. The promenade on the river embankment was built in 1949 and steps lead down to it from Budyonnovsky Prospekt. Attractive woods can be seen across the river and also one of the best river beaches in the South of Russia.

New blocks of flats and whole new residential areas are springing up throughout the town and around it. There are plans to build a 16-storey hotel. Among other impressive new buildings is the Rostselmash Palace of Culture built in 1961—Selmashevsky Prospekt 3. There is a theatre of opera and ballet here for the use of amateur groups.

✿ CATHEDRAL OF THE NATIVITY OF THE VIRGIN *Stanislavsky Street 58*. The cathedral is open for service.

ALL SAINTS' CHURCH *Dolomanovsky Pereulok 70*. This church is open for service.

ARMENIAN CATHEDRAL *Nakhichevan.* Built in the 19th century by Starov and now used as a young technicians' club.

SYNAGOGUE *Gazetnyi Pereulok.*

Also in Rostov are churches of the *Old Believers* and the *Baptists* and six other Russian Orthodox churches.

LOCAL HISTORICAL MUSEUM *Engels Street 79. Open 10–6; closed on Mondays.* The stone idols worshipped by nomads in 11th–12th centuries are of interest. The *Rostov Planetarium* is located in the same building.

FINE ART MUSEUM *Pushkinskaya Street 115. Open 10–6; closed on Mondays.* Here are paintings by Repin and other Russian and Soviet realists.

MUSEUM OF THE REVOLUTIONARY PAST AND THE GLORY OF LABOUR *Gusev Street 2.*

LENIN MONUMENT *At the entrance to Gorky Park.* This statue by Nyeroda was unveiled in 1929.

LENIN MONUMENT *Lenin Prospekt.* Unveiled in 1963.

KIROV MONUMENT *Kirov Square.* By Vilenski, unveiled in 1939.

PUSHKIN STATUE *Pushkin Street, where it is crossed by Karl Marx Street.* The 4 m (13 ft) statue by Schultz was unveiled in 1959.

GORKY'S STATUE *On the embankment.* The well known writer, Maxim Gorky, worked here as a docker in 1891. The 3·5 m (12 ft) statue was unveiled in 1961.

GORKY DRAMA THEATRE *Teatralnaya Square 1.*

YOUTH THEATRE *Engels Street 170.*

MUSICAL COMEDY THEATRE *Serafimovich Street 88.*

OPENAIR THEATRE (ZELENYI TEATR) *Oktyabrsky Park Revolutsii.* Built in 1962 with 3000 seats.

CIRCUS *Budyonnovsky Prospekt 45.* Completed in 1957, this is the biggest permanent circus building in the Soviet Union.

GORKY PARK *Engels Street 45.*

FIRST OF MAY CITY GARDEN *Engels Street 129.*

ZOO *Zoologicheskaya Street 3.*

BOTANICAL GARDEN *Zheloznodorozhnyi Raion.*

ULYANOVOY PARK *Oktyabrskaya Street.* Here is the Rostov Exhibition of Agricultural and Industrial Achievements. There is a children's railway in the park.

ROSTSELMASH STADIUM *Oktyabrskaya Street.* Room for 33,000 spectators. At the entrance is a monument commemorating the launching of the first Soviet sputnik.

DYNAMO STADIUM *Tekuchev Street.*

HIPPODROME RACECOURSE *Maluginoy Street 233.*

BATHING BEACH *From the centre of Rostov the main road to the Caucasus crosses the Don. After the bridge one can turn left to the beach on the river bank.*

DON HOTEL AND RESTAURANT *Gazetnyi Pereulok 34; tel: 23–40.*

YUZHNAYA (SOUTH) HOTEL *Karl Marx Prospekt 20; tel: 6–54–38.*

MOSKOVSKAYA HOTEL AND RESTAURANT *Engels Street 62; tel: 99-77-00.* The Intourist office is also in this hotel, tel: 53-91.

TSENTRALNY RESTAURANT *Engels Street 76.*

VOLGODON RESTAURANT *Beregovaya Street 31.*

TEATRALNYI (Theatre) RESTAURANT *Oktyabrskoi Revolutsii Park.*

DRUZHBA (Friendship) CAFE *Engels Street 90.*

ZOLOTOY KOLOS (Golden ear) CAFE *Engels Street 45.*

COSMOS CAFE *Engels Street 128.*

MOLODYOZHNOYE (Youth) CAFE *Teatralnaya Square 1, upstairs in Gorky Drama Theatre.*

G.P.O. *Podbelskov Street 24.*

TELEGRAPH OFFICE *Serafimovich Street 62.*

TELEPHONES *Semashko Street 34.*

BANK *Sokolov Street 26.*

DEPARTMENT STORES *Engels Street 46 and 65.*

JEWELLER'S *Engels Street 43 and 58.*

BOOKSHOP NO. 1 *Engels Street 69.*

PODARKI (Gifts) *Engels Street 60.*

ART SALON *Engels Street 128.*

MARKET *Oborony Street.*

FILLING STATION *Pushkin Street and Oktyabrskaya Chaussée 6; the latter provides round the clock service. To find it, on the way into town along Oktyabrskaya Chaussée do not take the left turn to the centre but keep straight on for 1 mile; the filling station is on the left.*

REPAIR STATION *Suvorov Street 80 and Oktyabrskaya Chaussée 6; the latter is open 8 a.m.–4 p.m. Tel: 6-15-55.*

CAMPING SITE *At the entrance to the town, on the right.*

There is a *Rostov By-pass*. Driving to the south from Kharkov, there is a sign indicating the way to Ordzhonikidze 2 km before Rostov and this leads on to the By-pass. Alternatively, to reach the town centre, follow the signs to the Caucasus (Kavkaz).

TANAIS

Tanais was the ancient Greek name for the Don and also for the town at the river mouth. Now there is a museum and an archaeological reservation. Open between 25th April and 10th November 9–5; closed on Tuesdays. Tanais is near the village of Nedvigovka, about 30 km (18 miles) from Rostov on the way to Taganrog.

For more than six centuries—3rd B.C.–4th A.D.—Tanais was the economical and cultural centre of the area. Excavations to date have revealed the remains of a fortress and towers and a number of streets.

STAROCHERKASSKAYA STANITSA

Founded about 1570, this is the oldest Cossack settlement. Formerly known as Cherkassk, it was named after the Cossack, Avgust Cherkas. Between 1644 and 1805 it was the capital of the Don Cossacks. The town was well fortified with earth walls and wooden towers where eighty guns were mounted.

It is well known in Russian history for its capture in 1670 by the Cossack and peasant leader, Stepan Rasin and again in 1708 by Kondrat Bulavin. Peter the Great came here several times and on one occasion he noticed a naked Cossack with a rifle riding on a barrel. It was explained to him that a Cossack can drink away everything except his rifle, and the tsar was so delighted that he approved as the design for the Cossack army a naked Cossack on a barrel holding a rifle.

St. Ephraim's Convent in Cherkassk was one of the richest in Russia.

Ataman (Cossack leader) Platov found a better place for the administrative centre and the capital was transferred to Novocherkassk in 1805. Cherkassk lost its importance and was given its present day name. The prominent Russian artist, Surikov, came here in 1893, looking for Cossack models for his painting, "The Conquest of Siberia by Yermak".

Today one can visit nine-cupola Voskresensky (Resurrection) Cathedral (1706–1719) which is now a branch of Novocherkassk museum. Some interesting fortified houses of the 18th century also remain.

The town is often flooded in the spring and the people use small boats to get about in. It still keeps its old name of the Cossack Venice. The road to Starocherkasskaya is very bad and visitors are recommended to go there by boat.

BATAISK

Population: 52,000 (1959)

From Rostov-on-Don the milestones start numbering from 0 again; the road is known as the Rostov–Baku road and goes via Ordzhonikidze.

Originally known by the old Tartar name of Batai, it was taken over by the Cossacks during the siege of the Azov fortress and in 1780 the new Cossack settlement was called Bataisk. It lies only 10 km (6 miles) from Rostov.

It became an important railway junction in the 1870's which is why in 1919 it was a stronghold against the Germans. It saw much fighting again in 1943. Today many of the inhabitants work on the railway junction.

Near by is a fruit farm of 2400 hectares (6000 acres) which is the largest in the region.

✿ SERVICE STATION *At the 79 km milestone.*

✿ CAFE *At the 98 km milestone.*

KRYLOVSKAYA

✿ KUBAN CAFE

✿ FILLING STATION *On the main road by the 113 km milestone.* Diesel oil is obtainable here; round-the-clock service.

REPAIR STATION *On the main road by the 113 km milestone; tel: 0–21. Open from 8 a.m. till 4 p.m.*

PAVLOVSKAYA

Here at the 136 km milestone the road forks to the right to Krasnodar and the Black Sea coast and to the left to the Caucasus mountains.

KROPOTKIN

Population: 54,000 (1959)

Kropotkin lies ½ km (¼ mile) to the left of the main road. In 1778 a look-out post, guarding the crossing of the River Kuban, was placed here. Until 1926, when it became a town, Kropotkin was known as Romanovsky-Khutor (founded in 1880 on the right bank of the river). It was renamed after Prince Pyotr Alexeyevich Kropotkin (1842–1921), a widely-travelled geographer, revolutionary, and theorist of anarchism. His ideas got him into constant trouble, and he resided in England from 1886 until the 1917 revolution, when he returned to Russia.

The town's food industries are important, as is also its railway junction; the station, built in 1875, was originally called Kavkazskaya, and in fact formed the basis of the town.

Krasnaya Street is the town's main thoroughfare, and the site of the best shops.

✿ POKROVSKY SOBOR (Cathedral of the Intercession) *Komsomolskaya Street 26*. The Cathedral was built in 1912.

✿ LENIN PARK *Krasnaya Street.*

Hotel *Vokzalnaya Street 15.*

A new hotel and the Kuban Restaurant are under construction on Krasnaya Street.

Restaurant *Krasnaya Street.*

Cafe *At the turning to the town from the main road.*

Bank *Krasnaya Street.*

G.P.O. *Krasnaya Street.*

Market *Komsomolskaya Street.*

Filling Station *On the left of the main road 1½ km (1 mile) before the turning to the town.*

ARMAVIR

Population: 111,000 (1959)

Armavir lies 4 km (2½ miles) to the left of the main road. It is situated on the left bank of the River Kuban and its tributary the River Urup. The best view of the town is from the right bank of the main river. The mountains are visible on the horizon.

The town was founded in 1849 by immigrant Armenians but only became known as a town in 1914 and that after a thirty-year struggle for such recognition. During the Civil War it was isolated from the central part of Russia and was unique in minting its own coins. Some of these dated 1918 can be seen in the local museum. During World War II the central part of the town was ruined.

The town is now one of the largest in the whole of the North Caucasus. There is a machine-building factory and light industries including food production. There is also a teachers' training college.

Trinity Church *Razin Street.* This was built at the beginning of this century.

Uspenskaya Church *Kirov Street 5.* This Armenian church was built in the 1840's.

Local Museum *Lenin Street 92. Open 10 a.m.–5 p.m.; closed on Tuesdays.* This museum was founded in 1904.

Lenin Monument *Kirov Street.*

Kirov Monument *Kirov Square.*

Lunacharsky Drama Theatre *Lenin Street 66.*

Stadium *Turgenev Street.*

The town's gardens are famous for their white acacias.

Severnaya (North) Hotel and Yug (South) Restaurant *Mir Street 24, opposite the railway station. There is no car park.*

Kavkaz Restaurant *Lenin Park.*

G.P.O. *Lenin Street 79.*

Bank *Lenin Street 54.*

Department Store *Kirov Street 66.*

Bookshop *Lenin Street 62.* There is a large market.

Filling Station *At the crossing of Engels and Kirov Streets.*

Repair Station *On the main road, at the turning to Armavir, 297 km (184 miles) from Rostov. Open daily 8 a.m. to 4 p.m.*

Filling Station *By the Repair Station.* Diesel oil is available; round-the-clock service.

———— ★ ————

10 km (6 miles) farther along the road there is a pleasant place to stop and rest, on the bank of River Urup, on the left of the bridge.

NEVINNOMYSSK

Nevinnomyssk lies on both sides of the River Kuban, at the point where it is joined by the River Bolshoi Zelenchug. The town is situated at the end of a great upland which runs down from Mount Elbruz far into the North Caucasian Steppe.

The road passes through the suburbs of the town, which is noted for its food industry and especially for the manufacture of dairy products.

KUBAN RESTAURANT *Komsomolskaya Street 2.*

BANK *Gagarin Street 114.*

MINERALNIYE VODY

There are over a hundred mineral springs in the Caucasus, but the most important are the group known as the Caucasian Mineral Waters. Here, within a distance of about 40 km (25 miles), those who are in need of them can find all the cures for which otherwise they would have to travel all over Germany and France. Some of the types of water here are even unique of their kind.

The territory is located in steppeland not very far from Mount Elbruz. It is on the same latitude as Genoa in Italy and it lies considerably farther south than Yalta, but as it is separated from the warm Black Sea by the main Caucasian mountain range it has a continental climate, and the summer here is cooler than in the southern part of the Steppes. One of the first explorers of the geology of the Caucasus, Abikh, called this region the "cliff archipelago". Now it has been confirmed that the isolated mountains here were in fact once islands when the low-lying steppeland to the north of the Caucasus was under the sea.

The first Russian records of the people living in the Pyatigory ("five hills") region date from the middle of the 16th century. After Kazan had fallen to Ivan the Terrible, in 1552, the local population (now known as Kabardintsi, but then called the Cherkessi of Pyatigory) asked the tsar's protection from the Turks and Tartars. A few years after this Ivan the Terrible married a local Cherkess princess, Maria, and the first Russian fortress, Terki, was built in 1567. However, it was only after the peace treaty with Turkey in 1774 that Pyatigorsk and the region surrounding it passed to Russia.

Russia had been searching for health resorts of her own since the time of Peter the Great, and in 1773 an Academy of Sciences' expedition confirmed the healing qualities of Pyatigory's mineral springs. It was noticed that wounded soldiers recovered much more quickly when they used the springs here; so the first Russian residents of Pyatigoıy were retired soldiers who stayed on, and in fact all the main buildings of the future spas were built by the soldiers.

Only in 1803 was Caucasian mineral water proclaimed to be of national importance. Two resident doctors were then appointed and the present spas really date from 1803. In 1810 Dr. Gaaz discovered the springs at Zheleznovodsk and Yessentuki quite by chance, because local people reported that in some places their horses drank especially greedily. Pyatigorsk was proclaimed a town in 1830.

Now over 70 springs have been developed in this region, yielding up to 6,000,000 litres (1,300,000 gallons) a day of 12 different types of water; Pyatigorsk is famous for its hot carbonic hydrogen sulphide springs, and it takes first place among the spas because of its greater variety of waters. Pyatigorsk alone has 34 springs yielding up to 2,000,000 litres (450,000 gallons) of water a day.

In spite of the different qualities of the waters from the various springs, all the towns in the vicinity are known collectively as the spas of the Northern Caucasus and all share the same emblem which is depicted everywhere; it shows an eagle with wings spread, perching on a mountain peak. There are statues of this eagle in the hilly parks that rise above each spa.

ZHELEZNOVODSK

Zheleznovodsk lies 7 km (4½ miles) off the main road to the right. It has a mountainous climate like that of the central Alps, and the average annual temperature is 10°C (50°F). The 23 springs give up to 1,000,000 litres (250,000 gallons) of water a day, the water includes carbonic acid, hydrocarbonate-sulphate, sodium and calcium. The springs have temperatures varying from 10–55°C (50–130°F). The town now has about 15 sanatoria, some located in old villas and some in new buildings.

The Zheleznovodsk waters are particularly useful in the cure of metabolic, digestive and kidney diseases, and since 1965 Intourist have organised special 26-day courses of treatment for foreign visitors.

Mount Zheleznaya (iron) is of typical laccolit rock. A famous park lies in the southern foothills of the mountain adjoining the natural forest. A spiral path leads up the mountain side and from the entrance of the park an attractive flight of steps leads up to the Verkhnaya Ploshchadka and the Pushkin Gallery. A chestnut avenue leading to the right from the Gallery brings one to the springs. A little farther on and to the left under a small bridge is a statue of a group of bears; this is the point at which to turn either up the mountain or around the ring path. Alternatively the same avenue leads on the Slavyanovsky Istochnik (Professor Slavyanov's Spring, discovered in 1913), located in a pleasantly designed pavilion. The spring itself looks like a. foaming fountain, and has a temperature of 50°C (132°F); water is served there.

Farther on, in the Bolshaya Ploshchadka (large square), is the colonnade of the three Smirnov Springs (45·5°C/114°F). Down from this point run the Cascade Stairs, a double staircase with mineral water running down the centre. At the bottom of the Stairs, through the trees, the surface of a large artificial pond can be seen. On the slope of the mountain to the left of the stairs is Nyezlobinsky Istochnik with pleasant tasting and fairly cold water (19°C/66°F). To the right are some other springs, and baths filled with mineral water, looking like small swimming pools.

The uphill spiral path by which one circles the mountain twice, leads past three springs; Kegamovsky (16·5°C/62°F), Vladimirsky (26°C/79°F) and Spring No. 1. The route is 3600 m (2¼ miles) in length. The second path leading to the top of the mountain (852 m/2775 ft) is 3300 m (2 miles) one way and takes about 1 hr 15 min to climb. From the top of the mountain theire is a good view of Mount Beshtau, and to the left Mount Mashuk can be seen.

✿ THEATRE *In Pushkin Gallery, in the park.*

✿ KAVKAZ HOTEL *Gorky Street 3.*

DRUZHBA (Friendship) HOTEL AND RESTAURANT *Along the main road.*

BESHTAU RESTAURANT *Chaikovsky Street.*

CAFE *Pushkin Street in the park.*

✿ BANK *Lenin Street 55.*

G.P.O. *Lenin Street 53.*

BOOKSHOP *Chaikovsky Street 9.*

PYATIGORSK

Population: 70,000 (1959)

This spa lies at 514 m (1685 ft) above sea level on the left bank of the River Podkumok. Its name means "five mountains", and the peaks referred to are:—Lysaya Gora (bald mountain) (758 m/2415 ft), Mashuk (994 m/3250 ft), Zmeika (snake) (994 m/3250 ft),

Beshtau ("five hills" in Turkish) and Zheleznaya Gora (iron mountain) (854 m/2800 ft). All these are of volcanic origin and, with the exception of Beshtau, have a layer of limestone over the lava. Other mountains in the vicinity are Razvalka (930 m/3051 ft), Byk (bull) (821 m/2693 ft), Verblyud (camel) (902 m/2959 ft) and Goryachaya (hot).

There are pedagogical and pharmaceutical colleges in Pyatigorsk and also Institutes of Physiotherapy and Oil. There are food, textile and associated light industries and an agricultural machinery repair plant.

The town is mainly located on the southern and south-western slopes of Mashuk. It has about 50 springs which can be divided into four types: carbonic acid-hydrogen sulphate, carbonic acid, salt-and-alkaline, and radon. Their temperatures range from 14–60°C (57 to 140°F). The majority of the springs are at the foot of the mountain, but another part of the resort, Proval, is on a terrace on the southern slope of the mountain.

The waters are particularly valuable in the cure of muscular, circulatory, digestive, metabolic, nervous, skin and gynaecological diseases and since 1965 Intourist have organised terms of treatment lasting for 26 days.

The Lermontov Baths, near Tsvetnik (the Flower Garden), were formerly called the Nikolaevsky Baths; they are fed by the Alexandro-Yermolovsky spring. The temperature of the water is 42°C (107°F) and it contains natron-chloride, bicarbonic lime, sulphuric natron, free carbonic acid and sulphuric hydrogen. The bath-house was built in 1826–31 and is the oldest of its kind in Russia.

Mikhail Lermontov (1814–41), after whom the baths were named, was a Guards officer of Scottish ancestry, and is famed for his novels and poems which earned him his position as the greatest Russian Romantic and which cost him his life. There are many mementos of Lermontov in Pyatigorsk, the more important of which are described below.

Proval is a great grotto, 27 m (68 ft) deep, on the slope of Mashuk. It was washed out many years ago by a subterranean sulphuric stream; later a hole appeared in the roof of the grotto and a lake 14 m (46 ft) deep was formed. It has a warm sulphur spring and the water is blue in colour from the sulphuric combinations. In the past it was one of the sights for visiting society to see, and in 1837 a suspension bridge was put up upon which six couples could dance a quadrille. The bridge only lasted for four years. Local legend says that Lermontov was cured of rheumatism by swimming in the Proval Lake. The grotto is entered by a 45 m (50 yd) gallery. Open 11–6; closed on Tuesdays.

On the road to Proval from the town is an imposing stone monument by Svetlitsky; it stands on the spot overlooking the valley where four Soviet commissars were shot in 1918.

There is a pleasant walk which starts from Proval and leads around Mt. Mashuk, passing Lermontov's duelling place and ending near the Tyoplyi (warm) Narzan spring.

✿ LERMONTOV MUSEUM *Buachidze Street 9.*

LERMONTOV'S HOUSE *Lermontovskaya Street 18.* The writer lived here for two months, and after the duel his body was brought back here.

The duel in which Lermontov was killed took place on the foothills of Mashuk, 4 km (2½ miles) from the centre of Pyatigorsk. Lermontov was challenged by a certain Martinov for mocking him in the presence of ladies. When they met at the appointed time Lermontov explained that he never intended to insult Martinov and what he had said had been meant as a joke; he said that if Martinov would not be offended he was ready to ask his pardon, not only there but at any other place he chose. Martinov replied "Shoot! Shoot!" Lermontov was to fire first and he fired into the air, but Martinov came closer and shot him through the heart so that he died instantly. The writer had been opposed to the tsar and sent to the Caucasus as punishment for his verses, especially those devoted to the death of Pushkin who was also killed in a duel. "Butchers of freedom, genius and glory" was how he described the members of the government in the offensive poem, referring to Pushkin's death. When Nicholas I learned of Lermontov's fate he said, "A dog deserves a dog's death" and Martinov, instead of being sentenced to hard labour (the punishment for duelling at that time), was simply ordered to seek religious absolution. Lermontov's death was understood by many Russians to be a murder planned by the authorities. Lermontov was buried in Pyatigorsk and later his body was transferred to his birthplace, Moscow.

LERMONTOV STATUE *Lermontov Garden, Ondzhiyevsky Street.* This bronze statue by Opekushin was unveiled in 1889. The terrace in front of it commands a fine view of the mountains with the snow-capped summit of the twin-peaked Elbruz (white breasts) 97 km (60 miles) distant as the crow flies.

LERMONTOV GROTTO *Opposite the Akademicheskaya Gallery in the Park.* This cave was called after the writer following his death. During his lifetime he visited it several times, and he has described it in *A Hero of Our Time*. A marble sign marks the entrance.

LERMONTOV MONUMENT *On the site of the duel.* The monument, which takes the form of a bust of the poet surrounded by mourning griffons on stone posts connected by chains, was designed by Mikeshin and unveiled in 1915.

CHURCH *On the hill top at the end of Andzhiyevskov Street.* It was built at the end of the 19th century.

LOCAL MUSEUM *Sacco-and-Vancetti Street 2; Open 10–4.30; closed on Tuesdays.* There are natural history and art sections. The museum was founded in 1905.

AKADEMICHESKAYA GALLERY *On the top of Goryachaya Mountain.* This white pavilion built 1847–49 has a good view of Pyatigorsk. It used to be known as the Elizabeth Gallery but was renamed in 1925 to celebrate the 200th anniversary of the Academy of Sciences.

RESTAURATSIA *Kirov Street, near Tsvetnik.* In Lermontov's time this used to be a very grand restaurant with frequent balls and dances. Now the building houses the Physiotherapy Institute.

EOLOVA ARFA (AEOLEAN HARP). This monument was built in 1830–31 and called after the Greek god of the winds, Aeolus. Originally there was a wooden column with two harps; when the wind blew a weather vane plucked the strings and made music. This was replaced by the present small pavilion in ancient Greek style which has the best view over the town and the region surrounding. It stands on the spot where, even in Lermontov's time, Cossack guards kept watch to protect patients from unexpected attack from the peoples living in the mountains.

HEALTH RESORT EXHIBITION *Proval Street 2, in the Mikhailovskaya Gallery* which was built in 1848.

OBELISK *On the top of Mt. Mashuk* commemorates the topographer, Pastukhov.

KIROV MONUMENT *Kirov Square.* This monument to the revolutionary and statesman is by Kondratev and was unveiled in 1959.

BUST OF ANDZHIYEVSKY *In the park on Kirov Prospekt.* Shotskikh made this bust in memory of the first local party chairman.

MUSICAL COMEDY THEATRE *Kirov Street 17.*

PHILHARMONIA CONCERT HALL *In Lermontov Gallery, Tsvetnik Park.* This gallery was brought from the fair in Nizhni-Novgorod (now Gorky) in 1899.

DIANA GROTTO *In Tsvetnik ("flower garden") Park.* This big artificial cave named after the goddess of hunting was excavated in 1830–31. It is cool inside, even on the hottest day. It was designed by Bernardazzi.

KIROV PARK *Dunayevsky Street 5.* Here is the planetarium, an open-air theatre, amusement grounds, a dance floor and a boat hiring station.

HIPPODROME RACECOURSE *Kursovaya Street 219. Open from 2nd May until October; racing on Saturdays at 4 and on Sundays at 12 noon. There is a totalisator and a restaurant.*

MASHUK HOTEL AND DRUZHBA (Friendship) RESTAURANT *Kirov Street 25.* The hotel was formerly known as the Bristol. The Intourist office is here, tel: 22-45.

PYATIGORSK HOTEL AND RESTAURANT *Krainyev Street 41a.* A new Intourist hotel is under construction in the town.

KOLOS (Ear of corn) RESTAURANT *Shoseinaya Street 101.*

TSENTRALNAYA RESTAURANT *Kirov Street 27a.*

YUG (South) RESTAURANT *Universitetskaya Street 34.*

MASHUK RESTAURANT *Kirov Street 60.*

TOURIST RESTAURANT *Kirov Street.*

LYESNAYA POLYANA (Glade) RESTAURANT *At Lermontov's duelling place.*

KAVKAZ RESTAURANT *Near Proval.*

GORKA (Hill) CAFE *Anisimov Street 3.*

OTDIKH (Rest) CAFE *Kirov Street 32.*

PROVAL CAFE *In the Proval area.*

YUNOST (Youth) CAFE *Kirov Prospekt 56.*

G.P.O. *Kirov Street 52.*

BANK *Kirov Street 25.*

BOOKSHOP *Kirov Street 48.*

JEWELLER'S *Dzerzhinsky Street 42.*

DEPARTMENT STORE *Oktyabrskaya Street 1.*

TAXI RANKS *At the central bus station, the railway station, the upper market and Proval.*

FILLING STATION *Naberezhnaya Street 15, by the central bus station.* Round the clock service.

SERVICE STATION *At the same address as the Filling Station, tel: 35-13. Open 8 a.m.–6 p.m.; closed on Sundays.*

MOTEL *Kalinin Street 2, Belaya Romashka region; on the right side of the road coming into town from Mineralniye Vody.* Also at Lumumba Street 17, on the way into town, is a new building under construction which will supplement the existing facilities.

CAMPING SITE *Beside the Motel.*

*

From Pyatigorsk a side road branches off to the right and leads to Yessentuki (17km/10½ miles) and then on to Kislovodsk (a further 20 km/12½ miles).

Tambukanskoye Lake is about 11 km (7 miles) along the main road from Pyatigorsk. The road passes by the shores of this famous lake, the mud of which is used for curative mud-baths at the spas.

YESSENTUKI

This spa lies off the main Intourist road, 17 km (10½ miles) to the right from Pyatigorsk, in a valley watered by two streams, the Bugunty and the Yessentik. It was founded as a military settlement in 1798, and after 1826 it was known as a Cossack settlement. It was developed as a spa in the late 1880's.

There are 16 springs yielding a total of 500,000 litres (110,000 gallons) of water daily. All the springs are cold and either carbonic ferruginous or alkaline. The best are No. 17 and No. 4, both of which have a high degree of mineralisation. The water cures here are augmented with mud baths, and recommended for the treatment of digestive and metabolic disorders. Intourist organise courses of treatment lasting 26 days.

The main street, Internatsionalnaya Street, runs down from the railway station and leads to a small square, unofficially known as "Pyatachok"—meaning "5-kopek coin" and indicating its small size and its liveliness; it is the real heart of the spa. The best hotel, the Mayak, and the entrance to Staryi Park which has a territory of 40 hectares (100 acres) and contains the springs, are in this square.

Just inside the park is a theatre, and nearby there stands a pavilion where the water from springs No. 17 and No. 19 is used for drinking in summer. Spring No. 17 is open 7–10, 12–3.30 and 5–8 so that one can drink before meals. When it was discovered over 100 years ago it was called the "pearl of Caucasian mineral waters, and the pride of the motherland". Its temperature is about 13°C (56°F). Behind the theatre is the main bath house supplied by these springs. There is a memorial plaque here with the dates of their discovery.

An asphalted avenue, Alkalichesky Prospekt, leads down through the park. To the right, opposite the theatre, is the building of the Lower Baths with 34 bathrooms, and birch trees in front of it. Further on, to the left of the avenue, is the summer pavilion of Spring No. 4 and on the right side is the corresponding winter pavilion. This spring is less mineralised than No. 17 and has a temperature of 10–12°C (50–54°F).

The avenue finally leads to the domed and columned Pavilion No. 1, which is still less mineralised that No. 4 and 17. To the right is a pile of stones with the local emblem of an eagle killing a serpent, and to the left, on the slopes of Alkali Hill, is a sculpture depicting a Russian peasant seated with a drinking cup in his hand, commemorating the first use of these waters. Above him can be seen a semi-circular colonnade from which there is a good view across to Mashuk and Pyatigorsk. Farther on the path leads past flower beds to stone steps and a small bridge. The big building of a sanatorium, one of the oldest buildings in Yessentuki and formerly a restaurant, is situated here. Near by is the building of the Upper Baths, built in 1898 with a fountain in front of it. This has 60 bathrooms, each bath being of solid marble. Not far away along another avenue are other baths which are used only in summer.

The avenue leads on to the centre of the park where there is a concert platform and a library. The metal column with a figure of a dove on it marks the place where the water of spring No. 17 was first tapped. A little aside from this an avenue of palms leads back to the lower park.

Three walks begin from the east gates of the park. The first is 1820 m (just over 1 mile) in length and is a gentle slope climbing up 23·5 m (77 ft); the second, more hilly than the first, is 2515 m (a little over 1½ miles) and rises to 42·4 m (139 ft). The third walk is of 2436 m (1½ miles), and is more hilly still, going up to 61·8 m (202 ft). The park was planted out in 1849. In the northern part of Yessentuki is another park on higher ground, originally known as English Park.

✿ SEMASHKO MUD BATHS *Semashko Street*. These baths were built in 1913–15 by Academician Shreter, and are called after Dr. Nikolai Semashko, Soviet Commissar of Health, 1918–

1930. The building is in the style of ancient Greek public buildings, decorated with lions, columns, and statues of heroes from Greek mythology.

MEMORIAL OBELISK *In front of the railway station.* This small obelisk is dedicated to those who fell during the revolution.

✿ THEATRE *In the park.*

✿ There is good bathing in the River Podkumok, near the town at Byeli Ugol' ("white coal", called after one of the oldest power stations in Russia) railway station.

✿ YESSENTUKI HOTEL *Karl Marx Street 26.*

MAYAK (LIGHTHOUSE) HOTEL *Internatsionalnaya Street 3.*

YALTA HOTEL *Internatsionalnaya Street 18.*

KAVKAZ RESTAURANT *Internatsionalnaya Street 26.*

EATING HOUSES *Lenin Street 12 and Vokzalnaya Square, in front of the railway station.*

MECHTA (Dream) CAFE *At Pyatachok.*

✿ BANK *Kislovodskaya Street 5.*

G.P.O. *Kislovodskaya Street 18.*

DEPARTMENT STORE *Internatsionalnaya Street 11.*

BOOKSHOP *Internatsionalnaya Street 5.*

KISLOVODSK

This spa lies off the main road to the right from Pyatigorsk; it is 20 km (12½ miles) past Yessentuki, and 37 km (23 miles) away from Pyatigorsk itself.

Kislovodsk is 822 m (2695 ft) above sea level, and lies at the bottom of a mountain valley crossed by the River Olkhovka and the River Berezovka. Surrounded by forestless mountains, it is protected from all winds, and late summer and autumn are its best seasons. Its winters are warm,—in fact it has more sunny days in winter than Davos, and only 60 or 70 rainy days in the whole year. The average annual temperature is 10°C (50°F), and the average winter temperature 2°C (35·5°F). The town is surrounded by terrace-like slopes of hard limestone which contain many caves.

There are 7 springs in Kislovodsk, the Narzan spring being the most famous of all in the region. It is the richest carbonic spring in the world and the Circassians called it the "drink of heroes". It is 818 m (2683 ft) above sea level and its temperature is 13°C (55°F). The spring has been known since the 18th century, and in 1848–58 a gallery was built in English Gothic style to house it. The Narzan Bath-house was built later in Indian style. In the centre of the town there is a factory where the water is bottled. The other springs in the town, including Dolomitic Narzan and Sulphate Narzan, are of similar type. The volume of water yielded daily by the Kislovodsk springs is only exceeded by those of Pyatigorsk.

The waters here have been found most effective in the cure of circulatory diseases, mild bronchial asthma and chronic (but non-tubercular) diseases of the respiratory organs. Since 1965 Intourist have organised 26-day courses of treatment for foreign visitors.

✿ ST. PANTILEMON'S CHURCH *Uritsky Street 16.* Built in 1905 in a good position with an excellent view over the town.

✿ YAROSHENKO MUSEUM *Yaroshenko Street 3. Open 11–6; closed on Tuesdays.* Nikolai Yaroshenko (1846–98) was a prominent Russian painter.

SERGO ORDZHONIKIDZE MUSEUM *In the Sergo Ordzhonikidze Sanatorium.*

STATUES OF LENIN AND DZERZHINSKY *By Lenin Prospekt.*

GORKY THEATRE *Krasnoarmeiskaya Street 5.*

CONCERT HALL *In Verkhny (upper) Park.*

KURORTNYI PARK. Following the right bank of the River Olkhovka the main path leads to a pool. A small pavilion stands here, and from under it the water flows from the pool in a steady stream. It is crystal clear and so much resembles molten glass that it is often called Glass Stream. From here the path goes on to Pine Hill (Sosnovaya Gorka), where there is a rosarium and an open air stage. Farther along through shady avenues the path comes to Krasniye Kamni (red stones), which are coloured by the iron content of the water and are often eroded by the weather into strange mushroom shapes. A bas-relief of Lenin has been carved on one of the stones. A flight of steps runs down from this point to Lenin Prospekt.

The path leads on to Seriye Kamni (grey stones) which stand at a height of 942 m (3090 ft). From this point there is a good view of Kislovodsk, and in fine weather the summit of Elbruz can be seen. Farther on is Pyervomaiskaya Polyana (Mayday Field), a meadow surrounded by mountain slopes to form a natural amphitheatre with room for 60,000 people. It is occasionally used as such. Nearby is Khram Vozdukha (Temple of air).

Krasnoye Solnishko (Red sun) gets its name from being the usual place to watch the sun rise and set. From here the road leads to Siniye Gori (Blue Mountains), so called because at sunset they take on a blueish colour. The spot commands a good view of Kislovodsk and Elbruz. It is prescribed that people with weight to lose walk on from this point up to Maloye and Bolshoye Sedlo (small and large saddle).

VERKHNYI PARK (UPPER PARK).

This park is usually at its liveliest in the evening. The Gorky Theatre, a cinema and a concert platform which is unique in its acoustics are all in it. The floor of the concert platform contains a layer of broken glass to reflect the sound, and the shell-shaped roof is double-layered and itself resounds like a musical instrument.

STADIUM *Pervomaisky Prospekt 34, on the left side of the road leading into town.*

KAVKAZ HOTEL AND RESTAURANT *Dzerzhinsky Prospekt 24; tel: 5-21-60.*

NARZAN HOTEL *Mir Prospekt 14.*

ZARYA (Dawn) RESTAURANT *Gertsen Street.*

CHAIKA (Seagull) RESTAURANT *Pervomaisky Prospekt 4.*

KHRAM VOZDUKHA (Temple of Air) RESTAURANT *Nizhni (lower) Park.*

TOURIST CAFE *By Lake Kislovodsk, just outside the town and near the Motel.*

KRASNOYE SOLNISHKO (Red sun) CAFE *In Lower Park, on Krasnoye Solnishko Hill.*

CHAINAYA (Tea room) CAFE *In the park, near the rosegarden.*

SOSNOVAYA GORKA (Pine hill) CAFE *Lower Park.*

PARK CAFE *In Lower Park, near the open-air theatre.*

KURZAL CAFE *In Upper Park, by the theatre.*

KISLOVODSK CAFE *In the garden on Mir Prospekt.*

MILK BAR *Mir Prospekt 17.*

DIETETIC CAFE *Mir Prospekt, just opposite the Narzan Gallery.*

Cosmos Cafe *By the railway station.*

G.P.O. *Krasnaya Street 3.*

Bank *Mir Prospekt 24.*

Bookshop *Karl Marx Prospekt.*

Jeweller's *Karl Marx Prospekt.*

Motel *3 km (2 miles) from the centre of the town, beside Lake Kislovodsk, which covers 10 hectares (25 acres).* Here there are facilities for bathing and boating. There is a café and a shashlik bar, and the "Tourist" Restaurant is near by, and also a Service station, carwash and filling station. 3 km (2miles) farther on is the "Zamok" ("Castle") Motel, where a two-storey building built to resemble an old castle is used as an annexe to the main Motel; it also has a restaurant, the Zamok Restaurant, which specialises in Caucasian dishes.

Camping Site *Beside the lake.*

Filling Station *At the entrance to the town, on the right-hand side.*

———— ★ ————

Lermontov Cliff *4·5 km (3 miles) from Kislovodsk.* This cliff is described in *A Hero of Our Time.* 430 m (500 yd) from here is the Lermontov Spring.

The Castle of Cunning and Love (Kovarstva i Lyubvi) *6 km (4 miles) from Kislovodsk.* This is really the name of a cliff strongly eroded by the weather. The actual castle which stands there and which is now used as a Motel was built long after the cliff got its name. The story about it runs thus:

Once upon a time the daughter of one of the mountain princes fell in love with a simple shepherd boy. Her father was angry at this and betrothed her to a rich relative of his own. When the young couple learned of his plans they decided to commit suicide by leaping from the cliff. The young man jumped first—and the girl was so terrified at the sight of his battered body that she thought better of her intention and returned home to marry the man of her father's choice. The cliffs alone were witness to the tragedy.

Medovyi Vodopad (Honey Waterfall). This is 10 km (6 miles) past the Castle, following the same beautiful road with gorge and valley landscapes.

Dolina Narzanov (Narzan Valley) *33 km ($20\frac{1}{2}$ miles) from town.* It is so called because there are 17 Narzan-type springs here. The valley which has the mountain rivers Khasaut and Mushta rushing through it can be reached by car.

Bermamuitskaya Skala *34 km (21 miles) from Kislovodsk. Skala* means "cliff". This point should be visited, because from here Elbruz can be seen in its entirety.

BAKSAN

In this village lying in the valley of the River Baksan there is an old Russian fortress dating from 1822.

Filling Station

CHEGEM

There are in fact two villages of this name in the valley of the River Chegem. The numerous mausoleums in the vicinity belong to the 18th century.

NALCHIK

Population: 88,000 (1959)

(off the main Intourist road)

This town lies on the left bank of the River Nalchik at a height of 554 m (1817 ft) above sea level. Its name, meaning "horseshoe", refers to the shape of the mountains around, for it is in the foothills of the northern spurs of the Black Mountains. It is famous for its picturesque environs and for its view of the Caucasus Mountains. One of the local sorts of mineral water,

Nartan, takes its name from a nearby mountain.

During the Caucasian War of 1822 a Russian military fortress was founded here, and by the end of the 19th century the number of inhabitants had already increased considerably. Now the town is the capital of the Kabardino-Balkarian Autonomous Republic, and the republic's university was opened in 1957. It is also the central point for tourists and mountaineers going to the central Caucasus.

✿ LOCAL MUSEUM *Lenin Prospekt. Open 11–6; closed on Saturdays.*

FINE ARTS MUSEUM *Lenin Prospekt 35. Open 11–6; closed on Saturdays.*

LENIN MONUMENT *Sovietov Square.* Made by Posyada and unveiled in 1957.

UNIFICATION MONUMENT *Lenin Prospekt.* This monument by Listopad and Makhtin was unveiled in 1957 to mark the 400th anniversary of the region's union with Russia.

JABAGI KAZANOKOV MONUMENT *In Svoboda Garden.* Kazanokov was a local philosopher of the 18th century.

Two busts, of BEKMURZA PACHEV (Kabarda poet) and of KYAZIM MECHIYEV (Balkar poet) *In the park.* The sculptors Tkhakumashev and Krym-Shakhalov were responsible for them both and they were unveiled in 1961.

✿ DRAMA THEATRE *In the park.*

✿ The large park begins *immediately outside the town on the way to Dolinsk, and continues for 3 km (2 miles).* Occupying an area of 800 hectares (2,000 acres) it is one of the biggest parks in the northern Caucasus. There is a collection of trees from the Caucasus, Europe and America and the avenue of pines and the rose gardens are especially worthy of note.

SPARTAK STADIUM *Sovietov Square.*

HIPPODROME RACECOURSE *Baksanskoye Chaussée.*

✿ ROSSIA HOTEL AND RESTAURANT *Lenin Street 32.*

NALCHIK HOTEL *Lermontov Street 2.*

KAVKAZ RESTAURANT *Kabardinskaya Street 13.*

DOROZHNY RESTAURANT *Osetinskaya Street 132.*

NALCHIK RESTAURANT *Respublikanskaya Street 2.*

ELBRUS RESTAURANT *In the park.*

KOSMOS CAFE *Lenin Prospekt 35.*

✿ G.P.O. *Teatralnaya Street 4.*

BANK *Teatralnaya Street 2.*

DEPARTMENT STORE AND SOUVENIRS *Kabardinskaya Street 15.*

BOOKSHOP *Lenin Prospekt 46.*

JEWELLER'S *Kabardinskaya Street 10.*

MOTEL AND CAMPING SITE *In the village of Dolinsk, 5 km (3 miles) from Nalchik.* The motel has a dining room, and the Dolinsk Restaurant is nearby, also a billiard room, garage, service station, filling station. There are many sanatoria at Dolinsk, also a swimming pool and the building of the Geophysical Institute of the Academy of Sciences.

Popular short excursions are those from Nalchik to Mount Nartan (1008 m/3300 ft) and Mount Sarai (1329 m/4700 ft), while 40 km (25 miles) away are the Blue Lakes and Chegemski Waterfalls. The largest of the lakes has an elliptical shape, and is 235 m (257 yd) long and 125 m (137 yd) wide. Its depth of 258 m (846 ft) makes it the sixth deepest lake in the U.S.S.R.

ARGUDAN

This village is at the 609/726 km milestone. There is a restaurant and the remains of the Alan fortress of 6th–7th centuries A.D. can be seen.

TATARTUP

At the 638/693 km milestone, on the left bank of the Terek. Little remains here of the 14th century Alan town of Upper Dzhulat except the minaret which is 35 m (114 ft) high. One can climb the stairs to the top. The place used to be an important central Caucasian trading town.

IR RESTAURANT *Opposite the minaret.*

BESLAN

Population: 23,600 (1963)

This town stands on the right bank of the Terek.

Here is Europe's largest maize processing plant, where starch, glucose and many other things are produced. There are other branches of the food industry as well.

HIPPODROME RACECOURSE *On the left side of the main road.*

SERVICE STATION.

ORDZHONIKIDZE

(formerly Vladikavkaz and Dzaudzhikau)

Population: 202,000 (1964)

The town was founded on either side of R. Terek on the site of the 18th century Ossetian village, Dzauga. It is guarded by the rocky cliffs of Table Mountain (3008 m/9870 ft) whose silhouette from the side resembles the sleeping princess in this local legend.

Long ago the Cyclops lived in caves in the thick forests. Each year one came down to the kingdom that lay to the north of where Table Mountain now stands, and demanded that the most beautiful seventeen-year-old girl be given him to eat. The people found out that the spell would be broken if the loveliest girl would sacrifice herself voluntarily. At last came the turn of the Princess to be devoured. Her father locked her away but she learned of the trouble and escaped. She rushed forward to sacrifice herself to the Cyclops and there was a howl, a flash and a cloud of smoke. When the air cleared the people saw the princess had turned into a mountain—but the monster had gone.

The princess's suitor, a brave shepherd called Kazbek, heard the sound and looked down from the hills upon the scene. He could not sacrifice himself as his beloved had done but turned immediately into the mountain now called Kazbek.

(There are some more legends of Mt. Kazbek in the section describing the village of Kazbegi, farther along the road, up in the mountains.)

A fortress was built here in 1784 to subdue the mountain peoples but in fact it was never used. In the second part of the 18th century the place became especially important for Russian trade with the Caucasus and Iran, and later because of its position on the Georgian Military Highway leading south through the mountains to Tbilisi. In 1860 it was proclaimed as the town of Vladikavkas (Mistress of the Caucasus) but was renamed in 1931 in honour of Ordzhonikidze. Grigory "Sergo" Ordzhonikidze (1886–1937) was a prominent Communist, a Georgian who concerned himself with the political life of the whole of the Soviet Union. When he was posthumously held in disgrace from 1944–54, the town was known as Dzaudzhikau, but was changed back to Ordzhonikidze

ОРДЖОНИКИДЗЕ
ORDZHONIKIDZE

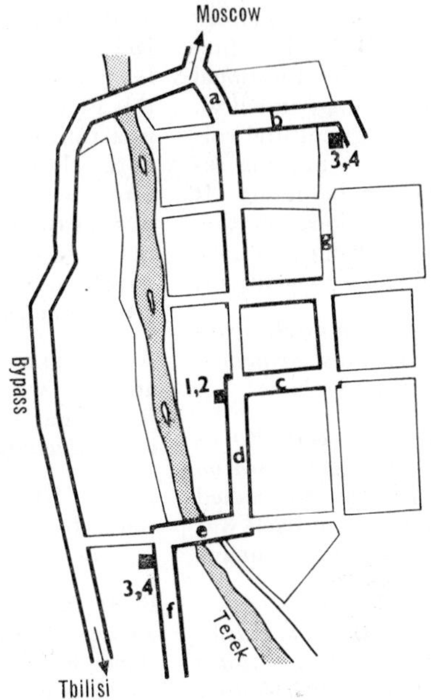

1 and 2 Hotel and Restaurant 3 Filling Station
4 Service Station

a Kitaiskaya ploshchad b Ul. Pozharskogo
c Ul. Kirova d Prospekt Mira
e Ul. Ordzhonikidze f Ul. Tbilisskaya
g Ul. Tel'mana

when the revolutionary was rehabilitated.

During World War II the German army was as close as 6 km (4 miles) to the town.

Ordzhonikidze is the capital of the North Ossetian Autonomous Republic. The Ossetian people themselves are a mixture of Caucasian and Persian; their predecessors were called the Alani and lived here at the beginning of the 1st century A.D. Today the population is mainly Russian and Ossetian, although there are also Armenians, Georgians, Persians and other minorities.

The town's main thoroughfare is Mir (formerly Alexandrovsky) Prospekt. It runs for 1 km (¾ miles), lined with many of the original old houses and with an avenue of fine lime trees. There are shops, hotels and restaurants here and it is a favourite strolling place.

Local industry includes metallurgy based on zinc and silver, a rolling stock repair station, factories producing tractor and car equipment, textiles, sewing machines, food products and the local mineral water known as "Karmadon". Before the revolution considerable Belgian capital was invested here and it was a Belgian company that installed the first trams. Among the town's educational establishments are mining, medical, teachers' training and agricultural colleges. Not far distant are hunting reserves where bears can be found. It is planned to extend the local hunting facilities and to organise fishing on Lake Bekan and pony-trekking expeditions.

ST. GEORGE'S CHURCH *Armyansky Pereulok 1*. This Armenian church was built in the 1840's.

LOCAL MUSEUM *Muzeinyi Pereulok 5. Open 10–6.30; closed on Tuesdays.* The building was constructed in 1902–06 but the museum itself was founded in 1897. This section contains the History Department.

BRANCH OF THE LOCAL MUSEUM *Katsoyev Street 64. Open 10–6.30; closed on Tuesdays.* Here is the Natural History Section of the museum. The building in which it is housed is one of the most impressive in Ordzhonikidze. It is the Mukhtarov Dzhuma Mosque, a Sunnite mosque built in 1906–08 with money donated by a Baku oil magnate called Mukhtarov. (The "Dzhuma" part of the mosque's name comes from the Arabic word for Friday.) It was designed as a small scale copy of a famous mosque in Cairo, as also were the mosques built in St. Petersburg and Kazan. It was closed in the 1930's but over 300 inscriptions from the Koran still adorn the walls. The majority of believers in Ordzhonikidze now are either Christian or Mohammedan.

KIROV AND ORDZHONIKIDZE MUSEUM *Kirov Street 48. Open 9–5; closed on Wednesdays.* These were both well known Bolshevik revolutionaries.

KOSTA HETAGUROV MUSEUM *Voikov Street 20. Open 10–6; closed on Thursdays.* Hetagurov (1859–1906) was called the Leonardo da Vinci of the Ossetian people. He was poet, artist, writer and playwright and is venerated as the founder of the Ossetian literary language. This museum which bears his name illustrates the development of this literature. The museum is housed in a 19th century Ossetian church and in the churchyard outside is Hetagurov Grove where there stands a black marble bust of the poet by Sanokoyev. Nearby is the grave of Arsen Kotsoyev (1872–1944), another Ossetian writer, who also worked as a translator.

ART GALLERY *Mir Prospekt 12.* There are some works by the Russian realists, Repin and Levitan. *Open 10–6; closed on Wednesdays.*

LENIN STATUE *Lenin Square.* This statue by Azgur stands 12 m high and was unveiled in 1957.

PUSHKIN'S BUST *In Pushkin Garden, Tsereteli Street.* The Russian poet stayed here in a hotel, now demolished, on his way down to the Caucasus in 1829.

PLIYEV BUST *In a garden on Mir Prospekt.* General Issa Pliyev (b. 1902) was twice acclaimed a Hero of the Soviet Union during World War II.

KOSTA HETAGUROV STATUE *Karl Marx Square.* The 13 m statue by Tavasiyev was unveiled in 1955.

ORDZHONIKIDZE STATUE *Svoboda Square.* By Ditrikh, 13 m high and unveiled in 1949.

GREY MARBLE OBELISK *Kitaiskaya Square, at the entrance to the town.* This is in memory of the Chinese soldiers who died here during the Civil War in 1918. Bitemirov was the architect and the obelisk was unveiled in 1960.

GRANITE OBELISK *Tbilisskoye Chaussée.* In memory of 17,000 Red Army soldiers who fell during the Civil War, in 1919.

The obelisk by Dziova and Poluyektov stands 24 m high and was unveiled in 1957.

OSSETIAN MUSIC AND DRAMA THEATRE *Naberezhnaya 18*. The theatre was founded in 1935 but the building was only completed in 1958.

RUSSIAN DRAMA THEATRE *Lenin Square 1*. The theatre was founded in 1869, and the building in 1872.

PUPPET THEATRE *Lenin Square 3*.

OPEN AIR THEATRE *Kirov Park*.

GREEN THEATRE (Open air) *Tbilisskoye Chaussée*. Seats for 10,000 people.

PLANETARIUM *Kirov Street 14, in an old mosque*.

KOSTA HETAGUROV PARK *Mir Prospekt*. This park is pleasantly situated beside the Terek. There are artificial lakes with islands linked by miniature bridges, and there is a puppet theatre here.

CHILDREN'S PARK *Kirov Street*.

DYNAMO STADIUM *Tramvainaya Street*.

SPARTAK STADIUM *Shmulevich Street*.

INTOURIST HOTEL AND RESTAURANT *Mir Prospekt 19; tel: 6-70*.

TEREK HOTEL *Mir Prospekt 56*.

IRISTON HOTEL *Mir Prospekt 24; tel: 32-74*.

KAVKAZ HOTEL AND RESTAURANT *Vatutin Street 50*.

TEREK RESTAURANT *Mir Prospekt 32*.

OTDYKH (Rest) RESTAURANT *Hetagurov Park*.

MILK BAR *Mir Prospekt 8*.

TSEY ICE-CREAM PARLOUR *Mir Prospekt 22*. The name is taken from that of a mountain.

OGONYOK CAFE *Mir Prospekt 7*.

GORKA (Hill) CAFE *On Mt. Lysaya*.

G.P.O. *Gorky Street 14*.

BANK *Kuibyshev Street 4*.

DEPARTMENT STORE *Mir Prospekt 31*.

BOOKSHOP *Mir Prospekt 12*.

JEWELLER'S *Mir Prospekt 26*.

SOUVENIRS *Mir Prospekt 33*.

FILLING STATION *Pozharsky Street, on the left side of the road when entering the town from Rostov*.

SERVICE STATION *At the same address; both provide round-the-clock service*.

CAMPING SITE AND MOTEL *7 km (4 miles) from Ordzhonikidze, at the beginning of the Georgian Military Highway, stands the first guard-tower known as the Redant. 1 km (½ mile) aside from this, beside an artificial lake with a boating station and a bathing beach, are the camping site and the motel. A by-pass runs around the west of the town to this point.* Redant Restaurant, an eating house, garage. Filling station and service station with carwash, tel: 11-64 and 21-00; round-the-clock service.

★

GORNY OREL (Mountain eagle) RESTAURANT *On the slopes of Mt. Lysaya, 11 km (7 miles) from town*. There is an excellent view of Ordzhonikidze and of the mountains. There is also a dendrarium here and a swimming pool and boat hiring station.

STALACTITE CAVE *15 km (9½ miles) from town, in one of the northern spurs of Mt. Stolovaya*. The cave is 6 m (20 ft) high.

DARGAVS *In the Dargava Ravine, 38 km (24 miles) from Ordzhonikidze, and about 3 km (2 miles) walk from the road, in the foothills of Mt. Shau-Khokh (4646 m./1524.3 ft)*. The name means "town of death". The Ossetians buried their dead in stone tombs because of the shortage of good arable land. It was an old Ossetian saying that every piece of good land big enough for a cow to stand on is worth a cow. So the villages were built only on poor ground and nearby grew up a second settlement, for the dead. Each house of the living in the village had its corresponding mausoleum in the "town of death", and each mausoleum had its own character, just as the ordinary houses had. Beside the bodies were placed the things their owners might need,—knives and tobacco for the men and needles, beads and mirrors for the women.

NIZHNY KOBAN *Another interesting village on the way to Dargavs.* It is best known for its burial places typical of the Koban Culture of the 2nd and 1st thousand years B.C. Excavations began here in 1876 and the graves were found to have been made in eight distinct layers, over a territory of two hectares (5 acres). This particular Bronze Age culture is distinguished by special axes, long, narrow and curved, as well as by a variety of ornaments including wide plated belts. These people had been hunters and primitive herdsmen. Items from this site are on exhibit in museums abroad as well as in the Soviet Union and there is naturally a good selection on display in the Ordzhonikidze Museum.

TATARTUP *On the left bank of the River Terek, near the village of Elhotovo.* In this ancient town there is a 14th century minaret 35 m (114 ft) high. The place is now deserted, and special permission from Intourist is required to go there.

NUZAL *In Alaghir Ravine.* Here there is a 12th century church with frescoes of Saint George and Saint Eustace.

THE GEORGIAN MILITARY HIGHWAY

This route became very important from the time the Russians first appeared in the North Caucasus. In 1766 the Russian army under Count Totleben was sent this way through the mountains to help the Georgians in their battle against the Turks. After the unification of Georgia and Russia in 1801 it was important to have a reliable route to Georgia as the easiest connection between the two countries. The road was accordingly built, with the help of "iron and powder". It involved the use of much labour and a great deal of money, but by 1817 it was already open to the public. It is 207 km (130 miles) long and derives its name from its strategical importance. The towers and fortress guarding the highway, the ruins of which are still to be seen, were built at the same time.

The mountain section of the road crosses five mountain ridges. The first is Forest Ridge; at the beginning of the road, Mount Lisaya (bald) (1037 m/3405 ft) rises in the west, and to the left is Mount Tarskaya (1224 m/4019 ft). 9 km ($5\frac{1}{2}$ miles) farther on, the highway crosses the second ridge, Pasture Ridge, and to the right is Mt. Fethur (1736 m/5698 ft) while on the left stands Mount Izvestkovaya (lime) (1270 m/4169 ft). The first village on the highway is Balta.

After 1·5 km (1 mile) following the wide valley of the River Terek, a route known to Pliny and Strabo in ancient times, the road reaches the Balta Gorge which crosses Rocky Ridge.

The pipeline running beside the road is the Stavropol–Ordzhonikidze–Tbilisi gas pipeline which was completed in 1963.

CHMI

Chmi is the Ossetian word for dogwood.

To the west stands Mount Arau-Hokh (2600 m/8532 ft) and to the east Stolovaya Gora (Table Mountain) (3008 m/9869 ft). When there is snow on the mountains the flat granite plateau of Stolovaya Gora looks as though it is covered with a white table-cloth.

The stalactite caves near the village are a tourist attraction.

LARSY

This village is 1100 m (3610 ft) above sea level; the remains of an old Russian fortress called Lars, dating from the time of the 19th century Caucasian wars and built to defend the road, lie here.

The Yermolovsky Kamen (Yermolov Stone) blocks the River Terek just to the south of Larsy. It takes its name from General Alexei Yermolov (1772 to 1861) who was appointed ruler of Georgia by Alexander I, and who is believed to have used the stone for a resting place. It weighs 1500 tons and measures 29 m (95 ft) long by 15 m (50 ft) wide by 13 m (42 ft) high. It was brought down the mountains by an avalanche in 1832 which blocked the traffic for 2 years and the amount of ice and snow was so great that it had to be blasted away, and in fact only finished melting in 1839.

"Beaten by jagged rocks to steam,
Before me pours the boiling stream;
Above my head the eagles scream,
The pinewood speaks,
And through the mist there faintly
gleam
The mountain peaks."

(From "The Avalanche" by Lermontov, translated by W. Morison.)

After Larsy and Chertov Most (this marked the border between Ossetia and Georgia; *cherta* means "border") the highway passes through Darialskoye Ushcheliye (Darial Ravine), or "the Gate of the Alani". In old Persian the name means "gate", and according to Pliny the Caucasian Gates (*Porta Caucasia* or *Portae Caspiae*) were here. They were of wood plated with iron and closed the mouth of the 8 km (5 miles) gorge, the rocky sides of which tower perpendicularly to a height of 1798 m (5900 ft).

"The cliffs in serried masses seem,
Replete with some mysterious
dream,
To bend their heads above the
stream
And watch the waters as they
gleam."

(From "The Demon" by Lermontov, translated by A. C. Coolidge.)

One cannot help but be impressed by this stretch. Some have said that this is not a road but a thrilling fairy tale; the narrow and curiously shaped rift is like a gigantic grave, and the traveller feels a poor helpless creature at the bottom. Everything in the ravine is dim and the southern sky looks like a narrow blue ribbon high up above.

The Darial Gorge has also been compared to the banks of the Rhine where similar romantic castles perch on the rocks. In the middle of the ravine on a small rock are the ruins of a particular old castle called Tamara's Castle which has, however, nothing to do with the famous Georgian Queen. It was mentioned in Lermontov's poems:

"Perched on the rock, the castle
tower,
That stands on Caucasus to wait,
A giant guardian at the gate,
Seems sternly through the mist to
glower."

(From "The Demon", translated by A. C. Coolidge.)

Some historians believe that it was built in 150 B.C. by king Mirian and restored by King David in the 12th century. The legend of the castle is a follows:

The castle was inhabited by the beautiful but wicked Queen Tamara, who enticed handsome young travellers into her castle with promises of love and happiness, but after a single night of pleasure the unfortunates were beheaded and their bodies thrown into the Terek.

It is this legend that Lermontov related in verse.

It is interesting to note that the home of the Amazons of whom the ancient Greek and Roman writers told was supposed to be here beside this very River Terek.

GVELETI

Just before the village of Gveleti is Gveleti Bridge over the River Terek. This marks the narrowest part of the gorge known as Chortovy Vorota (Devil's Gate) and also the beginning of the republic of Georgia. From here southwards the road passes successively through three ethnographical regions, Hevi, Mtiuleti and Kartli.

At this point the highway could be built only by cutting into the rock face. Some of the overhanging rocks have a threatening aspect, and most resemble some object from which their interesting names derive,—as for instance the Sphinx, Sentry and Bat. Another rock is known as "Carry us through, O Lord".

Nearby, in the valley of the River Kabakhi, are the remains of a 12–13th century church with fragments of frescoes, and also the ruins of a fortress.

KAZBEGI

(*known in the 19th century as Stepan-Tsminda*)

"Kasbek above with diamond light
Of everlasting snow shines blinding;
And deep below, a streak of night,
Like some dark cleft,
the snake's delight,
In endless curves the Darial's
winding.
And Terek, like a lion springing
With bristling mane, in fury roars;
The beast of prey, the bird high
winging
Its flight in azure, where it soars,
Have heard the cry his waves give
forth."

(From "The Demon" by Lermontov, Translated by A. C. Coolidge.)

Kasbegi is the centre of Mokhavia, a mountain region of Georgia, and the birthplace of the 19th century Georgian writer, Alexander Kazbegi (1848–93). From the town there is a good panoramic view of Mount Kazbek (5047 m/16,560 ft), and, to the left of the road, Mount Kuru (3790 m/13,420 ft).

On the mountain slope is the village of Gergeti and the Tsminda Samebo (Holy Trinity) Church. This was built in the 12th century in the time of Queen Tamara on the spot where it was believed the Apostle Andrew erected a cross. It was built with particular attention to the surrounding mountains and to snowy Kazbek itself.

✿ CHURCH. In the main square of Kazbegi is a church built in 1801 in Roman style. It belongs to a private family.

✿ KAZBEGI RESTAURANT *On the main road.*

✿ LOCAL MUSEUM *On the main square. Open 9–5.* The museum occupies the house where the writer Kazbegi, lived. It contains a section about him as well as arms and national costumes. There is a statue of Kazbegi in the Square which was unveiled in 1960 and nearby is his grave, with a tombstone carved out of solid marble in the shape of the two-peaked Mount Kazbek. Alexander Kazbegi was of a princely line, and the mountain was called after his family.

In the Ossetian language Mount Kazbek is called the Mountain of Christ. According to legend the top of the mountain is inaccessible, and God Himself dwells on the summit. Anyone approaching it will be stopped by unseen forces or by a terrible storm. Abram's tent is said to be there, and a cradle supported by unseen hands with a sleeping child in it. There is also a tree surrounded with scattered treasure which no-one has ever seen. The only people able to see these marvels were an old priest and his son, both being pure in body and spirit. The old man died on the return journey, but the son brought back a bit of unknown wood from the tree and a piece of material from the tent, and the soles of his boots were stuck with silver coins.

In spite of the legends, members of the London Alpine Club (Freshfield, Tucker and Moore) managed to climb to the top of the mountain from the south-east slope in June 1868. From 1900 onwards the Russian mountaineer Mrs. Preobrazhenskaya made the ascent nine times, obviously finding it a pleasant walk. In 1913 at a height of 3962 m (13,000 ft) ruins of a church with a cross on the top were found.

Here is another picturesque description of the mountain:

"He turned to stone and like a wise old man sat silent for centuries, his snow-white curls falling in a single mass, fringed with the delicate hairs of the mountain streams. The crown upon his royal head twinkles and sparkles with diamonds under the bright rays of the sun, or turns to pale opal under a transparent silver veil and then begins to shine again. At sunset his crown is covered with blood, burning with the last sad lights before dying and being extinguished by the darkness. Kazbek is great as only the ruler and master of the world can be."

SIONI

In this village there are mineral springs of the Narzan type, and amidst the picturesque woody scenery stands an 8th–9th century domeless church.

From Sioni the road climbs steeply along the side of Mount Kabardzhin (3141 m/10308 ft) towards Kobi.

KOBI

Kobi lies at 1932 m (6340 ft) above sea level at the junction of four ravines. Nearby is a building with a mineral water bath.

After this village the road climbs again. In 3 km (2 miles) one can cross a stone bridge over the River Baidarka and climb a mountain where there is a mineral lake so rich in gas that it looks as though it is boiling. The lake overflows, and the rocks have turned yellow from the high iron content of the water. Above the lake are alpine meadows full of forget-me-nots, harebells, mountain violets and cornflowers.

From this point the road climbs on its final ascent to Krestovi Pereval (Cross Pass) (2388 m/7837 ft) the highest point on the road, marked by an obelisk. The pass used to be so dangerous that sometimes people preferred to get out of their carriages and walk, and it is recorded that a certain foreign ambassador was so frightened that he asked to be blindfolded and was then led through by the hand. When the bandage was taken from his eyes he fell down on his knees to thank God for his survival. From here there is a wonderful panorama of the Caucasus. To the left is the old part of the road, where at a distance of about a kilometer ($\frac{1}{2}$ mile) one can see a cross of red stone which was, according to legend, placed there by King David the Builder (grandfather of Tamara) and repaired by General Yermolov in 1824. The tops of the mountains Nepis-Kalo (3536 m/11604 ft) and Shvidi-Dzma (Seven Brothers) (3150 m/10341 ft) among others can be seen.

After this point the slope down to the valleys of Georgia begins, and the road winds in zig-zags through heaps of rock known as the Stone Chaos. Then it runs above the Gudaur Abyss (500 m/1642 ft) and affords a good panoramic view over the southern mountains.

GUDAURI

At 2158 m (7080 ft) this is the highest sited village on the Highway.

Legend runs that long ago a daughter, Nina, was born to a poor family living in this village. She was the most beautiful baby there had ever been in the whole of Ossetia and as she grew up everyone, the villagers and anyone who happened to be travelling through the mountains, loved her for her beauty. Not least among her admirers was the spirit of Mount Gud; when she walked on the slopes he smoothed her path, and when she tended her father's five sheep he made sure that no harm came to them.

Nina grew up into an incomparably lovely girl and the ancient Gud, who in all his many years had never seen anyone like her, became more and more devoted to her. He wondered whether a powerful spirit could take on the form of a poor Ossetian peasant,—but Nina herself was already attached to Sasiko, the good-looking son of a neighbouring family.

In his jealousy, Gud tried to harm the young man by sending him hunting in the most difficult places and giving him bad weather. This was of no avail, but then, when Nina and Sasiko were alone together in a hut, he buried them beneath an avalanche of snow. As the days passed their love was overshadowed by hunger. Sasiko paced the hut and turned suddenly, and rushed at Nina and bit her on the shoulder like a starving beast. Her terrified screams were heard by the neighbours who quickly dug through the snow to release the young couple. Their lives were saved, but their love had died entirely and old Gud could not restrain his laughter and shook down a great mass of stones in his delight.

From Gudauri begins the Zemo-Mletsky Spusk which zig-zags 640 m (2100 ft) down the mountains in six great bends. After passing Kumlis-Tsikhe the road again runs along the edges of precipices to the bridge over the River White Aragvi. "Probably there is no other place on the Highway which can compare with this in its beauty and sharp changes of atmosphere." The *spusk* is built on the sheer rocks of the left bank of the Aragvi, and is a rare example of skilful engineering. In some places one side of the road is supported over the slope by a high artificial wall, and there are 18 sharp corners. The road was built between 1857 and 1861 following the project of Colonel Statkovsky, and under his personal supervision.

On arriving in Mleti the tourist feels as though he has come from north to south, from the severe, cold mountain world into the joyful southern country.

"Before him now another scene,
Had living beauties to display,
Where Georgian valleys robed in green
Stretched outward like a carpet lay."

(From "The Demon" by Lermontov; translated by A. C. Coolidge.)

MLETI

This village stands at a height of 1412 m (4635 ft). After the previous quick descent one feels that it is impossible to go any lower, but still from here the road continues by easy slopes down to the River Kura.

KVESHETI

On the rocks at the side of the road near the village is an old signal and guard tower.

This part of the Highway may be blocked by masses of sand and stones brought down from the mountains by the small streams which swell and rush across the road. It is wise to examine the flooded places as the road itself may have been washed away and one's car might be swept over into the river below.

PASSANAURI

In old Persian *Passanauri* means "Holy height". The place is 1014 m (3335 ft) above sea level, in a narrow valley at the confluence of the Black and the White Aragvi Rivers. There is here an interesting natural phenomenon, in that the waters of the two rivers do not mix for some distance, until the village of Bibliani. The dark water of the Black Aragvi keeps to the left side of the stream and the light-coloured White Aragvi stays on the right.

THE 19TH CENTURY CHURCH is closed.

PASSANAURI HOTEL AND RESTAURANT *Beside the main road from the north.*

RESTAURANT *Beside the main road from the south.*

FILLING STATION

★

Up in the valley of the Black Aragvi live three tribes of Caucasians which have puzzled ethnologists for many years. They are the Hefsurs, the Tushins and the Pshavs, and are now considered by some to be descendants of the Crusaders. Certain of the families still possess unusual national costumes which some Hefsurs wore even as late as the 1930's. These are decorated with a large white or coloured cross, and consist of chain-mail shirts, helmets with chain-mail and broad-swords. The shields bear inscriptions in Latin letters,—"Vivat Stephan Batory" (a Polish king), "Souvenir", "Genoa", "Vivat Husar" and "Sollingen". Some have images of eagles and crowns. Linguists, however, have discovered that the tribes belong to the Kartli peoples. The Hefsurs are good hunters and are famed for their kindness and hospitality; the greatest dishonour is to beat a child or to insult a guest, and even if the offender is the host's own brother he risks his life.

After Passanauri a region of vineyards and orchards begins.

ANANURI

The name means "Holy Mother".

There is a 16th–18th century fortress and within its walls stands the Assumption Church, built in 1689. There is a fine carved cross on the outside of the west wall and inside some 17th and 18th century frescoes remain. The iconostasis is of Moscow workmanship and dates from the 19th century. Nearby is the 16th century Bteba Church and the small buildings up the hill, to the left as one goes through the entrance gate, were bath houses. Below is a ridged domed Armenian Church of the 19th century.

In 1737 this village was the scene of an exceptionally bloody battle between the members of two families, during which barricades were made of corpses. During the fray someone sought sanctuary for himself and his family in a church, but the building was surrounded with logs and burnt to the ground.

ZHINVALI

In the vicinity of this village are the remains of a 7th century town and a castle called Bebris-Tsikhe. The castle consists of two parts, the upper and the lower. In some places the thickness of the wall is as great as 2 m (6 ft 6 in.). No exact date is known for its foundation, but it is probably of the 9th or 10th century.

NATAKHTARI

On the hill nearby are the ruins of Natskhor (Girl's Tower), and on the other side of the river is a monastery of the 6th century called Dzhevris-Sandari.

Further on the road forks to the right to the Black Sea via Kutaisi and to the left to Mtskheta and Tbilisi (30 km/18½ miles). Visitors to Tbilisi have afterwards to retrace their tracks as far as this point.

MTSKHETA

Mtskheta stands at the confluence of the Aragvi and Kura rivers. On the right bank of the River Kura, on the slopes of Mount Kartli, the mythological father of the Georgian people, Kartlos, was buried, according to legend. He was said to be a direct descendant of Japhet, and it was his son Mikhetos who founded this town and gave it his name. It became the cradle of Georgian culture, and up till the 5th century it was the capital, where the ancient religious and political life was concentrated. It was also the residence of the Patriarchs.

On Mount Kartli, which is a holy mountain, stood the shrine of an idol called Armaz, the Georgian version of the Persian god Ormuzd, the god of compassion and life. On the mountainside east of Mtskheta above the left bank of the River Aragvi was another idol's shrine. This idol's name was Zaden, and these two were the chief gods worshipped by pagan Georgia. On the other hills around Mtskheta were shrines to less important gods with names and characters derived from the gods of the various peoples upon whom Georgia had depended at different times. At the entrance to the town, for example, stood a statue of Aphrodite. Armaz and Zaden, however, were the most highly esteemed, being the gods who spread the sun's rays and in general protected the country from all harm. They were the gods of fertility, too, and were sometimes offered human sacrifices.

The Armaz Monastery was so called because it was founded on the site of the pagan temple. Now only a bell-tower remains among the ruins.

The centre of the town was at the point where the two rivers converge; a fortress and the tsar's palace were built there and the rest of the town spread farther up the river valleys. From the 3rd century B.C. the citizens of Mtskheta had been highly cultured, and during the town's early history they had military and trade connections with Greece, Rome, Persia and Parthia.

✿ SVETI TSKHOVELI CATHEDRAL. This cathedral was dedicated to the Twelve Apostles but was also known as the Church of the Pillar of Life. According to legend a local Jew called Elioz was summoned to Jerusalem to participate in the trial of Christ. He was present at the Crucifixion and after the drawing of lots for Christ's clothes he won the Robe and brought it back to Mtskheta. There he was met by his sister Sidonia, herself a secret Christian. When she learned of the Crucifixion of Christ she fell down dead, clutching the robe. None could wrench it from her grasp,—it was as though it had grown onto her flesh, and all the city was witness to the strange occurrence. That night during an earthquake a crevasse opened and Sidonia was buried together with the Robe. Later a cedar tree grew up on the spot.

About 250 years after this there lived in Jerusalem a certain Nina, the daughter of a Roman general. She had been born in Capadocia, but when she was twelve her parents took her to Jerusalem. There she was taught by an old woman called Nianfora who told her that the Robe had been taken to pagan Iberia (the old name for Georgia). Inspired by this story Nina prayed constantly to the Virgin asking to be able to go to the place where the Robe had been taken, and finally she was told by the Virgin in a dream that she should go to Iberia and that Christ Himself would help her.

Simply clad, and carrying a cross of vinerods tied with her own hair, Nina set off on the long difficult journey to Mtskheta, arriving in 314 A.D. At the moment of her arrival King Mirian was about to go up to Kartli to offer a human sacrifice to Armaz, but Nina prayed to God and in a violent storm the idol was overturned. She erected a cross on the slope of the mountain and then went down to begin her missionary work in the city. Even King Mirian himself came to the door of her hut to hear the story of Christ, and after ten years her sermons and her own holy life persuaded the King, his wife and children, and with them the whole population of the town, to be baptised.

The pagan temples and the idols were destroyed. According to the Georgian chronicles King Mirian said of his former religion, "I am the thirty-sixth King, and the first Christian king of Georgia. My fathers sacrificed children to idols. The mountains of Armaz and Zaden deserve to be destroyed by fire."

Among her other miracles Nina cured the Queen of sickness, and when Mirian was blinded by lightning she restored his sight. After her death Nina was canonised and is today, like Queen Tamara, remembered as one of the Georgian great.

In the year 328 King Mirian had the great cedar tree chopped down, and beneath it, still held in Sidonia's hands, the Robe of Christ was found. Mirian built a wooden cathedral over the spot. This was rebuilt in stone in the 5th century, but was robbed and damaged several times and finally destroyed during Tamerlane's invasion, on Tamerlane's personal order. The site of the legendary cedar tree is still marked by a stone column reputed to ooze holy oil. The column, which stands in the southern part of the cathedral, was decorated by Grigori Guldzhavarishvili in the 17th century with themes from the history of early Christianity in Georgia, and was originally embellished with gold and silver.

Christ's Robe was kept in Mtskheta until the 17th century when Shah Abbas captured the town and sent the Robe as a gift to the Russian Tsar Mikhail Fedorovich, who in turn placed it with great ceremony in the Uspensky Sobor in the Moscow Kremlin.

The present building of the Sveti Tskhoveli Cathedral is a perfect example of Georgian 15th century architecture surrounded by a great crenellated fortress wall with batteries and towers built in the 18th century. The Cathedral itself was erected in 1440 during the reign of Alexander I of Georgia, and under the supervision of Patriarch Melchisadek. The upper dome of the cathedral was restored in the 17th century, and in the 19th century some small outbuildings were pulled down and most of the frescoes whitewashed. The interior decorations still to be seen date from the 16th and 17th centuries. The iconostasis is 19th century work. On the southern wall is a 17th century fresco illustrating the words of Psalm 150, "Let every thing that hath breath praise the Lord".

The façade of the cathedral is carved. Over the arch of the northern façade there is a hand holding a set square, and the architect's name, Arsukidze, is inscribed there.

The coronation of the Georgian Kings took place in this building and near the altar are the tombs of the last Georgian Kings, Erekle II and Giorgi XII. In the southeast corner of the central aisle is the Patriarchs' stone throne decorated with 17th and 18th century frescoes. Also inside the cathedral is a small chapel, a copy of the Chapel of Christ's Sepulchre in Jerusalem. The stone font is that in which the King Mirian is said to have been baptised. The tombs include those of members of the royal and noble houses of Georgia. *Services are held in the Cathedral between 10 a.m. and 12 on Saturdays and Sundays and on all Church festivals.*

Samtavra Convent. The main church is dedicated to Saint Nina, "the Enlightener of Georgia" who was buried there, and it is similar in form to the Cathedral of the Twelve Apostles. It was built at the beginning of the 11th century in mediaeval Georgian baroque style, on the site of a 4th century church erected by King Mirian. Its name comes from *mtavara* meaning "ruler". Beside the cathedral to the northwest there is a three-storey 16th century belltower, and a small and ancient chapel on the place where Saint Nina's hut once stood.

The graves of King Mirian and of his wife, Queen Nina are still in the cathedral but the sepulchres date from the 19th century and are of little historic interest. The site is surrounded by walls. The cathedral was restored at the same time as the rest of the convent in 1903. There are now fifteen nuns in the convent.

DZHVARI CHURCH. Up on the hill on the other side of the river Aragvi are the ruins of a church built in 585–604, its name meaning "cross". It is designed to catch the attention, and from many points can be seen dominating the town. When Christianity was adopted in the 4th century a cross was erected here as a symbol of the religious victory. The present church was built to enclose the older one completely.

During its 1400 years of existence Dzhvari Church was damaged only once: in the 10th century, when it was set on fire by invading Arabs. The eastern and southern façades are lavishly decorated with reliefs, including images of patrons and people who gave money for, and organised, the building. There is a legend that this Church and the Sveti Tskhoveli Cathedral were linked by an iron chain, and that the monks used to leave their cells on the hilltop and climb down for services in the Cathedral, but when faith grew weaker among the people the chain broke and was lost.

This church, which is very old, has served as the prototype of many other Georgian churches.

✿ THE BEDRIS TZIKHE TOWER. This is another remnant of Mtskheta's past. Its name means "old man's fortress".

An ancient cemetery was found in 1871 beside the highway near Samtavra Convent. It had been used from the Iron Age until the 11th century, and during the excavations some coins of the time of Caesar Augustus were found. The upper row of graves are in the form of stone boxes.

Today Mtskheta is famous for the garden of one of the inhabitants named Mamulanshvili, who has a very rich collection of plants and flowers.

✿ MTSKHETA RESTAURANT *Near Samtavra Convent, open from 9 a.m. until midnight.*

★

By the road leading out of Mtskheta, where the River Kura joins the River Aragvi, is the Zemo-Avchalskaya dam and hydro-power station opened in 1927 and designed to generate 26,500 kilowatts. A large monument to Lenin stands here.

After passing through the Saburtalo suburb of Tbilisi the road comes to the capital of Georgia and so to the end of the Georgian Military Highway.

TBILISI

Old Russian: Tiflis

Population: 694,000 (1959)

The capital of the Georgian Soviet Socialist Republic is located in the eastern part of Georgia and the central part of the Caucasian isthmus. It is 350 km (220 miles) by rail from the Black Sea and 550 km (340 miles) from the Caspian Sea. The highest part of the town rises 91 m (nearly 300 ft) above the rest of Tbilisi, and altogether it covers over 6000 hectares (15,000 acres), twice as much as in 1921. On the west side of the town is Mtatsminda Mountain (Holy Mountain or Mount David) (727 m/2386 ft), to the east lies the Makhat Range (650 m/2133 ft) and to the south the Sololax (488 m/1602 ft).

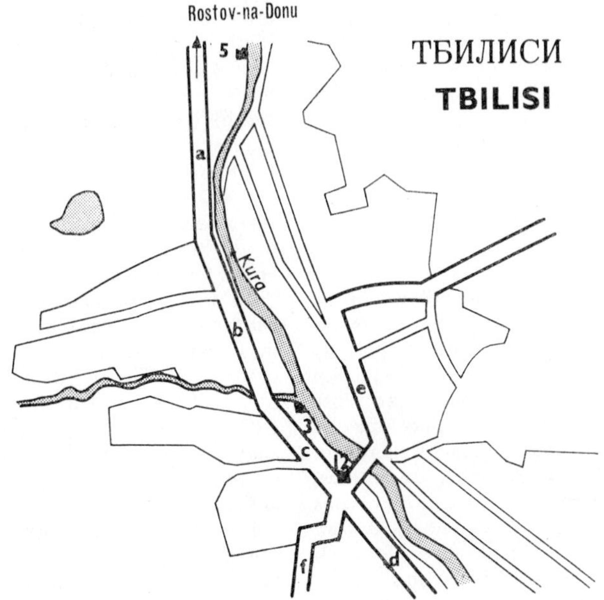

1 and 2 Hotel and Restaurant 3 Filling Station 5 Camping Site

a Voenno Gruzinskaya doroga
b Ul. Lenina
c Pr. Rustaveli
d Ul. Leselidze
e Ul. Sovetskaya
f Ul. Davitashvili

River Kura, the longest river in the Caucasus, rises in Turkey and flows through Tbilisi to the Caspian Sea. From ancient times the site of Tbilisi has been a trading point between Europe and India.

The climate is continental with an average annual temperature of 12·7°C (55°F). The summer is long, dry and hot with an average temperature of 24·5°C (76°F), but it may rise to more than 40°C (104°F). The winter is mild with little snow; the average winter temperature is 1·3°C (34°F) but if there is a north wind it may sink to −15°C (5°F). Autumn is considered to be the best season of the year, and in general the climate must be a healthy one, for in Georgia there are over 20,000 people who are more than 90 years old and over 600 of them live in Tbilisi.

The name Tbilisi came from the Georgian word *tbili* meaning "warm" and now it is understood to mean "the town of warm springs". The Georgians however have long called it simply *kalaki* meaning "town" because it is the biggest built-up area in Georgia. A legend, chronicled by Leonti Mraveli, says that long ago the Georgian King Vakhtang Gorgazali (452–502) was hunting in the place where Tiflis now stands, and he wounded a deer. While it was bleeding to death the beast fell into a warm sulphur spring where its wound was washed. It was cured and rushed from the spring and ran off into the forest. The King examined the spring, found its waters warm and curative, and ordered that a settlement be made on that spot. There is to be a monument to the king in Tbilisi, commemorating his discovery.

The first written mention of Tbilisi as a town dates from the 4th century and in the 5th century, under King Vakhtang Gorgazali (Vakhtang VI), it became the capital of Georgia instead of Mtskheta. During its history it has been pillaged by enemies forty times, and during the space of 1400 years was entirely devastated 29 times. Especially severe were the attacks by the Mongols at the end of the 13th century and those made at the end of the 18th century by the Persian Shah Aga-Mohammed. Khazars, Huns, Persians, Byzantines, Arabs, Mongols, Turks and numerous tribes from the mountains have all forced their way inside its walls. Each time it was rebuilt Tbilisi showed the influence of its new masters, and that of the Persians was especially strong.

Georgia has had contact with Russia since the 15th century. As the Georgians held the Orthodox faith in common with the Russians it was to them that they appealed for help in moments of crisis. Ivan the Terrible sent his Cossacks as reinforcements in the 16th century and Russo-Georgian relations were even closer in the 17th and 18th centuries when Peter the Great and Vakhtang VI established a military alliance. In 1736 Georgia was divided between Turkey and Persia, the Turks dominating West Georgia and the Persians East Georgia and Tbilisi. Since that time the Georgian Kings were appointed by the Persian shahs, but the Georgians frequently revolted and sought the protection of the Russian tsars. In the second half of the 18th century the Georgian King Erekle II came to power and in 1783, to save his country from military disaster from Persia and Turkey, signed an agreement passing supreme power to Russia. The last king, Georgi XII, passed practically all power to Russia after the massacres and seizure of Tbilisi by the Persians under Shah Aga-Mohammed in 1795. This warlike leader was a eunuch and was renowned for his ferocity; his men would take babies from their mothers and try to cut them in half at a single blow to test the sharpness of their swords. After this attack on Tbilisi nothing remained of the town except two caravanserais and a few houses.

In the second quarter of the 19th century many new houses appeared in Tbilisi, especially in the central part of the town. The architecture shows elements of Russian Classicism combined with the old Georgian style; for instance, on the traditional flat roofs appeared a second floor with balconies and carved columns. With its ancient culture and natural beauty Georgia attracted Russian intellectuals as visitors. These included the dramatist Alexander Griboyedov, Pushkin, Lermontov and Tolstoi. In 1851 Tolstoi wrote about it "Tiflis is a very civilised town, closely imitating Petersburg and doing it rather well. The high society is select and fairly large and there is Russian theatre and Italian opera". Tchaikovsky, Chaliapin, Chekhov, Rubinstein and Gorky all visited it with pleasure.

The first funicular railway, 501 m/548 yd in length was built on Mount David in 1905. It ends with a three-storey house, the top floor of which is used as a restaurant. Tbilisi's largest park is at the top of Mount David. The old Asian quarters of Tbilisi are not very extensive but their narrow streets and lanes form a labyrinth fascinating to tourists. The section known as Maidan may be reached by walking from Lenin Square along Leselidze Street. One of the old caravanserai buildings, now used as a depot, stands at the end of Sionskaya Street, to the south-east of the Sioni Cathedral. There are other similar buildings still in existence in Tbilisi. The palace at Rustaveli Prospekt 6 was built in 1807 and reconstructed in 1865. Before the revolution it was the residence of the governor of the Caucasus, and until 1941 when the new government building was put up nearby it was the seat of the Georgian government. Now it is a Palace of Pioneers, the Soviet equivalent of the Boy Scouts' and the Girl Guides' Associations. Ilyi Chavchavadze Street 33 is the building of the former seminary, and was erected in 1905; now it is used by the Agricultural Institute. The new Government building, Rustaveli Prospekt 8, was built between 1938 and 1953 by architects Kokorin and Lezhava; it is five storeys high and contains an unusual covered courtyard. The Georgian State Museum was designed by Severov and built between the establishment of Soviet rule in 1921 and the outbreak of the Second World War. A university and 12 institutes are among Tbilisi's educational establishments. An underground railway is being built to improve its communications and new housing is going up on all sides. Saburtalo on the city's northern outskirts is probably the best looking of the new residential areas. The main road to Mtskheta runs through it.

30 km (19 miles) from Tbilisi is the newly-built industrial town of *Rustavi*, which was founded in 1944 and now has a population of 60,000. It has a large metallurgical factory and chemical works.

The reservoir known as the *Sea of Tbilisi* was completed in 1951. There is a bathing beach there, and a regular bus route connects it with the city.

The town's greatest wealth has always been in its warm sulphur springs, but for many centuries only the Moslems used them. Most are to be found in the Maidan sector on the banks of the River Kura. Those on the right bank are similar to the springs of Bataglia and those on the left resemble the waters of Ems and Baden. The waters come from the Mtabori Hill and emerge from thermal cracks in the bituminous layers. Their temperatures fluctuate from 47·5°C (117·5°F) to 24°C (75°F). The old bath-houses, similar to the caravanserai in architecture, are mostly to be found in the old town in the Legvis Hevi Ravine. The oldest is the Erekle Bath, on the corner of Banaya and Akhundova Streets. It was long a bone of contention between the Kings and the clergy until King David gave it to Sioni Cathedral in 1549. Opposite this bath-house is another dating from the 17th century, known as the Sumbatovskaya Bath, and another of similar date is Bebutovskaya Bath on the southern side of Akhundov Street. Further on from this is Kazonnaya Bath which in the 18th century belonged to Tamara, daughter of King Georgi XII. The Seidabadskaya Bath in Mesnikov Street was built in 1840. There are several others, but these are the best and the most interesting. They are certainly worth a visit; there are Turkish baths with traditional massage and separate baths for men and women.

✿ SIONI OR ASSUMPTION CATHEDRAL *Sionskaya Street 4.* The original cathedral was built between 575 and 639. After the death of Queen Tamara it fell into decay. According to legend Sultan Gelal-Eddin tore down the dome in 1226. The local Metropolitan Saginashvili rebuilt the dome and redecorated the whole church. It was afterwards repeatedly restored, and in 1853–54 the cathedral was newly painted by the Russian artist Gagarin as a result of which the old frescoes were lost. At the same time the stone iconostasis was built. In 1882 the paintings in the dome were restored. The belltower stands nearby; it was built in 1425 and restored in 1939. To the west of the cathedral is another belfry in Russian Empire style, built between 1805 and 1812. Saint Nina's Cross, interwoven with vines and her own hair, was brought to the Sioni Cathedral from

Mtskheta and can be seen here. Among the cathedrals other treasures are two cherished icons, "St. Nina" and "Our Lady of Sioni".

UNCHISKHATI CHURCH *Shavteli Street 5/7*. This church standing beside the River Kura is called after the 11th century icon which was brought here in the 17th century from the village of Unchi in south-western Georgia. Now the icon hangs in the Art Museum. The church was founded in the 6th century, and reconstructed several times, extensively so in 1675 when new gateways and a bell-tower over them were added upon the orders of Catholicos Domenti. The external form of the basilica was spoiled by the 19th century reconstruction of the dome in Russian style.

SAINT DAVID'S CHURCH *Mtatsminda Mountain*. This church was founded in 1542, restored several times, and completely rebuilt, dome and all, at the end of the last century. Since 1929 it has been known as the Pantheon of prominent Georgian public figures and writers, including Nikoloz Baratashvili, Akaki Tsereteli, Vazha Pshavela and Ilya Chavchavadze. Saint David was one of the missionaries who came from Syria in the 6th century to preach Christianity, and he lived on Mount Mtatsminda where the church now stands. On the summit there used to be an observatory, built by the Arabs under whom Tbilisi rose to be the third most important town in the Caucasus. There is a second Pantheon of public figures and writers at Brdzola Street 40, in the Didubei region of Tbilisi. It was founded in 1939.

KVASHVETSKAYA CHURCH *Geordzhadze Street 2, just off Rustaveli Street. Kva* means "stone" and *shva*—"to give birth"; the church is so called, so the story runs, because long ago the daughter of a Tbilisi noble was expecting a child and she accused Saint David of being the father. He was summoned to court and touching her with his staff asked, "Who is the father of this child?" From within her a voice proclaimed the name of the real father, and thereupon the girl began to labour. She brought forth a stone which was used as the foundation of a new church. The present building was erected between 1904 and 1910.

DZHVARIS MAMA CHURCH *Leselidze Street*. The name means Holy Cross; the church was built in the 15th century and reconstructed in the first half of the 18th century.

METEKHI CHAPEL *Crowning the cliff above a bend in the River Kura*. This chapel is a good example of the efforts of an architect to harmonise a building with the landscape. It is designed with regard to its silhouette and placed so that it can be seen from many points in the town. Founded in 1278–83 and reconstructed several times, it was for some while the chapel of the Georgian Catholicos. A new dome was built at the beginning of the 18th century; then in the 1820's the chapel was turned into a prison, and the three buildings near it were part of the prison remaining, although the other buildings were demolished in 1937.

DIDUBI-PANTEON *Tsereteli Prospekt 38. Open 12–7; closed on Mondays*. Georgian writers, artists, actors and scientists are buried in this cemetery. In the Church of Our Lady of Didubi is a miracle-working icon of the Virgin.

LURDZHI MONASTERY *Near Kirov Park, at the end of Vasha-Pshavela Prospekt*. The name means "blue", referring to the blue glazed tiles which decorate it. The basilica dates from the 12th century although the dome is of more recent date.

SYNAGOGUE *Leselidze Street 37*.

MOSQUE *Botanicheskaya Street*.

SAINT JOHN THE BAPTIST'S CHURCH *Vasha-Pshavela Prospekt 21*. This

Russian orthodox Church which was built in 1901 is open for service.

SAINTS PETER AND PAUL ROMAN CATHOLIC CHURCH *Kalinin Street 55.* This church built in the 1860's is open for service.

✿ SHURIS TSIKHE *Komsomolskaya Alleya, Narikala.* The ruins of the "rival fortress", also known as Sololakski Citadel, can be seen above the old part of the town on Sololakski Hill. The oldest fortress in the town, it is supposed to have been founded by the Persians in 368 to counter-balance the power of nearby Mtskheta. It was reconstructed several times during its history, and was newly rebuilt in the 17th century; in the earthquake of 1827 it was severely damaged but some parts were again restored in 1909.

SACHINO (NOBLE) PALACE *Avlabari.* Formerly the castle of Queen Darya, wife of King Erekle II, the palace was built in 1776 and partly rebuilt in the 19th century. The chapel also survives. Nearby, in Avlabari, at *Metekhskaya Street 18*, stands a typical example of an old Tbilisi house.

THE ACADEMY OF ART. This was built in 1857/58, and was at that time the most beautiful building in Tbilisi. Balls and banquets were held here and the parquet floors, marbles and carved decorations are still well preserved.

TOWN HALL *Lenin Square.* The Town Hall was erected in the 1880's in Moorish style.

LENIN MUSEUM *Rustaveli Prospekt 29.* The museum is located in the large building of the Marxism–Leninism Institute, designed by Academician Shusev in 1938.

HISTORICAL AND ETHNOGRAPHICAL MUSEUM *Komsomolskaya Alleya 11.* This collection was founded on that of the old Municipal Museum.

GEORGIAN LITERARY MUSEUM *Georgiashvili Street 8.*

GEORGIAN ART GALLERY *Rustaveli Prospekt 13. Open 11–9.* The building was originally that of the Khram Slavi (temple of glory), built in the 1880's to commemorate the victories of the Russian Army in the Caucasus.

GEORGIAN ART MUSEUM *Ketskhoveli Street 1. Open 11–9; closed on Tuesdays.* There is an excellent collection of icons, frescoes and china and among the Georgian paintings worthy of note are those by the primitivist Niko Picosmanashvili (Picrosmani) (1862–1918).

Dating from the 1830's, this building once housed the Tbilisi Ecclesiastical Seminary and on the outside wall by the entrance is a plaque saying that J. Stalin lived and studied here from 1st September, 1894–29th May, 1899.

DZHANASHIYA GEORGIAN MUSEUM *Rustaveli Prospekt 3. Open 10–4; closed on Mondays.* Originally the Caucasian Museum founded in 1852, this museum was renamed after the Georgian Academician S. Dzhanashiya. It contains much of interest, especially in the ethnographical section.

CHAVCHAVADZE'S HOUSE *Ordzhonikidze Street 22. Open 10–6; closed on Mondays.* Alexander Chavchavadze (1786–1846) was an outstanding Georgian romantic poet who translated both Russian and French poetry.

MUSEUM OF CHILDREN'S TOYS *Rustaveli Street 6.*

MARX LIBRARY *Ketskhoveli Street 5.* The library was founded in 1846. On the façade of the building, only completed in 1913, ancient Georgian architectural motifs were used in decoration. The carving was executed by the famous Georgian stonemason brothers, Agladze.

New Funicular Railway. Entrance from Rustaveli Street up a spiral staircase.

This overhead railway is 906 m (992 yd) long and rises to a height of 287 m (942 ft). It can take 30 people at a time.

Obelisk *Vakhtang Gorgazali Street.* This commemorates the 300 warriors who lost their lives on 11th September, 1795 as they covered the retreat of the Georgian Army from the Persians.

Pushkin Monument *Pushkin Square.* This monument was designed by Hodorovich in 1892.

Lenin Monument *Lenin Square.* By sculptor Topuridze, the 18·5 m monument was unveiled in 1956.

General Leselidze Bust *Leselidze Street.* Leselidze was a hero of World War II, and this monument to his memory was unveiled in 1945.

Kamo Monument. This monument was erected in 1957 in memory of the revolutionary, Ter-Petrosyan, who used Kamo as his nickname. It was designed by Okropiridze.

Shota Rustaveli Monument *Rustaveli Square.* Designed by Merabishvili and unveiled in 1942 to commemorate the 750th anniversary of the appearance of Rustaveli's poem "The Knight in the Tiger's Skin".

Griboyedov's Grave *On Saint David's Mount, by the church.* This Russian writer was killed in 1829 while serving as Ambassador to Persia. His tomb is of black marble with a bronze crucifix and a mourning female figure on it. To the left is a monument to his wife, Nina, who was left a widow at the age of 16 and who never remarried although she lived on until 1857. A statue of Griboyedov by Merabishvili (1961) stands beside the River Kura.

Symbol of Georgia Statue *Komsomolskaya Alleya.* The 16 m figure of a woman holding out a sword for her enemies and a bowl to her friends was designed by Amashukeli and unveiled in 1958.

✿ Paliashvili Opera House *Rustaveli Prospekt 25.* The company was founded in 1851 and the building was completed at the end of the 19th century, in Moorish style. Zahari Paliashvili was a composer of Georgian national music. His grave is in the theatre garden.

Mardzanishvili Theatre *Mardzhanishvili Street 8.* The theatre bears the name of the well-known Georgian producer, Kote Mardzhanishvili, whose grave is in the garden of the Paliashvili Opera House.

Rustaveli Theatre. The company was established in 1920 on the basis of the old Georgian Theatre. The Rustaveli Georgian Theatre Institute is to be found in the same building.

Griboyedov Russian Drama Theatre *Rustaveli Prospekt 2.* The building dates from the 1850's and was originally constructed as a caravanserai.

Shaumyan Armenian Drama Theatre *Shaumyan Street 8.* This theatre was opened in 1936.

Russian Youth Theatre *In the same building as the Russian Puppet Theatre.*

Georgian Youth Theatre *Rustaveli Prospekt 37.* The Georgian Puppet Theatre is at the same address.

Georgian State Philharmonia Concert Hall *Plekhanov Prospekt 123.* This is the house of the State Symphony Orchestra, the Capella Choir, the national dance ensemble (which has earned high praise during its tours abroad, and is well worth seeing) and a string quartet.

VANO SARADZHISHVILI TBILISI CONSERVATOIRE *Griboyedov Street 8*. The conservatoire is named after the "nightingale of Georgia" who now lies buried in the garden of the Paliashvili Opera House.

CONCERT HALL *Melikishvili Street*.

ABASHIDZE MUSICAL COMEDY THEATRE *Plekhanova Prospekt 182*.

CIRCUS *Geroyev Sovietskovo Soyuza Square*. The building was completed in 1940.

✿ FUNICULAR PARK *Mount Mtatsminda*. The park lies 362 m (1188 ft) above the town and is reached by either of two funicular railways. It was opened in 1935.

ORDZHONIKIDZE PARK *Plekhanov Prospekt 180/182*. The park was laid out on the base of the old Mushtaid Garden, named after the one-time head of the Persian clergy in Tbilisi. There is a children's railway here.

KHUDADOVSKY PARK *Khudadovskaya Street*. The park was planted in 1893.

KIROV PARK *Lenin Street 37*. The park was opened in 1933 and there is a monument to Kirov in it.

KOMMUNAROV GARDEN *Rustaveli Prospekt 13*. This was formerly the Alexandrov Garden, founded in 1859. There is a Gogol Monument designed by Hodorovich in 1903 and other monuments to Georgian revolutionaries.

VAKEI PARK *Chavchavadze Prospekt*. The park covers 120 hectares (300 acres) and contains the Burevestnik Stadium which can take 35,000 people. *Burevestnik* is the Russian name for the stormy petrel or Mother Carey's chickens.

PARK OF PHYSICAL CULTURE AND SPORT *Patrisa Lumumby Naberezhnaya 1*. There is an open air swimming pool in the park.

DYNAMO STADIUM *Brdzola Street 2*. Completed in 1935, the stadium can seat 40,000. It also has a swimming pool.

PALACE OF SPORT *Ordzhonikidze Square 1*. There are seats for 10,000 people.

HEATED SWIMMING POOL *Chavchavadze Prospekt*.

ZOO *Geroyev Sovietskovo Soyuza Square*. Opened in 1927, the grounds cover 20 hectares (50 acres).

BOTANICAL GARDENS *Botanicheskaya Street*. These gardens were founded in 1845 and based on the old garden of Tbilisi fortress.

✿ INTOURIST HOTEL AND RESTAURANT *Rustaveli Prospekt 7; tel: 3-10-05*. This was formerly the Orient Hotel, built in the 1880's.

TBILISI HOTEL AND RESTAURANT *Prospekt Rustaveli 13; tel: 3-05-83*. This hotel was built in 1915.

ABKHAZIA HOTEL AND RESTAURANT *Vazha Pshavela Prospekt*.

GEORGIA HOTEL AND RESTAURANT *Melikishvili Street 12*.

RUSTAVI HOTEL *Plekhanov Prospekt 103*.

ARAGVI RESTAURANT *Pushkin Street 29*.

DARYAL RESTAURANT *Rustaveli Prospekt 22*.

DYNAMO RESTAURANT *Dynamo Stadium, Brdzola Street 2*.

ISANI RESTAURANT *Meshkishvili Street 3*.

SAMGORI RESTAURANT *Nekrasov Street 10*.

FUNICULAR RESTAURANT *In the Park, Mount David*.

NAD KUROY RESTAURANT *Ordzhonikidze Park, Plekhanov Prospekt*.

KAZBEK RESTAURANT *Elbazvidze Spusk 1.*

SULKHINO RESTAURANT *Sherozia Street 2.*

RESTAURANT *In Vakei Park.*

GEMO (Taste) RESTAURANT *Lenin Street.*

TSISKARI (Twilight) CAFE *Chavchavadze Street 52.*

GAZABKULI (Spring) CAFE *Melikishvili Street.*

G.P.O. *Plekhanov Prospekt 44.*

CENTRAL TELEPHONE AND TELEGRAPH OFFICE *Rustavelli Prospekt 12.*

BANK *Kirov Street 3/5.*

ART SALON *Rustaveli Street 19, next to the Tbilisi Hotel.* Handicrafts are on sale here.

GEORGIAN TEA SHOP *Rustaveli Street 20.*

SOUVENIR SHOP *Lenin Square.*

CENTRAL BOOKSHOP *Rustaveli Street 28.*

JEWELLER'S *Lenin Square 4.*

ANTIQUE SHOP *Rustaveli Street 2.*

DVORETS KNIGI BOOKSHOP *Mardzhanishvili Street 5.*

DEPARTMENT STORE *Mardzhanishvili Street 7.*

FILLING STATION *On the right embankment of River Kura.*

REPAIR STATIONS *Saburtalinskaya Street and Plekhanov Prospekt.*

CAMPING SITE *At the entrance to the town by the 196/11 km milestone.* A little farther on is a motel and a filling and service station.

Intourist is planning to open to foreign motorists the road from Tbilisi to Yerevan via Kazakh and Lake Sevan.

IGOYETI

This village stands on the bank of the River Lekhuri.

TSITELI-SAGDARI CHURCH. This mediaeval church is to the left of the main road.

SAMATAVISI *A small village 2 km (1¼ miles) to the right of the main road.* It has an 11th century church with beautiful stone carving and frescoes, and also the remains of the 11th century Bishop's Palace.

GORI

Population: 45,000 (1964)

The town stands on the left bank of the River Kura, at the point where it is joined by the River Leakhvi and the River Lidzhudi. There is a fruit cannery and textile manufacture here. The local white wine, Atenuri, can only be drunk in Gori as it travels badly. There is also a pedagogical institute in the town.

The ruins of the castle of Goris-Tsikhe stand above Gori on a hill. The name Gori itself means "mountain" in Georgian. The castle, which dates from the 12th century, contains a church. In 1123 it was inhabited by refugee Armenians. In the 16th century the Turks captured it, and then it continually changed hands between the Turks, the Georgians and the Persians until it was taken by Russia in 1801. If was restored in 1900, but suffered considerably in the earthquake of 1920.

Near the fortress is the Armenian church of St. Stephan, founded in the 12th century and restored in the 17th century.

SYNAGOGUE *Cheluskintsev Street.*

LOCAL MUSEUM *Stalin Street.*

STALIN'S HOUSE *Open 9–6; closed on Tuesdays.* Stalin was born in Gori on 21st December, 1879, and spent his childhood here until 1894. His father, Vissarion Dzhugashvili, was a local cobbler. The museum was opened in 1939, and is in the form of a special pavilion which was built to protect the hut where Stalin was born. All the surrounding buildings were demolished.

HISTORICAL-ETHNOGRAPHICAL MUSEUM

STALIN MONUMENT *Stalin Square.* This is now the only big monument to Stalin in the whole of the Soviet Union.

BUST OF CHAVCHAVADZE *Chavchavadze Street.* Chavchavadze was a Georgian writer.

DRAMA THEATRE *Chavchavadze Street.*

INTOURIST HOTEL AND RESTAURANT *Stalin Street 20; tel: 37-44.*

KARTLI HOTEL AND RESTAURANT *Lenin Street.*

DEPARTMENT STORE *Stalin Street.*

GIFT SHOP *Stalin Street.*

FILLING STATION AND REPAIR STATION *At the entrance to the town, coming in from Tbilisi.*

★

GORIS-DZHAVRI (Cross of Gori) MONASTERY *3 km (2 miles) from the town centre, on a hill above the right bank of the River Kura.*

The 16th century church is dedicated to Saint George. The legend of its foundation is as follows:

Queen Tamara was hunting in this region when her favourite falcon flew away and settled on the top of the mountain where the monastery now stands. In dismay she asked that the man in her party who loved her best should swim across the River Kura and recapture the bird for her. The river was in full spring flood and the young men hesitated to show their loyalty, but at last one plunged in. He reached the opposite bank, caught the falcon and began to swim back again, but halfway across he got into difficulties and it seemed that he would drown. Tamara prayed to Saint George for help, promising to found a monastery if her prayer were answered. Apparently it was, for she later founded the monastery on the mountain top where her falcon had alighted.

At the end of the last century it was a tradition of the cathedral that those women who wanted either a husband or a child should put an iron chain weighing more than 50 kg (more than a hundredweight) around their necks, and if they were then able to walk around the building three times their misfortunes would be over.

UPLIS-TSIKHE CAVE TOWN. *7 km (4½ miles) from Gori along a very bad road.* Also known as the Troglodite Town, this was inhabited before the time of Christ. Some scientists say it belongs to the period of Persian and Parthian influence in Georgia. The name means "the castle of Uplis"; Uplis was the son of the founder of Mtskheta, and was said to be a direct descendant of Japhet. The caves of this town rise up in tiers, and streets, a market place, swimming pools and houses of different sizes can be recognised. Some of the caves closely resemble churches. Also underground is the so-called Palace of Tamara; there is no evidence that Tamara ever lived there, but the Georgians are fond of calling anything unusually splendid after her.

ATENSKI SIONI (ATHENIAN SION) CATHEDRAL *11 km (7 miles) from Gori along a very bad road.* The cathedral was built by Bagrat IV in the 11th century and is considered to be one of the best examples of the architecture of its time. The village of Ateni stands on the site of a town founded in the 2nd century B.C. On the rocks on the other side of the ravine can be seen the ruins of the Sativis-Tsikhe Monastery, standing 274 m (900 ft) above the River Tana. The walls of the cathedral in this monastery are covered with carving, and have marble columns and good frescoes.

URBNISI

The names of this village and of the next, Ruisi, probably derives from "urbs" and "rus". Two villages were so called by the Romans when they occupied the plateau above.

✿ The Byzantine style church dates from the 5th or 6th century.

RUISI

This village lies a little to the right of the main road.

✿ In the village an ancient church, restored in the 15th century, can be seen.

ARADYETI

✿ Ishkhe-Byelis-Tzikhe Castle dates from the 17th century.

KHASHURI

✿ HOTEL

EATING HOUSE.

From this village a good road leads for 29 km (18 miles) to the spa of Borzhomi, and from there on to the mountain resort of Bakuriani.

SURAMI

High up on a cliff are the ruins of a fortress which, as legend tells us, was built about 200 B.C. and belonged to Prince Tavis. Many difficulties were encountered during its construction, as each night all the work of the previous day collapsed into the abyss below. It was then recognised that the wall was bewitched, and a Persian magician was called in to give advice. He said that the wall would not stand until the only son of a widow had been buried alive beneath it. Accordingly, one unfortunate Tsurab was found and buried in the foundations, and after that the wall stood firm. Its surface, however, never dried and was said to be wet with the wretched widow's tears. There is a Georgian folk song about the woman's plight.

✿ ARMENIAN CHURCH *Internatsionalnaya Street.*

SYNAGOGUE *Internatsionalnaya Street.*

✿ LENIN MONUMENT

✿ PARK

✿ HOTEL *Lenin Street.*

UGELTEKHIR (Pass) RESTAURANT *Lenin Street.*

✿ G.P.O. *Lenin Street.*

There are stalactite caves in the vicinity of the town.

After Surami the road climbs gradually and then alternative roads lead to a choice of two passes. Rykotsky Pass (996 m/3267 ft) is the better choice. At the top is the Iveriya (the old name for Georgia) Restaurant. The other road crosses Surami Pass (949 m/3113 ft), and the roads join again at the village of Dzirula.

SHORAPANI

Shorapani stands at the confluence of the River Kvirila and the River Dzirula.

It is said that the remains of the old fortress on the mountain top date back to the 3rd century B.C., as did the neighbouring town which has since vanished without trace.

ZESTAPHONI

Known until 1921 as Kvirili, Zestaphoni stands on the River Kvirila, a swift-flowing tributary of the River Rioni.

Here there is an experimental farm where American vine stock was introduced for the first time to combat parasitic diseases. The whole of the Trans-Caucasian vine-growing industry benefitted from the experiments.

✿ GEORGIAN DRAMA THEATRE *Lenin Square.*

✿ ORDZHONIKIDZE PARK

STADIUM

✿ HOTEL AND RESTAURANT *Lenin Street 65.*

✿ G.P.O. *Lenin Street.*

DEPARTMENT STORE *Lenin Street.*

✿ FILLING STATION *On the right side of the main road.*

KUTAISI

Population: 128,000 (1959)

Kutaisi is located on either side of the River Rioni, at the place where it leaves a ravine to flow over the Colkhidian Plateau. There is an excellent panoramic view from the height of the right bank where remains of one of the world's most ancient cities can still be seen. Some archaeologists are of the opinion that Kutaisi was in ancient times the town of Ea or Kitea, residence of the legendary King Aietes of Colchis who owned the Golden Fleece and whose daughter was Medea. With its great age of more than 3000 years, it is five centuries older than Rome itself and the classical geographers wrote of its importance. To start with the town was in the colony of Miletus, and then in the 6th century B.C. it became the capital of the ancient empire of Colchis. It stood in the most beautiful and fertile part of the country, on the cross road of three important trade routes,—one from Iberia (the old name of Georgia), one from the south and one from the Black Sea coast. Later it became the capital of Imeretia and the residence of the king.

In the time of the Eastern Roman Empire this territory was known by the name of Lazica and was nominally a dependant of the Greek emperors. The fortress was known as Ukhinerioni. At the beginning of the 6th century Imeretia was for about forty years the battlefield for the forces of Emperor Justinian and the Persian Shah Hozroi. In the first part of the 7th century was devastated by the Arabs and only recovered when it was united by Bagrat III (975–1014). Tbilisi at the time remained in enemy hands and so Kutaisi became the political and administrative centre and the capital of the whole of Georgia. It retained its position until 1122 when Tbilisi was finally recaptured. David the Builder transferred the capital from Kutaisi to Tbilisi and at the same time he founded the Gelati Monastery at Kutaisi. Bagrat III, Bagrat IV, David the Builder and the famous Queen Tamara each in the period of their reigns did much to rebuild the country, and a great deal of there construction remains to be seen. Kutaisi has suffered much but the ruins of towers, churches, bridges and chapels in the

Kutaisi region mostly belong to this time.

In 1510 the Turks burnt the town and the monastery too, again they seized the Kutaisi fortress in 1666. Only in 1770 Russian and Imeretian forces under Solomon I liberated Kutaisi from the Turks who had held it for 102 years. Kutaisi became an important trade centre, and when in 1810 Imeretia was joined to Russia it became the seat of the governor. After 1840 trade increased rapidly and industry began to develop. In the middle of the 19th century it was the centre of the revolutionary movement in the southern Caucasus.

Today Kutaisi is the second most important cultural centre in Georgia. There is the Tsulukidze Pedagogical Institute, an agricultural institute, the Balanchivadze Musical School and the Chavchavadze Library, founded in 1894 and now possessing 270,000 books. Kutaisi has inspired many Georgian writers, both by its beauty and its heroic past. The town's industrial position is also second only to Tbilisi. There is a lorry and bus factory and an electro-mechanical factory and mining equipment, silk cloth, chemicals and food products are also manufactured. The market is interesting as people from the farthest parts of the Caucasus gather there.

Part of the ruined walls of *Kutaisi fortress* can be seen on the high right bank of the Rioni. The road up to the top starts from Tsepnoy (Chain) Bridge. Here, in the old town, is a most impressive and ancient cathedral built by Bagrat III in 1003. King Bagrat paid great attention to its construction which was intended to symbolise the unification of Georgia. It was built in the shape of a cross. For seven centuries visitors marvelled at its splendour. It was partly ruined in 1691 during the Turkish attack and was damaged again in the war of 1770. Now some restoration work is in progress to prevent further dilapidation.

SAINT GEORGE'S CHURCH *Asatiani Street.* This church built in 1890 is not far from the cathedral; it is open for service.

At MTSVANEKVAVILA, *not far from the fortress but on the left bank of the river*, is a well preserved 17th century tower and a number of churches, mostly dating from 17th–20th centuries. Among them however are the remains of a church built in 1013. Since 1956 the cemetery here has been reorganised as a burial place (pantheon) for prominent people.

TSULUKIDZE GARDEN, *on the left bank of the Rioni*, was the garden of Alexander III of Imeretia. The royal buildings stood here, but only one has survived. It is famous for its hall called *Okros Chardakhi* (Golden Tent) which was built in the 17th century and was completely reconstructed in the 1830's. It was used for receiving ambassadors, holding feasts and other important occasions. In the Garden is a great plane tree, its trunk 10·6 m (35 ft) in circumference. According to tradition, the Imeretian kings conducted trials and executions beneath its branches. Also in the Garden is a monument to Tsulukidze (see below, Tsulukidze Museum) by Tvavadze and Merabishvili which was unveiled in 1935.

SAINT PETER AND PAUL CATHEDRAL *Kommisarov Street 26.* The Cathedral is open for service.

TAVAR-ANGELOGIS (Archangel) CHURCH *Tkibuli Street.* This was built in the 16th century.

ROMAN CATHOLIC CHURCH *Telmann Street.* The building has now been put to secular use, but its very existence points to the fact that the foreign colony here must have been of considerable size.

SYNAGOGUES *Shaumyan Street.* These are located in the old quarter of the town which has long been inhabited by Jews. The synagogues stand close to each other. They were built about 150 years ago and are in good condition.

HISTORY AND ETHNOGRAPHY MUSEUM *Tbilisi Street 1. Open 10–6; closed on Tuesdays.* In the museum's rich collection are 10th–13th century icons; some of them of gold and silver came from Gelati Monastery as did many manuscript books. There are 700 manuscripts dating from 11th to 19th centuries and including an 11th century gospel. Other items include armour and old musical instruments.

TSULUKIDZE MUSEUM *Tsulukidze Street 21. Open 10–6; closed on Mondays.* Kutaisi was the birthplace of Alexander Tsulukidze (1876–1905), a Georgian revolutionary. The Museum is located in the house that used to be his home. The monument to him that stands in the museum courtyard is by Nikoladze.

LENIN MONUMENT *Lenin Square.* The 6·40 m (21 ft) bronze figure by Merabishvili was unveiled in 1958.

1905 REVOLUTION OBELISK *Town Garden.* This was unveiled in 1955 to mark the 50th anniversary of the 1905 revolution. It stands on the place where demonstrators clashed with the Cossacks.

KIKVIDZE MONUMENT *Avtozavodskaya Street.* Vasili Kikvidze (1895–1919) was a hero of the civil war. Unveiled in 1959, the 2·5 m (8 ft) bronze figure is by Mizandari and Nikoladze.

MESKHISHVILI DRAMA THEATRE *Rustaveli Square.* The theatre was founded in 1861.

PUPPET THEATRE *Revolutsiya Street 11.*

OPEN-AIR THEATRE *In the park.*

PARK *On the banks of the Rioni.*

CENTRAL STADIUM *Engels Street.*

TBILISI HOTEL AND RESTAURANT *Tsulukidze Street; tel: 26-29.*

KUTAISI HOTEL AND RESTAURANT *Rustaveli Street 5; tel: 42-77.*

GELATI RESTAURANT *On the left of the main road, at the 46/204 km milestone.*

IMERETIA RESTAURANT *Rustaveli Street 15.*

TSKHALTSITELA (Red river) CAFE *On the right, on the way into town.*

G.P.O. *Kirov Street 64.*

BANK *Pushkin Street 18.*

DEPARTMENT STORE *Paliashvili Street 18.*

JEWELLER'S *Near the market.*

MARKET *Paliashvili Pereulok 2.*

FILLING STATIONS *Beside the main road both as you enter and as you leave the town.*

★

GEGUTI *To the south of the town, near Rioni Railway Station.* Ruins of Geguti Palace which was built during the reign of Georgi III (1156–1184) as a winter and hunting palace. It had twenty-one rooms. Excavations have been going on since 1953.

RIONI POWER STATION *5 km (3 miles) from the town.* The Rioni was dammed here in 1934 and the very attractive reservoir is known locally as the Sea of Kutaisi. The power station has a capacity of 50,000 kilowatts. Two more power stations were completed in 1956 in the nearby village of Gumati, and they have a joint capacity of 66,500 kilowatts.

SATAPLIA *lies 6 km (3½ miles) to the south-west of the town and is accessible by road.* The name means "honey-bearing" and refers to the wild bees that nest in the hills there. Sataplia is a reservation of 500 hectares (1250 acres), famed since 1933 when a local scientist, Peter Chabukiani, found traces of dinosaurs here. There is a huge karst cave, about 600 m (650 yds) long, with stalactites and stalagmites; another, with an open arch, is called Yazom Grotto. In 1914 some tools belonging to Paleolithic Man were found in the Sakazhia Cave.

MOTSAMETA (Martyr) MONASTERY *6 km (3½ miles) to the east of Kutaisi, standing upon a cliff above the right bank of the Tskhaltsitela (red river). The road is not very good, but one can get there by train and it is only two stops from Kutaisi.*

The story of the monastery's foundation tells how in the middle of the eighth century there were in the royal house of Mkheidze two princely brothers called David and Constantine. They ruled this territory and were famed for their nobility and courage. When they were attacked by the Arabs they and their army defeated the vanguard of the invaders, but later fell before the main force. The Arab emir, surprised by their youth, bravery and uncommon beauty, offered them their freedom and honour if they would accept the Mohammedan faith. This they refused to do and so they were tortured and then with heavy stones around their necks they were thrown into the Rioni. The river cast the bodies up upon the shore where they were found by a peasant. He laid the brothers on his bullock cart and then gave the bullocks freedom to wander. The beasts made their way up the hills to where the monastery now stands. The princes were buried there and in 1040 the monastery itself was founded, while the sacred remains were the object of pilgrimage of the faithful.

GELATI MONASTERY *7 km (4½ miles) from Kutaisi on the road to Tkibuli and accessible by car. Open 10–6; closed on Tuesdays.*

The monastery was founded in 1106 on the left of the Tskhaltsitela river by King David II of Georgia (1089–1125), often referred to as David the Builder. He built the monastery in gratitude for his first victories and he was later canonised by the Georgian Church. From the day of its foundation King David and his successors always cared for the monastery and gave many presents of gold, silver and rare manuscripts so that at one time it was richest in the Caucasus. The monastery complex is a good example of Byzantine and Georgian architecture of the Georgian Golden Age, although much has crumbled away owing to the softness of the sandstone blocks used in the construction. Inside the thick wall are three churches, the main one dedicated to the Nativity of the Virgin. It is from this that the monastery itself takes its name, the Georgian word *genati* having changed to Gelati. Other buildings include the belltower and the refectory which until the 16th century was the academy hall.

King David was well versed in both Christian and Islamic culture and was at the same time a champion of Georgian culture. Besides founding Gelati, he assisted older Georgian monasteries, both in Georgia and abroad. When the monastery was founded, King David invited scholars from Georgia and from other countries too to come and join the brotherhood and he endowed it well. The academy soon became a centre of learning and art; histories, philosophy and scientific works were written here and almost all the most important literature in the world at that time was translated into Georgian. The mosaics and the work in precious metals created here were noted for their beauty. Even in the time of David the Builder the academy was called the New Athens and the New Jerusalem. The academy school was run on the lines of similar schools in Byzantium and geometry, arithmetic, music, rhetoric, philosophy and astronomy were taught. The monastery was sacked and burned by the Turks in 1510 but was soon rebuilt and restored and became the residence of the Patriarch of Western Georgia. The academy however did not survive, and the academy hall was rebuilt as a refectory. In 1759 the monastery was again pillaged, this time by the Lezgins, and the cathedral was burned again. However it was rebuilt and the monastery tradition continued until Gelati was closed in 1923.

Construction of the *Church of the Nativity of the Virgin* took nineteen years (1106–1125). It was consecrated in 1126 on the order of King David's son, Demetre. It is built in the shape of a cross and measures 29·2 m (96 ft) long, 20·2 m (66 ft) wide and 36·3 m (119 ft) high. The 13th–17th century frescoes inside the cathedral show the saints and portraits of various Georgian kings including on the north wall one painted in the 16th century which is the only surviving portrait of David the Builder himself; he is depicted as a giant dressed as a king with a crown and carrying a model of the church in his left hand. At the corner of the apse is a large 13th century mosaic of the Virgin and the Archangels Gabriel and Michael. Gelati Monastery was the burial place of both the Georgian and the Imeretian kings. It is believed that the famous Queen Tamara who ruled from 1184 to 1212 is buried on the right side of the cathedral. On the left are buried King Bagrat IV, Solomon I and others. *David the Builder's grave* is in the two-storey building, a combined chapel and entrance gate, which stands to the south of the main church. His tomb is covered with a stone slab bearing the inscription in Georgian:

"This is my resting place for all eternity
And I would not wish for anything more."

The slab of stone was set in the floor so that all who passed might tread it underfoot; it is said that this was David's own wish and a sign of his humility. Another of his epitaphs reads: "There was a time when seven kings were guests at my feasts; and I was so mighty that I swept the Persians, the Turks and the Arabs away from my borders and let the fish of one sea into another—but being so mighty, still I lie here with my hands folded upon my chest."

St. George's Church stands to the east of the main church and measures 11 m (36 ft) long, 5·5 m (18 ft) wide and 21·4 m (70 ft) high. Built in the 13th century, it was damaged in 1510, when the main church was burned by the Turks, but Bagrat III restored them both and he and his wife are buried here. The frescoes are of the 16th and 17th centuries and Bagrat III's portrait is on the south wall.

St. Nicholas's Church is to the west of the main church. It was built in the 14th century and has two storeys. It is 8·5 m (28ft) long and 6·5 m (21ft) wide. The belltower dates from the 12th–14th centuries; there is a spring of water under it. To the west of St. Nicholas's are the ruins of the *academy building* founded in the 12th century. It is roofless but inside the 10 m (33 ft) walls the stone benches remain. The other buildings in the compound are of the 19th and 20th centuries. Outside the monastery walls, near the eastern entrance, is a church over a spring; it was rebuilt in 1903. To the north-east are the ruins of the *Sokhasteri* (Hermitage).

TSKHALTUBO *is 12 km (7½ miles) by road to the north-west of Kutaisi.* The name of this spa means "warm water". It is said that once, long ago, an old shepherd stopped to rest beside an unknown stream. He bathed his feet as he sat there, and enjoyed the surprising warmth of the water. When at last he got up to continue on his way, he was amazed that all the aches and tiredness to which he had long been accustomed had gone from his legs. He returned as quickly as he could to his village to tell his story and the fame of the water soon spread far and wide. This may be only a legend but the collections of crutches and discarded walking sticks left behind by patients that have been cured at the various sanatoria here is proof of the water's powers.

The first written reference to Tskhaltubo dates from the 12th century. In ancient times it was a royal bathing place and many came to benefit from the water. Some thought that the longer they spent in the water, the quicker the cure, and they settled there for the night, comfortably warm and tied to a low hanging tree so that they would not drown or drift downstream while they slept.

Although it has been known for centuries, it only became a proper spa in the 1930's. The place is located in the picturesque valley of the Tskhaltubo river, surrounded by hills and mountains and protected by them from the wind. It is only 70 km (42 miles) from the Black Sea coast. The river now flows through two canals which meet again near the railway station and then it flows in the Gubis-Tskhali. The river is dammed not far from its source and forms a reservoir of 5 hectares (12½ acres). Visitors come here all the year round, but the best time is October and November. The winter is mild. The water maintains a steady temperature of 33–35°C (92–96°F) summer and winter because the river is fed by many warm springs which flow straight into it. The chemical content of the water is also constant; it contains rodon and nitrogen and is slightly radio-active (from 3 to 30 Maché Units) and is recommended for the cure of rheumatism, disorders of the metabolism, gynaecological diseases and diseases of the circulatory and nervous systems. Since 1965 Intourist have organised special courses of treatment lasting 20 days at Tskhaltubo. There are a number of sanatoria and bath-houses here.

THEATRE

THE PARK of 80 hectares (200 acres) contains some subtropical flora. There is an open-air stage.

TBILISI HOTEL AND RESTAURANT

CAFES

SAMTREDIA

The name means "dovecote"; in olden times Samtredia was frequented by royalty as a famous hunting ground for pigeons, which were overrunning the region.

Samtredia is the capital of Imeretia, which was once a dependant of Georgia, ruined several times by the Turks. From the 16th century onwards the tsars of Imeretia asked for protection from Christian Russia against the Turks and when Georgia was joined to Russia Imeretia's fate was also decided. In 1804 the last king, Solomon II, signed an act of subservience to Russia; he abdicated in 1810 and Imeretia then belonged entirely to Russia.

LENIN MONUMENT *In front of the railway station.*

THEATRE *Rustaveli Street.*

PARK

STADIUM

SAMTREDIA HOTEL AND RESTAURANT *Rustaveli Street 19.*

G.P.O. *Rustaveli Street.*

BANK *Telia Street.*

FILLING STATION *Across the river, on the way out of town.*

ZUGDIDI

Population: 32,000 (1959)

Zugdidi is the capital of Mingrelia, which in ancient times was a part of Colchis, and then part of Georgia, from which it separated in 1442. For about 400 years it was officially independent, although for most of that period it was subservient to Turkey, and had to pay considerable tributes in money and slaves. Only in 1774, with the peace treaty between Russia and Turkey did this relationship come to an end. The owner of Mingrelia, Prince Dadiyan, became a vassal of Russia in 1804, but the territory was officially united with Russia in 1867.

The Mingrels belong to the Georgian tribe and their language, which is a dialect of Georgian, is in fact two-thirds Georgian; they have long been under the cultural influence of Georgia. In appearance they are said to be the most beautiful people of the Caucasus; the French geographer, Elise Reclus (1830–1905) said, "One day's walk

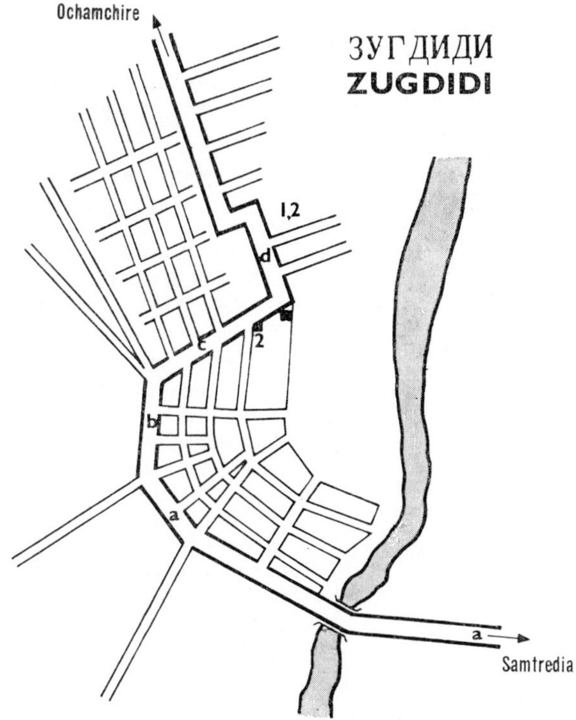

1 and 2 Hotel and Restaurant 2 Restaurant

a Sukhumskoye chaussée
b Zhdanova ul.
c Teatralnaya ul.
d Oktyabrskaya ul.

around Zugdidi or any other small town near the River Rioni is sufficient to prove that there is no other branch of the human race which has more beautiful representatives".

Local industry produces, among other things, paper, tea and wine.

MATSKOVRISKARI CHURCH *Rustaveli Street.* This church was built in the 15th century.

LOCAL MUSEUM (the Central Mingrelian Museum) *Oktyabr Street 2, on the territory of the old palace. Open 10.30–4.30; closed on Mondays.* The museum is located in the building of the palace of David Dadyani which was built in the 19th century. Nearby stands a church built in 1830 and also the ruins of another palace which was destroyed in 1854. Another of the palace buildings, standing near the museum, has fine wood carvings on the second floor. The way into the museum from the main road is through two large gate posts with the sign "Restaurant".

LENIN MONUMENT *In the boulevard beside Oktyabr Street.*

STADIUM

ODISHI (the ancient name for Mingrelia) HOTEL AND RESTAURANT *Oktyabr Street.*

ZUGDIDI RESTAURANT *On the top of the hill.*

RESTAURANT *In the park near the museum, Oktyabr Street.*

G.P.O. *Oktyabr Street.*

FILLING STATION *Beside the road that leads out of town.*

ILORI

At the time when the Greeks were influential on the coast, Ilori was a town of considerable size and importance.

THE CHURCH OF SAINT GEORGE OF ILORI. The church was built in the 11th century and restored in the 19th century. At one time the church's special feast-day was in November, and each year a bull appeared in the churchyard at this time. The bull was killed and the meat remained fresh the whole year round, and was beneficial in the curing of various diseases.

OCHEMCHIRE

Situated on the low bank of the River Galizga, near the river mouth, Ochemchire is a natural port and trading centre. In the 1860's it was the winter residence of the last owner of Abkhazia, Prince Mikhail Shervashidze, before his exile to Russia in 1864.

IRTSKHAKU (Abkhazia) RESTAURANT *On the embankment.*

FILLING STATION *On the road leading to Sukhumi.*

★

Near Ochemchire is a rubber plantation, and from the 834/550 km milestone a road leads down to a good sandy beach.

BEDIA. 13 km (8 miles) from Ochemchire along a very bad road off the Achigvare highway in the village of Agu-Bedia, once the residence of kings and bishops, is the ancient cathedral of Bedia. It was built in the 10th century by King Bagrat III (975–1014), who is himself buried here. Inside are the remains of frescoes, and the outside walls bear a pattern of leaves and crosses. On the west side of the cathedral lie 13th–14th century ruins, but there is no record to tell what the building was.

RESTAURANT

MOKVI *21 km (13 miles) from Ochemchire.* After crossing River Mokwa, take the right turn to Chyli. The road is bumpy and there is a ford to cross.

A large cathedral founded by the West Georgian King Leon II (955–967) and dedicated to Our Lady stands here. It has been restored several times, and the stone gate in front of it was erected at a later date. Like Dranda, Mokvi was in times past the residence of a bishop; it was also the birthplace of Prince Shervashidze, who restored the cathedral, and of his wife and son. The Prince died in 1865 while in exile in Voronezh, but he is buried here. His son, Georgi, who was a writer, died here in 1918.

From the road between Ochemchire and Sukhumi there is a good view of the mountains, and Mount Elbruz is sometimes visible.

KELASURI. *On the road to Sukhumi and approaching the town is the village of Kelasuri,* near which there are interesting caves, and also a wall which once ran for 160 km (100 miles). The construction of the wall was begun in the 6th century but it continued for many hundreds of years. The section between the River Kelasuri and the River Mokva is now in the best state of preservation. In other places there are simply the remains of the wall and sometimes only the towers; some of these are 35–50 m (40–55 yd) apart and some 200–250 m (220–275 yd). In many places the wall is 2 m (7 ft) high and 1·5 m (5 ft 6 in.) thick. Some historians think it was built by the ancient Greeks or by Justinian II. The wall closed all the mountain roads and protected the southern half of Abkhazia and other regions of Western Georgia from the peoples of the northern Caucasus, and was at the same time used as a defence wall against enemies from the sea.

DRANDA

Dranda lies on the bank of the River Kodori.

The monastery dates from the foundation of the cathedral, one of the oldest churches in Abkhazia, in the 6th century. Dranda used to be the residence of the bishops. In 1871 the monks from the Novi-Afon Monastery on the Black Sea Coast restored the cathedral and planned also to restore the rest of the monastery, but the buildings were badly damaged by the Turks in 1877 to 1878. The monastery was re-opened in 1883, and in 1886 the cathedral was again restored and consecrated in the name of the Virgin. During the last restoration the frescoes were whitewashed. The dome was reconstructed and raised in 1900, and its present height is 21 m (70 ft). The cathedral, which still preserves the shape of an ancient Byzantine type church, is 20·5 m (67 ft 6 in.) wide and 31 m (103 ft) long.

The monastery is surrounded by caves, and underground tunnels have been built into the hill beneath it; it is said that all these were constructed in ancient times by the monks to protect them from their enemies. There were still 300 monks in the monastery before the revolution, but it has been put to secular use, and visitors are not at present allowed inside.

About 2 km (1¼ miles) away from the monastery is a small stone church. This was a hermitage belonging to Dranda and dedicated to Saint Panteleomon and Feodor Stratilata. The church which stands on the banks of the River Mali Kotor, was founded in the 7th or 8th century and restored in 1892.

 EATING HOUSE

GULRIPSHI

This is a pleasant place to stop for a picnic, with the so-called Valley of Roses near by.

SUKHUMI

Population: 80,000 (1964)

Sukhumi is the capital of the Abkhazian Autonomous Republic, which has a population of 400,000 (1959) and covers an area of 3300 sq. miles. The people of the republic are Georgians, Abkhazians and Russians.

The coastal climate is subtropical, and tobacco, tea and citrus fruits are grown, and coal and honey produced. There are also some good health resorts in the region.

Along the sea coast, on the border between the strip of coastal lowland and the inland mountainous part of the country many stalactite caves in the limestone strata are to be found. A famous cave is Abrskilova Peshchera, about 45 km (28 miles) from Sukhumi on the Ochemchire road. Its galleries have a total length of 2 km (1¼ miles) and some of the halls are up to 30–40 m (100–130 ft) in length with stalactites in the form of curtains and palm tree crowns. Its name derives from a local legend similar to the legend of Prometheus. The Gumistinskiye Caves also deserve a visit, the most interesting being Jackal Cave which is divided into three parts by its stalactites.

Abkhazia belonged in turn to Colchis, Pontus, Rome and Byzantium before gaining its independence in 756. Christianity had begun to spread here in the 5th century. In 985 Abkhazia became a part of Georgia, but later regained its independence until taken by Turkey in 1578. Russia ruled it from 1810 and following local uprisings many Abkhazians emigrated to Turkey, especially after 1864.

Sukhumi Bay lies between the River Gumista and the River Kelasuri while the town itself is crossed by the River Besleti. Behind the town Sukhumi Hill stands 201 m (660 ft) high. There is no other place on the Black Sea coast with so much sun and warmth as Sukhumi; from April until November there are sea breezes during the day and a light wind from the mountains at night. Citrus, banana, palm and eucalyptus decorate the parks and streets of the town. "The Sukhumi Valley is a corner of Spain or Sicily dropped at the foot of Old Man Caucasus", wrote Russian travellers in the 19th century. In fact it lies on the same latitude as Nice and has an average annual temperature of 15°C (59°F), and approximately 270 sunny days during the year. It is at its best in autumn, winter and spring.

When the Argonauts sailed to faraway Colchis to claim the Golden Fleece, among the travellers who went with Jason were the Dioscuri brothers, the twins Castor and Pollux. Their name comes from "Dios Kouros"—"sons of Zeus". Legend has it that the brothers founded a rich and flourishing town in Colchis, which was called Dioscuria after them. A little way out to sea, and buried beneath 5·5 m (18 ft) of mud and fine silt, the ruins of this town have lain hidden for 1500 years. It is supposed to have been robbed and ruined by Pompey's Roman legions in 65 A.D., but an acropolis, a contemporary of the Parthenon, still stands under the water. The site is under investigation and exhibits, including an ancient marble tombstone, have begun to come to the local museum.

The Romans rebuilt Sukhumi in the 2nd century B.C. on the order of Emperor Adrian, and they knew it as Sevastopolis, while the Georgians spoke of it as Tukhomi. In 1455 it became Turkish and was called Su-Khum-Kale ("water-sand-fortress"). It was annexed to Russia in 1810, but it was held by the Turks again in both 1855 and 1877. It had previously been one of the chief slave markets on the Black Sea.

Local industry now deals with tobacco, sweets and food products. There is a pedagogical institute in the town.

✿ SUKHUMI FORTRESS *By the Sea.* Possibly this fortress was founded at the time of Colchis. In 1578 the Turks built a new fortress on the remains of the old one and there was a slave market outside the walls. In the 19th and 20th centuries it was used as a prison.

KING BAGRAT FORTRESS *Chelyuskintsev Street, in the south-eastern part of Sukhumi.* The fortress was founded in the 10th or 11th century either by the Georgian King Bagrat III (965–1014) or by Bagrat IV (1027–72). Only the ruins remain now and the entrance gateway shows traces of underground tunnels.

BESLEDSKI MOST (THE VENETIAN BRIDGE) *6 km (4 miles) to the north-east of Sukhumi along the Besledski Chaussée.* The bridge was built in the 10th–12th centuries and was from that time on of certain military importance, as the ruins of a defence tower near by show. 300 m (330 yd) from the bridge on the left bank of the River Besleti are the ruins of an old church. The bridge itself is 13 m (43 ft) long and varies in width from 5–7 m (17–23 ft); it has not yet been established whether it is of Venetian or local construction.

BLAGOVESHCHENSKY (Annunciation) CATHEDRAL *Leselidze Street 59.* The cathedral was built at the end of the 19th century and was formerly a Greek church.

MONKEY COLONY *Baratashvili Street.* Founded in 1927, this research enterprise under the auspices of the U.S.S.R. Academy of Sciences is situated on the slopes of Mount Trapetsaya. By 1962 there were over 1000 monkeys in this colony, 75 per cent of which were born there, and they had reached the eighth generation. The inmates are mostly baboons and macaque monkeys. They thrive out of doors in this southern climate and eat local grown fruit for which they each have a daily spending allowance of 70–80 kopeks. They are there for medical experiments. In 1948 after 9 years of experiments on cancer, artificial sarcoma were induced. The fifty scientists at the colony work in 7 laboratories.

LOCAL MUSEUM *Lenin Street 20. Open 9–5.*

SCIENTIFIC MUSEUM

LENIN MONUMENT *In front of the House of the Government.* By Asatiani and Georgadze and unveiled in 1959.

SHOTA RUSTAVELI MONUMENT *In Rustaveli Park.* Merabishvili made this monument to the Georgian poet which was unveiled in 1939.

DMITRI GULIA MONUMENT *Lenin Street 18.* Gulia (1874–1960) was an Abkhazian poet. Rukhadze made this monument which was unveiled in 1962.

AKAKI TSERETELI MONUMENT *In Tsereteli Garden.* By Razmadze and unveiled in 1954.

ORDZHONIKIDZE MONUMENT *In Ordzhonikidze Park.* By Eshba and unveiled in 1961.

S. CHANBA MONUMENT *Pushkin Street 1.* Chanba was a local writer. Gogoberidze was responsible for this monument, unveiled in 1959.

✿ DRAMA THEATRE *Pushkin Street 1.* Built in 1952 in Georgian style, decorated with stone carving, a waterfall in a grotto and griffin fountains. On the façade are busts of Georgian representatives of the arts.

SUMMER THEATRE *Kirov Street, in the park.*

✿ DYNAMO STADIUM *Ordzhonikidze Street 33.*

BOTANICAL GARDEN *Chavchavadze Street 18.* The gardens were founded in 1840, devastated by the Turks in 1878, and restored in 1894. There are four ponds for water plants, and many of them, including the Blue Water Lily, the Water Poppy and the giant Victoria Regia with leaves 2·5 m (8 ft) in diameter, are subtropical. The Indian Lotus is also grown, and the greenhouses contain many rare tropical plants and cacti.

PARK *Near Frunze Street.*

ORDZHONIKIDZE PARK *Kirov Street.*

SHOTA RUSTAVELI PARK *Teatralnaya Street.* There is a monument to Shota Rustaveli and the many palm trees include Blue Palms.

PARK ON SUKHUMI HILL *A road leads up to the carpark at the top.* The Amza (moon) Restaurant, which has a good view, is reached by a wide flight of steps.

The best *bathing beaches* are 1 km (½ miles) from town and reached by either car or motor boat. The Intourist beach has sand and shingle.

ABKHAZIA HOTEL AND RESTAURANT *Frunze Street 2.* Built in 1937, this is now an Intourist hotel. Tel: 33-11 and 3-91.

RITSA HOTEL *Rustaveli Prospekt 34.*

TKVARCHELI HOTEL *Lenin Street 1.*

ARAGVI RESTAURANT *Mir Prospekt 67.*

RITSA RESTAURANT *Lenin Street 2.*

KAVKAZ RESTAURANT *Frunze Street 2.*

PSOU RESTAURANT *Tbilisskoye Chaussée 15.*

AMZA (Moon) RESTAURANT *On the top of Sukhumi Hill.*

AMRA (Sun) RESTAURANT *Rustaveli Prospekt, by the sea.*

SHASHLIK BAR *In the open air, about 10 km (6 miles) along the Sukhumi Military Road.*

G.P.O. *Mir Prospekt 92.*

BANK *Lenin Street 14.*

DEPARTMENT STORE *Mir Prospekt 52.*

BOOKSHOP *Mir Prospekt 52.*

JEWELLER'S *Lenin Street 1.*

MARKET *Tarkhnishvili Street 7.*

FILLING STATIONS *Beside the road, both on the way into town and on the way out.*

SINOP MOTEL *1 km (½ mile) from Sukhumi along the Tbilisskoye Chaussée; near the road, among tropical and subtropical trees.* Eating house, carwash and service station. 100 m (100 yds) from the exit gate is the Medicinal Beach with carpark, a café and a shop.

★

A motor road is now under construction, linking Sukhumi with Pyatigorsk over the mountains.

ESHERI

There are dolmens (ancient tombs) to be seen near the road at this point.

ESHERA RESTAURANT *In the ravine.* This is a very modern establishment, and is one of the best restaurants on the coast.

NOVYI-AFON

Novyi-Afon stands near the sea on the River Psyrtskha. The bathing season here lasts for 6 or 7 months.

The ancient Greek colony here was called Nycopsia or Anacopia. The Romans were here in 2 A.D., and the remains of their constructions can be seen on Iverskaya Hill (350 m/1149 ft) which is a favourite walk for tourists. On the slope of the hill is a Byzantine wall with a tower, and on the hilltop are three other towers remaining from the Roman fortress, Aspar, supposedly built in the time of Emperor Trajan. In the late 6th century Anacopia became the seat of the Byzantine rulers of Abkhazia, and on the hilltop there are also the ruins of an 8th century Christian church, restored in the 11th–12th centuries, which contains ancient sepulchres with Byzantine decorations.

At the end of the ravine of the River Psyrtskha (4 km/2½ miles) is the Monk's Cave and the remains of the church of Simon the Canaanite (10th–11th centuries); Simon was the apostle who came here with Saint Andrew. The remains of a 13th century Genoese tower stand in the grounds of the Primorsky Sanatorium down by the sea; another walk leads to Armyanskaya Ravine and to the Spusk Hill (800 m/2625 ft) where there is a two-storey house known as the Swallow's Nest.

The name Novyi-Afon means "New Athos", for the monks of Mount Athos founded a large monastery here in 1875. The imposing cathedral dedicated to the Martyr Pantilemon was built in 1900. It is built in Byzantine style and is designed to take a congregation of 3000. The height of the main dome is 40 m (131 ft), and the cathedral's length 50 m (163 ft) and its width 32 m (105 ft). The frescoes decorating the interior were completed in 1914. Since 1959 the cathedral has been open to the public from 11–5 as a museum. Also in the monastery complex is the 9th century church of Simon the Canaanite, reconstructed from the ruins of a 4th century temple; this now contains a library. Of the three other churches, the most interesting is the Iberian Chapel, from which there is an excellent view of the surrounding countryside.

Originally there were 720 monks here, and Novyi-Afon was one of the richest monasteries in Russia, being granted 14,400 hectares (36,000 acres) at the time of its foundation. After the revolution the monastery was shut down and in 1924 most of the monastery buildings were turned into sanatoria. The monks' orchards and gardens grew into the Abkhazia Farm, which possesses the largest olive grove on the coast (65 hectares/162 acres) and which was also planted out by the monks.

GOLUBOYE OZERO (Blue lake) appeared after the monks had constructed Russia's first hydro-electric station in 1912. Since then the waterfall fed by the River Psyrtskha has provided electricity for the surrounding region. The power station was reconstructed in 1935.

Novyi-Afon's attractive park contains palms, magnolias, oleanders and cypresses.

✿ PSYRTSKHA RESTAURANT *In the town centre.*

RESTAURANT *Near Swan Lake by the sea.*

MOTEL *At the 27 km milestone (from Sukhumi), among cypresses and by an olive grove.* At the motel are the Gemo Restaurant and a café.

GUDAUTA

This resort is also known as Palm Haven or Box Bay. It spreads out on the high shore of a small bay and the sandy beach, especially at the eastern end, is one of the widest and best on the Abkhazian coast.

Inland on Mount Dzishra (2634 m/8640 ft), there are rich deposits of silver and lead, and there are also mineral springs nearby. Wine, tobacco, maize and fruit are produced locally and there is a tea factory in the resort.

In 1870–71, during the mass emigration of Armenians from Turkey a large settlement was founded here, and later the Armenians were joined by Abkhanazians, Greeks and other nationalities.

✿ ORDZHONIKIDZE PARK

HOTEL

✿ MARKET

———— ★ ————

LIKHNY *5 km (3¼ miles) from Gudauta.* This village, also called Souk-Su ("cold water"), was of great historic importance for Abkhazia. It has been inhabited since 600 B.C., and until 1863 it was the seat of the Abkhazian rulers, the Shervashidzes. The ruins of their palace still exist near a sacred grove, and nearby stands a 11th century church built in Byzantine style as a copy of the church at Pitsunda. There were several attempts to build the palace itself, but all efforts were successful only after a young couple had been buried alive under the foundations. The Lime of Truth, a tree which is hundreds of years old and under which the Abkhazian nobles used to dispense justice, can be seen at Likhny.

In 1866 the place was witness to a bloody uprising when a Russian civil servant was chopped into small pieces by the local inhabitants and his other assistants and some Cossacks killed.

In the meadow in front of the palace, on the third Sunday in October, an annual harvest holiday takes place, with horseback competitions that attract the best riders in the country.

The group of 40 small houses was formerly used by Stalin's guards when they protected his house nearby. Recently they have been used to put up visiting East Europeans.

ZOLOTOI BEREG (Golden Beach) *10 km (6 miles) from Gudauta.* In spite of the implications of its name, the beach here is pebbly.

MUSSERA

Mussera lies 12 km ($7\frac{1}{2}$ miles) off the road toward the sea. The turning to the left is at the 727/423 km milestone. Mussera is in one of the loveliest parts of this region, known as the Abkhazian Switzerland. The road leads through woods of beach and oak, groves of eucalyptus and palm, citrus and tea plantations. The soil here is very porous and the atmosphere in consequence unusually dry. There is an excellent park in Mussera and from here a 3 km (2 mile) motor road runs down to the beach.

✿ CAFE

PITSUNDA

This resort is also known by the Georgian name of Bichvinta (pinegrove). The turning to it is at the 706/422 km milestone, at a village called Alahadze. The road passes eucalyptus groves, and for a few miles goes through the Monk's Avenue, planted as a penance by the monks of the local monastery.

Pitsunda is on the same latitude as Nice and has a bathing season of 4 to 5 months. The pinetrees, the good harbour and the average of 216 sunny days each year make it a very pleasant place in which to stay.

In 700 B.C. settlers from Miletus had built among other towns and settlements the "great and rich town of Pitiunt". A Greek colony settled in 500 B.C., and excavations are today in progress. The name comes from Pitus, the Greek for "pinetree"; the particular pines that grow here are Pinus Pithysa, which in the past were felled for shipbuilding because they were so straight and made such strong masts. In 100 B.C. Pitiunt, with other towns near by, fell into the hands of Mithradates the Great of Pontus. It was known as one of the rich towns of Colchis; later Pitsunda came under Roman rule and was then invaded by the Persians. In 55 A.D. Saint Andrew and Simon the Canaanite visited Pitsunda on their missionary travels, and Saint Andrew was buried here.

It was Justinian I who finally converted the inhabitants to Christianity in the 6th century, and who built the large cathedral dedicated to Saint Sophia in 551. This cathedral played an important part in local life, and was for about 1000 years the seat of the Abkhazian patriarchs, until the 15th century when Pitsunda lost its former glory under the Turks. The church was restored in 1869, and was dedicated to the Assumption of the Virgin Mary. The surrounding wall had been built earlier, in the 17th century, from the ruins of Pitiunt. The cathedral is in Byzantine style, and local legend says that within it lies the grave of Saint John the Golden-Tongued who died here during his exile in the 5th century. The acoustics of the cathedral are such that the voices of a few singers sound like a full choir. The building is now open as a museum.

There are great plans for the future of Pitsunda, and 14-storey hotels are being built in the town instead of the usual sanatoria. It is eventually expected to cater for 10,000 holidaymakers, and will serve as a model for the laying out of other resorts.

Near the cathedral stretches Lake Inkit and here begins an area of 200 hectares (500 acres) running for 7 km (4½ miles) along beside the sea which is covered by ancient flora of the tertiary period. Lake Inkit, which is the largest of the three lakes in this region, has good fishing, and nutria are successfully bred on its shores.

The poultry farm near Pitsunda has a small restaurant with good fresh products.

✿ PITSUNDA MOTEL *Close to the sea on Pitsunda Cape.* Motorists should leave the main road by an asphalted road sign-posted to the Cape, and running towards the sea. After 12 km (7½ miles) at the end of an avenue of cypresses, they will arrive at the Motel. There is a sports ground by the motel.

FILLING STATION *At the 384/363 km milestone, back on the main road.*

REPAIR STATION *By the main road, at the entrance to the town of Gagra.*

RITSA

The turning inland from the main road to Ritsa (39 km/24 miles) is at the 713/429 km milestone, at a place called Bzipi. Ritsa can be visited from May to November; but in the winter the valley is blocked with snow. Sheep and goats are taken up to seek pasture in Ritsa in the summer, and bees are also transported there by night in their hives and are taken down to the sea again in the autumn.

The river at the turning is the River Bzipi, and the ruins of old watch towers stand at this point. There is also a factory producing prefabricated building parts for use in the growing town of Pitsunda. Near the turning is a large cave where Stone Age remains were found. Down a smooth cliff near the road there runs a little stream called "Maiden's Tears"; a little farther on is a second cliff and a stream known as "Man's Tears". To the left of the road are the ruins of a 10th–12th century fortress and an 8th century Christian church.

5 km (3 miles) farther is the village of *Shota Rustaveli*, and a little farther along the road on the left stand the ruins of a 13th century watch tower.

At the 14 km milestone lies *Goluboye Ozero* (Blue lake). The lake, supplied by underwater springs, really is blue. It is over 70 m (230 ft) deep and its temperature is never higher than 7–12°C (45–54°F). After the Blue Lake, the road follows the valley of the River Geggi; the river is yellow on one side and steel-blue on the other because the waters of the Geggi and the River Upshara flow, hardly mixing, along a single river bed, just as the Black and White Aragvi rivers do in the southern Caucasus. The road zigzags up through the narrow Upsharsky Ravine (25 m/82 ft wide), where the cliffs rise to over 400 m (1312 ft) on either side. After the last climb Mount Atsetuk (2455 m/8054 ft) and Mount Agepsta (3261 m/10701 ft) can be seen from the road, their summits covered with snow.

Lake Ritsa lies 925 m (3036 ft) above sea level. It is 2·6 km (1½ miles) long, 1 km (½ mile) wide and 115 m (378 ft) deep. The water is cold, and the temperature never rises above 15°C (59°F).

The lake appeared a few hundred years ago, after a great landslide from Mount Pshegishkha (Table Mountain) had dammed the River Lashipse. The story attached to its formation is as follows:

Once upon a time there were three hunter brothers who lived in the mountains beside a gentle stream. Their names were Atsetuk, Agepsta and Pshegishkha. Every evening their lovely sister Ritsa cooked for them in the high mountain valley that they had made their home.

One day they were very late in returning, but Ritsa sang happily to herself and to the stars while she waited. Her song was heard by the bandit brothers, Geggi and Upshara, and the latter rushed away on horseback to seek the owner of the sweet voice.

On seeing her he was filled with passion, and he seized her fiercely despite her cries for help. Her plight was seen by the mountain eagle who flew off to tell her brothers. They all ran back as fast as they could, without letting Upshara know of their approach. Pshegishkha threw his shield at the intruder, but missed him and the shield blocked the stream and caused the water to rise, quickly forming a lake.

Ritsa was so filled with shame that she plunged into the lake and the waters instantly turned as clear as teardrops. In dismay her three brothers pursued Upshara, caught him, and threw him into the lake too, where he would have drowned but for the bubbling and seething of the water which cast him over the shield-dam. He rushed madly down to join his brother Geggi, tearing down trees and boulders on his way; but Ritsa's three brothers turned to stone and still watch over the sparkling waters of the lake.

✿ Ritsa Hotel and Restaurant

Shashlik Bar *Across the lake, by motor boat.*

Motel. The buildings of this motel are interesting, being built in the style used by the boyars (Russian aristocrats) up till the 17th century.

Eating House

✿ Filling Station and Service Station.

From the lake, beside which Stalin had a country house, the road runs for 16 km (10 miles) along the valley of the River Lashipse until this river joins the valley of the River Avadhara, 1600 m (5250 ft) above sea level and containing mineral springs. A new spa called Avadhara is developing here.

GAGRA

This resort is located on a narrow strip of coastland, and at this point the mountains, which are of porous limestone, full of gorges and caves, come down very close to the sea. Some of the peaks rise to 2750 m (9000 ft). Gagra is the warmest place on the eastern coast of the Black Sea; roses bloom in the winter and the trees are nearly always green. From May till November the sea is between 16 and 23°C (61–73°F). The beach is of shingle with some sandy places. Thanks to the climate, experiments are being made with the cultivation of cacao and the first 700 trees were expected to yield their first crop in 1965.

This spot has long been known as a fortified place. In 600 B.C. it went by the name of Triglit, and its fate was closely linked with that of Rome and Greece, and later with Genoa. Gagra was then under Turkish rule, as was most of the Black Sea coast, until it was taken by Russia in 1830. It began to develop as a resort in 1901 when Prince Alexander Oldenburgsky decided to popularise it. In a short time hotels, a quay, and other tourist facilities were constructed, and the Prince built himself a palace which can still be seen.

Today there are about 30 sanatoria, mostly located on the steep slopes of the mountains. Paths, avenues and steps join them to the Marine Park, which runs for 3 km (2 miles) beside the sea, and covers 14 hectares (35 acres). Many of the trees and shrubs are subtropical and there are statues, fountains and an artificial lake with black and white swans in the park. At the eastern end of the park is a semi-circular colonnade and a carpark. To the west of the park the little River Gagripsh runs into the sea. In the grounds of the Zhoekvara Sanatorium are the remains of a 6th–7th century church. Gagra's plantation of cork oak was transplanted from Africa in the first half of the 19th century. The trees have now reached a height of 30 m (100 ft).

There are many pleasant walks in the vicinity. The ravine of the River Tsikherva, at the beginning of which there is a two-storey cave, is 3 km (2 miles) away. It is about 8 km (5 miles) to the picturesque ravine of the River Zhoekvara which is surrounded by cliffs, and has two waterfalls. By the road are the ruins of a watchtower known as the Marlinsky Tower. Another walk of about 10 km (6 miles) leads to a grotto with a spring in the ravine of the River Gagripsh; the path has a good view of the sea and goes through beechwoods.

Gagripsh (Beauty of Gagra) Hotel and Restaurant. It is said locally that this three-storey hotel was built without a nail.

Holodnaya Rechka Motel. The motel is 8 km (5 miles) from Gagra, inland from the main road; it has a cinema, a rest room, baths, showers, a shop, a post office, and an international telephone call box. There is also an open carpark, garage, service station, carwash and filling station. The motel is near the sea and has its own beach, and it is 70 km (43½ miles) from here to Lake Ritsa.

★

New Gagra is near Gagra. There is a big market, many small shops, a hotel and a filling station in the town.

Gagra Mountain Resort. A cable-car railway links the seashore with the mountain resort 5½ km (3½ miles) inland as the crow flies. A 28 km (17 miles) motor road is under construction.

GANTIADI

The ruins of a 5th–6th century church can be seen in this village. Motorists should turn towards the sea from the main road.

Motel. The motel is near the sea among eucalyptus trees, and has an eating house and showers and carpark. There is good bathing from June to October.

LESELIDZE

Camping Site

VESYOLOYE

Druzhba (Friendship) Restaurant

★

Camping Site *At the 416/331 km milestone.*

Shashlik Bar *At the 419/328 km milestone.*

Cosmos Restaurant *On the road leading into Adler.*

Filling Station *At the 428/319 km milestone.*

ADLER

Adler stands at the mouth of the River Mzymta ("fierce" in Georgian), which rises 1990 m (6500 ft) up in the mountains; the whole area used at one time to be a hotbed of malaria. The winter here is colder than in Sochi, and the summer hotter but with less rain. Now tea and tobacco, citrus fruits, plums, olives and vines are grown, and fruit trees and violets begin to flower in the middle of January. There are some sandy patches on the wide shingle beach.

In the north-western suburbs of Adler there is a big tea factory, and across the bridge over the River Mzymta is a large poultry farm which supplies all the resorts in this region. On the left bank of the River Mzymta, south of Adler, is the Yuzhniye Kultury Horticultural Research Station. A good park with attractive ponds was laid out here in 1910. There is a rose garden, and an avenue leading down to the sea. The station covers 20 hectares (50 acres) and includes 800 kinds of subtropical plants.

One of Adler's suburbs is being developed as a new resort for a further 5000 visitors. Adler is the southernmost point of the territory of the Russian Federation, and its airport also serves Sochi.

FORTRESS *By the sea.* These are the remains of a fortress built here in 1837.

LENIN MONUMENT

RUSSIAN SOLDIERS' MONUMENT *On the Boulevard.* This monument commemorates the Russian soldiers who fell in the Russo-Turkish War.

BESTUZHEV-MARLINSKY MONUMENT *In the Park.* The Russian writer Bestuzhev-Marlinsky was among the Russian soldiers shot here when they landed in 1837.

MOTEL *Pervomaiskaya Street 41, in the centre of Adler and 10 minutes walk from the sea.* This motel has shops, a café, and a fully equipped carpark. Filling Station and Service Station, both open 7 a.m.–6 p.m.

CAMPING SITE *On the road from Adler to Gagra; turn right towards the sea at the village of Vesoloye (Happy), 10 km (6 miles) from Adler.* The camping site is in a eucalyptus grove on the territory of the local state farm, and close to the edge of the sea.

★

KRASNAYA POLYANA, *where the territory of the Caucasus State Reservation begins, can be reached by a very spectacular road from Adler.* It was built in 1899 by engineer Konstantinov. Over the first hill and past the village of Golitsinka there are the ruins of a monastery and also some stalactite caves. Then the road runs through the Akhtsu Gorge with the River Mzymta roaring at the bottom. In the gorge the road runs through a tunnel, and travellers used to light large candles before entering it. The road just before the tunnel is called "Carry us through, O Lord", as is part of the Daryal Ravine in the northern Caucasus. The obelisk with a star on the top, which stands just before the tunnel, commemorates the Red Army men who died here in 1920, and the metal obelisk on the other side of the tunnel, on the river bank, is dedicated to the partisans who died here at the same time. The stream which gushes out from the rocks on the left of the road forms a waterfall known as "Maiden's Tears".

The road climbs on, passing mineral springs such as the Narzan, Borzhomi and Yessentuki springs, and finally reaches Krasnaya Polyana nestling in the hills. Here there is an average annual temperature of 21°C (70°F). The reservation itself covers 100,000 hectares (250,000 acres) and has about 1400 different kinds of trees and plants, and 60 species of mammals including deer, boars, panthers, bears and a herd of more than 60 bison.

Krasnaya Polyana has been inhabited since prehistoric times. In 1864 the Cherkassian inhabitants were the last in the whole of the Caucasus to hold out against the Russians, but on 21st May, 1864, a religious service was held for 25,000 soldiers, and afterwards a manifesto was read out announcing the end of the war and the conquest of the Caucasus. Following this most of the local Cherkassians moved to Turkey, and Krasnaya Polyana was developed by Russian-Greek families and Estonians.

The mountains surrounding Krasnaya Polyana are Mount Achishkho (2365 m/7759 ft), Mount Aibga (2380m/7808 ft) and Mount Shoogoos (3245 m/10,646 ft). The region was once an imperial hunting ground, and at that time Krasnaya Polyana was known as Romanovsk after the name of the imperial family. It is possible to walk to Mount Achishkho, to Lake Kardivach and through the Kutakheku Pass to Lake Ritsa (24 km/15 miles).

KHOSTA

The name comes from "kho" meaning "be careful" and "sta"—"river". The legend from which the name is derived tells of an outlaw who lived in the ravine and who used to scare people passing by. On Italian maps of the 13th–15th centuries, in the place of present-day Khosta, a Genoese settlement called "Kasto" is shown. In 1901–03 fertile plots of land were given to people on the condition that within three years they cleared the ground, where necessary, and began to build.

The little River Khostinka runs out of a deep ravine. Khosta is surrounded by mountains on three sides, and lies on the edge of a small bay with a good beach of mixed sand and shingle, better than the beaches at Sochi. The mountains protect the resort from the north-west winds, so that it is always calm and warm here; the temperature is 1 or 2 degrees warmer than in Sochi.

Khosta is famous for its marine park, founded in 1930, and near this is a box and yew park which covers 300 hectares (750 acres) and lies 3 km (2 miles) inland from the sea. In the middle of the park are the ruins of a 12th century fortress, supposedly Genoese.

A path leads up the valley to the White Rocks (200 m/650 ft high).

KHOSTA RESTAURANT *Kiparisovaya Street 5.*

VOLNA (Wave) RESTAURANT

FILLING STATION NO. 3 *At the 435/312 km milestone, tel: 56–83, round-the-clock service.*

SOCHI

Population: 95,000 (1959)

The name derives from that of a local tribe, the Shashe. The largest resort on the north-eastern coast of the Black Sea, Sochi stretches along the shore for 30·5 km (19 miles), and lies between the River Mamaika and the River Kudepsta. Its climate is as fine as that of Nice, San Remo and other popular places in Europe. The average summer temperature is 23°C (73°F), and the temperature of the sea rises from 18°C (64°F) in mid-June to 29°C (84°F) later in the summer and in the early autumn; the sea bathing season lasts for five months. Autumn is from October until December, and spring begins in March. The best time of the year is late summer, known in these parts as the "velvet season".

Compared with other places along this coast, Sochi is a young town. The fortress founded in 1838 used to be called Navagenskoye, and in 1840 it held out against a local uprising when it was besieged. The heroine of the occasion was the Commander's wife, Mme Posipkina, who even under fire walked with her parasol along the earth wall to encourage the men. The Commander was afterwards promoted and Mme Posipkina received a costly necklace as a personal gift from Tsaritsa Alexandra. At one time the fortress was called Alexandria after the Tsaritsa. In 1894, it was still the site of a military settlement, but received the title of town in 1896. Its curative properties were then recognised and in 1909 it became known as the Caucasian Riviera, and as a health resort it really dates from this time. The opening of the railway line in 1925 led to speedier growth, and since 1933, when it was decided to turn Sochi into a resort of national importance, millions of roubles have been spent on it and the best Soviet architects including I. Zholtovsky and A. Shusiev have been employed in the construction of the resort. The harbour building was completed in 1955; its spire is 37 m (122 ft) high.

Above Sochi stands the 180 m (590 ft) television tower, completed in 1958. Sochi Television Centre puts out 3–4 hours of programmes daily for viewers in the area between Tuapse and Gagra.

The Sochi Experimental Station of Subtropical and Southern Fruit Crops lies up the valley of the Bzugu river. It was first organised in 1894 when it dealt chiefly with garden crops, but now tea, vines and other fruits are studied here.

At present visitors to this area number over a million annually and there are fifty-eight palatial sanatoria with more being built. Since 1958 the Chaika (Seagull) Sanatorium has accepted visitors from abroad; it has a funicular railway connecting it with the beach just as the Lazurny Bereg (Azure coast) and the Ordzhonikidze Sanatoria have. The Ordshonikidze Sanatorium is among the largest and most splendid of all. It was built between 1935 and 1941 by Kuznetsov in Italian renaissance style, and part of the interior has been decorated by artists from the villages of Palekh and Mstera in traditional Russian style. Flights of white marble steps lead up to it. The Metallurg (Steel worker), Sochi and Rossia Sanatoria, among others, have heated sea-water swimming pools to attract people there in the winter. The Sochi and Dzerzhinsky Sanatoria are linked with the beach by tall lift towers and the Noviye Sochi Sanatorium has a lift inside the cliff going down 35 m (115 ft). It was built in 1961. From here a tunnel of 112 m (123 yds) leads to the beach.

Since the spring of 1961 the territory around has been known as *Greater Sochi*; it includes about 160 km (100 miles) of coastline, running from Vesyoloye to Shapse (near Tuapse). Included in the total accommodation of Greater Sochi are 60 sanatoria, 20 holiday homes, 10 tourist bases and over 20 Pioneer Camps for children.

✿ CATHEDRAL OF THE ARCHANGEL MICHAEL *Mayachnaya Street 14.* The cathedral was built in 1852, and is open for service.

✿ RUINS OF THE 16TH CENTURY FORTRESS *Mamai-Kale.*

RUINS OF THE FORTRESS OF 1838 *Not far from the lighthouse.*

LOCAL MUSEUM *Ordzhonikidze Street 29. Open 10–6; closed on Tuesdays.* Sections on the natural history of the Caucasus and the Black Sea.

OSTROVSKY MUSEUM *Ostrovskov Lane 4. Open 10–10; closed on Wednesdays.* Nikolai Ostrovsky (1904–36) served in the civil war and then at the age of 20 became paralysed, blind, and bedridden. He moved to Sochi in 1924 and wrote *How the Steel Was Tempered* and the greater part of *Born of the Storm*, now standard literature for Soviet youth. The museum is located in his house and in a new building completed in 1957; the street is called after him, as are a school and a library.

STATUE OF LENIN

SOVIET SOLDIERS' MONUMENT

CANNON AND ANCHOR *Primorskaya Naberezhnaya*. On the sea shore and near the Pushkin Library is a cannon on a concrete pediment, and in front of it stands an anchor weighing 2800 kg (nearly 3 tons) which was made in the Urals in 1719.

THEATRE *Teatralnaya Square*. Built in 1937 to seat 1100 people, by architect K. Chernopyatov.

OPEN-AIR THEATRE *Primorsky Park, Chernomorskaya Square*. Built in 1937.

CIRCUS *Deputatskaya Street 8*. This takes 1180 people.

During the summer season many touring performers and companies come to Sochi, and also exhibitions.

DENDRARIUM *Kurortny Prospekt. Open 10–6*. The Dendrarium covers an area of 16 hectares (40 acres) and is divided in two by Kurortny Prospekt. It contains as many as 1600 different shrubs and trees, including subtropical specimens, from all over the world and is really worth a visit. The upper part is the most decorative with a pavilion, sculptures and fountains while the lower part is more natural with bamboo groves and magnolias. It is planned to extend the territory to 60 hectares (150 acres).

RIVIERA PARK This covers 10 hectares (25 acres) and contains 100 different species of trees and bushes from all parts of the world; there is a subtropical section. There are a number of cafés here, a dance floor and an open-air variety stage.

There is a stadium in Sochi as well as three swimming pools, a boat hire station, tennis courts and as many as 400 sports grounds.

Other parks include Frunze Park and those belonging to the sanatoria.

INTOURIST HOTEL AND RESTAURANT *Kurortny Prospekt 91; tel: 82–82*. There is a Beryozka Shop in the hotel which accepts foreign currency and the hotel has its own bathing beach. The Intourist organisation also rents accommodation for foreign visitors at the Chaika, Kirov, Lazurny Bereg and Caucasians Riviera Sanatoria.

PRIMORSKAYA HOTEL AND RESTAURANT *Primorskaya Street 21/1; tel: 7-97-43; service bureau 9-91*. The hotel faces the sea.

YUZHNAYA (South) HOTEL *Teatralnaya Street 8; tel: 21–69; Intourist office tel: 28-29*.

KUBAN HOTEL *Gagarin Street 5*.

CHAIKA (Seagull) SANATORIUM *Kurortny Prospekt 98*.

SOCHI HOTEL AND RESTAURANT *Kurortny Prospekt; tel: 22–57*.

LENINGRAD HOTEL

KAVKAZ HOTEL

SVETLANA RESTAURANT *Pushkinskaya Street 10*.

GORKA (Hill) RESTAURANT *Voikov Street 22*.

GOLUBOYE (Light blue) RESTAURANT *Voikov Street 8*.

PRIMORYE (Seaside) RESTAURANT *Chernomorskaya Street 10*.

DIETICHESKI (Dietetic) RESTAURANT *Voikov Street 10*.

AKHUN RESTAURANT *On the slopes of Mt. Bolshoi Akhun*.

NOVIYE SOCHI RESTAURANT *Vinogradnaya Street*.

G.P.O. *Voikov Street 14*.

BANK *Ordzhonikidze Street 2*.

INTER-URBAN TELEPHONE OFFICE *Parkovaya Street 15.*

SOCHI INFORMATION BUREAU *Gorky Street 3; tel: 20–52.*

SAVINGS BANK *Voikov Street.*

SOUVENIRS *Gorky Street 40.*

HOLIDAYMAKERS' REQUIREMENTS *Kooperativnaya Street 6.*

BOOKSHOPS *Voikov Street 5 and 16.*

CHEMIST'S *Kurortny Prospekt 24.*

ART SHOP *Boulevarnaya Street, opposite Morskoi Vokzal.*

JEWELLER'S *Kurortny Prospekt 26.*

MARKET *Kirpichnaya Street 30.*

TAXIS BY PHONE *tel: 25–29.*

ADLER AIRPORT *36 km (22 miles) out of town; tel: 33–11.*

SPUTNIK INTERNATIONAL YOUTH CAMP *At the foot of Mt. Akhun.*

FILLING STATION NO. 2 *Kurortny Prospekt, Primorye.* Diesel oil also supplied; round the clock service.

LENIN SANATORIUM *3 km (2 miles) from the Rheumatics Institute.* The walk leads through a wooded park and across mountain streams and gorges with good views.

BITKHU HILL (305 m/1000 ft) *6·5 km (4 miles) from the Voroshilov Sanatorium.* There is a good view of Sochi from this hill.

———— ★ ————

RAVINE OF THE RIVER AGUR. The road begins 8 km (5 miles) south of Sochi, runs through forest land, and ends in a carpark. From here a path with pleasant views leads on across a small bridge over the River Agur to a little lake. Although it is 7 m (21 ft) deep, the bottom is clearly visible. The waterfall of the River Agur (27 m/89 ft high) is nearby, and a path leads up to a second waterfall.

MOUNT AKHUN. Near the turning to the Agur Waterfalls is another turning from which a good road leads to Mount Akhun (663 m/2176 ft). It is 22 km (14 miles) from the centre of Sochi to the mountain. 3 km (2 miles) up this mountain road are the ruins of a 13th century church. "Akhun" Restaurant is on the mountain and a lookout tower, 30 m (100 ft) high, built by Vorobyev in 1936, commands a good view of the snow-covered tops of the main Caucasus range, of Sochi, and of the whole region around. From near the tower a path runs down the mountain to the Agur Ravine and waterfalls.

MATSESTA *20 km (12½ miles from Sochi).* The name means "firewater", and refers to the mineral springs discovered in 1837 in the valley of the River Matsesta, the waters of which cause the skin to redden. Now new wells have been sunk to a depth of 1524 m (5000 ft) and the water is 38°C (100°F). It has nearly three times the highest sulphur content ever found in a natural spring and its supplies are inexhaustible.

The water is recommended for treating circulatory, muscular, nervous, gynaecological and skin diseases. Intourist's courses of treatment last for 26 days.

RESTAURANT *In the building of the Salt-water Baths.*

ORLINIYE SKALY (Eagle Rocks) *377 m (1240 ft) above sea level, walking from Matsesta.* The path leads through the orchards of the Matsesta Valley and then climbs steeply through the woods above the town. There are pits beside the trail, remains of naturally formed limestone caves. From the top there is a fine panorama of the Bolshoi Akhun and the Caucasus Mountains and below at the foot of the precipice is the Agura with its first waterfall and the little lake.

DAGOMYSS

There is a big tea factory here, and furniture is manufactured in another factory in the town.

PARK *On the western slopes of Mount Armyanka.* This park which was formerly imperial property, was founded in 1900, and many rare trees flourish in its Mediterranean climate.

KRASNODARSKY CHAI TEAROOM

DAGOMYSS MOTEL *23 km from Sochi, towards the sea on the left side of the road.* The motel is situated in wooded grounds where nut trees, crab apples and wild pears grow, and has 2 hotel-type buildings, an eating house, sports grounds, a reading room, television, an open-air cinema, a fully equipped and covered carpark, and carwash. The Filling Station and Service Station are also here, open 7 a.m. till 6 p.m.

CAMPING SITE *Near the Motel.* Motorboats leave for Sochi from this place.

LOO

(*Pronounced to rhyme with "door"*)

1·5 km (1 mile) from the main road are the ruins of an 11th to 12th century church.

GORIZONT (Horizon) CAFE

At the 253/494 km milestone is the TOURIST CAFE.

LAZAREVSKOYE

This resort is called after Admiral Mikhail Lazarev (1788–1851), who commanded the Black Sea Fleet between 1833 and 1850.

It stands at the mouth of the River Psezuapsye, which has a good bathing beach of sand and shingle, where the water gets deep quickly. The bathing season lasts from June to October, but is best in the autumn when the temperature of the water has risen to 22°C (72°F).

The place was originally founded as a fortress in 1839. Since the beginning of the 20th century tea has been cultivated in this region, which was in fact the first place in Russia to grow it. Now there are many tea farms in the neighbourhood.

CHURCH OF THE NATIVITY OF THE VIRGIN. Built at the beginning of the 19th century.

LAZAREV MONUMENT *Near the ruined fortress walls and the railway station.*

ODOYEVSKY MONUMENT. Alexander Odoyevsky (1802–39) was a poet who was sentenced to 10 years hard labour in Siberia for active participation in the 1825 St. Petersburg revolt, and who was afterwards sent here as a soldier; it was here that he died of malaria in 1839. The Monument was unveiled in December, 1952.

HOTEL

VOLNA (WAVE) HOLIDAY HOME. This home is for young foreign visitors.

PRIBOI RESTAURANT *At the Motel, Pobeda Street 2.*

CAFE

MOTEL, SERVICE STATION AND FILLING STATION *Pobeda Street 2.* On the right of the main road are small bungalows, and on the left is the carpark, service station and restaurant. 150 m (165 yd) from the Motel is a buffet. The Filling Station is open from 7 a.m. till 6 p.m.

Camping Site *Sochinskoye Chaussée 2 a, 79 km from Sochi, on the left of the main road towards the sea.* This turning is the first on the left before the bridge over the River Psezuapsye, and the camping site is at the mouth of the river, near the sea. There is a buffet, shop, self-service kitchen and other facilities.

The Mamedovo Ravine is near Lazarevskoye. There are small waterfalls here and some ancient tombs in the shape of old sea chests.

ASHEI

This is a pleasant little seaside resort.

TUAPSE

The name means "two waters" in the Cherkess language; it was so called because the River Tuapse and the River Pauk flow into the sea at this point.

The climate is more moderate than it is farther south, and makes this a good fruit farming area. What used to be a small seaside town has grown into a port and a manufacturing centre. A railway line and two pipelines link it with the oil fields of the north Caucasus. Oil refining, ship repairing, engineering and metal processing are carried on.

Karl Marx Street is the main thoroughfare of the town.

A small Russian fortress called Veliaminov Fort was founded here in 1838 (one of the 17 established in these parts to assist in the conquering of the Caucasus) but it was blown up by the Russians themselves in 1854; parts of the stronghold remained until 1897.

Local Museum *Politayeva Street 8. Open 10–6; closed on Tuesdays.*

Lenin Monument *Beside the main road.*

Seamen's Club *In the port, in the Palace of Seamen.*

Park *Ilicha Square.*

Yuzhnaya (South) Hotel *Vokzalnaya Street 8; tel: 3–12.*

Tuapse Restaurant *Karl Marx Street, beside the main road.*

Cafe *Pirovskoy Street 2.*

G.P.O. *Karl Marx Street 9/10.*

Bank *Karl Marx Street 22.*

Bookshop *Karl Marx Street 7/9.*

Jeweller's *Pirovskoy Street 2.*

Filling Station *Beside the main road out of town.*

Service Station *Beside the main road out of town.*

NOVO-MIKHAILOVSKOYE

The part of the coast between Tuapse and Ghelendzhik is known as Zolotaya Dolina (Golden Valley); it has a sandy beach and the sea is shallow. The Orlyonok (Eaglet) Pioneer Camp is situated here in grounds of 300 hectares (750 acres). There is to be a swimming pool, a stadium for 4000 and a school for 1000.

White Stone Statue *On a nearby hilltop.*

Primorsky (Seaside) Restaurant

On the road out of Novo-Mikhailovskoye to the north there is a turning leading to a tourist base and to the sea.

DZHUBGA

This resort lies in the valley of the River Dzhubga among sweet chestnut woods and large tobacco plantations. Although Dzhubga was founded as long ago as 1832, it has not grown to be a large resort. The beach is of sand and shingle; there is a boat hire station in the town, and the fishing is good.

A prehistoric tomb can be seen in the vicinity.

DRUZHBA RESTAURANT

MOTEL *In the village, on the left of the main road.* Accommodation is in 2-storey buildings, with an eating house, and a kitchen garden. It is 124 km (77 miles) from here to Novorossisk.

FILLING STATION AND REPAIR STATION WITH CARWASH *Both at the Motel.*

Just outside the village at the 141/425 km milestone is a path with a convenient slope running down to the Golden Beach; this is a sandy beach 6 km (4 miles) long and 50–75 m (55–82 yd) wide.

ARKHIPO-OSIPOVKA

This place stands on the bank of the River Vulcan. In 1840 there was an uprising of a large army of 12,000 locals against the Russian garrison of 59 who held the fortress. The garrison fought back and finally in despair asked for a volunteer to set fire to the powder room. A certain Arkhip Osipov came forward and as he rushed to his doom with a blazing torch he shouted "Brothers, remember Arkhip Osipov!" The explosion was so great that there was but a single survivor to tell the story afterwards. A white cross, commemorating the event, stands on a small hill near the sea. It was erected in 1876 at the order of Alexander II.

There is a fruit preserving factory in the town.

From the suspension bridge over the River Vulcan a paved path runs down for 1300 m (¾ mile) to the sea. The beach in the bay is pebbly with patches of sand; it has a boat hiring station.

KAVKAZ RESTAURANT *By the turning to the camping site.*

RUSSKIYE KVAS I AKROSHKA SNACK BAR *Kvas* is a drink made from fermented rye bread and flavoured with raisins. It is a good thirst-quencher in summer and is also used as the base of *akroshka*, a cold, summer soup containing meat, hard-boiled egg, cucumber, radishes, spring onions, dill and other herbs.

VOLNA (Wave) CAFE *By the beach.*

POST AND TELEGRAPH OFFICE.

CAMPING SITE *On the edge of the sea, among pine trees and sheltered by the hills.* It is 63 km (39 miles) from here to Ghelendzhik.

PSHADA

OBELISK *Main square.* This obelisk was erected to commemorate the heroes of the Civil War.

EATING HOUSE. Pshada forms the beginning of the Pshadsky Pass (546 m/1825 ft above sea level).

Farther along the main road, by a statue of a she-bear with two cubs, is a sign "100 m" indicating the way to one of the biggest tombs in the region.

★

From the highway another side road runs down to the seaside villages of *Krinitsa* and *Betta.*

Krinitsa: At the end of the last century a group of intellectuals following Leo Tolstoi's teaching decided to take up manual labour, and founded a farm colony here. The Tolstoi Monument was erected in 1910. The beach is pebbly, and 3–4 m (10–14 ft) from the shore the water reaches a depth of 1·5–2 m (5–6 ft).

Betta: This village founded in the 1890's is 8 km (5 miles) south of Krinitsa. It has a shingle beach and a sandy seabed.

The orchards in the valley of the mountain River Dougab and in the surrounding area belong to one of the biggest farms in the region, the Mikhailov Pass Farm, with 1350 hectares (3375 acres) mostly under fruit and vines.

At the bottom of the hill there is a spring and a statue of a girl with her hair in plaits. She is kneeling down and the stream runs out of her water jar.

The road, lined with azaleas, now climbs to the Mikhailovsky Pass, 325 m (1065 ft) above sea level. The highest mountain is Mount Tkachegochuk (Land of the Gods). A curative mineral spring discovered 100 years ago can be seen on the right side of the road, on the way down the 4 km (2½ miles) long steep hill.

✿ CAFE *At the 689/58 km milestone.*

At the 57 km milestone stands a large Bronze Age stone tomb. The main road now runs further back from the sea, following the Novorossisk-Sukhumi Highway. Work on this road was begun in 1891 when 300,000 peasants eagerly volunteered to work on it because of famine in parts of Russia at that time. It was accordingly known as Hungry Highway.

DIVNOMORSK

The turning to this place is 7 km (4½ miles) before reaching Ghelendzhik from Sochi. The name meaning "marvellous sea" was given to this place in 1964. The old name of Falshivy (False) Ghelendzhik is more curious. It arose because the bay is so similar in appearance to that of Ghelendzhik that ships find it hard to know where they are.

The good beach is of sand and fine shingle; and the sea bed is sandy and slopes gently, reaching a depth of 1·5 m (5 ft) 8–9 m (9–10 yd) from the shore.

3 km (2 miles) south of this point is the most picturesque part of the region called Dzhankhot after a local noble of the last century and meaning "born-with-a-silver-spoon-in-the-mouth".

Near by is a grove of pine trees. The Russian writer Korolenko lived here at the beginning of the 20th century and called it "a basket of greenery".

GHELENDZHIK

The name means "white bride", possibly because it was once a centre of the slave trade. Ghelendzhik is situated in an oval bay hemmed in by two capes, the rugged Tolstyi (thick) and the gently sloping Tonky (thin). The beach is stony except for a sandy patch known as Solntsedar, below Cape Tonky. It is a sunny place, with excellently pure and dry air and strong winds. The average annual temperature is 13°C (55°F) and the average temperature in July and August is 24°C (75°F); the bathing season lasts from June until October.

The Greek town of Toricos was situated here in the 6th century B.C. This was succeeded by other towns—Pagri and after a further few hundred years, Eptala. In the time of the Turkish occupation Eptala was the chief port for the export of local girls to the Turkish harems. In 1864 Kazaks were settled here, but they were used to working steppe soil and were unable to live off this forest land; and later foreigners were invited to settle in their place. Greeks and Czechs arrived in 1877 and made their homes in the surrounding region.

Now Ghelendzhik is a flourishing seaside resort with Lenin Street as its main thoroughfare. It is planned, by 1980, to provide accommodation for 1,000,000 summer visitors instead of the current 250,000 in the 100 km (62 miles) of coastline on either side of the resort.

Nearby, in the valley of the River Ashampe, is the Black Sea Oceanology Research Settlement.

Beside the bay burial mounds of the 6th and 10th centuries B.C. have been found, as well as a settlement of primitive man with implements of the Late

Stone Age and the Bronze Age. 5 km (3 miles) away near the River Aderba are some ancient barrows.

LOCAL MUSEUM *Lenin Street 23. Open 8–1 and 2–5; closed on Mondays.*

PARTISANS' MONUMENT *Lermontov Boulevard.* This statue of a seaman, a factory worker and a peasant was erected to commemorate the partisans of the Civil War.

LERMONTOV MONUMENT *On the Promenade.*

WORLD WAR II VICTORY MONUMENT *On the sea shore, near the town stadium.*

GHELENDZHIK HOTEL AND RESTAURANT.

PLATAN (Plane tree) RESTAURANT.

MAYAK (Lighthouse) RESTAURANT.

CAFE *Lenin Street.*

G.P.O. *Lenin Street.*

GHELENDZHIK MOTEL *Lunacharsky Street on the right and 5 km (3 miles) from Ghelendzhik town centre.* The motel has a 2-storey hotel, small bungalows, an eating house, garage, and a Service Station and Filling Station.

CAMPING SITE *Lunacharsky Street, opposite the Motel on the left side of the road, and even nearer to the sea.* The site has a café, shop and a hiring depot.

Ghelendzhik has a boat hire station and boats take trips to *Golubaya Bukhta* (Blue Bay), north of Cape Tonky, and one of the prettiest places on this part of the coast.

KABARDINKA

This village runs for about 3 km (2 miles) on either side of the main road amidst orchards and chestnut trees. It owes its origin, as do so many places along the coast of the Black Sea, to the foundation of a military fort here in the 1830's. The Kabardinsky Regiment was stationed here. The average temperature in July and August is 24°C (75°F).

The beach itself is pebbly, but the sea bed here is sandy and the water very shallow.

KABARDINKA CAFE

NOVOROSSISK

Population: 93,000 (1959)

North-east winds blow into Novorossisk from the mountains. These winds sometimes blow at gale force for days on end during the winter, and are then known as the "bora".

In ancient times there was on this spot a Greek town called Bati. During the 13th and 14th centuries the place was in the possession of the Genoese, and the Turks built a fortress called Sundzhuk-Kale in the 16th century. The Russians first took the fortress in 1808, and it has belonged to Russia continuously since 1829. In 1838, when the Black Sea Fleet under Admiral Lazarev docked here, a temporary fortification called Tzemesskaya was built, and was soon renamed Novorossisk. Tsemes Bay, from which the fortress derived its first name, is deep enough for ocean-going vessels to dock. The Genoese called it Calo Limena (Beautiful Bay), and it has been used as a port since 1848. Novorossisk itself is sometimes called the Sea-Gate of Kuban. The port played an active part in both world wars, and it now deals widely in cement, grain, oil, fish and fruit. Near the port is a 9-storey grain elevator which is the highest in Europe and the second highest in the world, built in 1894 by engineer Kerbedz. In 1854 the fortress was blown up and deserted, as were many other small fortresses in this region, but was restored in 1858. During the first Russian revolution of 1905 a Novorossian Republic was in existence for two weeks.

On the 18th June, 1918, the Russian Black Sea Fleet was sunk in Tsemes Bay to avoid the approaching Germans, and to commemorate the event there stands a memorial saying, "In Tsemes Bay which lies before you, in 1918, by the order of V. I. Lenin, the Black Sea Fleet was sunk so as not to surrender to the German imperialists."

The Sugar-Loaf Mountain of the Markotkhsky Range yields high quality marl from which cement is made locally. This was first exploited in 1879, and the first cement factory was completed in 1881. Now the industries also include fish curing, wagon repairing, flour milling and slate quarrying. The principal streets of Novorossisk are Sovietov, Svobodi and Zhdanova, all of which contain a number of new houses. The main road follows the coast past the port, then goes along Mir Street and Sovietov Street.

✿ CHURCH OF THE ASSUMPTION *Vidov Street.* This church dates from the end of the 19th century.

✿ LOCAL MUSEUM *Sovietov Street 58.*

PICTURE GALLERY

GAGARIN PLANETARIUM *In Lenin Park.*

WAR MEMORIAL *Heroes-of-World-War-II-Square.* Here beside the sea are war graves, and between two graves with monuments to Heroes of the Soviet Union, Cesar Kunikov and Nikolai Sipiagin, burns an eternal flame. Tape-recorded music by Shostakovich is played each hour. Another monument is dedicated to an Unknown Seaman. An obelisk commemorates the 20th anniversary of the liberation of the town from the White Guards.

On the Cape of Love stands a monument to twelve fishermen who died in a storm in 1959.

LIBERATION MONUMENT *Svoboda Square.* "Svoboda" means "Freedom". The 13 m (43 ft) monument commemorates the liberation of Novorossisk from the Germans in 1943, and depicts a sailor, a soldier and a partisan, symbolising the unity of the armed forces with the civilians; the sculptors were Timoshin and Shmagun, and the monument was unveiled in 1961.

THE RAILWAY CARRIAGE *In the grounds of the October Cement Factory.* The remains of this shot-through railway carriage are all that is left of the carriage that formed part of the battle front which was held for a year in World War II.

OBELISK WITH SCULPTURED GROUP *On the road out of town.* This commemorates the soldiers and civilians shot here in 1943.

✿ DRAMA THEATRE *Letny Sad, Sovietov Street.*

FOREIGN SEAMEN'S CLUB *In the port.*

✿ FRUNZE PARK There is a swimming pool here.

TRUD STADIUM *Sovietov Street 55.*

LENIN PARK *Sovietov Street 53.*

✿ CHERNOMORSKAYA (Black Sea) HOTEL AND RESTAURANT *Sovietov Street 42; tel: 33-34.*

PRIBOI (Surf) RESTAURANT *Michurinsky Pereulok 3.*

VOLNA (Wave) RESTAURANT *At the port.*

YUZHNY (South) RESTAURANT *By the beach.*

MIR (Peace) CAFE *Naberezhnaya Street 23.*

UYUT (Cozy) CAFE *Svoboda Street 4.*

CHAIKA (Seagull) CAFE *Sovietov Street.*

✿ G.P.O. *Sovietov Street 36.*

BANK *Sovietov Street 47.*

DEPARTMENT STORE *Svoboda Square.*

BOOKSHOP *Sovietov Street 38.*

JEWELLER'S *Sovietov Street 40.*

TAXI RANK *On the corner of Sovietov and Mir Streets.*

FILLING STATION *Kozlov Street 1.* Diesel oil is for sale; and there is round-the-clock service.

★

25 km (15½ miles) to the north of Novorossisk is *Abrau-Durso,* the birthplace of Soviet champagne. This is a small village surrounded by mountains with a lake lying 84 m (276 ft) above sea level. The lake is rich in fish, especially carp. Both its climate and its soil resemble those of the champagne country of France; in 1870 the first vineyard was planted here on an area of 1 hectare (2 acres) with imported French vines. Since then it has grown to cover 500 hectares (1250 acres), producing nearly a million bottles of champagne a year. Other good Soviet wines are also made here.

EATING HOUSE

CAMPING SITE

MONUMENT TO CIVIL WAR HEROES *Near the 19/402 km milestone.*

AFIPSKAYA

FILLING STATION *At the 20 km milestone (from Novorossisk).* Diesel oil is on sale here; and there is round-the-clock service.

KRYMSK

Population: 30,000 (1959)

Known until 1958 as Stanitsa Krymskaya (Crimean Cossacks village).

The town lies 4 km (2½ miles) from the main road, beside the River Adagum, a tributary of the Kuban river.

Here is one of the largest fruit and vegetable preserving plants in Russia as well as wine factories and breweries.

RESTAURANT *In the town.*

FILLING STATION *Cross the railway which lies to the left of the main road and drive on for 1 km.*

ABINSK

This small town, founded in 1863, was formerly known as Abinskaya Stanitsa. There are tobacco plantations and a wine factory.

AKHTYRSKAYA

CAFE *Beside the main road.*

KHOLMSKAYA

At the 83/338 km milestone.

CAFE *Beside the main road.*

FILLING STATION *At the 87/334 km milestone.*

CAFE *Beside the main road, at the 93/328 km milestone at the turning to the village of Chernomorsky.*

ILSK

At the 98/323 km milestone. Ilsk was formerly known as Ilskaya Stanitsa. There are tobacco plantations and oil wells.

EATING HOUSE.

KRASNODAR

(formerly Yekaterinodar)

Population: 400,000 (1964)

The town stands on the high right bank of River Kuban which flows through the black earth plain that is one of the Soviet Union's most important areas for growing wheat, sugar beet and sunflowers, and often known as "the pearl of Russia".

It was founded in 1793 during the reign of Catherine II as a Cossack

1 and 2 Hotel and Restaurant   3 Filling Station
4 Service Station

a Krasnaya ul.   b Ul. Severnaya
c Kommunisticheskaya ul.   d Krasnoarmeiskaya ul.
e Sedina ul.   f Gogolya ul.

N.B. One-way street system in operation

settlement and fortress protecting the Russian frontier. It was called Yekaterinodar and became the Cossack army's headquarters. The buildings at that time consisted largely of mud huts roofed with reeds and straw. A traveller at the beginning of the 19th century wrote that the huts reminded him of the military command "at ease", because they all faced different ways, some even having their backs to the streets. In 1860 it was made the capital of the Kuban Cossacks but seven years later it was reorganised as a civilian town. At the end of the nineteenth century it began to develop rapidly, as did so many other towns, following the opening of the railway connections; in the 1890's it was already a large transport and trade junction.

Yekaterinodar was the centre of the area's revolutionary activities in 1905 and during the Civil War. It was renamed Krasnodar in 1920.

During the Second World War the Germans occupied the town from August, 1942, till February, 1943, and when they retreated they blew up or burned most of the principal buildings.

Local industry now produces machine tools, electrical measuring devices, chemical, textiles, oil products and food products. There are medical, agricultural and teachers' training colleges and a polytechnical institute as well as a number of scientific research institutes dealing with agriculture, oil and foodstuffs. Modern buildings now line the suburban streets and there are some new hotels under constructions.

ST. CATHERINE CATHEDRAL *Kommunarov Street*. Built at the beginning of the 20th century.

ST. GEORGE'S CHURCH *Severnaya Street*. This was built in the 19th century as part of a monastery.

LOCAL MUSEUM *Kommunisticheskaya Street 53*. Founded in 1879.

LUNACHARSKY PICTURE GALLERY *Krasnaya Street 11. Open 11–6; closed on Tuesdays*. In 1904 a local art collector, F. Kovalenko, presented his collection to the town and from this the present collection grew. West European art is represented downstairs by many old copies of famous works; Russian and Soviet art is shown upstairs. The gallery is particularly proud of its collection of 18th and 19th century miniatures.

LOCAL ARTISTS' GALLERY *Krasnaya Street 9*.

LENIN MONUMENT. Unveiled in 1956.

GORKY DRAMA THEATRE *Krasnaya Street 55*. Seats for 820 people.

MUSICAL COMEDY THEATRE *Krasnaya Street 44*. Seats for 830 people.

CONCERT HALL *Krasnaya Street 67*.

PUPPET THEATRE *Ordzhonikidze Street 30*.

GORKY PARK *Telmann Street 34*. Opened in 1850 as the town garden, there is now a boat hiring station by the pond. Other attractions include a small zoo.

MAY DAY PARK in Roscha Region.

DYNAMO STADIUM *Krasnaya Street 174*. This stadium can hold 12,000.

KUBAN STADIUM *Zheleznodorozhnaya Street 35*. This one has room for 20,000.

KRASNODAR HOTEL AND RESTAURANT *Gogol Street 52; tel: 49-01*. The local Intourist office is here.

KUBAN HOTEL AND RESTAURANT *Kommunisticheskaya Street 51*.

SPORT HOTEL *Zheleznodorozhnaya Street 35*.

TSENTRALNY HOTEL AND RESTAURANT *Krasnaya Street 25*. A new hotel is under construction at *Krasnaya Street 170*.

OGONEK RESTAURANT *Gorky Park, Telmann Street 34*.

MIR (Peace) CAFE *Mir Street 29/11*.

SVETLYACHOK (Glow-worm) CAFE *Corner of Krasnaya and Sverdlova Streets*.

EXPRESS CAFE *By the railway station*.

G.P.O. *Shaumyan Street 60*.

BANK *Ordzhonikidze Street 35*.

TELEGRAPH OFFICE *Sverdlov Street 64*.

DEPARTMENT STORE *Gogol Street 69*.

SURPRISE GIFT SHOP *Krasnaya Street 84*.

BOOKSHOP *Krasnaya Street 23*.

JEWELLERY *Krasnaya Street 75*.

PHOTOGRAPHIC DEVELOPING *Krasnaya Street 86 and Druzhba Street 81*.

MARKET

FILLING STATIONS *Zheleznodorozhnaya Street 17 and Brigadnaya Street 32*. Both supply Diesel oil and give round-the-clock service.

REPAIR STATION *Severnaya Street 31; open from 8 a.m. till 4 p.m.*

KORENOVSKAYA

RESTAURANT

FILLING STATION *At the 59 km milestone (from Krasnodar)*. Diesel oil is for sale here, and there is round-the-clock service.

INDEX

(The **bold figure**(s) in brackets after each town indicate(s) the road(s) upon which it lies)

MADE IN GREAT BRITAIN

10 TOURIST ROUTES IN THE SOVIET UNION

CONVERSION TABLE

MILES	KILOMETRES
0	0
25	40
62	100
100	161
124	200
186	300
200	322
250	402
300	483
311	500
400	644
500	805

1Kilometre = 0·62137 Miles

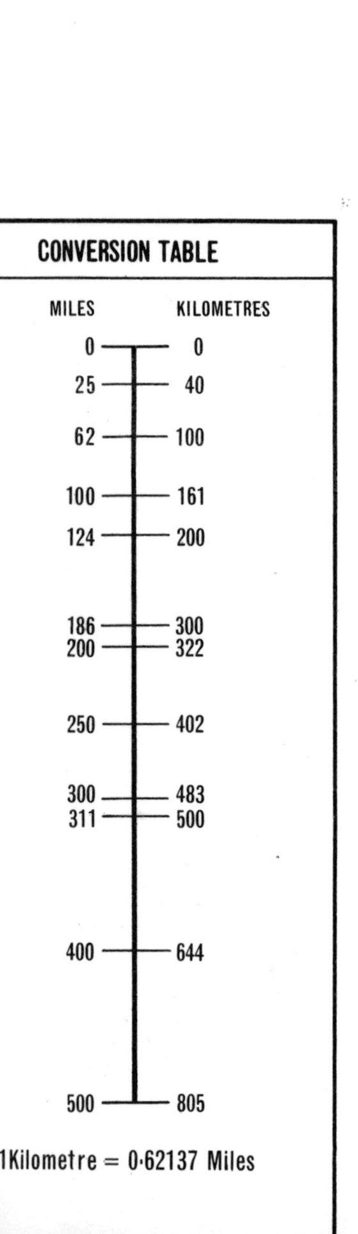

EAST
GERMANY
CZECHOSLOVAKIA
AUSTRIA
HUNGARY
JUGOSLAVIA
Adriatic
Sea
ALBANIA

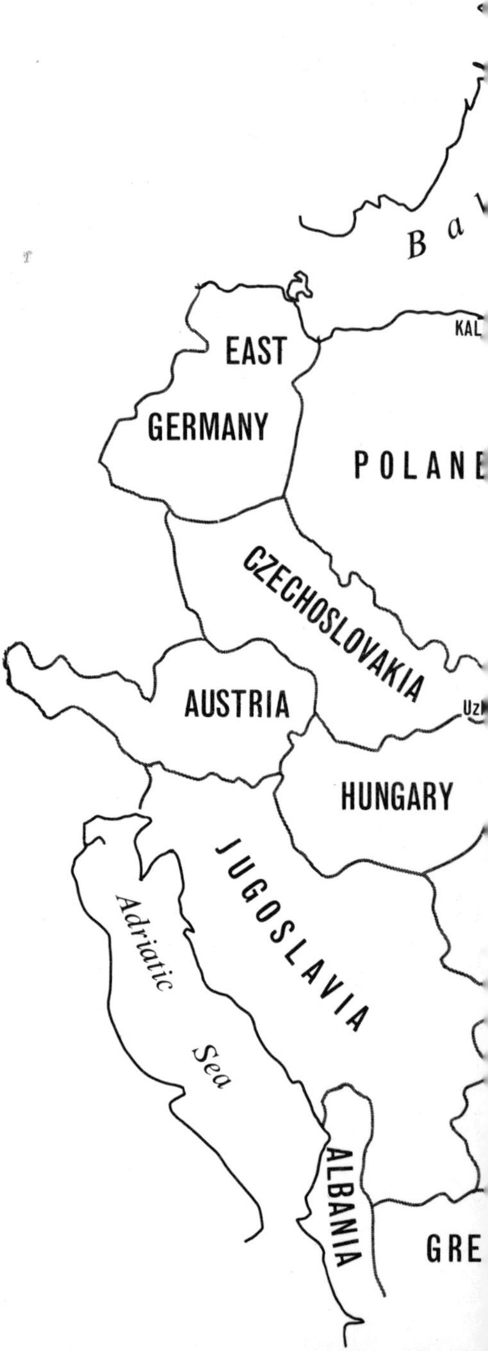